on the Justice *of* Roosting Chickens

REFLECTIONS ON THE CONSEQUENCES OF U.S. IMPERIAL ARROGANCE AND CRIMINALITY

WARD CHURCHILL

INTRODUCTION BY CHELLIS GLENDINNING

AK PRESS
EDINBURGH • LONDON • OAKLAND

*On the Justice of Roosting Chickens—
Reflections on the Consequences of U.S. Imperial Arrogance and
Criminality*
by Ward Churchill
ISBN 1-902593-79-0

AK Press
674-A 23rd Street
Oakland, CA 94612-1163
USA
(510) 208-1700
www.akpress.org
akpress@akpress.org

AK Press U.K.
PO Box 12766
Edinburgh, EH8 9YE
Scotland
(0131) 555-5165
www.akuk.com
ak@akedin.demon.uk

The addresses above would be delighted to provide you with the latest complete AK catalog, featuring several thousand books, pamphlets, zines, audio products, video products and stylish apparel published and distributed by AK Press. Alternatively, visit our websites for the complete catalog, latest news and updates, events and secure ordering.

Library of Congress Control Number 2003112215

Library of Congress Cataloging-in-Publication data
A catalog record for this title is available from the Library of Congress

Printed in Canada

Author Photo by Leah Renae Kelly
Cover design by John Yates

For Yuri Kochiyama
whose vision and consistency have been an
inspiration to us all

Contents

Other Works by Ward Churchill

Authored:

Perversions of Justice: Indigenous Peoples and Angloamerican Law (2003)

Acts of Rebellion: The Ward Churchill Reader (2003)

Fantasies of the Master Race: Literature, Cinema and the Colonization of American Indians (1992, 1998)

Struggle for the Land: Native North American Resistance to Genocide, Ecocide and Colonization (1993, 1999)

Indians Are Us?: Culture and Genocide in Native North America (1994)

From a Native Son: Selected Essays in Indigenism, 1985–1995 (1996)

Que Sont les Indiens Devenus? (1994)

Since Predator Came: Notes from the Struggle for American Indian Liberation (1995)

A Little Matter of Genocide: Holocaust and Denial in the Americas, 1492 to the Present (1997)

Coauthored:

Culture versus Economism: Essays on Marxism in the Multicultural Arena (1984)
with Elisabeth R. Lloyd

Agents of Repression: The FBI's Secret Wars Against the Black Panther Party and the American Indian Movement (1988)
with Jim Vander Wall

The COINTELPRO Papers: Documents from the FBI's Secret Wars Against Dissent in the United States (1990)
with Jim Vander Wall

Pacifism as Pathology: Reflections on the Role of Armed Struggle in North America (1998)
with Mike Ryan

Edited:

Marxism and Native Americans (1983)

Critical Issues in Native North America (1989)

Critical Issues in Native North America, Vol. 2 (1990)

Das indigene Amerika und die marxistiche Tradition: Eine kontroverse Debatte über Kultur, Industrialismus und Eurozentrismus (1993)

Coedited:

Cages of Steel: The Politics of Imprisonment in the United States (1992)
with Jim Vander Wall

Islands in Captivity: The Record of the International Tribunal on the Rights of Indigenous Hawaiians, 2 vols. (2003)
with Sharon H. Venne

Spoken:

Doing Time: The Politics of Imprisonment CD (2001)

In a Pig's Eye: Reflections on the Police State, Repression and Native America CD (2002)

Pacifism and Pathology in the American Left CD (2003)

Life in Occupied America CD (2003)

Speaking Truth in the Teeth of Power

Reflections on Ward Churchill's *On the Justice of Roosting Chickens*

> We have sown the wind: he is the whirlwind.
>
> —Jean Paul Sartre
> Preface to *The Wretched of the Earth*

September 11, 2001. The date, the devastation, the meaning—they reside in historical context.

To understand that context, we Americans might do well to remember that, just a century ago, 85 percent of the landmass of this planet existed under forced domination by the governments of European peoples. We might also remind ourselves that the decades to follow saw fiery uprisings in the form of decolonization and liberation movements—with a peak of activity after World War II, when over 100 new nations made of formerly colonized peoples arose and groups within colonizer countries challenged their oppression.

Let me be candid: the foremost political and psychological legacy of today's world is not the battle between "democracy" and "evil" as conceived by dominant-society philosophers. No. The foremost political and psychological legacy of our times is the tragic short-circuiting of these efforts at liberation. Political in the sense that every people today—both of the "liberated" nations and within colonial powers—does not reside in the sought-after state of self-determination. Psychological in the sense that demise after a period of pure hope presents arduous hurdles indeed.

At this point, purity of hope is a rare find. The postwar reforging of political and economic structures into the contemporary version of empire—corporate globalization—perpetuates inequality on a scale that Alexander the Great, Queen Victoria, or Hitler himself might envy. The ecological devastation made evident from resulting abuses pushes the Earth to the point of no return. And the endless perpetration of violence, with its continuous display via telecommunications spectacle, has spawned a feat of unimaginable distress: the globalization of trauma. As Newe (Western Shoshone) natives, Russian citizens, and U.S. environmentalists chanted together at a Nevada Test Site protest in 1992, "We are all wounded."

If there is any purity left, it is in the stark understanding that social systems based on oppression imprint seemingly irresolvable conflicts

1

onto every sphere of human endeavor. If there is a perspective shared by peoples around the world, it is that at this moment in history there are no easy solutions.

In the midst of this confusion of expectation and means comes a voice that is so definitive that it echoes the leaders of the era gone by. Perhaps Ward Churchill is a bit of a descendant of Ché Guevara. Fierce in his dedication to autonomy in Latin America and willing to risk everything to achieve it, Guevara was deeply caring. "Déjeme decirle, a riesgo de parecer ridículo," he said, "que el revolucionario verdadero está guido por sentimientos grandes de amor." "Let me tell you, at the risk of appearing ridiculous, that the true revolutionary is guided by great feelings of love." And indeed, if you excavate beneath Churchill's rhythms of urgency, you will uncover palpable love.

Perhaps too, he is the child of Malcolm X, the daring leader of African American liberation in the 1960s. Actor Ossie Davis described Malcolm X in this way: "You can imagine what a howling, shocking nuisance this man was. Once he fastened on you, you could not escape." And indeed, if Churchill is anything, he is a howling nuisance to whatever equilibrium one thinks one possesses.

And most definitely, Churchill stands in lineage with the Martinique intellectual Frantz Fanon, whose post-World War II training as a doctor ironically provided him with the tools for turnabout: psychiatric language to deconstruct racism and define the experience of the colonized. As Jean-Paul Sartre wrote in his preface to Fanon's best-known work, The Wretched of the Earth, Fanon "certifies that [Europe] is dying, on external evidence, founded on symptoms he can observe. As to curing her, no; he has other things to think about; he does not give a damn whether she lives or dies. Because of this, his book is scandalous."

So, too, is On the Justice of Roosting Chickens scandalous, for herein blows a fury that gusts right through the issues of relative justice and comfort that tend to infuse leftist political endeavor in the U.S. The U.S. was born and maintains itself through the perpetration of violence, asserts Churchill, and this legacy will be no more denied by seemingly reasonable rationales like "Twin Towers: Never Again!" and "Liberate Iraq!" than it was in 1637 in Pequot country. Or 1776 against the Cherokee. Or 1848 in Mexico. Or 1898 against the Cubans and Filipinos. Or 1966 in Ghana. Or 1993 in Haiti.

Rampaging through the Left's propensity to analysis that, he insists, leaves people in a paralysis of complexity, Churchill calls for action as blunt as the village stock: criminal proceedings conducted by international institutions against individuals who have executed policies of genocide. And he exhorts the citizens of American Empire to recraft their society that it may participate in the restoration of a broken humanity and a devastated planet. If we do not, he prophesizes, the "recrafting" will come via the violent expression we have come to know—from without.

My own responsibility as the writer of the preface to this book has made me reflect on Sartre's task in his preface to *The Wretched of the Earth*. Sartre was French; Fanon was a man whose people had been colonized by France. I am European American; Churchill is native Creek and Cherokee. I feel the weight of my responsibility in this configuration. My lesson is to understand the earnestness of oppressed peoples and to honor the politics of sovereignty.

And yet, since the U.S. has crystallized its role as CEO to international hegemony, the clarity of category forged during the days of classical empire—of "colony" and "metropole," of oppressed and oppressor—has blurred. Today we are wantonly zapped by the electromagnetic radiation of the telecommunications industry. We are wage-slaves to the economic machine together, plied by drugs both prescription and illicit, fed genetically-engineered foods, made to find the means of our survival in corporate fantasias. If any one of us dares to protest, we risk being maced and stun-gunned, or corralled in a concentration camp. In today's world, we are all colonized.

While Churchill most definitely directs his message to the American reader, like Fanon, he also stops. His end point is a proclamation: it is well past time to reclaim power. For Churchill, such a reconstruction surely entails the re-empowerment of international humanitarian law over the current U.S.-led reign of corporate jurisdiction. But what might such a reclamation take to succeed? A massive focus of public will upon institutions of justice conducted in a legalistic manner? A reiteration of the functional seizure of power sought in the former decolonization movements? The phenomenological, and anarchist, revolt described in Zapatista philosophy—revolution in every moment, in every situation, resulting in a literal revolving back to "power to the people" and "an end to the dialectic"?

That these and other details of Churchill's proposal are not made entirely clear in a work of otherwise perfect clarity is to its credit. By what means? Towards what end? With what outcome? The reader may think that, by the strength of implication, Churchill's politics are scandalous. Whatever you think, in a time of no easy solutions, this book will awaken you to the pure necessity to put an end to empire.

—Chellis Glendinning
Chimayó, New Mexico
February 2003

The Ghosts of 9-1-1

Reflections on History, Justice and Roosting Chickens

> As ye sow, so shall ye reap.
>
> —*Galations,* 6:7

September 11, 2001, will now and forever be emblazoned in the short-hand of popular consciousness as a correlation to the emergency dialing sequence, "9-1-1." On that date, a rapid but tremendous series of assaults were carried out against the paramount symbols of America's global military/economic dominance, the Pentagon and the twin towers of New York's World Trade Center (WTC), leaving about one-fifth of the former in ruins and the latter in a state of utter obliteration. Initially, it was claimed that as many as 5,000 U.S. citizens were killed, along with 78 British nationals, come to do business in the WTC, and perhaps 300 other "aliens," the majority of them undocumented, assigned to scrub the floors and wash the windows of empire.[1]

Even before the first of the Trade Center's towers had collapsed, the "news" media, as yet possessed of no hint as to who may have carried out the attacks, much less why they might have done so, were already and repeatedly proclaiming the whole thing "unprovoked" and "sense-less." Within a week, the assailants having meanwhile been presumably identified, *Newsweek* had recast the initial assertions of its colleagues in the form of a query bespeaking the aura of wide-eyed innocence in which the country was by then, as always, seeking to cloak itself. "Why," the magazine's cover whined from every newsstand, "do they hate us so much?"

The question was and remains boggling in its temerity, so much so that after a lifetime of spelling out the reasons, one is tempted to respond with a certain weary cynicism, perhaps repeating Malcolm X's penetrating observation about chickens coming home to roost and leav-ing it at that.[2] Still, mindful of the hideous human costs attending the propensity of Good Americans, like Good Germans, to dodge responsi-bility by anchoring professions of innocence in claims of near-total igno-rance concerning the crimes of their corporate state, one feels obliged to try and deny them the option of such pretense. It is thus necessary that at least a few of those whose ravaged souls settled in upon the WTC and the Pentagon be named.

At the front of the queue were the wraiths of a half-million Iraqi children, all of them under twelve, all starved to death or forced to die for lack of basic sanitation and/or medical treatment during the past

5

ten years.[3] These youngsters suffered and died because the U.S. first systematically bombed their country's water purification, sewage treatment and pharmaceutical plants out of existence, then imposed a decade-long—and presently ongoing—embargo to ensure that Iraq would be unable to repair or replace most of what had been destroyed.[4] The point of this carefully calculated mass murder, as was explained at the outset by then-President George Herbert Walker Bush, father of the current Oval Office occupant, has been to impress upon the Iraqi government—and the rest of the world as well—that "what we say, goes."[5]

In other words, though no less bluntly: "Do as you're told or we'll kill your babies."

Much has been made, rightly enough, of how U.S. governmental agencies, corporate media and academic élites collude to provide only such information as is convenient to the status quo.[6] It is thus true that there is much of which the public is unaware. No such excuse can be advanced with respect to the fate of Iraq's children, however. Not only was the toll publicly predicted before U.S. sanctions were imposed, but two high UN officials, including Assistant Secretary General Denis Halliday, have resigned in protest of what Halliday described in widely-reported statements as "the policy of deliberate genocide" they reflected.[7] Asked by an interviewer on *60 Minutes* in 1996 whether the UN's estimate of child fatalities in Iraq was accurate, U.S. Ambassador to the UN *cum* Secretary of State Madeleine Albright confirmed it before a national television audience.[8]

"We've decided," Albright went on in a remark prominently displayed in the *New York Times* and most other major newspapers, "that it's worth the cost" in lives extracted from brown-skinned toddlers to "set an example" so terrifying in its implications that it would compel planetary obedience to America's dictates in the years ahead.[9] Such were the official terms defining the "New World Order" George Bush the elder had announced in 1991.[10]

One wonders how information about what was happening in Iraq could have been made much clearer or more readily accessible to the general public. Claims that average Americans "didn't know" what was being done in their name are thus rather less than credible. In reality, Americans by-and-large greeted Albright's haughty revelation of genocide with yawns and blank stares, returning their attention almost immediately to what they considered far weightier matters: the Dow Jones and American League batting averages, for instance, or pursuit of the perfect cappuccino. Braying like donkeys into their eternal cell-phones, they went right on arranging their stock transfers and real estate deals and dinner dates, conducting business as usual, never exhibiting so much as a collective flicker of concern.

In effect, the U.S. citizenry as a whole was endowed with exactly the degree of ignorance it embraced. To put it another way, being ignorant is in this sense—that of willful and deliberate ignoration—not synonymous with being uninformed. It is instead to be informed and then *ignore* the information. There is a vast difference between not knowing and not caring and if Good Americans have difficulty appreciating the distinction, it must be borne in mind that there are others in the world who are quite unburdened by such intellectual impairments. They, beginning with those most directly targeted at any given moment for subjugation or eradication at the hands of American "peacekeepers," know above all else that professions of ignorance inherently preclude claims of innocence in such circumstances.

There was a time, oddly enough, when it could be said that the U.S. stood at the forefront of those endorsing the same principle. How else to explain its solemn invocation at the time of the Nuremberg Trials of a collective guilt inhering in the German populace itself?[11] One would do well to recall that the crimes attributed by Americans to Good Germans were that they'd celebrated a New Order of their own, looking away while the nazi crimes were committed, never attempting to meet the legal/moral obligation of holding their government to even the most rudimentary standards of human decency.[12] For these sins, it was said, they, the Germans, civilians as well as military personnel, richly deserved the death and devastation that had been rained upon them by America's "Mighty Eighth" Air Force and its British counterpart.[13] In sum, they'd "brought it on themselves."

Some People Push Back

To be sure, I've "oversimplified," committed "reductionism" and "compared apples and oranges" in offering the preceding analogy. That was Germany, after all, while this is the U.S. The situation here is of course much more "complex." America today, unlike Germany a half-century ago, is a "democratic," "multicultural" society. Its courts offer a prospect of "due process" in dispute resolution absent under the nazis.[14] Most importantly, unlike the situation in nazi Germany, there is a discernible opposition in the U.S., an active counterforce to the status quo through which progressive social, political and economic change can ultimately be accomplished without resort to the crudities of bullets and bombs, never mind the scale of atrocity witnessed on 9-1-1.[15]

These things duly remarked, it must also be said that the implications embodied in such counterforces must be tested by their effectuality rather than their mere existence. On this score, the practical distinction between formal and functional democracy has been remarked by numerous analysts over the years.[16] As to the merits of the U.S. judicial system, one might do well to begin any assessment by asking Leonard Peltier, Mumia Abu-Jamal, Geronimo ji Jaga (Pratt), Dhoruba Bin Wahad or any of the hundreds of other political activists who have been entombed on false charges or are now serving dramatically inequitable sentences in American prisons.[17] One might ask as well those sent to death row on racial grounds,[18] or who number among the two million predominately dark-skinned people—a proportion of the population larger than that of any country save Russia—consigned to the sprawling archipelago of forced labor camps forming the U.S. "prison-industrial" complex.[19]

Turning to America's vaunted "opposition," we find record of not a single significant demonstration protesting the wholesale destruction of Iraqi children. On balance, U.S. "progressives" have devoted far more time and energy over the past decade to combating the imaginary health effects of "environmental tobacco smoke"[20] and demanding installation of speedbumps in suburban neighborhoods[21]—that is, to increasing their *own* comfort level—than to anything akin to a coherent response to the U.S. genocide in Iraq. The underlying mentality is symbolized quite well in the fact that, since they were released in the mid-1990s, Jean Baudrillard's allegedly "radical" screed, *The Gulf War Did Not Take Place*, has outsold Ramsey Clark's *The Impact of Sanctions on Iraq*, prominently subtitled *The Children are Dying*, by a margin of almost three-to-one.[22]

The theoretical trajectory entered into by much of the American left over the past quarter-century exhibits a marked tendency to try and justify such evasion and squalid self-indulgence through the expedient of rejecting "hierarchy, in all its forms." Since "hierarchy" may be taken to include "[any]thing resembling an order of priorities," we are faced thereby with the absurd contention that all issues are of equal importance (as in the mindless slogan, "There is no hierarchy to oppression").[23] From there, it becomes axiomatic that the "privileging" of any issue over another—genocide, say, over fanny-pinching in the workplace—becomes not only evidence of "elitism," but of "sexism," and often "homophobia" to boot (as in the popular formulation holding that Third World anti-imperialism is inherently nationalistic, and nationalism is inherently damaging to the rights of women and gays).[24]

Having thus foreclosed upon all options for concrete engagement as mere "reproductions of the relations of oppression," the left has largely neutralized itself, a matter reflected most conspicuously in the applause it bestowed upon Homi K. Bhabha's preposterous 1994 contention that writing, which he likens to "warfare," should be considered the only valid revolutionary act.[25] One might easily conclude that had the "opposition" not conjured up such "postmodernist discourse" on its own initiative, it would have been necessary for the status quo to have invented it. As it is, postmodernist theorists and their postcolonialist counterparts are finding berths at élite universities at a truly astounding rate.[26]

To be fair, it must be admitted that there remain appreciable segments of the left which do not subscribe to the sophistries imbedded in postmodernism's "failure of nerve."[27] Those who continue to assert the value of direct action, however, have for the most part so thoroughly constrained themselves to the realm of symbolic/ritual protest as to render themselves self-nullifying. One is again hardpressed to decipher whether this has been by default or design. While such comportment is all but invariably couched in the lofty—or sanctimonious—terms of "principled pacifism," the practice of proponents often suggests something far less noble.[28]

Nowhere was this more apparent than during the 1999 mass demonstrations against a meeting of the World Trade Organization (WTO) in Seattle.[29] There, notwithstanding much vociferous rhetoric denouncing the spiraling human and environmental costs attending the American-led drive to economic globalization, droves of "responsible" protesters served literally as surrogates for the police, forming themselves into cordons to protect major corporate facilities from suffering such retaliatory "violence" as broken windows.[30] Although this posture was ostensibly adopted because of a commitment to *non*violence on the part of the volunteer cops, adherence to such ideals was peculiarly absent when it came to their manhandling of Black Block anarchists bent upon inflicting minor property damage or otherwise disrupting business as usual in some material sense.[31] In truth, the only parties who appear to have been immunized against the physical impositions of the self-anointed "peacekeepers" were the police, WTO delegates, and other government/corporate officials.[32]

Tellingly, although the fact goes mostly unmentioned by the "peaceful protesters" involved, no less than President Bill Clinton went on television in the aftermath to complement that "great majority of the demonstrators" who, he said, did nothing at all to "interfere with the rights" of WTO delegates to coordinate an acceleration of the planetary rape and mass murder the demonstrations were supposedly intended to forestall.[33] Over the next several months, meetings and workshops were conducted among "dissidents" nationwide, most of them dedicated in whole or in part to devising ways of better containing and controlling Black Blockers at future demonstrations.[34] For its part, the government formed a special state-local-federal "counterterrorism task force" in Oregon, targeting anarchists in the cities of Eugene and Portland—each reputedly a locus of Black Block activity—for "neutralization."[35]

A tidier and more convivial arrangement is hard to imagine. All that was missing was something resembling a realization by participants on either side of the equation that their waltz could be continued neither indefinitely nor with impunity. So intoxicated had they been rendered by their mutual indulgence in the narcotic of American exceptionalism,[36] that they'd lost all touch with laws as basic and natural as cause and effect. "Out there," in the neocolonial hinterlands where the body count of the New World Order must mostly be tallied, no one really cares a whit that a sector of the beneficiary population has chosen to bear a sort of perpetual "moral witness" to the crimes committed against the Third World. What they *do* care about is whether such witnesses translate their professions of "outrage" into *whatever* kinds of actions may be necessary to actually put an end to the horror.[37]

When such action is not forthcoming from within the perpetrator society itself—when in fact those comprising that society's purported opposition can be seen to have mostly *joined* in enforcing at a bedrock level the very order from whence mass murder systematically emanates—a different sort of rule must inevitably come to govern.[38] There is nothing mysterious in this. The proposition is so obvious, uncomplicated and fundamentally just that it has been often and straightforwardly articulated, usually to the accompaniment of cheers, before mass audiences in the U.S. Recall as but one example the line delivered by the actor Lawrence Fishburn, portraying Prohibition-era Harlem gangster Bumpy Johnson in a 1984 movie, *The Cotton Club*: "When you push people around, *some* people [will eventually] push back."[39]

As the makeup of the historical figure upon whom Fishburn's celluloid character was based should have made equally clear, those finally forced into doing the (counter) pushing are unlikely to be "nice guys." Indeed, whoever they might otherwise have been or become, the sheer and unrelenting brutality of the circumstances compelling their response is all but guaranteed to have twisted and deformed their outlooks in some truly hideous ways.[40] Be it noted, moreover, that there is an undeniable symmetry involved when their response is in-kind.[41] "What goes around comes around," it has been said.[42] In the end, "Karma is unavoidable."[43] So it was on September 11, 2001.

Trails of Tears

True, my depiction of the situation remains reductionist. This is so in many respects, perhaps, but no doubt most importantly because the ghosts of Iraq's wasted children were by no means alone in their haunting. There were others present on 9-1-1, *many* others, beginning with the 800,000 Iraqi adults—the great majority of them either elderly or pregnant—known to have died along with their youngsters as a direct result of U.S. sanctions. This makes a total of 1.3 million dead among a population of fewer than twenty million in the decade since the Gulf War supposedly ended.[44] To these must be added another 150,000-or-so Iraqi civilians written off as "collateral damage" during the massive U.S. aerial bombardment defining the war itself.[45]

Then there were the soldiers, conscripts mostly, butchered in the scores of thousands as they fled northward along what became known as the "Highway of Death," out of combat, in full compliance with U.S. demands that they evacuate Kuwait, effectively defenseless against the waves of aircraft thereupon hurled at them by cowards wearing American uniforms.[46] Also at hand were some 10,000 Iraqi guardsmen retreating along a causeway outside Basra, killed in another "turkey shoot" conducted by U.S. forces 24 hours *after* the "war-ending ceasefire" had taken effect.[47] Untold thousands of others were there as well, terrified teenagers, many of them wounded, refused quarter by advancing American troops who disparaged them as "sand niggers," then buried them alive while they pleaded for mercy, using bulldozers specially prepared for the task.[48]

Neither the litany nor the count ends with the suffering of Iraq, of course. Present on 9-1-1 were the many thousands of Palestinians shredded over the years by Israeli pilots flying planes purchased with U.S. funds and dropping cluster bombs manufactured in/provided by the USA.[49] There, too, were the "Intifadists," rockthrowing—or simply fist-waving—Palestinian kids mowed down with numbing regularity by Israeli troops firing hyperlethal ammunition from American-supplied M-16 rifles.[50] Also in the throng were the hundreds massacred in refugee camps like Sabra and Shatila under authority of Israel's onetime defense minister, now prime minister, and always fulltime U.S. accessory, Ariel Sharon.[51] Countries, no less than individuals, will—indeed, must—be judged not only by what they do but by the company they elect as a matter of policy to keep and support (ask the Taliban).

Compared to others with whom the U.S. has bonded since 1950, moreover, the appalling Mr. Sharon might well purport to saintliness. Consider the 300,000 Guatemalans exterminated after the CIA destroyed their democratically-elected government in 1954, installing in its stead a brutal military junta dedicated to making the country safe for the operations of U.S. corporations.[52] Consider, too, the million or more Indonesian victims of a CIA-sponsored 1965 coup in which the Sukarno government was overthrown in favor of a military régime headed by Suharto, a maneuver that led unerringly—and with uninterrupted American support—to the recent genocide in East Timor.[53] The ghosts of these victims were surely present, along with their Iraqi and Palestinian counterparts, on 9-1-1.

No less apparent are the reasons for the presence of the multitudes subjected to numerically lesser but nonetheless comparable carnage by an array of other U.S. client governments: persons tortured and murdered by Shah Mohammad Reza Pahlavi's secret police, the SAVAK, after the CIA-engineered dissolution of Iran's parliamentary system in 1954;[54] more thousands "disappeared" and summarily executed after the CIA-instigated 1973 overthrow of Chile's Allende government and installation of a military junta headed by Augusto Pinochet;[55] thousands more murdered by agents of the ghastly "public safety" programs implemented with U.S. funding and supervision throughout South America during the 1960s;[58] still more who lost their lives to the U.S.-sponsored and orchestrated "contra" war against Nicaragua's Sandinista government during the mid-1980s.[57]

Although the list of such malignancies is still and rapidly lengthening, it is appropriate that we return to the roster of those whose fates were sealed by the U.S. in a far more direct and exclusive fashion. Of them, there is certainly no shortage. They include, quite conspicuously, three million Indochinese, perhaps more, exterminated in the course of America's savage and sustained assaults on Vietnam, Laos and Cambodia during the 1960s and early 1970s.[58] To those claimed by the war itself must be added the ongoing toll taken by America's "stay behind" legacy of landmines, unexploded artillery rounds and cluster bomblets, as well as an environment soaked in carcinogenic-mutogenic defoliants.[59] Added, too, must be those lost to the U.S. default on its pledge to pay reparations of $4 billion in exchange for being allowed to escape with "honor" from a war it started but could not win.[60] America has never been known for paying its bills, either literally or figuratively.

Present, too, on 9-1-1 were the uncounted thousands of noncombatants massacred by U.S. troops at places like No Gun Ri amidst the "police action" conducted in Korea during the early 1950s.[61] As well, there were the hundreds of thousands of Japanese civilians deliberately and systematically burned alive by the Army Air Corps during its massive fire raids on Tokyo and other cities conducted towards the end of World War II.[62] And, to be sure, these victims were accompanied by the dead of Hiroshima and Nagasaki, indiscriminately vaporized by American nuclear bombs in 1945—or left the slow, excruciating deaths resulting from irradiation—not to any military purpose, but rather to the end that the U.S. might demonstrate the technological supremacy of its "kill-power" to anyone thinking of questioning its dominance of the postwar world.[63] For all its official chatter about the necessity of preventing weapons of mass destruction from "falling into the hands of rogue states and terrorists," the U.S. remains the only country ever to use nuclear devices for that reason.[64]

Then there were the Filipinos, as many as a million of them, "extirpated" by American troops at the dawn of the twentieth century, as the U.S., having wrested their island homeland from the relatively benign clutches of the Spanish Empire, set about converting the Philippines into a colony of its own.[65] Nor was there an absence of "Indians," people indigenous to America itself, whose unending agony was enunciated in the silent eloquence of several hundred Lakota babies, mothers and old men dumped into a mass grave—a crude trench, really—after they'd been annihilated by soldiers firing Hotchkiss guns at Wounded Knee in 1890.[66] Punctuating their statement were the victims of a hundred comparable slaughters stretching back in an unbroken line through Weaverville and Yrika to the Washita and Sand Creek, through the Bad Axe to Horseshoe Bend and beyond, all the way to General John Sullivan's campaign against the Senecas in 1794, a grisly affair from which his men returned proudly attired in leggings crafted from the skins of their victims.[67]

Intermixed with those massacred wholesale were many thousands of native people slain piecemeal, hunted down as sport or for the bounties placed upon their scalps at one time or another by every state and territory in the Lower Forty-Eight.[68] Many more thousands could be counted among those who'd perished along the routes of the death marches—the Cherokee "Trail of Tears," for instance, and the "Long Walk" of the Navajos—upon which they were forced at bayonet-point, "removed" from their land so that it might be repopulated by a self-anointedly superior race busily importing itself from Europe.[69] Then there were the millions dead of disease, smallpox mostly, with which they'd been infected, often deliberately, as a means of causing them more literally to "vanish."[70]

In the end, the grim column of stolen lives reached such length that it threatened to disappear into the distance. Towards its end, however, could still be glimpsed a scattering of Wappingers, a small people now mostly forgotten, eradicated by the Dutch in their founding of New Amsterdam, now New York, the victims' severed heads used for a jolly game of kickball along a street near which the WTC would later stand.[71] As for the street upon which this gruesome event took place, it is now named in honor of a prominence by which it would long be flanked, the wall enclosing the city's once-thriving slave market.[72] The lucrative trade in African flesh—that, and extraction of discount labor from such flesh—were, after all, ingredients nearly as vital to forming the U.S. economy as was the "clearing" and expropriation of native land.[73]

Thus, the millions lost to the Middle Passage took their places among their myriad Asian and Native American cousins.[74] They, and all who perished under slavers' whips after being sold at auction in the "New World," were worked or tortured to death on chain gangs after slavery was formally abolished,[75] or were among the thousands lynched during a century-long "festival of violence" undertaken by white Americans—there were six million active members of the Ku Klux Klan in 1929—to ensure that ostensibly "free" blacks remained "in their place" of subjugation.[76] The atrocious record of apartheid South Africa always came in a feeble second to the malignancies of Jim Crow.[77]

Intermixed, too, were a great host of others: the thousands of Chinese coolies imported during the nineteenth century, none of them standing "a Chinaman's chance" of surviving the brutal conditions into which they were impressed while laying track for America's railroads and digging its deep shaft mines throughout the West;[78] the millions of children consigned in each generation to grinding poverty and truncat-ed lifespans across America's vast sprawl of ghettoes, barrios, Indian reservations and migrant labor camps;[79] millions upon millions more assigned the same or worse in the neocolonies of the Third World, the depths of their misery dictated by an unremitting demand for super-profits with which to fuel America's "economic miracle."[80] Truly, there seems no end to it.

Why should "*they*" hate "*us*"? The very question is on its face absurd, delusional, revealing of an aggregate detachment from reality so viru-lent in its evasiveness as to be deemed clinically pathological. Setting aside the wholly-contrived "confusion" professed in the aftermath as to who might be properly included under the headings "we" and "they," the sole legitimate query that might have been posed on 9-1-1 was—and remains—"How could 'they' possibly *not* hate 'us'?" From there, honest interrogators might have gone on to frame two others: "Why did it take 'them' so long to arrive?" and "Why, under the circumstances, did they conduct themselves with such obvious and admirable restraint?"

On Matters of Balance, Proportion and "Security"

There can be no defensible suggestion that those who attacked the Pentagon and WTC on 9-1-1 were seeking to "get even" with the U.S. Still less is there a basis for claims that they "started" something, or that U.S. has anything at all to get even with them for. Quite the contrary. For the attackers to have arguably "evened the score" for Iraqi's dead children alone, it would have been necessary for them to have killed *a hundred times* the number of Americans who actually died.[81] This in itself, however, would have allowed them to attain parity in terms of real numbers. The U.S. population is about fifteen times the size of Iraq's. Hence, for the attackers to have achieved a proportionally equivalent impact, it would have been necessary that they kill some 7.5 *million* Americans.

Even this does not apprehend the reality at issue. For a genuine parity of proportional impact to obtain, it would have been necessary for the attackers to have killed 7.5 million American *children*. To inflict an overall parity of suffering for what has been done to Iraq since 1990—taking into account the million-odd dead Iraqi adults—they would have had to kill roughly 22.5 million Americans. The instrumentality by which such carnage would have been dispensed would presumably have been not just the three "300,000 pound cruise missiles" employed on September 11,[82] but also the other 49,997 airborne explosives necessary for the attackers to break even in terms of the number of bombs and missiles the U.S. expended on Iraq's cities *after* their air defense systems had been completely "suppressed."[83]

The targets, moreover, would not have been restricted to such obvious elements of what America's general staff habitually refer to as "command and control infrastructure" as the Pentagon and the WTC. Rather the attackers of 9-1-1 would have followed the well-established U.S. pattern of "surgically" obliterating sewage, water sanitation and electrical generation plants, food production/storage capacity, hospitals, pharmaceutical production facilities, communications centers and much more upon which Americans are no less dependent than Iraqis for survival.[84] The result, aside from mass death, would be a surviving population wracked by malnutrition and endemic disease (just as in Iraq today).

Framed in these terms, it is immediately obvious that, were the U.S. somehow forced to compensate proportionally and in lives for the damage it has so consistently wrought upon other peoples over the past two centuries, it would run out of people long before it ran out of compensatory obligation. Indeed, applying such standards of "pay back" vis-à-vis American Indians alone would require a lethal reduction in the U.S. population, using biological agents and comparable means, of between 96 and 99 percent.[85] Hence, no one other than the most extravagant of America's many network propagandists has claimed that the attacks upon the Pentagon and WTC were carried out as part of an effort to extract anything remotely resembling a genuine equivalency in suffering.[86]

It follows that 9-1-1 was a mostly symbolic act, a desperate bid to command attention on the part of those so utterly dehumanized and devalued in the minds of average Americans that the very fact of their existence has never been deemed worthy of a moment's contemplation. On the basis of the September 11 "wake up call"—and perhaps *only* on this basis—could they position themselves to "send a message" standing the least chance of being heard by the U.S. body politic. Whether it might be understood is an altogether different matter, given the media's predictable, craven and across-the-board compliance with official demands that the attackers' carefully-articulated explanations of their actions *not* be placed before the public.[87]

Still, at one level, the message delivered was uncensorably straightforward and simple, assuming the form of a blunt question: "How does it feel?" The query was and remains on its face one well worth posing. Not since its own Civil War ended in 1865, after all, has the U.S. been directly subject to a serious taste of what it so lavishly and routinely dishes out to others (no, Pearl Harbor doesn't count; it is located in Polynesia, not North America).[88] Small wonder that, for most Americans, including even a decided majority of the troops who've served in "combat" since Vietnam, the grisly panoramas of war, mass murder and genocide have become sanitized to the point of sterility, imbued with no more concrete reality than any other "home entertainment" offering.[89]

How else to explain the popularity of increasingly technicalized military jargon like "kill ratios," "force degradation" and "collateral damage" among the general public?[90] How else to understand the public's willingness to accept the absurd proposition that a teenager safely ensconced at a computer console while launching missiles meant to slaughter unseen/unknown others at a thousand miles distance somehow or another qualifies as a "hero"?[91] Americans have in effect collectively lost their grip, and with it all sense of the charnel stench wafting from the policies, procedures and priorities they've consistently endorsed. The attacks of 9-1-1, while certainly designed to inflict the maximum material damage possible, given their very limited scope,[92] were even more clearly intended to force U.S. citizens into some semblance of reacquaintence with the kind of excruciation their country—

and thus they themselves—have become far too accustomed to dispensing with impunity.

This brings a second level of the attackers' message into focus. If it could be anticipated that Americans would find it exceedingly painful to undergo a heavy bombing of even the most token sort—as surely they would—it could also be expected that they would begin casting about with considerable urgency for a way of ensuring that such "terrorism" would not be repeated. This, in turn, suggested that U.S. citizens might at last be receptive to embarking upon the only route to attainment of this worthy objective, a trajectory marked by Noam Chomsky's formulation, advanced shortly after the attacks, that "if you really want to put an end terrorism, you have to begin by no longer participating in it."[93] Or, more sharply, "stop killing their babies," as the matter was framed by Georgia State law professor Natsu Saito a short while later.[94]

At base, what the attackers communicated was the proposition that, from now on, if Americans wish their own children to be happy and safe, they going to have to allow the children of other peoples an equivalent safety and chance for happiness. In effect, Americans will have to accord a respect for the rights of others equal to that which they demand for themselves, valuing "Other" youngsters as much as they do their own.[95] Finally, and emphatically, the U.S. is going to have to abide by the rules of civilized behavior articulated in international law (its own citizens shouldering the responsibility of seeing to it that this is so).[96] The character of a society rejecting such eminently reasonable terms as being "unfair" should be to a large extent self-revealing.

Unfortunately, this is precisely what the preponderance of Americans have done. Refusing the prospect that the collectivity of their own attitudes and behavior made something like 9-1-1 inevitable, they have instead bleated their "innocence" for all to hear, meanwhile reacting like a figurative Jeffrey Dahmer, enraged because the latest of his many hapless victims has displayed the effrontery of slapping his face.[97] Witness, if you will, the frenzied demands accruing from every major media outlet that those suspected of involvement in the 9-1-1 attacks—or of supporting the attackers in some fashion—be subjected to "complete extermination."[98] Witness as well the winks and chuckles with which commentators from "right" and "left" alike greeted photographic evidence that American surrogates in Afghanistan have been gleefully castrating and otherwise mutilating captured enemy soldiers before summarily executing them.[99]

Once again—this time in the name of a "crusade" to "rid the world of evil"[100]—Americans have enthusiastically embraced a policy devolving upon the systematic and potentially massive perpetration of war crimes and crimes against humanity. Here, a sublime irony presents itself: Since by no morally-coherent standard—moral assessment being necessary since the term employed is exclusive to the vernacular of theology/morality[101]—can the policy at issue be construed as anything *but* "evil," claims that it has been implemented for the above-stated purpose amount to little other than announcements of suicidal intent.[102] Still more ironic is the fact that the situation in many ways requires a more literal than metaphorical interpretation.

"Out there," amidst the seething, bleeding psychic wastelands spawned by the unspeakable arrogance of U.S. imperial pretension, someone is quietly awaiting the definitive answers to questions of whether and to what extent Americans might respond constructively to the warnings posted on the WTC and Pentagon. A grim smile upon his face, her finger upon the trigger, s/he is almost certainly mouthing words to the effect of, "Go ahead, punk. Make my day."[103] What will it be next time? A far larger and more destructive wave of suicide bombings? Dispersal of biological or chemical agents? Detonation of one or more portable nuclear devices? All of these?[104] The object, no doubt, will be to attain something much closer to bona fide payback for what the U.S. has done, and is doing even now.

The straw-like "option" at which the great majority of Americans are presently grasping in a transparent attempt to restore their sense of exemption from responsibility—the notion that a combination of military force, intelligence gathering and "tightened domestic security" can ultimately immunize them from the consequences of their country's actions (or their own inactions)—is purely delusional.[105] Short of setting out to kill every man, woman and child in the Third World, little can be expected of the military in terms of preventing "terrorist" responses to its own crimes. Suggestions that the CIA can somehow alter the situation, rendering applications of military force "surgically" effective against "the terrorist infrastructure" are laughable, as should be evident from the abysmal failure of the agency's Phoenix program, undertaken for precisely the same purpose in Vietnam.[106]

Claims that measures like those described in the recent "Homelands Security Act" will produce the desired prophylactic effect are the most vacuous of all.[107] The "internal security model" most often cited by "experts" for emulation by the U.S. is that of Israel, a country which, although it has converted itself into a veritable garrison state over the past thirty years, has been spectacularly *un*able to prevent determined attackers from striking almost at will.[108] All that can be expected of such "defense" initiatives is repression of what little actual political liberty had been left to residents of "the land of the free" by the dawn of the new millennium.[109]

The "Miracle of Immaculate Genocide"

In the final analysis, it is quite reasonable that fulfillment of America's now fervent quest for security be made contingent upon its willingness to commence a process of profound national introspection that, alone, will enable it to fundamentally rework its relationship(s) with those upon whom it has heretofore proven so cavalier in visiting the worst sorts of oppression. There is much militating against attainment of so positive a development, however, not least the fact that, in the U.S., a pathology often associated with clinical disorder has mutated long since into what can best be described as a normative social condition.[110] "There are," as Susan Griffin has observed, "whole disciplines, institutions, rubrics in [American] culture which serve as categories of denial."[111]

The mentality involved is in some respects multifaceted and complex, but always self-serving and convenient, each facet serving mainly to augment or complete its ostensible antithesis, producing a whole remarkable for nothing so much as the virulence of its intractability.[112] Writing of the holocaust perpetrated by U.S. troops in the Philippines a century ago—an onslaught entailing orders that every male Filipino over the age of ten be slaughtered, and the resulting deaths of one in every six inhabitants on the island of Luzon[113]—historian Stuart Creighton Miller describes "the tendency of highly patriotic Americans...to [vociferously] deny such abuses and even to assert that they could never exist in their country."[114] The pattern is unmistakably similar to that exhibited by severe alcoholics who, despite all evidence of the damage their behavior has caused, chronically insist that "the opposite of everything is true."[115]

More subtle than the characteristic refusal of "conservatives" to allow mere facts to in any way alter their core presumptions was/is the complementary nature of the "alternative" interpretation(s) most often posed by their "progressive" opponents. Noting that the Philippines genocide was a matter of public knowledge by 1901,[116] Creighton Miller goes on to observe that collective "amnesia over the horrors of the war of conquest...set in early, during the summer of 1902."[117] He then concludes by reflecting upon how "anti-imperialists aided the process by insisting that the conflict and its attendant atrocities had been the result of a conspiracy by a handful of leaders who carried out, through deceit and subterfuge, the policy and means of expansion overseas against the will of the majority of their countrymen."[118]

> By refusing to acknowledge that most Americans had been bitten by the same bug that afflicted Roosevelt, Lodge, and Beveridge, anti-imperialists were letting the people off the hook and in their own way preserving the American sense of innocence. Unfortunately, the man in the street shared the dreams of world-power status, martial glory, and future wealth that would follow expansion. When the dream soured, the American people neither reacted with very much indignation, nor did they seem to retreat to their cherished political principles. If anything, they seemed to take their cues from their leader in the White House by first putting out of mind all the sordid episodes in the conquest, and then forgetting the entire war itself.[119]

So it was then, the more so today. Contemporary conservatives, whenever they can be momentarily boxed into conceding one or another unsavory aspect of America's historical record, are forever insisting that whatever they've admitted can be "properly" understood only when viewed as an "exception to the rule," an "aberration," "atypical" to the point of "anamolousness."[120] None have shown a readiness to address the question of exactly how many such "anomalies" might be required before they can be said to comprise "the rule" itself. When pressed, conservatives invariably retreat into a level of diversionary polemic excusable at best on elementary school playgrounds, arguing that anything "we" have done is somehow excused by allegations that "they" have done things just as bad.[121]

Progressives, on the other hand, while acknowledging many of America's more reprehensible features, have become far more refined in offering hook-free analyses than they were in 1902. No longer much preoccupied with such crudities as "conspiracy theory,"[122] they have become quite monolithic in attributing all things negative to handy abstractions like "capitalism," "the state," "structural oppression," and, yes, "the hierarchy."[123] Hence, they have been able to conjure what might be termed the "miracle of immaculate genocide," a form of genocide, that is, in which—apart from a few amorphous "decision-making élites"[124]—there are no actual perpetrators and no one who might "really" be deemed culpable by reason of complicity. The parallels between this "cutting edge" conception and the defense mounted by postwar Germans—including the nazis at Nuremberg—are as eerie as they are obvious.[125]

The implications of this were set forth in stark relief during the aftermath of 9-1-1, when it was first suggested that a decided majority of those killed in the WTC attack might be more accurately viewed as "little Eichmanns"—that is, as a cadre of faceless bureaucrats and technical experts who had willingly (and profitably) harnessed themselves to the task making America's genocidal world order hum with maximal efficiency—than as "innocents."[126] The storm of outraged exception taken by self-proclaimed progressives to this simple observation has been instructive, to say the least. The objections have been mostly transparent in their diversionary intent, seeking as they have to focus attention exclusively on janitors, firemen and food service workers *rather than* the much larger number of corporate managers, stock brokers, bond traders, finance and systems analysts, etc., among those killed.[127]

A few have complained of the "cold-bloodedness" and "insensitivity" embodied, not in the vocations pursued by the latter group, but in describing their attitudes/conduct as having been in any way analogous to Eichmann's. Left unstated, however, is the more accurate term we should employ in characterizing a representative 30-year-old foreign exchange trader who, in full knowledge that every cent of his lavish commissions derived from the starving flesh of defenseless Others, literally wallowed in self-indulgent excess, playing the big shot, priding himself on being "a sharp dresser" and the fact that "money spilled from his pockets...flowed like crazy...[spent] on the black BMW and those clothes—forgetting to pack ski clothes for a Lake Tahoe trip, dropping $1,000 on new stuff," and so on.[128] As a "cool guy" with a "warm heart"? A "good family man"? Just an "ordinary," "average" or "normal" fellow who "happened to strike it rich"?[129] How then are we to describe Eichmann himself?[130]

Clearly, either the devastating insights concerning "the banality of evil" offered by Hannah Arendt in her 1963 study, *Eichmann in Jerusalem*, have yet to penetrate the consciousness of many American progressives,[131] or American progressives are in the main every bit as mired in the depths of denial as the most hidebound of their conservative counterparts.[132] Irrespective of whether there is an appreciable segment of the U.S. population prepared to look the matter in the face, however, the same condition of willful blindness cannot be said to prevail throughout much of the rest of the world.[133]

Excusing one's self for one's crimes is never a legitimate prerogative, nor are attempts to hide or explain them away. This is all the more true while the crimes are being repeated. Neither justice, forgiveness nor exegesis can be self-administered or bestowed. Of this, there should be no doubt in a country where the principle of "victims' rights" has lately been enshrined as an article of juridical faith.[134] Those who comprised the "chickens" of 9-1-1 will have their say, and it will ultimately be definitive. In this connection, the only real question confronting the U.S. polity is how in the future it will be necessary for them to say it. And that, rightly enough, will be entirely contingent upon the extent and decisiveness with which Americans prove capable of factoring such voices into the calculus of their personal and national self-concepts.

In the Alternative

In 1945, addressing a strikingly similar context of national criminality and denial—albeit one in which the state and its collaborating corporate institutions had been pounded into physical submission by external forces—the philosopher Karl Jaspers set forth a schematic of culpability, acceptance of which he suggested might allow both Germans and Germany to redeem themselves.[135] Internalizing Jaspers' four-part formulation stands to yield comparable results in America, for Americans, and thus for everyone else as well. It is therefore well worth summarizing here (in a somewhat revised form reflecting enunciation of the Nuremberg Doctrine and other subsequent developments).[136]

• First, there is the matter of *criminal guilt*. States, corportions and other such entities, while they may be criminally-conceived, and employed for criminal purposes, do not themselves commit crimes. Crimes—that is, violations of customary or black letter law—are committed by individuals, those who conceive, employ or serve state and corporate institutions. Those alleged to have committed specific offenses are subject to personal prosecution and punishment.[137] If the transgressions of which they stand accused are of a sort sanctioned either explicitly or implicitly by the state under which authority they've acted, their prosecution cannot as a rule occur before tribunals controlled by that same state.[138] Nor, if mere vengeance is to be avoided, can such tribunals be placed as a rule under control of the immediate victims. Where crimes of state and/or state-sanctioned crime are at issue, the only appropriate judicial forum is an impartially-composed international court.[139]

• Second, there is the matter of *political guilt*. It is the collective responsibility of the citizens in a modern state to ensure by *all* means necessary that its government adheres to the rule of law, not just domestically but internationally.[140] There are no bystanders. No one is entitled to an "apolitical" exemption from such obligation.[141] Where default occurs, either by citizen endorsement of official criminality or by the failure of citizens to *effectively* oppose it, liability is incurred by all. Although degrees of onus may be assigned along a continuum traversing the distance from those who most actively embraced the crime to those who most actively opposed it, *none* are "innocent."[142] The victims thus hold an unequivocal right to receive reparation, compensation and, where possible, complete restitution in ways and amounts deemed equitable and fair, not in the estimation of those liable, but in the judgment of an impartial international court.[143]

• Third, there is the matter of *moral guilt*. While it may prove impractical in settings where crimes of state are at issue to try all who have committed offenses (whether by way of perpetration, or by complicity), those who go unprosecuted are not thereby absolved.[144] To them belongs the public stigma associated with their deeds and consequent existential confrontation with themselves. In this, there can be no recourse to the supposed mitigation embodied in the apology that one has "merely done one's job" or "just followed orders."[145] Still less can exoneration be found in prevarications concerning "human nature"; if it were the "nature" of humans to engage in such acts, *everyone* would do so, and, self-evidently, not everyone does.[146] Each individual is thus personally responsible for his/her acts, "including the execution of political and military orders," and thus socially/morally accountable for them.

• Finally, there is the matter of what Jaspers termed *metaphysical guilt*. This rests most heavily upon those who, while not guilty of any specific offense, averted their eyes, sitting by while crimes against humanity were committed in their name.[147] It encompasses as well all who, while we may have registered opposition in some form or degree, did less than we might have—failing thereby to risk our lives unconditionally—in our struggle to prevent or halt such crimes. Therein, incontestably, lies the guilt shared by all who opt to remain alive while Others are systematically subjugated, dispossessed, tortured and murdered.[148]

Those who would reject such criteria out-of-hand might do well to bear in mind that they join company thus with Carl Schmitt, a leading light among the nazi legal philosophers, who was among the first to pronounce them "beneath attention."[149] Others, seeking to neutralize the implications by equivocation, insisting that while a Jasperian schema "makes sense for Germans," the "good offsets the bad" where America and Americans are concerned, should be aware that this is precisely the argument offered by Germany's "New Right"—neonazis, by any other name—with regard to the Third Reich itself.[150] If it can be agreed that the *Hitlerstaat* remains impervious to rehabilitation, regardless of its well-documented instigation of expressways and Volkswagens, the same holds true for the U.S., irrespective of the supposed triumphs of "American civilization."[151]

Such issues must be faced straightforwardly, without dissembling, if Americans are ever to hold rightful title to the "good conscience" they've so long laid claim to owning. How they are to respond to what stares back at them from the proverbial mirror is an altogether different question, however. Transformation from beastliness to beauty can be neither instantaneous nor, in terms of its retroactive undoing, complete.[152] There is no painless, privilege-preserving pill that can be taken to effect a quick fix of what ails the U.S., no petition, no manifesto, no song or candle-lit vigil that will suffice. The terms of change must and will be harsh, inevitably so, given the propensity of those who seek to prevent it to gauge their success by the rotting corpses of toddlers.[153] This truth, no matter its inconvenience to those snugly situated within the comfort zones of political pretense,[154] is all that defines the substance of meaningful struggle.[155]

It cannot happen all at once, but it must begin somewhere, and for this there is need of nothing so much as a focal point. That, and external assistance, given Americans' abject inexperience in undertaking projects entailing the least hint of humility. Fortunately, an "action-agenda" combining both elements readily presents itself. Americans must demonstrate, conclusively and concretely, that they have at last attained a sufficient degree of self-awareness to subordinate themselves both individually and *as a country* to the rule of law.[156] Such an initiative, *only* such, and then only if it is pressed by every available means, is likely to reassure those who came on 9-1-1 that the seeds of Jaspers' wisdom have at last taken root in the U.S. to an extent making future such attacks unnecessary.

All who fancy themselves progressive—in common with every conservative who has ever mouthed the lofty rhetoric of "law enforcement"—can start by inaugurating a concerted drive to compel their government to reverse its 1986 repudiation of the compulsory jurisdiction previously held over U.S. foreign policy by the International Court of Justice (ICJ).[157] Concomitantly, Americans can set about such action as is necessary to ensure that their country joins the rest of the world in placing itself under the jurisdiction of the newly-established International Criminal Court (ICC).[158] Massive international support and assistance is virtually guaranteed to accrue to any such U.S. citizen initiative.

Following a parallel track, although much of it falls within the domain of *jus cogens* ("customary law") and are thus enforceable against the U.S. without its agreement,[159] an important gesture would be embodied in Americans taking such action as is necessary to compel their government to ratify those elements of international public and humanitarian law it has, often alone, heretofore refused to endorse. High on this lengthy list,[160] is the 1948 Convention on Prevention and Punishment of the Crime of Genocide, to which the U.S. presently claims a "sovereign right" to self-exemption from compliance.[161] Recent additions include the International Convention on the Rights of the Child (1989)[162] and the International Treaty Banning the Use, Production, Stockpiling and Transfer of Anti-Personnel Mines (1998).[163]

Most important of all—given the abysmal record of the U.S. when it comes to bringing even those *acknowledged* to have perpetrated war crimes and crimes against humanity before its domestic bar of justice,[164] given the fact that only the most token punishments have ever been visited upon those few who have for cosmetic reasons been domestically tried and convicted of such offenses,[165] and given the imperative of establishing that Americans are finally serious about adhering to the law—such action as is necessary must be taken to compel delivery of an initial selection of present/former U.S. officials for prosecution by the ICC.[166]

Here, although the list of imminently eligible candidates is all but overwhelming, a mere threesome might constitute an adequate preliminary sample. The first, on the basis of her earlier-noted statement concerning the fate of Iraq's children and administration of attendant policies, should be former Secretary of State Albright. Second, for reasons explained quite well by Christopher Hitchens and others, should be former Secretary of State Henry Kissinger.[167] The third should be current North Carolina Senator Jesse Helms, the bellicosity of whose threats to visit "dire consequences" upon the world community "in the event a single American is ever indicted" for violating the laws of war and/or international humanitarian law exemplifies the manner in which the U.S. has for decades thwarted implementation of procedures for the peaceful resolution of international disputes (this in itself offers prima facie evidence of Helms' complicity in the more direct crimes perpetrated by his codefendants).[168]

Prosecution of these three major U.S. criminals before the ICC would pave the way for a series of such trials, targeting as in the Nuremberg proceedings representative defendants drawn from each of the interactive "classes" of American offenders—governmental, military, corporate, scientific and so on—comprising the élite decisionmaking stratum of America's New World Order.[169] Collaterally, the criminal trials would in themselves lay a superb evidentiary groundwork for consideration of international tort claims by the ICJ, in many cases the sole procedure through which issues concerning indemnification of America's proliferate victims are likely ever to be satisfactorily addressed.[170] It may also be anticipated that, under these conditions, the principles realized in international fora will be absorbed by the U.S. judiciary, as they were in postwar Germany, to an extent sufficient for bona fide prosecutions of America's war criminals and other such terrorists to at last commence in domestic courts.[171]

Against this backdrop, otherwise preposterous assertions that recourse to "the World Court is the way to proceed" in halting America's persistently murderous aggression take on a certain coherence. The question begged in such formulations, as they stand, and as they've stood all along, concerns enforcement. A court is not a police force. Less, is it an army. Neither its jurisdiction nor its judgments are self-executing. Its decrees are vacuous without a means of exacting compliance.[172] Should it turn out that Americans were prodded by the pain inflicted on 9-1-1 to finally begin shouldering the responsibility of forcing their government to obey the law—with *all* that this implies—it may be said that a world historic corner was turned on that date. Should this not prove to be the case, however, others, especially those Others most egregiously victimized by American lawlessness, will have no real alternative but to try and do the job themselves. And, in the collectivity of their civic default, Americans, no more than the Good Germans of 1945, can have little legitimate complaint as to how they may have to go about it.[173]

To See Things Clearly

If the prescription sketched out in the preceding section offers the prospect of improving the level of security enjoyed by all Americans—mainly by drastically reducing the need for it—it contains a range of other benefits as well. Salient among them is what, with respect to Germany, Harvard political scientist Daniel Jonah Goldhagen has described as an "internationalization of the 'national' history."[174] By this, he meant a process through which the country's apprehension of its past has been subjected to such intensive and sustained scrutiny/contributions by others that the "collective, narcissistic self-exaltation" typically marking such narratives has been preempted. This, Goldhagen concludes, has enabled contemporary Germans to attain a far more accurate—and thus healthier—conception of themselves than they were likely ever to have achieved on their own.[175]

It is exactly this kind of aggregate self-understanding that Jaspers posited as being essential to a process through which the varieties of guilt he'd so carefully delineated could be transformed into their antithesis, creating what he hoped might constitute an insurmountable psychointellectual barrier against any wholesale resurgence of the mentality from which Germany's communality of guilt had emerged.[176] There is no reason to assume that the idea holds less utility for Americans today than it did for Germans then, or that the rewards for the world of America's figurative denazification would be any less substantial than those manifest in the more literal German process.

A wealth of information necessary to redefining the character of the "American experiment" can be expected to take center stage in the above-described judicial proceedings, whether international or domestic, criminal or civil. Much of it will prove to have been available all along, publicly displayed but usually distorted beyond recognition, its meaning neatly buried in the texts, rendered alternately in terms of triumphalism or apology, that from the first have comprised America's historical canon and its popular counterpart(s).[177] Reinterpreted through the lens of law, detailed at trial by those charged with assessing the culpability of individual defendants and/or the degree of responsibility inhering in the polity that empowered them, even that which was "known" will stand exposed in the glare of an entirely different light.

Such developments represent a good start, but by no means an end point or culmination. Even the most honest and penetrating of prosecutorial presentations is by nature erratic and uneven, skewed by the parameters of its purpose to focus in fragmentary fashion upon certain usually topical matters, emphasizing, deemphasizing or ignoring issues of wider historical concern without regard to historiographical requirements.[178] The record made during the course of any trial, and the conclusions formally drawn from it, must therefore be compared to/combined with those obtained in related proceedings to create a composite. This overarching iteration of what has been "discovered" through adjudication must then be broken down again in various ways, sifted and refined, its implications adduced and contextualized (that is, reinterpreted by way of their connection with/dissimilarity from "broader"— i.e., historically deeper and more diverse—processes or sequences of events).[179]

Plainly, it will be forever premature to proclaim the consummation of such a project before the most thoroughgoing reconstruction of American history, and thus a complete resignification of the codes of meaning and value residing within it, has been achieved. With this in mind, the problem confronting those who would accept it is how best to approach so monumental a devoir. A method is needed by which to deal with the surfeit of data at hand, arranging it in ways which lend coherence to its otherwise nebulous mass, tracing not just its outer contours but the inner trajectories that gave them shape, coaxing it to divulge truths too long denied.

Notes

1. All told, citizens of 86 different countries are reported to have numbered among the dead; U.S. Attorney General John Ashcroft, press briefing carried on CNBC, Nov. 29, 2001.

2. Malcolm X with Alex Haley, *The Autobiography of Malcolm X* (New York: Ballantine, 1973) pp. 300–1.

3. Ramsey Clark, *The Impact of Sanctions on Iraq: The Children are Dying* (Washington, D.C.: Maisonneuve Press, 1996).

4. Ramsey Clark and Others, *War Crimes: A Report on U.S. War Crimes Against Iraq* (Washington, D.C.: Maisonneuve Press, 1992) pp. 22, 35, 53–4. Also see Jack Calhoun, "UN: Iraq Bombed Back to Stone Age," Manchester Guardian, Apr. 3, 1991; Patrick E. Tyler, "Disease Spirals in Iraq as Embargo Takes Its Toll," *New York Times*, June 24, 1991; Barston Gellman, "Storm Damage in the Gulf: U.S. Strategy Went Beyond Strictly Military Targets," *Washington Post Weekly*, July 8–14, 1991.

5. Quoted by Noam Chomsky in his essay, "'What We Say Goes': The Middle East in the New World Order," in Cynthia Peters, ed., *Collateral Damage: The New World Order at Home and Abroad* (Boston: South End Press, 1992) p. 52.

6. Among the more noteworthy of such efforts is Edward S. Herman's and Noam Chomsky's *Manufacturing Consent: The Political Economy of the Mass Media* (New York: Pantheon, 1988). Also see Chomsky's *Necessary Illusions: Thought Control in Democratic Societies* (Boston: South End Press, 1989); Herman's *The Myth of the Liberal Media: An Edward Herman Reader* (New York: Peter Lang, 1999); Noam Chomsky, Laura Nader, Immanuel Wallerstein, R.C. Lewontin, Ira Katznelson and Howard Zinn, *The Cold War and the University: Toward an Intellectual History of the Cold War Years* (New York: New Press, 1998).

7. Halliday's actions, statements, and the data upon which they were based form the core of Ramsey Clark's *Challenge to Genocide: Let Iraq Live* (Washington, D.C.: International Action Center, 1998); see esp. pp. 79, 127, 191.

8. The interview aired on May 12, 1996.

9. Quoted in William Blum, *Rogue State: A Guide to the World's Only Superpower* (Monroe, ME: Common Courage Press, 2000) pp. 5–6.

10. See Holly Sklar, "Brave New World Order," in Peters, *Collateral Damage*, pp. 3–46.

11. Eugene Davidson, *The Trial of the Germans, 1945–1946* (New York: Macmillan, 1966).

12. For a good overview of the arguments, see Karl Jaspers, *The Question of German Guilt* (New York: Fordham University Press, 2001).

13. See the chapter entitled "The Triumph of the Bombers" in H. Bruce Franklin's *War Stars: The Superweapon and the American Imagination* (New York: Oxford University Press, 1988) pp. 101–11.

14. For purposes of comparison, see Michael Stolleis, *Law Under the Swastika: Studies on Legal History in Nazi Germany* (Chicago: University of Chicago Press, 1998).

15. For theory, see David Dellinger, *Revolutionary Nonviolence* (Indianapolis: Bobbs-Merrill, 1971); Gene Sharp, *The Dynamics of Nonviolent Action*, 3 vols., (Boston: Porter Sargent, 1973); Barbara Epstein, *Political Protest and Cultural Revolution: Nonviolent Direct Action in the 1970s and 1980s* (Berkeley: University of California Press, 1991).

16. This is covered rather well in the chapter entitled "The Home Front" in Chomsky's *Deterring Democracy* (New York: Hill and Wang, 1992) pp. 69–88. Also see the chapter entitled "Power in the Domestic Arena," in his *Rogue States: The Rule of Force in World Affairs* (Cambridge, MA: South End Press, 2000) pp. 188–97.

17. Former Black Panther Bin Wahad served 19 years in a New York maximum security prison after being falsely convicted of attempted murder in 1971; Dhoruba bin Wahad, "War Within," in Jim Fletcher, Tanaquil Jones and Sylvère Lotringer, eds., *Still Black, Still Strong: Survivors of the U.S. War Against Black Revolutionaries* (New York: Semiotext(e), 1993) pp. 9–56. Ji Jaga, another former Panther, served 27 years in California before his false conviction was overturned; Jack Olsen, *Last Man Standing: The Tragedy and Triumph of Geronimo Pratt* (Garden City, NY: Doubleday, 2000). American Indian Movement member Peltier continues to served a life sentence in federal prison despite official admissions that the evidence used to convict him was false; Peter Matthiessen, *In the Spirit of Crazy Horse: The Story of Leonard Peltier* (New York: Viking, [2nd ed.] 1991). Former Panther Abu-Jamal is on death row in Pennsylvania; Daniel R. Williams, *Executing Justice: An Inside Account of the Case of Mumia Abu-Jamal* (New York: St. Martin's Press, 2001). Overall, see my and J.J. Vander Wall's *Cages of Steel: The Politics of Imprisonment in the United States* (Washington, D.C.: Maisonneuve Press, 1992).

18. See the section entitled "Race and the Death Penalty," in Amnesty International, *The United States of America: Rights for All* (New York: Amnesty International, 1998) pp. 108–12.

19. For comparative incarceration rates, see Marc Mauer, *The Race to Incarcerate* (New York: Free Press, 1999) pp. 21–2. On corporatization, see Daniel Burton-Rose, Dan Pens and Paul Wright, eds., *The Celling of America: An Inside Look at the American Prison Industry* (Monroe, ME: Common Courage Press, 1998); Joel Dyer, *The Perpetual Prisoner Machine: How America Profits from Crime* (Boulder, CO: Westview Press, 2000).

20. At the point American yuppies launched their drive to abolish smoking in public places—a social norm mainly among poor people/communities of color—it was estimated that "passive smoking" resulted in the deaths of as many as 3,000 people per year. The number could have as easily been set 3 or 3 million since there was at the time no scientific confirmation of any negative effects attending exposure to "environmental" tobacco smoke; see the chapter entitled "Smoke Exposure and Health," in Roy J.

Shephard, *The Risks of Passive Smoking* (New York: Oxford University Press, 1982) pp. 95–108. After twenty years of intensive and well-funded research—attended by increasingly stringent bans on ash-trays—the situation remains essentially the same; see Peter N. Lee's "Difficulties in Determining Health Effects Related to Environmental Tobacco Smoke," in Ronald A. Watson's and Mark Seldon's coedited and currently definitive *Environmental Tobacco Smoke* (Washington, D.C.: CRS Press, 2001) pp. 1–24.

21. Stephen Burrington and Veronika Thiebach, *Take Back the Streets: How to Protect Communities from Asphalt and Traffic* (Boston: Conservation Law Foundation, [3rd ed.] 1998).

22. Clark, *Sanctions*; Jean Baudrillard, *The Gulf War Did Not Take Place* (Bloomington: Indiana University Press, 1995).

23. Terry Eagleton, *The Illusions of Postmodernism* (Oxford, UK: Blackwell, 1996) esp. pp. 93–5.

24. The eurofeminist equation of nationalism to "masculinist dominance" commenced at least as early as Barbara Burris' "The Fourth World Manifesto," in Anne Koedt, ed., *Radical Feminism* ([Chicago: Quadrangle, 1973] pp. 322–57), and has seen continued refinement in essays such as those collected by Miranda Davis in her *Third World/Second Sex: Women's Struggles and National Liberation* (London: Zed Books, 1983); those collected by Roberta Hamilton and Michèle Barrett in their *The Politics of Diversity: Feminism, Marxism and Nationalism* (London: Verso, 1987); and, most recently, attempts to discredit the work of Third World anticolonial theorists like Frantz Fanon spearheaded by main-streamers such as Diana Fuss (see, e.g., her "Interior Colonies: Frantz Fanon and the Politics of Identification," in Nigel C. Gibson, ed., *Rethinking Fanon: The Continuing Dialogue* [Amherst, NY: Humanity Books, 1999] pp. 294–328).

25. Homi K. Bhabha, "Interrogating Identity: Frantz Fanon and the postcolonial prerogative" in his *The Location of Culture* (New York: Routledge, 1994) pp. 40–65. Also see Bart Moore-Gilbert, *Postcolonial Theory: Contexts, Practices, Politics* (London: Verso, 1997) pp. 138–9.

26. Bhabha himself—who has yet to produce a booklength manuscript—was recently hired as a reigning "star" by the literature department at Harvard; New York Times, Nov. 11, 2001.

27. Terry Eagleton, *The Illusions of Postmodernism* (Oxford, UK: Blackwell, 1996) p. 19. For a different and even sharper framing, see John Zerzan's "The Catastrophe of Postmodernism," *Anarchy*, Fall 1991.

28. For a reasonably substantial critique, see my and Mike Ryan's *Pacifism as Pathology: Reflections on the Role of Armed Struggle in North America* (Winnipeg: Arbeiter Ring, 1998).

29. The WTO was prefigured by the Trilateral Commission during the 1970s; see Holly Sklar, ed., *Trilateralism: The Trilateral Commission and Elite Planning for World Government* (Boston: South End Press, 1980). On its evolution during the 1990s, see Bernard Hoekman and Michael Kostecki, *The Political Economy of the World Trading System: From GATT to WTO* (New York: Oxford University Press, 2001).

30. See generally, Janet Thomas, *The Battle for Seattle: The Story Behind and Beyond the WTO Demonstration* (Golden, CO: Fulcrum, 2001); Alexander Cockburn, Jeffrey St. Clair and Allen Sekula, *Five Days That Shook the World: Seattle and Beyond* (London: Verso, 2001).

31. The inconsistency is not especially unusual; see my and Ryan's *Pacifism*, p. 124 (note 135).

32. This, too, is by no means unusual; ibid., pp. 21–2.

33. The statement was made in remarks carried by the major television networks on the evening of Dec. 1, 1997, and quoted in *USA Today* the following morning.

34. Some of this is mentioned in concluding chapters of Thomas, *Battle for Seattle*, and Cockburn, St. Clair and Sekula, *Five Days*; also see the essays collected in George Katsiaficas and Eddie Yuen in their coedited volume, *The Battle for Seattle: Debating Capitalist Globalization and the WTO* (New York: Soft Skull Press, 2001). It is worth noting that, while "dissidents" were spending their time trying to figure out ways of preventing a repeat of the Black Block's actions, establishmentarian news organs were acknowledging that "the protesters' message was heard...because of...the violence [sic, emphasis added]"; see "The Siege of Seattle," *Newsweek*, Dec. 13, 1999.

35. Rob Thaxton, an individual associated with Eugene's Anarchist Action Collective (AAC), shortly received a 7-year prison sentence for throwing a rock during a street demonstration. By June 2001, two others, Craig Marshall ("Critter") and Jeffrey Luers ("Free"), had been sentenced to 5 and 22 years respectively, ostensibly for setting fire to several SUVs at a local car dealership; see "Free Sentenced to 22 Years," *Green Anarchy*, No. 6, Summer 2001. The draconian penalties, especially that meted out to Luers, are plainly at odds with the relatively trivial nature of the offenses of which the three were convicted. They are, however, quite consistent with the sorts of pretextual sentencing guidelines sug-gested in the Antiterrorism and Effective Death Penalty Act of 1996 (10 Stat. 1214). Although it has never targeted humans—as opposed to property—the Earth Liberation Front (ELF), with which the AAC is allegedly overlapped, has been officially designated a "terrorist organization"; see "Ecoterrorism in the United States," *ERRI Intelligence Report*, Vol. 6, No. 262, Sept. 18, 2000. This ren-ders those involved either directly or indirectly open to extraordinary—that is, extraconstitutional—measures of repression; see Kenneth J. Dudonis, David P. Schulz and Frank Bolz, Jr., *The Counterterrorism Handbook: Tactics, Procedures, and Techniques* (Washington, D.C.: CRC Press, [2nd ed.] 2001). On the origins of the kind of "Joint Terrorist Task Force" now operating in Oregon, see my and Jim Vander Wall's *The COINTELPRO Papers: Documents from the FBI's Secret Wars on Dissent in the United States* (Boston: South End Press, 1990) pp. 309–11.

36. This goes to the notion that America is not only unique but entitled to play by a set of rules complete-ly different from those applying to the rest of the world; Deborah L. Madsen, *American Exceptionalism* (Oxford: University of Mississippi Press, 1998) pp. 1–14.

37. This is by no means a novel concept; see Malcolm X, *By Any Means Necessary* (New York: Pathfinder

Press, 1992); Peter Stansill and David Zain Mairowitz, eds., *BAMN* [by any means necessary]: *Outlaw Manifestos and Ephemera, 1965–1970* (New York: Autonomedia, 1999).

38. It is a testament to the extent to which Third Worlders are discounted in the minds of U.S. policymak-ers that the latter for the most part don't bother to observe the cardinal rule of domination holding that to prevent popular revolt it is necessary to present an illusion that relief is possible by other means. See generally, Michael Sawad, *Co-Optive Politics and State Legitimacy* (Hanover, NH: Dartmouth, 1991).

39. Interestingly, while there is a rather vast literature detailing the activities of white—primarily Italian, Jewish and Irish—gangsters of the 1920s and '30s, there is virtually nothing in print concerning blacks like Johnson, who not infrequently fought their more celebrated counterparts to a standstill.

40. There has been a veritable avalanche of denunciations since 9-1-1—by leftists as much as establish-mentarians—of the Islamic fundamentalists in the al-Qaida organization, which allegedly carried out the attacks on the WTO and Pentagon, as well as Afghanistan's Taliban government, which supported al-Qaida, as "theo-nazis." While there is undoubtedly much truth to such depictions of extreme funda-mentalism—Christian and Judaic, no less than Islamic—the question is how, given the manner in which the West has and continues to impose itself upon Islam, anyone might have expected things to have turned out otherwise. For the psychology at issue, see Frantz Fanon's *The Wretched of the Earth* (New York: Grove Press, 1966) esp. pp. 249–310. On the Taliban and al-Qaida, see Ahmed Rashid, *Taliban* (New Haven, CT: Yale University Press, 2001); Yonah Alexander and Michael S. Swetman, *Usama bin Laden's al-Qaida: Profile of a Terrorist Network* (Ardsley, NY: Transnational, 2001).

41. For theory, see Fanon, *Wretched of the Earth*, pp. 35–106. Also see B. Marie Perinbam, *Holy Violence: The Revolutionary Thought of Frantz Fanon* (Washington, D.C.: Three Continents Press, 1982).

42. Yes, I'm quoting Charlie Manson, who, unmistakably, exemplifies the sort of systemically-induced psy-chointellectual deformity at issue; see generally, Ed Sanders, *The Family: The Story of Charles Manson's Dune Buggy Attack Battalion* (New York: E.P. Dutton, 1971).

43. Rajenda Prasad, Karma, *Causation and Retributive Morality: Conceptual Essays in Ethics and Metaethics* (Calcutta: South Asia Books, 1990); Mary Evelyn Tucker and Duncan Ryuken Williams, eds., *Buddhism and Ecology: The Interconnection Between Dharma and Deeds* (Cambridge, MA: Harvard University Press, 1998).

44. Actually, since the figures used here accrue from 1998, the present toll stands to be far higher; Allan Connolly, M.D., "The Effect of Sanctions: A Medical Examination," in Clark and Others, *Challenging Genocide*, p. 106.

45. For the estimate, see Ramsey Clark, "Fire and Ice: The Devastation of Iraq by War and Sanctions," in Clark and Others, *Challenging Genocide*, p. 20. For use and contextualization of the term, see Peters, *Collateral Damage*. The manner in which Iraq's cities were attacked clearly violated the 1923 Hague Rules of Aerial Warfare (Article 22) and the 1949 Geneva Convention IV Relative to the Protection of Civilian Persons in Times of War (Article 3).

46. William A. Arkin, Damian Durant and Marianne Cherni, *On Impact: Modern Warfare and the Environment—A Case Study of the Gulf War* (Washington, D.C.: Greenpeace, 1991) pp. 105–15; Ramsey Clark and Others, *War Crimes: A Report on U.S. War Crimes Against Iraq* (Washington, D.C.: Maisonneuve Press, 1992) pp. 50–1, 90–3. Killing soldiers who are clearly out of combat is a war crime under terms of the Geneva Convention Common Article III. The attacks were carried out under a "no quarter" directive issued by George Bush a few days earlier; Edward Cody, "U.S. Briefers Concede No Quarter," *Washington Post*, Feb. 14, 1991. This is also a war crime under terms of the 1907 Hague Convention (Article 23 (d)).

47. Clark, War Crimes, p. 30; citing Patrick J. Sloyan, "Pullback a Bloody Mismatch: Route of Iraqis became Savage 'Turkey Shoot'," *New York Newsday*, Mar. 31, 1991; "Massive Battle After Ceasefire," *New York Newsday*, May 8, 1991. Also see Clark, "Fire and Ice," pp. 18–9. Launching an assault on opposing troops after a ceasefire has taken effect is a war crime under both the Hague and Geneva Conventions.

48. Clark, *War Crimes*, p. 35; citing Patrick J. Sloyan, "U.S. Officers Say Iraqis Were Buried Alive," *San Francisco Chronicle*, Sept. 12, 1991. Also see Clark, "Fire and Ice," p. 19. On use of the term "sand nig-gers," see Sklar, "Brave New World Order," p.8. As observed in note 46, refusal of quarter to opposing troops—especially the wounded—is a war crime.

49. The best overview is provided in Noam Chomsky's *The Fateful Triangle: The United States, Israel and the Palestinians* (Cambridge, MA: South End Press, [classics ed.] 1999).

50. Don Peretz, *Intifada: The Palestinian Uprising* (Boulder, CO: Westview Press, 1990); Middle East Watch Staff, *The Israeli Army and the Intifada: Policies that Contribute to the Killings* (New York: Middle East Watch, 1994); Roan Carey, ed., *The New Intifada: Resisting Israel's Apartheid* (London: Verso, 2001).

51. On the 1982 massacres at Sabra and Shatila, see Naseer Aruri, *Palestinian Refugees: The Right of Return* (London: Pluto, 2001) pp. 3, 127, 159. It is worth noting that Sharon "defended himself against charges of...complicity in the massacres by citing a similar Israeli role in [earlier massacres such as that at] Tal al-Za'tar" refugee camp in 1976; Rashid Khalidi, *Palestinian Identity: The Construction of Modern National Consciousness* (New York: Columbia University Press, 1997) p. 264.

52. On "Operation Success," as the CIA's Guatemalan intervention was codenamed, see John Prados, *Presidents' Secret Wars: CIA and Pentagon Covert Operations Since World War II* (New York: William Morrow, 1986) pp. 98–106. For insight into the consequences for grassroots Guatemalans, see Stephen Schlesinger and Stephen Kinzer, *Bitter Fruit: The Untold Story of the American Coup in Guatemala* (Garden City, NY: Doubleday, 1982); Ricardo Falla, *Massacres in the Jungle: Ixcán, Guatemala, 1975–1982* (Boulder, CO: Westview Press, 1994).

53. On the coup, see Noam Chomsky and Edward S. Herman, *The Political Economy of Human Rights, Vol.*

1: The Washington Connection and Third World Fascism (Boston: South End Press, 1979) pp. 205–9. On East Timor; John G. Taylor, *Indonesia's Forgotten War: The Hidden History of East Timor* (London: Pluto Press, 1991).

54. Prados, *Secret Wars*, pp. 91–8.

55. Armando Uribe, *The Black Book of American Intervention in Chile* (Boston: Beacon Press, 1975). For details of what happened after the coup, see Mary Helen Spooner, *Soldiers in a Narrow Land: The Pinochet Regime in Chile* (Berkeley: University of California Press, [2nd ed.] 1999); Hugh O'Shaughnessy, Pinochet: *The Politics of Torture* (New York: New York University Press, 2000).

56. A.J. Languuth, Hidden Terrors: *The Truth About U.S. Police Operations in Latin America* (New York: Pantheon, 1978); Martha K. Huggins, *Political Policing: The United States and Latin America* (Durham, NC: Duke University Press, 1998).

57. Reed Brody, Contra *Terror in Nicaragua: Report of a Fact-Finding Mission, September 1984–January 1985* (Boston: South End Press, 1985); Holly Sklar, *Washington's War on Nicaragua* (Boston: South End Press, 1988).

58. On the number killed, see H. Bruce Franklin, *Vietnam and Other American Fantasies* (Amherst: University of Massachusetts Press, 2000) p. 111. On the manner in which they were killed, see John Duffett, ed., *Against the Crime of Silence: Proceedings of the International War Crimes Tribunal, Stockholm-Copenhagen* (New York: Simon and Schuster, 1968); Vietnam Veterans Against the War, *The Winter Soldier Investigation: An Inquiry into U.S. War Crimes in Vietnam* (Boston: Beacon Press, 1972); Citizen's Commission of Inquiry, *The Dellums Committee Hearings on War Crimes in Vietnam* (New York: Vintage, 1972).

59. According to Israeli journalist Amnon Kapeoliouk, about a quarter-million Vietnamese children, all born during the war or after, have died of cancers or "hideous birth defects: resulting from the effects of American chemical warfare"; quoted in Noam Chomsky, "Rogue States," in his and Edward Said's *Acts of Aggression: Policing "Rogue" States* (New York: Seven Stories Press, 1999) pp. 41–2. Also see Barry Weisberg, *Ecocide in Indochina: The Ecology of War* (San Francisco: Canfield Press, 1970); John Lewallen, *Ecology of Devastation: Indochina* (New York: Penguin, 1971); Rajev Chandrasekaran, "War's Toxic Legacy Lingers in Vietnam," *Washington Post*, Apr. 18, 2000. On land mines, and the ongoing U.S. refusal to accept their prohibition under international law, see Blum, *Rogue State*, p. 101.

60. Franklin, *Vietnam*, p. 161.

61. I.F. Stone, *The Hidden History of the Korean War, 1950–51* (Boston: Little, Brown, [2nd ed.] 1988); Charles J. Hanley, Sang-Hun Choe and Martha Mendoza, *The Bridge at No Gun Ri: A Hidden Nightmare from the Korean War* (New York: Henry Holt, 2001).

62. Against Germany, with the exception of its participation in the notorious 1945 incendiary attack on Dresden, the U.S. restricted itself to daylight "precision" bombing raids using high explosives. There, the stated objective was to avoid unnecessary civilian deaths. Against Japan, on the other hand—about which U.S. officials openly announced that they favored "the extermination of the Japanese people in toto"— the preferred method was nighttime saturation bombing by masses of aircraft dropping incendiaries to create "firestorms" in which vast numbers of noncombatants were deliberately cremated. In the great Tokyo fire raid on the night of March 9–10, 1945, to give but one example, more than 267,000 buildings were destroyed, a million people rendered homeless, and upwards of 100,000 burned alive. Under such conditions, more Japanese civilians were killed in only six months than among all branches of the Japanese military during the entirety of World War II; H. Bruce Franklin, *Star Wars: The Superweapon and the American Imagination* (New York: Oxford University Press, 1988) pp. 107–11. The public statement by U.S. War Manpower Commissioner Paul V. McNutt is quoted by John W. Dower, *War Without Mercy: Race and Power in the Pacific* (New York: Pantheon, 1986) p. 55.

63. Ronald Takaki, Hiroshima: *Why America Dropped the Atomic Bomb* (Boston: Little, Brown, 1995); Gar Alperovitz, *The Decision to Drop the Bomb* (New York: Alfred A. Knopf, 1995).

64. The same can be perhaps be said with respect to biological warfare, which the U.S. attempted in Korea; Stephen Endicott and Edward Hagerman, *The United States and Biological Warfare: Secrets from the Early Cold War and Korea* (Bloomington: Indiana University Press, 1998). There is also a much longer history of it being selectively conducted against American Indians (see note 70), and the threat of it being employed for terrorist purposes by U.S. diplomats in their negotiations with native peoples; Elizabeth A. Fenn, *Pox Americana: The Great Smallpox Epidemic of 1775–82* (New York: Hill and Wang, 2001).

65. Stuart Creighton Miller, *"Benevolent Assimilation": The American Conquest of the Philippines, 1899–1903* (New Haven, CT: Yale University Press, 1982).

66. For a very accurate—and sickening—description of what was done at Wounded Knee, see Ralph K. Andrist, *The Long Death: The Last Days of the Plains Indians* (New York: Collier, 1964) pp. 351–2.

67. All of these are covered in the essay entitled "'Nits Make Lice': The Extermination of American Indians, 1607–1996," in my *A Little Matter of Genocide: Holocaust and Denial in the Americas, 1492 to the Present* (San Francisco: City Lights, 1997) pp. 129–288.

68. On the origin and history of scalp bounties, see my "Nits Make Lice," pp. 178–88. On the hunting of Indians as sport, see David E. Stannard, *American Holocaust: The Conquest of the New World* (New York: Oxford University Press, 1992) p. 116.

69. On the Trail of Tears and related atrocities, see Grant Foreman, *Indian Removal* (Norman: University of Oklahoma Press, [2nd ed.] 1952); Russell Thornton, "Cherokee Population Losses During the Trail of Tears: A New Perspective and a New Estimate," *Ethnohistory*, No. 31, 1984. On the Navajo experience, see L.R. Bailey, *The Long Walk* (Los Angeles: Westernlore, 1964). Regarding the explicitly racist attitudes underlying these policies, see Reginald Horsman, *Race and Manifest Destiny: The Origins of*

Racial Anglo-Saxonism (Cambridge, MA: Harvard University Press, 1981).

70. Suspected instances of smallpox epidemics being deliberately unleashed among the native peoples of North America begin with Capt. John Smith's 1614 foray into Massachusetts in behalf of the Plymouth Company. Confirmed—that is to say, documentable—cases include Lord Jeffrey Amherst's order that infested blankets and other such items be distributed among the Ottawas in 1763, the U.S. Army's duplication of Amherst's maneuver at Fort Clark in 1836, and several repetitions by "private parties" in northern California during the 1850s (other examples accrue from British Columbia and the Northwest Territories in Canada during the later nineteenth century); see my "Nits Make Lice," pp. 151–7, 169–70; Peter McNair, Alan Hoover and Kevin Neary, *The Legacy: Tradition and Innovation in Northwest Coast Indian Art* (Seattle: University of Washington Press, 1984) p. 24. It should be noted that even some rather staunch apologists for the status quo have lately begun to admit that "the history of the western hemisphere has a few examples of whites deliberately releasing the [smallpox] virus among Indians"; R.G. Robertson, *Rotting Face: Smallpox and the American Indian* (Caldwell, ID: Caxton, 2001) p. 301.

71. Alan Axelrod, *Chronicle of the Indian Wars from Colonial Times to Wounded Knee* (Engelwood Cliffs, NJ: Prentice-Hall, 1993) p. 39.

72. See the first chapter of Charles R. Giesst's *Wall Street: A History* (New York: Oxford University Press, 1999).

73. "Largely overlooked, neglected, or brushed off as a youthful indiscretion by our people is the enormous fact of slavery for over two centuries of our history," notes one progressive Euroamerican analyst, "and its role as a central determinant of our economic development until at least the mid-nineteenth century"; Douglas Dowd, *U.S. Capitalist Development Since 1776: Of, By, and For Which People?* (Armonk, NY: M.E. Sharpe, 1993) p. 77. That truism uttered, he makes passing reference to slavery on exactly four other occasions in his 542 page text (American Indians are not mentioned at all, even in a section titled "Land policy"; pp. 274–5). For useful information, see Jim Marketti, "Black Equity in the Slave Industry," *Review of Black Political Economy*, Vol. 44, No. 2, 1972; Boris Bittker, *The Case for Black Reparations* (New York: Random House, 1973); Richard America, *Paying the Social Debt* (New York: Praeger, 1993).

74. Estimates as to the number of blacks who died during the Middle Passage run as high as 30 million; see generally, the essays collected by David Eltis and David Richardson in their coedited *Routes to Slavery: Direction, Ethnicity and Mortality in the Transatlantic Slave Trade* (London: Frank Cass, 1997). Also see Hugh Thomas, *The Slave Trade: The Story of the Transatlantic Slave Trade, 1440–1870* (New York: Simon and Schuster, 1997).

75. Matthew J. Mancini, *One Dies, Get Another: Convict Leasing in the American South, 1866–1928* (Columbia: University of South Carolina Press, 1996); David M. Oshinsky, *"Worse Than Slavery": Parchman Farm and the Ordeal of Jim Crow Justice* (New York: Free Press, 1996); Alex Lichtenstein, *Twice the Work of Free Labor: The Political Economy of Convict Labor in the New South* (London: Verso, 1996).

76. Stewart Emory Tolnay, *A Festival of Violence: An Analysis of the Lynching of African Americans in the American South, 1882–1930* (Urbana: University of Illinois Press, 1995); Ralph Ginzberg, *100 Years of Lynchings* (Baltimore: Black Classics Press, 1997). On Klan membership, see Wyn Craig Wade, *The Fiery Cross: The Ku Klux Klan in America* (New York: Simon and Schuster, 1987).

77. Much of what was worst about South African apartheid was based upon preexisting U.S. models; George M. Frederickson, *White Supremacy: A Comparative Study of American and South African History* (New York: Oxford University Press, 1981).

78. Ronald Takaki, *Strangers from a Different Shore: A History of Asian Americans* (Boston: Little, Brown, 1989) pp. 80–7, 130, 240; Suchen Chan, *Asian Americans: An Interpretive History* (New York: Twayne, 1991) pp. 28–32.

79. See, as examples, Andrew Hacker, *Two Nations: Black and White, Separate, Hostile, and Unequal* (New York: Ballantine, [rev. ed.] 1995); Rodolfo Acuña, *Occupied America: A History of the Chicanos* (New York: Longman, 2000) esp. pp. 350–5, 400–10.

80. Gunder Frank, *Capitalism and Underdevelopment;* Harrison, *Third World;* Vogelsang, *Global Nightmare;* Falk, *Predatory Globalization.*

81. The actual number seems to be a matter of no small controversy. In the immediate aftermath, the official estimate stood at 4,500. A week later, it was ratcheted up to 5,000—the most commonly cited figure—ultimately cresting at nearly 6,000 before starting a sharp drop. By Dec. 11, the tally, as reported on Fox News, stood at 3,040 (this should be contrasted to Sen. Orin Hatch's assertion the same evening on *Larry King Live* [CNN] that "7,000 innocent Americans" were killed on 9-1-1). As of Jan. 10, 2002, the number of dead at the WTC reported by both Fox and CNN, including hundreds of dead "foreigners" (note 1), has fallen to 2,883. Adding in the now never-mentioned toll at the Pentagon, this would leave somewhere around 3,000 American fatalities.

82. This description of the attack was offered by Secretary of Defense Donald Rumsfeld in a televised press briefing conducted on Sept. 13, 2001.

83. The estimate is official; Clark, *War Crimes*, pp. 17–8, 85. Bombardment of "undefended population centers"—which is what Iraq's cities were, once their "Triple A" (antiaircraft artillery) was suppressed—has been formally defined as a war crime since the Hague Convention of 1907 (Article 25). Also see note 45.

84. For early reports on this pattern, see Jack Calhoun, "UN: Iraq Bombed Back to Stone Age," *Manchester Guardian*, Apr. 3, 1991; Barton Gellman, "Storm Damage in the Persian Gulf: U.S. strategy against Iraq went beyond strictly military targets," *Washington Post Weekly*, July 8–14, 1991. More comprehensively, see Clark, *War Crimes*, 22, 35, 53–8. It's worth noting that a strategy deliberately targeting anything

other than "strictly military targets" constitutes a major war crime; see note 45.

85. The preinvasion indigenous population of North America has been credibly estimated as somewhere between 12.5 and 18.5 million, the great bulk of it in what is now the Lower 48 States portion of the continent. By the time the 1890 U.S. census was taken, there were barely 237,000 survivors; Russell Thornton, *American Indian Holocaust and Survival: A Population History Since 1492* (Norman: University of Oklahoma Press, 1987).

86. A hue and cry was raised in the days following 9-1-1, by Fox News commentators and others, about Usama bin Laden's alleged instruction that his followers should "kill Americans wherever they may be found." While this was cast by the pundits as a desire to "exterminate" the U.S. citizenry as a whole, bin Laden's underlying intent was subsequently explained by more careful analysts—including even U.S. Secretary of State Colin Powell—as being to make things so decisively uncomfortable for Americans that they would eventually demand a general withdrawal of the U.S. presence from Islamic countries. Problematic as the scheme may be in itself, it is a very far cry from a call for genocide.

87. Segments of a videotaped statement in which Usama bin Laden explicitly linked 9-1-1 to the ongoing genocide in Iraq and the situation of the Palestinians was aired briefly, about a week after the attacks. Such broadcasts were abruptly halted when the government announced "national security" concerns, i.e., the contention that bin Laden might be using the tapes to send "coded instructions" to his followers in North America. On this ludicrous pretext, the idea that the motives underlying 9-1-1 warrant even a pretext of objective scrutiny have been abandoned in favor of official platitudes, delivered by-and-large in soundbite form, concerning the nature of "evil." It is quite possible that Americans would have rejected bin Laden's explanation, had they been allowed a chance to consider it. As things stand, we'll never really know, since the U.S. polity—uniquely, among its counterparts around the world—has been denied the possibility of hearing what he has to say. So much for "democratic decision-making" by an "informed citizenry." The principle/process at issue is explored very well in Chomsky's *Necessary Illusions*.

88. As noted Hawaiian rights activist Haunani-Kay Trask puts it, "Japan did not attack U.S. 'home territory' on December 7, 1941. It attacked the military forces of a foreign power engaged in the illegal occupation of my homeland. Hawaiians are not 'Native Americans,' we are Polynesians. Our country, Hawai'i, is not American, it is Polynesian. Hawai'i is not part of the U.S., it is a colony of the U.S. These things were true in 1941, and they are just as true today. Anyone saying otherwise is either ignorant or a liar"; lecture at the University of Colorado/Boulder; Mar. 14, 1993 (tape on file).

89. This is intended more literally than not; see, e.g., "Reagan Says Video Games Provide the Right Stuff," *Wall Street Journal*, Mar. 9, 1983.

90. George Cheney, "Talking War: Symbols, Strategies and Images," *New Studies on the Left*, Vol. XIV, No. 3, 1991; Douglas Kellner, *The Persian Gulf TV War* (Boulder, CO: Westview Press, 1992).

91. Lynda Boose, "Techno-Muscularity and the 'Boy Eternal': From the Quagmire to the Gulf," in Amy Kaplan and Donald E. Pease, eds., *Cultures of United States Imperialism* (Durham, NC: Duke University Press, 1993) pp. 581–616; Dana L. Cloud, "Operation Desert Comfort," in Susan Jeffords and Susan Rabinovitz, eds., *Seeing Through the Media: The Persian Gulf War* (New Brunswick, NJ: Rutgers University Press, 1994) pp. 155–70.

92. The fact is that in less than two hours, 19 men equipped with nothing more sophisticated than box cutters leveled a key command and control hub of globalization, eliminated around 2,000 of its most accomplished technical personnel, put a $100-billion hole in the global economy, and knocked down a chunk of the Pentagon in the bargain. In purely military terms—as defined by U.S. strategic doctrine since at least as early as 1942—the attacks were wildly successful; see George E. Hopkins, "Bombing and the American Conscience During World War II," *Historian*, No. 28, 1966. Also see Ronald Schaffer, *Wings of Judgment: American Bombing in World War II* (New York: Oxford University Press, 1965); Michael Sherry, *The Rise of American Air Power: The Creation of Armageddon* (New Haven, CT: Yale University Press, 1987).

93. Znet Commentaries, Sept. 17, 2001.

94. Interview on NPR's *Powerpoint*, broadcast on Atlanta radio station WCLK, Nov. 4, 2001.

95. For explication of the term used, see Tzvetan Todorov, *The Conquest of America: The Question of the Other* (New York: Harper & Row, 1984); Homi K. Bhabha, "The Other Question: Stereotype, discrimination and colonial discourse," in his *The Location of Culture* (New York: Routledge, 1990) pp. 66–84; Roger Bartra, *Wild Men in the Looking Glass: The Mythic Origins of European Otherness* (Ann Arbor: University of Michigan Press, 1994).

96. This principle was set forth by the U.S.-instigated tribunal at Nuremberg in 1945; see Quincy Wright, "The Law of the Nuremberg Trials," *American Journal of International Law*, No. 41, Jan. 1947.

97. For those unfamiliar with the case, see Anne E. Schwartz, *The Man who Could Not Kill Enough: The Secret Murders of Milwaukee's Jeffrey Dahmer* (New York: Carol, 1992).

98. It has been widely asserted, for example, that members of al-Qaida should be gunned down on the spot, even if attempting to surrender. Those making such statements are guilty of advocating criminal acts of the sort discussed in note 46. They may thus be technically subject to prosecution for war crimes in their own right. Whether or not this is so, they are certainly guilty of advocating—and thereby supporting—terrorism.

99. The photo spread appeared on p. B-1 of the *New York Times* on Nov. 15, 2001. The response mentioned occurred on CNN's *Crossfire* the following evening. Wayne Veysey, "I saw the killing of a Taliban Soldier," *Scottish Daily Record*, Nov. 16, 2001

100. Televised statements of U.S. President George W. Bush, Sept.12–Sept. 15, 2001. All mention of a "crusade" was quickly dropped, when it became evident that the word served more than anything to vali-

date in the eyes of Islam as a whole a 1997 al-Qaida manifesto announcing the organization had undertaken jihad against "Crusaders"; Rashid, *Taliban*, p. 134. Rhetoric concerning "evil" has been escalated to compensate.

101. See Paul Ricouer, *Symbolism of Evil* (Boston: Beacon Press, 1969). Interestingly, insofar as the pentagon is the penultimate symbol of evil among satanists, the attackers of 9-1-1 could make a far better—or at least more literal—case for attempting to rid the world of it than can the U.S.; Genevieve Morgan and Tom Morgan, *The Devil: A Visual Guide to the Demonic, Evil, Scurrilous, and Bad* (San Francisco: Chronicle Books, 1996) p. 148.

102. Edwin S. Schneidman, *Definitions of Suicide* (New York: John Wiley, 1985).

103. For younger readers, it should be noted that the lines quoted—wildly popular among rightwingers everywhere—were delivered by actor Clint Eastwood during his portrayal of a homicidal San Francisco police detective in the movie, *Dirty Harry* (1972).

104. On these potentials, see Jonathan B. Tucker, ed., *Toxic Terror: Assessing Terrorist Use of Chemical and Biological Weapons* (Cambridge, MA: MIT Press, 2000).

105. According to a poll reported on CNBC on Dec. 7, 2001, 86% of Americans favored this recipe. For implications, see, e.g., Pamela J. Taylor, Philippa Garety, Alec Buchanan, Alison Reed, Simon Wessely, Katarzyna Ray, Graham Dunn and Don Grubin, "Delusions and Violence," in John Monahan and Henry J. Stedman, eds., *Violence and Mental Disorder: Developments and Risk Assessment* (Chicago: University of Chicago Press, 1994) esp. the section entitled "The Nature of Delusions," pp. 161–3.

106. As many as 40,000 Vietnamese were murdered and another 30,000 imprisoned by Phoenix program operatives between 1968 and 1971, with no discernable impact on the "Viet Cong infrastructure." This was in large part because the program, which functioned on the basis of "hearsay [and] malicious gossip...fueled by feuds and political maneuvers," usually eliminated the wrong people; Prados, *Secret Wars*, pp. 309–11. Also see Stuart A. Herrington, *Stalking the Vietcong: Inside Operation Phoenix—A Personal Account* (San Francisco: Presidio Press, 1997).

107. Office of Homeland Security Act of 2001 (H.R. 3026, Oct. 4, 2001). Also see the Antiterrorism and Effective Death Penalty Act of 1996 (110 Stat. 1214).

108. Witness the wave of suicide bombings that has swept Israel since mid-November, 2001.

109. See generally, James X. Dempsey and David Cole, *Terrorism and the Constitution: Sacrificing Civil Liberties in the Name of National Security* (Los Angeles: First Amendment Foundation, 1999).

110. For an analogous context, see Wilhelm Reich, *The Mass Psychology of Fascism* (New York: Farrar, Straus and Giroux, 1970).

111. "There are whole disciplines, institutions, rubrics in our culture which serve as categories of denial"; Susan Griffin, *A Chorus of Stones: The Private Life of War* (New York: Anchor, 1993) p. 19. Also see E.L. Edelstein, Donald L. Nathanson and Andrew Stone, eds., *Denial: A Clarification of Concepts and Research* (New York: Plenum, 1989); Stanley Cohen, *States of Denial: Knowing About Atrocities and Suffering* (Cambridge, UK: Polity Press, 2001).

112. In simplest terms, the condition has much in common with Sadistic Personality Disorder, that is, a "pervasive pattern of cruel, demeaning and aggressive behavior" disguised behind a sophisticated matrix of rationalization and denial. Diagnostic criteria include "(a) the use of physical cruelty or violence in establishing dominance in a relationship (e.g., not merely for the purpose of theft); (b) a fascination with violence, weapons, martial arts, injury, or torture (c) treating or disciplining others unusually harshly; (d) taking pleasure in the psychological or physical suffering of others (including animals); and (e) getting others to do what he or she wants through terror or intimidation"; Thomas A. Widiger and Timothy J. Trull, "Personality Disorders and Violence," in Monahan and Steadman, *Violence and Mental Disorder*, pp. 213–5.

113. The widely-reported "one-in-6" estimate of fatalities on Luzon—a total 616,000 people—was offered by Brig. Gen. J. Franklin Bell during a 1902 appearance before Congress; U.S. Senate, Committee on the Philippine Islands, *Hearings Before the Senate Committee on the Philippine Islands* (Washington, D.C.: 57th Cong., 1st Sess., 1902). Bell was openly referred to, both by his troops and in the press as "The Butcher of Batangas"; U.S. Department of War, *Letter from the Secretary of War Relative to the Reports and Charges in the Public Press of Cruelty and Oppression Exercised by Our Soldiers Towards Natives of the Philippines* (Washington, D.C.: 57th Cong, 1st Sess., 1902). It should be noted that, these facts being known, Bell received a Presidential Commendation for his "service" in the islands, and was later promoted Army Chief of Staff; Creighton Miller, *"Benevolent Assimilation"*, pp. 237, 260.

114. Ibid., pp. 1-2.

115. William H. Chrisman, *The Opposite of Everything is True: Reflections on Denial in Alcoholic Families* (New York: William Morrow, 1991).

116. For a clear indication of how much was known, and in what detail, see Moorfield Storey and Julian Codman, *"Marked Severities" in Philippine Warfare* (Boston: George H. Ellis, 1902).

117. Creighton Miller, *"Benevolent Assimilation"*, p. 253.

118. Ibid.

119. Ibid. The individuals named—President Theodore Roosevelt, Massachusetts Senator Henry Cabot Lodge and Indiana Senator Albert Beveridge—were key leaders among what was referred to as "The Imperialist Clique"; Richard H. Miller, *American Imperialism in 1898: The Quest for National Fulfillment* (New York: John Wiley, 1971). On the contemporaneous "anti-imperialist movement," see Robert L. Beisner, *Twelve Against Empire: The Anti-Imperialists, 1898–1900* (Chicago: University of Chicago Press, [2nd ed.] 1985). Overall, see Thomas G. Patterson, ed., *American Imperialism & Anti-Imperialism: Problem Studies in American History* (New York: Thomas Y. Crowell, 1973).

120. A cornerstone articulation came in the contention that imperialism should be treated as a "great aber-

ration in American history" advanced by Samuel Flagg Bemis in his magisterial *Diplomatic History of the United States* (New York: Henry Holt, 1936).

121. Often, the compensatory allegations amount to outright falsehoods, as with the much-publicized 1990 claim that Iraqi soldiers had killed hundreds of Kuwaiti babies in order to steal their incubators; Boose, "Techno-Muscularity," p. 593.

122. There are, of course, significant exceptions to this, notably those like Mark Lane and Dick Gregory who have lost themselves forever in the mazes surrounding the Kennedy and King assassinations; see, e.g., Mark Lane and Dick Gregory, *Code Name "Zorro": The Assassination of Martin Luther King, Jr.* (Englewood Cliffs, NJ: Prentice-Hall, 1977); Mark Lane, *Plausible Denial: Was the CIA Involved in the Assassination of JFK?* (New York: Thunder's Mouth Press, 1991).

123. This is not to argue that such concepts have no analytical value. Obviously, they do (which is why I employ them myself). Their insufficiency in and of themselves should be equally obvious, however. The "nazi state" committed none of the crimes of nazism; *people* subscribing to nazi "ideals" and thus embracing their manifestation in statist form committed and/or were complicit in the crimes. Questions of popular culpability, accountability and even responsibility have been all but expunged from contemporary progressivist discourse, leaving it in some respects as sanitized—or disingenuous—as the conservative disquisitions it purports to critique.

124. To my knowledge, the only person attempting to define with any degree of precision who should be identified by the term "élite" has been the sociologist G. William Domhoff, in his *Who Rules America? Power and Politics in the Year 2000* (Mountainview, CA: Mayfield, 1998). Of additional interest, see Domhoff's *The Power Elite and the State: How Policy is Made in America* (Chicago: Aldine de Gruyter, 1990).

125. This is the famous stew composed in equal parts of "I didn't know," "I was only following orders"—or "I had no choice but to follow orders"—and "if I hadn't done it, someone else would have" ladled up by everyone up to and including ranking members of the nazi government. That the argument held no legal merit was clearly established at Nuremberg. Philosophically, it was rebutted rather firmly by Karl Jaspers and others at about the same time. Subsequently, it has been refuted chapter and verse both sociologically and on the grounds of historical evidence; see, e.g., Julius H. Schoeps, "From Character Assassination to Mass Murder," in Robert R. Shandley, *Unwilling Germans? The Goldhagen Debate* (Minneapolis: University of Minnesota Press, 2000) pp. 79–80. In essence, knowledge of the nazi crimes was widespread, orders could be—and sometimes were—refused without personal consequence, and, had a sufficient number of Germans simply declined to go along, the Hitler régime would have had to adjust its policies accordingly. The fact is that a lopsided majority of Germans were quite comfortable with—and to a considerable extent openly celebratory of—nazism's "triumphs and accomplishments" right up to the point that the war turned decisively against them (1942–43); Ian Kershaw, *Hitler, 1936–1945: Nemesis* (New York: W.W. Norton, 2000) pp. 311, 367, 375, 421, 551; Michael Burleigh, *The Third Reich: A New History* (New York: Hill and Wang, 2000) pp. 266–7, 759–60.

126. The piece generating such controversy is my own "Some People Push Back: Reflections on the Justice of Roosting Chickens," *Pockets of Resistance*, No. 27, Sept. 2001. The term "little Eichmanns," however, was borrowed from John Zerzan's "He Means It. Do You?" *Anarchy*, No. 44, Fall-Winter 1997–98.

127. Although not one of the many who raised this issue ventured a guess as to what proportion of the fatalities actually fit their description, most spoke as if there was no one in the WTC *but* such people. Alternately, their arguments imply that it is impermissible to attack a target if there is a chance any clean-up or food service personnel might suffer as a result. By this standard, of course, *no* targets are permissible, a principle precluding, for example, NLF mortar attacks on U.S. military compounds in Vietnam. Since none of the objectors has suggested that the latter restriction should hold true—several have in fact angrily repudiated it—their position ultimately reduces to the sort of double standard marking any other variety of American exceptionalism. For the record, using the standard media figure of about 4,500 dead at the WTC, my own arithmetic is as follows: Subtracting 300 undocumented workers, 600 documented workers, 100 temp workers, 100 bystanders and 300 firemen from the toll leaves approximately 3,100 little Eichmanns (a tally in which 200-odd police and FBI personnel are most emphatically included).

128. Obituary, *New York Times*, Dec. 9, 2001. I wish to emphasize that by using this young man as an illustration I do not mean to single him out as having been in any way more repugnant than his peers. As I said, he is representative. I could as easily have used the obituaries in the same *NYT* spread for the 32-year-old bond trader who had already purchased an extravagantly-expensive apartment on upscale West 72nd Street and, "although it was perfectly livable"—obviously enough—had it "gutted to the slab and girders" and reassembled in a personal fashion statement costing enough to sustain an entire Third World community for years. Then there was the older corporate vice president who, at 48, already owned his country estate, vacation cottage, cars, boat and collection of race horses, and was preparing to take early retirement so that he might better enjoy the "fruits of his labor." As easily, I could have used the obit spread run by the *NYT* on any other day since it began publishing them in September to obtain the same results.

129. The first three characterizations accrue from the obituary cited above, the last three from polemics e-mailed to me by self-styled progressives. Note how, in the second set, the wealth enjoyed by the individual in question is imputed more-or-less to chance, as if he'd won the lottery, rather than to the specific activities in which he'd actually engaged. The purpose of this dodge—the writer was plainly aware that happenstance played no role in the subject's income generation—is to exonerate the deceased from the onus of choices he himself had been "proud" to make, as well as from the implications of the values revealed thereby.

130. Actually, comparing him to the group in question may be in some ways unfair to Eichmann. Whatever else may be said of his motivations, they appear to have devolved upon some hideous combination of "professionalism" and perverted idealism rather than anything so crass as material greed. The "little Eichmanns" of 9-1-1, on the other hand, seem to have been suffering in varying degrees of acuteness from Antisocial Personality Disorder, a pathology marked by extreme displays of "hedonism, irresponsibility [and] indifference to the suffering" of anyone other than themselves and/or a narrow circle of family and friends; Thomas A. Widiger and Timothy J. Trull, "Personality Disorders and Violence," in Monahan and Steadman, *Violence and Mental Disorder*, pp. 208–13, 215. While many words come to mind in describing such a condition, neither "cool" nor "warm hearted" are among them. That they might go unchallenged when used in this way is evidence of the much broader pattern of dissociation/denial afflicting American social consciousness.

131. Much of the negative correspondence I've received has seemed rather visceral, as if the writers were reacting to the name, with no real clue as to who Adolf Eichmann was, what he did, and thence his significance in the present context. Let it be observed, then, that he was a mere mid-level officer in the SS, by all accounts a good husband and devoted father, apparently quite mild-mannered, and never accused of having personally murdered anyone at all. His crime was to have to sat at several steps remove from the holocaustal blood and gore, behind a desk, in the sterility of an office building, organizing the logistics—train and "cargo" schedules, mainly—without which the "industrial killing" aspect of the nazi Judeocide could not have occurred. His most striking characteristic, if it may be called that, was his sheer "unexceptionality" (that is, the extent to which he had to be seen as "everyman": an "ordinary," "average" or "normal" member of his society); see Hannah Arendt, *Eichmann in Jerusalem: A Report on the Banality of Evil* (New York: Viking, 1963); Bernard J. Bergen, *The Banality of Evil* (Lanham, MD: Rowman & Littlefield, 1998).

132. I am perhaps using the term "progressive" a bit too broadly. It should be noted that every hostile comment I've received—or heard—has come from relatively privileged whites, mostly men, self-described as a "peace activist." Such favorable commentary as I've encountered—and it's been considerable—has come mostly, though by no means exclusively, from people of color. The pattern is entirely consistent with that discussed in conjunction with notes 20–34, and one I've explored more thoroughly in *Pacifism as Pathology*.

133. Witness the oft-remarked and truly global sentiment of "anti-Americanism" which has become ever more pronounced over the past half-century; see, e.g., Alvin G. Rubinstein and Donald E. Smith, eds., *Anti-Americanism in the Third World: Implications for U.S. Foreign Policy* (New York: Praeger, 1985). Facile attributions of such resentments to "envy" are as pathologically delusional—or diversionary—as any other facet of American denial.

134. U.S. Senate, Committee on the Judiciary, *Hearing on a Proposed Constitutional Amendment to Protect Crime Victims* (Washington, D.C.: 105th Cong., 2d Sess., Apr. 28, 1998). Also see Sara Flaherty and Austin Sarat, eds., *Victims and Victims' Rights: Crime, Justice and Punishment* (New York: Chelsea House, 1998).

135. Jaspers, *German Guilt*, pp. 25–6. A further elaboration of the Jasperian schematic, reframed in terms of "responsibility" rather than "guilt," is developed by David H. Jones, in his *Moral Responsibility in the Holocaust: A Study in the Ethics of Character* (Lanham, MD: Rowman & Littlefield, 1999) esp. pp. 15–32.

136. See generally, Geoffrey Robertson, Crimes *Against Humanity: The Struggle for Global Justice* (New York: Free Press, 2000). More technically, see Ian Brownlie, *Principles of Public International Law* (New York: Oxford University Press, [5th ed.] 1998).

137. "The idea that a state, any more than a corporation, commits crimes, is a fiction. Crimes are committed only by persons... It is quite intolerable to let a legalism become the basis for personal immunity"; U.S. Supreme Court Justice Robert H. Jackson in his role as Nuremberg prosecutor (1945); quoted in Robertson, *Crimes Against Humanity*, p. 218. Also see Lyal S. Sunga, *Individual Responsibility in International Law for Serious Human Rights Violations* (The Hague: Martinus Nijhoff, 1992).

138. A major reason the Nuremberg Tribunal was convened was because Germany had rather spectacularly defaulted on its the authority allowed it under Articles 228 and 229 of the Treaty of Versailles to prosecute its own war criminals after World War I. Of 901 individuals against whom evidence was provided by the allied powers, 888 were acquitted in German courts. Only token sentences were imposed upon the remaining 13, several of whom were shortly "allowed to escape by prison officials who were publicly congratulated for assisting them"; Robertson, *Crimes Against Humanity*, pp. 210–1. As will be discussed in notes 163 and 164, the U.S. record is no better.

139. The idea is neither new nor novel. See Wright, "Law of the Nuremberg Tribunal"; Manley O. Hudson, *The Permanent Court of International Justice* (New York: Macmillan, 1943); Maynard B. Golt, "The Necessity of an International Court of Justice," *Washburn Law Review*, No. 6, 1966; Leo Gross, "The International Court of Justice: Enhancing Its Role in the International Legal Order," in Leo Gross, ed., *The Future of the International Court of Justice* (New York: Oceana, 1973) pp. 22–104; Rosenne Shabatti, *The World Court* (Leiden: A.W. Sijhoff, 1973).

140. There were those who "foresaw the disaster, said so, and warned; that does not count politically...if no action followed or it had no effect... To be content with paper protests [or] to play riskless politics...is evasion of responsibility"; Jaspers, *German Guilt*, pp. 56, 85. Also see Malcolm X, *By Any Means Necessary* and Mike Ryan's "On Ward Churchill's 'Pacifism as Pathology': Towards a Consistent Revolutionary Practice," in our *Pacifism as Pathology*, pp. 131–68.

141. "Politically everyone acts in the modern state, [if only] by voting, or failing to vote, in elections... One might think of cases of wholly non-political persons who live aloof from all politics... Yet they, too, are included among the politically liable, because they, too, live by the order of the state. There is no such

aloofness in modern states"; Jaspers, *German Guilt*, p. 56. Also see Frank Harrison, *The Modern State: An Anarchist Analysis* (Montréal: Black Rose Books, 1984).

142. "A people answers for its polity [because] political conditions are inseparable from a people's whole way of life... We are responsible for our régime, for the acts of our régime...for the kinds of leaders we allowed to arise among us... Hence there is a two-fold guilt—first in the unconditional surrender to a leader as such, and second, in the kind of leader submitted to. The atmosphere of submission is a kind of collective guilt"; Jaspers, *German Guilt*, pp. 55, 70, 72.

143. "There is liability for political guilt, consequently reparation is necessary and...loss or restriction of political rights on the part of the guilty (emphasis original)"; Jaspers, *German Guilt*, p. 30. Also see Istvan Vasarhelyi, *Restitution in International Law* (Budapest: Hungary Academy of Science, 1964).

144. In some cases, the number of actual perpetrators may run into the hundreds of thousands, those culpable by reason of active complicity into the millions. In such instances, the likelihood of everyone involved being brought to trial is nil. For logistical reasons, if nothing else, the best hope is that a few thousand "key players" be prosecuted and punished. This was more-or-less the pattern established at Nuremberg; John Alan Appleman, *Military Tribunals and International Crimes* (Westport, CT: Greenwood Press, 1971 reprint of 1954 original).

145. "Blindness for the misfortune of others...indifference toward the witnessed evil—that is moral guilt. The moral guilt of outward compliance, of running with the pack, is shared to some extent by a great many of us. To maintain his existence, to keep [her] job, to protect his [or her] chances, a man [or woman] would...carry out nominal acts of conformism. None will find an absolute excuse for doing so—notably in view of [those] who, in fact, did not conform, and bore the consequences... It is never simply true that 'orders are orders.' Rather—as crimes even though ordered...so every deed remains subject to moral [and criminal] judgment"; Jaspers, *German Guilt*, p. 64,

146. "It would, indeed, be an evasion and a false excuse if we Germans tried to exculpate ourselves by pointing to the guilt of being human"; Jaspers, *German Guilt*, p. 94. For a current rehash of the bilge at issue, see Francis Fukuyama, *The Great Disruption: Human Nature and the Reconstruction of Social Order* (New York: Simon and Schuster, 2000).

147. "Each one of us is guilty insofar as [s/he] remained inactive... The conditions out of which both crime and political guilt arise [consist of the] commission of countless little acts of negligence, of convenient adaptation, of cheap vindication, and the imperceptible promotion of wrong; the participation of the creation of a public atmosphere that spreads confusion and thus makes evil possible—all that has consequences that partly condition the political guilt involved in the situation and events"; Jaspers, *German Guilt*, pp. 63, 29.

148. I've consciously switched from "they" to "we" in this passage. This is because, despite my sustained, always vociferous and at times physical opposition, and the fact that I am a citizen only by virtue of the U.S. imposition of itself upon my people, I am nonetheless here, in the belly of the beast, still alive and at liberty, and have thus done less than I could have. Hence, I share in the political guilt of all Americans. It follows that had I been in aboard one of the fatal aircraft on 9-1-1—or should I be similarly extinguished in the future, as is entirely possible, under present circumstances—I will have no more basis for complaint than any other American.

149. Quoted in Jürgen Habermas, "Goldhagen and the Public Use of History: Why a Democracy Prize for Daniel Goldhagen?" in Shandley, *Unwilling Germans?*, p. 265. On Schmitt's decisive role in the formulation of nazi legal theory, see Stolleis, *Law Under the Swastika*, esp. pp. 13, 92–3, 97–8, 100.

150. This concerns "attempts of the New Right ideologues around Ranier Zitelmann as well as among some of the more naive social historians to relativize the horrors of the Third Reich by reference to the supposedly 'good aspects' of the regime, which is said to have promoted a sort of 'progressive social policy,' or even have become a kind of 'welfare state' in which 'only minorities and marginal groups' were persecuted"; Wolfgang Wippermann, "The Jewish Hanging Judge? Goldhagen and the 'Self-Confident Nation'," in Shandley, *Unwilling Germans*, p. 243.

151. The level of argumentation here descends to that embodied in claims that the lethal thugs rostering Brooklyn's Murder, Inc., during the 1930s really "weren't so bad" because, whatever else they may have done, they were always "good to their mothers"; see Robert A. Rockaway, *But He Was Good to His Mother: Lives and Crimes of Jewish Gangsters* (New York: Gefen, 2000). Like it or not, the evaluative principle by which such virtues are discounted to the point of irrelevancy in assessments of Lepke Buchalter and Allie Tannenbaum—or Adolf Eichmann—is equally applicable to many of those killed on 9-1-1, as much to Cantor Fitzgerald as to Murder, Inc., to the U.S. no less than to nazi Germany.

152. The past does not simply "go away," nor can America's myriad victims just "get over it," no matter how convenient it would be for Americans if they did; see analogously, Charles S. Maier, *The Unmasterable Past: History, Holocaust, and German National Identity* (Cambridge, MA: Harvard University Press, 1988).

153. In a sense, the same could be said of America's own troops, disproportionately drawn as they are from impoverished communities of color and poor sectors of the white populace, once their more privileged countrymen have used them as fodder. Witness the ongoing official refusal to acknowledge—and thus accept responsibility for—the well-established link between dioxin exposure and the cancers/other serious health maladies suffered at extraordinarily high rates by Vietnam veterans and their offspring; Fred A. Wilcox, *Waiting for an Army to Die: The Tragedy of Agent Orange* (Santa Ana, CA: Seven Locks Press, 1989); Institute of Medicine, *Veterans and Agent Orange: Update 1998* (Washington, D.C.: National Academy Press, 2000). Much the same thing is now occurring with the "Gulf War Syndrome" suffered at high rates by soldiers exposed to depleted uranium and other toxins in 1991; Akiro Tashiro, *Discounted Casualties: The Human Costs of Depleted Uranium* (Hiroshima: Chigoku Chimbum, 2001).

Needless to say, the mostly affluent "progressives" of the "antismoking movement"—for all their shrieking about the illusory "health effects" of environment tobacco smoke in open air sports stadia (see note 20)—have maintained a thundering silence vis-à-vis these substantive problems.

154. See the sections titled "The Comfort Zone" and "Let's Pretend" in *Pacifism as Pathology*, pp. 46–69.

155. It should be noted that Americans are by-and-large as self-contradictory on this score as anything else. Although there is endless clucking about the "moral impropriety" of armed resistance to state power in the U.S., exactly the opposite is held to be true with respect to Germany. Although it is true that, as Jaspers observes, many thousands of Germans were imprisoned for resistance by the nazis—"every month of 1944 political arrests exceeded 4,000"—it is also true that these "anonymous martyrs," offered no "dangerous opposition." They resisted almost exclusively "by word" and were therefore "ineffective"; Jaspers, *German Guilt*, pp. 77, 55. Also see Peter Hoffman's magisterial study, *The History of the German Resistance, 1933–1945* (Montréal: McGill-Queen's University Press, [3rd ed.] 1996). The sole group consequential enough to be recollected at all in the U.S.—and quite approvingly so—are the group of plotters who attempted to assassinate Hitler late in the war; see, e.g., Giles MacDonogh, *A Good German: A Biography of Adam von Trott zu Solz* (Woodstock, NY: Overlook Press, 1992).

156. The "traditional Washington stance [has been] that the U.S. is above international law"; Robinson, *Crimes Against Humanity*, p. 327. Suffice here to observe that the "unilateralist" policy pursued by the U.S. in international affairs draws much of its inspiration from the theory of a "prerogative state"—a "governmental system which exercises unlimited arbitrariness and violence unchecked by any legal guarantees" other than those it elects on the basis of expedience or transient self-interest to observe—described by legal philosopher Ernst Fraenkel, in his *The Dual State: A Contribution to the Theory of Dictatorship* (New York: Oxford University Press, 1941) p. xiii.

157. "U.S. Terminates Acceptance of ICJ Compulsory Jurisdiction," *Department of State Bulletin*, No. 86, Jan. 1986.

158. The U.S. refused to join 120 other states voting to affirm the ICC Charter in 1998, and continues to insist it will never do so until the Charter is revised to grant Americans "100 percent protection" against—that is, blanket immunity from—indictment and prosecution; Blum, *Rogue State*, p. 77; Robertson, *Crimes Against Humanity*, pp. 327–8.

159. On the binding effect of customary law on all states, see Wright, "Law of the Nuremberg Tribunal."

160. For a fairly comprehensive itemization, see Blum, *Rogue State*, pp.187–97.

161. Lawrence J. LeBlanc, *The United States and the Genocide Convention* (Durham, NC: Duke University Press, 1991); the text of the U.S. "Sovereignty Package" appears as Appendix C, pp. 253–4.

162. Article 37 of the "Convention on the Rights of the Child," which has been ratified by every U.N. member state but the U.S. and Somalia, makes it illegal to impose the death penalty on persons who were under 18 years-of-age at the time their crime was committed. In *Tompkins v. Oklahoma* (108 S.Ct. 2687 (1988)) and *Stanford v. Kentucky, Wilkins v. Missouri* (492 U.S. 361 (1989)), however, the U.S. Supreme Court has upheld the executions of persons who were as young as 16 when their offenses occurred. In effect, the U.S. refusal of the Convention, is expressly intended to preserve a legally-fictional "sovereign right" to kill children.

163. The "Land Mine Convention," which took effect on Mar. 1, 1999, has been affirmed by 131 states and formally ratified by more than 70. The U.S. has stated repeatedly that it will endorse the law only if it—and it alone—is exempted from compliance; Blum, *Rogue State*, p. 101.

164. A classic example concerns Col. John Chivington and other perpetrators of the 1864 Sand Creek Massacre. Although 3 separate federal investigations—one by the House, another by the Senate, the third by the Department of War—each concluded that violations of the Army's Lieber Code, several of them capital offenses, had been committed deliberately and on a massive scale, no one was prosecuted; see the final chapter of Stan Hoig's *The Sand Creek Massacre* (Norman: University of Oklahoma Press, 1961). Another concerns the 1968 My Lai Massacre in Vietnam. Only 4 of an already much-circumscribed list of 30 responsible officers were ever taken to trial; Joseph Goldstein, Burke Marshall and Jack Schwartz, *The My Lai Massacre and Its Cover-Up: Beyond the Reach of the Law* (New York: Free Press, 1976) pp. 3–4. The litany could continue, but there should be no need. The parallel to the interwar German performance discussed in note 138 is obvious.

165. Lt. William Calley, the only man ultimately convicted in the massacre of "at least 102 Oriental human beings" at My Lai, served only 3.5 years as a result. Several other officers received reprimands, demoted one rank, stripped of a medal, and/or directed to take early retirement; Goldstein, Marshall and Schwartz, *My Lai*, pp. ix-x, 465–7. The same pattern prevailed in 1902–03, with respect to the handful of officers found guilty of atrocities in the Philippines; Creighton Miller *"Benevolent Assimilation"*, pp. 236–8. Again, there is a striking similarity to the performance of interwar Germany (note 138).

166. Once again, the idea is by no means new. It was first seriously proposed in 1969, as part of a broader strategy to force a halt to the U.S. war against Indochina; see Judith Cockburn and Geoffrey Cowan, "The War Criminals Hedge Their Bets," *Village Voice*, Dec. 4, 1969; Townsend Hoopes, "The Nuremberg Suggestion," *Washington Monthly*, Jan. 1970.

167. Christopher Hitchens, *The Trial of Henry Kissinger* (London: Verso, 2001).

168. Robertson, *Crimes Against Humanity*, pp. 446–8.

169. See Telford Taylor, *Anatomy of the Nuremberg Trials* (New York: Alfred A. Knopf, 1992).

170. The notion of "voluntary" remedies, in which offenders themselves establish either the form or the equity involved, has long since proven more than inadequate; see Hubert Kim, "German Reparations: Industrialized Insufficiency," and Roy L. Brooks, "What Form Redress?" in Roy L. Brooks, ed., *When Sorry Isn't Enough: The Controversy over Apologies for Human Injustice* (New York: New York University Press, 1999) pp. 77–80, 87–100.

171. Although the dispensation of justice was far from perfect or complete, more than 6,000 criminal cases were brought against former nazis in Germany's domestic courts between 1951 and 1981; Diane F. Orentlicher, "Settling Accounts: The Duty to Prosecute Human Rights Violations of a Prior Regime," *Yale Law Journal*, No. 2588, 1991. One major barrier to a still more thorough process was the protection provided by the U.S. to thousands of potential defendants its CIA and military establishment saw as being useful for their own purposes; Christopher Simpson, *Blowback: America's Recruitment of Nazis and Its Effect on the Cold War* (London: Weidenfeld and Nicholson, 1988).

172. Shortly after 9-1-1, Noam Chomsky presumed to inform the attackers of what they "should" have done instead. Astonishingly, he then goes on to posit as a "precedent" for "how to go about [obtaining] justice" the 1985 *Nicaragua v. U.S.* case in which a people "subjected to violent assault by the U.S....went to the World Court, which issued a judgment in their favor condemning the U.S. for what it called 'unlawful use of force,' which means international terrorism, ordering the U.S. to desist and pay substantial reparations." What is bizarre is that Chomsky also observes how "the U.S. dismissed the court judgment with contempt, responding with an immediate escalation of the attack [in which] tens of thousands of people died. The country was substantially destroyed, it may never recover." This is the way victims "should proceed"? There's something seriously missing in the formulation; Noam Chomsky, interviewed by David Barsamian, "The United States is a Leading Terrorist State," *Monthly Review*, Vol. 53, No. 6, 2001, pp. 14–5.

173. "A state [polity] which has violated natural law and human rights on principle—at home from the start, destroying human rights and international law abroad—has no claim to recognition, in its favor, of what it refused to recognize itself"; Jaspers, *German Guilt*, p. 38.

174. "By 'national history,' I do not mean just the history of a given country or nation. I refer to the dominant framework for understanding that history. This is not confined to or necessarily governed by how academic history is written, though it may include that. It encompasses how a national history is represented more generally in the public sphere—in newspapers and magazines, on television and film, in textbooks and popular works of history. These shape a people's images of its past far more than do the scholarly books of academic historians"; Daniel Jonah Goldhagen, "*Modell Bundesrepublik: National History, Democracy, and Internationalization in Germany*," in Shandley, *Unwilling Germans?*, pp. 275–6.

175. Ibid., pp. 277–80.

176. Jaspers, *German Guilt*, pp. 96–117. I've given a secular reading to the decidedly theological cant exhibited by Jaspers in these pages.

177. For exemplars of the canonical approach, see Samuel Eliot Morison, *The Oxford History of the American People* (New York: Oxford University Press, 1965); James McGregor Burns, *The American Experiment*, 3 vols. (New York: Alfred A. Knopf, 1983–86). On its pop counterparts, see, as examples, Peter C. Rollins, ed., *Hollywood as Historian: American Film in a Cultural Context* (Lexington: University Press of Kentucky, 1983); Robert Brent Toplin, *History by Hollywood: The Use and Abuse of the American Past* (Urbana: University of Illinois Press, 1996).

178. Although overlapping, there are significant differences between the legal and historical arenas not only with regard to the rules of evidence, but concerning the purposes to which it is put. Put most simply, the emphasis of the former is to demonstrate culpability, the latter to explain it. See generally, Graham C. Lilly, *An Introduction to the Law of Evidence* (St. Paul, MN: West Wadsworth, 1996); Walter Prevenier and Martha C. Howell, From *Reliable Sources: An Introduction to Historical Methods* (Ithaca, NY: Cornell University Press, 2001).

179. This is more-or-less the process that has occurred with respect to Germany; see Maier, *Unmasterable Past*.

That "Most Peace-Loving of Nations"

A Record of U.S. Military Actions at Home and Abroad, 1776–2003

> We go to war but grudgingly and then only when compelled
> by the requirements of restoring the peace, justice, and good
> order, for we among all the peoples of the world comprise the
> most peace-loving of nations.
>
> — Woodrow Wilson, 1917

One of the paramount difficulties in achieving constructive change in the U.S. is, and has always been, the country's patently false image of itself. A particularly bizarre aspect of the "American exceptionalism" by which the collective self-concept has been defined is what analyst Stuart Creighton Miller has termed "radical innocence."[1] Put most simply, this is the notion that the U.S. is the "most peace-loving of nations," its populace—especially those of European descent—composed of essentially "peace-loving citizens" who go to war only when the aggressive irrationalities of other countries or peoples have left them "no choice," and then in a uniquely altruistic and humane fashion.[2]

The manner in which such mythology has been both packaged and embraced is as circular as it is self-congratulatory: a small range of "lapses," "excesses" and other such "aberrations" or "anomalies" is first nobly acknowledged, this "honest admission" of "regrettable exceptions" then advanced to "prove the rule" of America's exceptionally innocent nature. Thus, if not exactly perfect, it is concluded, both the U.S. record and the outlooks attending it must be seen as adding up to the best that is humanly attainable. Since improvement is impossible, there is no point in attempting it.[3]

To some extent, the mindset at issue derives from a pervasive public ignorance of American history, only the most simplified and sanitized version of which is taught in the country's schools. Asked to recite a list of America's wars, the average respondent, and more than a few who fancy themselves "historically-inclined," will typically reply with a list including only those conflicts fought on a grand scale: after the "Revolution," there were the War of 1812, the War with Mexico, the Civil War, the Spanish-American War, the First and Second World Wars, Korea, Vietnam and the Persian Gulf.[4] Most will include mention of the forty-odd "Indian Wars"[5]—usually without knowing how many were actually fought—and, mainly because they are so recent, the campaigns in Kosovo and Afghanistan. Some may also, mainly because of the currently ongoing appearance in theaters of Ridley Scott's *Black Hawk*

Down, make mention of Somalia, although most will not see this as having been an "actual" war (a view with which Somalis are guaranteed to vehemently disagree).

At least Americans are aware that something of a military nature happened in Somalia. Bringing up America's 1871 "Little War with the Heathens" in Korea, however, or the vastly brutal "Indian War" pursued against the "Moros" of the Philippines thirty years later, will produce blank stares from all but a handful of U.S. citizens.[6] The more so, such things as the hundreds of military "landings" on—invasions, really—other countries' territory to "protect American interests" around the world, and the participation of naval forces, including marines, in overthrowing the friendly and entirely legitimate government of Hawai'i (an act accurately described by then-President Grover Cleveland as violating international law).[7] The more so still when a recounting is attempted with respect to the numerous times and places where troops were used, often in direct violation of U.S. domestic law (e.g., the 1877 Posse Comitatus Act (18 USCS § 1385)), to repress opposition to socioeconomic inequities and unpopular policies at home.[8]

The chronology offered below, to my knowledge the most comprehensive of its sort ever assembled, is designed to set the record straight in certain respects. Not only does it provide the most complete itemization of U.S. military actions possible, it assigns motives either explicitly or implicitly to each action (often by quoting those directly involved). Here, altruism—the idea that America fights for ideals like "preserving freedom" or "ending war"—plays no part at all. The goals involved—outright expansionism, subordination of other countries' assets and economies, nullification of alternatives to U.S. hegemony abroad, and pacification of domestic opposition—tend increasingly over time to overlap and intertwine, with the result that as unimpeachable an expert as Major General Smedley Butler would frankly admit in 1935:

> I spent 33 years and 4 months in active service as a member of our country's most agile military force—the Marine Corps... And during that period, I spent most of my time being a high-class muscle man for Big Business, for Wall Street and for the bankers. In short, I was a racketeer for capitalism... I helped make Mexico and especially Tampico safe for American oil interests in 1914. I helped make Haiti and Cuba a decent place for the National City Bank boys to collect money in. I helped in the raping of a half a dozen Central American republics for the benefit of Wall Street... I helped purify Nicaragua for the international banking house of Brown Brothers in 1909–12. I brought light to the Dominican Republic for American sugar interests in 1916. I helped get Honduras "right" for American fruit companies in 1903. In China in 1927 I helped see to it that Standard Oil went its way unmolested. Looking back on it, I feel I might have given Al Capone a few hints. The best *he* could do was operate in three city districts. We Marines operated on three *continents*.[9]

What emerges from the chronology, then, and unmistakably so, is the portrait of a country which has not experienced a time when it was actually "at peace" since its inception. Each and every year for the past 226 years, the U.S. military has been in action somewhere, and quite often in a lot of places simultaneously. Far from comprising the history of "the most peace-loving of nations," the record is that of one of the most consistently belligerent countries—perhaps *the* most—in the annals of humankind. Far from "fighting for freedom and democracy," moreover, the U.S. has with equal consistency fought to repeal it anywhere and everywhere, not excluding the domestic sphere of the U.S. itself, they've threatened to take hold.[10] The American public may be conveniently oblivious to these realities, but the rest of the world is not.

A Genocidal Mentality

No less, are people elsewhere on the planet acutely conscious of other things of which Americans prefer to remain oblivious, or which they actively deny, and which can only be hinted at in these pages. These go to the ferocity—the sheer inhumanity, as it were—with which the U.S. has waged its wars. While the bodycounts provided here and there may impart something of this, the reality, to the extent that it can be conveyed at all, will be found in the "details," glimpsed in the mutilated corpses of women, children and old men strewn about massacre sites like Sand Creek,[11] in John Sullivan's troops returning from their campaign against the Seneca's wearing leggings made from the tanned skins of their opponents,[12] in Andrew Jackson's slicing the noses off slain Red Sticks at Horseshoe Bend to confirm their number of kills,[13] in General J. Franklin Bell's reduction of the Filipinos' densely-populated Batanga Province to a "howling wilderness" at the dawn of the twentieth century.[14]

Nor do such nightmarish scenes end with the "bad old days" of the "Wild West" (even though the "West" was as often situated in upstate New York or the far side of the Pacific as it was in Arizona, Colorado or the Dakotas). They are readily discernable among the letter-openers fashioned by marines from the thigh bones of their Japanese opponents during World War II and the ears of dead "gooks" commonly strung as trophy necklaces by GIs in Vietnam a generation later.[15] The revulsion with which the myriad massacres perpetrated by American soldiers at places like My Lai and No Gun Ri during the twentieth century are remembered should be no less than that attending recollection of their earlier counterparts at Bear River and Wounded Knee.[16] The truth is, as an army colonel put it in Vietnam, that "nothing kills like an Iowa farm boy."[17] The observation remains no less accurate today, or than it would have been 150 years earlier.

In the end, such things—each of them conventionally depicted, when it is mentioned at all, as an "anomaly" or "exception" to the rule— blend into a broad and continuous stream of atrocity, all of it committed in the most up close and personal manner by "the flower of America's young men and women." This stream, in turn, merges with another, detached, impersonal, increasingly prominent and vastly more lethal. Here, we encounter a world of technicians sitting in air-conditioned comfort at computer consoles while launching cruise missiles to obliterate untold numbers of people at hundreds of miles remove, of bombardiers in aircraft thousands of feet above their teeming and effectively defenseless targets, delivering endless "payloads" of hyperlethal ordnance—napalm, white phosphorus, aerosol bombs designed to suck all the oxygen out of underground shelters, cluster bombs spewing clouds of plastic shrapnel undetectable to x-rays (thus producing, as they were carefully designed to do, wounds extraordinarily resistant to medical treatment)—upon the faceless masses of humanity huddled below.[18]

An answer to the question of how many anomalies are needed to make a norm thereby presents itself: in "the American way of war," the supposed "exceptions" *are* the rule. To apprehend its meaning, we must enter not the humbly gallant mental domain of Gary Cooper's Sergeant York, but of the torturer's lust to inflict agony with impunity, the rapist's to dominate his victims at the most intimate of levels, the sociopath's sense of divine entitlement to dehumanize those s/he views as being less consequential than herself; the true psychopath's compulsion to transform dehumanization into the outright eradication of "lesser" beings.

America's time-honored "rhetoric of extermination"[19] is in the last connection utterly revealing: "Nits make lice," explained Colonel John Chivington, when instructing his troops to slaughter everyone, elder and baby alike, at Sand Creek in 1864;[20] U.S. policymakers' habitual figurations of the Vietnamese as "termites," "ants" and "flies" during the "war of attrition" waged in their country a century later are no less clear;[21] so too "our" pilots' leering characterizations of the scores of thousands of Iraqis (and others) butchered along the "Highway of Death" in 1991.[22] Undeniably, the outlook embodied in such verbiage is in kind with that of SS Reichsführer Heinrich Himmler when he likened his minions' extermination of Jews and Gypsies to "delousing."[23] Small wonder that much of the world, including even some of the more oppressed sectors of the U.S. population itself, have long since come to understand "Americanism" and nazism as synonyms. The "genocidal mentality" involved is,[24] after all, in either case indistinguishable, other than by way of the far more sustained and technologically-greater U.S. capacity to impose itself than was enjoyed by the Third Reich.

Some Notes on Method

A chronology such as that which follows can never be definitive. No matter how elaborately detailed, as much or more is inevitably left out as is included. In this case, the existence and duration of a welter of garrisons established by the U.S. at various points around the globe—e.g., the tiny island of Diego Garcia, in the Indian Ocean—have been deliberately excluded in order to keep the material presented from becoming overwhelming. For similar reasons, only the operations of the federal military establishment, including the Central Intelligence Agency (heavily overlapped as it is with the military's Special Forces units), are represented. The hundreds of domestic actions carried out by state and local militias—later the National Guard—over the past two-and-a-quarter centuries are therefore excluded.[25]

The same applies to operations carried out by the Special Weapons and Tactics (SWAT) teams—essentially military units within federal, state and local police agencies—which have proliferated over the past three decades in every city in the U.S. with a population of 50,000 or more.[26] In addition, no mention is made of the operations conducted by the literal private armies retained by American industrialists, especially during the second half of the nineteenth and early twentieth centuries, which waged "labor wars," unparalleled elsewhere in either their scale or their bloodiness, against the country's working men and women.[27] The chronology, lengthy as it is, amounts to no more than a "short list," the barest tip of the American militarist iceberg.

Aside from that attending the preceding introductory text, and the brief conclusion, no annotation accompanies the material contained herein. It would of course have been possible to provide it, but to do so would have dramatically increased the length of an already long piece. The idea of adding notes to what already amounts to a series of notes also seems rather awkward. Hence, a bibliography of the primary sources used in compiling the chronology is provided at the end. Presumably, readers will be able to match titles therefrom to matters of particular interest within the chronology itself and follow up accordingly.

Finally, it will be noticed that, apart from the earlier-mentioned Posse Comitatus Act, little or no attention is paid to the legality of what is depicted below. This undoubtedly seems peculiar, given my framing the implications of U.S. military comportment by way of comparison to the Third Reich (by all accounts a preeminently criminal state). Here again, the additional length and complexity involved in incorporating the additional information would have rendered the present exposition overly cumbersome. Questions of legality are therefore addressed in a separate chronological itemization, entitled "A Nation of Laws?", which also appears in this volume.

Chronology of U.S. Military Actions

1776–83: An élite group within thirteen of England's North American colonies, chafing at King George III's Royal Proclamation of 1763, an edict foreclosing upon their speculative interests in Indian land west of the Appalachian Mountains, instigates an armed insurrection against Crown authority. A "Continental Army" under overall command of General George Washington, "the richest man in North America," is organized on the promise that victory will result in soldiers being rewarded with land parcels west of the proclamation line. English forces are defeated after protracted fighting, and the colonies are granted independence in the 1783 Treaty of Paris.

1776: Three columns, totaling more than 6,000 men, are sent against the Cherokees in Georgia and Tennessee, leveling more than two dozen towns, destroying crops, inflicting serious casualties on noncombatants and sweeping much of the population into Spanish Florida. Only the cessation of about a third of all Cherokee territory brings the annihilatory campaign to a halt.

1777–94: Rangers commanded by General George Rogers Clark and others conduct raids against the Shawnees, Miamis, Mingos, Ottawas and other peoples indigenous to Kentucky and the "Northwest Territories" (Ohio, Indiana, Michigan and Illinois).

1779: An army commanded by General John Sullivan undertakes a campaign against the Senecas and other members of the Haudenosaunee (Six Nations Iroquois Confederacy) in upstate New York to "punish" the Indians for siding with England. Sullivan orders "a war of extermination waged against even the very orchards" and his men comply with gusto, laying waste to every native town, field and human being they encounter. Much weakened by the onslaught, the Haudenosaunee are rapidly dispossessed of their land.

1780: An offensive similar to that conducted against the Haudenosaunee a year earlier, and against the Cherokees in 1776, is undertaken against the Muskogees (Creeks) and Chickamaugas. The Muskogees suffer damage comparable to that incurred by their predecessors. The Chickamaugas are all but totally exterminated.

1790–91: Troops commanded by General Josiah Harmar are sent to "chastise" the Shawnees and their allies, led by Blue Jacket, for refusing to allow white settlers to encroach upon their traditional territories. Harmar's column is routed on October 21, 1790. The following spring, a much larger force under General Arthur St. Clair, is sent to avenge this humiliation. On November 4, St. Clair is handed a defeat that, in "proportion to the number of men fielded that day, stands as the worst loss the U.S. Army has ever suffered."

1793–94: The U.S. faces off with Great Britain over a British proposal to convert the Northwest Territories into an American Indian free state. The U.S. contends that England "ceded" the area to the U.S. in the 1783 Treaty of Paris. Britain counters, quite accurately, that since it could not be reasonably viewed as transferring title to land it had never purported to own, it had merely quitclaimed its acquisitive interest in the property (thereby leaving unclouded title in native hands). Although troops are mobilized in preparation for a war to assert U.S. "rights" in the matter, it is resolved—for everyone but the Indians—through Jay's Treaty in mid-1794.

1794: An army commanded by General "Mad Anthony" Wayne, after engaging in operations similar to Sullivan's in 1779, finally defeats the Shawnees at Fallen Timbers (in present-day Toledo, Ohio). The U.S. takes most of the Indians' territory as a condition for "peace." Meanwhile, George

Washington, now president, musters 15,000 troops to put down the so-called Whiskey Rebellion—which is not an armed revolt, but rather a group of citizens exercising their supposed constitutional right to assemble and publicly protest the federal government's recently-proclaimed excise tax on whiskey and other such "spirits"—in Virginia.

1796–99: Future president Alexander Hamilton is appointed Inspector General of the Army. In this capacity, he engineers a 16,000-man expansion of the service, lays the groundwork for adding another 20,000, and advances a secret plan in which he will assume command of 40,000 troops and invade South America. Although the plan, as such, never reaches fruition, its very articulation figures heavily in the subsequent formulation of the Monroe Doctrine.

1798–1800: An undeclared naval war is fought with France to prevent subordination of American shipping to conventional maritime law. Marines are landed in Puerto Plata (Dominican Republic) to seize French shipping, while black revolutionary Toussaint L'Ouverture is funded in the amount of $6 million to undermine French authority in Haiti. Tied up in an ongoing conflict with Britain in Europe, France declines further engagement. This outcome confirms the War Department in an already-stated belief that to "make war, and call it self-defense" is sound policy.

1799: President John Adams sends troops to put down Fries Rebellion, an "insurrection" of about 180 individuals upset by the levying of property taxes, in Pennsylvania.

1800: Troops are deployed to put down an incipient slave revolt led by Gabriel Prosser in Virginia. Prosser and 35 conspirators are summarily executed, as a "deterrent example" to others inclined to try and free themselves from chattel slavery, under orders of Governor (*cum* U.S. President) James Monroe.

1801–05: America's refusal to comply with the laws of the sea results in a declaration of war by Tripoli, on North Africa's "Barbary Coast" (Libya), and its capture of the U.S. frigate, *Philadelphia*. Although the U.S. fails to respond with its own declaration of war, an agent, William Eaton, is dispatched to raise a force of mercenaries. Marines are then landed, Tripoli stormed, and terms dictated.

1803: President Thomas Jefferson purchases French interests in the vast Louisiana Territory, west of the Mississippi River. Military reconnaissance begins almost immediately, with an eye towards constructing forts securing overland routes to the Pacific through unceded Indian territories. The first proposals also surface concerning possible use of the area as a dumping ground for indigenous populations resident to areas east of the Mississippi.

1806: Captain Zebulon Pike, commanding a platoon of U.S. troops and acting on orders of General James Wilkenson, invades Spanish territory at the headwaters of the Río Grande, apparently to test the Spanish response. The captain is captured and taken to Mexico, but later released.

1806–10: A force of U.S. gunboats operating out of New Orleans conducts operations against French and Spanish shipping in the Caribbean. This is an early phase of the drive, eventually articulated in the Monroe Doctrine, to assert U.S. military/commercial hegemony over the entire Western Hemisphere.

1807: President Thomas Jefferson formalizes the national policy of "exterminating" or "driving beyond the Mississippi River" all American Indians residing in the eastern U.S. Jefferson also proposes an invasion of Canada, but the army deems itself too weak to proceed.

1810: A force of troops sent by Louisiana Governor William Claiborne, acting on the instructions of President James Madison, invades the western portion of Spanish Florida, occupying it as far eastward as the Pearl River (whch then becomes the eastern boundary of Louisiana).

1811: Troops under future presidents John Tyler and William Henry Harrison complete yet another war against the Shawnees and allied peoples, now led by Tecumseh, defeating them at Tippecanoe. The U.S. takes the remainder of their territory and pushes most of the survivors into areas west of the Mississippi. Meanwhile, troops are deployed to put down a major slave revolt in Louisiana; 66 "insurgents" are shot dead, 16 "ringleaders" summarily executed as "deterrent examples" in the aftermath.

1812–15: General George Matthews, acting on orders from President Madison, seizes Amelia Island and adjacent parts of eastern Florida. Although the troops are quickly withdrawn under pressure from Britain and other powers, the foray is a contributing factor in the War of 1812, which begins shortly thereafter and lasts until 1815.

1813: In April, General James Wilkinson, acting on instructions from Congress, seizes Mobile Bay, in Spanish West Florida (now Alabama) with a force of 600 men. More-or-less simultaneously, an army under future president Andrew Jackson takes to the field to suppress resistance by the "Red Stick" faction of the Muscogee (Creek) Confederacy to further invasion by U.S. "settlers" of the Muscogees' Alabama homeland. Jackson obtains victory by massacring about 800 Red Sticks at the Horseshoe Bend of the Talapoosa River. The survivors are forcibly "removed" to Oklahoma.

1813–14: Troops invade Nukahiva, in the Marquesas Islands, where they build a fort and establish the first U.S. naval base in the Pacific.

1814: Troops under Andrew Jackson capture the town of Pensacola, in Florida, which has been occupied by the Briish with Spanish permission.

1814–25: Ostensibly to combat the depredations of pirates, a squadron of warships under Commodore James Biddle asserts U.S. naval primacy in the Caribbean, engaging in a lengthy series of altercations with Spanish, French and British vessels. In 1823, President Monroe asserts the doctrine that the U.S. enjoys a "right" to dominate the Americas, free from "interference" by European competitors.

1815: The "Second Barbary War" is undertaken, with a large fleet under Captain Stephen Decatur attacking Algiers. "Indemnities" are thereupon collected for the enforcement of Algerian maritime law against U.S. commercial shipping. Decatur then moves on to Tripoli, forcing payment of a similar fee from that country.

1816–18: Troops attack and destroy Nicholls' Fort—called "The Negro Fort" because it serves as a refuge for runaway African slaves from Georgia, Alabama and Louisiana plantations—in Spanish Florida. Generals Jackson and Edmund P. Gaines then launch the "First Seminole War" against the area's indigenous people, partly because they too offer sanctuary to runaway slaves. Several Spanish posts, including Amelia Island, are attacked and occupied, while a number of British citizens are summarily executed.

1818: In August, the territory of Oregon, claimed by Russia and Spain, is invaded by a detachment of troops at the mouth of the Columbia River. The U.S. then asserts "ownership" of the area.

1819: Under threat of yet another military confrontation, Spain finally transfers its claims in Florida and Oregon to the U.S.

1820–23: Naval units, acting on the instruction of Congress, conduct a series of raids against Portuguese slave shipping along the west coast of Africa.

1822: Troops are deployed to put down a slave revolt led by a freedman named Denmark Vesey in South Carolina. Thirty-five blacks, including Vesey, are hanged in the aftermath, their bodies left on public display for some time thereafter as a "deterrent" to others inclined to display similar "uppitiness."

1822–25: Marines under Commodore Biddle are landed in the Spanish colony of Cuba (at Escondito, Cayo Blanco, Siquapa Bay, Cape Cruz, Camrioca, Matanzas Sagua La Grande and elsewhere), while another detachment, under Commodore David Porter, occupies the town of Fajardo, in Puerto Rico. Ostensibly undertaken to combat pirates, the actions appear designed more to punctuate the Monroe Doctrine.

1827: Marines invade the Greek islands of Argentiere, Miconi and Andross, establishing a U.S. military presence in the eastern Mediterranean. The pretext for this offense against Greek sovereignty is once again a need to "combat pirates."

1828–39: Andrew Jackson is elected president and calls for "the scurging [sic] of the whole Cherokee Nation" (a U.S. ally against both the Red Sticks and Britain during the War of 1812). The army is then used to effect the forced removal of the so-called "Five Civilized Tribes"—the Cherokee, Creek, Chickasaw, Choctaw and Seminole Nations—to Oklahoma, a policy continued after Jackson leaves office.

1831: Troops are deployed to put down a slave revolt led by Nat Turner in Virginia. Turner and 18 of his 70-odd "co-conspirators" are hanged in the aftermath.

1831–32: A naval force is dispatched to the Falkland (Malvinas) Islands off Argentina to "investigate" the capture of three U.S. ships engaged in illegal sealing operations in Argentine waters. This double violation of maritime law is "justified" to the public by a "need to protect American interests" under the Monroe Doctrine. Another batch of ships is sent to Sumatra to punish the natives of the town of Quallah Battoo for seeking to enforce their own laws vis-à-vis American merchant shipping.

1832: Troops under General—and future president—Zachary Taylor are sent to forcibly remove the Mesquaki (Sac and Fox) people from their Illinois homeland precipitating the "Black Hawk War." After suffering a largescale massacre along the Bad Axe River in southern Wisconsin, the surviving Mesquakis are pushed across the Mississippi, their territory incorporated into the U.S. Future president Abraham Lincoln serves as a volunteer militia captain during the campaign.

1833: Troops are put ashore in Buenos Aires to "protect American citizens" during a popular insurrection in Argentina. The troops' actual role is to reinforce an emergent local élite, which is acting as a partner to U.S. business interests.

1834–42: Troops under Zachary Taylor are sent to forcibly relocate the Seminole Nation from Florida to Oklahoma. Most go, but a "recalcitrant" faction led by Osceola refuses. The Second Seminole War then begins, dragging on until, his men exhausted with trying to defeat the Indians in swampy terrain, Taylor simply declares "victory" and abandons the fight. The bulk of the Seminole homeland is, however, absorbed by the U.S.

1835–36: Marines are twice dispatched to put down Peruvian insurgents during an attempted revolution there, thus preserving a local élite useful to U.S. business interests.

1836: A campaign is undertaken in the Alabama/Mississippi area to ensure removal of the Muscogee "hold-outs" to Oklahoma. Meanwhile, General Gaines occupies Nacogdoches, Texas, to support American immigrants seeking to force the province's secession from Mexico. The army's presence assists the secessionists in winning their "War of Independence" and establishing what they call the "Republic of Texas." At Fort Clark, on the upper Missouri River, army officers distribute as "gifts" blankets taken from a smallpox infirmary among Mandan leaders assembled at a parlay requested by the military. When the Indians show early symptoms of the disease, army surgeons tell them to seek "sanctuary" in the villages of healthy relatives. A pandemic is thus unleashed which decimates the indigenous population of the Great Plains from Canada to the Gulf of Mexico. At least 100,000 Indians die as a result, making subsequent conquest of the region by the U.S. much easier.

1837: A border clash with Canada leaves the U.S. navy's river vessel *Caroline* destroyed at Navy Island, near Buffalo, New York. The boat, it turns out, has been transporting weapons and munitions to Canadian insurgents bent on overthrowing the government. Nonetheless, U.S. militias are mobilized under federal authority, thousands volunteer to invade Canada, and Congress votes to provide $10 million to raise an army of 50,000 men for the purpose. Fullscale war is narrowly averted.

1838–39: Naval forces are sent to Sumatra for the second time, landing marines at Quallah Battoo and Mukki to ensure that U.S. commercial vessels are free to operate outside the constraints of local law. Meanwhile, in a culmination of Jacksonian removal policy, troops under General Winfield Scott invade the Cherokee Nation (north Georgia and western Tennessee), round up the population and force-march them to Oklahoma. About half of all Cherokees die as a result of this "Trail of Tears." The Cherokee homeland is absorbed into the U.S.

1840–41: Naval forces are dispatched to Fiji to punish "the locals" for attempting to expel an American expedition sent to establish a military base there. Other ships are sent to Drummond Island, in the Kingsmill Group, and Samoa, to avenge the deaths of two American seamen killed as a result of offenses against native people. Again, the U.S. agenda is to override local law through force of arms.

1842: Commodore T.A.C. Jones, assigned to "show the colors" off California, decides that a war has broken out between the U.S. and Mexico (why he thinks this is mysterious, but suggests planning for the conquest that will occur six years later is already underway). He thereupon invades and occupies the towns of Monterey and San Diego. Upon learning of his "error," Jones salutes the local authorities and withdraws (no official apology is issued to the unoffending Mexicans). Meanwhile, President John Tyler uses troops to put down "Dorr's Rebellion," an effort to gain suffrage for landless tenant farmers and thereby transform a virtually feudal system prevailing in Rhode Island.

1843: Marines and sailors are landed from the warship *St. Louis* after a clash between Americans and Chinese over prices at a U.S. trading post in Canton. Four warships also land about 200 marines and sailors on the Ivory Coast in Africa to "punish" local blacks who have attacked American slave traders there.

1844: President Tyler deploys troops to protect Texas from forcible reintegration into Mexico, pending the republic's expected annexation by the U.S. Only when the Senate declines to ratify Tyler's proposed treaty with the Texans are American soldiers temporarily withdrawn.

1846–48: President James Polk sends U.S. troops to occupy an area of Texas still disputed by Mexico. When Mexico responds by sending an army to re-occupy all of Texas, the U.S. declares war, invades Mexico and assaults its capital. As a condition of "peace," Mexico is required by the Treaty of Guadelupe Hidalgo to cede the entire northern half of itself to the U.S. This includes all of the present-day states of New Mexico, Arizona, California, Nevada, Utah and part of Colorado.

1848: A campaign is fought in Oregon to subdue the indigenous Cayuse and allied Palouse peoples prior to the territory's being proclaimed a U.S. territory on August 14.

1849: A naval force is dispatched to Smyrna to compel release of an American agent arrested by Austria for violations of local law.

1850: An expedition is mounted in May against the native Pomos in the Russian River area of California. Trapped on an island where they'd sought to hide, the main body of Pomo noncombatants—"not less than 75"—are massacred by U.S. troops.

1851: A squadron of warships is sent to Johanna Island, east of Africa, to extract "redress" for the treatment of an American ship's captain imprisoned for engaging in whaling operations in violation of local law.

1851–56: A series of three "Rogue River Wars" are fought in rapid succession to subordinate the indigenous peoples of the northern California and southern Oregon (Rogues, Klamaths, Shastas, Modocs, Tunis, Chinooks, Mollalas, Tillamooks, Calapooias and others). Survivors are aggregated on tiny reservations while the balance of their land is occupied by white "settlers."

1852–53: Marines are landed for a second time in Buenos Aires to bolster the Argentine élite against a popular insurrection. Again, the stated reason is "protection of American interests."

1853: Marines are landed in Nicaragua to shield local oligarchs collaborating with U.S. businessmen against a popular insurgency. Meanwhile, an "Indian War" is briefly proclaimed near Sacramento, California, after Ben Wright, a militia captain operating under military authority, orders his troops to massacre a group of about fifty area Indians he'd invited to a "peace parley."

1853–54: Commodore Matthew C. Perry takes a fleet to Japan, using the threat of overwhelming force to compel the emperor to open the previously insular islands to penetration by U.S. business interests. Meanwhile, marines are landed in both the Bonin Islands and Okinawa to secure portage for the envisioned "Japan Trade."

1854: A group of peaceful Lakotas encamped in Kansas is attacked by Lieutenant William Grattan, supposedly as punishment for their "theft" of a cow abandoned by a passing group of Mormons (the Indians had offered to pay for the animal). The Lakotas respond by annihilating Grattan and his men. General William S. Harney then takes to the field with a substantial force and ends up assaulting a completely different group of Lakotas camped along the Blue Water River in Nebraska. Some 150 Indians are massacred.

1854–55: A war is fought in eastern Washington Territory to pacify the Yakima Nation. Meanwhile, marines are landed in Shanghai to protect American profiteers from antiwestern demonstrations by the Chinese in response to Britain's opium trade. In Nicaragua, the entire village of San Juan El Norté is leveled by marines as punishment for the residents' having "insulted" the U.S. ambassador to that country. Marines are also landed in Hong Kong to "fight pirates."

1855: Marines are landed in Montevideo to avert a revolt meant to depose the local élite—which, as usual, has been actively collaborating with American commercial interests at the expense of its own people—in Uruguay. In Paraguay, a U.S. gunboat sent up the Parana River to "persuade" the government to similarly accommodate American businessmen is fired upon and withdraws.

1855–58: A third campaign is undertaken against Seminole "recalcitrants" in Florida. The supposed mop-up operation proves unsuccessful, as the Indians retreat to sanctuary deep in the Everglades. Technically, the Florida Seminoles remain at war with the U.S. until 1967.

1856: Marines are landed in the Panama region of Columbia to help put down a popular revolt "threatening U.S. interests" there. Others are dispatched to Canton, China, to protect American businessmen put at risk by ongoing antiwestern demonstrations. Naval forces seize tiny Jarvis, Baker and Howland Islands in the Hawaiian Archipelago, mainly as a source of the guano used in manufacturing munitions.

1857: Marines are sent to Nicaragua again, this time to put down a coup undertaken by an American adventurer, William Walker, which would have upset the order of U.S. commercial relations in that country. A second motive is to prevent Walker's being punished under Nicaraguan law for his criminal conduct (he was removed to the U.S. over the protests of Nicaraguan officials). Walker was similarly protected after heading an unsuccessful "private" invasion of Baja California a few years previously, apparently attempting to repeat the Texans' achievement of "independence" *cum* annexation by the U.S. Meanwhile, in New York City, marines are used to break up large demonstrations by unemployed workers demanding jobs.

1857–58: A war is fought in eastern Washington and Idaho to pacify the indigenous Coeur d'Alenes and allied Walla Wallas, who have become increasingly resistant to the encroachment of white "settlers" on their land. Several Indian leaders are summarily executed after surrendering.

1858: Marines and sailors are landed in Montevideo again, to help quell a resurgence of revolutionary activity in Uruguay. Others are sent to Fiji, to "chastise" the natives for a second time (in this instance, for having punished two American nationals guilty of abusing indigenous Fijians).

1859: Congress authorizes the sending of a large naval force to intimidate Paraguay because of the 1855 Parana River incident; Paraguay apologizes, although the U.S. had plainly provoked the confrontation. Additional marines are landed in Shanghai, and 200 cavalry troops invade northern Mexico, allegedly in pursuit of a bandit named Cortina. Marines commanded by army Captain Robert E. Lee recapture a federal arsenal at Harper's Ferry, Virginia, after it is seized by the abolitionist John Brown in hopes of sparking a slave revolt. Brown and two blacks are hanged in the aftermath, while 3,000 federal troops are posted to the area for several months to ensure that there are no further "outbreaks."

1860: To "protect American lives and property" from local people who have grown "troublesome" under the yoke of European domination, troops are sent to Kissembo, Portuguese West Africa (Angola). Others are sent to the Bay of Panama in Columbia to ensure that an incipient revolt does not interfere with U.S. business interests there.

1861–65: The great internal adjustment of the U.S. economy and consolidation of the central authority of the federal government called the Civil War is fought, mainly between industrializing, "unionist" northern states and agrarian southern slaveholding states east of the Mississippi. The eventual northern triumph sets the stamp on future projections of American power from a foundation of true continental cohesion.

1861–72: A false accusation by a rancher and rash actions by the army sets off a protracted war with the Chiricahua Apaches in Arizona. Led by Mangus—assassinated by U.S. "peace negotiators" in 1863—and Cochise, the Chiricahuas wage a guerrilla campaign which the army proves ineffectual in combating. A transient "peace" is finally arranged in late 1872.

1862: Starving, and with their treaty-guaranteed Minnesota homeland literally overrun by whites, Santee Dakotas led by Little Crow attempt to clear the invaders from their territory. Troops under Colonel Henry Sibley put down their "revolt" with extreme brutality, culminating in the mass execution of 38 native leaders at Mankado. Santee lands are thereupon absorbed into the U.S. In New Mexico, a brief campaign results in the mass internment of the Mescalero Apaches at the Bosque Redondo, adjoining Fort Sumner, in eastern New Mexico.

1863: Troops are landed at Shimonoseki, Japan, to "redress an insult to the American flag" embodied in shots being fired across the bow of an American warship. In Utah, a volunteer cavalry unit based near Salt Lake City takes to the field against the Shoshones, perpetrating the Bear River Massacre of about 500 Indians in southern Idaho. To the south, in Arizona, troops under Colonel Kit Carson conduct a concerted campaign against the Navajo. When the Indians surrender a year later, they are force-marched to the Bosque Redondo. Interned there until 1868, about half of all Navajos die of starvation and disease. Meanwhile, President Abraham Lincoln orders troops used to quell antidraft riots in New York, Newark, Boston, Toledo, and elsewhere. About 400 people are killed in New York alone—the greatest number of any single incident in U.S. history—lesser numbers in other cities.

1864: Troops are landed at Yedo, Japan, to underscore U.S. demands for payment of commercial claims; naval units then forcibly "open" the Straits of Shimonoseki to foreign shipping. In Colorado, a special unit of volunteer cavalry is raised for the expressed purpose of "exterminating" all Cheyennes and Arapahos residing within territorial boundaries. The main result is the Sand Creek Massacre of about 150 Indians—mostly women, children and old men—camped at an assigned location under "protection" of the army. Cheyenne territory is then largely absorbed by the U.S. Meanwhile, President Lincoln orders troops used to break strikes by workers on the Reading Railroad, as well as machinists in St. Louis and Cold Springs (New York), and miners in Tioga County, Pennsylvania.

1865: Marines are landed in Panama again to prevent popular "interference" with U.S. business interests. Meanwhile, a campaign under Colonel Samuel Walker is mounted against the Lakota and allied peoples of the northern plains. After attacking a peaceful Arapaho village on the Tongue River (in present-day Montana), Walker's command is routed and driven out of "Sioux" country.

1865–77: Troops are deployed throughout the southeastern U.S. at the end of the Civil to maintain order during "reconstruction" of the vanquished confederacy of insurgent states. This leads to passage of the Posse Comitatus Act, prohibiting use of the military for such purposes (other than in cases where civil law enforcement authorities are demonstrably unable or unwilling to do so).

1866: A hundred troops under General Matthew Sedgwick invade and occupy Matamoros, Mexico, only to be withdrawn after three days under intense international protest. In China, marines are put ashore to protect the American consul at Newchwang from antiwestern demonstrations.

1866–68: Troops invade the Lakota Nation in present-day Wyoming and begin construction of a line of forts meant to protect a new transport route to Montana, known as the Bozeman Trail. This action touches off what is called "Red Cloud's War," lasting two years and resulting in the first genuine defeat of American arms. In the spring of 1868, the U.S. sues for peace and a treaty recognizing Lakota ownership of an area encompassing about five percent of the continental U.S. is signed at Ft. Laramie.

1867: Marines occupy Managua and Léon, Nicaragua, to intimidate dissidents. Others are landed on the island of Formosa (Taiwan) to punish "savages" who supposedly murdered the crew of a shipwrecked American vessel (this turns out to be a hoax). Marines from the *U.S.S. Lackawanna* occupy Midway Island in the Hawaiian Archipelago, claiming it as an American naval base. Secretary of State William H. Seward proposes taking all of Canada west of Ontario in order to connect Alaska, the purchase of which had just been consummated, to the rest of the U.S. (alternately—or additionally—Seward thinks it a nice idea to add the rest of Mexico to U.S. holdings)

1867–68: A war is undertaken to pacify the Comanches, Kiowas, Cheyennes and other indigenous peoples of the southern plains. Although the army proves singularly unsuccessful at defeating Indian combatants, "victory" is finally obtained when the 7th U.S. Cavalry, commanded by Lt. Colonel George Armstrong Custer, manages a dawn attack on a noncombatant Cheyenne village encamped for the winter along the Washita River in western Oklahoma. Hundreds of ponies as well as people are slaughtered. General Phil Sheridan makes his famous observation that "the only good Indian is a dead Indian."

1868: Naval forces are sent to Osaka, Hiogo, Nagasaki, Yokohama and Negata, Japan, to influence the outcome of a civil war fought to abolish the Shogunate. Marines and sailors are landed in Montevideo "to secure U.S. interests" during yet another Uruguayan insurrection against the local élite favored by American businessmen.

1870: Gunboats are sent about forty miles up the Río Tecapan in Mexico to destroy the pirate ship *Forward*. Troops are landed at Aspinwall to protect U.S. commercial assets upon the death of the Columbian president. A campaign is undertaken to "chastise" the indigenous Blackfeet, Bloods and Piegans in northern Montana for their "aggressions" against whites encroaching on their territories. Cavalry under Major Eugene Baker attack a peaceful encampment of Piegans camped along the Marias River, massacring at least 175.

1871: A force is landed to punish Korea for defense of its national territory, specifically for having killed the crew of the *U.S.S. General Sherman* and burning the vessel when it refused to leave Korean waters, and for firing on American small boats making unauthorized soundings on the Salee River. Marines assault several forts, kill about 400 Koreans, and "open the country to trade." Simultaneously, army concentrates the Aravaipa Apaches under its "protection" at Camp Grant, Arizona. The Aravaipas are then massacred by a group of civilian volunteers from Tucson.

1872–73: A campaign is mounted in Arizona to force the Tonto Apaches onto a reservation. The army also launches a campaign in northern California to clear indigenous Modocs from their land, with the intent of depositing them on the Klamath Reservation in southern Oregon. A group led by Captain Jack resists, but is defeated after a lengthy battle in local lava beds. Captain Jack and three others are then hanged, their homeland absorbed by the U.S., and the 153 surviving members of their people exiled to Oklahoma.

1873: Marines are landed at the Bay of Panama to quiet civil unrest. Troops repeatedly invade northern Mexico, ostensibly in pursuit of "bandits." Protests of the Mexican government are ignored. General Sheridan advocates extermination of the buffalo by commercial hunters as a means of destroying the economic basis for continuing resistance by peoples indigenous to the Great Plains to absorption into the U.S.

1874: Sailors and marines are landed in Hawai'i to "preserve order" during the coronation of a new king supported mainly by American businessmen and missionaries. An expedition headed by Lt. Colonel Custer invades the Lakota Nation in search of gold in the Black Hills. Although this is a clear violation of the 1868 Ft. Laramie Treaty, the Indians do not respond militarily. On the southern plains, meanwhile, the Kiowas and Comanches leave their reservation because of gross treaty violations by the U.S. The army mounts a major campaign against them, attacking their main encampment at Palo Duro Canyon (Texas) on Sept. 26, burning the Indians' winter provisions and slaughtering their ponies. The last of the "hostiles" surrender the following spring, their homelands incorporated into the U.S.

1875: Irregular troops mustered by Kansas but operating under sanction of the army massacres a group of Cheyennes camped peacefully along the Sappa Creek, near the Colorado/Kansas boundary.

1876: The army occupies the town of Matamoros, Mexico again, claiming to be "protecting" it during a transition in local government.

1876–77: The "Centennial Campaign" is mounted against the Lakota and allied nations to compel them to relinquish the Black Hills. General George Crook's column is defeated at the Rosebud Creek in mid-June, and Custer's regiment is decimated on the Little Big Horn River shortly thereafter. Only a winter campaign, attacking more-or-less defenseless villages, allows the army to win. About 90 percent of the Lakota homeland is then quickly stripped away. General Sheridan announces that, henceforth, U.S. military policy against Indians will be one of "extermination."

1877: General O.O. Howard heads an army force sent to take the Nez Percé homeland in eastern Oregon. The Indians resist and then attempt to retreat into Canada. Pursued by troops, they are finally cornered at Bear Paw Mountain in Montana and surrender. Chief Joseph and other principle leaders are subsequently interned in Oklahoma. In Nebraska, troops are also used to force the peaceful Poncas from their territory; the entire people is relocated to Oklahoma. Meanwhile, President Rutherford B. Hayes orders troops deployed to Chicago, St. Louis, Indianapolis, Philadelphia and elsewhere to break a strike against the B&O Railroad. This blatant violation of the newly-effected Posse Comitatus Act results in 30 deaths and several hundred serious injuries among the strikers.

1877–80: Conditions on the Arizona Apache reservations are so bad that a group of Mimbres led by Victorio leaves, vowing to "make war forever." The U.S. and Mexico mount a joint military response which results in annihilation of the "renegades."

1878: About 15,000 troops spend weeks chasing fewer than 500 Cheyennes who have escaped internment in Oklahoma and are attempting to return to their homeland in southern Montana. The bulk of the Cheyennes finally surrender, and are thereupon massacred at Camp Robinson, Nebraska. Meanwhile, in Idaho and northeastern Oregon, a campaign is undertaken to "pacify" the Bannocks and allied Umatillas.

1878–79: A campaign is undertaken in Idaho to pacify the so-called "Sheepeaters," reinforced by Bannock, Umatilla and Yakima "recalcitrants."

1879: Troops are sent against the Utes in western Colorado, after they kill government agent Nathan Meeker, who has been attempting to starve them into ceding their land. Colorado Governor Frederick Pitkin calls for the Indians' extermination, but settles for compressing survivors into a tiny fraction of their original territory.

1881–84: A group of Chiricahuas, including Geronimo, leave their reservation and join a band led by Nana, a Mimbres survivor of Victorio's group. Together, they renew the Arizona Apache resistance. General George Crook, unsuccessful at running them to ground, finally manages to negotiate a truce.

1882: Troops are sent to Egypt to protect American commercial interests during fighting between Egyptians and British colonial forces.

1885: Marines are landed in Panama, occupying portions of Colon and Panama City, to secure the isthmus from revolutionary upheaval. Warships are sent to Samoa to ensure the U.S. is granted the right to establish a naval base in Pago Pago Harbor.

1885–87: Embittered by U.S. violations of the agreement under which they laid down their arms, Geronimo and his Chiricahua band leave the San Carlos reservation and resume fighting. The second "Geronimo Campaign" is then undertaken, with several thousand troops under General Crook used to track down the group of about fifty Indians. After surrendering, Geronimo and other principles are first imprisoned in Florida, then permanently exiled to Oklahoma.

1887: The navy gains exclusive use of Pearl Harbor, on the Hawaiian island of Oahu, as a "forward basing area" in the Pacific. The U.S. signs a treaty of perpetual peace and friendship with the Kingdom of Hawai'i as part of the arrangement.

1888: Troops are landed in Haiti to recover an American commercial steamer seized by the government for violating Haitian maritime law. Marines are also landed in Samoa to protect U.S. commercial interests during civil disturbances.

1889: A direct confrontation between American and German warships occurs in Apia Harbor, Samoa, over control of the islands. Only a tremendous storm, which completely disables the potential combatant vessels, averts a significant naval battle. At about the same time, marines and sailors from ships in Pearl Harbor are landed in Honolulu to protect U.S. business interests—a major source of local discontent—from political turmoil in Hawai'i.

1890: Sailors are put ashore in Buenos Aires to protect U.S. facilities against Argentine protests of American actions in their country. In late

December, the army massacres about 350 unarmed Lakotas—mostly women, children and old men—at Wounded Knee Creek, in South Dakota. The ostensible purpose is to end the "insubordination" embodied in the Indians' practice of the Ghost Dance. More likely, the troops are intent on revenging themselves for the fate of Custer fourteen years earlier. In either case, three-dozen medals of honor are bestowed upon participating troops.

1891: Marines are landed on Navassa Island, off Haiti, to establish a forward base for further action. Naval forces are dispatched to the Bering Sea to repel Russian sealers plying their trade off the former Russian possession of Alaska. Troops are also put ashore in Valpariso, Chile, to "restore order" during a popular insurrection deemed "threatening to American interests."

1892: Troops are sent to Coeur d'Alene, Idaho, to break a mining strike organized by the American Federation of Labor (AFL). Strikers are first placed in concentration camps, then "deported" from the area.

1893–98: Marines and sailors are again landed in Honolulu from ships in Pearl Harbor, this time to support the overthrow by U.S. businessmen of the Hawaiian monarchy. Although President Grover Cleveland quite accurately describes the action as a violation of both U.S. treaty commitments and international law, Congress quickly recognizes the resulting American-run "Republic of Hawaii" as "legitimate." The "republic" then requests annexation by the U.S. as a "permanent trust territory." The island of Oahu is thereupon converted into *the* major basing area for overall U.S. military operations in the Pacific (a distinction it still holds).

1894: Naval force is displayed off Río de Janeiro to influence the outcome of a Brazilian civil war. Marines are landed at Bluefields, Nicaragua, to secure American commercial property against threats of impoundment by the local populace. In May, President Cleveland orders troops used to prevent "Coxey's Army" from conducting a peaceful protest in Washington, D.C. In July, another 16,000 soldiers are deployed—2,000 in Chicago alone, others in Los Angeles, Sacramento and elsewhere—to break the American Railway Union's Pullman Strike. Hundreds of strikers, as well as numerous bystanders, are wounded by gunfire and bayonets.

1894–96: Marines are stationed at Tsientsin, China, and conduct a foray as far inland as Peking, to demonstrate "American resolve" during the Sino-Japanese War. Subsequently, a warship is beached at Newchwang and used as a fort for the same purpose. Meanwhile, another marine detachment is posted to Seoul, Korea, to protect U.S. commercial interests from possible disruption by the Japanese.

1895: Marines are sent to the town of Bocas del Toro, Columbia, to "maintain order." More accurately, they are sent to protect American business interests from attack by a "local bandit" (actually, a popular insurgent leader).

1896: Marines are sent to Corinto, Nicaragua, to protect U.S. commercial interests during ongoing "political unrest" in that country.

1898: A war is fought against Spain, with the result that the U.S. acquires Puerto Rico, Guam and the Philippines outright, and converts Cuba into a virtual satellite. Marines are again sent into Nicaragua, this time to San Juan del Sur, for the usual reasons. In Minnesota, troops are used to put down an "uprising" of indigenous Ojibwes at Leech Lake.

1898–99: Marines are posted again to Tsientsin and Peking to protect American business interests during a contest between the dowager empress and her son.

1899: Troops are landed to quell a "crisis" in Samoa (in actuality, all that was happening was that the Samoans had been attempting to require American businessmen to operate in conformity with local law). Construction of the Pago Pago naval base begins. In Cuba, General William Ludlow uses troops to break strikes among dock and railway workers. A general strike is then called in Habana, causing Ludlow to agree to a compromise.

1899–1901: Major U.S. forces are committed in the Philippines to put down a generalized independence movement. Operations conducted by Brigadier Generals J. Franklin Bell and "Hell Roaring Jake" Smith are consciously genocidal, especially with regard to tribal "Moros" in the southern islands. Upwards of 600,000 Filipinos are killed. The island of Luzon then becomes the primary basing area for U.S. military operations in Far East (a distinction it retained into the early 1990s).

1900: A regular "presence" of U.S. forces in China is initiated in response to the threat to American business interests posed by the antiwestern Boxer Rebellion.

1901: Marines are landed in Panama again, as always to protect U.S. commercial interests, during a popular insurrection. The navy begins the process of converting Guam's Apra Harbor into a permanent installation from which to base its operations in the northern Pacific (a purpose it continues to serve to this day).

1901–04: President Theodore Roosevelt engineers a rapid buildup of U.S. naval power signified in an increase in the number of battleships from 9 to 24. Articulating a policy based upon "big stick" diplomacy, he orders a battle fleet painted white—the symbolism is unmistakable—and sent on a tour of Latin American ports. The purpose, openly stated, is to intimidate the "Dagoes," as Roosevelt calls Latinos, with their North American neighbor's burgeoning strength.

1902: Troops are sent into Bocas de Toro again, as the Columbian insurgency spreads. Armed guards are posted the length of the rail line in Panama, to keep the trains moving for U.S. business.

1903: Marines are put ashore at Puerto Cortez, Honduras, to occupy a steamship wharf for U.S. commercial purposes during a period of civil strife. Marines are also landed in Santo Domingo to protect American business interests during a revolutionary outbreak in the Dominican Republic.

1903–04: A detachment of marines is sent to Abyssinia to "assist" U.S. diplomats in negotiating a treaty of commerce. A major marine contingent is landed in Panama to provide security during construction of the isthmian canal. They remain until 1914, when the army replaces them on a permanent basis.

1904: A large force is landed in the Dominican Republic, to "restore order" and protect U.S. commercial interests in the cities of Santo Domingo, Puerto Plata and Sousa.

1905: Marines are sent to Seoul, Korea, to reinforce U.S. "open door" trade policies in the country.

1906–09: A major intervention is undertaken in Cuba to prevent a popular revolution from succeeding. The U.S. resultingly secures a major naval base at Guantanamo Bay—which it still holds—augmenting the Caribbean facilities it is already building in Puerto Rico.

1907: Troops are introduced to the Honduran towns of Trujillo, Ceiba, Puerto Cortez, San Pedro, Laguna and Choloma to protect U.S. business interests and influence the outcome of a border war between Honduras and Nicaragua. As a result, the border is fixed along the Río Coco. Meanwhile, in July, President Theodore Roosevelt sends troops to break a mining strike in Goldfield, Nevada, organized by the Industrial Workers of the World (IWW).

1910: Marines are sent to Bluefields and Corinto in Nicaragua to help stave off another popular revolt against local oligarchs supported by U.S. business interests.

1911: Marines are injected into the Honduran civil war to "protect American lives and interests." Others are positioned for the same purpose in Hankow, Shanghai, Nanking, Chinkaing, Taku and elsewhere in China on the eve of the nationalist (Kuomintang) revolution. Army troops are sent in at Camp Nicholson, and at Kentucky Island, off the Chinese coast.

1912: Marines are landed briefly in Honduras again, this time to prevent the government from "seizing" railroad facilities at Puerto Cortez. Army troops are introduced in Panama to ensure the outcome of the national election. Others are sent into Constantinople during the Balkan War, and into Orienté Province and Habana, Cuba, to combat insurgents in those locales.

1912–25: Marines intervene in Nicaragua during yet another revolutionary upheaval. They remain for 13 years, ensuring "governmental stability" against popular insurrection.

1912–41: With the Kuomintang revolution succeeding in China, the U.S. undertakes a military buildup there, maintaining a force of 5,000 troops ashore and a fleet averaging 44 vessels patrolling China's coast and rivers. Myriad small actions result.

1913: Marines are landed at Ciaris Estero, Mexico, to help put down a "rebellion" of the area's indigenous Yaquis (who are actually trying to defend themselves against Mexico's effort to subordinate them for the first time). The "regional stability" of Mexico is deemed essential to U.S. business interests.

1914: Naval forces fire on insurgent positions in the Dominican Republic to "protect" the town of Puerto Plata from its own people. Troops are also put ashore to guard Santo Domingo from rebels. Simultaneously, troops are landed in Haiti to quell unrest in that country. "Peace-loving" President Woodrow Wilson justifies such actions on the basis that the U.S. is merely exercising its "inalienable right" to engage in "the conquest of foreign markets."

1914–17: U.S. forces intervene repeatedly in the Mexican revolution, waging what amounts to an undeclared war. Vera Cruz is occupied and General John J. "Black Jack" Pershing invades northern Mexico for an extended period, in pursuit of the revolutionary leader Pancho Villa.

1915–34: An extended military presence is established in Haiti to prevent further popular insurrections there. The move is explicitly intended to create the conditions necessary for U.S. commercial development in the country.

1916: Additional marines are landed in China to put down a riot in Nanking.

1916–24: An extended military presence is established in the Dominican Republic to forestall further popular insurrections there. The stated rationale is identical to announced with regard to Haiti a year earlier.

1917: Additional marines are landed in China to influence the outcome of a political crisis in Chunking. The Dutch Virgin Islands are acquired for potential use as yet another Caribbean naval base.

1917–18: The U.S., having waited long enough to ensure that it was choosing the winning side—and that its own loses would be comparatively minor—declares its participation in the great reordering of capitalist power relations known as World War I (which began in 1914). General Ralph Van Deman, charged with building up the War Department's Office of Military Intelligence (OMI), begins wholesale surveillance of U.S. citizens suspected of "disloyalty."

1917–21: In March 1917, troops under General Omar Bradley are used to break a mining strike in Butte, Montana, engaging in "vicious beatings" and jailing 70 strikers without charge. It is later shown that the strike was instigated by OMI operatives as a pretext for "cracking down" on the IWW, an anarchosyndicalist union deemed especially "subversive" by the War

Department. The army's campaign against the IWW is nonetheless expanded and sustained, with troops deployed in Arizona, Montana, Washington and Oregon. By late 1921, when the operation wraps up, "the army had put down twenty-nine 'domestic disturbances' without any resort to constitutional procedures."

1918–19: The army invades Mexico a total of nine times, precipitating numerous clashes and a substantial battle with Mexican troops at Nogales in August 1918.

1918–20: Troops are sent to Panama to oversee an election, then stationed in Chiriqui to ensure the public "accepts" the unsavory results. In the newly-constituted Soviet Union, marines are landed at Vladivostok to support counterrevolutionary forces in Siberia. They are quickly reinforced by 7,000 army personnel. Another 5,000 troops are put ashore at Archangel, suffering 10 percent causalities in combat with Soviet forces. Another marine unit participates in a British landing on the Murman Coast of the USSR. These aggressive actions by the U.S. mark the beginning of an anti-communist Cold War—undertaken quite explicitly to protect the position/further the interests of America's capitalist élite—which will last, uninterruptedly, into the 1990s (arguably, given current U.S. policy towards Cuba and North Korea, it is ongoing in 2003).

1919: Troops are landed at Trau, in Dalmatia, to "maintain order" during a conflict between Italians and Serbs which threatens U.S. commercial interests. Marines are landed from the U.S. battleship *Arizona* for the same purpose during the Greek occupation of Constantinople. Others are landed in Honduras during yet another attempted revolution there, while a thousand men are sent to Seattle to break a general strike organized by the AFL in that city. General Leonard Wood places Gary, Indiana, under "modified martial law" as part of an overall campaign to break another AFL general strike, this one throughout the entire steel industry.

1920: Troops are sent in to Guatemala to put down labor unrest. Marines are meanwhile landed in Kiukiang, China, to quell a riot threatening U.S. business interests there. Others are deployed in West Virginia to quell a coalfield strike organized by the United Mine Workers (UMW).

1920–22: A marine garrison is established on Russian Island, in Vladivostok Bay, to guard a radio transmission facility located there. The army's campaign against the UMW is also expanded, as troops are used to break strikes in ten states.

1921: Naval forces are posted on both sides of the Panamanian Isthmus to influence a border dispute between Panama and Costa Rica.

1922: A landing force is sent to "preserve order" when Turkish forces enter the city of Smyrna.

1922–23: Marines are put ashore five times to handle localized "emergencies" in China (all but invariably involving Chinese attempts to seize U.S. business assets).

1922–2002: OMI head Deman, at the request of FBI Director J. Edgar Hoover, establishes a policy of secretly and illegally providing "political intelligence information" gathered by his operatives on the activities of U.S. citizens to the civilian Bureau. The arrangement, in a highly evolved form, is ongoing at present.

1924–25: Troops are sent to oversee the Honduran national election. Marines are landed in Shanghai to restore order during a dispute between Chinese political factions.

1925: Marines are sent to La Ceiba, Honduras, to counter popular rebellion against outcome of the U.S.-supervised national election a year earlier. In Panama, the army intervenes to end a national strike and other symptoms of labor unrest deemed threatening to American business interests.

1926: Increased forces are put ashore in Hankow and Kiukiang, China, to protect American business interests during the nationalist incorporation of these cities into the Kuomintang state.

1926–33: A *coup d'etat* by General Emiliano Chamorro provokes an upsurge of revolutionary sentiment in Nicaragua. Marines are sent to the country to reinforce the government, especially against the activities of insurgent leader Augusto César Sandino.

1927: Increased naval and marine forces are sent to Shanghai, Nanking and Tientsin, China, during the ongoing Kuomintang consolidation. Naval gunfire is directed at Chinese troops near Nanking.

1932: Marines are put ashore to protect American property during the Japanese occupation of Shanghai. In July, a detachment of 600 troops commanded by Army Chief of Staff Douglas MacArthur is used to forcibly disperse the "Bonus Army"—a group of impoverished veterans seeking to claim long-promised but still unpaid bonuses for their military service during World War I—who are peacefully encamped in Washington, D.C.

1933: Naval forces are sent to Cuba to make a show of support for President (and U.S. puppet) Gerardo Machado during an attempted revolution.

1934: Marines are put ashore at Foochow, China, to protect American property during Japan's occupation of the city.

1937: The U.S. gunboat *Panay*, "showing the colors" in China, is attacked by Japanese warplanes. The incident comes close to precipitating a war with Japan.

1940: "Lend-Lease" air and naval bases are established in Newfoundland, Bermuda, St. Lucia, the Bahamas, Jamaica, Antigua, Trinidad and British Guyana. Their purpose is to facilitate transfer of U.S. military material to Great Britain, then at war with Germany.

1941: U.S. troops occupy Greenland, Iceland and Dutch Guyana (Surinam). Naval forces commence active escort duty protecting British convoys, engaging in antisubmarine operations which constitute a state of undeclared war against Germany. President Franklin D. Roosevelt violates the Posse Comitatus Act by using troops to break a strike at an aircraft plant in Los Angeles.

1941–45: U.S. participation in World War II is declared, with American forces fighting in alliance with the British, French and Soviets against Germany, Italy and Japan. In August 1945, atomic bombs are dropped on Hiroshima and Nagasaki as both the finale of this second global conflagration and the opening postwar salvo of America's ongoing Cold War against its erstwhile Soviet allies and "communism" more generally. In Asia, the U.S. occupies Japan, reoccupies the Philippines and Guam, and sets up permanent installations in southern Korea, Okinawa, Formosa (Taiwan), the Marshall and Bonin Islands, and elsewhere. In Europe, American troops occupy a portion of Germany and establish longterm bases in England, France and Italy. U.S. military advisors begin to actively collaborate in the (re)imposition of colonial or otherwise antidemocratic régimes worldwide.

1945: Troops occupy the northern Italian city of Trieste to prevent its absorption by "communist" Yugoslavia as reparation for damages suffered at the hands of Mussolini's Italy during World War II.

1945–46: Troops are stationed in Iran as a hedge against Soviet influence in that oil-rich country. Others are sent to northern China to block "Soviet ambitions" in that region. Meanwhile, even as U.S.-instigated trials of German and Japanese war criminals are conducted in Nuremberg and Tokyo, OMI, in collaboration with the War Department's Office of Strategic Services (OSS), implements a secret policy shielding thousands of egregious offenders who are deemed useful to America's own military endeavors. Those protected include nazi intelligence chief Reinhard Gehlen and his network of operatives, SS officer Werner von Braun and his team of rocket scientists (guilty of using thousands of slave laborers to build V-2 cruise missiles) and Gestapo officials like Klaus Barbie. In the Far East, the members of Japan's infamous Unit 731, guilty of using an untold number of human guinea pigs while conducting bacteriological warfare experiments near Harbin, China, are exempted from punishment in exchange for sharing what they'd learned.

1945–52: As an expedient to obtaining the quantity "fissionable materials" necessary for a rapid buildup of its nuclear weapons inventory, the War Department—renamed the "Department of Defense" (DoD) in 1947—arranges for destitute Navajos living along the Grants Uranium Belt in New Mexico and Arizona to receive small business loans to become self-employed uranium miners. Information concerning the extreme health hazard associated with the radon gas naturally emitted by uranium ore is deliberately withheld from the Navajos, and hundreds of small, unventilated shaft mines are soon operating, Lung cancer mortality among the miners, almost none of whom were ever smokers, eventually nears 100 percent.

1945–54: The military's nuclear weapons production facility near Hanford, Washington, conducts 7 highly-secret experiments involving the massive release of radioactive iodides into the atmosphere for purposes of "studying dispersal patterns." Epidemic thyroid cancer and other such ill-effects upon the downwind civilian population results. Similar experiments are conducted during the same period at the Los Alamos Scientific Laboratory in New Mexico, while thousands of troops are exposed to the direct radiation of nuclear blasts so that the War Department *cum* DoD can assess the "effects on combat efficiency attending commitment to the atom-ic battlefield." On the remote north slope of Alaska, indigenous Inuits are coerced into swallowing capsules filled with pure uranium, in order that DoD researchers can "study the effects of massive contamination on the human organism."

1945–58: The U.S. uses the "trust authority" it asserts over the Marshall Islands at the end of World War II to convert its "protectorate" into a test range for nuclear weaponry. The previously populated islands of Bikini, Kwajalein and Enewetak in particular are rendered uninhabitable. Residents of the islands of Utirik and Rongelap are used as human guinea pigs to study the effects of fallout (the results, especially in terms of con-genital mutation, are horrific).

1945–2002: After the "temporary" partition of Korea between the U.S. and USSR at the end of World War II, the American-installed régime in the south, backed by about 50,000 U.S. troops, begins a systematic program of armed incursions across the 38th parallel into the north. In 1949 alone, there are 2,617 such incidents, several of them involving well over a thou-sand troops. In 1950, the north finally responds with a fullscale invasion of the south. There follows a bloody three-year UN "police action" organized by the U.S., during which China intervenes in support of the north. A stalemate is finally reached in 1953, and a massive U.S. military presence has been maintained in "South Korea" ever since.

1946: Using the financial inducements of its Marshall Plan, the U.S. engi-neers the North Atlantic Treaty Organization (NATO) and begins a (re)deployment of troops to confront the Soviets in Europe and "contiguous areas" such as Turkey. The OSS is converted into the Central Intelligence Agency (CIA) and secretly places a heavy emphasis upon conditioning the American public to embrace Cold War outlooks, systematically propagan-dizing the citizenry through means ranging from the "news" media, through academic publishing, to movies, television and other modes of popular entertainment. The new agency also establishes a "clandestine services" component, officially "paramilitary" in nature, but trained, equipped and tasked to perform operations indistinguishable from those later assigned such élite military units as the army's Special Forces and navy SEALS.

1946–54: Philippines "independence" leaves the U.S. in possession of 23 military bases, control of the islands' economy and "oversight" of national defense. The response is an insurgency by Hukbalahap guerrillas, coun-tered by a U.S.-coordinated counterinsurgency campaign. Colonel Edward Lansdale takes charge in 1950 and runs a high-intensity effort which leaves the Huks decimated. Meanwhile, a program of military support for resurgent French colonialism in Indochina is begun and grows steadily throughout the period.

1946–73: The U.S.-backed army of Chaing Kai-shek—aside from material assistance, there are in 1946 about 100,000 American troops in China—wages a bitter but unsuccessful counterinsurgency war against Mao Zedong's "people's liberation army." After China "falls to the Reds," remnants of Chaing's forces are ensconced on the off-coast U.S. bastion of Formosa. Thereafter, a combination of CIA and military clandestine forces conduct an array of low intensity operations against China, lasting until at least as late as 1973.

1947–48: As part of a comprehensive CIA-orchestrated program to subvert free elections in Italy, the U.S. threatens "another world war" if the communist party wins at the polls. Such pressure is largely responsible for the success of a host of corrupt anticommunist officials. Meanwhile, the CIA organizes and supports Albanian émigrés in an unsuccessful attempt to bring about the armed overthrow of the communist régime of Enver Hoxha.

1947–1951: The U.S. takes over the role of waging a counterinsurgency campaign against Greek communists who had sought power by parliamentary means. The brutal repression works, and Greece is pushed into an anticommunist dictatorship.

1947–57: Using the nazis' "Gehlen Apparatus," the CIA undertakes a program of organizing and supporting guerrilla forces—most of whom had fought for the Germans during World War II—in the Baltic states, the Ukraine and elsewhere in eastern Europe. During ten years of substantial activity, the Baltic units alone claim to have killed some 80,000 Soviet troops and as many as 12,000 "communist officials and collaborators." Meanwhile, the CIA expands the earlier OSS program of shielding "useful" nazi war criminals from punishment to include members of collaborating organizations in other countries—e.g., the Croatian Ustasha—many of them guilty not only of war crimes but of direct participation in the wartime genocide of Jews and Gypsies. Hundreds are provided false identities and imported to "bolster anticommunist sentiment" within East European immigrant communities in the U.S. and Canada. Some, mostly veterans of SS campaigns in the USSR, are used to build up Special Forces units in the U.S. Army.

1948–49: Increasingly bad relations with the USSR results in the Soviets sealing off the partitioned city of Berlin, well within their postwar occupation zone of Germany. The U.S. deploys combat units and "lifts the siege" via an extended airlift of supplies.

1950: In keeping with Cold War priorities, strategic planners prepare a secret study, NSC-68, outlining the requirements for converting the U.S. into a fullfledged "National Security State." Adopted as policy by the Truman Administration, the document calls for curtailment of political expression, comprehensive indoctrination of the citizenry concerning the "danger of communist subversion and aggression" (NSC-68 is quite candid in suggesting falsified data should be used to this end), the consequent "need" for U.S.

"military preparedness" to be placed on a perpetual wartime footing, and thus to harness the country's economy to developing what President—and former General of the Army—Dwight D. Eisenhower would soon call the "military-industrial complex" rather than bona fide social welfare initiatives.

1950–2002: The military converts its Las Vegas (Tonopah) Bombing and Gunnery Range, established in 1940 by executive order, into the Nellis Test Range, for purposes of conducting nuclear weapons testing. Although the 3.5 million acres eventually encompassed within the boundaries of the facility are part of Newe Segobia, the territory recognized as belonging to the Western Shoshones under the 1863 Treaty of Ruby Valley, and never relinquished by that people, approximately 1,000 nuclear devices are detonated there over the years, making the unoffending Shoshones "the most bombed nation on earth." Fallout from testing on the Nellis Range, meanwhile, creates radioactive "hot spots" in locales as far away as upstate New York, precipitating, among other maladies, immune system degeneration and endemic lung cancer within a substantial segment of the U.S. population. By 1990, the ill-effects have become so ubiquitous that a national "public health campaign" is launched, attributing them to "environmental tobacco smoke."

1953: CIA operative Kermit Roosevelt engineers the overthrow of the democratically-elected Mossadegh government, reinstalling the decisively antidemocratic régime of the Shah of Iran. Military equipment and advisors are quickly sent to consolidate Roosevelt's "achievement" in bringing this economically/strategically vital country into the "Free World" of U.S. client states.

1953–54: The CIA, in collaboration with reactionary local military leaders, undertakes a campaign which results in the overthrow of the democratic government of Jacobo Arbenz in Guatemala. It is replaced with a military dictatorship "friendlier" to U.S. corporate interests. A military airlift is also undertaken to supply French troops besieged by Vietnamese forces at Dien Bien Phu. Vice President Richard Nixon proposes using tactical nuclear weapons to prevent the decolonization of Indochina. The Vietnamese nonetheless prevail and France is expelled.

1953–67: The CIA undertakes a secret and ultimately unsuccessful project, MK-Ultra (later MK-Search), intended to discover "scientific methods of mind control." Using prison inmates, psychiatric patients, and unwitting bystanders as guinea pigs, the agency experiments with LSD and other powerful hallucinogens, as well as a variety of psychosurgical and "psychic driving" techniques, in both the U.S. and Canada. Several suicides result, and an unknown number of victims suffer severe—and in many cases lasting—psychosis before the failed effort is terminated.

1954–55: The CIA attempts to replicate its Guatemalan feat in Costa Rica. A program is also initiated to subvert the Geneva Accords, which partition the former French colony of Indochina into four countries: North and South Vietnam (to be reunified by general election in 1956), Laos and

Cambodia. The first U.S. military advisers are posted to Laos, Edward Lansdale and other CIA personnel to South Vietnam.

1954–62: A series of air and naval confrontations are undertaken to prevent mainland Chinese occupation of the islands of Quemoy and Matsu, off Taiwan.

1955–61: CIA and Special Forces personnel create and lead an "indigenous guerrilla force" in Tibet, ostensibly to liberate the country from China. The operation, which proved rather costly to the Tibetans, may have been continued in one form or another into the present.

1956: Troops are sent to Morocco to prevent formation of a leftist government. Others are sent to the Suez to manifest U.S. interest in the disposition of the canal there, at the time being nationalized by Egypt's President Abdul Gamal Nasser. CIA propaganda and infiltration operations help instigate an armed revolt in Hungary. Once Soviet troops move in to crush it, however, the U.S. abandons the insurgents, capitalizing on the "moral value" of their fate. Thousands are killed.

1956–57: Kermit Roosevelt fails in an attempt to repeat his Iranian success, this time against "leftist" Ba'athists in Syria. The U.S. installs a régime headed by Nguyen Vo Diem in South Vietnam and backs his boycott of elections required by the Geneva Accords. The CIA begins a major program to develop a "comprehensive national police infrastructure in South Vietnam," and the first U.S. military advisers are introduced. Military advisers are also sent to Thailand, with the result that Thai troops shortly invade Cambodian border areas to "prevent the country from going communist."

1957–58: The CIA makes eight separate attempts to bring about the overthrow of the "leftist" Nasser government in Egypt. In collaboration with dissident elements of the Indonesian military, the CIA also sets out to assassinate Indonesia's President Sukarno. When various murder schemes fail, a *coup d'etat* is unsuccessfully attempted. In Indochina, Thai incursions into Cambodian territory are augmented with penetrations by CIA-backed Khmer Serei irregulars based in South Vietnam.

1957–1988: The Eisenhower Administration enters into a compact to build nuclear reactors for the staunchly anticommunist—and virulently racist—apartheid régime in South Africa. This allows the South Africans to secretly launch a nuclear weapons development within five years, and to begin production of the weapons themselves by 1979. Meanwhile, the DoD maintains a more conventional program of military assistance, covertly continued despite a UN embargo until the régime's effective collapse in 1988.

1958: 14,000 marines and army troops—more than the total strength of the entire Lebanese military—are put ashore in Lebanon to "keep order" during that country's civil war. Some 70 naval vessels and hundreds of aircraft also take part in the operation. Lebanon is kept safely "out of the hands of the communists." The CIA coordinates a coup d'etat in Laos to prevent participation by the communist Pathet Lao in a coalition government.

President Eisenhower sends troops to quell a crisis over school desegregation in Little Rock, Arkansas.

1958–2002: The Eisenhower Administration enters into a compact to build a nuclear reactor for Israel, and to train Israeli nuclear physicists, with the predictable result that the country now known as "America's firmest ally in the Middle East" had established its own nuclear weapons development program with two years, the weapons themselves by 1974. Simultaneously, the DoD launches an ongoing assistance program which makes Israel—with the exception of South Vietnam from 1965–75—the recipient of by far the largest infusion of U.S. military hardware and other support of any country in the world. In dollar terms, the annual appropriation for such purposes is sufficient to establish Israel as a veritable "51st state" of the U.S. The costs and consequences to the Palestinians, upon whose land Israel established itself, are self-evident, as are those to the Arab states which have supported the liberation of Palestine.

1959: Special Forces "White Star Mobile Training Teams," assigned to create an irregular army of H'mong highlanders to fight the Pathet Lao, begin secret combat operations in Laos. Marines are landed in Haiti to prevent the overthrow of the brutal régime of "Papa Doc" Duvalier, a U.S. ally.

1959–1979: The Eisenhower Administration enters into a compact to build nuclear reactors for its newly-installed ally, the Shah of Iran, giving him the capacity to produce nuclear weapons by some point in the early-70s. Ironically, these reactors, and thus the capacity to produce "weapons of mass destruction," fall into the hands of the emphatically antiwestern insurgents who overthrow the Shah in 1979.

1959–2002: Troops are put ashore to bolster Cuban dictator Fulgencio Batista against popular insurrection. When Batista is nonetheless overthrown in 1959, the troops remain for several months to oversee the removal of transportable American assets and evacuation of U.S.-aligned Cubans. The latter are immediately organized and equipped by the CIA to begin irregular but protracted warfare against the newly-constituted government of Fidel Castro. These include numerous landings of special operations units on Cuban soil—as well as an outright invasion attempt at the Bay of Pigs in April 1961—assassination plots (several involving the Mafia), as well as multiple uses of bacteriological and chemical warfare. It is quite probable that this effort continues in some form at present.

1960: Kong Le, a CIA-backed army colonel stages another coup in Laos, pulling the country still further to the right. In Guatemala, CIA-led, -trained, and -equipped Cuban irregulars put down an insurrection meant to restore democratic governance.

1960–63: The CIA oversees a counterinsurgency campaign in Ecuador to quell a leftist guerrilla movement threatening to "recreate the Cuban experience" in that country.

1960–64: The CIA moves into the decolonizing "Belgian" Congo, deliberately exacerbating rivalries and ideological differences among the new country's leadership to prevent consolidation of a leftist government. A bloody and protracted "civil war" results, culminating in the assassination of Patrice Lumumba, the Congo's only truly capable leader.

1960–65: The CIA and Special Forces personnel create and lead an élite counterinsurgency force against "Cuban-backed guerrillas" in Peru.

1961: President John F. Kennedy escalates military commitment in South Vietnam, and Special Forces personnel begin to forge an irregular army of indigenous Montagnards in the country's central highlands area. In France, the CIA is involved in a plot by disgruntled army colonels to assassinate President Charles DeGaul so that they can resume fighting for control over the former French colony of Algeria. Across Europe, combat units are placed on full alert because of yet another "Berlin Crisis."

1961–64: General Vernon Walters undertakes a "project" for the CIA, using disgruntled Brazilian army colonels to overthrow the liberal government of President Joao Goulart. After a *coup d'etat* in March 1964, General Costa e Silva, the new head-of-state, allows the Agency to establish an irregular political police apparatus which serves as the prototype for the U.S. "Office of Public Safety" (OPS), the mechanism through which Latin American death squads are created on a wholesale basis later in the decade.

1962: U.S. forces are placed on full alert and a naval blockade is imposed upon Cuba to force withdrawal of Soviet missiles based on the island. Frustrated that President Kennedy has not ordered a fullscale invasion, the Joint Chiefs of Staff secretly initiate "Operation Northwind" to manufacture the pretext necessary to force him into doing so. Among the methods actively considered to "whip up public sentiment against Castro" are blowing up a U.S. warship anchored at Guantanamo Bay and blaming it on "Cuban saboteurs," launching a "Cuban terror campaign" involving bombings and murders in Miami and Washington, D.C., and having "Cuban agents" hijack airliners to Habana. Meanwhile, a force of 1,800 Marines is positioned off the coast of the Dominican Republic in an attempt to influence the election of a replacement for President Rafael Trujillo, assassinated the year before. "Left-leaning" Juan Bosch is nonetheless elected.

1962–96: The CIA launches what becomes its most sustained counterinsurgency effort, supporting the military dictatorship it installed in Guatemala after the 1954 Arbenz coup. By 1994, the Agency's devotion to "preserving freedom" in this country had resulted in the deaths of at least 200,000 people, mostly Maya Indians, and the creation of about a quarter-million refugees.

1963: Troops are put ashore in Haiti to oversee evacuation of U.S. nationals—and certain business assets—during a period of civil strife.

1963–93: The Kennedy Administration enters a 30-year compact to build nuclear reactors for India, a matter which allows the "strongest U.S. ally in South Asia" to begin nuclear weapons production in 1974. This sets off an arms race with India's regional rival, Pakistan, with the result that the Pakistanis also begin producing nuclear weapons during the 1980s.

1964–85: The CIA collaborates in a rightwing coup against the Bosch government in the Dominican Republic. A naval force is concentrated near the Panama Canal Zone, and army units within it are placed on full alert, to deter an initiative by Panama to nationalize the canal. Major U.S. military forces begin moving into Thailand, initiating a counterinsurgency campaign which lasts through 1985.

1964–72: The OPS pilot project is inaugurated for use against the Tupamaro guerrillas in Uruguay in December 1964. Over the next five years, an estimated 10–20,000 Uruguayans are murdered and/or subjected to increasingly sophisticated torture. Thousands more are arbitrarily arrested and jailed for indefinite periods, often extending into years. In 1972, a CIA-coordinated drive finishes off what's left of the Tupamaros.

1964–74: The CIA intervenes in Greece, sponsoring a series of military plots against the democratic—but insufficiently anticommunist—government of George Papandreau, culminating in an April 1967 coup which brings a junta led by Colonel Georges Papadopoulis to power. Over the next seven years, hundreds of Greek opposition leaders are murdered and thousands of dissidents are tortured and imprisoned by "The Colonels," all of it with unwavering U.S. support.

1965: The CIA assists the Indonesian military in finally overthrowing Sukarno, precipitating a liquidation of "communists" which ultimately claims as many as a million lives. After a provoked and in large part fabricated "engagement" with North Vietnamese naval forces in the Gulf of Tonkin, President Lyndon Johnson orders the first marine maneuver battalions into South Vietnam (setting off a chain of events that will cost the lives of an estimated 3.2 million Indochinese over the next decade). In Laos, a "secret" bombing campaign is begun which results in more than two million tons of explosives being dropped on that tiny country by 1973. In the Dominican Republic, 23,000 U.S. troops are used to put down a popular revolt meant to restore democratic governance.

1966: In Ghana, panafricanist President Kwame Nkrumah is overthrown in a CIA-sponsored coup. An anticommunist dictatorship is then established with U.S. military and economic support.

1966–69: A series of naval confrontations result from the U.S. practice of illegally sending intelligence-gathering vessels into North Korean territorial waters. Finally, in 1968, the Koreans seize an American spy ship, the *Pueblo*, and intern her crew. War is narrowly averted.

1967: A combined CIA/Special Forces group in Bolivia, operating with an élite Bolivian ranger unit trained in counterinsurgency techniques from 1964 onward by the "green berets," destroy a guerrilla unit led by Ernesto "Che" Guevara (a hero of the Cuban revolution). Guevara is wounded, captured, and summarily executed on October 8. Meanwhile, a military airlift is undertaken to assist U.S.-aligned factions in ongoing fighting in the Congo.

The *U.S.S. Liberty*, a spy ship monitoring Arab radio traffic in behalf of Israel during the latest of that country's many wars with its neighbors, is strafed by Israeli jets in the Mediterranean, resulting in the deaths of several sailors. The mysterious incident is never adequately explained. About 4,000 troops are sent to quell a rebellion in Detroit's inner city. Several thousand others are deployed in October, at the Pentagon, to "maintain order" during a massive protest of the war in Vietnam (about 100,000 participants, by most estimates).

1967–74: In a repeat of OMI operations during World War I, the Army Security Agency and other military intelligence units begin Operation Minaret, illegally surveilling the communications and activities of U.S. citizens expressing opposition to the Vietnam War. The program is terminated when its existence is disclosed in 1973. Meanwhile, also beginning in 1967, the CIA launches three equally illegal operations—codenamed Chaos, Merimac and Resistance—for the same purpose. These are not ended until 1974.

1968: More than 70,000 troops are deployed in April to quell nationwide civil unrest following the assassination of celebrated civil rights leader Martin Luther King, Jr.

1969: In November, President Richard M. Nixon orders deployment of some 40,000 troops in Washington, D.C., to "maintain order" during a truly huge protest of the war in Vietnam (more than 500,000 participants, by most estimates).

1969–72(?): The CIA, with apparent DoD cooperation, undertakes a supersecret domestic operation to "neutralize" America's already acid-drenched "counterculture" of dissident white youth by rendering it "psychologically dysfunctional." The means employed is a flood, not only of LSD, but also methamphetamine and a variety of the army's chemical warfare substances—e.g., STP—passed off in tablet form as "recreational hallucinogens." Vast quantities of heroin, imported through military channels from Southeast Asia, are also released in the African American and Latino communities, as an expedient to undermining the then-burgeoning black/brown liberation movement. Simultaneously, Nixon declares "war on drugs" and launches a campaign aimed at halting the flow of marijuana—a "soft" alternative to the other drugs—smuggled across the U.S./Mexican border.

1969–1999: Partly in response to "instability" in neighboring Chile, the Nixon Administration enters into a 30-year compact to build nuclear reactors for the military régime in Argentina (considered the primary U.S. ally in South America's "southern cone"), with the result that the country attains nuclear weapons production capability by 1985. DoD support to "the colonels" continues unabated during a "dirty war" waged against the Argentine population throughout the 1980s.

1970: A show of force is made to help convince the government of Jordan to accede to the territorial desires of Israel, which, despite the *Liberty* incident, has emerged as a primary U.S. ally in the Mideast.

1970–71: The CIA arms rightwing insurgents in Costa Rica in an effort to bring about the overthrow of liberal democratic government of Jose Figueres.

1970–72: On March 18, CIA and military intelligence consummate a coup against Prince Sihanouk while the neutralist Cambodian head-of-state is abroad. He is replaced by the U.S.-aligned Colonel Lon Nol. The U.S. shortly invades, in what President Nixon calls a "preventive incursion," following up with a secret but extended saturation bombing campaign along the Cambodia/Vietnam border.

1971: U.S. and South Vietnamese forces invade Laos in Operation Dewey Canyon II.

1972–2002: The Nixon Administration enters into a compact to build nuclear reactors for Taiwan (the arrangement is not scheduled to end until 2014), a matter providing the Taiwanese the capacity to produce their own nuclear weapons by 1979. An almost identical arrangement (ending in 2002) is affected with the same result with Brazil. Meanwhile, the DoD maintains major programs of conventional military assistance in both countries.

1973: A military airlift of advanced weaponry and other material is undertaken to bolster Israel in still another of its endless wars against its Arab neighbors. Counterinsurgency specialists from Ft. Bragg, North Carolina, are sent to assist the FBI and U.S. Marshals Service in putting down an "uprising" of the American Indian Movement at Wounded Knee, on the Pine Ridge Sioux Reservation in South Dakota.

1973–6: A group of CIA-supported military conspirators, headed by Colonel Augusto Pínochet, overthrows Chile's democratically-elected marxist president, Salvador Allende (himself killed during the bloody coup). U.S. military advisers then join Agency personnel, assisting the Pínochet régime in consolidating its power, a process which results in the liquidation of several thousand Chilean liberals and leftists over the next three years. Spain later files genocide charges against Pínochet.

1973–86: Despite ironclad evidence of its carcinogenic/mutogenic effects, and in the face of mounting evidence of these maladies among Vietnam combat veterans, the DoD steadfastly denies any link to their often massive wartime exposure to defoliants laced with dioxin—"the most toxic substance ever created by man"—such as "Agent Orange." As with the earlier generation of "atomic veterans," this policy of "waiting for an army to die" before acknowledging the obvious minimizes official liability for the fate of those who "did their duty" and "served their country honorably." A similar pattern is evident with regard to Vietnam vets suffering from combat-induced posttraumatic stress disorder (PTSD).

1973–2002: Partly in response to the 1968 *Pueblo* incident, the Nixon Administration enters a compact to build nuclear reactors for South Korea, giving its ally the capability of producing its own nuclear weapons by 1985. This sets off an arms race with North Korea, which appears to have attained a similar capability by the mid-90s, a matter presently being used by the Bush Administration as a pretext for a possible war against the North Koreans.

1974: Troops are landed on Cyprus to protect U.S. business assets and evacuate nationals during Greek/Turkish fighting on the island. Others are sent to Ethiopia for the same reason after the reactionary Emperor Haile Salassi—long the largest recipient of U.S. military aid in all of subsaharan Africa—is overthrown by a military council known as the Dergue.

1974–2002: As part of a gambit designed to keep the newly-installed "socialist" régime of Portugal in NATO, the Nixon administration enters a compact to build nuclear reactors for Portugal (it does not expire until 2014), with the result that the Portuguese attain nuclear weapons production capability by 1984. Meanwhile, the DoD builds up and sustains a conventional military assistance program in Portugal.

1975: Marines are put ashore in Cambodia after the collapse of the Lon Nol régime, engaging in combat with Khmer Rouge troops. The CIA, in conjunction with the Shah of Iran and the Mossad (Israeli intelligence), launches a program to arm Kurdish guerrillas in northern Iraq. Later, when its interests change, the U.S. abandons the Kurds to their fate (it is estimated that more than 50,000 are killed by Iraqi and Turkish counterinsurgency forces).

1975–78: The CIA intervenes in Zaire (formerly the Congo) to reinforce dictator Mobutu Sese Seko against secessionists. Moroccan troops are used as surrogates for Americans in Zaire. In exchange, the U.S. provides equipment and other military support for Morocco's war against Polasario guerrillas at home.

1975–79: The CIA, using mercenaries, undertakes an increasingly substantial effort to bolster the régime of Anastasio Samosa, a U.S. client, in Nicaragua. The dictator is finally overthrown by leftist Sandinista guerrillas, but at the cost of 60,000 lives.

1975–91: The CIA and a force of mercenaries undertake operations supporting prowestern factions seeking to seize power in recently decolonized Angola. Upwards of 60,000 people are killed in the fighting, which continues to flare up from time to time.

1976: Troops are put ashore in Lebanon to secure key facilities and evacuate personnel during a civil war fomented in part by the Mossad.

1976–80: The CIA intervenes in Jamaica, subverting military and police officials into undermining and ultimately deposing the liberal left government of Michael Manley.

1977: Troops are sent briefly to Uganda in a show of force against the country's anti-Israeli dictator, Idi Amin.

1978–80: Troops are sent to Iran to evacuate personnel as the U.S. client régime there collapses. The deposed Shah, wanted for multitudinous crimes against his own people, is provided sanctuary in the U.S. Iranian revolutionaries therefore seize the American embassy in Teheran, holding its staff and marine security detachment for exchange purposes. Instead, the U.S. unsuccessfully attempts to use Delta Force—a then-newly created "super-élite" Special Forces unit—to free the hostages, who are finally released when the Shah dies.

1979–81: The CIA employs the veteran mercenary commander "Mad Mike" Hoare—who had worked for the Agency in the Congo during the 1960s—to stage an unsuccessful coup attempt in the Seychelles Islands. The islands are desired as a site for an electronic intelligence-gathering operation.

1979–91: CIA and Special Forces personnel undertake a counterinsurgency campaign in El Salvador which eventually costs the lives of well over 150,000 Salvadorans.

1980–91: CIA and Special Forces personnel provide increasingly extensive support to Mujahadeen guerrillas fighting Soviet forces after their invasion of Afghanistan. Among those trained is Ramsey Yousef, the demolitions expert who later prepares the device used for the 1993 World Trade Center bombing in New York.

1981: Libyan aircraft, seeking to protect the country's claimed territorial waters in the Gulf of Sidra from incursion by U.S. naval vessels, are shot down. A military clash is narrowly averted in an incident concerning a Czech national attempting to defect to the U.S. at Panmunjon, in the Korean demilitarized zone.

1981–91: An expanded program of "military assistance" is undertaken in Honduras. Its primary purpose is to establish the infrastructure necessary to support a secret and protracted campaign of low-intensity warfare against Nicaragua's leftist Sandinista government. The operation, which is prohibited by Congress, is funded in part by CIA-sponsored drug sales in the U.S., in part by the equally-illegal sale of advanced military technology to Iran. The Sandinistas are eventually deposed at the cost of an estimated 85,000 lives, and a U.S. client régime installed.

1982: Logistical support is provided to Britain in its war to maintain control over the Argentine Malvinas (Falkland) Islands.

1982–84: Marines are put ashore in Lebanon to support an Israeli invasion and partial occupation of that country. The CIA uses the threat of major mercenary operations to coerce the government of Surinam into refusing Cuban aid, accepting increasing domination by the rightwing régime of neighboring Brazil instead.

1982–96: Troops are deployed as "peacekeepers" in the Sinai, mainly to ensure ongoing Israeli control over the Gaza Strip.

1983: Grenada is invaded and occupied by massive U.S. forces. A government acceptable to the U.S. is then installed. The Reagan administration orders a show of naval force and the transfer of sophisticated electronics technology to Saudi Arabia to support its antidemocratic government against popular sentiments.

1984–9: The CIA and Special Forces units undertake a prolonged counterinsurgency campaign to quell leftist guerrillas in the southern Philippines. The unsuccessful effort claims some 30,000 lives.

1985: Navy SEALs are deployed against members of the Abu Nidal terrorist organization who have seized the Italian liner *Achille Lauro* in the Mediterranean.

1986: U.S. aircraft bomb the Libyan cities of Tripoli and Benghazi, personally targeting Libya's antiwestern head of state, Muamar al Qadaffi, and killing hundreds (including Qadaffi's adopted baby daughter). The attack is ostensibly made in retaliation for the bombing of a German discotheque in which seven U.S. military personnel were killed. German and other European intelligence services had already concluded, however, that Libyan operatives were uninvolved in the disco bombing. Meanwhile, the Reagan administration repudiates jurisdiction of the International Court of Justice, after the ICJ enters an opinion declaring U.S. military operations against Nicaragua to be in violation of international law.

1986–2002: Special Forces units are posted to several Latin American countries—notably Columbia, Bolivia and Peru—to collaborate with the CIA, DEA and local military/police personnel in waging another "war on drugs." In actuality, this is a cover for U.S. participation in combat operations aimed at various leftist guerrilla groups. In the U.S. itself, the Posse Comitatus Act is revised to allow military participation in "drug interdiction" operations, as well the training and equipping of special police units tasked with enforcing drug laws (once trained and equipped, of course, such units can be assigned whatever other tasks local authorities might from time to time find convenient).

1987: A Delta Force sniper team is deployed to help quell a revolt by Cuban "detainees" held in the Atlanta Federal Prison.

1987–88: Naval forces are posted in the Persian Gulf during a war between Iraq, at the time a U.S. client state, and Iran. An unarmed and clearly identified Iranian airliner is shot down by the *U.S.S. Vincennes*, killing 290. The captain of the *Vincennes* is subsequently decorated for his "bravery" during the incident, a matter thought to have provoked the Iranians to retaliate by planting the bomb on PanAm Flight 103 which detonated over Lockerbee, Scotland, killing all aboard *that* civilian airliner (an alternative scenario is that the Libyans destroyed Flight 103 in retaliation for the 1986 U.S. airstrikes on Tripoli and Benghazi).

1989: Libyan aircraft are again shot down while attempting to defend the Gulf of Sidra against U.S. naval incursion. Meanwhile, additional U.S. troops are dispatched to the Philippines to prevent a coup there.

1989–90: Massive forces are deployed in what is dubbed "Operation Just Cause" to invade, occupy, install a régime preferred by the U.S. in Panama. Nominal Panamanian head-of-state Manuel Noriega, a former CIA "asset," is arrested for violating U.S. drug laws and taken to Miami to stand trial (he is presently serving a life sentence in federal prison). Although the DoD and the media proclaim the affair "essentially bloodless," hundreds of Panamanians are killed.

1990: Troops are sent to Liberia in an operation dubbed "Sharp Edge" to protect business assets and evacuate U.S. nationals during a civil war.

1991–94: Troops are sent to Somalia to "restore order"—i.e., to protect U.S. interests in the strategic Horn of Africa—during a period of civil war. Unsuccessful, they withdraw. A smaller group of "peacekeepers"—actually, élite ranger and Delta Force units—are then inserted to eliminate "warlords" unfriendly to the U.S. This gambit results in the "Black Hawk Down" bloodbath in which a handful of U.S. soldiers—and several thousand Somalis—are killed.

1991–2002: Under the pretext of "rolling back naked aggression" manifested by Iraq's occupation of Kuwait, an American client state, the U.S. assembles a military coalition to "secure" the economically/strategically crucial Persian Gulf region. In what is dubbed "Operation Desert Storm," Iraq's military and civilian infrastructures alike are obliterated by sustained aerial bombardment. About a quarter-million Iraqis, at least a third of them noncombatants, are killed in the process. Thereafter, the U.S. conducts regular airstrikes throughout the country, continuously "degrading" efforts to rebuild. Simultaneously, economic warfare is waged against Iraq, with the U.S. enforcing an embargo resulting in the deaths of an additional million people—half of them children under 12-years-of-age—a toll described by various U.S. officials as "worth the price," if it means that "those who hate freedom" will come to accept the advent of a "new world order" in which "what we say, goes." U.N. high commissioner Denis Halliday publicly terms this "a policy of deliberate genocide."

1992: President George Bush sends troops to help put down a rebellion in Los Angeles sparked by an all-white jury's "not guilty" verdicts ending the trial of police officers videotaped beating black motorist Rodney King. Delta Force specialists are secretly sent to advise and provide other, unspecified, "services" to the FBI during an armed stand-off with white separatist Randy Weaver at Ruby Ridge, Idaho. Weaver's wife and son are killed.

1992–99: Another "peacekeeping" force is sent to the former Yugoslavia in an effort to ensure that the governments emerging within this strategic locale adopt postures acceptable to the U.S.

1992–2002: In a replay of the earlier atomic veterans and Agent Orange "controversies" the DoD, despite clear evidence to the contrary, denies any connection between the military's massive use of depleted uranium ammunition against Iraqi armored formations and a mysterious "Gulf War Syndrome" evident among large numbers of combat veterans.

1993: Delta Force sniper teams and reconnaissance specialists are secretly assigned to assist the FBI in its protracted siege of the Branch Davidian Compound, near Waco, Texas. As at Wounded Knee in 1973, this violation of the Posse Comitatus Act is compounded by the army's provision of weapons, equipment and sophisticated munitions to civilian law enforcement personnel. Ultimately, 76 people, including 23 children, are massacred. Subsequent litigation reveals the existence of a highly classified "Praetor Protocol" under which it is presumed that the president holds authority to (secretly) "waive" Posse Comitatus constraints at his/her discretion, being thus self-empowered to employ military force against the domestic populace whenever, wherever, and for whatever purpose s/he decides.

1993–6: Troops are sent to Haiti to pave the way for a U.S.-supported government. They are then reinforced to "maintain order" and "teach Haitians about democracy."

1994: A show of force is mustered to intimidate North Korea into abandoning policies of nuclear development which might underpin weapons production (the U.S. took no such action to deter either Israel or South Africa from earlier doing the same thing). A tense confrontation occurs when the Koreans shoot down an American helicopter which has penetrated their airspace. Meanwhile, troops are sent to Rwanda to evacuate U.S. nationals during a "civil war." No attempt is made to interfere with the blatant genocide occurring there at the time.

1995–2002: Troops are deployed along the U.S./Mexican border to fulfill functions assigned the civilian Immigration and Naturalization Service. The ongoing operation, dubbed "Gatekeeper," is yet another violation of the by now routinely-ignored Posse Comitatus Act.

1996: "Operation Assured Response" is conducted in oil-rich/corporate friendly Liberia to impress local dissidents with the idea that the U.S. is prepared to react quite forcefully in the event things "get out of hand" during ongoing civil unrest.

1997: U.S. air power is used to destroy the only pharmaceutical manufacturing facility in the Sudan, purportedly because it is being used to produce explosives employed by the al-Qaida terrorist network to attack American embassies and other such installations abroad. The U.S. then attempts to quash a UN investigation that reveals the plant had been used for no such purpose (no apology, much less reparation, has ever been offered the Sudanese).

1998–2002: The Joint Chiefs of Staff demonstrate the extent to which they believe their doctrine and the consequent methods employed by their troops conform to legality by recommending that the U.S. refuse jurisdiction of the newly-created International Criminal Court—modeled on the Nuremberg precedent—until the international community agrees to guarantee, in the immortal words of Senator Jesse Helms, that "no American serviceman or woman will ever be brought before it."

1999: President Bill Clinton relies on the Praetor Protocol to bring in Delta Force personnel to provide advice and "backup" to local police during demonstrations protesting a meeting of the World Trade Organization in Seattle.

1999–2001: U.S. naval and air units are deployed, ostensibly to force Yugoslavia's Milosevic régime to halt a "campaign of genocide" against ethnic Albanians in Kosovo (a province within the Yugoslavian domain). Belgrade is heavily bombed and the Chinese embassy located there destroyed in the process. In the aftermath—and in stark contrast to the slaughters in Rwanda (1994) and Bosnia-Herzegovina (1991–96), where the U.S. stood by and watched, or East Timor (1975–1999), where the U.S. functioned as a de facto sponsor—no evidence of genocide against the Albanians is produced. To all appearances, the assault was intended to bring about the old-line communist Milosevic's replacement by a U.S.-preferred head-of-state. Ironically, the deposed president is currently—and rightly—standing trial before the Hague Tribunal on charges of genocide stemming not from his policies in Kosovo, but Bosnia-Herzegovina.

2001–2003: On September 11, 2001, the al-Qaida network, citing among other things the ongoing U.S. policy of genocide towards Iraq as its reason, employs three "300,000 pound cruise missiles" to "degrade" the U.S. military's "command and control infrastructure" in Washington, D.C., as well as its economic counterpart at the World Trade Center in New York. "Collateral damage" among civilians is about 1/30,000th as great as that inflicted by the military upon Iraq alone over the past decade. Predictably, the administration of President George W. Bush seizes the opportunity to launch a "war on terror," not against al-Qaida—all assertions to the contrary notwithstanding, there is no indication it has suffered appreciably as a result—but instead against the Islamicist Taliban régime in Afghanistan, an entity guilty of interfering with U.S. corporate ambitions to exploit lucrative oil fields in central Asia. Some 4,700 Afghanis are killed in the blitzkrieg—dubbed "Operation Infinite Justice"—which culminates in installation of a "democratic government" handpicked by the U.S. Substantial U.S. forces are then committed to an ongoing military occupation—this one is called "Operation Enduring Freedom" and described as a "nation-building exercise"—ensuring that the new puppet government remains in place.

2002–03: Special Forces troops are sent to the southern Philippines to destroy the allegedly "al-Qaida-linked" Abu Sayyaf guerrilla group (itself believed by many Filipino dissidents to be a CIA front). Others are sent to "stabilize" Chechnya and the Republic of Georgia. President Bush makes a speech designating three mutually-hostile countries—Iraq, Iran and North Korea—an "axis of evil" which comprises the "top priority" for U.S. attack in the "war on terror" (Sudan, Libya, Somalia and Syria are also mentioned by DoD officials as possible "secondary" targets, while the quasiofficial Rand Corporation recommends occupation of Saudi oil fields). Preparations for an invasion of Iraq are begun. Meanwhile, selected Taliban and al-Qaida fighters, captured during the war in Afghanistan, are drugged, brought by aircraft to a prison camp at Guantanamo Bay, and housed in open cages. In response to international criticism, the U.S. takes an extraordinarily confused position, arguing that the captives are both "prisoners of war," and thus not subject to the protection of U.S. domestic law, and "illegal combatants" who are outside protection of the Geneva Convention. In effect, the prisoners are said to occupy a status in which *no* rule of law applies, their treatment therefore becoming a matter of U.S. "discretion." Variations of the same convoluted—and entirely illegal—"logic" is increasingly applied not only to foreign nationals residing in the U.S., but to citizens as well.

2003: Claiming that it is imperative to do so because the country is maintaining illegal stockpiles of chemical and biological weapons, that it is in the process of developing nuclear weapons, the U.S. launches a massive air campaign against and then invades Iraq on Mar. 19. Although the conquest is swift, and relatively bloodless, the U.S. is unable to demonstrate that Iraq was possessed *any* of the allegedly offending weaponry. The campaign nonetheless puts the U.S. in control of the country's vast oil reserves, and in a position to dictate a "new economic, political and military order for the Middle East."

Alternatives

In light of the above, Americans are clearly faced with a choice. On the one hand, they can continue in their collective pretense that "the opposite of everything is true,"[28] prattling on about "innocent Americans" being "the most peaceful people on earth" while endorsing the continuous U.S. dispensation of death, destruction and domination in every quarter of the globe. On the other, they must at last commence the process of facing up both to the realities of their national history and to the responsibilities that history has bequeathed. In effect, Americans will either become active parts of the solution to what they and their country have wrought, or they will remain equally active parts of the problem. There is no third option. Imagining the contrary, that certain "complexities" create "unique circumstances" in the U.S., circumstances that preclude doing what would be obviously necessary and appropriate in any other context ("out there" in the Third World, for instance),[29] is simply to embrace an especially insidious variant of American Exceptionalism, remaining part of the problem rather than acting as part of the solution while pretending that the opposite of that, too, is true.[30]

There is no place for either spectators or bystanders at a holocaust. Here, the mere "bearing of moral witness" is irrelevant or worse, as is the expression of "opposition" through modes deemed acceptable by the perpetrating entity.[31] Only the undertaking of whatever course of action proves necessary to actually halt the genocidal process—action that can by definition be sanctioned by neither the perpetrators nor those complicit in the perpetration by virtue of their acquiescence or the "principled" ineffectuality of their opposition to it—is acceptable in any defensible moral schema (no, the Jews who in 1944 overpowered and killed a few of the SS men at Auschwitz had *not* in the process become "just as bad" as their nazi exterminators).[32] The only relevant question is thus which among a range of possible courses of action is most likely to obtain the desired outcome, not whether undertaking it will allow those who do so to remain comfortable (much less "pure," in some idealized sense).

Admittedly, even this singular query can be—indeed, has been—used as a means by which to block action through endlessly digressive speculation.[33] Fortunately, things are not really so nebulous or subjective as those whose oppositional politics amount more to a fashion statement than substance would have it. History does offer a lens, embodied in Germany's experience during the Third Reich, of what is required to nullify the genocidally militaristic posture of a major state. This did not, and *could not*, come about through a "reform," no matter how "fundamental," of the perpetrating entity. Rather, the desired result was obtained, as it *had* to be, through outright destruction of the state apparatus itself.[34]

True, in the case of nazi Germany, it was necessary that this be accomplished by a saturation bombing campaign followed by a massive invasion and occupation of the country by other countries, a procedure that left not only Germany but most of Europe devastated and some forty million people dead. As was noted even at the time, however, both the fact and the nature of the cataclysm resulted primarily from a default on the part of the German people themselves to shoulder the burden of abolishing the nazi régime.[35] Such an undertaking would not have been painless for the Germans, of course. On the contrary, given the inherently brutal nature of nazism, any effective effort to repeal it would necessarily have been quite violent. *But*, and this is really the point, the level of violence involved, and the consequent degree of pain suffered by the Germans—not to mention everybody else—would have been *far less* had they simply done what was so obviously necessary in the first place.[36]

That the Germans did not rise to the occasion, saving themselves and others untold misery, was the result neither of apathy nor of cowardice. Rather, their collective failure to meet even the most rudimentary of their obligations to humanity accrued from the fact that they, afflicted with their own Teutonic version of America's triumphant exceptionalism, overwhelmingly applauded nazism's imposition of a "new order" both at home and abroad, turning at best a blind eye to its "flaws" until Germany began to incur its first significant defeats during the winter of 1941–42 (for most Germans, the "turning point in morale" did not really set in until the disaster at Stalingrad a year afterwards, and for many later still).[37] Thereafter, they were reduced first to fighting with increasing desperation to stave off a collective punishment they knew full well the lethal arrogance of their own behavior had earned them, then by-and-large—in a striking parallel to Americans' perpetually sweeping assertions of "national innocence"—to denying that the punishment was warranted.[38]

Those today who are serious in seeking to come to grips with U.S. militarism would do well to heed the lessons provided by the experience of their German predecessors. Leashing the North American Reich will not be attained through petition campaigns, candle-lit vigils, marches, rallies, mass demonstrations or any other such state-sanctioned method of "swaying" policy formation/implementation. It will not be attained through electoral efforts to "throw the bums out" of office or in support of "the lesser of two evils" (the result of which is always and by definition an endorsement of evil), by litigation in judicial fora integral to the offending entity, or by lobbying for the enactment of new laws. Still less will it come through the writing of better books, poems and movie scripts, taking the right drugs, alterations in diet and hair styles, fetishizing the significance of gender parity, establishing alternative radio stations, ridding society of ashtrays or riding bicycles rather than driving cars. With all due respect to Pete Townsend, music is *not* "the revolution."[39]

If any or all of these "lines of action" combined were in the least threatening to the stability of the status quo, they'd simply be declared illegal on their face, or, as has often happened, militarily-repressed long before they reach the point of inflicting discernable damage.[40] Each, or at least most, of these approaches yield a discernable utility, but only when their functional limits are properly understood: petition drives and electoral campaigns, litigation and mass protests are of value only to the extent that their organizers consciously employ them as vehicles upon which to demonstrate the impossibility of achieving meaningful change through such means.[41] In the sense, and this sense only, involvement in state-sanctioned modes of political activity can be useful, not as "solutions" or ends in themselves, but as tactical expedients necessary to developing the "critical mass" necessary to eradicate the U.S.

The objective, attainable if approached correctly (which means, first and foremost, framing issues clearly), is to facilitate a popular reappraisal of the "American character," engendering thereby a generalized assessment moving ever closer to a genuine apprehension of reality. Concomitantly, a revision in the self-concept held by individuals, most pronouncedly among those situated within communities of color and elsewhere along the lower third of the socioeconomic spectrum, stands to be set in motion.[42] This, in turn, will all but inevitably precipitate a profound reconceptualization of what must be done if "things are to be set right" in the U.S., as well as the obligation of "average Americans" to do it. A dynamic duality is thus unleashed, signaled in the first instance by a mounting refusal to serve in the military and other enforcement mechanisms by which the present order is sustained,[43] in the second by a growing willingness to confront and defeat these steadily-weakening institutions on their own terms, ultimately overpowering and discarding them.

There was a time, barely three decades past, when such a scenario came near to fruition. In the moment, however, many of those best positioned to carry America's "coming apart" through to its culmination blinked at the prospect,[44] shying away from the very real personal jeopardy entailed in their station, abruptly abandoning applied politics for the privileged sanctuary of academia, a few trading the currency of their repentant radicalism for elected office within the very system they'd built their reputations opposing, others opting for the subterfuge of embracing a "revolutionary" catechism so rigid as to preclude revolution altogether.[45] Thus, on the shoals of internal contradiction and failed nerve, the "almost revolution" of the early-70s quickly faded.[46]

The task at hand is to recapture the energy, imagination of that period, adding to it a broadbased and unequivocal acceptance of the proposition that the dissolution of state power here can be no more "nonviolent" here than it would have been—in fact, *was*—in nazi Germany, and that pretending otherwise simply increases the overall level of violence involved in the process. Can this happen? Of course it can. Whether it will, however, is an entirely different matter. One thing is nonetheless certain: there is absolutely no basis—moral, ethical or otherwise—upon which to expect those bearing the hyperlethal brunt of U.S. aggression abroad to continue to die in their millions, politely and perpetually out of sight and mind, while Americans dither over the questions of whether fundamental change is "really" necessary or "realistic," and, if so, how it might be accomplished in manner entailing no inconvenience—much less sacrifice—to themselves.

If "Good Americans" will not finally undertake the steps necessary to euthanize the genocidal instrumentalities of U.S. power projection, those on the receiving end will henceforth increasingly assign themselves the job, using any and all means available to accomplish it. That they wield a right to do so is a fact made incontrovertible by the magnitude and duration of the suffering inflicted upon them, not just by U.S. governmental/military/corporate élites but by the unending ranks of average Iowa farm boys who have so willingly pulled the triggers, launched the missiles and dropped the cluster bombs (or performed the technical functions necessary to converting the systematic starvation of brown-skinned children into the finance capital and lush stock dividends of the U.S. economy). Should it prove necessary that the right of the victims be translated into a program best framed as "two, three, many 9-1-1s," Good Americans, all whining pretenses to wounded innocence notwithstanding, will be entitled to no more complaint than were their Good German counterparts before them.

Notes

1. .Stuart Creighton Miller, "*Benevolent Assimilation*": *The American Conquest of the Philippines, 1899–1903* (New Haven, CT: Yale University Press, 1982) pp. 253–67. On American exceptionalism more generally, see Deborah L. Madsen, *American Exceptionalism* (Jackson: University of Mississippi Press, 1998).
2. For a representative taste of such bilge, see the chapter entitled "We Take Nothing by Conquest, Thank God" in Howard Zinn's *A People's History of the United States, 1492 to the Present* (New York: HarperPerennial, 1980) pp. 147–66.
3. This process is analyzed quite well by Noam Chomsky in his *Necessary Illusions: Thought Control in Democratic Societies* (Boston: South End Press, 1989).
4. This is standard stuff; see, e.g., T. Harry Williams, *The History of American Wars from 1745–1918* (Baton Rouge: Louisiana State University Press, 1981).
.5. This is the official count, as reported by the U.S. Bureau of the Census in its *Report on Indians Taxed and Not Taxed*(1890) (Washington, D.C.: U.S. GPO, 1894) pp. 637–8.
6. On Korea, see Edwin P. Hoyt, *America's Wars and Military Incursions* (New York: McGraw-Hill, 1987) p. 284. On the Philippines, see Creighton Miller, "*Benevolent Assimilation*".
7. Grover Cleveland, "Special Message to Congress on Recent Events on the Kingdom of Hawaii," Dec. 18, 1893. For background, see Noel J. Kent, *Hawaii: Islands Under the Influence* (Honolulu: University of Hawaii Press, [2nd ed.] 1993).
8. See generally, Robert Justin Goldstein, *Political Repression in Modern America, 1870 to the Present* (Cambridge/New York: Schenkman/Two Continents, 1978).
9. Butler's statement was made in congressional testimony, then published in *Common Sense*, Vol. 4, No. 1, Nov. 1935, p. 9.
10. See Noam Chomsky, *Deterring Democracy* (New York: Hill and Wang, 1992).
11. Stan Hoig, *The Sand Creek Massacre* (Norman: University of Oklahoma Press, 1961) pp. 177–92.
12. Anthony Wallace, *The Death and Rebirth of the Seneca* (New York: Alfred A. Knopf, 1970) pp. 141–4.
13. David E. Stannard, *American Holocaust: Columbus and the Conquest of the New World* (New York: Oxford University Press, 1992) p. 121.
14. Moorfield Storey and Julian Codman, "Marked Severities" in *Philippine Warfare* (Boston: George H. Ellis, 1902) esp. pp. 26–7.
15. On letter openers, see John W. Dower, *War Without Mercy: Race and Power in the Pacific War* (New York: Pantheon, 1986) p. 64. On ears, see Michael Herr, *Dispatches* (New York: Alfred A, Knopf, 1978) pp. 34–5, 198–9.
16. Michael Bilton and Kevin Sim, *Four Hours at My Lai* (New York: Viking, 1992); Charles J. Hanley, Sang-Hun Choe and Martha Mendoza, *The Bridge at No Gun Ri: A Hidden Nightmare from the Korean War* (New York: Henry Holt, 2001); Brigham M. Madsen, *The Shoshoni Frontier and the Bear River Massacre* (Salt Lake City: University of Utah Press, 1985); Ralph K. Andrist, *The Long Death: The Last Days of the Plains Indian* (New York: Macmillan, 1964) pp. 351–2.
17. The observation is attributed to Colonel George S. Patton III, grandson of the legendary World War II general, who also described his men as a "bloody goddamned good bunch of killers"; "The Colonel Speaking of His Men," excerpts from an interview on WABC-TV (New York), in Mitchell Goodman, ed., *Movement Towards a New America* (Philadelphia/New York: Pilgrim Press/Alfred A. Knopf, 1970) p. 625.
18. See generally, Sven Lindqvist, *A History of Bombing* (New York: Free Press, 2001); on the advent of napalm in particular, see pp. 104–9. For a more technical overview of such munitions, see Stockholm International Peace Research Institute (Malvern Lumsden), *Incendiary Weapons* (Stockholm/Cambridge, MA: Almquist & Wiksell International/MIT Press, 1975).
19. David Svaldi, *Sand Creek and the Rhetoric of Extermination: A Case-Study in Indian-White Relations* (Landham, MD: University Press of America, 1989).
20. Hoig, *Sand Creek Massacre*, p. 47.
21. The quotes will be found in Francis Fitzgerald, *Fire in the Lake: The Vietnamese and the Americans in Vietnam* (New York: Vintage, 1973) p. 460; Richard Drinnon, *Facing West: The Metaphysics of Indian-Hating and Empire-Building* (Minneapolis: University of Minnesota Press, 1980) p. 451; in Stanley Karnow, *Vietnam: A History* (New York: Viking, 1983)p. 325.
22. For a concise survey of such epithets, see Holly Sklar, "Brave New World Order," in Cynthia Peters, ed., *Collateral Damage: The "New World Order" at Home and Abroad* (Boston: South End Press, 1992) p. 8. On the Highway of Death itself, see Michael Kelly, "Highway to Hell," *New Republic*, Apr. 1991; Ramsey Clark, et al., *War Crimes: A Report on United States War Crimes in Iraq* (Washington, D.C.:Maisonneuve Press, 1992) pp. 50–1, 90–3.
23. Quoted in Stannard, *American Holocaust*, p. 131.

24. For explication of the term, see Robert Jay Lifton and Eric Markusen, *The Genocidal Mentality: Nazi Holocaust and Nuclear Threat* (New York: Basic Books, 1990).
25. Overall, see William H, Riker, *Soldiers of the States* (Washington, D.C.: Public Affairs Press, 1957). For an excellent case study, see Robert M. Gephart, "Politicians, Soldiers and Strikes: The Reorganization of the Nebraska Militia and the Omaha Strike of 1882," *Nebraska History*, No. 46, 1965.
26. Peter B. Kraska and Victor E. Kappler, "Militarizing American Police: The Rise and Normalization of Paramilitary Units," *Social Problems*, Vol. 44, No. 1, Feb. 1997.
27. Goldstein, *Political Repression*, pp. 3–236. Also see Sidney Lens, *The Labor Wars: From the Molly Maguires to the Sitdowns* (Garden City, NY: Doubleday, 1973).
28. Such posturing is both common and plainly delusional; see William H. Chrisman, *The Opposite of Everything is True: Reflections on Denial in Alcoholic Families* (New York: Quill, 1991). More directly on target here, see Donald L. Nathanson, "Denial, Projection and the Empathic Wall," in E.L. Edelstein, Donald L. Nathanson and Andrew Stone, eds., *Denial: A Clarification of Concepts and Research* (New York: Plenum, 1989) pp. 37–55.
29. Examples of such perspectives being advanced by "oppositionists" are legion. A classic illustration is Todd Gitlin's *The Sixties: Years of Hope, Days of Rage* (New York: Bantam, 1987).
30. I develop this theme much more thoroughly in my essay, "Pacifism as Pathology: Notes on an American Pseudopraxis," in my and Mike Ryan's *Pacifism as Pathology: Reflections on the Role of Armed Struggle in North America* (Winnipeg: Arbiter Ring, 1998).
31. Again, examples of professed oppositionists—and even self-styled "revolutionaries"—advancing arguments to the contrary are legion. For what is probably the definitive articulation in this vein, see Gene Sharp's *The Politics of Nonviolent Action*, 3 vols. (Boston: Porter Sargent, 1973).
32. The point is made quite well by Bruno Bettelheim in his foreword to Miklos Nyiszli's *Auschwitz* (New York: Fawcett, 1960).
33. For a succinct but thoroughgoing critique of this tendency in one of its more faddish guises, see Terry Eagleton, *The Illusions of Postmodernism* (Oxford, UK: Blackwell, 1996).
34. While the nazi edifice represents a rather crystalline example, and is therefore useful for illustrative purposes, the point here can, with justice, be applied far more broadly; see Jens Bartelson, *The Critique of the State* (Cambridge, UK: Cambridge University Press, 2001).
35. See, e.g., Karl Jaspers, E.B. Ashton and Joseph W. Koterski, *The Question of German Guilt* (New York: Fordham University Press, 2002).
36. The truth of this is plainly imbedded in the fact that the only group much remembered for mounting any sort of effective attempt to put a stop to the nazi insanity were the so-called Plotters of 1944, who attempted to assassinate Hitler and otherwise employ military means to seize control of the government; see Giles MacDonough, *A Good German: A Biography of Adam von Trott zu Solz* (Woodstock, NY: Overlook Press, 1992). Far more broadly, see Peter Hoffman's *The History of the German Resistance, 1933–1945* (Montréal: McGill-Queens University Press, [3rd ed.] 1996).
37. Richard Grunberger, *The 12-Year Reich: A Social History of Nazi Germany, 1933–1945* (New York: Holt, Rinehart and Winston, 1971) pp. 39–40; Michael Burleigh, *The Third Reich: A New History* (New York: Hill and Wang, 2000) pp. 758–9.
38. "I keep hearing the opinion that we shouldn't burden the younger generation with the so-called guilt question... Life is hard enough, and we shouldn't make it harder for the young. And whenever I hear this sort of thing, I always ask myself: In whose interest is this really being said? Do the young really resist this burden? Or is it really we older people who would like to hide behind the young in order not to have to admit our own [crimes]?"; Hans Graf von Lehndorff, quoted in Hannah Vogt, *The Burden of Guilt: A Short History of Germany, 1914–1945* (New York: Oxford University Press, 1964) p. xiii. Relatedly, see Charles S. Maier, *The Unmasterable Past: History, Holocaust, and German National Identity* (Cambridge, MA: Harvard University Press, 1988); Robert E. Shandley, ed., *Unwilling Germans? The Goldhagen Debate* (Minneapolis: University of Minnesota Press, 1998).
39. Townsend, guitarist for a decidedly mediocre British rock band called The Who, made this assertion during an on-stage altercation with anarchist agitator Abbie Hoffman during the 1969 Woodstock music festival in upstate New York; for context, see Abbie Hoffman, *Woodstock Nation* (New York: Vintage, 1969) pp. 140–5.
40. A third possibility, actually the norm, is that at a certain point the state will mount an actively cooptive response (usually in combination with the enactment of repressive legislation and selective applications of physical force). This is what Marcuse had in mind in his important essay, "Repressive Tolerance"; in Robert Paul Wolff, Barrington Moore, Jr., and Herbert Marcuse, *A Critique of Pure Tolerance* (Boston: Beacon Press, 1965) pp. 81–123. For illumination of how such techniques have been employed, see George Katsiaficas, *The Imagination of the New Left: A Global Analysis of 1968* (Boston: South End Press, 1987) pp. 161–4, 186–98.
41. This was a strategy employed by the Student National Coordinating Committee (SNCC) during the mid-60s. The late Kwame Turé (Stokely Carmichael) once told me that although he'd been arrested 38 times for asserting the right of blacks to vote in the Deep South, he himself had never bothered. The point of SNCC's voter registration drives was in Turé's view twofold: first, to empower disenfranchised blacks with the realization that they could in fact force the white supremacist power structure to allow them to do things previously forbidden, and, second, by achieving black suffrage, to impress upon them how little such formal systemic adjustments would actually accomplish in terms of changing the material circumstances of their lives. With those lessons gleaned from direct experience, SNCC organizers believed, grassroots blacks, already activated during the registration drives, would be much more receptive to the idea that revolutionary change rather than mere reform was both necessary and pos-

sible than would otherwise have been the case. The analysis was in large part correct, although SNCC itself proved incapable of following through; see Manning Marable, *Race, Reform and Rebellion: The Second Reconstruction in Black America, 1945–1982* (Jackson: University Press of Mississippi, 1984) esp. pp. 168–99.

42. The idea is by no means dissimilar to that embodied in the Black Pride/Black Power concepts espoused by SNCC and other activists during the mid-to-late 1960s. See, e.g., Robert L. Scott and Wayne Brockbriede, eds., *The Rhetoric of Black Power* (New York: Harper & Row, 1969).

43. This is not only possible, it was well underway during the early 1970s; see Richard Boyle, *Flower of the Dragon: The Breakdown of the U.S. Army in Vietnam* (San Francisco: Ramparts Press, 1972); Cincinnatus, *Self-Destruction: The Disintegration and Decay of the United States Army during the Vietnam Era* (New York: W.W. Norton, 1972).

44. The phrase used is borrowed from William L. O'Neill's *Coming Apart: An Informal History of America in the 1960s* (Chicago: Quadrangle, 1971). Also see Goodman, *Movement*; Katsiaficas, *Imagination*.

45. The classic example, of course, is Tom Hayden, a founder of SDS, author of the seminal *Port Huron Statement* and other important tracts, defendant in the Chicago conspiracy trial and all-round "revolutionary leader" of the 1960s, who, when the going got really rough during the early-70s, converted to liberal politics and a seat in the California state legislature (for a good taste of the apologetics he's indulged in ever since, see his *Reunion: A Memoir* (New York: Random House, 1988)). Others who moved in the same direction include SNCC leaders like Julian Bond and John Lewis, Black Panther founder Huey P. Newton and Chicago Panther leader Bobby Rush. Among those who opted for academia at the expense of politics are early SDS leaders Todd Gitlin and Richard Flacks. On the revolutionary catechist vector, see Max Elbaum, *Revolution in the Air: Sixties Radicals Turn to Lenin, Mao and Che* (New York: Verso, 2002).

46. The descriptor used accrues from Max Priaulx and Sanford J. Ungar, *The Almost Revolution: France-1968* (New York: Dell, 1969). On failed nerve, see Eagleton, *Illusions*, p. 19.

"A Government of Laws"?

U.S. Obstructions, Subversions, Violations and Refusals of International Legality Since World War II

> The government of the United States has been emphatically termed a government of laws, and not of men. It will certainly cease to deserve this high appellation, if the laws furnish no remedy for the violation of a vested legal right.
>
> —Chief Justice John Marshall
> *Marbury v. Madison* (1803)

Sanctimony is one of the more repulsive attitudes. In league with such attendant character defects as smugness, duplicity, hypocrisy, and that steadfast denial of uncomfortable or inconvenient information usually referred to as "ignorance," it forms a squalid composite defining what might, for lack of a better term, be called "the American point of view." Taken as a whole, the outlook constitutes nothing so much as a collective and intractable mental disorder, a netherworld of self-absorbed fantasy in which, as with those suffering the effects of alcoholism and kindred maladies, "the opposite of everything is true."[1] Unlike alcoholics, however—no matter *how* much pain individual drunks may prove capable of causing their families, friends and communities—those afflicted with the mass psychosis of Americanism[2] are uniquely positioned both to attempt the reshaping of reality itself in conformity with the demands of their dementia, and to employ genuinely genocidal modes of force against all who might seek to prevent their having their way in the matter.[3] In this sense, the lunatics really *have* assumed a kind of tentative control over the planetary asylum.

Apart from the bizarre fable that Americans, who've wrought a country that has after more than two centuries yet to evidence a single year during which it was not making war upon someone, somewhere, for some reason, comprise "the most peace-loving of peoples" (see the chronology bearing that title in this volume), the inversions of reality imbedded at the very core of America's delusional self-concept comprise a cluster of four interlocking myths: 1) the U.S. was the first democracy since that of the Athenian Greeks, and remains the world's foremost exemplar of "democratic values"[4]; 2) given its standing as the world's leading democracy, the U.S. presents the benchmark realization of "human freedom"[5]; 3) both of these things are true, and will forever remain so, because, as Chief Supreme Court Justice John Marshall put it as early as 1803, the "government of the United States

[is] a government of laws...not of men";[6] 4) so integral is this last feature in configuring America's sociopolitical existence that, as Justice Henry Brown observed nearly a hundred years after Marshall, even in situations where the law is silent, failing to address particular sets of circumstances at given moments, "certain principles of natural justice inherent to the Anglo-Saxon character" ensure that the U.S. can inevitably be counted upon to do right, without recourse to the "need [for] constitutions and statutes."[7]

In America, then, "law" is presumed—uniquely so, Justice Brown's formulation having served merely to epitomize his country's time-honored and hubristic belief in its own exceptionality[8]—*always* to prevail, despite the fact that law, as such, may be conspicuous solely on the basis of its absence (either figurative or literal). Put another way, this is to assert that, whenever America's "government of laws" does or says something, whatever has been said or done *must* by virtue of its source be considered "legal." To rephrase the proposition yet again, it is contended that the U.S., or, more accurately, the state-corporate amalgam that has long since come to preside over it,[9] is, in and of itself, "The Law." Thus, far from exhibiting the lofty ideals to which John Marshall pretended in its behalf, we find that the American system ultimately displays itself as something far more nearly resembling what was once described by German scholar Ernst Fraenkel, while trying to explain the structure of nazi governance to those unfamiliar with or confused by it, as a "Prerogative State."[10] By this, he meant any system consisting at base of a politicojudicial arrangement in which the "men" who rule, whether personally or institutionally, employ illusions of legality as a means by which to impose their will upon the populace in a relatively unfettered manner.[11]

The extent to which Fraenkel's description is applicable to the U.S. may in some ways be readily discerned in the country's classic wedding of the terms "law" and "order," forging a union so complete that the pair have become fused as a single four-syllable word in popular parlance, one half virtually inconceivable without the other.[12] From there, it is but a short step to perceiving order not just as synonymous with law—as though the two were incapable of conflicting—but as its most tangible manifestation. A shorter step still takes us to the point where order is seen as being all-important, law as naught but a contrivance through which it is achieved, maintained and perfected.[13] Conceptions of law as being codified in accordance with fundamentally humanitarian principles and order constructed only in conformity with legal requirements/constraints are thereby completely reversed.[14] At that juncture, to paraphrase Antonio de Nebrija's fifteenth-century pronouncement on the relationship of language to empire, law becomes the "a perfect instrument of subjugation,"[15] the medium for transmission of what has more recently been referred to as an "unjust legality."[16]

This, for obvious reasons, can never be admitted, either by the law-makers who harness their product to the service of order, or by the much broader but mostly privileged and affluent sector of the public embracing their efforts. Hence, the promulgation of each new statute regulating the activities and behaviors of the population as a whole is attended by an "explanation"—usually devolving upon outright disinformation and often advanced through a wholesale media blitz—of why it is in the "best interests" even of those most adversely affected ("public health and safety," as well "national security," are mainstays in this regard).[17] The same dynamic is apparent whether the point of reference is the sweeping curtailments of constitutional rights/civil liberties contained in measures such as the 1996 Antiterrorism and Effective Death Penalty Act and the 2001 USA PATRIOT Act,[18] or, far more ubiquitously—and thus insidiously—the rapidly proliferating pile of socially-repressive/regimenting legislation involving everything from smoking[19] to homelessness[20] to "pedestrian control."[21] And, to be sure, augmentation of the mechanisms of enforcement available to the state—a description applying not only to the burgeoning U.S. police/penal apparatus,[22] but to a rampant expansion in the range and severity of fines, fees and penalties attaching to all manner of petty "offenses"[23]—proceeds apace.

As things stand, persons residing in the U.S. are subject to a greater proliferation of rules effecting a far broader range of their day-to-day activities than any people in the world.[24] To the degree that "freedom" may, as it must, be socially defined as the latitude of personal autonomy retained by individuals—or, again to put it another way, by the relative absence of an overarching authority regulating/regimenting the minutia of each person's daily existence—U.S. citizens now enjoy the least freedom of any people.[25] In the "land of the free," one is "free" to do exactly what one is told in virtually everything one does, every waking moment[26]—and, for the most part, every *sleeping* moment as well[27]—of every single day. Either that, or continuously run the risk of "suffering the consequences" assigned by the state to any and all deviations, no matter how seemingly slight or insignificant. The situation is one which has, of course, been witnessed before, conforming as it does in all too many respects to that prevailing in Germany during the 1930s.[28]

On the Matter of Legal Equity

Unlike nazi jurisprudence, that of the U.S. has always laid explicit claim to redemption through an ironclad constitutional embrace of a principle of consistency articulated as "equal justice before the law."[29] Realization of this lofty standard has from the outset been decidedly incomplete, however, and hotly contested by many of those in power (i.e., subject to deliberate and systematic subversion by those responsible for enforcing it). At the beginning, although it was generally agreed that the appearance of legal equity must preclude establishment of a

formal aristocracy within the U.S.,[30] the idea that the poor and unprop-
ertied might hold the same legal rights as their rich and propertied
counterparts was—and remains—a highly "controversial" proposition.[31]
That anything resembling equal rights might be vested in Euroamerican
women, or nonwhite persons of either sex, was, and, especially with
regard to the latter, continues to be denied outright.

   The history is sordid. In 1856, for example, Chief Justice Roger B.
Taney, writing for the Supreme Court, opined that a black man possessed "no rights which the white man was bound to respect."[32] It was
not until 1879 that a federal court finally conceded that an American
Indian might be considered a "person" for purposes of law.[33] Beginning
in 1889, with the *Chinese Exclusion Case*, the Supreme Court held that
East Asian immigrants were not vested with the same rights as persons
emigrating to the U.S. from Europe.[34] The same logic was still being
applied by the federal judiciary a century later, with regard to Haitians,
Salvadorans, and others.[35] Women, irrespective of race, were not only
not accorded suffrage in the U.S. until 1920, and were, at least when
married, formally disallowed under the Common Law of Coverture and
other such devices from managing businesses and owning most forms
of property until very nearly as late.[36] When viewed against the backdrop of Jim Crow legislation and the like,[37] the famous guarantee of
"separate but equal protection" extended by the U.S. high court to
African Americans and other "out groups" in *Plessy v. Ferguson* stands
revealed both for what it was, and for what to all intents and purposes
it continues to be.[38]

   The routine imposition of disparate sentences for conviction of similar offenses is one sure signifier of legal inequality. A notorious example is that of George Jackson, an 18-year-old black youth sentenced in
1960 to a life term in prison after pleading guilty to acting as the get-
away driver in a $70 gas station stickup (considerable evidence indicat-
ed that he was merely waiting in the car, unaware that a robbery was
occurring).[39] Jackson's fate must be contrasted to that of corporate
raider Michael Milken, a white man sentenced to ten years imprisonment in 1990—he actually served far less—after he pled guilty to having
engaged in massive stock fraud involving the theft of several *billion* dollars (the evidence indicates that Milken was guilty of far more than he
admitted).[40] Such inequities are standard. A 1997 study concluded that
in Massachusetts an Afroamerican convicted of a "drug-related offense"
was 39 times, and a Latino *81* times, more likely to be sentenced to
prison than a Euroamerican found guilty of the same charge, an "incon-
gruity" prevailing, albeit to varying extents, in all U.S. jurisdictions.[41] In
the same vein, a person convicted of murdering a Euroamerican is,
overall, 4.3 times as likely to be sentenced to death as a person convicted of murdering an Afroamerican (in some states—Georgia, for
instance—the ratio exceeds 10:1),[42] while the rate at which capital pun-

ishment is meted out to blacks who murder whites is some 40 times that of whites who murder blacks.[43]

Small wonder, all things considered, that peoples of color in the U.S. are incarcerated at several times the rate experienced by the "mainstream"—the official euphemism for "white"—population, with the number of Afroamerican men imprisoned for "drug offenses" alone increasing by 707 percent between 1985 and 1995 (the number of black women imprisoned for the same reason rose by an even more astonishing 828 percent during the same period).[44] Black males aged 18–25 in the U.S. now face a one-in-three probability of imprisonment, more than double the prospect confronted by their South African counterparts under apartheid.[45] Latinos and American Indians are also sentenced to prison at rates approximately four times that of whites.[46] In the U.S., which currently imprisons a greater proportion of its population than any country except Russia,[47] nonwhites are extravagantly "overrepresented"[48]—meaning that whites are just as extravagantly *under*represented, given that they demonstrably perpetrate crimes at rates as great or greater than persons of color[49]—and all but a tiny fraction of white prisoners come from the lower socioeconomic brackets.[50]

Another question, inherently necessary in a system purporting to treat corporations and the state itself as entities imbued with "the rights of persons under the law,"[51] is whether such institutions, or those serving as executors and functionaries within them, are held to the same standards of legal accountability as everyone else. Some sense of the answer was undoubtedly gleaned from comparing the wildly disparate punishments meted out to George Jackson and Michael Milken. The accuracy of this perception is rapidly borne out by even the most cursory examination of the record, replete as it is with such examples as Ivan Boesky,[52] Charles Keating[53] and Warren Anderson,[54] to name but three more of the worst white collar offenders to be effectively let off the hook during the 1980s and '90s. And, to be sure, an all but identical process is currently underway with regard to the executives and board members of Enron, WorldCom, Quest, Arthur Anderson, Freddie Mac and other major corporations whose fraudulent accounting practices have resulted in artificially-inflated stock prices/immense personal profits derived from the resultantly catastrophic losses absorbed by the general public.[55] The story is as old as that of the U.S. itself, and surely as much a matter of "organized crime"—in this case all but unpenalized—as anything undertaken by Al Capone, John Gotti, the Crips and Bloods, or the much-reviled cabal of "Columbian drug lords."[56]

If it may be said that the U.S. corporate élite has to purposes been immunized against the ostensible legal consequences of its criminal comportment, the same is even more true with respect to those engaged in the activities of state. In terms of corruption, this was plainly so with the Yazoo land swindle during the earliest days of the republic,[57] the various influence-peddling schemes besetting the Grant administration during the 1870s,[58] the Harding administration's Teapot Dome Scandal during the early 1920s,[59] Richard Nixon's involvements with Beebe Rebozo and others a half-century later,[60] and much more.[61] One of the more glaring denominators common to all such examples is that, with painfully few exceptions, the offenders went unprosecuted, and, in those rare instances where a penalty was imposed, it has tended to be far more of the token than the genuinely punitive—much less exemplary—variety.[62] By and large, the worst a U.S. official has ever had to fear, should s/he prove inept enough to be caught violating the public trust for purposes of personal gain, has been to suffer the "humiliation" of exposure in the press and consequent removal from his/her place at the trough. Typically, those thus deposed have been allowed to retain some part—and in many instances all—of what they've stolen, and, their moral/ethical qualifications for such jobs abundantly demonstrated during their stints in "public service," are quickly ushered into lucrative positions in the private—read, corporate—sector.[63]

The same applies to officials guilty of crimes committed out of political rather than pecuniary motives. Witness the figurative slaps on the wrist dispensed to H.R. Haldeman, John Erlichman and other ranking members of the Nixon administration involved in the Watergate conspiracy during the early 1970s,[64] and the veritable replay acted out with regard to John Poindexter, Oliver North and other Reaganites convicted as a result of the Iran-Contra affair a decade later.[65] Witness as well the fact that in 1975, a Senate investigating committee documented how the FBI had for fifteen years conducted a secret operation codenamed COINTELPRO, designed to "neutralize" individuals and organizations the Bureau considered to be politically objectionable.[66] Although the senators correctly concluded that COINTELPRO was by definition illegal, and filled their multivolume final report to the overflowing with illustrations of criminal activities by Bureau personnel running the gamut from false arrests and imprisonments to complicity in murder, not a single FBI agent or official ever spent a minute behind bars as a result.[67] An identical outcome pertains to congressional findings, revealed in 1997, that the vaunted FBI crime lab has long been systematically tailoring—and in many cases fabricating—the "physical evidence" used in court to convince juries to convict and imprison thousands of quite possibly innocent people.[68]

The FBI is by no means unique in this regard. Perjury by police witnesses in every judicial venue from traffic court to capital murder trials is as endemic as it is unpunished,[69] while the number of cops doing time as a result of their ubiquitous dispensation of that form of curbside punishment known as "police brutality" is truly laughable.[70] Police officers, as Amadou Diallo could readily testify, *don't* go to prison in the U.S., even when it's conceded that they fired a barrage of bullets at very close range into the body of an unarmed man whose only "offense," aside from being black, was to have responded to their demand that he produce ID by reaching for his wallet.[71] The number of corroborating witnesses on this point, all of them with the sort of firsthand experience suffered by Diallo, might easily run into the thousands.[72] Similarly, although the record of U.S. war crimes is staggering, not least in official renderings,[73] no American military officer of field grade or above has ever served time in prison as a result.[74] Meanwhile, the handful of junior officers and enlisted men who've been convicted of such offenses over the years have, like the infamous Lt. William Calley, under whose immediate command the 1968 My Lai Massacre was perpetrated, typically enjoyed reduction or outright commutation of their already paltry sentences.[75]

Clearly, the notion that the U.S. system produces anything resembling "equal justice before the law" is at best a grim farce. So too, then, the idea that this "government of laws" embodies the principles of freedom and democracy, representative or otherwise. Instead, the U.S., all pretensions to the contrary notwithstanding, and no matter how long and carefully these may have been cultivated, remains what it's always been: a plutocracy—a political construction, that is, wherein the wealthy rule—marked by distinctly racist and sexist overtones.[76] It follows that, as in any such configuration, U.S. domestic law serves primarily to rationalize inherent disequilibria of power and privilege, creating the illusion rather than the equality of justice.[77] And that, in turn, is just another way of saying that legal codification in the U.S. takes as its objective the preservation and perfection of a structure of *in*justice.

All the World a Stage

It is, of course, one thing for a government to employ law to such purposes within the framework of its own jurisdiction, quite another for it to seek to impose the arrangement on other countries. Thus, it is noteworthy that, insofar as it has lately undertaken to ensure that promulgation of international legality will henceforth "conform to the doctrines of [its own] domestic law that have been so laboriously crafted over the past two centuries,"[78] it is the latter trajectory that the U.S. is presently and increasingly pursuing. Actually, the trend is more than a half-century old, commencing in earnest during World War II with U.S. initiatives to lay the groundwork for a permanent international body composed of its allies to serve both as a primary diplomatic forum in the postwar context and, more importantly, to anchor the new planetary order in a "progressive development and codification of international law."[79] Unequivocally, the U.S. took the helm in founding the entity that became known as the United Nations, arranging for it to be chartered in San Francisco on June 26, 1945.[80]

The concept underpinning the UN was far from new, certainly, a precursor, the League of Nations, having existed from 1919-1939. Significantly, however, although President Woodrow Wilson had been a catalyst in the League's creation,[81] the U.S. had never deigned to join, a matter that all but guaranteed its ineffectuality.[82] More significantly still, the U.S. embarked upon establishment of the UN at a moment when it was not only decisively victorious in a war of global proportions, but genuinely ascendant in both military and economic terms. It's monopoly on nuclear weapons, moreover, combined with the fact that it alone of the prewar major powers had escaped devastation of its industrial base during the fighting, seemed to guarantee that the decisiveness of its advantages could be sustained against all potential rivals over the foreseeable future.[83] All that remained was to create a medium through which to cast an aura of legitimacy over the reality of U.S. world dominance, and to regularize activities among the various components of the resulting empire.

The project proceeded along several tracks. Even as the initial UN meetings were convened to begin the process of codifying the elements of international customary law that would serve, it was said, to "outlaw war as a means of resolving disputes between nations,"[84] a series of show trials were launched in Nuremberg and Tokyo to set the precedent for what would happen to anyone, heads of state included, who deviated.[85] Slightly earlier, a meeting had been conducted at Bretton Woods, New Hampshire, between U.S. representatives and those of several countries closely aligned with it. The result was establishment of several institutions—notably the World Bank and the International Monetary Fund—as well as a General Agreement on Trade and Tariffs (GATT, used as the cornerstone for creating the World Trade Organization in the mid-90s), designed, when taken together, to "coordinate"—read, regiment—the global economy.[86] Rounding out the package was the lodging of a "law enforcement" mechanism called the Security Council within the UN itself.

> The U.S. organizational blueprint [for the UN], among other things, included special privileges for itself and its powerful allies. Specifically, this meant permanent seats on the Security Council; Security Council control over all vital issues of international peace and security; and, of enormous tactical significance, a veto over any proposed Council action by any of the five permanent members... It was the viewpoint of the U.S. and its World War II allies that they alone would determine the nature of the post-war peace... In other words...a deliberate decision was taken to establish a collective security system which could not be applied to the permanent members themselves... There was no illusion that smaller countries, let alone nations still colonized by the great powers, would have an equal voice.[87]

Given the degree of material primacy wielded by the U.S., it could be expected that the "Big Five" Security Council members would largely to defer to its wishes, a matter effectively vesting the "legitimate" use of force in international affairs exclusively in the U.S. and/or its surrogates.[88] Better yet, since all UN member-states were committed by the body's Charter not only to support but "contribute" to such actions as the Security Council *cum* U.S. might decide, the list of U.S. surrogates could in a tangible sense be taken to include every country in the world other than such "rogue" states as might comprise the target(s) of America's ire at any given moment.[89] For a member-state to refuse to go along would, in this framing, itself constitute an illegality warranting the offending country's subjection to, if not "corrective action" in a military form, then at least the ravages of collective trade sanctions and the like.[90] A handier vehicle for extending the reach of U.S. plutocrats to universal dimensions than that envisioned by the UN's American founders is difficult to imagine.

Fortunately, consolidation of the intended U.S. position as an unchallenged—and virtually unchallengeable—planetary hegemon was shortly blocked by two momentous events. First, on September 23, 1949, the Soviet Union test-detonated a nuclear weapon of its own, thus, while establishing a rough military parity with the U.S., creating a potent political counterbalance in the Security Council, and in world affairs more generally.[91] Second, also in 1949, Mao Zedong's communist guerrillas defeated the forces of Chiang Kai-shek's U.S.-aligned régime in China, thereby eliminating at a stroke one of the Big Five and demonstrating conclusively that the peoples of various countries, notably those of the Southern and Far Eastern regions long colonized by the European powers, were not especially accepting of the new order of Northern/Western state-corporatist subjugation the U.S., through the instrumentality of the UN, had in mind to impose upon them.[92] The era of "people's war"—that is, of armed struggles manifested *within* rather than between countries—had begun,[93] and it was a mode of combat the UN structure was ill-designed to contain.

One of the more problematic aspects of what was happening in the areas soon be known as the "Third World" was that the peoples situated therein tended to take the UN's articulations of international legality quite seriously.[94] U.S. officials and diplomats, ever prone to the sort of self-flattery embodied in espousing noble-sounding principles, even—or especially—when they believe and practice the exact opposite, ensured that a great deal of the UN Charter was devoted to affirming the "right of all peoples to self-determination" and laying out the procedures by which decolonization would occur within the welter of "non-self-governing territories" encompassed by the classic European empires.[95] Those thus formally assured of such rights as independence and "permanent sovereignty over their lands and resources" were for the most part unaware of—still less impressed by—the fact that the U.S. intended such verbiage rather less than literally; that, indeed, the American emphasis on self-determination was more than anything a subterfuge designed to nullify the "lawful dominion" over Africa and Asia exercised by the old order of colonialism, thereby opening these rich realms to domination/exploitation by U.S. neocolonial enterprises (i.e., the plan was to replicate the U.S. relationship to Latin America on a global basis).[96] Instead, the Third Worlders, not content to simply trade one master for another, took the newly-revised law of nations at face value, asserting their entitlement to bona fide liberation by any and all means available to them.[97]

In this, given that their actions seriously impaired consummation of U.S. imperial ambitions, the revolutionaries received substantial material and diplomatic assistance from America's Soviet rival, against which, because of its capacity to reply with nuclear weapons, there could be no direct retaliation.[98] There followed, from roughly 1950 onwards—in truth, the process had already begun before the Second World War was over—a protracted contest of proxies, with the U.S. quietly but continuously intervening in the internal affairs of other nominally sovereign states for purposes of creating the "stability" deemed essential to expanding its corporate "investment" (i.e., extraction of extraordinary profits).[99] Stripped of its trappings, U.S. foreign policy reduced to a systematic reinforcement of anticommunist régimes, no matter how virulently fascistic, wherever they could be found or installed, a matter translating into the U.S. becoming far and away the world's largest purveyor of arms, munitions and military equipment, most of it appropriate only to the task of domestic repression.[100]

All of this engendered intense resentment among those victimized, fertile ground for an ongoing succession of popular insurgencies throughout the Third World.[101] Much of it was also illegal from the outset, becoming steadily more so as the number of UN member-states grew over the years—from 51 in 1945 to 185 four decades later, most of the additions being former European colonies[102]—and the pace at which international legality was committed to black letter form correspondingly picked up. The process has been one in which the U.S. has moved from a stance of consistently conducting itself in a manner contrary to the broad principles of international customary law to one in which it is just as consistently violating the particulars articulated in specific covenants and conventions.[103] Along the way, as they have within the arena of their domestic jurisprudence, those presiding over U.S. policy formation/implementation have become ever more adept at evading, distorting and otherwise obfuscating legal meaning, often standing it squarely on its head.[104]

To anyone familiar with the U.S. record vis-à-vis the indigenous nations encapsulated within its claimed borders, and the juridical convolutions through which this has been rationalized, its contemporary performance on the wider stage of world affairs is unsurprising. Both the arguments and the methods presently at issue have been present in U.S. relations with American Indians from virtually the first day, and were largely worked out, both in theory and in practice, by the end of the nineteenth century.[105] These include entry into myriad treaties with which the U.S. held not the least intention to comply;[106] senatorial refusal to ratify treaties already signed by the federal executive, meanwhile holding that the other party/parties to such compacts are bound by them;[107] the pretense that subsequent domestic statutes can have the legal effect of unilaterally nullifying U.S. obligations under existing treaties without abrogating the treaties themselves;[108] assertions that its own domestic law is enforceable at the discretion of the U.S. in the jurisdictions of other countries;[109] the pretense that a legitimate sphere of federal "plenary" authority exists outside the boundaries of all law, whether domestic or international;[110] and refusal by the federal executive to accept decisions of the courts, or the authority of the courts themselves, in matters pertaining to U.S. foreign policy.[111] A parallel to the basic presumption uniting the whole—that the U.S. is/can be bound by no laws other than those it has itself formulated or expressly accepted—was advanced as their first line of defense by the nazi defendants at Nuremberg. [112]

It was not until the unraveling and ultimate collapse of the USSR during the late-80s,[113] by which time the energy and enthusiasm fueling the Third World liberation struggle had also largely spent itself,[114] that the U.S. could return to its original plan of utilizing the UN's structural/procedural/legal attributes as a primary means through which not only to propel the American plutocrats' drive to absolute global hegemony, but to cast an aura of legitimacy upon both the process and its outcome. Evidence of such a shift has accrued rapidly, and with increasingly blatancy, over the last thirteen years, beginning in 1990, when the U.S. was able to obtain a Security Council resolution authorizing its heading-up of a multinational war against Iraq, the first such endorsement since a temporary Soviet boycott of the Council allowed it to gain a similar license for its "Korean police action" of 1951–53.[115] During the past decade, American spokespersons in the General Assembly, representatives in the various UN organs, as well as delegates to a host of conferences convened under UN auspices to hammer out the elements of international law, have also become increasingly insistent not only that the law of nations be written—in many cases rewritten—in conformity with the requirements of U.S. domestic law, but that the U.S. be explicitly accorded "special" status—usually in the form of a unique exemption from compliance, to be exercised at its own discretion—if the law itself is to be considered "valid."[116]

In the alternative, as is made clear by the openly "unilateralist" rhetoric emanating from American officialdom with ever greater emphasis since 1995, the U.S. is prepared to "go it alone," discarding the UN and its framework of international legality altogether.[117] This was the message punctuated quite forcefully in March 2003, when, in the face of active opposition by virtually the entire General Assembly, and the prospect of a veto in the Security Council of any resolution meant to approve such action, the U.S. proceeded "on [its] own authority" to launch an outright war of conquest against Iraq.[118] The UN—in effect, the entire rest of the world—has thus been confronted with a stark

choice: either to accept its U.S.-assigned role as a "tool of American foreign policy,"[119] or to be relegated, like the League of Nations before it, to
the realm of utter "irrelevancy."[120] No third option—maintaining and
perfecting a genuinely equitable system of international legality, for
instance—is, from the U.S. perspective, to be allowed a place at the
table of international consideration. So much for that "fundamental
respect for the law" supposedly enshrined at the core of America's
"democratic values." So much as well for the "freedom" of anyone not
already admitted to the exceedingly narrow ranks of the American
élite.

A Chronology of Criminal Comportment

A picture, they say, is worth a thousand words. Unfortunately, the
topic at hand does not lend itself to such representation. That being so,
the next best thing is to offer the following itemization, chronologically-
arranged, of exactly what has been under discussion in the preceding
section. Thus, and perhaps *only* thus, is it possible to convey a clear
sense of the consistency with which the U.S. has actively obstructed,
subverted, refused and/or violated virtually every articulated/articula-
ble element of international legality over the past half-century. Simply
put, a statement like "the U.S. cast...65 vetoes [of Security Council draft
resolutions] between 1973 and 1990,"[121] while completely accurate,
yields far less psychointellectual impact than seeing these vetoes listed,
item by item. Viewed in the latter fashion, the real magnitude of what
the U.S. has done—and how very far it is from actually being a country
administered by "a government of laws"—takes on an obviousness not
otherwise possible. Indeed, the sheer weight of the evidence threatens
to become overwhelming.

At some levels, the chronology is intended as a handy reference
guide. Those encountering ambiguous mention elsewhere of U.S.
actions vis-à-vis the UN in certain connections or given years will be
able to quickly pin down the details in snapshot form herein.[122] The
same applies to the correct but vague assertions of illegality attending
all too many historical analyses of the U.S. performance in places like
the Marshall Islands, Korea, Iran, Guatemala, Vietnam, Laos,
Cambodia, Indonesia, Chile, Angola, El Salvador, Grenada, Nicaragua,
Panama, Iraq—in effect, the entire Third World—since 1945.[123] Herein, it
is not merely contended that laws were broken, but, in each case, *which*
laws, specifically. Taken together with any of the numerous volumes in
which the texts of the various covenants, conventions and declarations
cited are compiled,[124] the chronology thereby provides anyone willing
to invest a minimal degree of effort the basic "ammunition" necessary
to build a well-grounded rather than merely rhetorical argument concerning the criminality of U.S. postwar comportment in almost any context.

Developing a coherent political analysis is any many respects contingent upon an ability to connect one context to another, a process not dissimilar to playing the kid's game of dot-to-dot. There are thus advantages to giving the entire chronology a more than cursory read. Close inspection of the record reveals, quite unmistakably, that in the very repetitiveness with which certain maneuvers have been undertaken by the U.S., administration after administration, generation after generation, lurk certain patterns imbued with a substantial explanatory power in their own right. Returning to the matter of U.S. vetoes of Security Council resolutions, for example, we find that 27 of the 65 mentioned above—34 of 76, if we begin with the first U.S. veto in 1970 and carry the count through June 2003—concern efforts by the other member-states represented in the Council to force Israel's compliance with some of the more fundamental requirements of international law.[125] About half the remainder (20)—apart from a dozen instances in which the U.S. has vetoed attempts to accomplish the same feat with regard to its own conduct—have served to extend an identical protective shield over the myriad and glaring illegalities perpetrated during the 1970s and '80s by the white supremacist régimes of South Africa and Rhodesia.[126]

A country's character can, of course, be judged both by that of the company it keeps, and by the intimacy of such relationships. Here, veto patterns reflect but the tip of the proverbial iceberg. The U.S. made sure that *none* of the 23 Security Council resolutions aimed at South Africa it *did* endorse between 1960 and 1985 contained effective enforcement provisions (sanctions, first imposed in 1963, were always very narrowly drawn, made voluntary rather than compulsory until 1977, etc.).[127] During the same period, the U.S., alone or joined only by Israel, voted against literally scores of General Assembly resolutions condemning South Africa's criminal actions and policies. Small wonder that in 1985 Archbishop Desmond Tutu was wont to depict the U.S. posture as being "objectively racist," pointing out that if it had not blocked the Security Council's undertaking measures against Pretoria similar to those the U.S. was itself imposing, not only without authorization but *in defiance* of both the Security Council and the World Court against the entirely lawful government of Nicaragua, South Africa's engagement in apartheid and related crimes against humanity would have ended in a heartbeat.[128]

The lengths to which the U.S. has gone to immunize the Israelis from the consequences of their criminality have been even more striking. In addition to those it's vetoed, the U.S. has ensured that all 43 Security Council resolutions it's endorsed with regard to Israel since 1948 have included no enforcement provisions at all, and could thus be safely ignored. Beyond that, the U.S., alone or in tandem with Israel itself, has on 206 occasions cast votes opposing General Assembly resolutions condemning Israeli actions/policies and/or affirming the rights of or services to Palestinians.[129] The sanctimonious pontifications

recently spewed by George Bush, Donald Rumsfeld and other U.S. officials concerning the "necessity" of going beyond a murderous embargo
that had already resulted in the deaths of well over a half-million Iraqi
children,[130] indulging in a fullscale war against the country because of
its ostensible failure to comply with "14 Security Council resolutions"—
or 17, the number kept changing—are thereby exposed to the full glare
of their own hypocrisy, no such need being voiced with regard to Israel's
ongoing refusal of 77 (counting U.S. vetoes), or having been, with
respect to apartheid South Africa's of 43.[131]

Nor can it be reasonably claimed that the nature of the issues
involving Iraq, even assuming that U.S. spokespersons actually believed
their oft-repeated suspicions—unfounded as they've turned out to be—
that the target country possessed illegal weapons of mass destruction
("WMD"), were somehow more serious than those pertaining to Israel or
South Africa, thereby justifying the blatant double-standard otherwise
presenting itself. South Africa, with considerable Israeli collaboration,
was, during the decade before the collapse of the apartheid régime,
well-known to have been heavily engaged in the illicit development of
nuclear weaponry.[132] More to the point, it is unquestionable that Israel,
with active U.S. assistance commencing at least as early as 1963, has
been for a full generation in possession not only of a nuclear arsenal,
but of the aircraft and missiles necessary to employ it with devastating
effectiveness.[133] More to the point still, the country possessing by far the
greatest quantities of WMD—not just nuclear weapons, but the very
types of prohibited chemical and biological weaponry Iraq was accused
of hording—is the U.S. of America.[134]

Ba'athist Iraq, it was asserted with rather more justification, was
also guilty of a bellicosity that had led it twice in a decade to invade and
in one case attempt to occupy its neighbors, to consistently abuse the
Kurdish minority in the northern reaches of its dominion, and to
viciously repress the democratic aspirations of its own Arabic populace.[135] The truth of these charges is more than offset, however, when
juxtaposed to South Africa's invasion/protracted occupation of
Namibia, its frequent military aggressions against such neighbors as
Angola, Zambia and Botswana, and the relentless savagery of the
apartheid system imposed for four decades by the white minority upon
the black majority within its own borders.[136] As concerns Israel, the first
occupation by military force of Palestinian lands beyond the boundaries
quite dubiously assigned the new state by the UN in 1947 came within
the first months, and remains very much in effect 55 years later.[137] To
this must be added the temporary occupation of the Egyptian Sinai in
its entirety on two occasions, occupation of the remainder of Palestine
and the Syrian Golan, beginning in 1967 and continuing to this day—
despite numerous Security Council and General Assembly resolutions
ordering withdrawal—and the invasion/protracted occupation of southern Lebanon.[138] At issue, too, is the frankly antidemocratic and

apartheid-like construction of Israel's "domestic" polity,[139] as well as its monumental and sustained abridgements of Arab rights in the occupied territories.[140]

The records of this squalid duo of U.S. client states blanches, moreover, in comparison to that of the sponsor itself. Here, any honest appraisal must begin with the recognition that, by its own admission, fully a third of U.S. continental territoriality consists of unceded—and therefore illegally occupied—land seized from a host of indigenous nations.[141] The same is true, perhaps in even greater proportion, in Hawai'i.[142] Then there are the ongoing occupations of Puerto Rico, Guam, "American" Samoa and the "U.S." Virgin Islands.[143] Barely a year had elapsed at the time of George Herbert Walker Bush's 1990 announcement of a "legal and moral imperative" for the U.S. to utilize "all due force" in driving Iraq's invading army out of Kuwait,[144] since the U.S. had itself invaded and occupied Panama,[145] less than a decade since it had done the same to Grenada,[146] and the smoke was still clearing from a lengthy low-intensity war waged by U.S. surrogates to topple the Sandinista government of Nicaragua.[147] Another proxy campaign had barely wrapped up in El Salvador,[148] while still others remained ongoing in Indonesia, Angola, Guatemala and elsewhere.[149]

The duplicity with which the U.S. pursued the most draconian kinds of sanctions against Iraq during the 1990s, meanwhile continuing to run interference for far more egregious offenders like Israel is easily matched by that displayed in other cases. Consider by way of illustration the embargo imposed at U.S. insistence upon Libya in January 1992, to coerce it into handing over to their accusers a pair of intelligence officers said to have orchestrated the 1988 bombing of Pan Am flight 103, in which 286 people—189 of them Americans—were killed.[150] Omitted from most recountings of this "terrorist act," is that, assuming they were involved at all, the Libyans were likely retaliating in the only way open to them after a U.S. airstrike on their capitol city killed more than a hundred civilians on April 14, 1986.[151] The U.S. attack, unauthorized through UN Charter procedures, was thus flatly illegal, but the U.S., having already repudiated the jurisdiction of the International Court of Justice (ICJ or "World Court") over its conduct, quickly vetoed a Security Council resolution condemning its crime and ordering payment of compensation (U.S. courts also dismissed Libyan and other complaints in the matter, both official and individual).[152] Likewise unmentioned in conventional accounts are such inconveniences as the facts that the U.S. was simultaneously—and still is—ignoring India's requests for the extradition of Union Carbide CEO Warren Anderson, accused of criminal culpability in the 1984 deaths of some 16,000 people near Bhopal,[153] or that Libya had, well before sanctions were ordered, repeatedly offered to provide the alleged culprits for trial before an impartial—read, international—tribunal.[154]

Cuba, against which the U.S. unilaterally imposed an ongoing "total" embargo in 1960, provides an even more telling example.[155] Indeed, aside from casting off the yoke of northern corporate domination and charting a course for itself independent of U.S. approval at the conclusion of its revolution in 1959,[156] Cuba is accused of no specific "crime" at all. True, American officials are prone to emitting periodic rumblings about the "atrocious human rights situation" on the island,[157] but the nature of such charges is ambiguous at best. Every Cuban child is guaranteed adequate nutrition, after all, while in the U.S. one in five is left to go hungry and their government regularly votes against UN resolutions to declare food a basic human right.[158] All Cubans are also guaranteed high quality medical attention—the Cuban health care system is by all standards the best and most comprehensive in the hemisphere—while in the U.S. an estimated 40 million people are presently left without such services altogether, and their government, when it's not busily "privatizing" what little remains of its once promising public health infrastructure, is staunchly opposing General Assembly efforts to include adequate health care among the fundamental rights delineated in international law.[159] There are no homeless persons cast out of mental institutions wandering the streets of Havana, as there are in every major U.S. city.[160] The Cuban populace, all but illiterate in 1960, now evidences by a decided margin the highest literacy rate of any country in the Americas,[161] and substantial progress has been made towards ensuring that every citizen enjoys decent housing (a goal *never* embraced by the U.S., even during the "Great Society" period presided over by Lyndon Johnson during the mid-1960s).[162]

And, to be sure, there is much more. Unlike the U.S., where such atrocities are documentedly ubiquitous, there is no record of Cuban police routinely clubbing, macing and otherwise assaulting citizens—much less shooting them to death—and no indication that its police force has been militarized à la the U.S. SWAT model.[163] No one has contended that prison construction has become a growth industry in Cuba,[164] that its architects have been commissioned to design penal design facilities for the express purpose of reducing those lodged within them to a state of "psychological jelly,"[165] or that its "totalitarian" government has devoted itself to making incarceration a profit-making enterprise.[166] There is no hint that, as is standard in the U.S. "business community," the head of any Cuban business concern "earns" several hundred times the wage paid his/her workers.[167] Nor has anyone suggested that government-chartered Cuban entities have sought to increase their profitability by establishing sweatshops throughout the Third World wherein twelve-year-olds are conscripted to fulltime labor under abysmal conditions and for as little as a dollar per day.[168] Cuba, by all indications, has not even endeavored to "persuade" other countries to dismantle their own social welfare systems, whatever they may be, in favor of the type of "order" implied by prioritizing their police/military capabilities.[169] To the contrary, sugar, cigars and rum notwithstanding, the island's largest export over the past quarter-century has been pharmaceuticals and trained medical practitioners.[170]

To all appearances then, Cuba, in stark contrast to the U.S., has treated its legal/moral obligations relative to human rights with the utmost seriousness, and has done a superb job of programmatically addressing them despite the impact of U.S. sanctions that have cost its already small economy at least $20 billion in potential revenues.[171] It is undoubtedly for this reason that in 1992 the General Assembly finally, over strenuous U.S. objections, approved for the first time a resolution affirming "the necessity of ending the economic, commercial and financial embargo imposed by the U.S. of America upon Cuba."[172] The U.S., of course, has steadfastly refused to comply with the resolution which, upon being introduced for the eleventh time in 2002, was endorsed by UN member-states—only the U.S. and Israel, joined by Uzbekistan, cast opposing votes—arguing, in a truly bizarre logical contortion, that, since the UN never approved the embargo in the first place, it has "no authority" to require its termination.[173] Putting the best possible face on it, the U.S. position is that the embargo is and has always been strictly definitive of its own trade policy—a sovereign prerogative exercised, with certain constraints under the UN Charter, by all states[174]—never intended to bind the international community, and is thus exempt from repeal by the General Assembly.

The falsity of this pretense is, however, amply demonstrated by the fact that the U.S. has done everything in its considerable power over the years—including even the occasional sabotage of their ships and cargos—to force other countries into adopting its own "Cuba trade policy."[175]

> One manifestation of the effort to internationalize the embargo took the form of the so-called "Cuba Democracy Act" [1992], known as the Toricelli Bill, which called for punishment of any ships from any country who called at Cuban ports by denying them access to U.S. ports for up to six months. Further congressional efforts during the same period tried to directly internationalize the embargo by threatening U.S. corporations with financial punishments if wholly foreign-owned subsidiaries conducted any trade with Cuba. What that meant was that a British company, for example, owned and operated and incorporated in England, but a subsidiary of a larger U.S. corporation, was forbidden to sell its goods to Cuba, even if that refusal violated British law, on threat of penalties being exacted on [its] U.S.-based corporate headquarters.[176]

Plainly, the motives underlying such conduct have nothing to do with upholding international law or furthering democracy and human rights. If they did, U.S. officials would not find it necessary to consistently misrepresent—that is, lie about—the nature of their policies. Instead, as Noam Chomsky and others have pointed out, the U.S. objective has all along been that of "deterring democracy" wherever it threatens to break out.[177] In this script, those countries coming closest to realizing the democratic ideal, and of achieving a decent standard of living for their citizenry as a whole, have, given that such things by definition require both political and economic independence from the U.S., been either abolished outright, through internal subversion or direct invasion by U.S. forces—sometimes referred to as "constructive bloodbaths"[178]—or subjected to whatever other forms of abuse might be deemed most expedient to demonstrating the cost prohibitive nature of their attempts at attaining a modicum of freedom and dignity.[179] One need not look only to the holocaustal "excesses" perpetrated by the U.S. in Indochina during the 1960s and '70s, or to Iraq from 1990 through 2003, to find proof of this proposition.[180] The examples of Cuba and Libya will do quite well, as will those of Greece in 1949 and 1967,[181] Iran in 1953,[182] Guatemala in 1954,[183] the Congo in 1961,[184] Indonesia and the Dominican Republic in 1965,[185] Ghana in 1966,[186] Chile in 1973,[187] Angola during the mid-1970s,[188] Nicaragua during the 1980s,[189] and scores of others.[190]

By the same token, those of Israel and South Africa are only the most visible examples of the kinds of allies—openly fascistic in many cases—the U.S. has embraced, installed and supported in the course of its global crusade to thwart the spreading "infection" of democratic aspirations. Here, one encounters the likes of Rhee in South Korea,[191] Chiang in Taiwan,[192] Cuba's Fulgencio "The Butcher" Batista,[193] Mobutu in Zaire,[194] the Shah of Iran,[195] the Duvaliers in Haiti,[196] Nicaragua's Somoza,[197] Trujillo in the Dominican Republic,[198] the régimes of Pinochet and Suharto in Chile and Indonesia,[199] Stroessner in Paraguay,[200] the Greek and Guatemalan colonels,[201] the white supremacists of Rhodesia,[202] the Argentine junta,[203] the Salvadoran oligarchs,[204] and so on and on, in seemingly endless refrain (yes, Saddam, the "new Hitler" of the Middle East, and Manuel Noriega, the "drug dealer" of Panama, numbered among America's clients, so long as they were useful[205]). Having "fought the wrong opponents" during World War II, as many on the right declaimed in its aftermath,[206] the U.S. has in effect been compensating for its imagined error ever since, stepping into the vacuum created by the vanquished Reich, often employing not only the sorts of imitators mentioned above, but real nazi fugitives for the purpose.[207] The purportedly long shadow of Nuremberg's gallows never reached further than those in whom U.S. officials could find no utility.[208]

It follows that, no more than those of the nazis, both literal and figurative, it has for so long and so avidly embraced, can the government of the U.S. be viewed as a lawful entity. Quite the opposite. What emerges most clearly from the following chronology is the picture of a world community struggling with the vigor of increasing urgency to forge an equitable and humane rule of law, while the U.S., with the arrogance born of an ever-increasing and utterly cynical sense of self-absorption, stymieing their efforts at every turn.[209] If, as U.S. Defense

Secretary Rumsfeld has observed, the world continues to be an exceedingly "rough neighborhood,"[210] it is mainly because he and his ilk have insisted—indeed, guaranteed—for their own purposes that it be so. And this, notwithstanding the insufferably smug delusions afflicting the great and mostly mindless mass of "law-abiding Americans," is the signature characteristic of the variety of criminal enterprise commonly referred to as an "outlaw" or "rogue" state.[211]

1945

June 26: While the U.S. endorses the Charter of the United Nations, an entity it has been instrumental in creating, and its acceptance becomes a matter of U.S. domestic law on Oct. 24, the thrust of America's postwar foreign policy has already been formulated in direct contradiction to the lofty principles enunciated therein. By Sept. the U.S. has already divided the former Japanese colony of Korea along the 38th Parallel, for example, and shortly deposes an autonomous government in the southern zone—which, unlike its northern counterpart, falls under ostensibly temporary U.S. administrative authority—installing Syngman Rhee, a dictatorial and unabashed American client, as premier. Although Article I(2) of the UN Charter requires that all member-states "respect the equal rights and self-determination of peoples," the U.S. quickly makes it clear that reunification of their country is contingent upon Koreans accepting economic and governmental forms determined by the U.S. Rhee does not hold even a pretense of an election until 1950. Meanwhile, the U.S. pours in assistance to build up his police apparatus, used mainly to repress those politically opposed to his régime (there are an estimated 14,000 political prisoners in "South Korea" by the end of 1949). U.S. occupation troops are also used to intimidate and physically repress those attempting to exercise their self-determining rights; between 1945 and 1950, U.S. soldiers "fired on crowds, conducted mass arrests, combed the hills for suspects, and organized posses of Korean rightists, constabulary and police for mass raids" to prevent anything resembling democracy from breaking out in the south.

Aug. 6: Although the 1923 Hague Convention on the Rules of Aerial Warfare make it patently illegal to deliberately destroy civilians and their property—and/or use bombing for purposes of terrorizing civilians—the U.S. drops an atomic bomb on the Japanese city of Hiroshima, a decisively nonmilitary target, killing an estimated 100,000 people. Three days later, it does the same to the city of Nagasaki, killing another 50,000 or more. It has since been officially argued that the nuclear bombings were carried out for the "humanitarian" purpose of compelling a Japanese surrender without the U.S. having to invade the country, an operation supposedly projected to cost the lives of a half-million Americans and perhaps three times that many Japanese. Leaving aside the fact that no such casualty estimates existed at the time, this scenario begs the fact that Japan had been attempting to surrender for several months, asking only that its emperor be left in his position (a condition ultimately accepted by the U.S. in any event). In actuality, then, the obliteration of Hiroshima and Nagasaki had nothing at all to do with ending the Second World War, everything to do with sending a *polit-ical* message to the Soviet Union—which at the time lacked a nuclear weapons capacity—as to who would be "in charge" of the planet during the postwar era. They should thus be viewed, not as the last act of World War II, but rather as the first act of a renewed "Cold War" waged by the U.S. against "International Communism" from 1945 onward. In any event, arguments to "military necessity" not really obtaining, the U.S. atomic bombings consti-tute war crimes of the very highest magnitude.

Sept.–Oct.: Pres. Harry S. Truman, ignoring Chapter I of the UN Charter, orders the rearming of recently-surrendered Japanese troops to prevent large areas of northern China from "falling into the hands" of Chinese led by Mao Zedong, an erstwhile U.S. wartime ally. Some 50,000 marines are also posted to the region, adding to another 100,000 American troops stationed in China. Over the next three years, the U.S. expends $2 billion in cash and another $1 billion in military hardware in a futile effort to sustain its preferred brand of Chinese "leadership"—the venal régime of Generalissimo Chiang Kai-shek—against Mao's highly-popular insurgency. Ultimately, Chiang is defeated, his government forced to seek refuge in 1949 on the offshore island of Taiwan (Formosa), a locale made safe for his com-ing by the employment two years earlier of U.S. weapons to slaughter about 20,000 local nationalists (a glaring breach of the Charter's Chapter XI). In the aftermath, despite requests by foreign minister Chou en-Lai for the establishment of a relationship based in mutual aid and friendship, the U.S. refuses to recognize Mao's government, pretending instead that Taiwan *is* China, and blocking representation of the Chinese mainland population in the UN for more than 20 years. Meanwhile, a mockery is made of the Chapter I provisions requiring that UN member-states "settle their interna-tional disputes by peaceful means" (Article 2(3)) and "without threat or use of force against the territorial integrity or political independence of any state" (Article 2(4)), as the U.S. arms, trains, equips, financially-supports and in many cases commands Chiang's residual forces as they engage in an end-less series of cross-border raids and aerial attacks on Chinese towns that last into the early 1960s. As of this writing, the question of *Taiwanese* self-determination remains entirely unaddressed, while their homeland contin-ues to serve as a major U.S. basing area in East Asia.

Nov. 20: Pursuant to the London Charter of Aug. 8, 1945 (Agreement for the Prosecution and Punishment of the Major War Criminals of the European Axis Powers and Charter of the International Military Tribunal), which it has been uniquely instrumental in negotiating, the U.S. participates in the initiation of the criminal prosecution of two-dozen nazi leaders at Nuremberg. Although Supreme Court Justice Robert H. Jackson, in his opening remarks, makes a point of asserting that the defendants are being tried for gross violations of international law, both customary and conven-tional, and that they are not being held to a legal standard his own country is unprepared to subscribe to, the precise opposite is true. Throughout the 11-month trial (verdicts were read on Oct. 1, 1946), each time a defendant is able to demonstrate conclusively that the U.S. and its allies engaged in the same pattern of legal violation with which he is charged—of conducting unrestricted submarine warfare, for instance, or engaging in the indiscriminate "terror" bombing of civilian population centers—the charge is simply dropped. Much the same procedure applies in the "Tokyo Trials" of Japanese leaders and, albeit to a much lesser extent, the trials of Italian fascists during the same period. The only real "principle" thus established in practice is that criminal acts are to be considered criminal only if a country other than the U.S. commits them.

1946

Jan. 24: While the U.S. endorses United Nations General Assembly (UNGA) Res. 1 (I), calling for international control of atomic energy by establishment of an International Atomic Energy Commission, it clearly views the mechanism as applying only to countries other than itself (and, on occasion, its allies). Starting from a posture of "nuclear monopoly," it formulates policy in a thoroughly unilateralist manner, "cooperating" with the IAEC only when and where doing so seems likely to reinforce its own military/technological primacy.

July 1: Although it is supposedly exercising only a temporary "trust" authority over the Marshall Islands, seized from Japan during World War II, pending the islanders' realization of the genuinely self-determining status guaranteed them under Chapters XI and XII of the UN Charter, the U.S. conducts an experimental detonation of a nuclear device on Bikini Atoll, rendering it uninhabitable. This is but the first of a decade-long series of such tests in the Marshalls, a process which devastates the atolls of Kwajalein and Enewetak as well as Bikini, meanwhile precipitating a wave of stillbirths, mutations, cancer and other significant maladies among the indigenous population.

July 4: The U.S. grants "independence" to the Philippines, thereby avoiding its obligation under Chapter XI of the UN Charter to inscribe the islands, an outright American colony since 1898, on a list of "non-self-governing territories" maintained by the Secretariat for purposes of overseeing their timely decolonization. Thus freed from UN supervision, the U.S. imposes terms by which it retains effective control over the form/composition of the Filipino national government, a trade agreement ensuring American corporate domination of the islands' economy, and more-or-less permanent usage of its sprawling—and strategically vital—Clark Air Base and naval complex at Subic Bay (a neocolonial arrangement, by any definition). Meanwhile, the U.S. does inscribe many of its other territorial holdings—the island of Guam, in the northern Marianas, for example, and other areas of Micronesia, as well as Hawai'i and Puerto Rico—on the Secretariat's list. The present disposition of these holdings is taken up elsewhere in this chronology. One that is not, however, is the Ryukyu island of Okinawa, colonized by Japan in 1895 and seized by the U.S. in 1945. Cast by the U.S.—in an interestingly selective endorsement of Japan's imperial pretensions—as a "Japanese home island" in the postwar context, Okinawa was never inscribed on the Secretariat's list. Today, it continues to serve as a major military basing area for the U.S.—by agreement with the government of Japan, not the Okinawans—while the self-determining rights of the Ryukyuans, like those of the Taiwanese, remain totally unaddressed. Until the situation is corrected, a condition of illegal occupation will continue to exist in both the Ryukyus and Taiwan.

Aug. 11: Pres. Truman signs the Indian Claims Commission Act, a measure designed to distinguish the U.S. record of territorial acquisition from that of the nazi defendants even then being tried at Nuremberg by retroactively "purchasing" lands expropriated from American Indians over the preceding 160 years. Under the Act's provisions, the U.S., not the native owners, decides if, when and how much land was unlawfully taken from specific peoples; native people cannot recover property found to have been unlawfully taken from them (they thus have no option but to "sell"); the U.S., not the owners, sets the "fair price" of each "sale" (i.e., compensation); and, in many cases, a concomitant to "settlement" is withdrawal of U.S. recognition that the people in question continues to exist at all (i.e., their existence is officially "terminated"). By the time the Claims Commission wraps up its proceedings in 1978, it has been thoroughly documented that the U.S. has no claim to ownership of or jurisdiction over approximately one-third of its gross "domestic" territoriality other than this transparently illegitimate procedure (all the nazis would have had to have done by this definition was to have issued a check to the Poles after their 1939 conquest of Poland to "legitimate" their aggression). Plainly, the entire procedure was undertaken in violation of Chapters I, VI, VII, IX, XI and XII of the UN Charter, Chapters II, IV, V and VII the Charter of the Organization of American States (OAS), and a number of other important elements of international law. The attendant policy of compulsory tribal dissolution, initiated in 1953, was/is also violative of Article II(b) and Article II(c) of the 1948 Convention on Prevention and Punishment of the Crime of Genocide, meaning that those who participated in formulating and implementing the plan were/are guilty of a range of Article III violations. In any event, the U.S. continues, as of this writing, to contend that title to much of its purported national territory was "quieted" by the Commission process. At least one-third of the U.S. portion of North America can thus be said to be in a state of illegal occupation at the present moment.

Dec. 11: The U.S. joins the rest of the General Assembly in endorsing UNGA Res. 95(I), the Affirmation of the Principles of International Law Recognized by the Charter of the Nuremberg Tribunal. At the same time, the U.S. Office of Strategic Services and other agencies are busily violating those very principles by in effect immunizing whole categories of nazis and their collaborators believed useful to the U.S. in its rapidly-intensifying Cold War with the Soviet Union (or "Communist Bloc," as the "enemy" will shortly be called). Among those protected by the U.S. in these illegal programs are Werner Von Braun and his team of rocket scientists, subject to prosecution for their massive use of slave labor and other crimes against humanity while producing Germany's V-2 missiles during World War II, but instrumental in creating the postwar U.S. ICBM capability; Gen. Reinhard Gehlen and his eastern Europe-focused Abwehr intelligence apparatus, subject to prosecution for all manner of war crimes and crimes against humanity during the war, but of value to the OSS (later CIA) in its development of espionage/sabotage assets in the USSR and its "satellites"; selected members of the Waffen SS, all of them subject to prosecution for war crimes and crimes against humanity, who are incorporated into the U.S. Army for purposes of developing its capacity to conduct irregular warfare in Soviet territory (this is the origin of the Army's Special Forces units); prominent members of the Ustasha, Arrow Cross and other eastern European fascist organizations, all of them wanted for major crimes against humanity but imported to the U.S. under false identities for purposes of instilling what U.S. policymakers view as an "appropriate" degree of anticommunist sensibility among the immigrant communities situated in North American cities. In the Far East, similar programs are conducted, as with the immunization of Japan's notorious Unit 731, subject to prosecution for war crimes and crimes against humanity because of its use of prisoners in conducting biological warfare experiments from 1935–1945, in exchange for its sharing of technical information facilitating the development of U.S. biowarfare capabilities.

1947

Jan. 12: Beginning with a state visit by Italian Premier Alcide de Gasperi, the U.S. State Dept. sets about a systematic violation of Chapter I of the UN Charter by interfering directly with the Italian national election, upcoming in April 1948. The U.S. goal, fully achieved, was to displace candidates from Italy's Communist Party—a mainstay of antifascist activity during the Mussolini era, and immensely popular as a result—in favor of an amalgam of "collaborators, monarchists and unreconstructed fascists" describing themselves as "Christian Democrats." Both the carrot (promising to cancel Italy's debt, increased aid and restoration of its African colonies) and the stick (threatening to suspend aid, foreclose the debt, and reduce immigration quotas) were used overtly to coerce the electorate, while the CIA covertly expended more than $1 million on propaganda inside Italy itself. Thus was democracy not-so-subtly subverted in the name of "freedom" by the self-proclaimed "leader of the Free World."

Jan. 24: The U.S. endorses Security Council (SC) Res. 18, calling for regulation of the international arms trade, with the goal of an overall reduction in the proliferation of armaments, worldwide. These noble-sounding sentiments expressed, America not only maintains but expands its position as the world's leading arms merchant over the next half-century. Such sales are by no means restricted to conventional weaponry. The U.S. both sells the poison gas and provides the training in how to use it, that is employed to lethal effect by Egypt against Yemen in 1967. From 1985-1989, to offer an even more striking example, U.S. firms, operating under State Dept. license—and in direct violation of the 1971 Biological Weapons Convention—also sell to Iraq significant quantities of anthrax, botulin toxin, E.coli virus and dozens of other microbes basic to the development of inexpensive weapons of mass destruction. Other U.S. exports during the period "included the precursors to chemical-warfare agents, plans for chemical and biological warfare production facilities and chemical warhead filling equipment... [Transactions that continued until] at least November 28, 1989, despite the fact that Iraq was [known to be] engaging in chemical and possibly biological warfare against Iranians, Kurds and Shiites since at least the early 1980s." Such actions, in which the U.S. has been obviously and fully complicit, have been illegal since at least as early as the 1925 Geneva Protocol for the Prohibition of the Use in War of Asphyxiating, Poisonous or Other Gases, and of Bacteriological Methods of Warfare.

Mar. 10: The U.S. endorses SC Res. 20, affirming UNGA Res. 1 (I) concerning the need for international control of nuclear proliferation through an International Atomic Energy Commission. While holding that other countries should be open to IAEC inspection, however, the U.S. insists that its own strategic interests preclude unfettered access by inspectors. Both Israel and Iraq, among others, later model their own postures after the U.S. precedent.

Apr. 2: A tacit agreement between the U.S. and the USSR wherein the Soviets accept U.S. assertion of a special "strategic trust relationship" to Micronesia in exchange for U.S. acceptance of comparable Soviet authority over the Kuril Islands is approved by the UN Security Council (SC Res. 21). No attempt is made by any of the parties involved to ascertain the sentiments of either the Micronesians or the Kuril Islanders in the matter. All parties thus act in violation of Chapters XI and XII of the UN Charter.

June 14: Raphaël Lemkin and others finalize the "Secretariat's Draft" of the proposed United Nations Convention on Genocide, which is then turned over to the United Nations Economic and Social Council (ECOSOC) for review. The U.S. delegation, prominent among those of other member-states, raises a number of "concerns" with the document's scope, whereupon ECOSOC refers the matter to the UN General Assembly.

July 25: The U.S., having complied with Chapter XI of the UN Charter by inscribing Hawai'i on the Secretariat's list of non-self-governing territories in 1946, transmits the first of the reports required under Article 73(e) on conditions in the islands. No move is made by the U.S., however, to meet its obligation as "trustee" to "promote the political, economic, social, and educational advancement of the [native Kanaka Maoli] inhabitants" (Article 76(b)) with an eye towards their "progressive development towards self-government [and] independence" (Article 76(c)). Instead, U.S. military/corporate control over the islands is rapidly expanded, while the native Hawaiians are rendered more dispossessed, disenfranchised and destitute than ever.

Nov. 29: The U.S. joins in approving UNGA Res. 181 (II), establishing the boundaries of what will be the State of Israel within the area already known as Palestine, a British "protectorate." Insofar as no formal poll is taken of Palestinians as to whether they in any sense accept this partitioning of their homeland—and given that all informal indications suggest that they are strongly opposed—the resolution violates Chapters XI and XII of the UN

Charter by ignoring the Palestinians' fundamental right to self-determination.

1948

Feb.–Mar.: The General Assembly refers the draft Genocide Convention back to ECOSOC with instructions that the Council form a working group to revise the document. The U.S. assumes control of the working group and oversees a thorough gutting of the draft Convention. The final product is then resubmitted by ECOSOC to the General Assembly, where it is scheduled for a vote.

Mar. 5: Although the idea of partitioning Palestine to create Israel has already resulted in open warfare between Jewish settlers and local Arabs, the U.S. endorses SC Res. 42, calling for implementation of UNGA Res. 181 (II). Violations of Palestinian rights contained therein remain unaddressed.

Apr. 1: The U.S. endorses SC Res. 43, calling for a UN-brokered truce between Arabs and Jews in Palestine, with an eye towards legitimating the boundaries of Israel within Palestine. The territorial rights and aspirations of the Palestinians themselves continue to be ignored.

Apr. 1: The U.S. endorses SC Res. 44, calling upon the UN Secretariat to convene a special session of the General Assembly to decide the future governance of Palestine. No mention is made of the fact that the wishes of the Palestinians are legally paramount. The violations of Chapters XI and XII of the UN Charter entailed in UNGA Res. 181 (II) are thus compounded.

Nov. 4: The U.S. endorses SC Res. 62, calling for a ceasefire between Arab and Jewish forces fighting in Palestine, and for all parties to withdraw to the positions they occupied on Oct. 4. The Jewish forces make no effort to do so, thereby considerably enlarging the area demarcated by the General Assembly for inclusion within the incipient State of Israel. Although this "acquisition of territory by force of arms" is in patent violation of the so-called Stimson Doctrine adopted by the U.S. prior to World War II and subsequently incorporated into the UN Charter's Articles 2(4) and 2(6), no action is taken to compel compliance.

Dec. 29: The U.S. endorses SC Res. 66, calling for another immediate ceasefire in Palestine, and for all parties to comply with previous Security Council resolutions. Israel again ignores the resolution, holding fast to its expanded territoriality, and, again, no UN enforcement action is forthcoming.

Dec. 9: Although the U.S. joins in the General Assembly's unanimous endorsement of the Convention on Prevention and Punishment of the Crime of Genocide, the Senate—leaving the U.S. alone among UN member-states as a nonsignatory—thereafter refuses to ratify it for a period of 40 years. A primary motivator, readily apparent in periodic Senate debates, is that the federal government continues to pursue policies—and to protect policies undertaken by various states and actions by "private individuals and organizations"—against American Indians, African Americans and other "minorities" which are construed as genocidal even by the Convention's considerably circumscribed definition. A majority of the Senate insists that perpetration of genocide falls within the domain of U.S. "sovereign prerogatives."

1949

Feb. 15: The U.S. refers the "Republic of Korea"—the country's southern zone—to the General Assembly for admission to the UN as a member-state separate from the north. Insofar as no country-wide referendum to determine the preferences of the Korean people in the matter has ever been conducted, the action is contrary to Chapters XI and XII of the UN Charter. It also makes clear to the north that the U.S. intends its partitioning of the country to be permanent.

Mar. 4: Although the new state remains blatantly noncompliant with SC Resolutions 62 and 66—and despite the fact that the Charter-guaranteed rights of the Palestinian people to self-determination remain completely unaddressed—the U.S. endorses SC Res. 69, approving Israel for UN membership. A pattern is thus established at the outset wherein U.S. recognition of Israel's "legitimacy" is perpetually separated from Israeli adherence to international law, and the rights of Palestinians are perpetually treated as if they are "optional" (or ignored altogether).

Mar 9: Although the UN Charter protects organizational employees from being hired, fired, or otherwise screened on the basis of their personal political sympathies, the State Dept. extracts a secret agreement from Sec.-Gen. Trygve Lie to allow those working at the UN headquarters in New York to be subjected to precisely such scrutiny by U.S. intelligence agencies. While the overall effects of this clandestine arrangement are unknown, at least three American citizens "guilty" of nothing more than standing on their Fifth Amendment rights when interrogated by Senator Joseph McCarthy's investigating committee are quietly dismissed from their UN staff positions by 1952.

Apr. 22: The Inter-American Convention on the Prevention, Punishment and Eradication of Violence Against Women enters into force, with 18 state parties. As of this writing, 54 years later, the U.S. continues to refuse ratification, claiming that its own domestic statutory codes provide "all necessary protections" (and thereby purporting to reserve unto itself the "sovereign right" to withhold at its own discretion protections guaranteed to all women under international law).

Aug. 11: Although Israel continues to defy SC Resolutions 62 and 66, the U.S. is instrumental in pushing through SC Res. 73, approving Israeli/Arab armistice agreements that are then used by Israel to "confirm" its illegally expanded borders. With these gains in hand, Israeli PM David Ben-Gurion sets about consolidating his newly-founded state and developing its capacity to create what he refers to as "Greater Israel," a regionally dominant and ethnic-specific political/military entity, the territory of which he sees as eventually encompassing a huge expanse including the entirety of the Egyptian Sinai, all of Jordan west of the Jordan River, and all Lebanese territory south of the Litani River. Realization of this "fantastic plan," as Ben-Gurion calls it, of course necessitates his steering Israel along a course, not of rapprochement, but rather of endless conflict with neighboring Arab states. Although the general contours of Israeli ambitions are known, the U.S. undertakes no particular effort to curb them. Instead, a zionist propaganda infrastructure is allowed to develop and flourish in the U.S. itself (during a period when other varieties of "un-Americanism" are being subjected to the severe repression of "McCarthyism"). The cornerstone for what will become America's "special relationship" with Israel is thus laid at the outset.

Oct. 21: The U.S. orchestrates passage of UNGA Res. 293, finding the government of South Korea to be "lawfully established" and admitting the "country" to the UN. *None* of the Charter issues raised by Korea's history of colonization by Japan and subsequent U.S. military occupation of the southern zone have been addressed, much less resolved in a manner allowing for an exercise of the Korean people's right to self-determination. The resolution is thus invalid.

Dec. 5: The U.S. joins in endorsing UNGA Res. 300 (IV), calling for international regulation and general reductions of the arms trade, as well as reductions in the armaments and armed forces of all UN member-states. The U.S., however, is then in the process of a military *buildup* that has lasted to the present day. It has also positioned itself as the world's leading arms exporter, a position it still holds.

1950

Jan. 17: The U.S. joins in endorsing SC Res. 79, affirming UNGA Res. 300 (IV) and calling for creation of an International Arms Control Commission.

Apr. 13: The National Security Council completes a document, referred to as NSC-68, in which it is proposed that the U.S. be converted into a "national security state" and placed on a permanent wartime footing in terms of expenditures and other domestic policies/priorities, in order that it might prosecute its Cold War strategies of first "containing," then "rolling back World Communism." Embraced from this point on as formal—if usually unstated—U.S. policy, the economic components of NSC-68 are not fully realized until the Reagan era of the 1980s, its political dimension until passage of the so-called PATRIOT Act in 2001 (attendant deformities of America's internal fabric had begun to accrue steadily long before the document's completion, however). Suffice it here to say that the logic embodied in NSC-68 stands in direct contradiction to the purpose of the United Nations, as articulated in the UN Charter, and categorically at odds with the imperatives encompassed by international law (both customary and conventional).

June 25: The Koreans in the northern zone, responding to U.S. initiatives to consolidate the south as a permanently separate state, set out to reunify their country militarily. Announcing that it is necessary to oppose "a return to the rule of force in international affairs," Pres. Truman demands and receives Security Council authorization—SC Resolutions 83 (June 27) and 84 (July 7)—for the U.S. to "repel the aggression" embodied in the Koreans' attempt to (re)assert control over Korea, and thus "restore peace and security to the area." Some 2 million Koreans are slaughtered in the ensuing U.S. "police action," during which American troops drive all the way to the Chinese/Korean border along the Yalu River. Only a massive military response by China—after Chinese towns are repeatedly bombed and Gen. Douglas MacArthur, commander of all "UN" forces in Korea, threatens to invade China itself (apparently for no other reason than because he personally dislikes its form of government)— prevents the U.S. from swallowing up the entire peninsula. Finally, after much foot-dragging by American negotiators, an armistice is signed in 1953, restoring both sides to their original positions. As of this writing, 50 years later, Korea remains partitioned along the 38th parallel, its southern half occupied by U.S. troops (China has never occupied the north).

Aug. 1: Pres. Truman signs the Organic Act of Guam, conferring a much-qualified form of U.S. citizenship upon indigenous Chamorros without moving to incorporate their island as a state of the union. Disposition of the Chamorro right to self-determination was deferred indefinitely, under a provision in the Organic Act indicating that the native people would have the option of approving a constitution at such time as they decided they were ready to do so. In the interim, however long it might be, they would be governed under U.S. authority. It would not be until Jan. 1982 when, without UN supervision, a referendum was conducted to allow the Chamorros to indicate their desires with regard to Guam's political status. When the results of this poll, which included the option of full independence, was deemed "indecisive" by U.S. authorities, a second referendum was scheduled for September. This time, with the choices restricted to commonwealth status or statehood, 73 percent of the electorate opted for the former. As of this writing, two decades later, there has been no appreciable change in Guam's standing vis-à-vis the U.S.; its internal affairs remain subject to external control, and it continues to serve as a primary basing site for U.S. military operations in the Pacific.

Sept. 20: The Army conducts the 1st of 6 clandestine biowarfare experiments in San Francisco during the week of Sept. 20-7, in which *Bacillus globigii* and *Serratia marcescens* microbes are released in aerosol form from a ship offshore, at one point forming a cloud 2 miles long. An unknown number of persons are resultantly infected—many of them in hospitals as far away as Palo Alto—and at least 1 person dies. The Army later admits that, between 1949 and 1969, 239 populated areas in the U.S. were unknowingly subjected to comparable bio- and chemical warfare experiments. Although precision is impossible, given the secret nature of the experimentation, at least 13 other U.S. citizens are known to have died, and many hundreds, perhaps thousands, sickened as a result. Every single test was conducted in violation of the Nuremberg Code, promulgated in 1949 in responses to the medical experiments conducted by the nazis at Dachau and other such camps, which makes "the voluntary consent of the human subject[s]" employed in any sort of scientific experiment not just an ethical or moral consideration, but a legal requirement.

Nov. 3: The U.S. endorses UNGA Res. 337A (V), otherwise known as the "Uniting for Peace Resolution." Needless to say, the endorsement is contradicted by the U.S. Cold War posture in its entirety.

Nov. 17: The U.S. joins in endorsing SC Res. 89, noting Israel's massive and systematic displacement of Palestinians into Egyptian territory and calling for the first time for their repatriation. The resolution is once again written, at the suggestion of the U.S., without enforcement provisions, allowing the Israelis to simply ignore it.

Dec 17: The U.S. joins in endorsing UNGA Res. 380 (V), condemning as aggression the fomenting by any country of civil strife in another. At that point, the U.S. is engaged in a number of such activities worldwide, not least by way of its "hands-on" participation in a counterinsurgency campaign designed to destroy a popular leftist movement in Greece while installing a viciously antidemocratic rightist régime composed of military officers (several of whom were known nazi collaborators). In another operation, begun in 1949, the CIA creates what it calls the "Albanian National Liberation Front," trained on Malta and headed by collaborators with Mussolini's wartime occupation government, to sow internal discord and engage in armed insurrections against Albania's leftist Hoxha government. In addition to the violations of UNGA Res. 380 (V) involved, all such undertakings violate both the letter and spirit of UNGA Res. 337A (V).

1951

May 18: The U.S. joins in endorsing SC Res. 93, calling upon Israel to "immediately cease" its violation of the 1949 armistice by building in the demilitarized zones separating it from its Arab neighbors. Unlike the U.S.-engineered Security Council resolutions pertaining to North Korea, SC Res. 93 contains no enforcement provisions, and the Israelis ignore it. Structurally, this is the origin of the problem of "Jewish settlements" that continues at present to plague the Mideast peace process. Although always the recipient of at least tacit U.S. support, Israeli settlement policies have never for a moment been legal.

June 4: The people of Puerto Rico, which had been an outright American colony since 1898, approve a constitution under which, given authorization by the U.S. Congress (conveyed in July 1952), they would assume commonwealth status. Although the referendum through which the new constitution was seemingly ratified had not been supervised by the United Nations, as is required under Chapter XII of the UN Charter—and despite the constitution itself taking a form directly contradicting the fact that the U.S. had found it necessary as recently as October 1950 to utilize military force in quelling a popular insurrection aimed at attaining nothing less than complete independence—the commonwealth arrangement was put forward as a basis for removing Puerto Rico from the Secretariat's list of territories scheduled for timely decolonization. On Nov. 27, 1953, although all parties agreed that the island hadn't really attained self-governing status within the meaning of the Charter, Puerto Rico "became the first colony to be removed from the United Nations list of non-self-governing territories." As of this writing—40 years later, and all U.S. contentions to the contrary notwithstanding—the island's political disposition has never been legally resolved (nor will it be until a UN-administered plebiscite is conducted).

July 28: The U.S. refuses to endorse the UN Convention Relating to the Status of Refugees, which comes into force on Apr. 22, 1954. For the next 35 years, the U.S., contrary to international law, limits eligibility for asylum from political or religious persecution to those fleeing designated "communist" countries (those trying to escape fascism or other such manifestations of the "free world" need not apply). As of this writing, the U.S. has not joined 127 other UN member-states in ratifying the Convention.

1952

Apr. 5: Ignoring UNGA Res. 380 (V) and most of the articles under Chapters I, VI and VI of the UN Charter, Pres. Truman approves a CIA initiative to organize a coup by Guatemalan army officers to topple the democratically-elected government of Jacobo Arbenz, which is "guilty" of nationalizing the holdings of United Fruit and other U.S. corporations (thereby improving both the national economy and quality of life experienced by Guatemala's grassroots citizenry). Self-evidently, the U.S. intervention in Guatemala also violates UNGA Res. 337A(V).

1953

Apr. 13: CIA Director Allen Dulles authorizes initiation of MK-ULTRA, a top secret project designed to test the utility of LSD-25, an extraordinarily powerful hallucinogen, in achieving "mind control." The Agency purchases 10 kilograms of the substance—enough for 100 *million* doses—and conducts a range of parallel experiments, some of them in concert with the Army, concerning the use of LSD in interrogations and as a chemical weapon causing both selective and mass psychoses: the inmates at 15 mental institutions are used as unwitting guinea pigs, many of them subjected to electroshock and/or "ice pick lobotomies"—a psychosurgical technique in which brain tissue is removed through the eye socket, without leaving a telltale scar—while under the influence of the drug; at least 1,500 active duty soldiers are administered LSD without their knowledge, confined to sensory deprivation chambers, then subjected to hostile questioning to "test the effects on combat-ready personnel"; a secret multiyear program is funded at McGill University in Montréal wherein another batch of psychiatric patients are subjected to a hideous process of mental "depatterning" and "psychic driving" under the influence of LSD; a cloud of LSD is reputedly released over San Francisco at one point, to test whether the substance can be used effectively as a military aerosol. Given their secrecy, the overall toll taken by MK-ULTRA and related projects, psychologically and otherwise (there was at least 1 suicide, and several of the Montréal victims have sued successfully), is impossible to pin down. What is absolutely clear, however, is that *all* of this was done in blatant contravention of the Nuremberg Code (see the entry for Sept. 20, 1950). There is strong indication, moreover, that, during the mid-to-late 1960s, the CIA, adopting a pharmaceutical approach to domestic pacification, may have dumped a few million "hits" of the LSD it had acquired into the then-flourishing white youth "counterculture" as a means of quashing its more concrete tendencies towards rebellion (a variation of this approach seems to have been adopted with regard to the contemporaneous black liberation movement in the U.S.; see the entry for Apr. 5, 1971).

June 17: Continuing to ignore UNGA Res. 380 (V) and most of the articles under Chapter I of the UN Charter, CIA-administered radio stations in the western zone of Berlin seize the opportunity presented by an uprising of East Berliners to broadcast appeals for the insurrectionists to escalate the turmoil. Other Agency operations of the period include the contamination of milk destined for East German schools, the smuggling of a virulent toxin called cantharidin to East German dissident groups so that they can attempt the assassination of the country's leaders by poisoning their cigarettes, kidnapping/murdering activists prominent in several leftist organizations, regularly disrupting political meetings with fires or stink bombs, and engaging in a concerted campaign of industrial sabotage. Plainly, a violation of UNGA Res. 337A (V) is also involved.

Aug. 19: In gross disregard of both UNGA Res. 380 (V), as well as the UN Charter's first chapter, the CIA consummates a coup in which Iran's democratically-elected and staunchly independent government of Mohammed Mossadegh is replaced by that of the dictatorial Mohammed Reza Shah Pahlavi. Some 300 Iranians are killed in the process, and, over the next quarter-century, while the Shah serves as the "preeminent U.S. ally in the Third World," thousands more die at the hands of SAVAK, his American-trained and equipped political police. Not unnaturally, the experience inculcates an abiding "anti-Americanism" among the grassroots population, and thus shapes the Iranian revolution of 1978–79.

Nov. 2: Israeli PM Ben-Gurion, 68-years old and "exhausted by the demands of his job," announces his "temporary retirement from politics." Although Moshe Sharett, a moderate, replaces Ben-Gurion as PM, de facto control remains in the hands of Ben-Gurion's own faction, notably represented by army chief-of-staff, and later defense minister, Moshe Dayan. Before his departure, Ben-Gurion, relying upon Dayan as executor, set in motion a plan to absorb the demilitarized zones established by the 1949 armistice to separate Israel from Syria. Dayan unleashes a program of forcibly relocating Arab inhabitants from the DMZ, installing Israeli troops disguised as "settlers" in their villages, and, most provocatively of all, initi-ates a construction project to divert the flow of the Jordan River to the Negev region of Israel (this in itself is contrary to international law, since all the riparian states along the Jordan share interest in its water; Dayan delib-erately compounds the offense by situating the construction site well within the DMZ despite the availability of better sites outside the disputed territo-ry). Syria, which has already offered to give up 70% of its interest in the DMZ to resolve the issue, protests to the UN. The U.S. then brokers an arrange-ment wherein Israel abandons its water diversion project in exchange for virtually total control over the DMZ (only a Soviet veto prevents Israel from getting the water, too). The U.S. further rewards Israel's illegalities with a $26-million grant-in-aid, thus violating the spirit, if not the letter of UNGA Res. 337A (V).

Nov. 24: The U.S. endorses SC Res. 101, registering the Security Council's "strongest censure" of Israel's massacre of 69 Jordanian civilians at the village of Qibya, in the West Bank region, on the night of Oct. 14–15, 1953. Although the identities of the perpetrators is known—the massacre was carried out by what was thereafter designated "Unit 101," in sardonic reference to the resolution condemning its action, an élite commando force headed by future Israeli PM Ariel Sharon—the U.S. argues that it would be "counterproductive" to include provisions requiring their prosecution for the war crimes, and makes its vote contingent upon such requirements not appearing in the resolution. Nor is the U.S. willing to allow the imposition of sanctions or other methods of compelling Israel not to repeat its perform-ance.

1954

Feb. 28: Sharon's Unit 101 follows up on the Qibya Massacre by con-ducting "Operation Black Arrow," an attack on an Egyptian army head-quarters in the outskirts of Gaza City, killing 37 and wounding 31 more. Although the raid is ostensibly conducted in retaliation for the killing of an Israeli bicyclist by an unidentified Arab civilian a week earlier—establishing a template for the sort of disproportionality which has remained embodied in Israeli "responses to terrorism" through the present moment—internal documents later reveal that it is actually a celebration of PM David Ben-Gurion's return to power and thus a precursor to his later policy of more openly "prodding" Egypt into an outright war (see the entry for Nov. 2, 1954). Although Egypt protests Israel's gross violation of international law at the UN, the U.S. forestalls a response by the Security Council. The U.S. maneu-ver plainly violates the spirit, if not the letter of UNGA Res. 337A (V).

May 8: The U.S., U.K., France and the Soviet Union jointly convene a conference in Geneva to address "the problem of restoring peace in Indochina" after several years of colonialist warfare waged by the French. The resulting Agreement on the Cessation of Hostilities in Vietnam ("Geneva Accords"), signed by France on July 20, provides for the with-drawal of French forces not only from Vietnam, but from Laos and Cambodia as well, divides Vietnam into two reorganizational zones—north and south—pending general elections and national reunification to be conducted in 1956, and prohibits foreign military intervention. While the rest of the guarantors accept these provisions as written, the U.S. alone purports not to be bound by them in any way.

June 18: In gross disregard of both UNGA Resolutions 380(V) and 337A (V), Chapter I of the UN Charter, and Article 18 of the OAS Charter, which states that "No State or group of States has the right to intervene, directly or indirectly, for any reason whatever, in the internal or external affairs of another State," the CIA launches its coup against the Arbenz government in Guatemala. On June 21, Guatemala's foreign minister appeals to the UN for help. American UN Ambassador Henry Cabot Lodge first attempts to block a Security Council vote on the matter, then engages in a campaign of coercing negative votes from other Council members so blatant that Sec.-Gen. Dag Hamarskjöld nearly resigns in protest (the Security Council initiative to conduct a UN investigation of the events in Guatemala is defeated by a 5-4 vote, with Britain and France abstaining). By June 30, a régime headed by Col. Carlos Diaz is installed, initiating a country-wide purge of "leftists" that involves the arrest and torture of thousands, the murder of several hundred more.

July 23: A group of Israeli intelligence operatives are apprehended in Cairo while attempting to plant a bomb in a theater frequented by American and British nationals. The object of the exercise, which is intended to be merely the first of several such atrocities, is to derail Egypt's relations with the U.S. and U.K. by attributing the resulting carnage to "Arab terrorists." In marked contrast to the intensity with which actual Arab bombers will later be reviled, even when U.S. citizens are not targeted—and demands that the perpetrators be handed over to U.S. authorities whenever Americans *are* killed—the U.S. maintains a stony silence throughout the whole affair.

Sept. 8: The U.S., U.K., France, Australia, New Zealand, Pakistan, the Philippines and Thailand, meeting in Manila, sign the Southeast Asian Collective Defense Treaty, creating the Southeast Asia Treaty Organization (SEATO). Although no such entity yet exists, and to create one would constitute a patent violation of the just-finalized Geneva Accords, the U.S. inserts a protocol into the SEATO Treaty extending military protection over what would shortly become the "separate country" of South Vietnam ("Republic of Vietnam").

Dec. 8: A team of 5 Israeli soldiers engaged in an espionage mission miles deep in Syrian territory are captured. In response, Israeli Defense Minister Pinhas Lavon orders the world's first hijacking of an airliner—a pair of IAF fighters are assigned to force a Syrian airliner out off its flight path, and to land in Israel—taking the passengers and crew hostage in hopes of exchanging them for the Israel Defense Force (IDF) troopers. International uproar over this unprecedented act of air piracy foils the plan, forcing release of the plane and its occupants with 48 hours—the Israeli soldiers remain in Syrian custody—and leads to passage of the Convention on Offenses and Certain Other Acts Committed on Board Aircraft in 1963 (as well as the 1970 Convention for the Suppression of Unlawful Seizure of Aircraft and the 1971 Convention for the Suppression of Unlawful Acts Against the Safety of Civil Aviation). The U.S., in sharp contrast to the position it will take with regard to Arab hijackings only a decade later, maintains a remarkable silence throughout the entire affair.

1955

Feb. 7: The Supreme Court enters its opinion in the case of *Tee-Hit-Ton v. U.S.*, asserting that the U.S. holds title to American Indian territories and other property within its claimed boundaries by "right of conquest." The opinion not only contradicts the historical record—the U.S. recognizes the existence of more than 400 indigenous peoples within the same area, but fought, by its own count, only 40 "Indian Wars"—but the entire sweep of American judicial opinion since Chief Justice John Marshall entered his 1823 opinion in *Johnson v. McIntosh* and Pres. Truman's statement when signing the Indian Claims Commission Act in Aug. 1946. The *Tee-Hit-Ton* opinion, moreover, violates not only the "Stimson Doctrine" of not recognizing territorial titles acquired by force advanced by the U.S. vis-à-vis Japan, Italy and other countries prior to World War II, but the 1928 Kellogg-Briand Pact (or "Treaty Providing for the Renunciation of War as an Instrument of National Policy," as it is formally titled), the 1932 Chaco Declaration, the 1933 Saavedra Lamas Pact, the 1933 Montevideo Convention on the Rights and Duties of States, the Declaration on Non-Recognition of the Acquisition of Territory by Force adopted by the 8th Pan-American Conference in 1938, Article 2(3) of the UN Charter, Articles 3 and 18-21 of the OAS Charter, and the 1946 Affirmation of the Principles of International Law Recognized by the Charter of the Nuremberg Tribunal, to all of which and more the U.S. was/is a signatory. Nonetheless, the *Tee-Hit-Ton* opinion remains unnullified by subsequent courts, and therefore continues to form an element of the domestic jurisprudence concerning native territorial rights (or lack of them).

Feb. 12: Sec. of State John Foster Dulles secretly offers to commit the U.S. to a formal mutual defense pact with Israel in exchange for an Israeli agreement to cease cross-border provocations and abandoning plans for territorial expansion. Israel declines. Despite this rather clear signal that the Israelis are bent upon a course prohibited under both the London and UN Charters, U.S. relations with the offending state remain unimpaired.

Mar. 29: The U.S. endorses SC Res. 106, condemning the "prearranged and planned attack ordered by Israeli authorities [and] committed by Israeli regular armed forces against Egyptian armed forces in the Gaza Strip" on Feb. 28, 1955. As is becoming a habit, the U.S. makes its affirmative vote contingent upon the absence of provisions involving penalties, sanctions, or other means of compelling Israeli compliance with the law. In response to this act of Israeli aggression, and the ineffectuality of the UN response,

Egyptian Pres. Gamel Abdel Nasser, who has until then acted to constrain the desire of the hundreds of thousands of Palestinian refugees displaced into Egypt to engage in guerrilla operations against Israel, reverses his position. In June, he also begins providing material assistance to Palestinian fighters operating out of Jordan.

July 7: A Protocol amending the 1927 Slavery Convention, to which the U.S. is a signatory, and which has been duly ratified by the Senate, enters into force. The Senate, attaching only a single reservation, ratifies the additional protocol as well, and it becomes U.S. law on Mar. 7, 1956. The maneuver is more illusory than substantive, however. As of mid-2003, the 13th Amendment to the U.S. Constitution still advances the invalid premise that slavery is "permissible" when imposed on persons duly convicted of a crime. Approximately 2 million persons are thus "legally" enslaved in the U.S. at any given moment, none of them more guilty of violating the law than are those who force involuntary servitude upon them.

Aug. 5: Newly-installed "premier" of the southern zone of Vietnam, Nguyen Vo Diem, a U.S. client, following his sponsor's lead, proclaims that his "country" does not "consider itself bound in any way by the Geneva Agreements which it did not sign." The U.S. has by then also entered into the early phases of training and equipping Diem's military and police, another clear violation of the Accords' prohibition on the introduction of "additional military personnel, or arms, munitions or war material...into either regrouping zone in Vietnam." U.S. policy in Vietnam plainly violates both the letter and the spirit of UNGA Res. 337A (V).

Oct. 26: Although the partitioning of Vietnam is clearly cast as a temporary measure in the Geneva Accords, Diem declares the southern zone an "independent republic." The U.S., following up on the groundwork laid in the SEATO Treaty, immediately conveys de facto recognition of the entity's status as a "legitimate state," entitled to defend the demarcation line separating it from the north as a permanent border, and internally, against segments of the population determined to achieve the (re)unification guaranteed by the 1954 agreement.

Nov. 2: Israeli PM Ben-Gurion announces a policy of "confrontation" with Egypt. That night, Israeli troops assault and destroy Egyptian positions in al-Sabha, killing 50 soldiers and capturing 50 more. Internal documents later reveal that the unprovoked attack is part of a strategy of "prodding [Egyptian Pres.] Nasser to go to war." Despite this clear violation of the London Charter—Israel's action constitutes a "Crime Against Peace"—and Chapter VI of the UN Charter, the U.S. neither imposes sanctions on the Israelis nor allows the Security Council to do so.

1956

Jan. 19: The U.S. endorses SC Res. 111, condemning yet another unprovoked Israeli attack, this one on Syrian military positions on the Golan Heights on Dec. 11, 1955—the action, code-named "Operation Kinneret," is again carried out by Ariel Sharon and his now notorious Unit 101—and calls upon Israel to comply with its obligations under the 1949 armistice agreements. Typically, the trade-off for U.S. cooperation is that there be no enforcement provisions, allowing Israel to simply ignore the resolution. The only tangible "consequence" imposed upon the Israelis is a cosmetic postponement of U.S. arms transfers, and this is offset by Sec. of State John Foster Dulles' back-channel encouragement of both Canada and France to take up the slack. France shortly follows through by providing $100 million in munitions and equipment, including 72 Mystère fighter aircraft and 200 AMX tanks.

July: Although the 1954 Geneva Accords plainly specify that the two "regrouping zones in Vietnam" are to be unified through a general election conducted in this month, and the U.S. has orally pledged to facilitate this process of "free elections supervised by the United Nations," Diem, with full U.S. backing, cancels the south's participation. The reason posited in the internal documents of the Eisenhower administration is that, given Diem's considerable unpopularity, the only conceivable victor of a nationwide ballot would be northern zone leader Ho Chi Minh, a "communist" who'd led the decolonization struggle against the French. The north, which has begun to refer to itself as the Democratic Republic of Vietnam, responds by launching a concerted campaign of agitation in the south, aimed at forcing the election issue to a head. The U.S. position remains in contradiction to Chapters I, VI, VII and XI of the UN Charter, as well as UNGA Resolutions 337A (V) and 380 (V).

July 26: Egypt nationalizes the Suez Canal. Although the move is perfectly legal, and fair compensation is offered stockholders in the British/French corporation that has previously "owned" the strategic seaway, both France and Britain initiate planning to retake "their" canal by military force. Israel then offers its services in the endeavor. On Oct. 21, a secret agreement known as the Protocol of Sèvres is reached wherein Israel will launch a surprise offensive and drive across the Sinai to the canal itself. At that point, British and French troops are to occupy key positions along the canal in the name of "restoring peace and good order." In the aftermath, it is envisioned that Israel will retain such portions of the Sinai as it desires, while Britain and France will regain joint control of the canal (to which Israeli shipping will have full access). The plan, implemented on Oct 29, is a stunning success and, on Nov. 7, Ben-Gurion delivers a victory speech. The transparent nature of the "secret" alliance is sufficient to provoke a threat of direct Soviet intervention, however, and both Britain and France quickly relinquish their hold on the canal. At that point, Israel, which has acted independently of the U.S., is forced to give up its gains as well. The U.S. nonetheless shields the Israelis from suffering the consequences of having waged an obviously aggressive war—there is serious discussion in the UN of both expelling Israel and imposing severe sanctions—and further solidifies the two countries' military/diplomatic relationship. By every measure then, the IDF, with considerable U.S. assistance, emerges from the war as the strongest military power in the Mideast.

1957

Apr. 30: The Supplementary Convention on the Abolition of Slavery, the Slave Trade and Institutions and Practices Similar to Slavery enters into force without U.S. ratification, although the Senate eventually ratifies the Convention, allowing the U.S. to ostensibly join 114 other UN member-states in accepting the law as binding on Dec. 6, 1967. As is the case with the 1927 Slavery Convention and its 1955 amending protocol, the maneuver is far more illusory than substantive, largely because enslavement is still deemed a "permissible" punishment of those "duly convicted of a crime" under the 13th Amendment to the U.S. Constitution. As has been noted, some 2 million persons in the U.S. thus remain in a condition of involuntary servitude as of this writing. In addition to violating the antislavery conventions, this situation violates Article 4 of the Universal Declaration of Human Rights and Article 8 of the International Convention on Civil and Political Rights, among other elements of international law.

July 1: ECOSOC adopts the Standard Minimum Rules for the Treatment of Prisoners. Although the U.S. does not openly contest the rules, its penal policies routinely violate them from the outset (see, e.g., the entry for May 13, 1987).

Aug, 31: "Smokey," the above-ground ("atmospheric") detonation of a nuclear weapon is conducted at the Nevada Test Site. Over 1,000 U.S. troops are ordered to gather in nearby positions—and are thereby exposed to extraordinary concentrations of radiation—as part of an Army experiment to assess "the effects of blast proximity on the combat-readiness of units operating on the nuclear battlefield." Scores of such "exercises" are carried out between 1951 and 1958, impacting not only the troops, but the civilian population residing in adjacent locales. Meanwhile, "longitudinal studies" are conducted concerning the longterm effects of more diffuse radiation exposure on islanders unwillingly subjected to fallout from U.S. nuclear test detonations at Bikini, Kwajalein and Enewetak during the 1940s and early 1950s (see the entry for July 1, 1946), unwitting Inuits on Alaska's North Slope are fed capsules of pure uranium in order for the military to assess the "effects of such ingestion on the human organism," and "downwinders" near the Hanford nuclear weapons complex in Washington State are deliberately/repeatedly exposed to the gaseous release of radioactive iodides in order for the effects of *that* to be studied (see the entry for Aug. 5, 1963). Suffice it to observe that each of these experiments—and there were many more—was conducted in blatant violation of the Nuremberg Code (see the entry for Sept. 20, 1950).

1958

Jan. 22: The U.S. endorses SC Res. 127, condemning Israeli impoundment of Jordanian property in the demilitarized zone separating the two countries, as well as Jewish settlement activities therein, and calls upon both countries to abide by the 1949 armistice agreements (peculiar, since there is no indication that Jordan has violated them). Since the U.S. has allowed no inclusion of enforcement provisions, Israel simply ignores the resolution, continuing both impoundments and the construction of settlements.

July 16: Following the Ba'athist coup in Iraq on July 14, which effectively ends British dominance in that country, Pres. Eisenhower orders U.S. marines and airborne troops into Lebanon to shore up the tottering—but decisively prowestern—régime of Pres. Camille Chamoun; Britain simultaneously maintains the status quo in Jordan by sending several thousand paratroopers to Amman. The U.S. intervention, which plainly violates the self-determining rights of the Lebanese, and thus Chapter I of the UN Charter, sets in motion a process of internal fragmentation and periodic civil war in that country which has lasted into the present moment. Another upshot of these explicitly anti-Arabist interventions is an upgrading of both the quantity and the quality of British/U.S. arms transfers to Israel.

Dec. 12: The U.S. endorses UNGA Res. 1314 (XIII), establishing a UN Commission on Permanent Sovereignty over Natural Resources, instructed to conduct a global survey of local assets and conditions. More than anything, the U.S. appears to view the body as a vehicle for intelligence-gathering (certainly, it does not view the Commission as being imbued with an authority to alter or constrain its own trade practices).

1959

Jan. 1: The U.S.-backed régime of Cuban dictator Fulgencio Batista is abolished by Fidel Castro's insurgent nationalist movement. In the weeks following, the CIA responds by launching a protracted and utterly illegal campaign of international terrorism which, although somewhat abated in recent years, remains ongoing. Beginning at least as early as Oct. 1959— despite a provision in Title 18 of the federal statutory code making it a felony to undertake a "military enterprise or expedition" from U.S. soil against a country with which the U.S. is not formally at war—Florida-based aircraft piloted by a combination of self-exiled Batistites and CIA clandestine services operatives make the first of what become hundreds of strafing and incendiary bombing raids on Cuban cane fields, sugar mills and other targets—in Jan. 1960, 3 Americans are killed and 2 others captured when their planes are shot down during such missions—and literally hundreds of small seaborne attacks conducted as part of "Operation Mongoose." In 1962, an entity known as Omega 7 emerges as the preeminent organization among CIA-sponsored Cubans, carrying out well over a hundred major terrorist actions—bombings (including that of a Cuban airliner on Oct. 6, 1976, that claimed 73 lives), airplane hijackings, murders—during the next 15 years. Attempts are also made to assassinate Castro (repeatedly), his brother Raul, Ché Guevara—who, in Dec. 1964, is subjected to an Omega 7 bazooka attack at the UN headquarters in New York—and other ranking members of Cuba's revolutionary government. Not content with its own terrorist apparatus, the CIA also enlists the services of the Mafia in its efforts to murder

Cuba's head of state. A complete itemization of the international laws violated by the U.S. in its protracted effort to terrorize Cuba into submission could obviously go on for pages. Suffice it here to observe that Chapters I, VI and VII of the UN Charter, and Chapters IV and V of the OAS Charter, would necessarily top any such list. Violations of UNGA Resolutions 337A (V) and 380 (V) are also at issue.

Jan. 17: The Abolition of Forced Labor Convention enters into force without U.S. ratification. Ultimately, the Senate does ratify the Convention more than 30 years later, ostensibly allowing the U.S. to join 117 prior signatories in accepting the rule of law on Sept. 25, 1992. At the time of its formal acceptance, however, the U.S. is well on its way to consolidating an internal "prison-industrial complex"—and reintroducing literal chain gangs to many penal contexts—wherein forced labor is standard. Given the proportion of its population it incarcerates—second only to Russia as of 1999—the U.S. remains as of this writing among the world's most flagrant violators (far worse than China, whose human rights violations in this regard the U.S. routinely condemns). In addition to violating the Forced Labor Convention, current U.S. penal policy violates the 1927 Slavery Convention as well as its additional protocol and supplement, Article 4 of the Universal Declaration of Human Rights and Article 8 of the International Convention on Civil and Political Rights, among other elements of international law.

June 27: The U.S. proclaims Hawai'i to be "decolonized" by virtue of a statute incorporating the islands into America's "home compartment" as the "50th State of the Union." Although the U.S. claims its action results from the sort of referendum required under Chapters XI and XII of the UN Charter to ensure that "peoples who have not yet attained a full measure of self-government" are afforded the self-determining right to do so, the process has been subverted by including not only the colonized native population, but the islands' much larger settler population in the vote on whether Hawai'i should become a state. The plebiscite was, moreover, not supervised by the UN, as is required under Chapter XII of the Charter. Nonetheless, the U.S. has Hawai'i removed from the Secretariat's list of non-self-governing territories and declares its political status to have been "permanently resolved." It should be noted that British and French attempts to perform very similar maneuvers in Malta and New Caledonia were subsequently—the former in 1964, the latter in 1986—held to be legally invalid.

1960

Jan. 20: From the day of his inauguration, Pres. John F. Kennedy picks up and tightens his predecessors' economic embargo of Cuba, a sanctions régime intended solely to force an alteration of Cuba's internal political priorities. Although the U.S. will later claim that the embargo is simply a matter of its own "trade policy," thus falling within the range of its sovereign prerogatives rather than the realm of international action subject to UN intervention, this is clearly not the case at the outset. Not only does the Kennedy administration seek to enlist other countries in its plan to starve the Cubans into submission, it employs sabotage and other such methods in its effort to accomplish the desired result. Already, in Mar. 1959, a French freighter docked in Havana had been bombed by members of the CIA's incipient Omega 7 terror network, killing 75 and wounding 200. Then, in Aug. 1962, the cargo—Cuban sugar bound for the Soviet Union—of a British freighter that had put in for repairs at San Juan, Puerto Rico, is chemically contaminated by CIA operatives there. Two years after that, in Oct. 1964, the CIA arranges the collision of a Japanese freighter with an East German vessel in British waters as a means of preventing the latter's delivery of 42 busses to Cuba. Such actions—and there are numerous others—violate not only Chapters I, VI, VII, and IX of the UN Charter, but Chapters IV, V and VI of the OAS Charter, UNGA Resolutions 337A (V) and 380 (V), several articles of the Convention on the High Seas (signed by the U.S. on Apr. 29, 1958, and entering into force on Sept. 30, 1962) and other elements of international law.

Apr. 1: The U.S. endorses SC Res. 134, deploring the recent "large-scale killings of unarmed and peaceful [antiapartheid] demonstrators by South African police and military units, and calling upon the Pretoria régime to abolish apartheid. The U.S., however, unlike its posture towards Cuba—where no such reprehensible policies and attendant atrocities have occurred—maintains perfectly cordial relations with South Africa, both diplomatically and commercially. It must be remembered, of course, that America's own well-established system of formal apartheid—referred to as "Jim Crow"—is in full flourish during this period, as was attendant racial violence. The U.S., moreover, is just on the verge of unleashing a substantial wave of official repression, including physical repression of the most lethal sort, against civil and human rights activists.

Dec. 14: With its Hawaiian, Puerto Rican, Micronesian and other external holdings "legitimated," the U.S. abstains from opposing UNGA Res. 1514 (XV), the Declaration on the Granting of Independence to Colonial Countries and Peoples. Although the Declaration merely clarifies the intent underlying Chapters XI and XII of the UN Charter, the U.S. refuses to accept it as a binding policy guide. One result is that the U.S. repeatedly and all but solitarily opposes final implementation of the Declaration's—and thence the Charter's—basic decolonization provisions during the 1990s.

Dec. 14: The UNESCO Convention Against Discrimination in Education is passed, prohibiting policies "depriving any person or group of persons [defined by] race, colour, sex, language, religion, political or other opinion, national or social origin, economic condition or birth...of access to education of any type or at any level...limiting any [such] person or group of persons to education of an inferior standard [or] establishing or maintaining separate educational systems or institutions for [such] persons or groups of persons." The Convention enters into force on May 22, 1960. At the time, despite the Supreme Court's ruling in *Brown v. Board of Education* a few years earlier, the bulk of America's public school system remains formally segregated on the basis of race. For a brief period during the 1960s and '70s, it appears that a combination of desegregation initiatives, increased federal funding and—perhaps most importantly—affirmative action programs may eventually bring the U.S. into a posture of legal conformity. Today, however, the results of a quarter-century of retrenchment on all fronts has effectively restored much of the pre-1960 order.

Dec. 15: The U.S. endorses UNGA Res. 1515 (XV), asserting the right of all states, including those of the 3rd World, to dispose of their resources as they see fit. U.S. foreign/trade policy, however, increasingly contradicts this noble-sounding gesture.

1961

Jan. 17: CIA counterinsurgency ace Edward Lansdale submits a report recommending that clandestine operations against the northern zone of Vietnam be intensified. Lansdale, who served as the Agency's Saigon station chief from 1954–1956, had himself initiated a program in early 1955 through which highly-trained Vietnamese operatives were infiltrated from the southern into the northern zone aboard a specially-assembled "junk fleet" for purposes of engaging in sabotage and subversion (it should be noted that this operation began *4 years* before the oft-mentioned 1959 Party Congress at which the Hanoi government decided to begin infiltrating guerrilla cadres into the south). On May 11, 1961, Pres. Kennedy signs NSAM-52, authorizing then Saigon station chief William Colby to undertake a significant escalation in the still-ongoing operation inaugurated by Lansdale, to expand it to include infiltration of operatives by parachute, and to employ selected Army Special Forces personnel and Navy SEALs in the process. This is the origin of the U.S. Special Operations Group (MACV-SOG) in Indochina (see entries for Dec. 15, 1963 and Aug.4, 1964). Suffice it here to observe that the SOG activities were conducted in violation of the 1954 Geneva Accords and UNGA Resolutions 337A (V) and 380 (V), as well as numerous articles falling under Chapters I, VI, VII, XI and XII of the UN Charter.

Jan. 17: Congolese premier Patrice Lumumba is murdered by Moise Tshombe, a secessionist leader in the country's Katanga Province, into whose hands he was delivered a few hours earlier by CIA-backed forces under the command of Gen. Mobutu Sese Sekou (Joseph Mobutu). Mobutu himself is later shown to have been able to "arrest" Lumumba on Dec. 1, 1960, mainly as the result of intelligence information provided on the premier's whereabouts following a failed CIA attempt to assassinate him by use of a "bacteriological agent." After Lumumba's murder, CIA personnel dispose of his corpse. Lumumba's major "sin" is that he has attempted—during the barely two months in which he is allowed to hold power in the newly-decolonized Congo—to chart a truly independent course for his country, free of neocolonial economic domination by the U.S. and its former western European colonizers. When these "Free World" countries act as a bloc to prevent the Congo from receiving aid from the UN—their idea is to force Lumumba into "moderating" his anticolonialist attitudes—he requests assistance from the Soviet Union, and his fate is sealed: both he and his people are to be made examples of the costs and consequences of any Third World country attempting to exercise genuinely self-determining prerogatives. In the wake of Lumumba's assassination, the Congo disintegrates into a bloody "civil war" in which Tshombe seeks to follow through on his plan to break away, only to be crushed by Mobutu's troops (supplied and equipped by the western powers and augmented by hefty contingents of foreign mercenaries). The outcome is typically "democratic": Mobutu is installed in 1965 as "President for Life," inaugurating a 30-year reign during which the Congo, renamed Zaire, proves to be one of the most lucrative locales in Africa for U.S. corporate penetration while the people starve. The list of illegalities bound up in America's clandestine Congo operations—and policy—could be extended for pages. Suffice it here to observe that, as of 1961, it included violation of Chapters I, VI, VII, IX, XI and XII UN Charter, the Universal Declaration on Human Rights and the 1949 Geneva Conventions I and IV, as well as UNGA Resolutions 337A (V), 380 (V) and the 1960 Declaration on the Granting of Independence to Colonial Countries and Peoples. Given the human costs involved, and their sheer predictability as of 1961, it is also quite reasonable to suggest that the U.S. was, at the very least, in violation of Article III(b) and III(e) of the 1948 Genocide Convention.

Apr. 11: The U.S. endorses SC Res. 162, urging Israel to comply with decisions rendered by the UN commission overseeing compliance with the 1949 armistice agreements. Since the U.S. has prevented inclusion of enforcement provisions in the resolution, Israel simply ignores it.

Apr. 16: The CIA, with the express authorization of Pres. Kennedy, consummates "Operation Pluto," putting an invasion force of American-supported Cuban exiles ashore at the Bay of Pigs, on Cuba's southern coast, with the goal of forcibly dissolving the Castro government. The invasion fails spectacularly—in addition to several hundred killed, 1,241 members of the landing force are captured, and there is no "rising of the Cuban people to throw off the yoke of tyranny," as U.S. planners had confidently predicted— and Castro becomes more popular with his constituents than ever before. Apart from the individual charges of murder that might be levied with respect to the more than 1,700 Cubans who died defending their country against the aggression of this proxy army, U.S. actions and policy vis-à-vis the Bay of Pigs represent glaring violations of the 1928 Kellogg-Briand Pact, numerous articles falling under Chapters I, VI, VII and IX of the UN Charter and those found in Chapters I, II, IV and V of the OAS Charter, as well as UNGA Resolutions 337A (V) and 380 (V).

Nov. 1: Responding to a request from a key military advisor, Gen. Maxwell D. Taylor, that he secretly insert "a force of 9 or 10,000 combat troops disguised as flood control officers" to bolster the position of U.S. client Ngo Dinh Diem in the southern zone of Vietnam, Pres. Kennedy orders the first regular military units to Vietnam (they field 300 helicopter pilots to conduct "Eagle Flights" delivering Vietnamese troops into battle). By early 1962, U.S. personnel in Vietnam, referred to as "advisors," had "increased ten-fold to 4,000. These included detachments of Green Berets, or Special Forces, as the main cutting-edge Counter-Insurgency Council chaired by...Taylor." The Council is shortly redesignated as a "Military Assistance Group" (MAG), and then, as the U.S. presence expands to over 20,000, as the "Military Assistance Command, Vietnam" (MACV). All of this is, of course, undertaken in direct violation of the 1954 Geneva Accords, not to mention UNGA Res. 337A (V) and numerous articles of the UN Charter.

Nov. 24: UNGA Res. 1653 (XVI)—the Declaration on the Prohibition of the Use of Nuclear and Thermo-Nuclear Weapons—is adopted, making the employment of such armaments under *any* circumstances a crime against humanity. The Declaration coincides closely with Pres. Kennedy's public announcement—false, as it turns out (the U.S. at that point had 5,100 warheads capable of reaching the Soviet Union, the Soviets only 300 with which to reciprocate)—that the U.S. has fallen behind in its "arms race" with the Soviet Union, and he orders that U.S. inventories of thermonuclear warheads, as well as the number of "delivery systems" with which to use them, be radically expanded. Shortly, U.S. strategic theorists like Harvard's Henry Kissinger have perfected the concept of MAD—Mutually Assured Destruction—in which a balance of power formula guaranteeing veritable species suicide is passed off as being a better "guarantor" that nuclear weaponry will not be used than would disarmament itself. Variations of MAD remain predominant in U.S. strategic thinking until the demise of the USSR during the early 1990s. Presently, although there is no longer a Soviet counterbalance, the U.S. continues to develop its nuclear arsenal at a steady rate, ultimately presenting the prospect of AD—Assured Destruction—to any country unheeding of Pres. George Bush's 1991 observation that "what we say, goes" (an outlook often referred to as the "New World Order"). Although the U.S. is not known to have used nuclear weapons against an opponent since 1945, it is known to have seriously considered doing so on several occasions—for Pres. Richard Nixon, this seems to have been routine—and its ongoing evolution of such weaponry must be viewed as contrary to the spirit, if not the letter of the law. Its possession of such ordnance has, moreover, long since translated into a form of international blackmail, and blackmail is of course a crime.

1962

Apr. 9: The U.S. endorses SC Res. 171, reaffirming SC Res. 111 (1956) and condemning Israel's "flagrant violation" in attacking Syrian positions on the Golan Heights on the night of Mar. 16–17, an action carried out as usual by Ariel Sharon and his Unit 101. The U.S. once again ensures that no penalties or enforcement measures are included in the resolution.

May 13: A Canadian technician is hired by the CIA to infect Cuban turkey flocks with the Newcastle disease (some 8,000 birds die before the outbreak is contained). This is but the first "incident" in what turns out to be a protracted campaign of chemical/biological warfare intended to wreck Cuba's economy, thereby compelling the country to adopt a form of governance approved by the U.S. Throughout the 1960s, there appear to have been attempts, using a variety of aerosol sprays, to damage the island's sugar crop. In both 1969 and 1970, "cloud-seeding" and other experimental weather modification techniques are used in an effort to obtain the same result. In 1971, Cuban pigs are deliberately infected with the swine fever virus (more than a half-million animals have to be destroyed in order to contain the epidemic). In 1981, mosquitoes carrying dengue fever are released, causing an epidemic in which more than 300,000 people are infected (158 die, more than 100 of them children under 15). Leaving aside the patent violations of numerous articles falling under Chapters I, VI, VII and IX of the UN Charter, all of the articles falling under Chapters IV, V and VI of the OAS Charter, and UNGA Resolutions 337A (V) and 380 (V), the entire campaign was conducted in violation of the 1925 Geneva Protocol for the Prohibition of the Use in War of Asphyxiating, Poisonous or Other Gases, and of Bacteriological Warfare, and the 1949 Geneva Convention IV.

July 9: At the conclusion of a protracted conference begun in May 1961, a second set of Geneva Accords on Indochina, this time formally endorsed by the U.S., are adopted. Titled "A Declaration of the Neutrality of Laos and Additional Protocol," the agreement prohibits deployment of foreign troops within the Laotian Kingdom, as well as provision of munitions and military equipage to the various warring factions therein. In practice, U.S. special operations personnel, introduced to Laos at least as early as 1958, continue and in some ways accelerate their activities. Such operations violate not only the 1961 Accords, but several articles concerning the rights of neutral states included in the 1899 Hague Convention II on Land Warfare, the 1907 Hague Convention V Respecting the Rights and Duties of Neutral Powers and Persons in Case of War on Land, numerous articles falling under Chapters I, VI, VII, XI and XII of the UN Charter, UNGA Resolutions 337A (V) and 380 (V), as well as the 1960 Declaration on the Granting of Independence to Colonial Countries and Peoples.

Oct. 14: A U-2 spy plane collects photographic evidence the Soviets are engaged in the perfectly legal activity of installing medium and intermediate-range missile bases in Cuba, setting off 13 days of U.S.-instigated nuclear brinksmanship. When challenged by the U.S., the Soviets respond that the missiles have been requested by the Cuban government, which, reasonably enough, is interested in defending itself against further U.S. or U.S.-sponsored invasions (à la the Bay of Pigs, a year earlier). When the U.S. points out that the missiles are essentially offensive rather than defensive weapons and that their positioning so close to the U.S. thus poses an "inordinate threat" to its national security, the Soviets answer that this is no different than the threat posed to it by missile batteries the U.S. has had positioned in Turkey for several years. Pres. Kennedy then orders Cuba placed under naval blockade—U.S. vessels are instructed to stop and board Soviet ships on the high seas, an outright act of war—in an effort to force the Soviets to back down unilaterally. At the last moment Kennedy secretly commits to withdraw the U.S. missiles from Turkey in exchange for Soviet reciprocation in Cuba—and to guarantee that the island will suffer no further invasions, as such, at the hands of the U.S.—and Soviet Premier Khrushchev orders his missile-laden cargo ship to turn around short of the U.S. blockade line. Leaving aside the illegality inherent to the U.S. violation of Cuban airspace involved in U-2 and other such reconnaissance over-flights, the steadfast American refusal to negotiate withdrawal of its missiles from Turkey in any context other than a head-on military confrontation is plainly contrary to the intent of the UN Charter's first chapter, the letter of Article 18 of the OAS Charter, and UNGA Res. 337A (V).

Nov. 6: The U.S. endorses UNGA Res. 1761 (XVII), condemning the "racist [apartheid] régime" in South Africa. U.S. relations with Pretoria remain warm, however, and the investments of its corporations in South Africa actually increase over coming months.

Dec. 14: The U.S. endorses UNGA Res. 1803 (XVII), asserting the sovereignty of all states, including those of the Third World, over natural resources within their borders. U.S. foreign/trade policy continues to evolve in direct contradiction to the principles articulated in the resolution, however.

1963

Mar. 13: The U.S. compounds its violations of UNGA Resolutions 337A (V) and 380 (V), Chapter I of the UN Charter, and Article 18 of the OAS Charter vis-à-vis Guatemala with a CIA-sponsored coup in which a junta headed by Col. Enrique Peralta Azurdia displaces that of Gen Miguel Ydigoras Fuentes, who had announced his intention to hold free elections in 1964. In 1966, Peralta steps aside to make way for a U.S.-selected civilian "liberal," Julio Cesar Mendez, who, in open defiance of the Genocide Convention—but with unstinting American military, financial and diplomatic support—inaugurates a campaign of outright extermination against the Mayan population of the Guatemalan north. At least 200,000 indigenous people are slaughtered over the next quarter-century as Mayan territory is cleared of both its inhabitants and its rainforest, creating "industrial development zones" for use by primarily U.S. corporations. This last places the U.S. in the position of having, at the very least, violated Article III(e), Complicity in Genocide, under provision of the 1948 Convention.

May 27: Israeli PM Ben-Gurion, who has refused the IAEC inspections of his country's recently-completed reactor complex at Dimona mandated under SC Res. 20 (1947), writes a letter to Pres. Kennedy proposing periodic U.S. inspections as an alternative. Although Ben-Gurion's proposal clearly represents a legal circumvention, Kennedy agrees. While it has been known since 1959 that the Dimona facility is capable of producing substantial quantities of the plutonium necessary to manufacture nuclear weapons, and that preventing such production requires comprehensive inspections twice annually, Kennedy's successor, Lyndon Johnson, allows the Israelis to restrict oversight to a single day's "visit" by not more than 3 American "observers" once per year (the U.S. representatives are not allowed to bring their own instrumentation, and there is evidence the Israelis constructed a false control room for them to "monitor"). U.S. participation in this transparent subterfuge, allows its "de facto ally"—as Kennedy puts it in 1961—

both to develop the bomb and to share its weapons technology with other rogue states (see the entry for Sept. 22, 1977).

Apr. 7: The U.S. endorses SC Res. 181, calling for member-states to participate in a voluntary arms embargo on South Africa, because of the racist nature of its apartheid domestic order and the general bellicosity with which it relates to the prospect of black African self-determination. The U.S. remains a major supplier of weaponry and weapons technology.

July 11: A CIA-sponsored military junta seizes power in Ecuador, toppling the government of Pres. Carlos Julio Arosemana. Ironically, Arosemana, who had been elected vice pres. in the 1960 election, was himself installed in the top seat by a military coup that had deposed the elected president, José Maria Velasco Ibarra, in Nov. 1961. Both coups, as was later revealed, are "necessitated" by the failure of a CIA operation undertaken in 1960 to prevent the centrist Velasco's election by introducing "left-wing terror" to Ecuadorian politics (the CIA literally manufactured several "violence-prone leftist organizations" for this purpose). In the wake of the 1963 coup, national elections are suspended indefinitely, allowing Ecuador to remain in the "Free World," its American-supported junta protecting the country from the "threat of dictatorship" posed by democratic processes for more than a decade. That these U.S. actions and attendant policies stood in gross violation of UNGA Resolutions 337A (V) and 380 (V), Chapter I of the UN Charter, and Article 18 of the OAS Charter is self-evident.

Aug. 5: The U.S. signs the Treaty Banning Nuclear Weapons Tests in the Atmosphere, in Outer Space, and Under Water, which is quickly ratified by the Senate and enters into force in U.S. law on Oct. 10. Although the U.S., which had recently wrapped up "Operation Dominic," a series of 24 atmospheric detonations conducted in 1962 on Hawai'i's Johnson Island, complies with the letter of the treaty, it accelerates its underground testing program, mostly under treaty-reserved Western Shoshone territory in Nevada. This leads to an unknown number of "ventings" in which clouds of radioactive debris are released into the atmosphere (e.g., the "Banebury" test of 1970). By the mid-1990s, when Pres. Bill Clinton supposedly halted further testing, the homeland of the unoffending Shoshones has been subjected to nearly 1,000 above and below-ground nuclear detonations, making theirs by far "the most bombed nation on earth." Given the likely longterm effects upon the Shoshone population of this massive irradiation of their landbase, the U.S. nuclear weapons testing program in Nevada constitutes a violation of Article II(c) of the 1948 Genocide Convention. It should also be noted that the U.S. regularly circumvented the Test Ban Treaty by regularly and deliberately releasing "plumes" of radioactive gases from its Hanford nuclear weapons production facility in Washington so that dispersal patterns—and perhaps the effects on downwind humans—could be studied. As of 2003, moreover, the U.S. has resumed the atmospheric testing of nuclear weapons by experimenting with "dirty bombs" at the military's White Sands Test Range in New Mexico.

Oct. 11: The U.S. abstains from voting on UNGA Res. 1881 (XVII), which condemns South Africa's policy of apartheid and calls for voluntary sanctions to "encourage" the Pretoria régime to abandon it. U.S. diplomatic and commercial relations with South Africa nonetheless remain as cordial as ever.

Nov. 20: The U.S. abstains from voting on UNGA Res. 1904 (XVIII), which points to the need for a convention banning all forms of racial discrimination. In combination with its then-prevailing domestic racial policies, this posture earns the U.S., alongside apartheid South Africa, a resolution of condemnation at the First Assembly of the Heads of State and Government of the Organization of African Unity (OAU) in July 1964.

Dec. 15: Defense Sec. Robert S. McNamara approves a plan to create what is cover-named the "Studies and Observation Group"—actually a Special Operations Group—combining CIA clandestine operations with those of selected U.S. and South Vietnamese special warfare units in a coherent structure under MACV. The primary purpose of the new unit is initially to render ongoing CIA-sponsored raids along the coastline of Vietnam's northern zone more effective (for background, see the entry for Jan. 17, 1961; for implications, see the entry for Aug. 4, 1964), to take over and expand longer-term operations designed to foster insurgency in the north (also ongoing; there have been 25 such since 1961), and to engage in cross-border reconnaissance missions in Laos. Insofar as SOG operations in and against Vietnam's northern zone are both secret and denied—indeed, they are undertaken in a context wherein the existence of a de facto state of war is officially disacknowledged by the U.S.—they have no recourse to legitimation under either the laws of war or the UN Charter. Instead, they are illegal on their face. SOG operations in Laos, moreover, are undertaken in violation of several articles concerning the rights of neutral states included in the 1899 Hague Convention II on Land Warfare, the 1907 Hague Convention V Respecting the Rights and Duties of Neutral Powers and Persons in Case of War on Land, the 1961 Geneva Accords and numerous articles falling under Chapters I, VI and VII of the UN Charter, as well as UNGA Resolutions 337A (V) and 380 (V).

1964

Mar. 31: Ignoring UNGA Resolutions 337A (V) and 380 (V), Chapter I of the UN Charter, and Article 18 of the OAS Charter, a CIA-sponsored coup is undertaken to remove Brazil's duly-elected socialist president, Joao Goulart. Although the junta is not yet in place by that point, the U.S. formally recognizes its "legitimacy" on Apr. 2. It is later revealed that, well before the fact, the plotters have been promised not only immediate recognition, but massive U.S. military and economic support in exchange for their undertaking to save Brazil from the "dictatorship" of free elections and other aspects of democratic governance. In the aftermath, the Castelo Branco régime is one of the first recipients of "assistance" from the State Department's Office of Public Safety (OPS), which by 1969 has trained more than 100,000 Brazilian police in such "technical matters" as the use of electric shock and other such methods of torture, how to arrange the "disappearance" of labor organizers and other political dissidents, and the proper organization of death squads (see entry for Aug. 10, 1970).

Aug. 4: A nonevent happens in the Gulf of Tonkin, off the coast of Vietnam, when a destroyer, the *U.S.S. Maddox*, reports that it has come under attack by North Vietnamese patrol boats. Quickly joined by a second destroyer, the *U.S.S. C. Turner Joy*, the *Maddox* soon announces a second attack. Although it is later revealed that the attacks are a hoax, and that the *Maddox* in any event invited retaliation by participating earlier the same evening in raids by U.S./South Vietnamese SOG personnel on the North Vietnamese islands of Hon Me and Hon Nieu, the discovery is not made until long after Pres. Lyndon B. Johnson misrepresents the "Tonkin Gulf Incident" as "unprovoked aggression against U.S. naval vessels on the high seas," thereby gaining congressional authorization for the overt use of force against the northern zone of Vietnam. Airstrikes commence on Aug. 5, and continue with only periodic interruption through the end of Johnson's presidency, 4 years later, then are picked up and intensified by his successor, Richard M. Nixon, for another 6 years (actually, they don't end altogether until 1975). The scale and ferocity of the bombing are beyond comprehension. By the end of 1969, 4.5 million tons of bombs have been dropped on Vietnam and contiguous areas of Laos and Cambodia—some 9 times the total tonnage expended in the entire Pacific Theater during World War II—leaving an area larger than the State of Connecticut's 5,000 sq. miles covered by huge, interlocking craters up to 30 ft. deep. From there, the intensity of the air campaign actually *increases*. By far the greater proportion of the estimated 2 million Indochinese civilians who are killed during America's undeclared "10,000 day war" against their very habitat, die as the result of high altitude saturation bombing and/or "precision" airstrikes. At an absolute minimum, the protracted U.S. air campaign against Indochina violates the 1923 Hague Rules of Aerial Warfare, the 1949 Geneva Convention IV, the 1954 Hague Convention for the Protection of Cultural Property and its Additional Protocol, most of the articles falling under Chapters I, VI and VII of the UN Charter, UNGA Resolutions 337A (V) and 380 (V) and, well before the end, UNGA Res. 2131 (XX). Given the indiscriminate approach taken to bombing heavily populated areas, including the stated objective in some locales of destroying the very land itself, the air campaign obviously violated Articles II(a), II(b), II(c), III(b) and III(d) of the Genocide Convention. As concerns the official U.S. fabrication of events in the Gulf of Tonkin on the night of Aug. 4, 1964, which served as the "predication" for all this, it plainly bears comparison to the "unprovoked attack by Polish forces upon German border installations" staged by the nazis on the night of Aug. 31, 1939, as a pretext for starting World War II the following morning. One firm indication of the aptness of such an assessment is the fact that by 1970 even Telford Taylor, U.S. Chief Counsel at Nuremberg, is prepared to acknowledge that under the standards applied against the nazis in 1945, the entire American leadership belonged in a similar defendants' dock.

Sept. 5–11: Following up on a preliminary summit conducted in Cairo a few months earlier, the Arab League meets in Alexandria to devise a common strategy for finally resolving the issue of Palestinian refugees and the more general problem of Israel. The Palestine Liberation Organization (PLO), recognized by both the League and the UN a decade later as being "the sole legitimate representative of the Palestinian people" (see the entry for Oct. 28, 1974), is established, and the mechanics of "a united front against zionist imperialism" hammered out. Another particular focus is how to undo the effects of a recently completed Israeli project, begun in 1959, diverting water from Lake Kinneret to the Negev region (this is a variation on the earlier Israeli effort to divert water from the Jordan River itself; see the entry for Nov. 2, 1953). Israel, joined by the U.S., responds by refusing to recognize the PLO—Israel in fact refuses to recognize even the existence of *Palestinians*, per se, claiming that they should as a group be considered "Jordanians"—thus precluding the possibility of a negotiated rather than military solution to the "Question of Palestine." The Israeli/U.S. posture in this regard is contrary to Chapters I, VI and XI of the UN Charter, as well as the 1954 Convention Relating to the Status of Stateless Persons. With respect to Arab complaints about water diversion, Israel undertakes—according to the posthumously published notes of no less than Moshe Dayan—a "policy of escalation" against Syria in the area of Lake Kinneret (according to Dayan, "80 percent" of all the clashes between Israel and Syria during this period are "deliberately provoked" by Israel). Despite Israel's consistent violation of the UN Charter's first Chapter, UNGA Res. 337A (V), and numerous other elements of international law, U.S. support remains unimpaired.

1965

Mar. 28: *The New York Times*, quoting Defense Sec. McNamara, reports that U.S. troops in Vietnam have been experimenting with the use of three types of gas—DM, CN and CS—against those inside suspected "enemy fortifications" (many of which turn out to be cellars in which terrified civilians have sought refuge from the fighting). In Sept., Gen. William Westmoreland, commander of all U.S. forces in Southeast Asia, is authorized to employ all three gases on a routine basis. Although military spokespersons insist that the gases are "nonlethal," all three, esp. when heavily concentrated in closed spaces, are well-known to cause asphyxia (esp. among small children, and elderly persons with lung ailments), cardiac arrest (esp. among those with preexisting heart conditions) and severe damage to the eyes and mucous membranes. The first report of civilian fatalities—26 women and 28 children asphyxiated in the village of Vinh Quang, when American soldiers flood their shelters with 48 canisters of CS—is reported in the Times on Oct. 5 (the incident actually occurred a month earlier). By Jan. 1966, both CS and CN are being massively deployed in "aerogel" form from low-flying aircraft. At about the same time, the "Mighty-Might"—a high-pressure pump designed to inject a toxic and highly volatile oxyacetylene mixture into bunkers and tunnels—also comes into use. There are also well-documented reports that, by 1970, sarin nerve gas is used by Army Special Forces units operating in Laos (see entry for June 7, 1998). It is impossible to estimate with any degree of precision how many Indochinese—combatants and non-combatants alike—are ultimately killed by the U.S. resort to gas warfare; certainly, the tally must run into the thousands, and perhaps tens of thousands. Irrespective of the number of fatalities, the employment of these obviously *lethal* gases was undertaken in flagrant violation of the 1899 Hague Declaration 2 Concerning Asphyxiating Gases, the 1925 Geneva Protocol for the Prohibition of the Use in War of Asphyxiating, Poisonous or Other Gases, and the 1949 Geneva Convention IV. Insofar as such gases were employed against targets known or suspected to contain enemy medical facilities, it was also undertaken in violation of the 1949 Geneva Convention I for the Amelioration of the Conditions of the Wounded and Sick in Armed Forces in the Field.

Apr. 29: Ignoring the 1928 Kellogg-Briand Pact, UNGA Resolutions 337A (V) and 380 (V), Chapter I of the UN Charter, and Article 18 of the OAS Charter, the U.S. lands the first 500 Marines in the Dominican Republic to ensure that a popular insurrection meant to reinstate leftist Pres. Juan Bosch, deposed 19 months earlier in a U.S.-backed military coup, is unsuccessful. U.S. forces quickly swell to over 23,000, winning a "smashing victory" over their nonmilitary opponents, occupying the country for months, and laying the groundwork for the rightist régime of U.S. client Joaquin Balaguer to remain in power for another dozen years. As *Newsweek* magazine puts it at the time, "democracy [is] being saved from Communism by getting rid of democracy."

Sept. 11: The 1st Cavalry Division (Airmobile) arrives in Vietnam. Unlike the 9th Marine Expeditionary Force, which arrived on Mar. 8, thus comprising the first U.S. maneuver battalions sent to Indochina, or the 3rd Marine Division that arrived on May 6, the "Air Cav" is equipped with M-16 rifles, a technological circumvention of the 1899 Hague Declaration 3 Concerning Expanding Bullets. The Hague Declaration prohibits use of unjacketed ammunition—especially dum-dum and hollow point bullets—in combat because of their tendency to flatten out on impact with the human body, causing "unnecessarily terrible" wounds and correspondingly inordinate death rates among those suffering them (this is the origin of the requirement that military ammunition be of the full-metal jacketed "ball" variety). The M-16, fires a very small, super-high velocity projectile which is extremely unstable in flight, a matter causing the bullet to tumble upon impact, thus inflicting the same sorts of wounds the Hague Declaration was meant to avoid. By early 1969, more than 240,000 M-16s have been issued to troops in Vietnam. Today, the M-16 is the standard issue rifle for all U.S. military personnel aside from snipers and members of special operations units.

Oct. 1: Ignoring UNGA Resolutions 337A (V) and 380 (V), as well as Chapter I of the UN Charter, the CIA brings to fruition a long-planned military coup to displace the government of Indonesia's duly-elected, left-leaning and staunchly independent president Sukarno, replacing it with a junta headed by Gen. Suharto, a deeply corrupt and openly fascistic U.S. client.

Over the next several years, the newly-installed régime, another recipient of immediate and sustained U.S. military/diplomatic support, indulges in the slaughter of somewhere between 500,000 and 1 million "communists," following up on Dec. 7, 1975, with an invasion of the tiny breakaway country of East Timor, quickly butchering about one-third of the entire population. Despite its grotesque violations of virtually every element of international humanitarian and human rights law, Suharto's Indonesia continues to receive unqualified U.S. support—and to be cast as an exemplar of the "Free World"—until the Indonesians themselves finally manage to bring the dictator down in 1995. In effect, since both Suharto's seizure of and maintenance in power was entirely contingent upon U.S. sponsorship, the U.S. was/is guilty of complicity in each of his myriad crimes against humanity.

1966

Feb. 24: Ignoring UNGA Resolutions 337A (V) and 380 (V), as well as Chapter I of the UN Charter, the CIA consummates a military coup, toppling Ghana's pan-Africanist president, Kwame Nkrumah. Although Nkrumah has been educated in the U.S., and has taken care to develop a "nonaligned" position for his government—i.e., neither pro-Soviet nor pro-U.S.—the very staunchness of his anticolonialism seems to be the major complaint against him. For U.S. policymakers, the "freedom" of Third World leaders extends only as far as their adoption of openly pro-U.S. postures.

Mar. 7: The U.S. declines to endorse UNGA Res. 2106 (XX), the International Convention on the Elimination of All Forms of Racial Discrimination, which enters into force on Jan. 4, 1969. Eventually, the Senate ratifies the convention, ostensibly allowing the U.S. to accept the law's binding effect on Nov. 20, 1994. The Senate attaches 3 reservations, 1 "understanding," 1 declaration, and 1 proviso to its ratification, however, all of which add up to a U.S. claim that it holds a "sovereign right" to exempt it itself from compliance when and however it desires to do so. As of this writing, police practices involving "racial profiling," as well as race-based disparities in incarceration rates and imposition of the death penalty, continue to offer ample evidence as to the form and extent of U.S. self-exemption.

Oct. 27: The U.S. endorses UNGA Res. 2145 (XXI), terminating South Africa's mandate in South West Africa (Namibia) and affirming the right of the Namibian people to self-determination under provision of the 1960 Declaration on the Granting of Independence to Colonial Countries and Peoples. The U.S., which views South Africa's virulently racist apartheid régime as a "bastion of the Free World," nonetheless lobbies against inclusion of enforcement provisions in the current resolution, and will use its Security Council veto prerogative as a means of preventing Namibian self-determination from being realized in anything resembling a timely fashion.

Nov. 25: The U.S. endorses SC Res. 228, censuring Israel for its "largescale and carefully planned attack" on the Jordanian town Samu, south of Hebron, resulting in considerable "loss of life and heavy property damage" on Nov. 13. Emphasis is placed on asserting that Israel's ongoing "actions of military reprisal cannot be tolerated." Although the U.S. is again successful in averting inclusion of actual penalty and enforcement provisions, other member-states finally force insertion of the threat that unless Israel desists in its aggression, "the Security Council will have to consider further and more effective steps as envisioned in the [UN] Charter to ensure against repetition."

Dec. 16: The U.S. declines to endorse UNGA Res. 2200 (XXI), the International Covenant on Economic, Social and Cultural Rights, which enters into force on Jan. 3, 1976. In 1977, Pres. Jimmy Carter finally signs off on the Covenant and transmits it to the Senate for ratification. The Senate declines to ratify, however, on the basis, best articulated by Reagan State Dept. official Elliot Abrams in 1981, that the U.S. does not acknowledge the existence of economic, social or cultural rights, as such. As of this writing, the U.S.—unlike 133 other countries—remains a nonratifying state.

Dec. 16: The U.S. declines to endorse UNGA Res. 2200 (XXI), the International Covenant on Civil and Political Rights (allowing the UN Human Rights Committee to hear complaints from individuals as well as state parties), which enters into force on Mar. 23, 1976. Although the Senate finally ratifies the Covenant on Sept. 8, 1992, the U.S.—unlike the 132 other countries having accepted the law as binding—qualifies its acceptance with 5 reservations, 5 "understandings," 4 declarations and 1 proviso, all of which add up to its claiming a "sovereign right" to exempt itself from compliance whenever it desires to do so.

Dec. 16: The U.S. declines to endorse UNGA Res. 2200A (XXI), the Optional Protocol Additional to the International Covenant on Civil and Political Rights, which enters into force on Mar. 23, 1976, with 87 state parties. As of the writing, the U.S. remains a nonsignatory state.

Dec. 21: The U.S. endorses UNGA Res. 2131 (XX), the Declaration of the Inadmissability of Intervention in the Domestic Affairs of the States and the Protection of Their Independence and Sovereignty, reaffirming and greatly amplifying the principles set forth in UNGA Res. 380 (V). Having made this noble gesture, the U.S. of course continues without interruption to do exactly what it had been doing all along, and was doing at the moment of its endorsement: intervening in the affairs of any country adopting policies not to its liking (which, over the years, has been virtually all of them).

1967

Apr. 13: A CIA-backed "Colonels' Coup" overthrows the government of liberal Prime Minister Georges Papandreou, the first ever to be elected by a majority of Greek voters (in 1964), two days before the start of a campaign that was all but certain to extend his term for another 4 years. In the aftermath, the junta, with full U.S. support, inaugurates a wave of repression against "leftists" so brutal that within months Norway, Denmark, Sweden and the Netherlands have all gone before the European Commission on Human Rights to argue that "The Colonels," as they continue to be called, have violated virtually every convention under the Commission's mandate; the régime is found guilty on all counts in early 1969, and only its walkout from the Council of Europe prevents Greece's expulsion by that body. Under these circumstances, American support to Greece rapidly *increases*, with Vice Pres. Spiro Agnew publicly extolling the régime's "achievements," as measured, presumably, by its "constant co-operation with U.S. needs and wishes." Ultimately, a falling out among The Colonels themselves in 1973, followed in July 1974 by their collective miscalculation in provoking a military confrontation with Turkey over control of the island of Cyprus, brings about the régime's collapse and resumption of civilian governance in Greece. Apart from its obvious complicity in virtually all the crimes of which The Colonels were found to be guilty, the U.S. role in installing them was undertaken in violation of Chapters I and II of the UN Charter and UNGA Resolutions 337A (V), 380 (V) and 2131 (XX).

May 10: The Russell Tribunal, an international body convened in Stockholm under authority of ECOSOC Res. 1503 (XLVIII), Article 38 of the Statute of the ICJ, and the 1946 Affirmation of the Principles of International Law Recognized by the Charter of the [Nuremberg] Tribunal concludes that the U.S. is engaged in the perpetration of aggressive war in Southeast Asia "under the terms of international law" enshrined in the Nuremberg Charter and that prosecution of the war has entailed "deliberate, systematic and large-scale bombing of civilian objectives in Vietnam" in violation of the 1923 Hague Rules of Aerial Warfare, as well as "repeated violations of the sovereignty, the neutrality and the territorial integrity of Cambodia" and Laos in violation of the 1907 Hague Convention V Respecting the Rights and Duties of Neutral Powers and Persons in Time of War. A multitude of other war crimes and crimes against the peace are also documented. The U.S. ignores these findings and continues with business as usual.

June 5: Without prior warning, the Israeli Air Force launches a predawn lightning attack that destroys its Egyptian counterpart on the ground. By mid-afternoon, those of Syria and Jordan have also been eliminated, and the only Iraqi airbase near enough to join the fray has been devastated. Over the next 5 days, Israeli army units seize the Golan Heights from Syria, the West Bank area—including the holy city of Jerusalem—from Jordan, and, once again, the entire Sinai from Egypt. Thus ends Israel's "Six Day War" of aggression. Although the Israeli blitzkrieg is conducted in flagrant violation of both the London and UN Charters, and is carried out in significant part with arms provided by the U.S., the U.S. neither severs relations nor offers any other appreciable response.

June 18: Israel formally annexes East Jerusalem, extending its domestic law over the inhabitants on June 27. Although such assertion of title by conquest has been repudiated in international law since at least as early as the 1928 Kellogg-Briand Pact—and in U.S. foreign policy pronouncements since the Stimson Doctrine was articulated in Jan. 1932—the U.S. again makes no move to alter its relations with Israel.

Nov. 22: The U.S. endorses SC Res. 242, calling upon Israel to immediately withdraw from all territories occupied during its recent war with contiguous Arab states. The U.S. delegation blocks inclusion of enforcement provisions, however, allowing the Israelis to simply ignore the resolution (albeit, at the behest of the U.S., they go through the motions of "formally accepting" it in Aug. 1970). Resultantly, Israel continues, 35 years later, to defy the law by occupying the West Bank, Gaza Strip and Golan Heights (the "Occupied Territories"). As of this writing, moreover, Israel, despite—or because of—its fundamentally illegal comportment, continues to receive by far the most U.S. military, economic and diplomatic support of any country in the world.

Nov. 25: Arthur W. Galston publishes an article entitled "Herbicides in Vietnam" in the *New Republic*, providing the first broad public exposure to "Operation Ranch Hand," a sustained project, begun under the codename "Hades" in late 1961, through which the Air Force has set about using aerosol sprays of herbicides to defoliate huge areas of Vietnam in an effort to "deny cover to the enemy." The defoliants, code-named "Agent Orange," "Agent White," "Agent Blue" and "Agent Purple," are all known to contain dioxin, along with plutonium among the most virulently carcinogenic/mutogenic substances ever synthesized. Before the Air Force suspends use of Agent Orange in 1970—it was by far the most used chemical—thousands of tons have been sprayed, and approximately 25% of the rainforest in the southern zone of Vietnam destroyed. Scores of thousands of U.S. troops and perhaps 2 million Vietnamese have also been exposed, many of them repeatedly and/or for prolonged periods. Among the latter group especially, postwar cancer rates prove catastrophic, as does the incidence of congenital birth defects among their children. Given that the likely effects of exposure to even minute quantities of dioxin are known before the fact, and that it is equally well-known that dioxin is present in the herbicides employed in "Ranch Hand," the entire operation is a violation of Article 23 of the 1907 Hague Convention IV Respecting the Laws and Customs of War on Land (prohibiting the use of "poison or poisoned weapons"), the 1925 Geneva Protocol for the Prohibition of the Use in War of Asphyxiating, Poisonous or Other Gases, and the 1949 Geneva Convention IV. In addition, given the express intent to destroy the very ecology of Vietnam involved in the operation, as well as the obvious willingness to visit incalculable human costs upon an entire population its planners exhibited, "Ranch Hand" unquestionably violates Articles II(c), III(b), III(d) and III(e) of the Genocide Convention.

Dec. 1: A second session of the Russell Tribunal (see the entry for May 10, 1968), this one conducted at Roskilde, Denmark, supplements the findings of the first session by concluding that the wanton use of incendiary ordnance, esp. napalm, in Vietnam violates the Martens Clause of the 1907 Hague Conventions, as well as the U.S. Army's own articulation of "The Laws of Land Warfare" (FM 27-10), in that it involves "a kind and degree of violence not necessary to military aims and objectives." The Tribunal also finds the overall U.S. military policy in Indochina to be in gross violation of the

1949 Geneva Convention III Relative to the Treatment of Prisoners of War and the 1949 Geneva Convention IV Relative to the Protection of Civilian Persons in Time of War. Most "controversially," the Tribunal unanimously endorses Jean-Paul Sartre's formulation that since the U.S. military engagement in Vietnam amounts in essence to a colonial war, and since colonialism is invariably tantamount to genocide, the U.S. is by definition guilty of violating the Genocide Convention. Apart from denouncing the Tribunal, the U.S. ignores its findings and continues with business as usual.

1968

Jan. 25: The U.S. endorses SC Res. 245, which reaffirms UNGA Res. 2145 (XXI), terminating South Africa's mandate in Namibia, and UNGA Res. 2324 (XXII), demanding the immediate release of all members of the South West African People's Organization (SWAPO) and other Namibian independence figures imprisoned by South Africa, and calling upon South Africa to comply. The U.S. prevents inclusion of enforcement provisions.

Mar. 14: The U.S. endorses SC Res. 246, expressing "dismay" that South Africa has not complied with UNGA Res. 2324 (XXII) or SC Res. 245, and calling upon UN member-states to bring appropriate "pressure" to bear in an effort to convince South Africa to do so. U.S. business with South Africa continues as usual.

Mar. 16: A company of the 23rd Infantry ("Americal") Division commanded by Lt. William Calley slaughters 347 unarmed civilians—including a dozen babies as young as 1 month of age—at the hamlet of Song My (My Lai 4), in Vietnam's southern zone. Although the massacre is observed from helicopters by Calley's superiors, and its true nature known to higher-ups, it is falsely cast as "an intense firefight" in which 128 "enemy soldiers" were killed. Only when a former soldier forces the incident into public view a year later is an extremely limited official investigation initiated; not only are all of Calley's superiors effectively exonerated, several other massacres perpetrated by Americal units in the vicinity of My Lai on the same day are hushed up (current Sec. of State Colin Powell, then a divisional staff officer, played a significant role in the coverup). In the end, Calley alone is charged with "murder of at least 102 Oriental human beings." Convicted, he ultimately serves 3.5 years under house arrest before his sentence is commuted by Pres. Richard Nixon. The My Lai case provides a lens through which to examine the de facto rules of engagement under which U.S. ground forces in Vietnam operate for nearly 7 years (1965-72). Known as the "Dead Gook Rule"—that is, if a corpse is Vietnamese it is counted as a slain "enemy combatant" on that basis alone—it points to a process of unremitting massacre, both largescale and small, of the civilian population. To illustrate: in one major 9th Infantry Division operation conducted in mid-1968, a body-count of more than 11,000 is claimed while only 748 weapons are recovered, indicating that more than 10,000 of the dead are peasant bystanders. More than a score of such operations are conducted during the course of the U.S. "commitment," and this is not even to begin to count the toll taken by such routine measures as the declaration of whole swaths of the country to be "free-fire zones" in which anything that moves can be killed with impunity. Unquestionably, the entire sweep of the U.S. "attrition" strategy employed in Vietnam embodies gross violations of numerous articles of the 1907 Hague Convention IV Respecting the Laws and Customs of War on Land and the 1949 Geneva Convention IV. It also constitutes violation of Articles II(a), II(b), II(c), III(b) and III(d) of the Genocide Convention. As is indicated by the My Lai criminal proceedings, no one is ever held to account for *any* of this. On the contrary, military personnel who attempted to meet their moral, ethical and legal responsibilities under the Nuremberg Doctrine to refuse participation in the overall pattern of war crimes and crimes against humanity are not infrequently prosecuted.

Mar. 24: The U.S. endorses SC Res. 248, condemning the "military action launched by Israel in violation of the United Nations Charter and [1967] cease-fire resolutions," and calls for Israeli compliance with both. The U.S. blocks inclusion of enforcement provisions in the resolution, allowing Israel to ignore it.

May 21: The U.S. endorses SC Res. 252, deploring Israeli noncompliance with UNGA Res. 2253 (ES-V) of July 4, 1967, and UNGA Res. 2254 (ES-V) of July 14, 1967, invalidating all Israeli land expropriations in the occupied territories of Palestine, and rejecting Israel's attempts to alter the legal status of Jerusalem. The U.S. prevents inclusion of enforcement provisions.

July 1: The U.S. signs the Treaty on Non-Proliferation of Nuclear Weapons, which is duly ratified by the Senate and enters into force on Mar. 5, 1970. Among the more important requirements is the Article V provision that a strict inspection régime will be maintained with regard to all countries to whom the nuclear powers provide reactor technology as a means of ensuring that it is not used for the purpose of weapons development. In the interim between signing and implementation, however, the U.S. "permanently suspends" its inspection of Israeli reactor sites (this, in full knowledge that Israel has been developing a nuclear weapons capacity at its Dimona reactor complex; see entry for May 27, 1963).

Aug. 16: The U.S. endorses SC Res. 256, reaffirming SC Res. 248 and condemning Israel's ongoing violation of the UN Charter. The U.S. is able to constrain the resolution to the level of a rhetorical flourish.

Sept. 18: The U.S. endorses SC Res. 258, reaffirming SC Res. 242 (1967). The U.S. once again blocks inclusion of enforcement provisions.

Dec. 31: The U.S. endorses SC Res. 262, condemning Israel's "premeditated attack" on the Beirut International Airport in violation of the UN Charter and numerous UN resolutions, and ordering restitution paid. The U.S. blocks inclusion of actual enforcement provisions, although the threat to employ "more effective measures," first made in SC Res. 228 (1966), is renewed. As of this writing, Israel has made no restitution.

1969

Feb. 9: Gen. Creighton Abrams, Westmoreland's successor as commander of MACV, requests permission from newly-elected Pres. Richard M. Nixon to order an "Arclight" airstrike by B-52 heavy bombers on a "Communist basing area" in neutral Cambodia. Nixon approves on Mar. 17, thus initiating "Menu," a top-secret bombing campaign against the hapless country that lasts until Aug. 1973. By Apr. 1972, 50,000 tons of bombs per month are being dropped on supposed "Communist sanctuaries" stretching a third of the way to Thailand. Ultimately, about half of Cambodia's 8 million people are left homeless and perhaps a half-million killed. From start to finish, the bombing of Cambodia is conducted in violation of several articles concerning the rights of neutral states included in the 1899 Hague Convention II on Land Warfare, the 1907 Hague Convention V Respecting the Rights and Duties of Neutral Powers and Persons in Case of War on Land, the 1923 Hague Rules of Aerial Warfare, the 1949 Geneva Convention IV, numerous articles falling under Chapters I, VI, VII, XI and XII of the UN Charter and UNGA Resolutions 337A (V), 380 (V) and 2131 (XX).

Mar. 20: The U.S. endorses SC Res. 264, condemning South Africa's refusal to comply with UNGA Resolutions 2145 (XXI), 2248 (S-V), 2325 (XXII), 2372 (XXII) and 2403 (XXII), as well as SC Resolutions 245 (1968) and 246 (1968), all of them declaring South Africa's continuing occupation of Namibia to be illegal and calling upon all UN member-states to bring "appropriate pressure" to bear in convincing South Africa to change its policies. The resolution ends by threatening to take "other steps or measures" under the UN Charter, if South Africa fails to do so, but the U.S. prevents inclusion of any less ambiguous formulation.

Apr. 1: The U.S. endorses SC Res. 265, condemning Israel's "preplanned air attacks" on Jordanian villages in violation of SC Resolutions 248 (1968) and 256 (1968), reaffirming both resolutions, and deploring the loss of life resulting from Israel's crimes. The U.S. blocks inclusion of any penalties or enforcement provisions.

May 23: While it is no more than a codification of customary international law and therefore attended by a Declaration of Universal Participation, the U.S. declines to accept the binding effect of the Vienna Convention on the Law of Treaties. Although the Convention entered into force on Jan. 27, 1980, and the State Department has all along recognized it as the definitive articulation of treaty law, the formal U.S. position as of this writing remains that its compliance is entirely "discretionary." A major motivator in this regard concerns the U.S. posture of gross violation vis-à-vis some 400 ratified treaties with indigenous nations now encapsulated within its claimed boundaries.

June 23: With Israel having made no move to comply with SC Res. 242, Egypt's Pres. Nasser warns that Egypt will if necessary use force to recover the Sinai. Israel, which has been erecting "settlements" in preferred portions of occupied Egypt, begins to construct fortifications along the east bank of the Suez Canal, and to employ the IAF as "flying artillery" to prevent Egypt's "incursion" into its own territory. In Dec., U.S. Sec. of State William Rogers presents a "peace plan" which consists mainly of Israeli compliance with SC Res. 242 in exchange for American guarantees of Israel's security. Israel rejects the proposition and, on Jan. 7, 1970, inaugurates a campaign of airstrikes deep in *unoccupied* Egyptian territory; by the time the campaign ends on Apr. 13, Israeli pilots—most of them flying F-4 Phantom aircraft provided by the U.S.—have flown more than 3,300 sorties and dropped upwards of 8,000 tons of ordnance on targets west of the Suez. On June 19, Rogers submits a second proposal, essentially reiterating the first, but adding significant increases in military aid as a side deal. This, Israel "accepts" (see the entry for Nov. 2, 1967), but then fails to follow through on. The U.S. nonetheless delivers the promised weaponry, thus violating the spirit, if not the letter, of SC Res. 18.

Aug. 26: The U.S. endorses SC Res. 270, condemning "premeditated" Israeli air attacks on villages in southern Lebanon in violation of SC Resolutions 233 (1967) and 234 (1967), reaffirming both resolutions, and renewing the threat of employing "more effective measures" of enforcement made in SC Resolutions 228 (1966) and 262 (1968). The airstrikes continue.

Nov. 22: The U.S. tentatively endorses, but fails to ratify the American Convention on Human Rights, which enters into force on July 18, 1978, with 25 state parties. As of this writing, the U.S. is the only OAS member-state not to have accepted the law's binding effect.

Dec. 18: The U.S. endorses UNGA Res. 2444, affirming Respect for Human Rights in Armed Conflicts, requiring that "a distinction be made at all times between persons taking part in the hostilities and members of the civilian population," and prohibiting "attacks against the civilian population as such." U.S. military policy in Indochina is plainly in flat violation of such provisions, and will remain so until 1975, however.

1970

Jan. 30: The U.S. endorses SC Res. 276, reaffirming the right of the Namibian people to self-determination under provision of UNGA Res. 1514 (XV)—the 1960 Declaration on the Granting of Independence to Colonial Countries and Peoples—and termination of South Africa's mandate in Namibia under provision of SC Res. 264 (1969), "strongly condemning" South Africa's refusal to comply with either resolution, and declaring South Africa's continued occupation of Namibia to be illegal. Unlike its earlier performance vis-à-vis Korea, and later with regard to Iraq, the U.S. insists that the best approach to the problem is for the Security Council to create a committee to study ways and means of enforcement.

Mar. 17: 9 of 15 Security Council member-states endorse draft res. S/9696 + Corr. 1,2, calling for an end to the white supremacist régime in Rhodesia. The U.S. joins the UK in vetoing the resolution (final vote: 9-2-4).

Mar. 18: Cambodia's neutralist head of state, Prince Sihanouk—viewed by the Nixon administration as being overly sympathetic to Hanoi—is deposed by a CIA-backed clique headed by the country's much more U.S.-oriented prime minister, Lon Nol. On May 1, Nixon orders a massive "preventive incursion" by U.S./South Vietnamese ground forces into the Cambodian border region in order to destroy "Communist sanctuaries"; Lon Nol protests that he'd neither been informed of nor approved the invasion (the troops are withdrawn on June 29). The U.S. "incursion" violates numerous articles of the UN Charter, UNGA Resolutions 337A (V), 380 (V) and 2131 (XX), several provisions of the SEATO Treaty, and numerous elements of the laws of war.

Mar. 19: CIA Dir. William Colby, testifying before the Senate Foreign Relations Committee, discloses the existence of the "Phoenix Program," initiated under his orders in 1967 to "eradicate the Communist infrastructure" in Vietnam's southern zone. "Under Phoenix, or Phung Hoang, as it was called by the Vietnamese, due process was totally nonexistent. South Vietnamese civilians whose names appeared on blacklists could be kidnapped, tortured, detained for...years without trial, or...murdered, simply on the word of an anonymous informer. At its height Phoenix managers imposed quotas of eighteen hundred neutralizations per month." Although Colby indicates that 1967 intelligence estimates indicated the presence of "about 75,000 Communist political cadres operating in the South," well over 50,000 people have been assassinated by Phoenix operatives at the time he testifies, and at least double that number arbitrarily arrested, subjected to prolonged "interrogation" and incarcerated for indeterminate periods under atrocious conditions; simple arithmetic thus suggests that, by the CIA's own estimates, at least 1 in every 2 persons "neutralized" are innocent bystanders (actually, there's little evidence that more than a few, if any, of the victims are actual "Communist cadres"). The Phoenix Program, which is continued until the collapse of "South Vietnam" in 1975, is unquestionably conducted in violation of the 1949 Geneva Convention IV, UNGA Res. 2444, the Universal Declaration of Human Rights, the UN Standard Minimum Rules for the Treatment of Prisoners, the International Covenant on Civil and Political Rights, and numerous elements of international law.

May 12: The U.S. endorses SC Res. 280, demanding the withdrawal of Israeli troops from southern Lebanon, condemning Israel's "premeditated military action" there in violation of SC Resolutions 262 (1968) and 270 (1969), reaffirming both resolutions, and declaring that further such actions "cannot be tolerated." The threat of resort to "more effective measures of enforcement, as provided in the [UN] Charter," already made in SC Resolutions 228 (1966), 262 (1968) and 270 (1969), is once again repeated. The U.S., however, blocks inclusion of any actual enforcement provisions. Israeli troops remain in Lebanon.

July 29: The U.S. endorses SC Res. 283, reaffirming SC Resolutions 264 (1969) and 276 (1970), expressing "deep concern" that South Africa has failed to comply with either resolution by withdrawing its troops from Namibia, and requesting that all UN member-states refrain from any relations with South Africa that might imply that its illegal occupation is legitimate. A comprehensive embargo is then proclaimed, not of South Africa but of *Namibia.*

Aug. 10: The body of former Richmond, Indiana, police chief Dan Mitrione is discovered in the trunk of a car in Montevideo. He had been kidnapped a few days earlier by Uruguay's Tupamaro guerrillas, interrogated at considerable length, then executed when the Uruguayan government, backed by the U.S., had refused to exchange imprisoned rebels for his release. Ultimately, the spectacular incident lifted the lid on a State Department program, dubbed the "Office of Public Safety," administered by U.S. AID with ample CIA collaboration, which, since Pres. John F. Kennedy approved it in 1961, had been systematically training and organizing key members of Latin American police forces to utilize such "countersubversive" techniques as torture, bombing and assassination. Mitrione, for example, who turned out to be a veteran OPS operative who served in Brazil before being posted to Uruguay, maintained a soundproofed torture chamber in the basement of his home as a "training facility." The OPS, which provided similar "services" in virtually every country south of the Río Grande, was largely responsible for creating the quasiofficial death squads so endemic to the Latin American context. It also violated virtually every clause in the Universal Declaration of Human Rights, the American Declaration on the Rights and Duties of Man, the American Convention on Human Rights, the UN Standard Minimum Rules for the Treatment of Prisoners, among numerous other elements of international human rights law, and UNGA Resolutions 380 (V) and 2131 (XX).

Sept. 13: Under strong pressure from the U.S., Jordan's King Hussein moves to disarm PLO guerrillas based in refugee camps along the east bank of the Jordan River. When Syria intervenes in behalf of the Palestinians, the U.S. requests mobilization of Israeli forces. A complete regional conflagration is averted only when the PLO announces that it will relocate the bulk of its personnel to Lebanon. Insofar as the U.S. secured no UN authorization before instigating a military conflict, its role in precipitating "Black September" constitutes violation of various articles falling under Chapters I, VI and VII of the UN Charter, as well as UNGA Resolutions 337A (V), 380 (V), 2131 (XX) and 2444.

Oct. 24: The U.S. declines to endorse UNGA Res. 2625 (XXV), the Declaration on the Principles of International Law Concerning Friendly Relations and Cooperation Among States in Accordance with the Charter of the United Nations. Among other things, the Declaration sets forth the duty of all states to "refrain from any forcible action which deprives people...of their self-determination, and freedom and independence." Setting aside the obvious U.S. pattern of doing just the opposite in Third World countries, the FBI and collaborating police agencies are even then engaging in repressive operations designed to destroy the Puerto Rican independence movement—on both the island and the mainland—by way of a "domestic counterintelligence program" (COINTELPRO) involving numerous assassinations and political imprisonments (including transparently false imprisonments). An entirely similar program is also being pursued with regard to elements of the black liberation movement, notably the Black Panther Party and the Republic of New Afrika (RNA), while another will shortly be undertaken against the American Indian Movement (AIM). COINTELPRO, by whatever name, violates Articles 6-10 of the Universal Declaration of Human Rights and Articles 9 and 14 of the International Covenant on Civil and Political Rights. Additionally, since the targets consist primarily of peoples of color, it violates Article 5 of the International Convention on the Elimination of All Forms of Racial Discrimination.

1971

Apr. 5: A package containing 7.7 kilograms of Double U-O Globe brand heroin, shipped via the U.S. military postal service in Bangkok, is seized at Ft. Monmouth, NJ. In Nov., another 13.5 kilos of Double U-O Globe is seized in possession of a Filipino diplomat posted to Vientienne, Laos, as he tries to clear customs in New York. These seizures correspond to a sharp increase in the quantity of opiates grown in the "Golden Triangle" of northern Burma and smuggled into the U.S. The massive influx triggers the "great heroin epidemic of 1971–72,"a phenomenon concentrated mainly in America's inner cities. In charge of the source is a "secret army" of Hmong ("Meo") tribesmen headed by Vang Pao, a CIA client, which is otherwise employed by the Agency to combat Pathet Lao guerrillas and attack North Vietnamese supply lines in Laos. Profits from sales are used to fund Vang's military operations, thus circumventing the need for the CIA to report them as a part of its annual budget. The Hmongs themselves have been convinced by the Agency, much as the Kurds at about the same time (see the entry for Mar. 24, 1974), that their sacrifices are being put towards establishment of their own free state (a "commitment" the CIA has neither the authority nor the inclination to honor). In the end, Hmong society, which is considered expendable by all parties to the conflict, is very nearly destroyed, while the polity of neutral Laos is severely destabilized. The flood of heroin into U.S. ghettos, meanwhile, appears to have been calculated to narcotize the country's then-burgeoning black liberation movement in much the same way that LSD and other hallucinogens were employed to undermine the white "new left" movement a few years earlier (see the entry for Apr. 13, 1953). CIA involvement in the opium trade violates an international protocol adopted in 1953 for purposes of eliminating it. U.S. operations in Laos more generally violate several articles concerning the rights of neutral states included in the 1899 Hague Convention II on Land Warfare, the 1907 Hague Convention V Respecting the Rights and Duties of Neutral Powers and Persons in Case of War on Land. The CIA's manipulation of the Hmongs violate Articles II(b), II(c) and III(e) of the Genocide Convention.

Apr. 14: 1st Lt. Michael J. Uhl, an intelligence officer with the Americal Div. from Nov. 1968–Apr. 1969, testifies before a congressional committee with regard to standard "interrogation techniques"—i.e., torture—applied to prisoners, both military and civilian, captured by U.S. forces in Vietnam.

These include not only endemic beatings, rapes and similar crudities, but the use of more sophisticated techniques like electric shock and the so-called water torture. Summary execution is also reported to be a regular occurrence. The performance of South Vietnamese forces is even worse, albeit what the Vietnamese do is all but invariably done under the watchful eyes of American "advisers" (and, in point of fact, the South Vietnamese forces would not exist, absent U.S. support). Worst of all is the sprawling prison compound on Con Son Island, nominally administered by the South Vietnamese, but built by the U.S. and actually presided over by a State Dept. employee, Frank Walton (former police commander in the Watts district of Los Angeles; the program is similar to that of the OPS in Latin America), in which thousands of Vietnamese scooped up by the CIA's Phoenix Program are held for years in open air "tiger cages" (on Phoenix, see the entry for Mar. 19, 1970). Overall, the treatment of prisoners by the U.S. and its Vietnamese clients is in violation of Articles 4–7 and 14–20 of the 1907 Hague Convention Respecting the Laws and Customs of War on Land, the 1949 Geneva Convention I for the Amelioration of the Conditions of the Wounded and Sick in Armed Forces in the Field, the 1949 Geneva Convention III Relative to the Treatment of Prisoners of War, the 1949 Geneva Convention IV Relative to the Protection of Civilian Persons in Time of War, UNGA Res. 2444, the Standard Minimum Rules for the Treatment of Prisoners (1955), and the Universal Declaration on Human Rights.

Apr. 16: Journalist Fred Branfman, who has spent the period Mar. 1967–Feb. 1971 in neutral Laos, testifies before a congressional committee concerning the "secret" U.S. saturation bombing of the country's Plain of Jars and contiguous areas, begun in earnest in 1969. Inundated in barely 2 years by the same bomb tonnage as was expended by the U.S. in all theaters during World War II, the roughly 50,000 sq. mile target zone has become "the most heavily-bombed area in the history of warfare" by the time Branfman's testimony is entered. By the end of 1969, more than 75 percent of the region's villages have been completely destroyed, the local civilian population of 900,000 forced to live mostly underground to avoid the white phosphorous and cluster bombs being rained upon them. At least 100,000 are dead by early 1971, score of thousands of others maimed, and the bombing continues with little interruption until May 1973. From start to finish, the bombing of Laos is conducted in violation of several articles concerning the rights of neutral states included in the 1899 Hague Convention II on Land Warfare, the 1907 Hague Convention V Respecting the Rights and Duties of Neutral Powers and Persons in Case of War on Land, the 1923 Hague Rules of Aerial Warfare, the 1949 Geneva Convention IV, numerous articles falling under Chapters I, VI, VII, XI and XII of the UN Charter, and UNGA Resolutions 380 (V), 2131 (XX) and 2444.

Sept. 25: The U.S. endorses SC Res. 298, noting Israel's noncompliance with SC Resolutions 252 (1968) and 267 (1969), as well as UNGA Resolutions 2253 (ES-V) and 2254 (ES-V), reaffirming both Security Council resolutions, and calling upon Israel to rescind its efforts to alter the political status of Jerusalem. The U.S. blocks inclusion of enforcement provisions.

Oct. 20: The U.S. endorses SC Res. 301, reaffirming SC Resolutions 264 (1969), 276 (1970) and 283 (1970), and renewing the call for member states to participate in the arms embargo of South Africa declared in SC Res. 282 (1970). The U.S. remains a major supplier of weaponry and weapons technology to the targeted country.

1972

Feb. 4: The U.S. endorses SC Res. 310, condemning the ongoing refusal of South Africa to comply with UN resolutions pertaining to Namibia and calling on member-states to honor the embargo of Namibia imposed under provision of SC Res. 283 (1970). Once again, the threat of a U.S. veto restricts the Council to threatening rather than imposing more "effective steps or measures in accordance with the [UN] Charter" if South Africa does not immediately comply.

Feb. 28: The U.S. endorses SC Res. 313, demanding that Israel "desist and refrain" from further ground or air action against Lebanon, which had begun a few months earlier in an effort to deny basing area to PLO guerrillas, and to immediately withdraw its troops from the southern portion of the country. The U.S. renders this reiteration of SC Res. 280 (1970) even more vacuous than the original. Israeli forces remain in southern Lebanon, and the airstrikes continue.

Mar. 16: Israeli PM Golda Meir, referred to as "Golda the Intransigent," rejects a proposal by Jordan's King Hussein to simultaneously resolve the issues of Israeli occupation of the West Bank and of Palestinian refugees, by creating a Palestinian state therein. Instead, in August, Meir's government publishes a position paper called the *Galilee Document*, announcing a policy of militarily reinforcement of accelerated Jewish settlement in the occupied territories, thereby establishing Israel's "permanent right" to them. Although this openly annexationist policy is enunciated in flat defiance of SC Res. 242 and numerous other Security Council resolutions, and thus constitutes a flagrant violation of the London and UN Charters, U.S. military and financial assistance to Israel continues unabated.

Apr. 10: The U.S. endorses the Convention on the Prohibition of the Development, Production and Stockpiling of Bacteriological (Biological) and Toxin Weapons and on Their Destruction. The Convention is duly ratified by the Senate and enters into force in U.S. domestic law on Mar. 26, 1975. To all accounts, however, U.S. development, and at least limited production and stockpiling, of such weapons continues without interruption. The U.S. has also been a major proliferator of the base stocks going into the development and production of such weapons by other countries (notably, Iraq; see entry for Jan. 24, 1947).

June 26: The U.S. endorses SC Res. 316, expressing "grave concern" over persistent Israeli violation of SC Resolutions 262 (1966), 270 (1969), 280 (1970), 285 (1970) and 313 (1972). The U.S. manages to hold the resolution to the level of a rhetorical statement.

July 21: The U.S. endorses SC Res. 317, condemning Israeli abductions of Syrian and Lebanese military and security personnel, and ordering their immediate return. The resolution also condemns Israeli violence more generally, and threatens "further action" if Israel fails to comply with the UN Charter and all relevant Security Council resolutions. The U.S. once again blocks inclusion of any tangible enforcement provisions, however, and Israel refuses to comply with the demand for release of its captives—until it is ready—and its broader policies remain unaltered.

Sept. 10: 13 of 15 Security Council member-states endorse draft res. S/10784, condemning persistent Israeli violations of its 1967 ceasefire agreement with neighboring states. The U.S. employs its veto to override them (final vote: 13-1-1).

Nov. 29: The U.S. abstains from voting on UNGA Res. 2932A (XXVII), deploring the use of napalm and other incendiary weapons in all conflicts. Although the frame of reference adopted by the Gen. Assembly includes the then ongoing use of substantial quantities of such ordnance by Portugal in its efforts to repress national liberation movements in its African colonies of Angola, Cape Verde, Mozambique and Guinea Bisseau—this was specifically condemned in UNGA Res. 2810 (XXVII) on Nov. 14—the main focus is upon the unprecedented quantity of incendiary munitions being used, often against civilian-populated targets, by U.S. forces in Indochina. All told, it is credibly estimated that about 400,000 tons of aerial incendiary ordnance— mostly napalm, but also including 70 mm white phosphorous rockets and thermite cluster bombs—are expended by U.S. fliers over the southern zone of Vietnam alone by 1973. In addition, U.S. ground forces use some 375,000 tons of incendiary thickening oil (mixed at a 10:1 ratio for usage), 600,000 XM-191 napalm rockets, 379 *million* white phosphorous hand grenades, an almost equal number of thermite grenades, and an untold—but huge—number of incendiary artillery rounds. Scores of thousands of Vietnamese civilians are thus subjected to a very literal holocaust—i.e., they are "consumed by fire"—while hundreds of thousands of others are maimed, rendered homeless, and so on. Although the use of such weapons is in itself not technically illegal at the time, it is certainly contrary to both the spirit of the 1907 Hague Convention IV Respecting the Laws and Customs of Land War, and the letter of the 1958 International Red Cross Draft Rules for the Protection of the Civilian Population from the Dangers of Indiscriminate Warfare. It is also undertaken in a manner violating the 1949 Geneva Convention IV, UNGA Res. 2444, and, arguably, Articles II(a), II(b), II(c), III(b) and III(d) of the Genocide Convention.

Nov. 29: The U.S. "accepts" UNGA Res. 2936, on the Non-Use of Force in International Relations and Permanent Prohibition of the Use of Nuclear Weapons. U.S. foreign policy, which is all but completely contingent upon the application of one or another "force increment"—or at least the threat of it—remains entirely unchanged.

Dec. 1: John Whitlam takes office as Australia's Prime Minister, reflecting the Labor Party's first significant electoral victory in 23 years. By Jan.

1973, Whitlam has recalled the last of his country's military forces from Vietnam, pointing out that the SEATO Treaty had never required their presence in the first place, and sets about extending Australia's formal recognition to the Hanoi government. The CIA, which had expended millions of dollars over preceding months in an effort to prevent such an outcome—i.e., attempting to subvert Australia's domestic political process—then goes to work to unseat Whitlam. Finally, in 1975, as the result of a convoluted procedure involving the channeling of additional millions to the Liberals and others of Australia's opposition parties, the Agency is able to bring about Whitlam's dismissal by John Kerr, a longtime CIA asset serving at the time as Australia's unelected Governor-General. Once again, in a gross violation of the 1970 Declaration on Principles of International Law Concerning Friendly Relations and Co-operation Among States in Accordance With the Charter of the United Nations (esp. Chapter I), as well as UNGA Resolutions 337A (V), 380 (V) and 2131 (XX)—not to mention the actual provisions of the SEATO Treaty—"democracy has been repealed in the name of preserving democracy."

1973

Jan. 23: Sec. of State Henry Kissinger initials the Paris Peace Accords, by which the U.S. finally acknowledges what was made abundantly clear in the Geneva Accords of 1954: Vietnam is one country, not two. The U.S. also agrees by way of a codicil attaching to Article 21 of the 1973 Accords to pay the Hanoi government some $4 billion in reparations as the result of damage inflicted during America's sustained effort to thwart the self-determining rights of the Vietnamese people (it is noteworthy that the Vietnamese had been offering exactly the same package since Nixon took office in 1969; he could have signed it at any point in the interim, thus sparing the lives of well over a million Indochinese, and about half of all U.S. personnel killed during the war). Having thus achieved "peace with honor," Nixon promptly reneges on the deal, setting out through massive infusions of military matériel and air support to sustain "South Vietnam" as a separate country (the policy is referred to as "Vietnamization"). He also announces that no reparations will be paid until every American serviceman missing in action during the war has been accounted for by the Hanoi government (no suggestion is made that the U.S. might account for any of the 200,000–300,000 Vietnamese soldiers missing by that point). Insofar as the 2,273 American MIAs—as compared to 78,794 still missing from World War II, and more than 8,100 from the Korean "police action"—are known to have been lost in aircraft that crashed into the South China Sea and other areas outside the northern zone of Vietnam, the demand is obviously impossible to fulfill. As of 2003, although only *one* U.S. serviceman is still listed as MIA in Vietnam, the agreed-to reparations remain unpaid.

Mar. 21: 13 of 15 Security Council member-states endorse draft res. S/10931/Rev. 1, affirming Panama's ultimate sovereignty over the U.S.-leased Canal Zone. The U.S. employs its veto to override them (final vote: 13-1-1).

May 22: 11 of 15 Security Council member-states endorse draft res. S/10928, calling for and end to the white supremacist régime in Rhodesia. The U.S. joins the UK in vetoing the resolution (final vote: 11-2-2).

July 26: 13 of 15 Security Council member-states endorse draft res. S/10974, calling for a "comprehensive examination of the Middle East situation." The U.S. employs its veto to override them (final vote: 13-1-0; China does not participate).

Sept. 11: Duly-elected Chilean Pres. Salvador Allende, a leftist, is killed during a military coup. Chile had been the target of an increasingly stringent U.S. embargo, meant to demonstrate that "socialism doesn't work," since almost the moment of Allende's election in 1970. When preliminary results show in 1973 that the Allende government has actually *gained* in popular support, the CIA begins to pass along sanitized weaponry and munitions to a group of military plotters headed by Gen. Augusto Pinochet. In the aftermath, operating on the premise that, "to remain pure, democracy must occasionally be bathed in blood," the Pinochet régime, with full U.S. support, inaugurates a liquidation of the left that claims thousands of dead, thousands more tortured and arbitrarily imprisoned. Under CIA tutelage, Pinochet's intelligence service, the DINA, interfaces with the Omega 7 group of Cuban émigrés to form a hemispheric terror apparatus designed to prevent further leftist victories at the polls. Probably the most spectacular action undertaken by this malignant combine was the Sept. 21, 1976, assassination by car bomb of former Allende diplomat Orlando Letelier—a U.S. national, Ronni Moffit, was also killed in the blast—in Washington, D.C. Suffice it here to observe that the U.S. campaign to eliminate the Allende government violated the 1970 Declaration on Principles of International Law Concerning Friendly Relations and Co-operation Among States in Accordance With the Charter of the United Nations (esp. Chapters I, VI, VII and IX), Chapters I, II, IV, V and VI of the OAS Charter and UNGA Resolutions 337A (V), 380 (V) and 2131 (XX), among many other elements of international law. U.S. support to the Pinochet régime during its brutal purge of the left—a matter amounting to complicity, if not more active participation—violated the Universal Declaration of Human Rights, and the CIA's involvement in the Letelier assassination violated the 1973 Convention on the Prevention and Punishment of Crimes Against Internationally Protected Persons, Including Diplomatic Agents, to which the U.S. was/is a signatory.

Oct. 6: Utterly frustrated with the failure of 6 years of diplomatic efforts to convince Israel to comply with SC Res. 242, and convinced by the *Galilee Document* that Israeli intentions run in exactly the opposite direction (see the entry for Mar 16, 1972), Egypt and Syria launch a joint attempt to resolve the issue militarily. The Arab armies are initially highly successful, and are brought to a halt only though desperate maneuvers overseen by Israeli Defense Minister Moshe Dayan. A ceasefire is effected on Oct. 22, in response to SC Res. 338, and confirmed a day later by SC Res. 339, which calls for both sides to return to the positions they occupied when the fighting broke out, and for an immediate implementation of SC Res. 242. Sec. of State Henry Kissinger, in whose hands U.S. policy had already been reduced to "support for Israel and for the status quo" of illegal occupation, begins a process of "shuttle diplomacy" to try and salvage the situation.

Oct. 25: The U.S. endorses SC Res. 340, noting Israel's continual violation of its ceasefire agreement with Egypt, and again calls upon both parties to return to the positions they occupied at 1650 hours GMT on Oct. 22. As usual, however, the U.S. ensures that no penalties are attached to Israel's violations.

Nov. 30: The U.S. abstains from voting on UNGA Res. 3068 (XXVIII), the International Convention on the Suppression and Punishment of the Crime of "Apartheid." The Convention is never submitted to the Senate for ratification, although it enters into force internationally on July 18, 1976. U.S. relations with South Africa, which is the immediate target of the Convention, remain unimpaired.

Dec. 6: The U.S. abstains from voting on UNGA Res. 3076 (XXVIII), which invites the International Conference on the Reaffirmation and Development of International Humanitarian Law Applicable in Armed Conflicts to seek agreement on the prohibition of napalm and other incendiary weapons. U.S. reliance upon such munitions in Indochina remains unaltered.

Dec. 12: The U.S. declines to endorse UNGA Res. 3103 (XXVIII), affirming that imprisoned members of bona fide national liberation movements, as defined by Article 1, Para. 4 of Protocol I Additional to the 1949 Geneva Conventions, "are to be accorded the status of prisoners of war." At the time—and now—the U.S. is incarcerating numerous members of the Black Panther Party, RNA, AIM and the Puerto Rican independence movement, all of whom qualify, but none of whom are treated as POWs (see the entries for Oct. 24, 1970, and May 11, 1976).

Dec. 14: The U.S. declines to endorse UNGA Res. 3151G (XXVII), which condemns *inter alia* the "unholy alliance" between South African racism and zionism.

Dec. 17: The U.S. declines to endorse UNGA Res. 3171 (XXVII), which augments the 1962 UNGA Res. 1803 (XVII) by reasserting the permanent sovereignty of all states, including those of the Third World, over natural resources within their borders. U.S. foreign/trade policy continues to evolve in contradiction to both resolutions.

1974

Jan. 18: The first of the Kissinger-brokered disengagement agreements resulting from Israel's latest war with its Arab neighbors (see the entry for Oct. 6, 1973) is signed by Egypt. By its terms, the Egyptians recover the east bank of the Suez Canal and all of the Sinai as far east as the Mitla Pass, while Israel (re)commits itself to implementation of SC Resolutions 242 and

338. It should be noted that Israeli "concessions" are greater than those required by Egypt in a 1971 proposal rejected by Israel. Had the 1971 proposal been accepted, Egypt's participation in the 1973 war would likely have been averted. In any event, the 1974 quid pro quo for Israel's partial compliance with SC Res. 242—and its renewed promise of full compliance at some nebulous "later date"—is Kissinger's side agreement to increase levels of U.S. financial/military aid. The entire U.S. posture under Kissinger is constructed in violation of UNGA Res. 337A (V); the arms provisions encompassed in his side agreement is a violation of the spirit, if not the letter, of SC Res. 18.

Mar. 22: A CIA memo reveals that since 1972, at the request of Iran's Reza Shah Pahlavi, the U.S.—in an operation not dissimilar to those run a few years earlier with regard to the Hmongs in Laos and the Montagnards of Vietnam—has been secretly arming and organizing a Kurdish revolt in northern Iraq. While, like the erstwhile tribal peoples of Indochina, the Kurds have been conned into believing they're being supported in their desire to (re)assert control over their own territory, the real objective is to use them to undermine the Iraqi position during a border dispute with Iran. Once Iran and Iraq reach an accord in Mar. 1975, the Kurds are immediately abandoned. The Iraqis move swiftly to crush their revolt and some 200,000 Kurdish refugees flood into Iran, from whence at least 40,000 are shortly pushed back into Iraq. Kurdish society suffers great damage in the process. Aside from its obvious violations of the 1970 Declaration on Principles of International Law Concerning Friendly Relations and Co-operation Among States in Accordance With the Charter of the United Nations (esp. Chapters I, VI and VII), as well as UNGA Resolutions 380 (V) and 2131 (XX), the U.S. initiative arguably contravenes Chapters XI and XII of the UN Charter. It is also undertaken in blatant violation of the 1949 Geneva Convention IV, UNGA Res. 2444, and Articles II(c), III(b) and III(e) of the Genocide Convention.

May 1: The U.S. declines to endorse UNGA Res. 3201 (S-VI), the Declaration of a New Economic Order. U.S. foreign/trade policy, and the ambitions of its transnational corporations, contradict virtually every aspect of the Declaration, especially those articles asserting the rights to sovereignty, self-determination and control over natural resources vested in Third World peoples.

May 31: The second of the Kissinger-brokered disengagement agreements resulting from Israel's latest war with its Arab neighbors (see the entry for Oct. 6, 1973) is signed by Syria. By its terms, Israel relinquishes all territory taken during the 1973 war, as well as a portion of the Golan Heights area seized in 1967, and (re)commits itself to implementation of SC Resolutions 242 and 338. The quid pro quo for Israel's partial compliance with the law has already been worked out vis-à-vis the earlier disengagement agreement with Egypt (see the entry for Jan. 18, 1974). It is a testament to Kissinger's skills as a self-promoting propagandist that the disengagement agreements—which really amount to a tacit sanction of ongoing

Israeli illegalities—are usually remembered as a major accomplishment in behalf of "international law and order."

Oct. 28: Meeting in Rabat, Morocco, the Arab League passes a resolution affirming the PLO as being "the sole legitimate representative of the Palestinian people," and reaffirming the right of Palestinians to national self-determination. In Nov., the UN General Assembly adopts a similar resolution after an address by PLO Chairman Yasser Arafat, with Israel and the U.S. casting the only negative votes. Although Arafat's Palestinian National Council had from its founding articulated a preference for a "political settlement" with Israel as early as 1964 (see the entry for Sept. 5–11, 1964)—a position clearly implying willingness to accept creation of a Palestinian state *alongside* Israel—the Israelis, backed by the U.S., adamantly refuse to recognize/negotiate with the PLO on the spurious basis that the organization "refuses to acknowledge the right of Israel to exist" (which, legally-speaking, it lacks, at least until such time as Palestine's self-determining rights are accommodated). Insofar as it thus leaves the Palestinians no alternative but to engage in armed struggle—i.e., to wage a bona fide "war of national liberation"—the Israeli/U.S. position constitutes a fundamental violation of both the UN Charter's first chapter and UNGA Res. 337A (V).

Oct. 30: 10 of 15 Security Council member-states endorse draft res. S/11543, revoking South Africa's UN membership. The U.S. joins the UK and France in vetoing the resolution (final vote: 10-3-2).

Nov. 16: The UN World Food Conference, meeting in Rome, unanimously adopts the Universal Declaration on the Eradication of Hunger and Malnutrition. The U.S. endorses the Declaration, but thereafter refuses to acknowledge food as a fundamental human right (see, as examples, the entries for Dec. 14, 1981; Dec. 18, 1982, Dec. 16, 1984, and Dec. 19, 2001).

Dec. 9: The U.S. abstains from voting on UNGA Res. 3255A (XXIX), expressing appreciation to the Red Cross for volunteering to compile information preparatory to the convening of an international conference to draft a convention outlawing napalm and other incendiary weapons. U.S. reliance upon such weapons in Indochina remains unaltered.

Dec. 9: The U.S. abstains from voting on UNGA Res. 3255B (XXIX), urging all UN member-states to refrain from using napalm and other incendiary weapons, pending an international convention prohibiting them. U.S. reliance upon such munitions in Indochina remains unaltered.

Dec. 12: The U.S. declines to endorse UNGA Res. 3281 (XXIX), the Charter of Economic Rights and Duties of States, most of which contradicts U.S. foreign/trade policy and the "global reach" increasingly displayed by American transnational corporations (what the U.S. had in mind at the time was already something along the lines of the General Agreement on Tariffs and Trade [GATT]).

Dec. 14: The U.S. "accepts" UNGA Res. 3314 (XXIX), on the Definition of Aggression, although a substantial portion of U.S. foreign policy falls within the scope of the definition, and thus violates the relevant articles in the UN Charter. U.S. foreign policy remains unchanged.

Dec. 17: The U.S. endorses SC Res. 366, which notes an International Court of Justice (ICJ) advisory opinion on Namibia entered on June 21, 1971, as well as a host of UN resolutions condemning the ongoing occupation and "illegal and arbitrary imposition" of South African laws in Namibia, and demands that the Pretoria régime immediately comply with all relevant UN resolutions and the Universal Declaration of Human Rights. As has become customary by this point, the resolution ends with the threat that the Security Council is considering employment of "other measures" in accordance with the UN Charter, but the prospect of a U.S. veto prevents the resolution from being more than just another rhetorical gesture.

Dec. 22: Pres. Gerald Ford signs Public Law 93-531, the Navajo-Hopi Land Settlement Act of 1974, authorizing the forced removal of approximately 13,500 American Indians from their traditional landbase. Primarily targeted are the Big Mountain Diné (Navajo), a "discrete human group" within the meaning of international law. Although the U.S. claims the relocation is undertaken for the humanitarian purpose of separating the Diné from the Hopis, with whom they are allegedly locked in a bitter land dispute, it turns out that no such dispute exists (indeed, many Hopis support Diné resistance to relocation). In actuality, the federal motive is to remove the Diné population from the Big Mountain area of Arizona in order that a rich coal vein can be stripmined. By 1995, the relocation is virtually complete, and the Big Mountain Diné, scattered to the winds, destroyed as an identifiable group. The relocation is thus a violation of Articles II(b), II(c), III(a) and III(b) of the 1948 Genocide Convention, as well as the Universal Declaration of Human Rights and the American Convention on Human Rights.

1975

Jan. 4: Congress passes the so-called American Indian Self-Determination and Educational Assistance Act of 1975. The statute stands the international legal meaning of "self-determination" squarely on its head by authorizing the federal government to preside over all matters of policy pertaining to Indian rights and status, Indians themselves responsible for implementing/administering resulting programs. This political formulation, which derives from John Marshall's *Cherokee* opinions of the early 1830s, serves not only to rationalize ongoing U.S. colonization of indigenous nations within its claimed borders, but as a template for the concept of "internal self-determination" advanced by U.S. representatives in UN fora as being appropriate and applicable to native peoples everywhere in the world (see the entry for Jan. 18, 2001).

Jan. 22: The National Security Council's "40-Committee" authorizes the CIA to pass $300,000 to Holden Roberto, head of the FNLA, the most rightward-leaning of 3 major political factions in recently-decolonized Angola which had come together a week earlier to form a coalition government.

The alliance immediately shatters as Roberto makes his bid for dominance, unleashing a "civil war" that has continued to erupt, intermittently, into the present moment. In 1976, after a contingent of Cuban soldiers had been introduced to the fray in order to offset the CIA's expenditure of more than $1 million to import 300 American and an equal number of European mercenaries—the U.S. also provided "off the books" air support and training for Roberto's troops—Congress abruptly orders the CIA to terminate its involvement. Aware by then that it is fighting a losing battle, the Agency grudgingly obeys, leaving a power vacuum into which South Africa will be pouring its regular military units within a few months. At a minimum, the U.S. gambit in Angola violates the 1970 Declaration on Principles of International Law Concerning Friendly Relations and Co-operation Among States in Accordance With the Charter of the United Nations (esp. Chapters I, VI, VII, XI and XII), as well as UNGA Resolutions 337A (V), 380 (V) and 2131 (XX). Also, insofar as mercenaries were employed, it violates the prohibition on mercenaries established by the Organization of African Unity in 1963.

June 6: 10 of 15 Security Council member-states endorse draft res. S/11713, condemning South Africa's illegal occupation of Namibia. The U.S. joins the UK and France in vetoing the resolution (final vote: 10-3-2).

Aug. 11: 14 of 15 Security Council member-states endorse draft res. S/11795, granting UN membership to South Vietnam. The U.S. employs its veto to override them (final vote: 14-1-0).

Aug. 11: 14 of 15 Security Council member-states endorse draft res. S/11796, granting UN membership to North Vietnam. The U.S. employs its veto to override them (final vote: 14-1-0).

Aug. 31: Sec. of State Kissinger and Israeli PM Yitzhak Rabin reach an "understanding" in which the U.S. will triple its transfer of armaments to Israel—the deal adds up to $4 billion per year for 3 years—mostly consisting of advanced F-16 fighter aircraft and Pershing missiles. In exchange, Israel agrees to relinquish a narrow strip of the Sinai adjoining the Suez Canal, and to engage in "continuing negotiations" with Egypt concerning its compliance with SC Resolutions 242 and 338. The arrangement, orchestrated by Kissinger, violates both resolutions, which call not for protracted discussions, but rather for immediate and unconditional Israeli withdrawal from all territories occupied in 1967. The U.S. arms transfers to Israel also violate the spirit, if not the letter, of SC Res. 18.

Sept. 30: 14 of 15 Security Council member-states endorse draft res. S/11832, granting UN membership to South Vietnam. The U.S. employs its veto to override them (final vote: 14-1-0).

Sept. 30: 14 of 15 Security Council member-states endorse draft res. S/11833, granting UN membership to North Vietnam. The U.S. employs its veto to override them (final vote: 14-1-0).

Nov. 10: The U.S. refuses to endorse UNGA Res. 3379, which concludes that "zionism is a form of racism and racial discrimination," and therefore contrary to the 1963 Declaration on Elimination of All Forms of Racial Discrimination. Intense U.S. pressure prevents key signatories from following up with sanctions against Israel similar to those already imposed on South Africa.

Dec. 8: 13 of 15 Security Council member-states endorse draft res. S/11898, condemning Israel's continuing violation(s) of SC Res. 242. The U.S. employs its veto to override them (final vote: 13-1-1).

Dec. 9: The U.S. endorses UNGA Res. 3452 (XXX), the Declaration on Protection from Torture. At the time, however, practices defined as torture in the resolution are endemic in U.S. prisons, especially where political prisoners are concerned. Former Black Panther leader Geronimo ji Jaga (Elmer Gerard Pratt), to offer but one example among many, is just beginning the third of what will be 8.5 consecutive years of solitary confinement. Ji Jaga, who was falsely convicted of murder as the result of a COINTELPRO operation directed against him (see the entry for Oct. 24, 1970), ultimately serves 27 years of a life sentence before being exonerated in 1996.

Dec. 22: The U.S. endorses SC Res. 384, which deplores the intervention of Indonesia in East Timor as a violation of the 1960 Declaration on the Granting of Independence to Colonial Countries and Peoples, calls upon Indonesia to immediately withdraw its military forces, and upon all UN member-states to respect the territorial integrity and self-determining rights of the East Timorese. Although the "intervention" is actually a fullscale invasion involving a wholesale slaughter that ultimately claims the lives of about 200,000 East Timorese—35% of the population—the U.S. blocks inclusion of enforcement provisions which might be applied against its Indonesian client. Under the circumstances, this may be construed as, among other things, a violation of Article III(e) of the Genocide Convention.

1976

Jan. 25: 9 of 15 Security Council member-states endorse draft res. S/11940, calling for compliance with international law in the Middle East, esp. with regard to the Palestinian Question. The U.S. employs its veto to override them (final vote: 9-1-3; China and Libya do not participate).

Jan. 26: *Christian Century* reports that between 1971 and 1975 approximately 40% of all American Indian women of childbearing age were subjected to involuntary sterilizations in clinics administered by the Bureau of Indian Affairs. A bit later it is revealed that about the same proportion of Puerto Rican women were sterilized during roughly the same period in federally-sponsored clinics on the island. Although the U.S. contends that those suffering involuntary sterilization were selected on the basis of economic rather than "national, ethnical, racial or religious" criteria, and that its actions were therefore not genocidal in a strictly technical sense, the argument is transparent to the point of absurdity. The U.S. involuntary sterilization programs targeting American Indian and Puerto Rican women constitute a conspicuous violation of Articles II(d), III(a) and III(b) of the 1948

Genocide Convention, as well as the Universal Declaration of Human Rights and the American Convention on Human Rights.

Jan. 30: The U.S. endorses SC Res. 385, expressing "deep concern" over South Africa's continuing refusal to comply with SC Resolutions 245 (1968), 246 (1968), 264 (1969), 276 (1970), 282 (1970), 283 (1970), 284 (1970), 300 (1970), 301 (1971), 310 (1972) and 366 (1974), over South Africa's "brutal repression" of the Namibian people's aspirations to self-determination, over its persistent violation of their most fundamental human rights, over its efforts to destroy the national unity and territorial integrity of Namibia, and its "aggressive military build-up" in illegally occupied Namibian territory. The resolution calls for the Pretoria régime to "immediately comply" with all the above-listed Security Council resolutions, notes that the Council will "remain seized of the matter" and "consider taking appropriate measures under the [UN] Charter" unless South Africa does so. Again, this U.S.-engineered stance bears comparison to that adopted by the Security Council vis-à-vis Korea and Iraq, or, for that matter, the unilateralist approach taken by the U.S. with regard to Cuba and Indochina. Plainly, even as it joins in denouncing them—mainly for PR purposes—the U.S. is actively preventing any sort of effective international intervention to put an end to South Africa's illegalities.

Mar. 25: 14 of 15 Security Council member-states approve draft res. S/12022, deploring the situation created by Israeli illegalities in the occupied territories of Palestine. The U.S. employs its veto to override them (final vote: 14-1-0).

Mar. 31: The U.S. endorses SC Res. 387, which condemns South Africa's invasion of Angola by way of Namibia and demands that the invaders "scrupulously respect [both countries'] independence, sovereignty and territorial integrity." As usual, the U.S. prevents inclusion of enforcement provisions in the resolution.

Apr. 22: The U.S. endorses SC Res. 389, which calls upon Indonesia to "withdraw without further delay all its forces from East Timor." The U.S. sees to it that there is no more reference in this resolution to enforcement than there was in SC Res. 384 (1975).

May 11: Representatives of the U.S. Dept. of Justice present "true copies" of an affidavit in Canadian court to obtain the extradition of Leonard Peltier, a member of the American Indian Movement wanted for killing 2 FBI agents a few months earlier. Peltier is extradited, convicted, and sentenced to 2 consecutive life terms in federal prison before the affidavit presented in Canada is revealed to be a fabrication. In 1986, much of the evidence presented against Peltier at trial is shown to have been equally falsified, and that the FBI was in fact conducting a campaign of outright counterinsurgency warfare against AIM at the time its agents were killed. Under those circumstances, 60 members of Canada's House of Commons vote to demand Peltier's repatriation to Canada, and, on the basis of the U.S. perpetration of "documented treaty fraud," recommend termination of Canada's extradition treaty with the U.S. The U.S. refuses repatriation,

Peltier remains in prison as of this writing—although his prosecutors conceded nearly 20 years ago that they really "have no idea" who committed the acts for which he was convicted—and the U.S./Canadian extradition treaty remains in effect. Nonetheless, the 1976 U.S. maneuver violated Article 49 of the Vienna Convention on the Law of Treaties. It was also, and rather obviously, contrary to the1970 Declaration on Principles of International Law Concerning Friendly Relations and Co-operation Among States in Accordance With the Charter of the United Nations. The treatment of Peltier, personally, contravenes Articles 7-11 of the Universal Declaration of Human Rights, Articles I and II of the American Declaration of the Rights and Duties of Man, Article 9 of the International Covenant on Civil and Political Rights, and UNGA Res. 3103 (XXVIII). The treatment to which AIM has been subjected more generally, insofar as it conforms to the definition of a bona fide national liberation movement advanced therein, constitutes a pattern of violation of Article 1, Para. 4, of Protocol I Additional to the 1949 Geneva Conventions, Articles 1-6 of Protocol II Additional to the 1949 Geneva Conventions, and UNGA Res. 3103 (XXVIII).

June 19: The U.S. endorses SC Res. 392, expressing "deep shock" and "strong condemnation" of South Africa's massacre of blacks at Soweto on June 16, reaffirming that apartheid is a crime under international law, and once again calling upon South Africa to abolish it. At the insistence of U.S. delegates, nothing resembling a penalty or enforcement provision is included in the resolution.

June 23: 13 of 15 Security Council member-states endorse draft res. S/12110, granting UN membership to North Vietnam. The U.S. employs its veto to override them (final vote: 13-1-0; China not participating).

June 19: 10 of 15 Security Council member-states approve draft res. S/121119, accepting the first annual Report of the Special Committee on the Rights of Palestinians. The U.S. employs its vote to override them (final vote: 10-1-4).

July 30: The U.S. endorses SC Res. 393, "strongly condemning" South Africa's air attacks on Zambia as a "flagrant violation of [the country's] sovereignty and territorial integrity," and demanding that South Africa "scrupulously respect [its neighbors'] independence, sovereignty and territorial integrity." As usual, the U.S. prevents inclusion of enforcement provisions in the resolution.

Aug. 23: Israeli PM Rabin meets with Lebanese Maronite leader Camille Chamoun, entering a deal wherein the Maronite Phalange will "secure" southern Lebanon in exchange for Israel's provision of $150 million in weaponry (small arms, TOW missiles and obsolete tanks). The U.S. backs Israel's position, agreeing to replace whatever is transferred to the Maronites from Israeli inventories, thereby upgrading Israel's armored forces. The Israeli/U.S. intervention in Lebanon's internal affairs violates UNGA Resolutions 380 (V) and 2131 (XX), and both levels of the arms transfer arrangement violate SC 18 (1950).

Oct. 19: 10 of 15 Security Council member-states endorse draft res. S/12211, condemning South Africa's illegal occupation of Namibia and calling for a tightening of sanctions to compel withdrawal. The U.S. joins the UK and France in vetoing the resolution (final vote: 10-3-2).

Nov. 15: 14 of 15 Security Council member-states endorse draft res. S/12226, granting UN membership to the Socialist Republic of Vietnam (i.e., North and South Vietnam combined). The U.S. employs its veto to override them (final vote: 14-1-0).

Dec. 10: The U.S. endorses the Convention on the Prohibition of Military or Any Other Hostile Use of Environmental Modification Techniques (outlawing not only the kind of chemical defoliation effort undertaken by the U.S. in Indochina, and the weather modification techniques employed against both the Indochinese and the Cubans, but the sort of sustained saturation bombing—also employed extensively in Indochina—that irrevocably alters landscapes and often renders the soil itself unproductive). The Senate duly ratifies the treaty and it enters into force in U.S. domestic law on Jan 17, 1980. The U.S. has nonetheless continued to experiment with weather modification technologies, and has made extensive use of "improved" defoliants in Mexico, Columbia and elsewhere as part of the Reagan, Bush and Clinton administrations' so-called War on Drugs.

1977

May 17: The Likud party is voted into power in Israel, and Menachem Begin assumes the position of prime minister. In the manifesto by which it sets forth its central tenets, Likud explicitly forecloses any possibility of Israeli compliance with SC Resolutions 242 and 338: "Judea and Samaria [the West Bank] shall...not be relinquished to foreign rule; between the sea and Jordan, there will be Jewish sovereignty alone. Any plan that involves surrendering part of Western Eretz Israel militates against our right to the Land, would inevitably lead to the establishment of a 'Palestinian State' [and] endanger the existence of the State of Israel." Begin announces that it is "impossible" to consider recognizing or negotiating with the PLO, since it is an "organization dedicated to terrorism and led by one of the world's foremost terrorists [Yasser Arafat]." Unmentioned, is the fact that Begin himself, as head of the Irgun, was designated as a "leading terrorist" by British authorities in Palestine during the years before Israeli statehood. Among other things, he was wanted in connection with numerous assassinations and the notorious 1946 bombing of Jerusalem's King David Hotel. Despite the Likud's hypocritical and expressly illegal posture, U.S. relations with Israel remain effectively unchanged.

Sept. 17: The U.S.-brokered "Camp David Accords" between Israel and Egypt are signed. On this basis, a formal Israeli/Egyptian treaty, again brokered by the U.S., is signed on Mar. 26, 1979. By its terms, Israel is allowed to retain the Gaza Strip, but withdraws all its military forces from the Sinai and destroys the settlements it has erected therein since 1967, while Egypt agrees not to deploy its military forces at any point further east than the Mitla Pass. At the point the Israeli withdrawal is complete, Egypt agrees to normalize diplomatic relations with Israel—thus becoming the first Arab state to recognize Israel's right to exist absent a resolution of the fundamental illegalities attending its creation—to allow transit of Israeli shipping through the Suez Canal, and to guarantee Israel's supply of oil for 15 years (the U.S., as always, adds increased economic/military support to Israel as a "sweetener"). Both the Accords and the treaty also require that Israel proceed to resolve all other issues related to full implementation of SC Res. 242, notably by effecting a speedy withdrawal from the West Bank, but, on this, Begin reneges from almost the moment Egypt's formal recognition of Israel is conveyed. His order to *accelerate* the building of Jewish settlements in occupied Palestine constitutes such a blatant violation of the treaty terms—not to mention SC Resolutions 242 and 338—that it precipitates the resignation of no less than Moshe Dayan, who has been serving as Begin's defense minister. As for Egypt, its breaking of ranks with the Arab League results in its immediate expulsion (its readmission occurs only after its head of state, Anwar al-Sadat, is assassinated by army officers disgruntled by the treaty on Oct. 6, 1981). It being a firm principle of international law that recognition of the legitimacy of one state by another is irrevocable, Begin's subterfuge creates a *fait accompli*. Hence, while Egypt has complied with its obligations under the treaty, it is plain that Israel has neither reciprocated in full nor ever held the least intention of doing so (such a posture is contrary to the Vienna Convention on the Law of Treaties, esp. Article 49). Since the U.S. both guaranteed the deal struck in the Accords/treaty, and insofar as Israel's violations of it have resulted in no impairment of its relations with the U.S., the U.S. must be viewed as being at the very least complicit in these Israeli illegalities.

Sept. 22: Israel, in collaboration with South Africa, conducts its first test detonation of a nuclear weapon in the Kalahari Desert, violating both the 1963 Treaty Banning Nuclear Weapons Tests in the Atmosphere, in Outer Space, and Under Water and the 1970 Treaty on the Non-Proliferation of Nuclear Weapons. While neither South Africa nor Israel is a signatory to either treaty, Israeli nuclear weapons development has plainly been facilitated by longterm U.S. assistance in avoiding IAEC inspections of its Dimona reactor, and a concomitant default by the U.S. on its obligation under the Non-Proliferation Treaty to conduct such inspections itself (see the entry for July 1, 1968). Israel's cooperation with South Africa in this instance points to a chronic violation of the UN imposition of a comprehensive arms/trade embargo of the apartheid régime dating back to SC Res. 121 in 1963 (Israeli trade with South Africa exceeds $100 billion in 1975). In any event, it turns out that Israel is by this point possessed of about 100 nuclear warheads, as well as Jericho I missiles with which to deliver them; by 1980, its "Samson Option" is endowed with 200 warheads; by 1985, it has added hundreds of low-yield nuclear artillery rounds and landmines to its arsenal. Self-evidently, Israel's technical knowledge of weapons production is passed along to South Africa, which in 1970 announces discovery of a new and more efficient uranium enrichment procedure, ideal for producing weapons-grade material. Most significantly, the U.S. maintains cordial relations with Israel—and South Africa, for that matter—as if nothing has happened (indeed, U.S. refusal to discuss Israel's "secret" possession of the bomb virtually destroys its ability to negotiate a nonproliferation arrangement with Pakistan a short time later).

Oct. 31: The U.S. joins the UK and France in vetoing three separate draft resolutions—S/12310/Rev. 1 (final vote: 10-5-0); S/12311/Rev. 1 (final vote: 10-5-0); S/12312/Rev. 1 (final vote: 10-5-0)— designed to impose a variety of compulsory sanctions on South Africa as an expedient to forcing an end to apartheid. All three countries then join in a unanimous endorsement of SC Res. 417, condemning apartheid and calling upon all UN member-states to "voluntarily" undertake "appropriate measures" to bring it to a halt. U.S. policy towards Pretoria remains unchanged, of course.

Nov. 4: The U.S. endorses SC Res. 418, which imposes a mandatory arms embargo of South Africa until such time as it complies with all relevant UN resolutions. From the outset, the U.S., along with Israel, is a major circumventor.

Nov. 30: The U.S. endorses SC Res. 420, which calls for immediate implementation of the Arab-Israeli ceasefire required under SC Res. 338 (1973). Israel is the only state party actually violating the ceasefire. SC Res. 338 also requires immediate implementation of SC Res. 242 (1967), calling for Israeli withdrawal from the Golan Heights and the occupied territories of Palestine. As always, the U.S. prevents inclusion of enforcement provisions in SC Res. 420, allowing Israel to simply ignore it.

Dec. 9: The U.S. endorses SC Res. 421, reaffirming SC Res. 418 and calling for a study of ways and means to make the arms embargo of South Africa more effective. The U.S., along with Israel, continues to violate the embargo.

Dec. 12: The U.S. signs (with 1 "understanding" attached), but then fails to ratify, Protocol I Additional to the Geneva Conventions of 12 August 1949, and Relating to the Protection of Victims of International Armed Conflicts, which enters into force on Dec. 7, 1978. As of this writing, the U.S. has not joined 143 other UN member-states in accepting the law. Especially problematic from the U.S. perspective is the fact that Article 1, Para. 4 of Protocol I extends the same rights and protections to members of bona fide national liberation movements as are accorded those fighting in state military forces.

Dec. 12: The U.S. signs (with 2 "understandings" attached), but then fails to ratify, Protocol II Additional to the Geneva Conventions, which enters into force on Dec. 7, 1978. As of this writing, the U.S. has not joined 134 other UN member-states in accepting the law as binding upon its own actions and policies. Especially problematic from the U.S. perspective is the fact that Protocol II acknowledges the legitimacy of national liberation movements, clearly specifying that combatants do *not* have to "wear the uniform of a recognized state" in order to be entitled to Geneva Convention protections. On this basis, the current U.S. policy of declaring al-Qaida fighters to be "illegal combatants" is extremely dubious, and applying the principle to Taliban personnel is illegal on its face.

1978

Mar. 9: The U.S. endorses SC Res. 425, which confronts cross-border operations ordered a week earlier by PM Begin to "root out PLO terrorists" by calling upon Israel to "immediately cease its military action against Lebanese territorial integrity and [to] withdraw forthwith." As usual, the threat of a U.S. veto prevents inclusion of enforcement provisions, and the Israeli action continues. Given the ineffectuality of the UN response, the PLO itself moves to counter Israel's aggressive operations by bombing a bus on the Haifa-Tel Aviv road, killing 35. Begin then orders an outright invasion of Lebanon as far north as the Litani River, claiming the bus bombing and attendant "deaths of innocent civilians" as a pretext, but conveniently omitting mention of the fact that the bombing was in retaliation for the fact that Israeli forces had already slaughtered upwards of 200 noncombatant Palestinians and Lebanese. While the post-Mar. 11 Israeli escalation has almost no effect on the PLO—it simply withdraws north of the Litani—the IDF goes on a rampage in which, as Israeli historian Avi Shlaim describes it, "villages were destroyed, [other] war crimes committed, and thousands of peaceful citizens [were driven] from their homes." Among myriad other violations of international law, the Israeli offensive qualifies as aggression under provision of UNGA Res. 3314 (XXIX), and thus constitutes an offense under the 1945 London Charter (i.e., the crimes for which the nazis were tried).

Mar. 19: The U.S. endorses SC Res. 427, which calls upon Israel to withdraw from all Lebanese territory "without further delay." Since the U.S. again blocks the inclusion of enforcement provisions, the Israelis simply ignore the resolution.

May 6: The U.S. endorses SC Res. 428, which "strongly condemns the latest armed invasion perpetrated by the South African racist régime against the People's Republic of Angola" and continued illegal occupation of Namibia, demanding immediate withdrawal. Typically, the U.S. blocks inclusion of enforcement measures.

Sept. 29: The U.S. endorses SC Res. 435, which declares the unilateral decision by South Africa's "illegal administration" in Namibia to conduct elections null and void. The U.S. prevents inclusion of measures by which the declaration can be enforced.

Nov. 13: The U.S. endorses SC Res. 439, again condemning South Africa's decision to conduct elections in Namibia in contravention of SC Resolutions 435 and 385 (1976). The U.S. continues to block inclusion of enforcement provisions.

Dec. 15: 119 member-states endorse UNGA Res. 33/75, which calls upon the Security Council to "take all necessary measures" to ensure that

that United Nations decisions on the maintenance of international peace and security are observed. The U.S., joined by Israel, cast the only opposing votes.

Dec.18: 110 member-states endorse UNGA Res. 33/110, calling for steps to improve the living conditions of Palestinians. The U.S. and Israel cast the only votes against the resolution, and thereafter ignore it.

Dec. 18: 97 member-states endorse UNGA Res. 33/113C, condemning Israeli human rights violations committed against Palestinians. The U.S. and Israel, joined by Guatemala (which is receiving Israeli military support), vote against the resolution.

Dec. 19: 119 member-states endorse UNGA Res. 33/136, calling upon developed states to increase the quantity and quality of developmental support to underdeveloped countries. The U.S. alone votes against the resolution.

Dec. 20: The U.S. endorses UNGA Res. 33/173, the Resolution on Disappeared Persons, calling upon all UN member-states and related entities to locate and account for all such persons. Undoubtedly the worst offender in the world in this regard is at the time Argentina, a U.S. client whose security police—primarily responsible for the disappearances there—have been trained in such methods by the State Department's OPS program (see entries for Mar. 31, 1964, and Aug. 10, 1970). The U.S. makes no effort to resolve the problem in Argentina. Rather, its relations—diplomatic, commercial and military—remain quite unaffected. Indeed, in 2001, the U.S. follows Argentina's example by adopting legislation permitting persons targeted for political reasons to be disappeared (see the entry for Oct. 26, 2001).

1979

Jan. 24: 114 member-states endorse UNGA Res. 33/183M, calling for an end to all military/nuclear collaboration with apartheid South Africa. The U.S., the U.K. and France cast the only opposing votes.

Jan. 29: 111 member-states endorse UNGA Res. 33/196, extending special protections over exports from developing countries. The U.S. alone votes against the resolution, arguing that such measures would thwart "free"—as opposed to fair—trade.

Feb. 11: The Ayatollah Ruhollah Khomaini assumes power as the U.S.-created and backed Iranian government of Reza Shah Pahlavi—who had fled the country on Jan. 16—is overthrown. The Shah, wanted in Iran for multitudinous crimes against his own people, and still in possession of several billion dollars of their wealth, is granted sanctuary in the U.S. on Oct. 22. When the U.S. refuses a request for extradition, Iranian students storm the American embassy in Teheran on Nov. 4, taking its occupants hostage and demanding not only the return of the Shah and his money but U.S. agreement to pay reparations for the crimes of its client in exchange for their release. After a badly bungled rescue attempt by the U.S. Army's Delta Force in April, 1980, the "hostage crisis" drags on for several more months, finally being resolved through secret negotiations conducted by representatives of U.S. president-elect Ronald Reagan (they agree to return a substantial part of the wealth stolen by the Shah, who, meanwhile, has died in the U.S.). The hostages are released on the day of Reagan's inauguration, Jan. 20, 1981. While the U.S. continues to make much of the fact that the assault upon its embassy and holding of its diplomats as hostages were violations of international law, it does so without acknowledgement that it was its own longstanding and far more serious pattern of criminal conduct in Iran that gave rise to the Iranian violations. The U.S. provision of sanctuary from Iranian jurisdiction to the Shah, moreover, should be viewed through the lens of recent U.S. policy towards Afghanistan because of its supposed harboring of Usama bin-Laden (see the entry for Sept. 11, 2001), and current U.S. threats to invade Syria unless it divests itself of Ba'athist officials and others wanted in Iraqi jurisdiction. Self-evidently, if providing sanctuary to bin-Laden and Saddam Hussein are crimes warranting the use of military force against Afghanistan and Syria, then U.S. provision of sanctuary to the Shah—and many other such figures—was/is equally criminal, and equally warranting of whatever retaliatory force can be mustered.

Mar. 22: SC 446 is passed, observing that Israeli settlements in the occupied territories of Palestine "have no legal validity" while presenting a "serious obstruction" to peace. The resolution also "strongly deplores" Israel's failure to comply with UNGA Resolutions 2253 (ES-V) and 2254 (ES-V), as well as SC Resolutions 237 (1967), 252 (1968) and 298 (1971), and calls once more for Israel to abide by the 1949 Geneva Convention IV. Having waived its veto in exchange for the exclusion of enforcement provisions, the U.S. abstains from voting.

Mar. 28: The U.S. endorses SC Res. 447, which "condemns strongly the racist régime of South Africa for its premeditated, persistent and sustained armed invasion of the People's Republic of Angola" and its continued illegal occupation of Namibia, while "commending" the peoples of both countries for their armed resistance to South African aggression. South Africa is, of course, ordered to "immediately withdraw," but, as always, the U.S. prevents inclusion of enforcement provisions in the resolution.

Nov. 23: 136 member-states endorse UNGA Res. 34/46, calling for the exploration of alternative approaches to further the enjoyment of human rights and fundamental freedoms by all peoples. The U.S. alone votes against the resolution, although the administration of Pres. Jimmy Carter, then in power, continues to claim that it holds a position of "world leadership" in championing human rights.

Nov. 23: 121 member-states endorse UNGA Res. 34/52E, asserting a right of return for Palestinians expelled from their homeland by Israel. The U.S., Israel and Australia cast the only dissenting votes, and Israel, with full U.S. military and diplomatic support, refuses to so much as consider compliance (a posture unchanged as of 2003).

Dec. 11: 120 member-states endorse UNGA Res. 34/83J, calling for general disarmament and a cessation of the nuclear arms race. The U.S., U.K. and France are the only countries voting against the resolution. The U.S. remains, by a significant margin, the world's foremost arms supplier.

Dec. 12: 111 member-states endorse UNGA Res. 34/90A, calling upon Israel to desist from specified human rights violations vis-à-vis Palestinians. The U.S. and Israel are the only dissenters, and Israel—again with full U.S. military and diplomatic support—actually increases the rate of its atrocities.

Dec. 12: 132 member-states endorse UNGA Res. 34/93D, calling for a strengthening of the international arms embargo against South Africa. The U.S., U.K. and France cast the only dissenting votes, and all systematically violate the terms of the resolution.

Dec. 12: 134 member-states endorse UNGA Res. 34/93I, calling for increased assistance both to the oppressed peoples of South Africa and their liberation movement (notably, the African National Congress). The U.S., U.K. and France cast the only dissenting votes, and the U.S. proclaims the ANC a "terrorist" organization.

Dec. 14: 104 member-states endorse UNGA Res. 34/100, opposing internal or external intervention by any country in the legitimate affairs of another state. The U.S., joined by Israel, cast the only dissenting votes.

Dec. 14: 120 member-states endorse UNGA Res. 34/113, commissioning a report on the living conditions of Palestinians displaced by Israel into other Arab countries. The U.S. and Israel cast the only dissenting votes.

Dec. 14: 112 member-states endorse UNGA Res. 34/133, calling for increased assistance to the Palestinian people. The U.S. and Israel, joined by Canada, cast the only dissenting votes.

Dec. 14: 118 member-states endorse UNGA Res. 34/136, confirming the permanent sovereignty of Arab countries over natural resources in territories militarily occupied by Israel. Only the U.S. and Israel vote against the resolution.

Dec. 17: 121 member-states endorse UNGA Res. 34/158, calling for an international conference on the rights and status of women. Only the U.S. and Israel cast dissenting votes.

Dec. 17: 122 member-states endorse UNGA Res. 34/160, specifically including Palestinian women in the already-approved UN Conference on Women. Again, only the U.S. and Israel cast dissenting votes.

Dec. 18: The U.S. endorses, but fails to ratify, UNGA Res. 34/180, the Convention on the Elimination of All Forms of Discrimination Against Women, which enters into force on Sept. 3, 1981. As of this writing, the U.S. has not joined 151 other UN member-states in accepting the law as binding.

Dec. 19: 112 member-states endorse UNGA Res. 34/199, extending special safeguards to the rights of developing countries in international trade negotiations. The U.S. casts the only dissenting vote, claiming that such safeguards would impair "free trade."

1980

Feb. 25: Journalist Les Payne reports in *Newsday* that "the Carter administration remains committed to driving [Jamaica's] socialist Prime Minister from office unless he moderates his pro-Cuban policies." Actually, the premier, Michael Manley, is not a "socialist" but a liberal democrat, presiding over a decidedly mixed economy. He is insufficiently bellicose towards Cuba, however, and his country's resources include bauxite, a mineral the U.S. considers strategically important. Thus, beginning at least as early as Manley's first reelection in 1976, the CIA mounts a steadily-escalating drive to unseat him, much of it devolving upon the importation of arms, munitions and selected anti-Castro Cuban "technicians" to wage a carefully-calibrated campaign of terrorism on the island. Unable to quell the violence, and deluged by CIA-orchestrated propaganda during the months leading up to his stand for a second reelection, Manley is defeated at the polls in Oct. 1980. The U.S. program in Jamaica violates the 1970 Declaration on Principles of International Law Concerning Friendly Relations and Cooperation Among States in Accordance With the Charter of the United Nations (esp. Chapters I, VI and VII) and Article 18 of the OAS Charter, as well as UNGA Resolutions 337A (V), 380 (V), and 2131 (XX).

Mar. 1: The U.S. endorses SC Res. 465, "deploring" the decision of the Israeli Knesset to officially support Jewish settlement in the occupied territories of Palestine in defiance of SC Resolutions 446 (1979) and 452 (1979), calling upon "all States not to provide Israel with any assistance to be used *specifically* in connexion with [such] settlements [emphasis added]." This U.S.-engineered "sanction," even more than those imposed against South Africa, is obviously endowed with loopholes wide enough to drive entire countries through (it should be compared to those unilaterally imposed against Cuba from the 1960s onward, and against Iraq during the 1990s, as but two examples).

Apr. 11: The U.S. endorses SC Res. 466, which expresses "grave concern at the escalation of hostile and unprovoked attacks by the racist régime of South Africa, violating the sovereignty, air space and territorial integrity of the Republic of Zambia," and demands that South Africa immediately desist. The resolution then "solemnly warns" South Africa that in the event of any further such armed incursions the Security Council "will meet to consider further appropriate action under provisions of the Charter of the United Nations, including Chapter VII." Undeterred by the threat of a meeting, and quite reasonably confident that the U.S. will continue to block any more concrete enforcement actions, South Africa simply ignores the resolution.

Apr. 30: 10 of 15 Security Council member-states endorse draft res. S./13911, affirming the rights of Palestinians under international law. The U.S. employs its veto to override them (final vote: 10-1-4).

May 8: SC Res. 468 is passed, which takes note of "the 1949 Geneva Convention IV Relative to Protection of Civilian Persons in Times of War," expresses "deep concern at the expulsion by Israeli military occupation forces of the Mayors of Hebron and Halhoul and the Sharia judge of Hebron," and calls upon Israel to immediately "rescind these illegal measures." Having threatened a veto if the resolution contains enforcement provisions, the U.S. abstains from voting.

May 14: Pres. Jimmy Carter orders a blockade of Cuba following Fidel Castro's announcement—made in reply to recent "concerns" expressed by Carter with regard Castro's human rights posture—that 125,000 of the island's more discontented citizens are free to leave for the U.S. by boat, from the port of Mariel. Unlike earlier waves of whiter, richer, and decisively more rightwing Cubans, the Marielitos are not welcomed with refugee status and government subsidies in "the land of the free." Instead, they are immediately placed in concentration camps. Those the INS deems deportable because of their medical or criminal histories in Cuba, or because of offenses allegedly occurring during their initial detention in the U.S., are consigned to federal prisons. In 1986, in *Garcia-Mir v. Meese*, federal courts rule that the hapless refugees can be held indefinitely, without hearings. As of this writing, several hundred Cubans remain incarcerated, some for over 2 decades, without trial or conviction, and in clear disregard of customary international law, the Universal Declaration of Human Rights, the American Convention on the Rights and Duties of Man, the American Convention on Human Rights, and the International Covenant on Civil and Political Rights. *Nothing* of which the Castro government is accused surpasses the abuse heaped by the U.S. upon the Marielitos.

May 20: SC Res. 469 is passed, essentially reiterating SC Res. 468. Satisfied that the resolution contains nothing new, the U.S. again abstains from voting.

June 13: The U.S. endorses SC Res. 473, expressing sympathy for the victims of apartheid and roundly condemning South Africa. U.S. policy towards the culprit remains unchanged.

June 30: SC Res. 476 is passed, which reaffirms that "all legislative and administrative measures and actions taken by Israel, the occupying power, which purport to alter the political status of Jerusalem constitute a flagrant violation of the 1949 Geneva Convention IV." Having once again threatened a veto to prevent inclusion of provisions to actually compel Israeli adherence to law, the U.S. abstains from voting.

Aug. 20: SC Res. 478 is passed, expressing "deep concern" over the enactment of a "basic law" by the Israeli Knesset proclaiming a change in the character and political status of Jerusalem. Its threat of a veto having prevented the inclusion of enforcement measures, the U.S. abstains from voting for the fourth time in 3 months.

Nov. 3: 96 member-states endorse UNGA Res. 35/13E, which calls upon Israel to facilitate the return of displaced Palestinians to their homeland. The U.S. and Israel cast the only votes against the resolution, and Israel, with undiminished U.S. support, continues to refuse to consider any such initiative.

Nov. 29: A team of 40 men headed by "Mad Mike" Hoare, one of the more notorious mercenaries contracted by the CIA to fight in the Congo during the early 1960s, arrive at the airport in the Seychelle Islands, in the Indian Ocean, about 800 miles off the coast of Kenya. When it is discovered that their baggage contains arms and munitions, they hijack an aircraft and escape to South Africa. In the ensuing investigation, it is discovered that they had come to overthrow the nonaligned government of Premier France-Albert Rene, which the CIA had been seeking to destabilize since it took power in 1977 (there had been an earlier attempt to employ mercenaries for this purpose in 1979, and would be still another in Dec. 1983).Rene's sin, it seems, had been to call for a nuclear-free zone in the Indian Ocean, including closure of U.S. strategic Air Force bases in the Seychelles and prevention of another being built on the island of Diego Garcia. Although it is unsuccessful, the CIA's operation clearly violates the 1970 Declaration on Principles of International Law Concerning Friendly Relations and Co-operation Among States in Accordance With the Charter of the United Nations (esp. Chapters I, VI and VII), UNGA Resolutions 337A (V), 380 (V) and 2131 (XX), and the International Covenant on Civil and Political Rights. Insofar as it is based from Africa, the fact that it employs mercenaries also violates the prohibition on such activities adopted by the OAU in 1963.

Dec. 5: 134 member-states endorse UNGA Res. 35/57, calling for establishment of a New International Economic Order to promote growth in underdeveloped countries and promote global cooperation. The U.S. alone votes against the resolution, citing its usual concern with "free trade."

Dec. 5: 118 member-states endorse UNGA Res. 35/75, condemning Israeli policy resulting in abysmal living conditions for Palestinians. The U.S. and Israel cast the only dissenting votes, and Israel, with full U.S. support, maintains business as usual.

Dec. 11: 134 member-states endorse UNGA Res. 35/119, implementing the UN's 1960 Declaration on the Granting of Independence to Colonial Countries and Peoples. The U.S., joined by the U.K. and France, cast the only votes against implementation.

Dec. 11: 118 member-states endorse UNGA Res. 35/122C, condemning Israeli human rights violations in the occupied territories. Only the U.S. and Israel cast dissenting votes. The same day, the dynamic duo cast the only votes against two related resolutions—UNGA Res. 35/122E (119-2 vote) and UNGA Res. 35/122F (117-2 vote)—and Israel continues its policy of intensified repression with full U.S. support.

Dec. 11: 132 member-states endorse UNGA Res. 35/136, proclaiming a Program for Action during the second half of the UN Decade for Women. The U.S., Israel and Canada cast the only dissenting votes.

Dec. 12: 111 member-states endorse UNGA Res. 35/145A, which calls for a cessation of all nuclear test explosions. Only the U.S. and U.K. vote against the resolution.

Dec. 12: 110 member-states endorse UNGA Res. 35/134, which calls for a prohibition on the use of nuclear weapons against non-nuclear states. Only the U.S. and Albania vote against such a prohibition.

Dec. 15: 120 member-states endorse UNGA Res. 35/169C, reaffirming the fundamental rights of Palestinians. The U.S. and Israel, joined by Australia, cast the only votes against the resolution.

Dec. 15: 120 member-states endorse UNGA Res. 35/174, affirming that development of both nations and individuals is a fundamental human right. Only the U.S. casts a dissenting vote, on the premise that acknowledgement of collective rights might "impair free trade and enterprise."

Dec. 16: 137 member-states endorse UNGA Res. 35/206J, which renews the call for increased assistance to the oppressed peoples of apartheid South Africa and to their liberation movements. The U.S., U.K. and France cast opposing votes, while the U.S. continues to insist that the ANC is a "terrorist" organization.

Dec. 19: The U.S. endorses SC 484, reaffirming SC Resolutions 468 and 469, as well as the binding effect of the 1949 Geneva Convention IV upon Israeli policies in the occupied territories of Palestine. U.S. affirmation is contingent upon the inclusion of no enforcement provisions.

1981

Feb. 23: The newly-installed administration of Pres. Ronald Reagan releases a document entitled *Communist Interference in El Salvador* (commonly referred to as "The White Paper"), in which it is claimed that Cuba and Nicaragua's Sandinista government have teamed up to provide some "200 tons" of arms and munitions to the FMLN guerrilla movement active in the tiny Central American country. Although not a shred of evidence is offered in support of this contention—less still, Reagan's bizarre assertion a few weeks later that the relative handful of rebels are plotting to take over the entire hemisphere—it is used as the pretext for the U.S. providing over $2 billion in military assistance to El Salvador's brutal military establishment over the next 5 years, while untold millions more go to the police, trained in OPS techniques during the early 1970s (see the entries for Mar. 31, 1964, and Aug. 10, 1970). During the same period, an estimated 40,000 Salvadorans are killed by death squads and in wholesale massacres carried out by the army (often accompanied by U.S. "advisors"); many thousands are maimed and tortured. By 1984, even El Salvador's Pres. José Napoleón Duarte admits that the U.S.—"[Who always] preaches to us of democracy while everywhere...support[ing] dictatorships"—is basically in control of everything happening on the "security" front. The U.S. counterinsurgency campaign in El Salvador violates the 1970 Declaration on Principles of International Law Concerning Friendly Relations and Co-operation Among States in Accordance With the Charter of the United Nations (esp. Chapters I, VI and VII), Article 18 of the OAS Charter, UNGA Resolutions 337A (V), 380 (V) and 2131 (XX), the Universal Declaration of Human Rights, the 1949 Geneva Convention IV and Additional Protocol II, UNGA Res. 2444, the 1978 Red Cross Fundamental Rules of International Humanitarian Law Applicable in Armed Conflicts, the 1978 Resolution on Disappeared Persons, the 1975 Declaration on Protection from Torture, and, before it ended, the 1984 Convention Against Torture and Other Cruel, Inhuman or Degrading Treatment or Punishment.

June 7: The Israeli Air Force, flying U.S.-supplied F-16 aircraft, conducts "Operation Babylon," the bombing of a nuclear reactor at Osirak, near Baghdad, totally destroying it and thereby creating a "dirty bomb" effect that irradiates a large swath of Iraq's more heavily-populated territory. Although it is common knowledge that Israel has illegally developed nuclear weapons of its own, and that the Osirak airstrike—intended to preserve its regional monopoly on such devices—is itself a form of nuclear attack, the U.S. is typically supportive. While Pres. Reagan enters a pro forma protest of Israel's gross violation of the UN Charter and a whole battery of other international laws, and temporarily suspends the transfer of still more advanced aircraft to the IAF, U.S. representatives prevent the Security Council from doing more than passing still another condemnatory resolution (no action is taken to even compel Israel to at last submit to IAEC inspections). By Nov. 30, the flow of armaments has not only resumed, but the U.S. has formalized a new strategic compact with Israel to "protect the peace and security" of the Mideast.

Aug. 19: U.S. fighter planes launched from the aircraft carrier *Nimitz* shoot down two Libyan reconnaissance aircraft flying in their country's own airspace in the Gulf of Sidra. The clash results from a decision by the Reagan administration, as part of a broader plan to "restore American pride" after the U.S. débâcle in Southeast Asia, by provoking lopsided military confrontations with weaker countries. In this case, the U.S. 6th Fleet has been ordered to conduct "training exercises" well within Libya's claimed territorial waters—which extend about as far as those claimed by the U.S. for military defense purposes—and there is strong evidence that American warplanes penetrated the airspace over the Libyan mainland itself, a matter virtually compelling a response. Libya appears to have been selected for such treatment because it is viewed as an exemplar of radical Arab nationalism, provides material/financial support to the PLO, and is aligned with the Iranian revolutionaries who had recently heaped humiliation upon the U.S. (see the entry for Feb. 11, 1979). In any event, the U.S. actions are taken in violation of the 1970 Declaration on Principles of International Law Concerning Friendly Relations and Co-operation Among States in

Accordance With the Charter of the United Nations (esp. Chapters VI and VII) and UNGA Res. 337A (V).

Oct. 10: The U.S. endorses the UN Convention on Prohibitions or Restrictions on the Use of Certain Conventional Weapons Which May be Deemed to be Excessively Injurious or to Have Indiscriminate Effects (outlawing certain of the technologies developed by the U.S. for use in Indochina, as well as the use of incendiary weapons against targets located in areas known to be populated by civilians). The Senate, however, refuses to ratify the treaty, claiming the U.S. enjoys a "unique right" to employ such ordnance and techniques.

Oct. 28: 145 member-states endorse UNGA Res. 36/12, once again condemning apartheid in South Africa and Namibia. Only the U.S. votes against the resolution.

Oct. 28: 124 member-states endorse UNGA Res. 36/13, condemning the collaboration of certain countries and transnational corporations with the South African government. Only the U.S. casts a dissenting vote.

Oct. 28: 114 member-states endorse UNGA Res. 36/15, demanding that Israel cease excavating specified archaeological sites in East Jerusalem. Only the U.S. and Israel cast dissenting votes. Israel continues its excavations "in the interests of science."

Nov. 9: 123 member-states endorse UNGA Res. 36/19, which calls for the promotion of cooperative initiatives in developing countries (mainly in the areas of agriculture, housing, savings and credit, consumer protection and social services). The U.S. alone casts a dissenting vote, claiming that such measures would "stifle the entrepreneurial spirit."

Nov. 9: 126 member-states endorse UNGA Res. 36/19, affirming the right of every country to choose its socioeconomic system in accordance with the will of its people, free from outside interference. Only the U.S., citing concern with "principles of freedom and democracy," votes against according all peoples the right to such basic freedoms.

Nov. 13: 109 member-states endorse UNGA Res. 36/27, condemning Israel for bombing an Iraqi nuclear facility. The U.S. and Israel cast the only votes against the resolution.

Dec. 1: 133 member-states endorse UNGA Res. 36/68, condemning the activities of transnational corporations in colonial/neocolonial territories. The U.S. and the U.K., joined by Guatemala, cast the only three dissenting votes. U.S. corporate dominance in Guatemala and other Third World countries continues to steadily expand in ways that directly contravene both the letter and the intent of the resolution.

Dec. 4: 109 member-states endorse UNGA Res. 36/73, renewing the UN's earlier condemnation of Israeli policies leading to degraded living conditions among Palestinians. Only the U.S. and Israel cast opposing votes. Meanwhile, Israel continues business as usual with full U.S. support.

Dec. 9: 118 member-states endorse UNGA Res. 36/84, renewing the UN's earlier call for a cessation of nuclear test explosions. Once again, only the U.S. and U.K. vote against the resolution.

Dec. 9: 107 member-states endorse UNGA Res. 36/87B, calling for the establishment of a zone free of nuclear weapons in the Middle East. Only the U.S. and Israel cast dissenting votes. It has by this point long since become an open secret that the U.S. has condoned, and in other ways facilitated, Israel's development of nuclear weapons in violation of the Nuclear Non-Proliferation Treaty and other elements of international law.

Dec. 9: 78 member-states endorse UNGA Res. 36/92J, calling for world-wide action to garner support for initiatives designed to curb the arms race and promote disarmament. Only the U.S., Canada and Brazil cast opposing votes. Pres. Reagan denounces such initiatives as "Soviet manipulation."

Dec. 9: 109 member-states endorse UNGA Res. 36/96B, urging negotia-tions on the prohibition of chemical and biological weapons. Only the U.S.—generally believed to be world's largest producer/stockpiler of such weapons, and the only country at the time conclusively documented to have used either in the post-World War II context—casts an opposing vote.

Dec. 10: 101 member-states endorse UNGA Res. 36/98, demanding that Israel comply with the Nuclear Non-Proliferation Treaty by renouncing pos-session of nuclear weapons. The U.S. and Israel cast the only two opposing votes, while Israel continues, with U.S. assistance, to perfect its nuclear arsenal.

Dec. 10: 121 member-states endorse UNGA Res. 36/120A, reaffirming Palestinian human rights. The U.S. and Israel enter the only two opposing votes, and jointly ignore the resolution.

Dec. 10: 119 member-states endorse UNGA Res. 36/120B, reaffirming the Palestinian right to self-determination. The U.S. and Israel, this time joined by Canada, cast the only three opposing votes, while Israel restates its basic position in the matter, denying the very existence of Palestine.

Dec. 10: 139 member-states endorse UNGA Res. 36/120E, rejecting foreclosure on the political status of Jerusalem. The U.S. and Israel cast opposing votes while Israel, with the usual U.S. support, continues its poli-cy of encircling its proclaimed capitol with an "iron ring" of illegal settle-ments (the obvious end goal being to simply absorb the city altogether).

Dec. 14: In blatant defiance of SC Resolutions 242 and 338, Israel for-mally annexes the Golan Heights, captured from Syria during its 1967 war of aggression. Syria immediately files a protest with the Security Council, and on Dec. 17, the U.S. goes along with SC Res. 497, declaring the imposi-tion of Israeli law on the Golan Heights to be illegal, demanding its imme-diate rescission, and asserting that the 1949 Geneva Convention IV is bind-ing upon Israel's administration of the occupied territories. As always, how-ever, the quid pro quo involved in U.S. cooperation on a resolution critical of Israel is that it contain no enforcement provisions. After another cosmetic suspension of arms transfers to the Israelis, U.S. support resumes as if nothing has happened.

Dec. 14: 135 member-states endorse UNGA Res. 36/133, declaring that education, work, health care and proper nourishment are basic human rights. The U.S. alone casts an opposing vote. At about the same time, Pres. Reagan opines that ketchup should be considered a "vegetable" for purposes of feeding poor children in the U.S..

Dec. 16: 141 member-states endorse UNGA Res. 36/146A, reaffirming the fundamental human, political and economic rights of Palestinian refugees in the Gaza Strip. The U.S. and Israel cast the only two opposing votes, and Israel openly defies the resolution by tightening its "security" in the area.

Dec. 16: 121 member-states endorse UNGA Res. 36/146B, reaffirming the right of displaced Palestinians to return to their homes. The U.S. and Israel, joined by Canada, cast the only three opposing votes, while Israeli officials proclaim a Palestinian right of return "unthinkable."

Dec. 16: 117 member-states endorse UNGA Res. 36/146C, denying Israel the prerogative of profiting from or making ultimate disposition of revenues deriving from Palestinian properties. As usual, the U.S. and Israel cast the only two dissenting votes. Israel, with full U.S. support, continues its policies of impounding and profiting from Palestinian-owned lands, homes and enterprises (meanwhile, quasiofficial Israeli efforts to recover Jewish properties/funds impounded by the nazis is intensifying).

Dec. 16: 119 member-states endorse UNGA Res. 36/146G, calling for the establishment of a university in Jerusalem to serve Palestinian refugees. The U.S. and Israel cast the only two opposing votes.

Dec. 16: 111 member-states endorse UNGA Res. 36/147C, condemning Israeli violations of human rights in the occupied territories. The U.S. and Israel cast the only two opposing votes, and Israel's violations continue unabated.

Dec. 16: 114 member-states endorse UNGA Res. 36/147F, condemning Israel's closure of Arab universities in the occupied territories. The U.S. and Israel cast the only two opposing votes, and the universities remain closed.

Dec. 16: 147 member-states endorse UNGA Res. 36/149B, calling for a more equitable world distribution of communications technology and free flow of information. The U.S. and Israel cast the only two opposing votes (the U.S. considers the news media to be private property rather than an integral aspect of the public domain).

Dec. 16: 139 member-states endorse UNGA Res. 36/150, opposing Israel's unilateral decision to build a canal linking the Mediterranean and Dead Seas. The usual pair cast the only two dissenting votes.

Dec. 17: 136 member-states endorse UNGA Res. 36/172C, condemning South Africa's aggression against Angola and other African countries. Only the U.S. casts an opposing vote.

Dec. 17: 129 member-states endorse UNGA Res. 36/172H, calling for an international conference of trade unions to strengthen the effects of sanctions on South Africa. The U.S. and U.K. cast the only two opposing votes.

Dec. 17: 126 member-states endorse UNGA Res. 36/172, encouraging an increased intensity of international actions against South Africa as a means of ending its external aggression and internal régime of apartheid. Only the U.S. and the U.K. cast opposing votes.

Dec. 17: 139 member-states endorse UNGA Res. 36/172N, renewing support for sanctions and other measures designed to end apartheid in South Africa. Only the U.S. casts an opposing vote. With the approval of the State Department, U.S. transnationals continue to violate the embargo.

Dec. 17: 138 member-states endorse UNGA Res. 36/1720, calling for cessation of further foreign investment in/loans to South Africa. Again, the U.S. casts the only opposing vote. U.S. financial dealings with the apartheid régime actually increase.

Dec. 17: 115 member-states endorse UNGA Res. 36/173, reiterating that the Arab owners retain permanent sovereignty over the natural resources within Israeli-occupied territories. The U.S. and Israel cast the only two opposing votes.

Dec. 17: 121 member-states endorse UNGA Res. 36/226B, asserting the nonapplicability of Israeli law to the occupied portion of the Golan Heights. There were, of course, two opposing votes.

Dec. 18: The U.S. goes along with SC Res. 498, calling for a ceasefire and immediate withdrawal of Israeli invasion forces from Lebanon. The quid pro quo for U.S. cooperation is that the resolution contains no enforcement provisions.

1982

Jan. 20: 9 of 15 Security Council member-states endorse draft res. S/14832/Rev. 2, calling upon Israel to comply with SC Resolutions 242 and 338 by withdrawing from the occupied territories of Palestine and the Golan Heights. The U.S. employs its veto to override them (final vote: 9-1-5).

Feb. 25: The U.S. declines to endorse, but does not veto, SC Res. 501, reaffirming Israel's obligation under SC Res. 425 to withdraw its military forces from Lebanon.

Mar. 10: Pres. Reagan proclaims an embargo on Libya's crude oil, 35% of which is consumed by the U.S. Although Reagan claims his action is taken in response to evidence that "Libyan hit squads" are operating in the U.S.— one of them allegedly assigned to assassinate Reagan himself—the FBI later admits that an exhaustive investigation has uncovered no trace of such a group. The embargo thus appears designed not to combat terrorism, but rather to coerce changes in Libya's domestic politics and international alliances, a clear violation of the 1970 Declaration on Principles of International Law Concerning Friendly Relations and Co-operation Among States in Accordance With the Charter of the United Nations (esp. Chapters I and IX), as well as Chapter I of the 1974 Charter of Economic Rights and Duties of States, and UNGA Resolutions 337A (V) and 3314 (XXIX). Despite the dearth of proof that Libya is underwriting international terrorism, it is inscribed on the State Department's list of "terror-sponsoring states" and continues more than 20 years later to be consistently (mis)represented to the public as such.

Apr. 2: 13 of 15 Security Council member-states endorse draft res. S/14943, calling upon Israel to comply with international law in its treatment of Palestinians in the occupied territories. The U.S. employs its veto to override them (final vote: 13-1-1).

Apr. 20: 14 of 15 Security Council member-states endorse draft res. S/14985, condemning Israeli violations of Palestinian rights to religious freedom at the al-Aqsa (Dome of the Rock) shrine in Jerusalem. The U.S. employs its veto to override them (final vote: 14-1-0).

Apr. 30: The U.S. joins the UK and France in vetoing 4 draft resolutions—S/14459 (final vote: 9-3-3); S/14460/Rev. 1 (final vote: 9-3-3); S/14461 (final vote: 11-3-1); S/14462 (final vote: 12-3-0)—designed to impose various compulsory sanctions on South Africa in order to force an end to its illegal occupation of Namibia.

May 26: The U.S. declines to endorse, but does not veto, SC Res. 508, approving PLO representation in discussions of the situation in Lebanon.

June 3: Palestinian gunmen attempt to assassinate the Israeli ambassador in London. Although it is known to Israeli intelligence that the assailants are part of a small group headed by Abu Nidal, a bitter foe of Yasser Arafat—the Mossad, Israel's equivalent of the CIA, correctly concludes that the attack is part of a scheme by which Nidal hopes to lure Israel into an assault upon his enemies in the PLO—the incident is used by PM Begin and his defense minister, Ariel Sharon, as the pretext for another fullscale invasion of Lebanon, in order, as Sharon put it, "to destroy the PLO [both] militarily...and politically" (a second objective is to install a "Lebanese" government acceptable to Israel). On June 6, following airstrikes on PLO targets as far north as Beirut, Sharon launches "Operation Peace for Galilee" by ordering 4 armored columns to cross into Lebanon while an amphibious assault is mounted on Sidon. While Sharon is supposedly authorized to penetrate only 40 kilometers into Lebanese territory, he is by the afternoon of the first day already making secret arrangements with Maronite Phalangist leader Bashir Gemayel for joint IDF/Phalange operations in Beirut. Preparations have also been made for a head-on confrontation with Syria, once the 40 kilometer line has been passed. On its face, Israel's invasion of Lebanon violates the 1970 Declaration on Principles of International Law Concerning Friendly Relations and Co-operation Among States in Accordance With the Charter of the United Nations (esp. Chapters I, VI and VII), as well as UNGA Resolutions 337A (V), 380 (V), 2131 (XX) and 3314 (XXIX). Given the facts that the campaign is preplanned, initiated on the flimsiest of pretexts, and, as is later revealed, incorporates an intention to retain a considerable portion of Lebanon's territory in the aftermath, it also constitutes a violation of the London Charter. Insofar as the U.S., according to no less than Gen. Alexander Haig, received advance notice from Sharon of Israel's intentions, the U.S. can only be seen as complicit in these crimes.

June 8: 14 of 15 Security Council member-states endorse draft res. S/15185, condemning the Israeli invasion of Lebanon, and demanding immediate withdrawal. The U.S. employs its veto to override them (final vote: 14-1-0).

June 9: Israel attacks Syrian positions in Lebanon's Bekaa Valley. Numerous air defense installations are destroyed and 23 Syrian aircraft shot by the IAF, while Israeli armored units drive the Syrian army back as far as Lake Karaoun. Given that Syria has made no offensive gesture towards Israel, the Israeli assault upon Syrian military forces compounds Israel's violation of the 1970 Declaration on Principles of International Law Concerning Friendly Relations and Co-operation Among States in Accordance With the Charter of the United Nations and UNGA Res. 337A (V). That the U.S. makes no move to sanction Israel under such circumstances—much less sever relations with it—speaks for itself.

June 11: With Israeli troops on the outskirts of Beirut, the U.S. sponsors a "cease-fire between all states parties." The wording, clearly designed to exclude the PLO, which has fallen back into the city, allows the Israelis to lay siege to the Lebanese capitol for the next 2 months, bombarding it with some 400 tank cannon and more than 1,000 artillery pieces, as well as endless airstrikes. On July 4, water and power are also cut off to the beleaguered city, filled as it is with Lebanese and Palestinian noncombatants. An estimated 12,000 unoffending civilians are killed, and scores of thousands more undergo immense suffering, before it can be arranged for the bulk of the surviving PLO fighters to be transported to Tunisia on Aug. 21 (others are dispersed to Syria, Iraq and Yemen). On Aug. 23, Bashir Gemayel is installed as Lebanese head of state, prompting Mossad operatives in Beirut to hold a wild celebration. PM Begin then announces that Operation Peace for Galilee has met "most" of its objectives. Despite the obvious Israeli violations of the 1949 Geneva Convention IV and both the 1977 Additional Protocols, as well as UNGA Resolutions 337A (V), 380 (V), 2131 (XX), 2444, and 3314 (XXIX) involved in all this, U.S. support for Israel remains unstinting.

June 26: 14 of 15 Security Council member-states endorse draft res. S/15255/Rev. 2, condemning Israel's ongoing aggression in Lebanon and imposing sanctions in the event Israel fails to immediately comply with a demand to withdraw. The U.S. employs its veto to override them (final vote: 14-1-0).

Aug. 6: 11 of 15 Security Council member-states endorse draft res. S/15347/Rev. 1, condemning Israel's ongoing aggression in Lebanon and calling for the introduction of UN forces to supervise a withdrawal. The U.S. employs its veto to override them (final vote: 11-1-3).

Aug. 17: The U.S. joins in approving SC Res. 519, condemning Israeli violations of the Lebanon ceasefire agreement and demanding immediate compliance. The U.S. ensures that the resolution lacks enforcement provisions, however. The violations continue.

Aug, 31: 13 of 15 Security Council member-states endorse draft res. S/14664/Rev. 2, condemning the U.S. intervention in Angola. The U.S. employs its veto to override them (final vote: 13-1-1).

Sept. 14: Bashir Gemayel is assassinated (probably by Syrian agents), temporarily ruining Sharon's plan for a "new political order" in Lebanon. On Sept. 15, Sharon orders his troops to occupy West Beirut, near which the Palestinian refugee camps of Sabra and Shatilla are located. He then gives the Phalangists a green light to "clean out the camps," with the result that hundreds of noncombatant Palestinians are massacred while IDF "security forces" stand by and watch. Gemayel is then replaced as head of state by his younger brother, Amin. Under even the most charitable interpretation, Israel's performance vis-à-vis Sabra and Shatilla embodies a gross default on its responsibilities under the 1949 Geneva Convention IV and both the 1977 Additional Protocols, as well as UNGA Res. 2444. Israel's intervention in Lebanon's internal political affairs, moreover, continues in violation of UNGA Resolutions 380 (V) and 2131 (XX).

Sept. 17: The U.S. joins in approving SC Res. 520, condemning continuing "Israeli incursions into Beirut in violation of the ceasefire agreement and various Security Council resolutions," and demanding immediate "withdrawal to the positions occupied by Israel before 15 September 1982." Since the U.S. once again blocks inclusion of enforcement provisions, Israel effectively ignores the resolution, withdrawing only when it is ready.

Oct. 28: 111 member-states endorse UNGA Res. 37/7, calling for a world charter to protect the ecology. Only the U.S. casts an opposing vote, claiming that such measures would "impair economic development."

Nov. 15: 136 member-states endorse UNGA Res. 37/11, authorizing an international conference on the succession of states with regard to state property, archives and debts. The U.S. casts the only opposing vote.

Dec. 3: 124 member-states endorse UNGA Res. 37/47, calling for universal ratification of the Convention on Abolition and Punishment of Apartheid. The U.S. casts the only opposing vote.

Dec. 8: A CIA-backed coup attempt fails in Surinam, among the results of which is that a pair of U.S. "diplomats" are quickly expelled for "destabilizing activities." As it turns out, CIA Dir. William Casey had actually informed Congress before the fact that he'd been instructed by Pres. Reagan to bring about the overthrow of Surinam's premier, Col. Desi Bouterse, because he'd "led his country into the Cuban orbit" (actually, Bouterse was much more the client of his rightwing neighbor, Brazil). Although, like that in the Seychelles in 1980, the operation is unsuccessful, it clearly violates the 1970 Declaration on Principles of International Law Concerning Friendly Relations and Co-operation Among States in Accordance With the Charter of the United Nations (esp. Chapters I, VI and VII), Article 18 of the OAS Charter, UNGA Resolutions 337A (V), 380 (V) and 2131 (XX), and the International Covenant on Civil and Political Rights.

Dec. 9: 141 member-states endorse UNGA Res. 37/69E, calling for an international mobilization against apartheid. The U.S. enters the only opposing vote. The same day, the U.S. alone opposes resolutions 37/69G (138-1 vote) and 37/69H (134-1 vote), calling for an international conference on the elimination of apartheid in sports and reaffirming the duty to cease making loans to South Africa's apartheid régime.

Dec. 9: 111 member-states endorse UNGA Res. 37/73, proclaiming the need for a comprehensive nuclear-test-ban treaty. The U.S. enters the only opposing vote.

Dec. 9: 114 member-states endorse UNGA Res. 37/78A, calling upon the U.S. and the Soviet Union to submit reports on the status of their nuclear arms negotiations. The U.S. casts the only opposing vote.

Dec. 9: 138 member-states endorse UNGA Res. 37/83, calling for the prevention of an arms race in outer space. The U.S., citing "unique security needs," casts the only opposing vote.

Dec. 10: 131 member-states endorse UNGA Res. 37/94B, supporting UNESCO's efforts to promote a new world information and communications order. The U.S. casts the only opposing vote.

Dec. 13: 95 member-states endorse UNGA Res. 37/98A, proclaiming the necessity of prohibiting chemical and biological weapons. The U.S. enters the only opposing vote.

Dec. 16: 113 member-states endorse UNGA Res. 37/103, calling for the development of legal norms and standards expressly relating to a new world economic order. The U.S., arguing that such measures would "impair trade," casts the only opposing vote.

Dec. 17: 146 member-states endorse UNGA Res. 37/137, calling for a ban on products harmful to health and the environment. The U.S., again claiming that such measures would "impair trade," casts the only opposing vote.

Dec. 18: 131 member–states endorse UNGA Res. 37/199, declaring that education, employment, health care, proper nourishment and national development are fundamental human rights. The U.S. casts the only opposing vote.

Dec. 20: 141 member-states endorse UNGA Res. 37/204, calling for a review of the implementation of the Charter of the Rights and Duties of States. The U.S. casts the only opposing vote.

Dec. 21: 132 member-states endorse UNGA Res. 37/237/XI, guaranteeing the adequacy of conference facilities to be used by the Economic Commission for Africa at Addis Ababa. The U.S. casts the only opposing vote.

Dec. 21: 146 member-states endorse UNGA Res. 37/251, calling for the development of energy resources in underdeveloped countries. The U.S., concerned about "trade implications," casts the only opposing vote.

Dec. 21: 124 member-states endorse UNGA Res. 37/252, calling for the restructuring of international economic relations in the interest of forging a new world economic order. The U.S., for its usual reasons, casts the only opposing vote.

1983

Feb. 7: The Kahan Commission, a body convened by an embarrassed Knesset to investigate Israel's role in the Phalangist massacres at Sabra and Shatilla (see the entry for Sept. 14, 1982), delivers its final report. Although it is widely hoped that the results will serve to exonerate the IDF, the exact opposite proves true. Appropriately enough, the commission finds Defense Minister Sharon to be the official primarily responsible. On Feb. 14, Sharon is removed from his position as defense minister—no thought is given, of course, to the possibility of prosecuting him for the mass murder over which it's been officially conceded he presided—but PM Begin immediately appoints him "minister without portfolio." Even as this charade is being carried out, the U.S. accepts the role of guarantor in an agreement between Israel and the Israeli-installed Gemayel régime, signed on May 17, wherein Israeli "security forces" will be allowed to remain indefinitely in southern Lebanon. For its part, the U.S. assumes Israel's "responsibility" of preserving the newly-fashioned "status quo" in northern Lebanon. Thus does the U.S. reward its "friends" for their commission of crimes against the peace and the waging of aggressive war, as well as violation of both the UN Charter and the Geneva Conventions.

Apr. 2: 12 of 15 Security Council member-states endorse draft res. S/14941, condemning the U.S. policy of aggression towards Nicaragua as violating international law. The U.S. employs its veto to override them (final vote: 12-1-2).

Apr. 18: The U.S. embassy in Beirut is attacked by a suicide bomber driving a truck filled with explosives at the very hour a high-level meeting of CIA personnel is being conducted therein. 36 Americans are killed and a number of others wounded. The attack is carried out by Islamic Jihad, an

Iranian-supported group spawned by Israel's ongoing refusal to comply with international law and the U.S. role in making it possible for the Israelis to persistently engage in aggression, war crimes and crimes against humanity. The Jihad dedicates itself to imposing consequences upon both parties (i.e., "zionists and crusaders"). At about the same time, another group, the Syrian-backed Hizbullah (Party of God), is established for purposes of reconstructing the Muslim sectors of Lebanese society and conducting irregular military operations against the IDF until such time as Israel, in accordance with SC Res. 425, fully withdraws from southern Lebanon. It is not until Mar. 10, 1985, however—after the Israelis assassinate several of its leaders—that Hizbullah conducts its first suicide bombing, targeting an IDF convoy outside the "Jewish settlement" at Metullah (at least 12 soldiers are killed, 14 wounded). It is important to emphasize that the Islamic Jihad and Hizbullah are differently-focused organizations, albeit both emerge in direct response to Israeli's 1982 invasion/partition of Lebanon and attendant imposition of policies devolving upon "control by terror."

June 4: 9 of 15 Security Council member-states endorse draft res. S/15156, deploring Britain's resort to military force in the Malvinas (Falkland) Islands. The U.S. joins the UK in vetoing the resolution (final vote: 9-2-4).

Aug. 2: 13 of 15 Security Council member-states endorse draft res. S/15895, condemning Israel's persistent violation of Palestinian human rights in the occupied territories, and imposing sanctions to compel Israeli compliance with international law. The U.S. employs its veto to override them (final vote: 13-1-1).

Aug. 28: Menachem Begin resigns as Israeli PM and is replaced by Yitzhak Shamir, a man whose record is equally unsavory. Shamir is a ranking veteran of LEHI, otherwise known as the "Stern Gang," a zionist terrorist sect that expressed strong profascist sentiments and actually explored the possibility of allying with nazis against Britain during World War II. In 1948, he was wanted by authorities in connection with the murder of Count Folke Bernadotte, a Swedish diplomat *cum* UN mediator who had earlier devoted himself to saving Jews from the Holocaust. The new administration nonetheless ratchets up the volume of Israel's "antiterrorist" rhetoric against the PLO, although Shamir's main goal appears to be mainly that of a caretaker (that is, to "give up nothing" prior to the Israeli general elections in 1984). While this posture is in itself illegal—defiant as it is of SC Resolutions 242, 338 and 425, among numerous others—Shamir receives solid backing from the U.S.

Oct. 23: A U.S. Marine barracks in Beirut is attacked by a suicide bomber belonging to the Islamic Jihad and driving a truck filled with explosives. 241 Marines are killed and many wounded. The attack is carried out in retaliation not only for the general U.S. policy of sending troops to serve as Israeli surrogates in northern Lebanon, but, more specifically, in response to U.S. naval vessels having fired more than 300 shells into positions occupied by Druze (Muslim) militiamen on Sept. 19 (the bombardment, undertaken in direct support of Maronite forces removes all pretense that the U.S. military presence is intended to fulfill a "neutral peacekeeping" function; far from keeping the peace, U.S. troops have in any event followed the Israeli practice of standing aside while the Phalangists indulge in a seemingly endless series of "mini-massacres" of Palestinian refugees). The Reagan administration, apparently shaken at the realization that it will not in this instance be allowed to engage in its customary range of illegalities with impunity, begins a rapid withdrawal of U.S. personnel from Lebanon.

Oct. 25: In an operation dubbed "Urgent Fury," an overwhelming U.S. military force abruptly invades the tiny Caribbean island of Grenada, quickly installing a government selected in Washington. At the outset, Pres. Reagan claims that he had been "requested" to mount the assault by several members of the Organization of East Caribbean States, including Jamaica, Barbados and Grenada itself (all British protectorates), a matter quickly and emphatically denied both by British Foreign Sec. Sir Geoffrey Howe and by Prime Minister Margaret Thatcher. Reagan then switches to claiming that the invasion was necessary to "rescue" several hundred Americans residing on the island—most of them medical students—from turmoil following the overthrow/murder of Grenada's prime minister, Maurice Bishop, a few days earlier. When it comes out that there was no known threat to the students, that military exercises preliminary to the invasion were being conducted well before the coup, and that the CIA had in any event been engaged in an effort to destabilize Bishop since 1979, Reagan switches again, this time averring that the presence of about 650 mostly middle-aged Cuban laborers helping construct a longer runway at the island's civilian airport "proved" Grenada had become "a Soviet-Cuban colony being readied as a major military bastion to export terror and undermine democracy, but we got there just in time." When this, too, is refuted by astonished officials at Plessey, the British construction firm contracted to build the strictly commercial runway for purposes of facilitating tourism— most of the investment had come from the European Common Market—the pres. at last falls silent. There was in essence, *no* justification—aside from the legally irrelevant fact that the U.S. preferred it have a different government—for the "Conquest of Grenada." Operation "Urgent Fury" thus embodies gross violations of the 1970 Declaration on Principles of International Law Concerning Friendly Relations and Co-operation Among States in Accordance With the Charter of the United Nations (esp. Chapters I, VI and VII), virtually every article found under Chapters I, II, IV and V of the OAS Charter and UNGA Resolutions 337A (V), 380 (V), 2131 (XX), and 3314 (XXIX), as well as the International Covenant on Civil and Political Rights.

Oct. 27: 11 of 15 Security Council member-states endorse draft res. S/16077/Rev. 1, condemning the U.S. invasion of Grenada as violating international law. The U.S. employs its veto to override them (final vote: 11-1-3).

Nov. 22: 110 member-states endorse UNGA Res. 38/19, the International Convention on Suppression and Punishment of the Crime of Apartheid. The U.S. casts the only opposing vote.

Nov. 22: 131 member-states endorse UNGA Res. 38/25, reaffirming the right of every state to choose its own socioeconomic system, free of outside interference. The U.S. casts the only opposing vote.

Dec. 5: 149 member-states endorse UNGA Res. 38/391E, calling for a step-up in the international campaign against apartheid. The U.S. casts the only opposing vote. Much the same result pertains later in the day with regard to resolution 38/39K (145-1 vote), authorizing a continuation of activities under provision of the International Convention Against Apartheid in Sports.

Dec. 5: 140 member-states endorse UNGA Res. 38/39I, calling upon the Security Council to consider imposing sanctions against South Africa's apartheid régime. The U.S. casts the sole opposing vote.

Dec. 15: 147 member-states endorse UNGA Res. 38/70, stipulating that outer space should be used only for peaceful purposes. The U.S. casts the only opposing vote.

Dec. 16: 132 member-states endorse UNGA Res. 38/124, declaring that education, employment, health care, proper nutrition and national development are basic human rights. Once again, this time noting that it "does not recognize a right to food," the U.S. casts the only opposing vote.

Dec. 19: 110 member-states endorse UNGA Res. 38/128, calling once again for the development of legal norms and standards facilitating a new world economic order. The U.S. casts the sole opposing vote.

Dec. 19: 137 member-states endorse UNGA Res. 38/150, declaring a "Transport and Communications Decade" for Africa. The U.S. casts the only opposing vote.

Dec. 20: 116 member-states endorse UNGA Res. 38/182, calling for a prohibition on new types of weapons of mass destruction. The U.S. casts the sole opposing vote.

Dec. 20: 133 member-states endorse UNGA Res. 38/183M, calling upon nuclear arms states to submit annual reports on steps taken to prevent nuclear war and end the nuclear arms race. The U.S. casts the only opposing vote.

Dec. 20: 98 member-states endorse UNGA Res. 38/187A, calling for intensification of negotiations leading to an accord prohibiting chemical and bacteriological weapons. The U.S. alone votes against the resolution.

Dec. 20: 113 member-states endorse UNGA Res. 38/188G, calling for a study of the naval arms race. The U.S. casts the only opposing vote.

Dec. 20: 132 member-states endorse UNGA Res. 38/188H, calling for establishment of an Independent Commission on Disarmament and Security Issues. The U.S., citing "unique defense needs" and "interference with [its] sovereignty," casts the only opposing vote.

Dec. 20: 126 member-states endorse UNGA Res. 38/202, calling for a strengthening of the capacity of the UN to respond to natural and other disasters. The U.S. casts the only opposing vote.

1984

Apr. 4: 13 of 15 Security Council member-states endorse draft res. S/16463, condemning the U.S. policy of aggression towards Nicaragua as violating international law. The U.S. employs its veto to override them (final vote: 13-1-1).

July 23: Shimon Peres is elected Israeli PM. Although supposedly more "centrist" than either Begin or Shamir, his platform includes rejection even "in concept" of a Palestinian state and of recognizing/negotiating with the PLO. Among his first acts is to order the construction of "five or six new Jewish settlements on the West Bank within a year" in open defiance of SC Resolutions 242 and 338. U.S. Sec. of State George Schultz announces increased U.S. support for such "moderation."

Sept. 6: 13 of 15 Security Council member-states endorse draft res. S/16732, condemning Israeli actions in southern Lebanon and demanding immediate withdrawal. The U.S. employs its veto to override them (final vote: 13-1-1).

Oct. 1: Using 8 U.S.-supplied F-16 fighter-bombers, the IAF conduct airstrikes on the PLO headquarters in Tunis, killing 56 Palestinians and 15 Tunisians, and wounding well over a 100 others, many of them Tunisian bystanders. Israel claims the attack is carried out in retaliation for the "murders of three innocent Israeli civilians vacationing in Cyprus"—who turn out to have been Mossad operatives—by the "Force 17" unit of Fatah (the PLO's military component). In actuality, it is intended to halt Jordanian efforts to arrange negotiations concerning the West Bank that include PLO representatives in exchange for official PLO recognition of Israel's "right to exist" and renunciation of armed struggle. Although the Israeli action embodies a clearcut violation of Tunisian sovereignty, and thus the 1970 Declaration on Principles of International Law Concerning Friendly Relations and Co-operation Among States in Accordance With the Charter of the United Nations (esp. Chapters I, VI and VII), as well as UNGA Resolutions 337A (V) and 3314 (XXIX), Pres. Reagan offsets a Security Council resolution condemning the attack as "unprovoked aggression" by sending PM Peres a telegram expressing his "personal satisfaction" at Israel's "response to terrorism."

Oct 12: Pres. Reagan signs the Bail Reform Act, under which the authority of federal judges to nullify the constitutional right of accused individuals to bail pending conviction and resolution of appeals is expanded to include all cases in which a prosecutor claims that the accused represents a "threat to the community." Allegedly necessary as a tool enabling federal authorities to more effectively combat "drug kingpins," bail denial under provision of the Act is being requested by prosecutor in more than 40% of all federal cases by 1986. Such requests are most conspicuous in proceedings against political targets like Puerto Rican independence activist Filiberto Ojéda-Ríos, accused in 1985 of shooting an FBI agent. Ultimately, Ojéda-Ríos serves 4 years of preventive detention, mostly in an isolation cell, before being acquitted of all charges on Aug. 26, 1989. Aside from the erosion of constitutional rights it entails, the Bail Reform Act conflicts with elements of the Universal Declaration of Human Rights, the American Declaration of the Rights and Duties of Man, the American Convention on Human Rights, the International Convention on the Elimination of All Forms of Racial Discrimination, and the International Covenant on Civil and Political Rights.

Nov. 8: 134 member-states endorse UNGA Res. 39/9, calling for greater cooperation between the UN and the League of Arab State. The U.S. and Israel cast the only opposing votes.

Nov. 16: 106 member-states endorse UNGA Res. 39/14, belatedly condemning the Israeli airstrike against the Iraqi nuclear facility at Osirak (see the entry for Nov. 13, 1981). The U.S. and Israel cast the only two opposing votes.

Nov. 23: 145 member-states endorse UNGA Res. 39/21, accepting the report of the Committee on the Elimination of All Forms of Racial Discrimination. The U.S. alone casts an opposing vote.

Dec. 5: 119 member-state endorse UNGA Res. 39/411, reaffirming the right of the island of St. Helena, a "British possession," to independence. The U.S. and the U.K. cast the only opposing votes.

Dec. 5: 121 member-states endorse UNGA Res. 39/42, condemning ongoing support by certain states to South Africa in its Namibian and other illegal endeavors. The U.S. and U.K. cast the only opposing votes. Both continue their support to South Africa's apartheid régime.

Dec. 10: The U.S. endorses UNGA Res. 39/46, the UN Convention Against Torture and Other Cruel or Degrading Treatment or Punishment, which enters into force on June 26, 1987. The Senate nonetheless refuses to ratify the Convention for 8 years before ostensibly allowing the U.S. to join 94 other countries in accepting the law's binding effect on Nov. 20, 1995. The gesture is largely a subterfuge, however, as the Senate attaches 2 reservations, 5 "understandings" and 2 declarations to its ratification, all of which add up to the claim that the U.S. retains a "sovereign right" to exempt itself from compliance when and however it desires to do so. As innumerable prison inmates, arrestees/subjects of police interrogation, and countless others can readily attest—and as Amnesty International has thoroughly documented—U.S. self-exemption remains in 2003 so ubiquitous as to constitute a normative official posture.

Dec. 11: 127 member-states endorse UNGA Res. 39/49A, reaffirming the rights of the Palestinian people. The U.S. and Israel cast the only opposing votes. Israel continues its violations of Palestinian rights with full U.S. backing.

Dec. 11: 121 member-states endorse UNGA Res. 39/49D, calling for a Middle-East Peace Conference. The U.S. and Israel, joined by Canada, cast the only opposing votes.

Dec. 12: 125 member-states endorse UNGA Res. 39/62, reaffirming the need for a prohibition on the development and manufacture of new types of weapons of mass destruction. Once again, the U.S. alone casts an opposing vote.

Dec. 12: 84 member-states endorse UNGA Res. 39/65B, reaffirming the need for a prohibition of chemical and biological weapons. Once again, the U.S. casts the sole opposing vote.

Dec. 13: 146 member-states endorse UNGA Res. 39/72G, reaffirming the need for concerted international action to abolish apartheid. The U.S. and the U.K. cast the only opposing votes.

Dec. 13: 138 member-states endorse UNGA Res. 39/73, calling for an updating of the law of the sea. Only the U.S. and Turkey cast opposing votes.

Dec. 14: 120 member-states endorse UNGA 39/95A, condemning Israeli human rights violations in the occupied territories. Only the U.S. and Israel cast opposing votes. Israeli violations continue, unabated and with full U.S. support.

Dec. 14: 143 member-states endorse UNGA Res. 39/95H, condemning assassination attempts against Palestinian mayors and calling upon Israel to arrest and prosecute the perpetrators. The U.S. and Israel cast the only two opposing votes. To date (2003) no such arrests/prosecutions have occurred.

Dec. 17: 94 member-states endorse UNGA Res. 39/147, condemning Israel's refusal to place its nuclear facilities under International Atomic Energy Commission safeguards. The U.S. and Israel cast the only opposing votes.

Dec. 17: 123 member-states endorse UNGA Res. 39/148N, reaffirming the needs for a nuclear weapons test ban, cessation of the nuclear-arms race and nuclear disarmament. The U.S. casts the only opposing vote.

Dec. 17: 141 member-states endorse UNGA Res. 39/151F, calling for a continuation of the UN study on military research and development. The U.S. casts the only oppsing vote.

Dec. 17: 143 member-states endorse UNGA Res. 39/161B, commemorating the 25th anniversary of the Declaration on the Granting of Independence to Colonial Countries and Peoples. The U.S. alone casts an opposing vote.

Dec. 18: 146 member-states endorse UNGA Res. 39/224, calling for social and economic assistance to the Palestinian people. Only the U.S. and Israel cast opposing votes.

Dec. 18: 118 member-states endorse UNGA Res. 39/232, extending support to the UN Industrial Development Organization. Only the U.S. and Israel cast opposing votes.

Dec. 18: 120 member-states endorse UNGA Res. 39/233, calling for an "Industrial Development Decade" for Africa. Only the U.S. casts an opposing vote.

1985

Mar. 12: 11 of 15 Security Council member-states endorse draft res. S/17000, condemning Israeli practices against civilians in southern Lebanon and calling upon Israel to comply with the requirements of the 1949 Geneva Convention IV. The U.S. employs its veto to override them (final vote: 11-1-3).

Apr. 9: The U.S. refuses to endorse UNGA Res. 29/248, calling for international consumer protection.

May 10: 13 of 15 Security Council member-states endorse draft res. S/17172/Rev. 1, condemning as criminal the U.S. policy of aggression towards Nicaragua as violating international law. The U.S. employs its veto to override them (final vote: 13-1-1).

May 13: Culminating a protracted series of confrontations between the group and city officials, Philadelphia police SWAT units, collaborating with the FBI, assault a home occupied by MOVE, an African American anarchist organization with strong spiritual leanings. Although it is known that there are several children inside, police pour copious amounts of asphyxiating and highly flammable CS gas into the building, then set it ablaze using a huge explosive charge lowered from a helicopter. The fire is left to burn for hours, and police are witnessed firing upon those attempting to escape the flames. 11 MOVE members, including 5 children, are killed and 2 city blocks burned to the ground. Not only the mass murder, but the pattern of official actions leading up to it violate a broad range of international law, including the International Declaration of Human Rights, the International Covenant on Civil and Political Rights, the International Covenant on Economic, Social and Cultural Rights, the International Declaration on Elimination of All Forms of Intolerance or Discrimination Based on Religion or Belief, and the American Convention on Human Rights. The use of CS gas and explosives under such circumstances also violates the spirit, if not the letter, of the 1928 Geneva Protocol for the Prohibition of Asphyxiating, Poisonous and Other Gases, as well as the 1949 Geneva Convention IV Relative to the Protection of Civilian Persons in Time of War and Additional Protocol II. In a prefiguration of a much larger replay conducted against Branch Davidians near Waco, Texas, 8 years later (see the entry for Apr. 19, 1993), only the surviving MOVE members are prosecuted.

July 25: 12 of 15 Security Council member-states endorse draft res. S/17354/Rev. 1, calling for imposition of mandatory sanctions in order to resolve the "South Africa Question." The U.S. joins the UK in vetoing the resolution (final vote: 12-2-1).

June 26: The U.S. abstains from endorsing, but does not veto, a French resolution to impose tighter voluntary sanctions against South Africa. U.S. policy towards Pretoria remains unchanged.

Sept. 13: 10 of 15 Security Council member-states endorse draft res. S/17459, deploring Israel's "repressive measures" in the occupied territories and calling upon Israel to comply with international law in its treatment of the Palestinians. The U.S. employs its veto to override them (final vote: 10-1-4).

Oct. 21: Following a speech before the General Assembly by Swedish PM Olaf Palme in which it is argued that no member-state should be allowed to underwrite more than 10% of the UN operating budget—the U.S. is at the time underwriting 25%—lest its influence overshadow that of other member-states, the Reagan administration seizes the opportunity to begun withholding payment of U.S. dues to the UN. Appearances to the contrary, however, the Reaganite objective is precisely the opposite of Palme's. Rather than reducing U.S. influence, Reagan's gambit is intended to amplify and expand it dramatically, with repeated announcements that America's back payments will be made only when the UN agrees to undertake a range of "structural reforms" unilaterally dictated by the U.S. By 1995, the U.S. is in arrears to the tune of $1.18 billion, thereby seriously impairing the UN's functioning.

Oct. 25: 133 member-states endorse UNGA Res. 40/4, calling for increased UN cooperation with the League of Arab States. Only the U.S. and Israel cast opposing votes.

Nov. 15: 12 of 15 Security Council member-states endorse draft res. S/17633, condemning South Africa's continuing illegal occupation of Namibia and calling for the imposition of tightened sanctions and other measures to force Pretoria to withdraw its forces. The U.S. joins the UK in vetoing the resolution (final vote: 12-2-1).

Nov. 29: 133 member-states endorse UNGA Res. 40/23, calling for economic and other changes necessary to promote social progress in the Third World. Only the U.S. casts an opposing vote.

Dec. 2: 125 member-states endorse UNGA Res. 40/52, condemning foreign economic interests impeding implementation of the Declaration on the Granting of Independence to Colonial Countries and Peoples in Namibia and elsewhere. The U.S. is 1 of 9 countries casting an opposing vote.

Dec. 9: The U.S. declines to endorse the Inter-American Convention to Prevent and Punish Torture, which comes into force on Feb. 28, 1987, with 13 state parties. As of this writing, the U.S. remains a nonsignatory state, mainly because certain policies and conditions in its own prisons are construed as torture within the Convention. The U.S. refusal thus adds up to an insistence upon its "sovereign right" to perpetrate torture, as defined in international law.

Dec. 10: Only the U.S. and Israel cast votes opposing UNGA Res. 40/64, which tightens sanctions against South Africa because of its continuing policy of apartheid.

Dec. 12: 101 member-states endorse UNGA Res. 40/93, calling for Israeli nuclear disarmament. Only the U.S. and Israel enter opposing votes.

Dec. 12: 131 member-states endorse UNGA Res. 40/96, reaffirming the Palestinian right to self-determination. Only the U.S. and Israel enter opposing votes.

Dec. 13: 134 member-states endorse UNGA Res.40/114, positing "the indivisibility and interdependence of economic, social, cultural, civil and political rights." Only the U.S. casts an opposing vote.

Dec. 13: 130 member-states endorse UNGA Res. 40/124, calling for the adoption of alternatives by the UN in furthering the enjoyment of human rights and fundamental freedoms. Only the U.S.—meanwhile, as always, proclaiming itself "the world's foremost champion of freedom"—casts an opposing vote.

Dec. 13: 100 member-states endorse UNGA Res. 40/139, deploring the human rights situation in El Salvador. Only the U.S. and Israel cast opposing votes.

Dec. 13: 121 member-states endorse UNGA 40/148, calling for measures to be taken to combat the spread of nazi, fascist and neofascist activities. Only the U.S. and Israel cast opposing votes.

Dec. 16: Only the U.S. and Israel cast votes in opposition to UNGA Res. 40/161, which conveys General Assembly acceptance of the annual Report of the Special Committee to Investigate Israeli Practices Affecting the Human Rights of the Population in the Occupied Territories.

Dec. 16: Only the U.S. and Israel cast votes opposing UNGA Res. 40/165, which approves continued funding for the UN Work and Relief Agency for Palestine Refugees in the Near East.

Dec. 16: 137 member-states endorse UNGA Res. 40/168, describing Israeli policy as a major barrier to peace in the Middle East. Only the U.S. and Israel cast opposing votes.

Dec. 17: 137 member-states endorse UNGA Res. 40/169, which approves expenditure of UN funds to sponsor economic development in the Palestinian territories. Only the U.S. and Israel cast opposing votes.

Dec. 17: 145 member-states endorse UNGA Res. 40/170, mandating the provision of humanitarian assistance to the Palestinian people. Only the U.S. and Israel enter opposing votes.

Dec. 17: 134 member-states endorse UNGA Res. 40/182, accepting the Draft Charter of the Economic Rights and Duties of States. Only the U.S. casts an opposing vote.

Dec. 17: 153 member-states endorse UNGA Res. 40/201, condemning the living conditions to which Palestinians are subjected. Only the U.S. and Israel enter opposing votes.

Dec. 17: 141 member-states endorse UNGA Res. 40/207, pointing to the need for changes in the longterm trends of economic development, esp. with regard to the Third World. Only the U.S., citing possible "impairment of free trade," casts an opposing vote.

Dec. 17: 133 member-states endorse UNGA Res. 40/445, calling for increased international cooperation in the areas of money, finance, debt, resource flow, trade and development. Only the U.S., again citing possible "impairment of free trade," casts an opposing vote.

1986

Jan. 17: 11 of 15 Security Council member-states endorse draft res. S/17730.Rev. 2, condemning Israeli treatment of civilians in southern Lebanon and calling upon Israel to comply with the requirements of the 1949 Geneva Convention IV. The U.S. employs its veto to override them (final vote: 11-1-3).

Jan. 30: 13 of 15 Security Council member-states endorse draft res. S/17769/Rev. 1, calling upon Israel to respect Muslim holy places in the occupied territories. The U.S. employs its veto to override them (final vote: 13-1-1).

Feb. 6: 10 of 15 Security Council member-states endorse draft res. S/17796, condemning Israel's shooting down of a Libyan airliner which has strayed off course. The U.S. employs its veto to override them (final vote: 10-1-4).

Mar. 16: Pres. Reagan makes the sensational allegation that Nicaragua's Sandinista leaders are involved in smuggling cocaine into the U.S. The charge, trumpeted in virtually every media outlet in the country, turns out, like Reagan's earlier "White Paper" (see the entry for Feb. 23, 1981), to be vacuous, a fact that goes rather less well reported. It also serves to eclipse a story appearing in the *San Francisco Examiner* the same day, recounting how it is not the Sandinistas, but rather the CIA-supported Nicaraguan contras who have been trafficking in cocaine, sustaining their low-intensity war effort against the Managua government in much the same way Vang Pao's Agency-sponsored Hmong army in Laos had been organized to use heroin for such purposes during the early 1970s (see the entry for Apr. 5, 1971). Considerable evidence confirms the magnitude, scope and duration of the CIA/contra/cocaine connection during subsequent "Iran-Contra Hearings" concerning another illicit mechanism with which the Agency's Nicaraguan proxies are funded (see the entry for June 27, 1986).

Domestically, the influx of CIA-connected cocaine, especially when converted into a form known as "crack," feeds a cynical "war on drugs" through which a preemptive counterinsurgency campaign is conducted against people of color who have become increasingly discontent with the administration's "trickle down" economic policies. By 1989, 1 in 4 African American males is resultantly caught up in the U.S. penal system, giving them a greater probably of imprisonment than that faced by their black counterparts in South Africa at the height of apartheid. This last is obviously contrary to the International Convention on the Elimination of All Forms of Racial Discrimination (1966), as well as the 1973 International Convention on the Suppression and Punishment of the Crime of "Apartheid," and the International Covenant on Economic, Social and Cultural Rights (1966). As concerns violations accruing from the Reagan administration's anti-Sandinista operations, see the entry for June 27, 1986.

Apr. 14: The U.S. launches an airstrike against the Libyan cities of Tripoli and Benghazi, resulting in massive damage and more than 100 civilian deaths. Libyan head of state Muamar al-Qadaffi is specifically targeted—in violation even of U.S. domestic law—with the result that his adopted infant daughter is killed. The attack is ostensibly carried out in retaliation for the earlier bombing by "Libyan terrorists" of a Berlin nightclub in which a U.S. serviceman was killed, although there is no evidence linking Libya to the incident, and German intelligence has concluded that no Libyans were involved (Pres. Reagan also alleges that Libya has sponsored bombings at the Rome and Vienna airports, although the Italian and Austrian intelligence services firmly deny it). The airstrike is thus conducted without Security Council authorization, and absent the least proof of any hostile action by Libya against the U.S., a blatant violation of the 1970 Declaration on Principles of International Law Concerning Friendly Relations and Cooperation Among States in Accordance With the Charter of the United Nations (esp. Chapters I, VI and VII) and UNGA 337A (V). It thus constitutes an act of aggressive war under provision of the 1945 London Charter. Given the nature of the U.S. attack, violations of the 1923 Hague Rules of Aerial Warfare, 1949 Geneva Convention IV and UNGA Res. 2444 are also apparent.

Apr. 21: 9 of 15 Security Council member-states endorse draft res. S/18016/Rev. 1, condemning the U.S. attack on Libya as a violation of international law. The U.S. employs its veto to override them (final vote: 9-1-5).

May 23: 12 of 15 Security Council member-states endorse draft res. S/18087/Rev. 1, calling for the imposition of punitive measures against South Africa because of its recent aggression against Botswana, Zambia and Zimbabwe. The U.S. joins the UK in vetoing the resolution (final vote: 12-2-1).

June 18: 12 of 15 Security Council member-states endorse draft res. S/18163, condemning South Africa's illegal intervention in Angola, and calling for the implementation of "all necessary measures" to force Pretoria to cease and desist. The U.S. joins the UK in vetoing the resolution (final vote: 12-2-1).

June 27: The ICJ enters an advisory opinion in the case of *Nicaragua v. U.S.*, finding the U.S. mining of Nicaraguan harbors to be illegal. The Reagan administration responds to this first-ever ruling against it by repudiating the court's jurisdiction, then vetoes a Security Council resolution designed to enforce the court's ruling. The dispute occurs amidst an undeclared but protracted "low-intensity" war waged by the U.S. against Nicaragua's leftist Sandinista government following the overthrow of long-time American client—and self-acknowledged dictator—Anastasio Somoza in 1979. In a replay of the strategy applied against Cuba during the early 1960s, the U.S. employs the "Contras," a surrogate force of expatriate rightwing Nicaraguans to do the actual fighting, providing weapons, munitions, equipment and "advisors." This is illegal even under U.S. law, making it necessary for officials not only to engage in the drug-trafficking discussed in the entry for Mar. 16, 1986, but in a series of convoluted transactions wherein U.S. weapons provided to Israel are secretly transferred to Iran in exchange for "off the books" cash with which to fund the war effort. Finally, in late 1988, after 6 years of relentless cross-border raids, 40,000 deaths, and the near-total destruction of their economy, Nicaraguans accept a "peace accord" resulting in the reinstatement of a government acceptable to the U.S. As is to some extent indicated in the ICJ opinion, the U.S. campaign to destroy the Sandinistas violates the 1970 Declaration on Principles of International Law Concerning Friendly Relations and Co-operation Among States in Accordance With the Charter of the United Nations (most esp. Chapters I, VI and VII), Article 18 of the OAS Charter, UNGA Resolutions 337A (V), 380 (V), 2131 (XX) and 3314 (XXIX), the Universal Declaration of Human Rights, the 1949 Geneva Convention IV and Additional Protocol II, UNGA Res. 2444, and the 1978 Red Cross Fundamental Rules of International Humanitarian Law Applicable in Armed Conflicts. U.S. repudiation of ICJ jurisdiction places the U.S. still further beyond the pale of international legality.

July 31: 11 of 15 Security Council member-states endorse draft res. S/18250, calling for enforcement of the ICJ advisory opinion in *Nicaragua v. U.S.* The U.S. employs its veto to override them (final vote: 11-1-3).

Oct. 26: By prearrangement, Israeli PM Peres hands the reigns of power back to Yitzhak Shamir, who promptly scuppers his predecessor's "moderate" initiatives. So popular is the old terrorist's hardline defiance of international law among Israeli voters that, on Nov. 1, 1988, Shamir is propelled into yet another term as prime minister, this one of 4 years duration (those who claim that LEHI was merely an "aberrant fringe" in pre-state zionist politics, and even more irrelevant after the attainment of Israeli statehood, would do well to note that this is Shamir's *third* stint as PM). Despite the absolute refusal of SC Resolutions 242 and 338 forming the core of Shamir's Likud ideology, and the fact that his positions and policies are formulated accordingly, the flow of U.S. support to Israel increases steadily during his tenure.

Oct. 27: 124 member-states endorse UNGA Res. 41/11, calling for establishment of a zone of peace and cooperation in the South Atlantic. Only the U.S. casts an opposing vote.

Oct. 28: 11 of 15 Security Council member-states endorse draft res. S/18428, calling once again for enforcement of the ICJ advisory opinion in *Nicaragua v. U.S.* The U.S. employs its veto to override them (final vote: 11-1-3).

Dec. 3: 148 member-states endorse UNGA Res. 41/68A, embracing UNESCO's "new world information order," designed to eliminate imbalances in the information and communications fields. The U.S. alone casts an opposing vote.

Dec. 4: 126 member-states endorse UNGA Res. 41/90, calling for a review of the implementation of the Declaration of the Strengthening of International Security. The U.S. alone casts an opposing vote.

Dec. 4: 117 member-states endorse UNGA Res. 41/91, calling for a multilateral "results-oriented dialogue" for purposes of "improving the international situation." The U.S. alone casts an opposing vote.

Dec. 4: 102 member-states endorse UNGA Res. 41/92, calling for establishment of a comprehensive system of international peace and security. The U.S., joined by France, cast the only opposing votes.

Dec. 4: 146 member-states endorse UNGA Res. 41/128, the United Nations Declaration of the Right to Development. Only the U.S. casts an opposing vote.

Dec. 4: 148 member-states endorse UNGA Res. 41/151, calling for measures to ensure the human rights and dignity of migrant workers. Only the U.S. casts an opposing vote. Meanwhile, U.S. domestic law and policy continues its rapid evolution in precisely the opposite direction.

Dec. 8: 146 member-states endorse UNGA Res. 41/450, calling for increased protection against products harmful to health and the environment. Only the U.S., citing its usual "trade" rationale, casts an opposing vote.

1987

Feb. 20: 10 of 15 Security Council member-states endorse draft res. S/18705, calling for imposition of mandatory sanctions against South Africa in order to compel its compliance with international law. The U.S. joins the UK in vetoing the resolution (final vote: 10-3-2).

Apr. 9: 9 of 15 Security Council member-states endorse draft res. S/18785, calling for the imposition of "all necessary measures" to compel South Africa to end its illegal occupation of Namibia. The U.S. joins the UK in vetoing the resolution (final vote: 9-3-3).

May 13: Amnesty International releases a report documenting that conditions in the federal "super-maximum" prison at Marion, Illinois, violate every one of the UN Standard Minimum Rules for the Treatment of Prisoners (1955). A year later, a second AI report indicates that the situation is even more extreme in the government's Lexington High Security Unit for Women, in Kentucky. By then, other human rights organizations have reached similar conclusions with respect to Shawangunk Correctional Facility in New York, the then-new Pelican Bay "supermax" in California, and others. Quite uniformly, the studies conclude that U.S. penal policy at both the state and federal levels has been formulated in conscious violation of the 1975 Declaration on Protection from Torture, the 1984 Convention Against Torture and Other Cruel, Inhuman or Degrading Treatment or Punishment, and the Universal Declaration of Human Rights. Subsequently, the offending U.S. policies have been intensified, as is witnessed by the regimen imposed from the outset at the newest federal supermax at Florence, Colorado.

July 3: The *U.S.S. Vincennes*, on patrol in the Persian Gulf, fires a surface-to-air missile at an Iranian commercial airliner, killing all 290 people aboard. Although the Pentagon pronounces the incident to have been "accidental," no official apology is issued, the U.S. officially refuses to indemnify the families of the victims, and both the ship's captain and the air defense officer who launched the missile are decorated for their performance in 1990. The U.S. posture in this instance bears obvious comparison to that it displayed vis-à-vis the Soviet Union after the Soviets shot down Korean Airlines Flight 007, which had illegally penetrated their airspace in 1983. Still more to the point, it bears comparison to the outpouring of outrage in the U.S.—and official insistence both upon prosecution of those responsible and billions in compensation for the families of those killed—when, in 1988, Libya is alleged to have blown up Pan Am Flight 103 in retaliation for the 1986 American bombing of Tripoli and Benghazi (see the entry for Apr. 14, 1986). While Libya eventually settles the claim against it, the equally meritorious claims of Libyan and Iranian families against the U.S. have, on the other hand, been dismissed out-of-hand by American courts and the U.S. refuses to accept ICJ jurisdiction in such matters (see the entry for June 27, 1986).

Oct. 14: The Senate finally votes to ratify the 1948 Convention on Prevention and Punishment of the Crime of Genocide. In doing so, however, it attached a "Sovereignty Package" consisting of 2 "reservations" and 5 "understandings," on the basis of which the U.S. claims the "right" to exempt itself from compliance at its own discretion. Thus, within weeks of the Reagan Administration's depositing of the ratification with the UN Secretariat in November, several prior signatories—Denmark, Finland, Ireland, Italy, the Netherlands, Norway, Spain, Sweden and the U.K.—all enter strong objections, challenging the legality of the Senate maneuver. The so-called Sovereignty Package has not been retracted, and the objections have not been withdrawn. As of this writing, the U.S. has still to become a valid signatory. In 1951, however, the ICJ declared the Genocide

Convention to have attained the force and status of customary international law. The U.S. is thus obliged to comply with the Convention's terms and provisions, whether or not it *ever* enters a valid ratification. The U.S. Senate has no more standing to alter that fact than did the nazi officials who made the same claim from the defendants' dock at Nuremberg.

Oct. 15: 153 member-states endorse UNGA Res. 42/5, reaffirming the need for greater cooperation between the UN and the League of Arab States. The U.S. and Israel again cast the only opposing votes.

Nov. 12: 94 member-states endorse UNGA Res. 42/18, asserting the need for compliance with ICJ rulings with regard to U.S. military and paramilitary operations against Nicaragua. The U.S. and Israel cast the only opposing votes.

Dec. 2: 145 member-states endorse UNGA Res. 42/69J, calling upon Israel to abandon plans to resettle Palestinian refugees away from their homes in the West Bank. Only the U.S. and Israel cast opposing votes. The resettlement continues with full U.S. support.

Dec. 7: 153 member-states endorse UNGA Res. 42/159, calling not only for measures to prevent international terrorism, but for a comprehensive study of its root causes, and for an international conference to define terrorism in such a way as to distinguish it from legitimate wars of national liberation. Only the U.S. and Israel cast opposing votes.

Dec. 8: 140 member-states endorse UNGA Res. 42/162B, calling for the training of journalists to strengthen communications services in the underdeveloped world. The U.S. alone casts an opposing vote.

Dec. 9: Beginning in the Jabaliya refugee camp, the Palestinian population of the Gaza Strip initiates a sustained mass revolt known as the Intifada. Although the demonstrators engage in no "violence" more serious than throwing stones, burning tires and waving the Palestinian flag, the IDF—complying with orders from Defense Minister Yitzhak Rabin to "break their bones"—responds with riot batons, tear gas, water cannons, rubber bullets and live ammunition. The population of the West Bank then joins in. Rabin replies with a still more sweeping program of repression, including "deportation of political activists, political assassination, administrative detention, mass arrests, curfews, punitive economic policies, the closing down of schools and universities, and the breaking up of communal structures." By the end of the first year, having itself sustained no fatalities in the process, the IDF has killed at least 390 unarmed Palestinian men, women and children; of these, more than 100 died upon being hit by "nonlethal" rubber bullets, 66 were asphyxiated by "nonlethal" CS gas (36 were children aged 12 or younger), and the demonstrations/killing continue for another 2 years. Despite these blatant crimes against humanity, the U.S. remains steadfast in its support to Israel, supplying ever-increasing quantities of weaponry and financial support, helping fend off meaningful action by the UN, and increasingly incorporating Israeli "crowd control" rationales/techniques into its own police procedures. A different result obtains, however, in that the Intifada galvanizes Arab support for the attainment of Palestinian statehood to an unprecedented degree; conversely, sentiments reviling the U.S. and Israel reach an all-time high on the "Arab street." The unremitting pattern of U.S.-supported Israeli atrocities attending the Intifada also gives rise, in 1988, to Hamas, an Islamicist group dedicated to the waging of "Jihad"—literally "struggle," meaning "Holy War" in this context—against Israel and its supporters. Like Hizbullah (see the entries for Apr. 18 and Oct. 23, 1983), Hamas adopts the tactic of suicide bombing in a desperate bid to offset the technological advantages enjoyed by their oppressors.

Dec. 11: 94 member-states endorse UNGA Res. 42/176, calling for an end to the embargo on Nicaragua. Only the U.S. and Israel cast opposing votes. The U.S. embargo continues, full-force.

Dec. 11: 154 member-states endorse UNGA Res. 42/198, calling for increased international cooperation with regard to the external debt problems of underdeveloped countries. The U.S. alone, claiming that Third World debt relief would "impair trade," casts an opposing vote.

Dec. 11: 131 member-states endorse UNGA Res. 42/441, authorizing the preparation of summary records for a UN conference on trade and development. The U.S. casts the only opposing vote on that as well.

Dec. 14: PLO Chairman Arafat, following up on resolutions passed by the Palestinian National Congress on Nov. 15, holds a press conference in Geneva. There, he confirms that the PLO has "totally and absolutely renounce[d] terrorism, including individual, group and state terrorism." He then goes on to clarify that the PLO has "unconditionally accepted Resolutions 242 and 338," and is therefore proposing a "two-state solution" to the Israeli/Palestinian conflict (a formulation implicitly following Sadat's much-reviled acceptance of Israel's "right to exist," even without resolution of the illegalities embodied in its founding; see the entry for Sept. 17, 1977). Israeli PM Shamir rejects Arafat's overture on its face, opining—perhaps projecting his own self-concept onto the Palestinians—that "those who have been terrorists will always remain terrorists." The U.S., however, is ensnared in the fact that then-Sec. of State Kissinger went on record in 1975 positing precisely the criteria Arafat has now addressed as the "essential preconditions" for U.S. recognition of the PLO as a legitimate negotiating partner (no such requirements were ever imposed upon Israel, of course). However grudgingly, the U.S. therefore opens a formal dialogue with PLO representatives. Concerned that a negotiated settlement may thus have been rendered inevitable, former Israeli PM Peres—now vice-premier— laments that the U.S. decision to at last allow the Palestinians themselves a voice in determining their fate represents "a sad day for all of us."

1988

Jan. 18: 13 of 15 Security Council member-states endorse draft res. S/19434, strongly deploring Israeli attacks against Lebanese territory and its treatment of civilians in the occupied areas of southern Lebanon. The U.S. employs its veto to override them (final vote: 13-1-1).

Feb. 1: 14 of 15 Security Council member-states endorse draft res. S/19466, calling upon Israel to accept the de jure applicability of the 1949 Geneva Convention IV to its policies in the occupied territories of Lebanon, Palestine and Syria. The U.S. employs its veto to override them (final vote: 14-1-0).

Mar. 8: 10 of 15 Security Council member-states endorse draft res. S/19585, calling for the imposition of mandatory sanctions as a means of compelling Pretoria to comply with international law. The U.S. joins the UK in vetoing the resolution (final vote: 10-2-3).

Apr. 15: 14 of 15 Security Council member-states endorse draft res. S/19780, condemning Israeli treatment of civilian populations in the occupied territories, calling upon Israel to rescind a recent order to deport Palestinians from certain areas, and demanding that the Israelis comply with the requirements of the 1949 Geneva Convention IV in its occupation policies. The U.S. employs its veto to override them (final vote: 14-1-0).

May 10: 14 of 15 Security Council member-states endorse draft res. S/19868, condemning another Israeli invasion of Lebanon and demanding immediate withdrawal. The U.S. employs its veto to override them (final vote: 14-1-0).

Oct. 18: 146 member-states endorse UNGA Res. 43/3, calling for greater UN cooperation with the League of Arab States. Only the U.S. and Israel cast opposing votes.

Oct. 25: 89 member-states endorse UNGA Res. 43/11, accepting the ICJ opinion in Nicaragua v. U.S. (see the entry for June 27, 1986). Only the U.S. and Israel cast opposing votes.

Oct. 25: 140 member-states endorse UNGA Res. 43/12, calling for greater UN cooperation with the Organization of African Unity. Only the U.S. casts an opposing vote.

Nov. 3: 130 member-states endorse UNGA Res. 43/21, describing the Intifada as a legitimate response to Israel's denial of Palestinian rights. Only the U.S. and Israel cast opposing votes.

Nov. 14: 144 member-states endorse UNGA Res. 43/23, calling for the declaration of the southern Atlantic as a zone of international peace and cooperation. Only the U.S. votes against the resolution.

Nov. 22: 133 member-states endorse UNGA Res. 43/29, condemning foreign economic interests impeding implementation of the 1960 Declaration on the Granting of Independence to Colonial Countries and Peoples in Namibia and elsewhere. The U.S. is 1 of 9 countries voting against the resolution.

Nov. 22: 147 member-states endorse UNGA Res. 43/45, calling for immediate implementation of the Declaration on the Granting of Independence to Colonial Countries and Peoples in all colonial territories. The U.S. and Israel cast the only opposing votes.

Nov. 22: 149 member-states endorse UNGA Res. 43/46, calling for increased dissemination by UN agencies of information on decolonization. Only the U.S. and Israel cast opposing votes.

Nov. 22: 135 member-states endorse UNGA Res. 43/47, calling for an "International Decade for Eradication of Colonization." Only the U.S. casts an opposing vote.

Dec. 5: 149 member-states endorse UNGA Res. 43/50K, condemning the continuation of apartheid in South Africa. Only the U.S. and Israel vote against the resolution.

Dec. 6: 143 member-states endorse UNGA Res. 43/54C, declaring Israeli policies to be the primary obstacle to peace in the Middle East. Only the U.S. and Israel cast opposing votes.

Dec. 6: 152 member-states endorse UNGA Res. 43/57E, calling for establishment of a UN Relief and Work Agency for Palestine Refugees. Only the U.S. and Israel cast opposing votes.

Dec. 6: 152 member-states endorse UNGA Res. 43/58D, accepting the Report of the Special Committee to Investigate Israeli Practices Affecting the Human Rights of the Population of the Occupied Territories. Only the U.S. and Israel cast opposing votes.

Dec. 7: 154 member-states endorse UNGA Res. 43/70, calling for prevention of an arms race in outer space. The U.S. alone casts an opposing vote.

Dec. 7: 99 member-states endorse UNGA Res. 43/80, calling for Israeli nuclear disarmament. Only the U.S. and Israel cast opposing votes.

Dec. 8: 154 member-states endorse UNGA Res. 43/146, calling for improved measures to "ensure the dignity and human rights of all migrant workers." Only the U.S. casts an opposing vote (Israel abstains).

Dec. 9: 117 member-states endorse UNGA Res. 43/160A, granting UN observer status to all national liberation movements recognized as such by the League of Arab States. Only the U.S. and Israel cast opposing votes.

Dec. 9: 137 member-states endorse UNGA 43/164, approving the Draft Code of Crimes Against Peace and the Security of Mankind. Only the U.S. and Israel cast opposing votes.

Dec. 14: 14 of 15 Security Council member-states endorse draft res. S/20322, strongly deploring an Israel attack against Lebanese territory on Dec. 9. The U.S. employs its veto to override them (final vote: 14-1-0).

Dec. 15: 138 member-states endorse UNGA Res. 43/176, affirming the right to self-determination of the Palestinian people. Only the U.S. and Israel cast opposing votes.

Dec. 20: 128 member-states endorse UNGA Res. 43/195, calling for increased international cooperation to eradicate poverty in developing countries. The U.S. alone votes against the resolution.

Dec. 20: 150 member-states endorse UNGA Res. 43/198, calling for an alleviation of the external debt crisis in order to facilitate development in Third World countries. The U.S. alone votes against the resolution.

Dec. 22: The U.S. signs and the Senate ratifies the Vienna Convention on Protection of the Ozone Layer. Although this makes compliance a domestic as well as international legal requirement, the U.S. persistently fails to fulfill its obligations in this respect, especially with regard to "co-operation in the legal, scientific and technical fields" (see, e.g., the entry for Nov. 10, 2001).

1989

Jan. 11: The U.S. endorses the Declaration on the Prohibition of Chemical Weapons adopted by the UN Conference of the same name. As of this writing, however, stockpiles at the Tooele Army Ordnance Depot in Utah remain intact.

Jan. 11: 9 of 15 Security Council member-states endorse draft res. S/20378, condemning a recent U.S. shoot-down of Libyan aircraft as a violation of international law. The U.S. employs its veto to override them (final vote: 9-4-2).

Feb. 1: The U.S. refuses to endorse ECOSOC's Draft Code of Conduct on Transnational Corporations.

Feb. 17: 14 of 15 Security Council member-states endorse draft res. S/20463, "strongly deploring" Israel's policies and practices in the occupied territories, as well as the ongoing Israeli refusal to comply with relevant Security Council resolutions and other requirements of international law. The U.S. employs its veto to override them (final vote: 14-1-0).

Apr. 20: 129 member-states endorse UNGA Res. 43/233, affirming the right to self-determination of the Palestinian people. Only the U.S. and Israel cast opposing votes.

May 14: With Israel's image badly tattered by its response to the Intifada—and with its confidence shaken by the inability of the IDF to quell it—PM Shamir advances a tentative "peace plan" in which, although the idea of a Palestinian state is rejected a priori, Israel will conduct preliminary discussions with non-PLO Palestinian representatives regarding disposition of the occupied territories. On May 20, Sec. of State James Baker embraces the idea, and, in Sept., Egyptian President Mubarak offers his services as host. In an unprecedented gesture, even the PLO agrees to temporarily step aside. Under severe pressure from his own Likud party, however, Shamir then abruptly reverses himself, announcing that Israel will not participate. Nonetheless, on Mar. 13, 1990—having been cast by Ariel Sharon and others as a "capitulationist"—he becomes the first prime minister in Israeli history removed by vote of the Knesset. Allowed to return to his position 12 weeks later, Shamir, lesson learned, fields the most rightwing cabinet ever assembled in a country noted for rightwing cabinets. Although such comportment is deeply embarrassing to the U.S., and despite the fact that the Israeli posture ends up to all appearances being more in conflict with the requirements of the UN Charter than it was at the outset, U.S. support to Israel continues without interruption.

June 9: 14 of 15 Security Council member-states endorse draft res. S/20677, condemning Israeli practices and policies in the occupied territories of Palestine and Syria. The U.S. employs its veto to override them (final vote: 14-1-0).

July 31: Jordan's King Hussein, weary of perpetual Israeli subterfuge, announces relinquishment of all legal and administrative claims to the West Bank, and that his country will no longer be party to negotiations "in behalf of" the Arab population there. Henceforth, to sustain even a pretense that it is seeking a means of complying with SC Resolutions 242 and 338, Israel will have no alternative but to negotiate directly with the Palestinians. Ignoring Arafat's clear statement in Geneva a few months earlier (see the entry for Dec. 14, 1988), Israeli PM Shamir responds that there can be no negotiation with "terrorists who deny the right of Israel to its very existence." Although the U.S. itself appears inclined to attempt a final cooptation of the PLO, its material support to Shamir's obstructionist régime remains undiminished.

Nov. 7: 14 of 15 Security Council member-states endorse draft res. S/20945/Rev. 1, deploring Israel's policies and practices in the occupied territories. The U.S. employs its veto to override them (final vote: 14-1-0).

Dec. 6: 151 member-states endorse UNGA Res. 44/42, calling for the implementation of SC Res. 242 (1967) and realization of Palestinian self-determination. Only the U.S. and Israel, joined on this occasion by Dominica, vote against the resolution.

Dec. 15: The U.S. refuses to endorse UNGA Res. 44/128, the Second Optional Protocol to the International Covenant on Civil and Political Rights, aimed at eliminating the death penalty. Although the protocol enters into force on July 11, 1991, with 29 state parties, the U.S. as of this writing remains a nonsignatory, purporting to reserve unto itself the "sovereign prerogative" of indulging in a form of state murder invalidated under international law.

Dec. 20: The U.S. launches "Operation Just Cause," the fullscale invasion of Panama. Although Pres. George Bush claims the assault is necessary to serve a warrant on the Panamanian head of state—military strongman Manuel Noriega, a former CIA asset whom U.S. intelligence agencies claim is involved in drug trafficking—the actual motive has far more to do with Noriega's increasing independence: refusing to extend U.S. "rights" to base troops in the Panama Canal Zone through the year 2000, to allow Panamanian territory to be used as a staging area for U.S. operations against Nicaragua, to participate in the ongoing U.S. embargo of Cuba, and so on. Having failed to coerce Panama's compliance with its desires through various means, including an ever more stringent embargo commencing in late 1985, the U.S. exercises its "military option," killing an estimated 4,000 Panamanians—their bodies are quickly buried in mass graves and their deaths officially denied by Washington—and wounding as many as 20,000 others in the process. Noriega is arrested and hauled off to the U.S., where he remains incarcerated in a federal maximum security prison, and his U.S.-installed successors have, understandably enough, proven far more deferential vis-à-vis their mighty neighbor to the north. "Just Cause" embodies blatant violations of the 1970 Declaration on Principles of International Law Concerning Friendly Relations and Co-operation Among States in Accordance With the Charter of the United Nations (including virtually every article falling under Chapters I, VI and VII), most of the articles falling under Chapters I, II, IV and V of the OAS Charter, UNGA Resolutions 337A (V), 380 (V), 2131 (XX), 2444 and 3314 (XXIX), as well as the 1949 Geneva Convention IV. The economic measures undertaken by the U.S. with regard to Panama prior to 1989 also violated numerous articles falling under Chapter IX of the UN Charter.

Dec. 23: 10 of 15 Security Council member-states endorse draft res. S/21048, condemning the U.S. invasion of Panama as a gross violation of international law. The UK and France join the U.S. in vetoing the resolution (final vote: 10-4-1).

1990

Jan. 17: 13 of 15 Security Council member-states endorse draft res. S/21084, condemning U.S. violations of international laws pertaining to diplomatic immunity during its invasion of Panama. The U.S. employs its veto to override them (final vote: 13-1-1).

Apr. 2: Mexican physician Humberto Alvarez-Machain is kidnapped and tortured at U.S. behest, then brought to the U.S. for prosecution on charges relating to the 1985 torture-murder of DEA agent Enrique "Kiki" Camarena. (Alvarez-Machain, whose cross-border abduction has been approved by the U.S. Att'ny Gen., is accused of keeping Camarena alive while he was being tortured). The Supreme Court then clears the way for Alvarez-Machain to be tried in the U.S., ruling that, since it does not *specifically* forbid the U.S. from kidnapping Mexican nationals, U.S.-Mexico Extradition Treaty has "no bearing" on the case. Ironically, a jury subsequently finds Alvarez-Machain to be innocent of the charges against him.

Apr. 13: Iraqi President Saddam Hussein, in a communication to his patron, George Bush, proposes a plan to eliminate weapons of mass destruction from all countries in the Middle East. Bush, undoubtedly with

Israel's nuclear arsenal in mind, "categorically rejects" the idea. Such a response is, of course, in flat contradiction, not only to the Nuclear Non-Proliferation Treaty and the conventions on chemical and biological weapons, as well as a host of UN resolutions. It also puts the lie to current U.S. assertions that Hussein was always hell-bent on preserving such weapons in his own arsenal.

May 13: The Phoenix Indian School, a residential facility, holds its final commencement ceremony. The school's closure marks the end of an era, lasting more than a century, during which the federal government utilizes such facilities—at one point there are nearly 100 of them—for the express purpose of destroying the cultural identity of every single American Indian child—and thus the viability of indigenous cultures themselves—within its claimed boundaries. In order to accomplish this, it was necessary to forcibly transfer thousands of youngsters from successive generations from their homes/communities/societies to the schools, where they were kept for years on end, often under conditions that can only be described as horrific (the death rates in many facilities was more than twice that of Dachau). Any such policy embodies patent violation of virtually every subpart of the 1948 Genocide Convention, esp. Articles II(b), pertaining to the causing of serious mental harm to members of the target group, and II(e), pertaining to the forced transfer of children. Systematic violations of the Universal Declaration of Human Rights, the American Declaration on the Rights and Duties of Man, and the American Convention on Human Rights is also self-evident.

May 31: 14 of 15 Security Council member-states endorse draft res. S/21326, condemning Israel's gross and ongoing violation of Palestinian rights. The U.S., arguing that the moment is "inopportune" for such a resolution, vetoes it (final vote: 14-1-0).

Aug. 2: Iraq, still very much a U.S. client state—Pres. Bush had approved the transfer of $5 million in advanced computers to the Iraqi military only the day before—occupies neighboring Kuwait, on the Persian Gulf. Although there is a strong case that Kuwait is actually Iraq's own 19th province, separated from the rest of the country by British fiat during the early 1920s—and that, in any event, the Kuwaitis have been using slant-drilling techniques to siphon Iraqi oil from the large fields situated west of Basra—its having undertaken such an action without explicit U.S. sanction prompts Bush to order an "immediate and unconditional withdrawal of Iraqi forces." When, on Aug. 12, Hussein communicates his willingness to leave Kuwait in exchange for a reciprocal Israeli withdrawal from the occupied territories of Palestine, Bush denounces him as being "worse than Hitler." Soon, absurd fables—e.g., Iraqi troops throwing hundreds of Kuwaiti babies out of incubators—are being trumpeted in the media to punctuate the point. Meanwhile, Bush has announced "Operation Desert Shield," the introduction of 425,000 U.S. troops to Saudi Arabia, ostensibly to guard against it too being overrun by Saddam's murderous hordes (there is no evidence that Iraq considered invading the Arabian peninsula). In short order, Bush has announced the advent of a "New World Order," in which "tyrants and dictators" must understand that "what we say, goes" (i.e., accept the tyranny of U.S. dictates). The U.S. refusal to negotiate a resolution to the "Crisis in Kuwait" violates the 1928 Treaty Providing for the Renunciation of War as an Instrument of National Policy (Kellogg-Briand Pact), the 1970 Declaration on Principles of International Law Concerning Friendly Relations and Co-operation Among States in Accordance With the Charter of the United Nations (esp. Article 33(1)) and UNGA Res. 337A (V).

Aug. 2: The U.S. secures passage of SC Res. 660, calling for an immediate withdrawal of Iraqi forces from Kuwait. Several countries, notably Cuba, wish to link the issue to enforcement of SC Resolutions 242 and 338 against Israel, but the U.S. refuses. Cuba then votes against SC Res. 660.

Oct. 8: What Saddam and Cuba have failed to accomplish, the Israelis do for them. An extremist group calling itself the "Temple Mount Loyalists" enters Haram al-Sharif (Noble Sanctuary), location of the Dome of the Rock and al-Aqsa Mosque—to Muslims, this is the most sacred site in all Jerusalem—to assert Jewish control. When infuriated Muslim worshippers pelt the "Loyalists" with rocks, an IDF security detachment opens fire, killing 21 Palestinians. International outrage is so great—especially in the Arab states, several of which have entered into a coalition with the U.S. to drive Iraq from Kuwait and threaten to withdraw unless something is done—that the U.S. is forced to join in two unanimous Security Council condemnations of the Israeli atrocity in as many days. In this case, the U.S. barely avoids having to go along with the imposition of tangible penalties against its "best friend in the Middle East."

Nov. 20: 113 member-states endorse UNGA Res. 45/17, condemning foreign economic and other activities impeding implementation of UNGA Res. 1514 (XV)—the 1960 Declaration on the Granting of Independence to Colonial Countries and Peoples—in Namibia and other non-self-governing territories. The U.S. is 1 of 11 countries casting opposing votes.

Nov. 20: 115 member-states endorse UNGA Res. 45/18, calling for implementation of the Declaration on the Granting of Independence to Colonial Countries and Peoples through specialized UN agencies. Only the U.S. and the U.K. cast opposing votes.

Nov. 20: 110 member-states endorse UNGA Res. 45/32, calling for resolution of the Question of Guam in conformity with the Declaration on the Granting of Independence to Colonial Countries and Peoples. The U.S., joined by Israel and the U.K., cast opposing votes.

Nov. 20: 131 member-states endorse UNGA Res. 45/34, calling for immediate implementation of the Declaration on the Granting of Independence to Colonial Countries and Peoples. Only the U.S. and the U.K. cast opposing votes.

Nov. 20: 133 member-states endorse UNGA Res. 45/35, calling for increased dissemination of information on decolonization by UN agencies. Only the U.S. and the U.K. cast opposing votes.

Nov. 27: 150 member-states endorse UNGA Res. 45/36, calling for declaration of the southern Atlantic as a zone of international peace and cooperation. Only the U.S. casts an opposing vote.

Nov. 28: 116 member-states endorse UNGA Res. 45/37, calling for conveyance of UN observer status upon all national liberation movements recognized as such by the League of Arab States. Only the U.S. and Israel cast opposing votes.

Nov. 29: The U.S. secures passage of SC Res. 678, authorizing the use of "all necessary force," beginning on Jan. 15, 1991, to compel Iraq's withdrawal from Kuwait. Several countries, again led by Cuba, seek to make the authorization contingent upon the adoption of similar measures to compel Israeli compliance with SC Res. 242. When the U.S. refuses to accept any such linkage, Cuba and Yemen vote against SC Res. 678, and China abstains.

Dec. 4: 127 member-states endorse UNGA Res. 45/49, calling for cessation of all nuclear test detonations. The U.S. and Israel are 2 of the 3 countries casting opposing votes.

Dec. 4: 116 member-states endorse UNGA Res. 45/50, calling for an amendment to strengthen the 1963 Treaty Banning Nuclear Weapons Tests in the Atmosphere, in Outer Space and Under Water. The U.S. is 1 of 3 countries casting opposing votes.

Dec. 4: 140 member-states endorse UNGA Res. 45/51, pointing to the urgent need for a Comprehensive Nuclear Test-Ban Treaty. Only the U.S. and Israel cast opposing votes.

Dec. 4: The U.S. alone casts a vote opposing UNGA Res. 45/58, calling for general and complete disarmament.

Dec. 4: 98 member-states endorse UNGA Res. 45/63, condemning Israel's illegal possession of nuclear weapons. Only the U.S. and Israel cast opposing votes.

Dec. 6: Only the U.S. and Israel cast votes opposing UNGA Res. 45/67, calling for resolution of the Question of Palestine in conformity with international law.

Dec. 6: 144 member-states endorse UNGA Res. 45/68, calling for an international conference to discuss reciprocal withdrawal of Iraq from Kuwait and Israel from the occupied territories of Palestine as a "necessary first step" towards achieving peace in the Middle East. Only the U.S. and Israel vote against the resolution, with the U.S. vociferously rejecting the idea of "linkage" between the postures of Iraq and Israel.

Dec. 6: 141 member-states endorse UNGA Res. 45/69, endorsing the Intifada as a legitimate response to the illegality of Israel's policies vis-à-vis Palestinians. Only the U.S. and Israel cast opposing votes.

Dec. 10: An international tribunal convened in New York under authority of ECOSOC Res. 1503 (XLVIII), Article 38 of the Statute of the ICJ, and the 1946 Affirmation of the Principles of International Law Recognized by the Charter of the [Nuremberg] Tribunal concludes that U.S. repression of national liberation movements within its borders violates Protocol II Additional to the 1949 Geneva Conventions, UNGA Resolutions 2625 (XXV) and 3103 (XXVIII), and several articles of the Universal Declaration of Human Rights, as well as Articles 9 and 14 of the International Covenant on Civil and Political Rights. The conditions under which members of such movements are imprisoned in the U.S. are found to be in violation of the UN Standard Minimum Rules for the Treatment of Prisoners, the Declaration on Protection from Torture, and the International Convention Against Torture and Other Cruel, Inhuman or Degrading Treatment or Punishment. The U.S. relationship to all peoples of color under its jurisdiction is found to be in violation of the International Convention on Elimination of All Forms of Racism and the International Covenant on Economic, Social and Cultural Rights. The U.S. relationship to Puerto Rico and Native North America is also found to be in violation of the 1960 Declaration on the Granting of Independence to Colonial Countries and Peoples. The U.S. ignores these findings and continues business as usual.

Dec. 11: 145 member-states endorse UNGA Res. 45/73K, commending and continuing activities undertaken by the UN Relief and Works Agency for Palestine Refugees in the Near East. Only the U.S. and Israel cast opposing votes.

Dec. 11: 145 member-states endorse UNGA Res. 45/74G, approving the annual Report of the Special Committee to Investigate Israeli Practices Affecting the Human Rights of Palestinians and Other Arabs of the Occupied Territories. Only the U.S. and Israel cast opposing votes.

Dec. 12: 128 member-states endorse UNGA Res. 45/77, calling for declaration of the Indian Ocean as an international zone of peace. The U.S. is 1 of 4 countries casting an opposing vote.

Dec. 12: 147 member-states endorse UNGA Res. 45/82, calling for greater cooperation between the UN and the League of Arab States. Only the U.S. and Israel cast opposing votes.

Dec. 14: 120 member-states endorse UNGA Res. 45/84, deploring the adverse consequences accruing from continuing political, military and economic assistance extended to the apartheid régime in South Africa. The U.S. is 1 of 9 countries casting opposing votes.

Dec. 14: 121 member-states endorse UNGA Res. 45/96, calling for the adoption of alternative approaches by the UN in its efforts to advance universal enjoyment of human rights and fundamental freedoms. The U.S. alone casts an opposing vote.

Dec. 14: 113 member-states endorse UNGA Res. 45/130, stressing the importance of the right to self-determination and calling for the immediate granting of independence to all non-self-governing territories. The U.S. is 1 of 15 countries casting opposing votes.

Dec. 14: 121 member-states endorse UNGA Res. 45/132, condemning the use of mercenaries to impede realization of the right to self-determination in non-self-governing territories. The U.S. is 1 of 10 countries casting opposing votes.

Dec. 18: 140 member-states endorse UNGA Res. 45/145, calling for implementation of the 1982 Law of the Sea. The U.S. is 1 of 2 countries casting opposing votes.

Dec. 18: The U.S. refuses to endorse UNGA Res. 45/158, the International Convention on the Protection of the Rights of Migrant Workers and Members of Their Families. As of this writing, the U.S. remains a nonsignatory state.

Dec. 21: 135 member-states endorse UNGA Res. 45/183, calling for increased nonmilitary assistance to the Palestinian people. Only the U.S. and Israel cast opposing votes.

1991

Jan. 2: Iraq again signals its willingness to withdraw from Kuwait, this time in exchange for a U.S. "agreement in principle" to take unspecified steps towards resolving the Palestinian refugee problem. Although several senior U.S. diplomats publicly describe the proposal as a "serious prenegotiating position," Pres. Bush dismisses it out of hand, insisting there can be no linkage of Iraq's conduct to that of Israel. Once again, the U.S. refusal to consider a diplomatic solution violates the 1970 Declaration on Principles of International Law Concerning Friendly Relations and Co-operation Among States in Accordance With the Charter of the United Nations (esp. Article 33(1)), as well as UNGA Res. 337A (V).

Jan. 16: The U.S. unleashes "Operation Desert Storm," an all-out air assault on Iraq. Over the next 43 days, some 67,000 combat sorties are flown—about 35,000 over military targets in the "Iraq-Kuwait Combat Theater," and the rest over Baghdad, Basra and other civilian-populated target areas—during which over 84,000 tons of ordnance is expended. Only about 7,400 tons of this total—less than 10 percent—consists of the "smart" munitions depicted continuously and all but exclusively in the American media. Along with the destruction of military targets, the U.S. takes as its stated objective the obliteration of Iraq's "infrastructure," a term including destruction of electrical power generation, water purification, sanitation and other such facilities, all of which the civilian population depends upon for survival. Given the very high proportion of "dumb bombs" used in the onslaught, it is entirely predictable that upwards of 20,000 Iraqi civilians will be killed in Baghdad alone. "Collateral damage" also includes the bulk of Iraq's food and medical supply stores, scores of hospitals and schools, even a home for the elderly (the destruction is *vastly* greater than anything even allegedly inflicted by Iraq upon Kuwait, and results, according to the

Jordanian Red Crescent Society, in about 120,000 civilian fatalities overall). There is simply no tenable interpretation of the nature/scope of the campaign mounted by the U.S. which brings it even remotely into conformity with the use only of such force as might be necessary to drive Iraq from Kuwait authorized by SC Res. 678. To the contrary, "Desert Storm" is expressly conducted in such a way as to destroy Iraq's military capacity, in the very broadest sense for "at least the next 10 years, [and] preferably, for the next generation," a goal vastly exceeding that set by the Security Council. Moreover, the tactics employed to this end incorporate systematic violation of the 1923 Hague Rules of Aerial Warfare, the London Charter, the 1949 Geneva Convention IV, UNGA Res. 2444, Protocol I Additional to the Geneva Conventions, and the 1978 Red Cross Fundamental Rules of International Humanitarian Law Applicable in Armed Conflicts. Insofar as both cluster bombs and a BLU-82 fuel-air bomb—that is, a huge incendiary device—are used on occasions where civilians are known to be present, violation of the 1981 Convention on Prohibitions or Restrictions on the Use of Certain Conventional Weapons Which May be Deemed to be Excessively Injurious or to Have Indiscriminate Effects is also at issue. Insofar as diplomatic solutions were deliberately and repeatedly avoided, the entire campaign constitutes patent violation of the 1928 Treaty Providing for War as an Instrument of National Policy, and qualifies as an aggressive war—thus a violation of the London Charter—under provision of UNGA Res. 3314 (XXIX).

Jan. 24: The U.S. bombs 2 oil tankers in the harbor at Kuwait City, releasing a gigantic oil slick into the Persian Gulf. A week later, the Pentagon concedes that U.S. planes have bombed the terminus points of 2 major oil pipelines, causing even more oil to spill—previously, Defense Dept. spokespersons had attributed this to Iraqi "environmental terrorism"—placing the entire Gulf ecosystem at risk. By this point, more than 500 combat sorties have been flown against Iraqi chemical plants and nuclear reactors. Hundreds of others have involved the dropping of napalm and white phosphorous ordnance on Iraq's southern oil fields (much is later made, and appropriately so, of the "ecological catastrophe" embodied in Iraq's firing of Kuwaiti oil fields during its withdrawal, but the U.S. was doing the same thing as a matter of course). *None* of this was prompted by the "military necessity" of winning the war; rather, it was, as U.S. officials candidly admitted, undertaken for the explicit purpose of shaping Iraq's postwar destiny. *All* of it, moreover, entailed gross violations of the 1978 Convention on the Prohibition of Military or Any Other Hostile Use of Environmental Modification Techniques.

Feb. 15: Iraq offers once more to withdraw from Kuwait, contingent only upon U.S. acceptance, "in principle," of a linkage of its doing so to the obligation of Israel, set forth in SC Res. 242 (1967), to withdraw its forces from the occupied territories of Palestine and Syria. The U.S. responds that Iraqi withdrawal must be "unconditional," a posture prompting even former Reagan officials like James Webb to opine that Bush is opting for "the rule of brute force" rather than diplomacy. Once again, the U.S. refusal to even consider a nonmilitary resolution violates the 1970 Declaration on

Principles of International Law Concerning Friendly Relations and Co-operation Among States in Accordance With the Charter of the United Nations (esp. Article 33(1)) and UNGA Res. 337A (V).

Feb. 23: The Soviets broker an Iraqi offer to begin withdrawing from Kuwait within 24 hours of a ceasefire, to which the U.S. replies that the withdrawal must be undertaken while the bombing continues. On Feb. 26, while Iraq attempts to comply, its retreating troops, heavily intermixed with fleeing civilians, are set upon full-force by U.S. airpower, armed for the occasion mainly with cluster and incendiary munitions (including napalm). Upwards of 25,000 people are annihilated within hours along the "Highway of Death" leading from Kuwait City to Basra. Setting aside the large numbers of civilians known to be present—a matter rendering the entire "target" illegitimate under terms of the 1923 Hague Rules of Aerial Combat, the London Charter, the 1949 Geneva Convention IV, UNGA Res. 2444, the 1977 Protocol I Additional to the Geneva Conventions, and the 1978 Red Cross Fundamental Rules of International Humanitarian Law Applicable in Armed Conflicts—the fact that the troops involved were plainly "out of combat" made them exempt from attack under provision of the 1949 Geneva Conventions, Common Article III. The use of incendiary and cluster ordnance under such circumstances is also a clear violation of the 1981 Convention on Prohibitions or Restrictions on the Use of Certain Conventional Weapons. Finally, by any rational assessment, the U.S. action plainly exceeds the use of "necessary force" authorized by SC Res. 678.

Feb. 27: Pres. Bush states publicly that "no quarter" will be given to Iraqi soldiers who continue to resist the U.S. invasion of their country. Such orders are illegal under provision of the 1907 Hague Convention IV Respecting the Laws and Customs of War on Land—not to mention the Nuremberg Charter—and have been outlawed in the U.S. Army's own rules of engagement since promulgation of its "Lieber Code" in 1863. Nonetheless, Gen. Norman Schwartzkopf, commander of all U.S. and allied forces in the Gulf, issues several comparable directives and says later that his one concern at the time was, "How long the world would stand by and watch the U.S. pound the living hell out of Iraq without saying, 'Wait a minute—enough is enough.'" It is thus unquestionable that those commanding U.S. military operations were well aware that their overall approach to the war vastly exceeded the use of "necessary force" authorized by SC Res. 678.

Mar. 2: Although a ceasefire has finally been announced by Pres. Bush two days earlier, Gen. Schwartzkopf orders the 24th Infantry Div. to attack an Iraqi Republican Guard unit as it moves defenselessly—and *away* from Kuwait—along a causeway near Basra. Over 2,000 Iraqi soldiers are slaughtered in a hail of fire from U.S. tanks, artillery and helicopter gunships using laser-guided weapons. Violation of a ceasefire in this fashion has been listed as a war crime under the U.S. Army's rules of engagement since 1863. Among other laws of war violated are the 1907 Hague Convention IV, the London Charter, Common Article III of the 1949 Geneva Conventions, and the1978 Red Cross Fundamental Rules of International Humanitarian Law Applicable in Armed Conflicts. Moreover, it is once again clear that, by any definition, the parameters of "necessary force" established by SC Res. 678 have been completely ignored.

Apr. 3: SC Res. 687 is passed, requiring Iraq to "submit to the United Nations a declaration disclosing the totality of its stockpile of weapons of mass destruction, the components of those weapons, and the means of their production." The resolution, reinforced in this regard by another a few months later, also requires Iraq to admit UN inspectors (UNSCOM) for purposes of verifying the accuracy of the Iraqi declaration, to oversee destruction of the offending weapons/materials, and then to oversee ongoing Iraqi compliance with prohibitions again reacquisition of them. The U.S., which assumes ascendancy over UNSCOM from the outset, soon converts the organization in part into an apparatus for gathering intelligence having nothing to do with its ostensible mission. Ultimately, in 1998, the persistence of espionage activity and other such provocations leads Iraq to expel all U.S. inspectors. His operation thus subverted by U.S. misconduct, UNSCOM head Richard Butler orders inspectors from other countries to leave as well (the Iraqi government thus did *not* "kick out [all] the UN weapons inspectors," as is now commonly asserted by U.S. officials and media pundits alike).

Apr. 5: SC Res. 688 is passed, extending UN protection over the Kurdish and Shi'ite minorities residing, respectively, in the northern and southern regions of Iraq. Although the U.S. and Britain claim that the Security Council has thereby imposed northern and southern "no-fly zones" over Iraqi territory, and authorized them to patrol the airspace involved to ensure compliance, such matters were never discussed by the Council, and SC Res. 688 contains no such language. In effect, the U.S. and Britain subvert the resolution to their own purpose of waging an unauthorized and undeclared but nonetheless continuous air war against Iraq from mid-1991 onward. For the most part the protracted assault is low-key enough to go mostly unnoticed—e.g., small airstrikes triggered by such "hostile" Iraqi actions as turning on a radar unit—but periodically involves largescale bombing and missile attacks (see, e.g., the entry for Dec. 16, 1998). Instructively, while the offenders claim their aggression is essential to the "humanitarian mission" of protecting Kurds from Iraqis, both U.S. and British pilots are assigned to provide air support to *Turkish* military forces conducting a largescale counterinsurgency campaign in northern Iraq against Kurdish guerrillas seeking to establish an independent state (from 1995-1997, and again in 2000, upwards of 50,000 Turkish troops are engaged in such operations; all told, some 30,000 Kurds are killed, hundreds of thousands of others displaced). Overall, the U.S./British air campaign against Iraq is conducted in violation of the 1928 Treaty Providing for Renunciation of War as an Instrument of National Policy (Kellogg-Briand Pact), the London Charter, the 1970 Declaration on Principles of International Law Concerning Friendly Relations and Co-operation Among States in Accordance With the Charter of the United Nations (esp. Chapters I, VI and VII), and UNGA Resolutions 337A (V), 380 (V) and 2131 (XX). With regard to air support missions flown in support of the Turks, violations of the 1923 Hague Rules of Aerial Combat, the 1949 Geneva Convention IV and

Additional Protocol I, UNGA Res. 2444, and the 1978 Red Cross Fundamental Rules of International Humanitarian Law Applicable in Armed Conflicts are apparent. In view of the non-self-governing status accorded the Kurds by both Turkey and Iraq, violation of UNGA Res. 1514 (XV)—the 1960 Declaration on the Granting of Independence to Colonial Countries and Peoples—is also at issue.

June 25: With U.S. backing, the Yugoslav republics of Croatia and Slovenia declare independence, precipitating a civil war within the Balkan state. Although each republic holds a self-determining right to do so— Yugoslavia was, after all, created not by its ostensible citizens, but by the League of Nations after World War I—U.S. intervention has seriously deformed the process and its implications. Especially in Croatia, substantial U.S. financial/political support accrues to overtly fascist groups, notably a faction headed by Franjo Tudjman, an unabashed Holocaust denier and admirer of Hitler who openly dedicates himself to the "ethnic purity" of Croatia. As incipient head of state, Tudjman adopts the flag of the nazi-aligned World War II Ustasha—a Croatian formation directly responsible for the deaths of as many as a million Serbs, Jews and Gypsies—as his country's emblem, and initiates a process of repatriating aging Ustashi to join his new government (see the entry for Dec. 11, 1946). When the Yugoslav government moves to prevent the Croatian/Slovenian breakaway—much as Abraham Lincoln moved to prevent the Confederate States of America from seceding in 1861—both the U.S. and the European Union impose stringent sanctions on Yugoslavia, while the U.S. channels significant military aid to the Tudjman régime. By Jan. 1992, both Slovenia and Croatia have been recognized by the U.S. and the EU as independent states and are scheduled for UN admission, despite the fact that no resolution to Yugoslavia's Charter-guaranteed right to maintain its territorial integrity has been achieved (this is usefully compared to an ongoing U.S. insistence that Iraq "must remain one country," despite the clear right of the Kurds to form a state of their own). The twisting of law to fragment Yugoslavia in a particular way allows for the direct incorporation of the country's northerly region into Germany's "sphere of immediate economic interest," and its southerly realm into the U.S. strategic dominion. Overall, U.S. policy in the Balkans violates the 1970 Declaration on Principles of International Law Concerning Friendly Relations and Co-operation Among States in Accordance With the Charter of the United Nations, as well as UNGA Resolutions 337A (V), 380 (V) and 2131 (XX). U.S. provision of armaments to Croatia also occurs in contravention of UNGA Res. 300 (IV).

Sept. 12: A story in *Newsday* reports the confirmation by U.S. officials that thousands of young Iraqi conscripts had been buried alive in 49 mass graves during the 4 days of "ground war" occurring towards the end of "Desert Storm." The victims had been given no more opportunity to surrender to their killers in this instance, than they were to the aircraft that had been relentlessly bombing and strafing them for weeks. Their fates, moreover, had been preplanned by U.S. strategists openly dedicated to "significantly impairing Iraq's military manpower availability for the next generation" (special plows had been built for the purpose of accomplishing mass live burials, operators trained for months in advance). Providing enemy combatants a reasonable opportunity to surrender has been a part of U.S. military law since 1863. It is also required under the 1899 Hague Convention II on Land Warfare, the 1907 Hague Convention IV Respecting the Laws and Customs of Land Warfare, the Nuremberg Charter, the 1949 Geneva Convention III, and the 1978 Red Cross Fundamental Rules of International Humanitarian Law Applicable in Armed Conflicts.

Oct. 28: The other 14 members of the Security Council approve a resolution condemning Israel's expropriation of Palestinian land around East Jerusalem, demanding that the impounded areas be returned. The U.S. vetoes the initiative, claiming that it has its own plans for resolving the issue.

Oct. 30: Having discovered the utility of Arab cooperation during the Gulf War, and therefore seeking to neutralize some of the effects of its ongoing bias in favor of Israel, the U.S. convenes a "comprehensive Mideast peace conference" in Madrid. In essence, the affair is merely a more grandiose version of the discussions earlier proposed, then refused by Israeli PM Shamir (see the entry for May 14, 1989). When Shamir attempts to avoid this conference as well, the U.S., which has to this point provided Israeli with $77 billion in outright subsidies, a sum that is increasing at the rate of $3 billion per year, quietly threatens to cut the flow of aid. While the PLO is expressly excluded as a sop to Israel, the star of the show nonetheless turns out to be Haidar Abdel Shafi, head of the Palestinian delegation, who proposes a phased Israeli withdrawal from Gaza and the West Bank overlapping with a transition period of "institution building" in the occupied territories, and, thereby, the "timely" realization of a Palestinian state confederated with Jordan. The plan, described as being "unreasonably reasonable" by one observer, is accepted in principle by all parties, including the PLO, except Israel.

Nov. 25: 141 member-states endorse UNGA Res. 46/19, calling for the declaration of the southern Atlantic as a zone of international peace and cooperation. Only the U.S. casts an opposing vote.

Dec. 4: In an effort to break the impasse presented by Israel at the Madrid conference, the U.S. attempts to host what are meant to be bilateral discussions between the Israelis and the Palestinians, with Jordanian and U.S. representatives sitting in, in Washington, D.C. Although the Palestinian and Jordanian delegations arrive as scheduled, the Israelis do not. Eventually, after considerable U.S. arm twisting, Shamir sends a delegation. After 5 rounds of talks, however, Israel still refuses to accept either the principle of exchanging "land for peace"—that is, of complying with SC Resolutions 242 and 338—or creation of a Palestinian state (in any form). Quite the opposite: in Feb. 1992, Shamir announces his intent, as a matter of policy, to *accelerate* the process of Jewish settlement in the West Bank. The U.S. nonetheless remains unwilling to deliver unto its ally anything resembling the sort of ultimatum presented to Iraq only 2 years before.

Dec. 5: 140 member-states endorse UNGA Res. 46/24, calling for greater UN cooperation with the League of Arab States. Only the U.S. and Israel cast opposing votes.

Dec. 6: 110 member-states endorse UNGA Res. 46/28, calling for an amendment to strengthen the 1963 Treaty Banning Nuclear Weapons Tests in the Atmosphere, in Outer Space and Under Water. Only the U.S. and Israel cast opposing votes.

Dec. 6: 147 member-states endorse UNGA Res. 46/28, pointing to the urgent need for a Comprehensive Nuclear Test-Ban Treaty. Only the U.S. and Israel cast opposing votes.

Dec. 6/9: 152 member-states endorse UNGA Res. 46/36D, calling for general and complete disarmament. Only the U.S. and Israel cast opposing votes.

Dec. 6: 76 member-states endorse UNGA Res. 46/39, condemning Israel's illegal possession of nuclear weapons. The U.S. and Israel cast opposing votes.

Dec. 9: 151 member-states endorse UNGA Res. 46/46L, commending and continuing activities undertaken by the UN Relief and Works Agency for Palestine Refugees in the Near East. Only the U.S. and Israel cast opposing votes.

Dec. 9: 150 member-states endorse UNGA Res. 46/47G, approving the annual Report of the Special Committee to Investigate Israeli Practices Affecting the Human Rights of Palestinians and Other Arabs of the Occupied Territories.

Dec. 9: 127 member-states endorse UNGA Res. 46/49, calling for implementation of a declaration proclaiming the Indian Ocean an international zone of peace. The U.S. is 1 of 4 countries casting an opposing vote.

Dec. 11: 137 member-states endorse UNGA Res. 46/77, calling for immediate implementation of the 1960 Declaration on the Granting of Independence to Colonial Countries and Peoples. Only the U.S. and the U.K. cast opposing votes.

Dec. 11: 143 member-states endorse UNGA Res. 46/72, calling for increased dissemination of information on decolonization by UN agencies. Only the U.S. and the U.K. cast opposing votes.

Dec. 11: Only the U.S. and Israel cast votes opposing UNGA Res. 46/74, calling for resolution of the Question of Palestine in conformity with international law. Only the U.S. and Israel cast opposing votes.

Dec. 11: 104 member-states endorse UNGA Res. 46/75, calling for an international conference on peace in the Middle East. Only the U.S. and Israel cast opposing votes.

Dec. 11: 142 member-states endorse UNGA Res. 46/76, embracing the Intifada as a legitimate response to the illegality of Israeli policies vis-à-vis Palestinians. Only the U.S. and Israel cast opposing votes.

Dec. 12: 140 member-states endorse UNGA Res. 46/78, calling for implementation of the 1982 Law of the Sea. Only the U.S. casts an opposing vote.

Dec. 13: 127 member-states endorse UNGA Res. 46/79E, calling for tougher sanctions against South Africa to end apartheid. The U.S. is 1 of 3 countries casting opposing votes.

Dec. 16: 119 member-states endorse UNGA Res. 46/84, calling for increased enforcement of the International Convention on Suppression and Punishment of the Crime of Apartheid. Only the U.S. enters an opposing vote.

Dec. 16: 122 member-states endorse UNGA Res. 46/89, condemning the use of mercenaries to impede the realization of self-determination in non-self-governing territories. The U.S. is 1 of 11 countries casting opposing votes.

Dec. 17: 123 member-states endorse UNGA Res. 46/117, calling for adoption of alternative approaches by the UN in its efforts to further universal enjoyment of human rights and fundamental freedoms. The U.S. and Israel cast the only opposing votes.

Dec. 19: 135 member-states endorse UNGA Res. 46/162, deploring the living conditions imposed upon Palestinians in the occupied territories. Only the U.S. and Israel cast opposing votes.

Dec. 20: 125 member-states endorse UNGA Res. 46/199, deploring the adverse economic and social effects on Palestinians caused by Israel's illegal settlements in the occupied territories. Only the U.S. and Israel cast opposing votes.

Dec. 20: 137 member-states endorse UNGA Res. 46/201, calling for increased nonmilitary assistance to the Palestinian people. Only the U.S. and Israel cast opposing votes.

1992

Feb. 19: The Israeli public finally gets a small taste of the interventionist diplomacy routinely visited by the U.S. on other countries. Sec. of State Baker "lets slip" at a news conference that the guarantee of a $10 billion loan to Israel is being "delayed" by Shamir's obstruction of the "Mideast peace process." The message is clear: if Israelis wish to continue to enjoy the benefits of U.S. financial support—military support is unmentioned, but it is implied—they will usher in a government acceptable to the U.S. On June 23, Shamir, and Likud more generally, are soundly defeated at the polls by Yitzhak Rabin and the Labor Party (the number of seats held by Likud in the

Knesset drops from 40 to 32, while Labor's increases from 39 to 44). It is important to note, however, that for all the "liberalization" the shift from Likud to Labor supposedly implied, the change was mainly cosmetic. Rabin had, after all, been Shamir's defense minister. "Both parties," moreover, "were deeply opposed to Palestinian nationalism and denied that the Palestinians had a right to national self-determination. Both always refused to negotiate with the PLO, and this refusal was absolute rather than conditional. Both were also unconditionally opposed to the establishment of an independent Palestinian state." That the U.S. would intervene in Israel's domestic affairs to install a Labor government does not therefore suggest a desire to ensure Israeli compliance with international law. Rather, it suggests merely that the U.S. was seeking a more sophisticated—and thus less embarrassing—partner with whom to project the illusion of legal compliance, while accomplishing a precisely opposite result.

Mar. 8: The Pentagon publishes what it calls its so-called *Defense Planning Guide*. Therein, it is explained that its "security" requires that the U.S. attain nothing less than complete domination of the world. Not only must U.S. strategy be designed to prevent the (re)emergence of a rival global power like the old Soviet Union, the document's authors assert, but it "must maintain the mechanism for deterring potential competitors from even aspiring to a greater regional role" than that they presently enjoy. While it is acknowledged that the U.S. "must account sufficiently for the advanced industrial nations" if this "New World Order" is to be viable, no mention at all is made of Third World interests. Nor is there so much as a cursory nod to any need for U.S. compliance with the rule of law. The U.S. position is constructed in direct contradiction to the 1970 Declaration on Principles of International Law Concerning Friendly Relations and Co-Operation Among States in Accordance with the Charter of the United Nations and UNGA Res. 337A (V).

Apr. 6: Although a satisfactory resolution to the issue of Yugoslav rights vis-à-vis Croatia and Slovenia has yet to be achieved, the U.S. and the EU recognize Bosnia as an independent state, unleashing an outright civil war there. On May 30, Pres. Bush issues Executive Order 12808, declaring the conflict there to be "an extraordinary threat to the national security, foreign policy, and economy of the United States"—exactly how any of this might be so is left unexplained—a formulation plainly implying that military force may be employed unless Yugoslavia simply accepts its dismemberment. The same day, a U.S.-engineered resolution—SC Res. 757—is passed by the Security Council, imposing "tough economic sanctions on the Yugoslav government" (Russia abstains rather than risk unilateral military action by the U.S.). On Sept. 22, with Bosnia now slated for membership, the U.S. orchestrates the General Assembly's expulsion of Yugoslavia from the UN, making it the first country ever ejected. On Nov. 16, the U.S. pushes through a second Security Council resolution, this one imposing a "total naval blockade...including the stopping of all ships approaching Yugoslavia on the Danube River as well as the Adriatic Sea." On Dec. 15, the U.S. arranges for economic sanctions to be tightened still further, as Yugoslavia is expelled from the International Monetary Fund. Meanwhile, U.S. aid pours into

Bosnia, supporting the Islamicist régime of Alija Izetbegovic, which has openly dedicated itself to converting the republic into a theocracy. U.S. Balkans policy remains in violation of the 1970 Declaration on Principles of International Law Concerning Friendly Relations and Co-operation Among States in Accordance With the Charter of the United Nations, as well as UNGA Resolutions 337A (V), 380 (V) and 2131 (XX).

June 4: The U.S. signs and the Senate ratifies the UN Framework Convention on Climate Change. Although this makes compliance a domestic as well as international legal requirement, the U.S. has consistently failed to meet its obligations, most spectacularly with respect to the follow-up implementation formula embodied in the 1997 Kyoto Protocol (see the entries for Dec. 11, 1997, and Nov. 10, 2001).

Aug. 5: A photograph is taken through barbed wire by British TV reporter Penny Marshall of a longterm tuberculosis victim named Fikret Alic, a Bosnian Muslim. The image of Alic's emaciated body is then deployed in the media by Ruder Finn, a public relations firm retained by Bosnia's Izetbegovic government, as well as the Tudjman régime in Croatia, to portray the treatment of Muslims by Bosnian Serbs—and, by extension, Yugoslavia—as being comparable to that of the Jews by the nazis, the Trnopolje camp in which Alic was photographed as "a new Belsen." No mention is made, needless to say, of Alic's TB, that Trnopolje is not a concentration camp but rather a refuge facility to which many Muslims had fled rather than being pressed into service by Izetbegovic's forces, or that it was Marshall, not Alic, who had been behind barbed wire when the photo was shot. Because it is under sanctions, Yugoslavia is barred from hiring a PR firm to make such things public. In one of history's more sublime ironies, Ruder Finn's propaganda blitz—passed off as "news" in U.S. outlets—is thus spectacularly successful in mobilizing the potent American Jewish lobby *in support* of Izetbegovic's Islamic fascists and, at least implicitly, Tudjman's literal nazis. The Serbs' supposed "genocide" of Bosnian Muslims is then used by the U.S., with broad international support, to organize a tribunal in the Hague for the explicit purpose of prosecuting Serbian leaders and soldiers (see the entry for May 2, 1996). This, in turn, serves as the "humanitarian" pretext for U.S.-organized NATO intervention in Kosovo (see the entry for Mar. 24, 1999). The U.S./British subterfuge is conducted in violation of UNGA Res. 337A (V). Implicit violations of UNGA Resolutions 380 (V) and 2131 (XX) are also at issue.

Oct. 4: An international tribunal convened in San Francisco under authority of ECOSOC Res. 1503 (XLVIII), Article 38 of the Statute of the ICJ, and the 1946 Affirmation of the Principles of International Law Recognized by the Charter of the [Nuremberg] Tribunal concludes that the U.S. relationship to Native North Americans, Native Hawaiians, Puerto Ricans, Mexican Americans and African Americans is fundamentally colonial in nature, and thus in violation of Chapters XI and XII of the UN Charter, as well as the 1960 Declaration on the Granting of Independence to Colonial Countries and Peoples. It is found that maintenance of the U.S. colonial régime, both internally and externally, entails a broad range of human rights abridgements perpetrated on a systematic basis. These include, but are not restricted to, violation of virtually every article in the Universal Declaration of Human Rights and the American Convention on Human Rights, the International Covenant on Economic, Social and Cultural Rights, the International Covenant on Civil and Political Rights, and the International Convention on the Elimination of All Forms of Racial Discrimination. Especially in the case of Native North Americans, clear violations of the Genocide Convention are found to have occurred. The U.S. ignores these findings and continues with business as usual.

Oct. 29: 119 member-states endorse UNGA Res. 47/12, calling for greater cooperation between the UN and the League of Arab States. Only the U.S. and Israel cast opposing votes.

Nov. 24: 59 member-states endorse UNGA Res. 47/19, calling for an immediate end to the U.S. embargo against Cuba. Only the U.S. and Israel cast opposing votes. The embargo continues.

Nov. 25: 127 member-states endorse UNGA Res. 47/23, calling for immediate implementation of the 1960 Declaration on the Granting of Independence to Colonial Countries and Peoples. Only the U.S. and the U.K. cast opposing votes.

Nov. 25: 132 member-states endorse UNGA Res. 47/24, calling for increased dissemination of information on decolonization by UN agencies. Only the U.S. and the U.K. cast opposing votes.

Nov. 25: 100 member-states endorse UNGA Res. 47/29, calling for the conveyance of UN observer status upon all national liberation movements recognized as such by the League of Arab States. The U.S. is 1 of 9 countries casting opposing votes.

Dec. 9: 118 member-states endorse UNGA Res. 47/46, calling for an amendment to strengthen the 1963 Treaty Banning Nuclear Weapons Tests in the Atmosphere, in Outer Space and Under Water. Only the U.S. and Israel cast opposing votes.

Dec. 9: 159 member-states endorse UNGA Res. 47/47, pointing to the urgent need for a Comprehensive Nuclear Test-Ban Treaty. Only the U.S. casts an opposing vote.

Dec. 9/15: 168 member-states endorse UNGA Res. 47/52, calling for general and complete disarmament. The U.S. alone abstains.

Dec. 9: 64 member-states endorse UNGA Res. 47/56, condemning Israel's illegal possession of nuclear weapons. The U.S. and Israel, joined by Turkey, cast the only opposing votes.

Dec. 9: 63 member-states endorse UNGA Res. 47/59, calling for the nuclear disarmament of Israel. Only the U.S. and Israel cast opposing votes.

Dec. 11: 140 member-states endorse UNGA Res. 47/63, describing Israeli policy as a major obstacle to peace in the Middle East. Israel alone casts an opposing vote, while the U.S. is 1 of 5 countries abstaining.

Dec. 11: Only the U.S. and Israel cast votes opposing UNGA Res. 47/64, which calls for resolution of the Question of Palestine in conformity with international law.

Dec. 11: 135 member-states endorse UNGA Res. 47/65, calling for implementation of the 1982 Law of the Sea. Only the U.S. casts an opposing vote.

Dec. 14: Only the U.S. and Israel cast votes opposing UNGA Res. 47/69, which commends and continues activities undertaken by the UN Relief and Works Agency for Palestine Refugees in the Near East.

Dec. 14: 143 member-states endorse UNGA Res. 47/70G, approving the annual Report of the Special Committee to Investigate Israeli Practices Affecting the Human Rights of Palestinians and Other Arabs of the Occupied Territories.

Dec. 14: 144 member-states endorse UNGA Res. 47/74, calling for the declaration of the southern Atlantic as a zone of international peace and cooperation. Only the U.S. casts an opposing vote.

Dec. 16: 113 member-states endorse UNGA Res. 47/81, calling for enforcement of the International Convention on Suppression and Punishment of the Crime of Apartheid. Only the U.S. and Israel cast opposing votes.

Dec. 16: 118 member-states endorse UNGA Res. 47/84, condemning the use of mercenaries to impede the expression of self-determination in non-self-governing territories. The U.S. is 1 of 10 countries casting opposing votes.

Dec. 17: In a move that "out-Shamires Shamir," Israeli PM Rabin orders the round-up and, though none of them are Lebanese, summary deportation of 416 Hamas activists to Lebanon. As is later observed by Israeli analyst Avi Shlaim, "the deportation order [is] without precedent and in flagrant violation of international law. None of the alleged Islamic activists [is] charged, tried, or allowed to appeal before being driven blindfolded into exile." Rabin's action, supposedly taken in response to the murder of a single Israeli border policeman, causes the Palestinian delegation to abruptly suspend their ongoing discussions with Israel, then in their eighth round. It is likely Rabin intended exactly this result, since continuing Israeli recalcitrance has brought the talks to a virtual stalemate. Precipitating a Palestinian walkout allows him to shift the onus of responsibility in the popular perception. The U.S. brings no particular pressure to bear upon Israel to bring its position vis-à-vis the Palestinian deportees into compliance with the Universal Declaration of Human Rights and/or the International Covenant on Civil and Political Rights.

Dec. 18: 106 member-states endorse UNGA Res. 47/116E, calling for tougher sanctions against South Africa because of its ongoing policy of apartheid. Only the U.S. and Israel cast opposing votes.

Dec. 22: 155 member-states endorse UNGA Res. 47/170, calling upon all states to render nonmilitary assistance to the Palestinian people. Only the U.S. and Israel cast opposing votes.

Dec. 22: 150 member-states endorse UNGA Res. 47/171, calling for a halt to the expansion of Israel's illegal settlements in the occupied territories. Only the U.S. and Israel cast opposing votes.

Dec. 22: 150 member-states endorse UNGA Res. 47/172, deploring the economic and social repercussions suffered by Palestinians as a result of Israel's illegal settlements in the occupied territories. The U.S. and Israel cast opposing votes.

1993

Mar. 13: Enraged by Israel's illegal mass deportation of its cadres (see the entry for Dec. 17, 1992), and by the failure of either the U.S. or UN to take tangible corrective action, Hamas declares open war against the offenders, killing 13 Jewish settlers in the West Bank. Although it is his own "get tough" posturing that has generated the violence, PM Rabin compounds the problem by ordering closure of Israel's borders *along their pre-1967 lines*—thus demonstrating conclusively what he himself actually believes to be the extent of Israel's legitimate territoriality—thereby depriving 120,000 Palestinian families of their livelihood. The number of Palestinians joining Hamas rises sharply as a result. The U.S. offers no comment on the self-evident human rights violations embodied in the Israeli action; U.S. material support to Israel continues without interruption.

Apr. 19: The FBI mounts an all-out assault on the home of a religious sect known as the Branch Davidians outside Waco, Texas. Although the Davidians are accused of having committed no violent acts prior to commencement of the federal offensive against them some 2 months earlier—it *is* alleged that they are in possession of illegal weapons, engaged in the manufacture of illegal drugs, and sexually abuse their children, all of which turns out to be false—and it is known that there are numerous youngsters, including infants, inside, the FBI uses tanks to inject massive quantities of asphyxiating and highly flammable CS gas into the structure (officially and misleadingly referred to as a "compound"). Incendiary flash-bang grenades are then fired into the building, igniting the gas. Snipers believed to be members of the FBI's "Hostage Rescue Team" and/or the army's élite Delta Force are then captured on film firing upon persons attempting to flee the flames. All told, 76 people—23 of them children—are killed, about half by burning alive. Not only the mass murder, but the pattern of federal actions leading up to it violate a broad range of international law, including the Universal Declaration of Human Rights, the International Covenant on Civil and Political Rights, the International Covenant on Economic, Social and

Cultural Rights, the International Declaration on Elimination of All Forms of Intolerance or Discrimination Based on Religion or Belief, and the American Convention on Human Rights. Insofar as the military provided much of the munitions and equipment used by the FBI—and insofar as Delta Force personnel were likely involved in a combat capacity—the use of CS gas and incendiaries also violated the 1928 Geneva Protocol for the Prohibition of the Use in War of Asphyxiating, Poisonous or Other Gases, the 1949 Geneva Convention IV Relative to Protection of Civilian Persons in Time of War and Additional Protocols, and the 1978 Red Cross Fundamental Rules of International Humanitarian Law Applicable in Armed Conflicts. Only the surviving Davidians are prosecuted, however, a fact that leads directly to the retaliatory bombing of the Alfred P. Murrah Federal Building in Oklahoma City on Apr. 19, 1995.

Apr. 27: The newly-elected Clinton administration attempts to finesse the Palestinian delegation at the beginning of the 9th round of Israeli/Palestinian discussions in Washington, D.C., passing out a working paper containing "new terms of reference" which, it claims, will allow the talks to "move forward more rapidly." The Palestinians immediately reject the maneuver, pointing out that the U.S. attempt to substitute the term "disputed" for "occupied" in describing the status of territory in the West Bank and Gaza is not new, but rather the regurgitation of a longstanding Israeli formulation designed to confuse the situation. Whether the territories in question are occupied is not "a matter of opinion," they conclude, but instead a matter of black letter law. Substitution of terms is thus neither analytically honest nor acceptable as a basis for discussion. With that, the talks collapse (a 10th round is conducted from June 15-July 1, but it goes nowhere).

June 21: The Supreme Court holds in *Sale v. Haitian Centers Council* that neither domestic nor international law prohibits the government from forcibly repatriating Haitian refugees intercepted on the high seas. In the decade following the 1981 coup which ousted Haiti's first democratically-elected president, Jean Bertrand Aristide, resulting in mass disappearances, imprisonment, torture and murder of Aristide supporters, the U.S. Coast Guard has intercepted 25,000 fleeing Haitians, allowing only 28 to land in the U.S., advancing the theory that they are "economic" rather than "political" refugees. Hundreds infected with HIV are arbitrarily and indefinitely detained at the U.S. naval base at Guantánamo Bay, Cuba. All of this violates the 1951 Convention Relating to the Status of Refugees and its 1980 Protocol, as well as the requirement of *nonrefoulement* prevailing under customary international law which forbids the forced return of persons to a countries where they are likely to be politically persecuted. Numerous violations of provisions contained in the Universal Declaration of Human Rights, the American Declaration on the Rights and Duties of Man, and the American Convention on Human Rights are also apparent.

June 27: The U.S. launches a cruise missile attack on the headquarters of Iraq's intelligence service. Although the action, which is not authorized by the Security Council, is allegedly undertaken in retaliation for an attempt to assassinate former Pres. Bush during a visit to Kuwait, no evidence is ever produced to confirm that Iraq was involved (or even that the supposed assassination attempt actually occurred). Among the many "collateral" victims of the missile strike is the prominent Iraqi painter, Leila Attar. The U.S. assault violates the 1970 Declaration on Principles of International Law Concerning Friendly Relations and Co-operation Among States in Accordance With the Charter of the United Nations (esp. Chapters I and VI), as well as UNGA Res. 337A (V), the 1923 Hague Rules on Aerial Warfare and the 1949 Geneva Convention IV.

Aug. 23: An international tribunal convened in Honolulu under authority of ECOSOC Res. 1503 (XLVIII), Article 38 of the Statute of the ICJ, and the 1946 Affirmation of the Principles of International Law Recognized by the Charter of the [Nuremberg] Tribunal finds the U.S. relationship to Hawai'i to be in violation of Chapters XI and XII of the UN Charter, as well as the 1960 Declaration on the Granting of Independence to Colonial Countries and Peoples. It is also found that maintenance of U.S. colonial control over the archipelago entails significant and systemic abridgements of human rights vis-à-vis the Kanaka Maoli (Native Hawaiians), including, but not restricted to, violation of virtually every article found in the Universal Declaration of Human Rights, the International Covenant on Civil and Political Rights, and the International Covenant on Economic, Social and Cultural Rights. With the exception of offering a formal apology to the Kanaka Maoli (see the entry for Nov. 23, 1993), the U.S. ignores the findings and continues with business as usual.

Aug. 23: Alarmed by rapid growth of Hamas and the Islamic Jihad in the occupied territories, Israeli PM Rabin startles his constituents by announcing for the first time that "there [is] no escape from recognizing the PLO." In actuality, Israeli representatives have been conducting secret negotiations with the PLO in Oslo, Norway, for several months. It is their assessment, backed by that of the Mossad, that Arafat's foreswearing of armed struggle and willingness to recognize the legitimacy of Israel even without resolving the legal issues attending its creation, have served to discredit him in the eyes of an increasingly number of Palestinian militants. The time is thus right in their opinion to coopt Arafat—and by extension the PLO—altogether, roping them into an agreement through which Israel can present the appearance of having at last granted the Palestinians their rights while actually effecting a final consolidation of its control of their lands and lives. A delighted U.S. endorses the arrangement.

Sept. 13: The Oslo Accords between Israel and the PLO are signed in a highly publicized ceremony on the White House lawn. Officially titled the "Declaration of Principles on Interim Self-Government Arrangements," the Accords require Israel to "relinquish" only the Gaza Strip and the Jericho area of the West Bank within 4 months, although it retains full authority over "external defense" and foreign policy. Authority over taxation and tourism in other portions of the West Bank are to be turned over to the PLO during the same period, along with sole responsibility for such things as education, health and social welfare (thereby letting Israel completely off the hook for the destitution its policies have fostered). Arafat is also charged with converting what remains of the PLO's military wing into a police force which will work directly with the IDF in suppressing Hamas and other such groups (in effect, the PLO is made responsible for securing Israel against the results of its own policies, both historical and current). More significantly still, further land returns are deferred for 2 years, made contingent on whether Arafat's "Palestinian Authority" performs to Israel's specifications, and rendered subject to "further negotiations" (as if Israel possesses a right to some portion of the territory it has been under a legally-binding order to relinquish since 1967). No mention at all is made of the right of Palestinians displaced from their lands from 1948 onward to return to it, or even to be compensated for it. Nor is there mention of the disposition of the many Israeli settlements illegally erected on Palestinian land after 1967. Finally, and most importantly, no mention is made of a timetable by which a Palestinian state will be acknowledged. *None* of this conforms in the least with the requirements embodied in the host of UN resolutions to which Israel is subject. But, as both Israel and its U.S. sponsor are quick to point out, no less than Yasser Arafat has accepted the deal.

Nov. 3: 84 member-states endorse UNGA Res. 48/16, calling for an immediate end to the U.S. embargo against Cuba. The U.S. and Israel, joined by Paraguay and Albania, cast opposing votes. The embargo continues.

Nov. 23: Pres. Bill Clinton signs Public Law 103-150, conveying an official apology by the U.S. government to native Hawaiians for America's illegal participation in the armed overthrow of their constitutional monarchy, subsequent annexation of their territory, and near-total dispossession of the people themselves. Having formally admitted its criminal culpability in the acquisition of Hawai'i, however, the U.S. makes no move to meet its legal obligations under international tort law to effect restitution, reparation or compensation to the victims. As of this writing, the status of both Hawai'i and native Hawaiians remains unchanged, while the U.S. continues its illegal occupation.

Nov. 24: 103 member-states endorse UNGA Res. 48/23, calling for the declaration of the South Atlantic as a zone of international peace and cooperation. The U.S. alone casts an opposing vote.

Dec. 9: 144 member states endorse UNGA Res. 48/28, calling for implementation of the 1982 Law of the Sea. The U.S. alone casts an opposing vote.

Dec. 10: Only the U.S. and Israel cast votes opposing UNGA Res. 48/40, commending and continuing activities undertaken by the UN Relief and Works Agency for Palestine Refugees in the Near East.

Dec. 10: Only the U.S. and Israel cast votes opposing UNGA Res. 48/41, approving the annual Report of the Special Committee to Investigate Israeli Practices Affecting the Human Rights of Palestinians and Other Arabs of the Occupied Territories.

Dec. 10: 113 member-states endorse UNGA Res. 48/47, calling for implementation of the Declaration on the Granting of Independence to Colonial Countries and Peoples through specialized UN agencies. The U.S. is 1 of 5 countries casting opposing votes.

Dec. 10: 141 member-states endorse UNGA Res. 48/52, calling for immediate implementation of the Declaration on the Granting of Independence to Colonial Countries and Peoples in all non-self-governing territories. Only the U.S. and the U.K. cast opposing votes.

Dec. 10: 141 member-states endorse UNGA Res. 48/53, calling for increased dissemination of information on decolonization by UN agencies. Only the U.S. and the U.K. cast opposing votes.

Dec. 14: 155 member-states endorse UNGA Res. 48/59, calling for the Middle East peace process to be conducted in conformity with international law. The U.S. and Israel, joined by the Federation of Micronesia, cast the only opposing votes.

Dec. 14: Only the U.S. and Israel cast votes opposing UNGA Res. 48/60, describing Israeli policy as a major obstacle to peace in the Middle East.

Dec. 16: 118 member-states endorse UNGA Res. 48/69, calling for an amendment to strengthen the 1963 Treaty Banning Nuclear Weapons Tests in the Atmosphere, in Outer Space and Under Water. The U.S. is 1 of 3 countries casting opposing votes.

Dec. 16: 144 member-states endorse UNGA Res. 48/75, calling for general and complete disarmament. The U.S. is 1 of 6 countries casting opposing votes.

Dec. 16: 130 member-states endorse UNGA Res. 48/82, to declare the Indian Ocean an international zone of peace. The U.S. is 1 of 6 countries casting opposing votes.

Dec. 16: 147 member-states endorse UNGA Res. 48/158C, calling for resolution of the Question of Palestine, in conformity with international law. Only the U.S. and Israel cast opposing votes.

Dec. 21: 164 member-states endorse UNGA Res. 48/182, calling for enhanced international cooperation towards achieving a "durable solution" of the problem of 3rd World debt. Only the U.S. casts an opposing vote.

Dec. 21: 143 member-states endorse UNGA Res. 48/212, deploring the economic repercussions suffered by Palestinians as a result of Israel's illegal settlements in the occupied territories. Only the U.S. and Israel cast opposing votes.

1994

Feb. 19: The interim agreement between Israel and the PLO called for in the Oslo Accords is initialed in Cairo (the formal signing occurs in

Washington, D.C., on Sept. 28, 1995). Israel has already begun to renege, specifying that it will "redeploy" IDF forces within the occupied territories rather than initiating their actual withdrawal. PM Rabin comes under intense domestic criticism even for that, with Likud leader Binyamin Netanyahu publicly denouncing him as having "signed an agreement with Hitler." The U.S., on the other hand, steps up its support to the Rabin government, despite its backsliding on legal compliance.

Feb 25: Dr. Bernard Goldstein, an American Jewish transplant to the Israeli settlement at Hebron, no doubt influenced by Netanyahu's "fiery oratory," and using a Galil assault rifle issued by the IDF, opens fire on Muslim worshippers at the Tomb of the Patriarchs, killing 29. In the aftermath, it is revealed that while the IDF has been busily disarming Palestinians in the occupied territories, it has been equally busy providing weapons to Israeli settlers there. Arafat demands removal of all settlers from Hebron. Rabin refuses, because he is "not required to do so by the Oslo Agreement." Although U.S. officials are quoted in the media decrying the "excesses" of certain "Jewish extremists" like Goldstein, his act is not categorized as being that of a *terrorist*. Less still is it concluded that, since the settler-extremists in question are supported as a matter of official policy—60% of the residential construction in the settlements is underwritten by the state, as compared to 25% in Israel proper—the Israeli government qualifies under U.S. guidelines as a "terrorist sponsor." Needless to say, Israel is not placed on the State Dept. list of terrorism-sponsoring states (as compared, say, to Libya, which was bombed on the basis of far less well-substantiated allegations; see the entry for Apr. 14, 1986). There having been no meaningful international response to Israeli settler terrorism—or the policies underlying it—Hamas for the first time launches a suicide bombing campaign; 50 Israelis are killed, another 340 wounded.

May 17: The U.S. endorses SC Res. 925, calling for a "ceasefire" between Hutus and Tutsis in Rwanda. The resolution is couched in terms designed quite deliberately to mask the fact that one side (Hutus), well-armed and organized, is systematically exterminating the other (Tutsis), who are effectively unarmed. A genocide is thus occurring. To describe it as such, however, would require an immediate intervention by UN forces to halt the process. Since no Security Council member can find a self-interest in effecting such an intervention in a "backwater" African country, the situation is carefully treated as if it were something other than what it is. Indeed, from April-June 1994, U.S. spokespersons are explicitly instructed *not* to use the word "genocide" in connection with the Rwanda slaughter, a matter bearing obvious comparison to the simultaneously cavalier usage of the term by these same officials when describing the situation in the former Yugoslavia (where the "genocide" at issue appears to have been largely invented). Ultimately, about 1 million Hutus are exterminated. At the very least, the U.S. performance in this case adds up to a violation of Article III(e), complicity in genocide.

July 18: Peace talks between Israel and Syria, conducted in Washington, D.C., under State Dept. sponsorship, end in stalemate. The main sticking points are that, while Syria insists that Israel must relinquish all territory in the Golan Heights area beyond the boundaries of June 4, 1967—as expressly required by SC Res. 242—Israel "prefers" the international border established by Britain and France to divide Syria from Palestine in 1923 (the difference in territory is small, but the 1923 border would effectively cut Syria off from water in the Sea of Galilee). Israel indicates that it may be willing to "consider" a pull-back to the 1967 line, but only if it is allowed to retain an "early-warning station" on the Golan Heights and Syria agrees to demilitarize its own territory as far north as Damascus (there is, of course, no offer of Israeli reciprocation). In any event, Israel would take 5 years to accomplish a complete withdrawal. Syria replies that the 1923 border has no bearing on Israel's obligations under SC Res. 242, that the resolution provides for no conditions such as the retention of an Israeli military presence in Syrian territory, that the demand for unilateral Syrian demilitarization violates Syria's sovereignty and security requirements—"We have far more to fear from you, than you from us," as one Syrian representative put it—and that, since it took Israel just 3 years to withdraw from the entire Sinai, 6 months would be a more reasonable timetable for the Israelis to remove themselves from the Golan Heights. Finally, Syria rejects Israel's proposition that the two countries normalize relations *before* any Israeli agreement to comply with the by now 27 year old UN decree that it immediately withdraw from occupied Syrian territory. The U.S. makes no discernible effort to persuade Israel to alter its fundamentally illegal position(s), a performance that again bears comparison to its performance vis-à-vis Iraq.

July 25: Israeli PM Rabin and Jordan's King Hussein sign the Washington Declaration in a highly publicized ceremony conducted in the U.S. capitol. The Declaration sets the stage for a treaty of peace between the two countries, signed at a border point in the Arava Desert on Oct. 26. Jordan thus becomes the second Arab state to formally accept the premise of Israel's legitimacy despite the still unresolved illegalities attending its creation. The treaty also commits Jordan to allowing Israeli settlers to retain property under Jordanian sovereignty. Israel recognizes Jordan's "special interest" in certain religious sites in Jerusalem—thus undermining the position of the PLO vis-à-vis the same sites—and commits itself to "working with" Jordan to resolve the problem of an estimated 1.7 Palestinian refugees displaced over the years into Jordanian territory. A beaming Pres. Clinton bestows his blessing on the arrangement.

Oct. 19: The Clinton administration enters into a "framework agreement" with North Korea, by which the latter will freeze its 1 functioning graphite-moderated nuclear reactor—from which weapons-grade material can be produced—and halt construction on 2 larger reactors. In exchange, the U.S. commits itself to provide heating oil to offset the country's loss of energy potential, complete construction of 2 new light water reactors—with which weapons cannot be produced—by 2003, and "move towards normalization of diplomatic and economic relations" within the same timeframe. North Korea immediately honors its end of the bargain. By the time Clinton leaves office more than five years later, however, the U.S. has delivered only on the heating oil. Given this patent U.S. default, and with relations worsening steadily under the new Bush administration, the Koreans resume construction on their own reactors, notifying the U.S. of this in Oct. 2002 (by which time Pres. Bush has already proclaimed them to be part of the "Axis of Evil"; see the entry for Jan. 31, 2002). The U.S. then has the audacity to claim that it is the *Koreans* who "violated the agreement." In actuality, it is the U.S. which is guilty of classic breach of contract. This, in turn, is a violation of the1970 Declaration on Principles of International Law Concerning Friendly Relations and Co-operation Among States in Accordance With the Charter of the United Nations (esp. Chapters I and IX).

Oct. 26: 101 member-states endorse UNGA Res. 49/9, calling for an immediate end to the U.S. embargo against Cuba. Only the U.S. and Israel cast opposing votes. The embargo continues.

Dec. 6: 130 member-states endorse UNGA Res. 49/28, affirming the principles embodied in the 1982 Law of the Sea. Only the U.S., claiming that the law impairs "private enterprise" on the sea floor, casts an opposing vote.

Dec. 9: 165 member-states endorse UNGA Res. 49/33, enlarging the UN Committee on the Peaceful Uses of Outer Space. Only the U.S. casts an opposing vote.

Dec. 9: Only the U.S. and Israel cast votes opposing UNGA Res. 49/35, authorizing continuation of activities undertaken by the UN Relief and Works Agency for Palestine Refugees in the Near East.

Dec. 9: Only the U.S. and Israel cast votes opposing UNGA Res. 49/36, approving the annual Report of the Special Committee to Investigate Israeli Practices Affecting the Human Rights of Palestinians and Other Arabs of the Occupied Territories.

Dec. 9: 119 member-states endorse UNGA Res. 49/41, calling for immediate implementation of the 1960 Declaration on the Granting of Independence to Colonial Countries and Peoples in all non-self-governing territories. Only the U.S. casts an opposing vote.

Dec. 14: Only the U.S. and Israel cast votes opposing UNGA Res. 49/62, reaffirming all relevant UN resolutions as well as the applicability of the 1949 Geneva Convention IV in the occupied territories of Palestine and the Golan Heights.

Dec. 15: 139 member-states endorse UNGA Res. 49/75B, calling for general and complete disarmament. The U.S. is 1 of 3 countries casting opposing votes.

Dec. 15: 131 member-states endorse UNGA Res. 49/82, proclaiming the Indian Ocean as an international zone of peace. The U.S. is 1 of 3 countries casting opposing votes.

Dec. 15: 161 member-states endorse UNGA Res. 49/83, proclaiming the southern Atlantic as an international zone of peace. The U.S. is 1 of 3 countries casting opposing votes.

Dec. 16: Only the U.S. and Israel cast votes opposing UNGA Res. 49/87, characterizing Israeli policies as a major barrier to peace in the Middle East.

Dec. 16: 149 member-states endorse UNGA Res. 49/88, calling for the Middle East peace process to be pursued in conformity with international law. Only the U.S. and Israel cast opposing votes.

Dec. 16: 130 member-states endorse UNGA Res. 49/90, calling for increased dissemination of information on decolonization. Only the U.S. and the U.K. cast opposing votes.

Dec. 19: 133 member-states endorse UNGA Res. 49/132, condemning the economic and social repercussions visited upon Palestinians and other Arab residents of the territories occupied by Israel in 1967. Only the U.S. and Israel cast opposing votes.

Dec. 23: 147 member-states endorse UNGA Res. 49/149, reaffirming the right to self-determination of the Palestinian people. Only the U.S. and Israel cast opposing votes.

Dec. 23: The U.S. is 1 of 5 member-states casting votes opposing UNGA Res. 49/151, reaffirming the importance of the right to self-determination and the need for a speedy granting of independence to all non-self-governing countries and peoples.

1995

May 19: The 14 other Security Council members approve a resolution to take whatever action might be necessary to halt Israeli expropriation of a large tract of Palestinian land in East Jerusalem for purposes of establishing yet another Jewish settlement there. The U.S., arguing that inclusion of enforcement measures would be "counterproductive," vetoes the resolution.

Apr. 14: The U.S. engineers passage of SC Res. 986, allowing Iraq to engage in what is generally touted as "oil-for-food program." According to the Memorandum of Understanding by which the resolution is implemented on May 20, 1996, however, Iraq is constrained to selling only $10 billion worth of oil each year, all of it to be paid into UN-administered accounts. There, 30% of the total is earmarked for payment of "reparations"—i.e., repaying the U.S. and its "coalition partners" for the expense incurred in waging the 1991 war against Iraq—and another 10-15% to underwrite "ongoing UN operations in Iraq" (i.e., weapons inspectors and continuing U.S./British overflights of the "no-fly zones"). By the time an additional 13% earmarked for the 3 million Kurdish residents of the country's northern region is subtracted, only about $4 billion is left to all other purposes (i.e., feeding and providing medical care to Iraq's 18 million Arab citizens, as well as rebuilding the country's devastated infrastructure). In sum, the U.S.-sponsored resolution is designed to "stabilize" the process of slow starvation/death by disease to which the Iraqi population is being subjected, while creating an appearance that the opposite is true. Aside from abuse of Security Council procedures, a violation of Chapter V of the UN Charter, the U.S. maneuver contravenes Article II(c) and all five criteria enumerated under Article III of the 1948 Convention on Genocide. Violations of the Universal Declaration of Human Rights are also self-evident.

May 17: 14 of 15 Security Council member-states endorse draft res. S/1995/394, confirming that the expropriation of Palestinian land is invalid and in violation both of relevant Security Council resolutions and provisions of the 1949 Geneva Convention IV. The U.S. employs its veto to override them (final vote: 14-1-0).

Aug. 4: In a massive exercise in "ethnic cleansing," the Croatian army—trained and equipped by the U.S. pursuant to a military agreement signed in Nov. 1994—launches "Operation Storm," a fullscale invasion of the Serbian district of Krajina. An estimated 14,000 people are quickly killed, another 170,000 pushed as refugees into neighboring Bosnia. U.S. aircraft, committed to NATO "peacekeeping" forces in the region, fly air support missions in behalf of the attackers, and the U.S. blocks a Russian attempt to pass a Security Council resolution condemning the offensive. In the aftermath, the U.S. rewards Croatia with a new and broader military compact, assisting in a thorough reorganization of the country's army based on lessons learned in Krajina.

Nov. 2: 117 member-states endorse UNGA Res. 50/10, calling for an immediate end to the U.S. embargo against Cuba. The U.S. and Israel, joined by Uzbekistan, cast the only opposing votes. The embargo continues.

Nov. 4: 148 member-states endorse UNGA Res. 50/21, calling for the Middle East peace process to be carried forward in conformity with international law. The U.S. and Israel cast the only opposing votes.

Nov. 4: Only the U.S. and Israel cast votes opposing UNGA Res. 50/22, describing Israeli policy as the major barrier to peace in the Middle East.

Nov. 5: Israeli PM Rabin is assassinated by Yigal Amir, described as a "young messianic Zionist" enraged by the prime minister's "coddling of the Palestinians." Rabin's widow afterwards refuses to shake hands with Likud leader Binyamin Netanyahu because, she says, "of the part he played in the incitement that led to the assassination of [her] husband." Nonetheless, Netanyahu is for the next several months spotlighted in American media talk shows as "one of the most promising of Israel's younger statesmen."

Nov. 21: The so-called Dayton Accords are signed at the Wright Patterson Air Force Base in Ohio, finalizing the dismemberment of Yugoslavia. The Accords are virtually identical to two earlier agreements—one brokered by the EU in Lisbon in Mar. 1992, and the "Vance-Owens Plan" put forward in May 1993—which the U.S. has not so much rejected as sabotaged, other than that the Dayton arrangement explicitly designates NATO as guarantor, thus preempting both the UN Security Council and any new European security formation while placing the U.S. in de facto control. In effect, the Dayton Accords are framed in a manner decisively at odds with the 1970 Declaration on Principles of International Law Concerning Friendly Relations and Co-operation Among States in Accordance With the Charter of the United Nations (esp. Chapters I, V, VII and VIII).

Dec. 5: 132 member-states endorse UNGA Res. 50/23, calling for implementation of the 1982 Law of the Sea. Only the U.S. casts an opposing vote.

Dec. 6: 147 member-states endorse UNGA Res. 50/29, accepting the annual Report of the Special Committee to Investigate Israeli Practices Affecting the Human Rights of Palestinians and Other Arabs of the Occupied Territories, calling upon Israel to accept *de jure* applicability of the1949 Geneva Convention IV in its administration of the occupied territories, reaffirming the right of Palestinians to return to their homes. Only the U.S. and Israel cast opposing votes.

Dec. 6: 146 member-states endorse UNGA Res. 50/38, raising the question of American Samoa, Anguilla, Bermuda, the British Virgin Islands, the Cayman Islands, Guam, Monserrat. Pitcairn Island, St. Helena, Tokelau, the Turks and Caicos Islands, and the U.S. Virgin Islands as non-self-governing territories within the meaning of the 1960 Declaration on the Granting of Independence to Colonial Countries and Peoples. The U.S. and U.K. cast opposing votes.

Dec. 6: 133 member-states endorse UNGA Res. 50/40, calling for increased dissemination of information on decolonization. The U.S. and U.K. cast opposing votes.

Dec. 12: 110 member-states endorse UNGA Res. 50/62, calling for an amendment to strengthen the 1963 Treaty Banning Nuclear Weapons Tests in the Atmosphere, in Outer Space and Under Water. The U.S. is 1 of 4 countries casting opposing votes.

Dec. 12: 139 member-states endorse UNGA Res. 50/70, calling for general and complete disarmament. The U.S. is 1 of 18 countries casting opposing votes.

Dec. 12: 56 member-states endorse UNGA Res. 50/73, positing Israel's possession of nuclear weapons as a major factor in the potential proliferation of such armaments in the Middle East. Only the U.S. and Israel cast opposing votes.

Dec. 12: 123 member-states endorse UNGA Res. 50/76, proclaiming the Indian Ocean an international zone of peace. The U.S. is 1 of 3 countries casting opposing votes.

Dec. 15: Only the U.S. and Israel cast votes opposing UNGA Res. 50/84, raising the Question of Palestine and calling upon Israel to comply with all relevant UN resolutions.

Dec. 20: 126 member-states endorse UNGA Res. 50/129, condemning the economic and social repercussions visited upon Palestinians and other Arab residents of the territories occupied by Israel in 1967. Only the U.S. and Israel cast opposing votes.

Dec. 21: 145 member-states endorse UNGA Res. 50/140, reaffirming the right to self-determination of the Palestinian people. Only the U.S. and Israel cast opposing votes.

1996

Jan. 5: Yahya Ayyash, an Hamas leader known as "The Engineer" and held to be the "mastermind" behind the organization's last major bombing campaign (see the entry for Feb. 25, 1994), is assassinated by Israeli intelligence operatives using a booby-trapped cell phone. The murder is widely applauded as being "a blow against international terrorism." No mention is made, however, of the facts that Ayyash's alleged offense resulted from the slaughter of more than 2 dozen Palestinians by an Israeli settler, of the Israeli policies that made the butchery possible/predictable, or that the Hamas leader's murder is itself a form of terrorism. Under these circumstances, Hamas unleashes a new wave of suicide bombings, shortly killing 60 Israelis and wounding scores of others. Israel's official response, fully supported by the U.S., is to once again seal off its 1967 borders, thereby penalizing the entire Palestinian population of the occupied territories and suspend talks with Arafat's newly-elected Palestinian Authority (which is bitterly opposed to its Hamas rivals). Beyond that, PM Shimon Peres, who has returned to power as a replacement for the slain Yitzhak Rabin, announces a policy of relying still more heavily upon the sort of operation that has claimed Ayyash, thereby guaranteeing a steady escalation of retaliatory "Arab violence."

Jan. 12: Ignoring the fact that the Knesset itself routinely seats representatives of terrorist groups like Gush Ecmunim—"Block of the Faithful," a Judaic fundamentalist sect prominent in the settler movement, and a participant in Israel's National Religious Party (both Bernard Goldstein and Yigal Amir were associated with the "Gush tendency"; see the entries for Feb. 25, 1994, and Nov. 5, 1995)—and that he himself has been a cabinet minister under world class terrorists like Begin and Sharon, PM Peres "indefinitely suspends" further talks with Syria on the grounds that it "harbors terrorists." At issue is the fact that Hamas, Hizbullah, the Islamic Jihad and the Popular Front for the Liberation of Palestine—the PFLP, a breakaway PLO faction headed by Georges Haddad, which refuses to be bound by Arafat's agreement with Israel—all maintain diplomatic offices in Damascus. Syria replies that while the U.S. accommodates Israeli diplomatic offices in its capitol city and elsewhere, Syria nonetheless maintains an open dialogue with the U.S. Although the Israeli position is plainly contrary to the 1970 Declaration on Principles of International Law Concerning Friendly Relations and Co-operation Among States in Accordance With the Charter of the United Nations—not to mention SC Resolutions 242 and 338—U.S. support to Israel, both material and diplomatic, remains undiminished.

Apr. 11: Still in violation of SC Res. 425 because of its ongoing occupation of southern Lebanon, which has been regularly confronted by Hizbullah, Israel launches "Operation Grapes of Wrath," a major offensive intended to clear the guerrillas from their basing areas further north. The IDF's major "accomplishment" is the shelling of a UN-sponsored refugee camp at Qana on Apr. 18, killing 102 Palestinian civilians. With Israel again subject to a torrent of international condemnation, the U.S., which has openly encouraged the operation, brokers a ceasefire on Apr. 27. Israel withdraws into its previous occupation zone, its violation of SC Res. 425 unaltered. U.S. support to Israel also remains unaltered.

Apr. 24: Pres. Clinton signs the Antiterrorism and Effective Death Penalty Act, a measure that expands the definition of "terrorism" to encompass a broad range of entirely legitimate political activities, normalizes the principle of guilt by association in its judicial application, greatly increases the scope of domestic intelligence-gathering activities, bolsters the ability of the government to utilize preventive detention of suspects as a "security" measure, and renders capital punishment a potentially common rather than exceptional punishment to be meted out by federal courts for political offenses. Aside from its severe erosion of rights and protections accruing under provision of the U.S. Constitution, the Act contains provisions contrary to the Universal Declaration of Human Rights, the American Declaration of the Rights and Duties of Man, the American Convention on Human Rights, the International Convention on the Elimination of All Forms of Racial Discrimination, the International Covenant on Civil and Political Rights and UNGA Res. 44/128 (the anti-death penalty protocol of 1989).

May 2: The trial of Dusko Tadic, a low level Serbian army officer accused of having participated in genocide, mass rape and other war crimes/crimes against humanity against the Bosnians begins before a U.S.-sponsored tribunal in the Hague (similar charges against a defendant scheduled for trial a bit earlier were quietly dismissed when it was proven that he'd been residing in Germany the whole time he'd supposedly been committing crimes in Bosnia). Ultimately, all the more sensational charges against Tadic are quietly dropped as well—indeed, it turns out that the Serbs' much-publicized mass rape of Bosnian Muslim women had itself never occurred—and he is convicted only of having beaten several prisoners, and of killing two Bosnian policemen. Instructively, of the 75-odd individuals docketed for prosecution before the Hague Tribunal, upwards of 60 are Serbs. None are drawn from the ranks of Croatian officials/military officers responsible for such largescale, well-documented and *U.S.-backed* atrocities against Serbs as Krajina (see the entry for Aug. 4, 1995). Still less is the tribunal authorized to take action against those guilty of perpetrating entirely comparable offenses outside the Balkans (e.g., Israeli officials and military personnel who'd bombed a Palestinian refugee camp, killing more than 100 civilians, barely a week before the Tadic trial began).

May 12: U.S. Ambassador to the United Nations Madeline Albright appears on the TV program *60 Minutes*. Asked about reports that more than 500,000 Iraqi children under 12 years of age have died since 1991 as the result of U.S.-orchestrated sanctions, she replies that she's well aware of the estimates and that the Clinton administration has determined that it's "worth the price" in other people's youngsters to force the Iraqi government to comply with U.S. dictates. UN Ass't Sec. Gen. Denis Halliday subsequently resigns in protest of what he publicly describes as America's "policy of deliberate genocide" against the people of Iraq.

June 18: Newly-elected Israeli PM Binyamin Netanyahu announces that he is reversing the half-hearted "peace initiatives" undertaken by his predecessors through the Oslo Accords and Cairo Agreement. Instead, in his own words, the Likud leader intends his régime to be "an expression of Zionist fulfillment." His program, as outlined to the Knesset, includes rejection of the idea of a Palestinian state, assertion of permanent Israeli sovereignty over the whole of Jerusalem, annexation of the Golan Heights, and an accelerated/expanded program of Jewish settlement in the West Bank and Gaza. Although Netanyahu's refusal of numerous UN resolutions—most especially SC Resolutions 242 and 338—could not be more explicit, U.S. support to Israel continues undiminished.

July 8: The ICJ enters an advisory opinion declaring the use or threat of use of nuclear weapons to be illegal. The U.S. not only refuses to accept the opinion as being in any way binding, but initiates production of a "whole new species" of tactical nuclear weapons within a few years (see the entry for Apr. 24, 2003).

Sept. 3–4: The U.S. launches a series of cruise missile attacks against targets in northern Iraq. Although the action, which is not authorized by the Security Council, is supposedly undertaken to protect the Kurdish population around Irbil from Iraqi depredations, the U.S. policy of supporting Turkish assaults against these same Kurds belies any such noble motive (see the entry for Apr. 5, 1991). On Sept. 14, Pres. Clinton admits that he actually "ordered the attacks in order to extend the no-fly zone." The U.S. missile strikes thus violate Chapter VII of the UN Charter, as well as UNGA Res. 337A (V) and a host of other elements of international law. Given the extent of "collateral" civilian casualties involved—not least among the very Kurds Clinton claimed to be trying to "save"—violations of the 1923 Hague Rules of Aerial Warfare and the 1949 Geneva Convention IV are also at issue.

Sept. 18: Sec. of State Warren Christopher, ignoring SC Resolutions 242 and 338, sends a "personal and confidential" letter to Binyamin Netanyahu, assuring the Israeli PM that the U.S. will support his absurd contention that there is "nothing binding from the standpoint of international law" with regard to Israel's obligation to withdraw from occupied Syrian territory on the Golan Heights. Christopher's successor as Sec. of State, Madeleine Albright, later attempts to persuade the Syrians to accept Netanyahu's proposal to "resume negotiations without preconditions"—thus nullifying what little progress was made in earlier talks (see the entry for July 18, 1994)—a subterfuge Syria flatly rejects. The Israeli/U.S. position is adopted in flagrant defiance, not only of the SC resolutions already mentioned, but the1970 Declaration on Principles of International Law Concerning Friendly Relations and Co-operation Among States in

Accordance With the Charter of the United Nations (esp. Chapters I, VI and VII).

Sept. 25: Netanyahu orders the opening of a "second gate" onto the plaza facing the Wailing Wall, at the base of the Dome of the Rock and very near the al-Aqsa mosque. When Palestinians respond to this "blatant Israeli violation of the pledge to resolve disputes over Jerusalem through negotiations [rather than] faits accompli" with largescale utterly predictable anger, Netanyahu orders the IDF deployed. In short order, the situation has escalated to the point that Israeli troops are engaged in firefights with Palestinian police. 15 Israelis and more than 80 Palestinians are killed in the 3-day confrontation.

Nov. 12: 137 member-states endorse UNGA Res. 51/17, calling for an end to the U.S. embargo of Cuba. The U.S. and Israel, joined by Uzbekistan, cast the only opposing votes. The embargo continues.

Nov. 19: The other 14 members of the Security Council vote to extend the appointment of Sec. Gen. Boutros Boutros-Ghali for 5 years. The U.S., having found Boutros-Ghali insufficiently malleable, vetoes the resolution, creating a vacancy in the UN's top position. Although a lopsided majority of member-states prefer that Salim Ahmed Salim be Boutros-Ghali's successor, Kofi Annan, the State Department's choice, is quickly installed.

Dec. 2: 133 member-states endorse UNGA Res. 51/22, calling for the elimination of economic coercion as a means of political/economic compulsion. The U.S. is 1 of 4 countries casting opposing votes.

Dec. 4: 104 member-states endorse UNGA Res. 51/23, calling for the creation of a committee to consider the inalienable rights of the Palestinian people. Only the U.S. and Israel cast opposing votes.

Dec. 4: 107 member-states endorse UNGA Res. 51/24, calling for establishment of a Division of Palestinian Rights within the UN Secretariat. Only the U.S. and Israel cast opposing votes.

Dec. 4: 152 member-states endorse UNGA Res. 51/26, calling for a peaceful resolution of the Question of Palestine, in compliance with international law. Only the U.S. and Israel cast opposing votes.

Dec. 4: 84 member-states endorse UNGA Res. 51/28, affirming Syria's legal right to recover the Golan Heights from Israel. Only the U.S. and Israel cast opposing votes.

Dec. 4: 159 member-states endorse UNGA Res. 51/29, calling for the Middle East Peace process to be conducted in conformity with international law. The U.S. and Israel cast opposing votes.

Dec. 9: The number of Israeli soldiers killed in southern Lebanon since the end of the 1982 war reaches 400; another 1,420 have been wounded. PM Netanyahu therefore proposes withdrawing the IDF from "that cursed place, on condition that the Israeli military presence be replaced by that of a multinational force of Egyptian, Jordanian and French troops. Lebanon, backed by Syria, rejects the proposition, pointing out that Israel has since 1978 been required by SC Res. 425 to withdraw its troops "unconditionally." Hizbullah's 400-odd fighters then declare a new offensive to force compliance. In Mar. 1998, with the death toll among IDF personnel rising steadily, an increasingly desperate Netanyahu tries again, this time proposing that Israeli forces be replaced by the Lebanese army, and that Lebanon undertake to "guarantee Israel's security" by destroying Hizbullah. This, too, is rejected, with Lebanon indicating that it will be prepared to negotiate its relationship to Israel only when the Israelis have demonstrated a willingness to "comply with all relevant United Nations resolutions." Netanyahu, joined by Sec. of State Albright, denounces as "unreasonable" the idea that Israel—like Iraq, for example—is obliged to obey the law.

Dec. 9: 138 member-states endorse UNGA Res. 51/34, calling for implementation of the 1982 Law of the Sea. The U.S. alone casts an opposing vote.

Dec. 10: 129 member-states endorse UNGA Res. 51/45B, calling for declaration of the southern hemisphere as a nuclear weapons-free zone. The U.S. is 1 of 3 countries casting an opposing vote.

Dec. 10: 129 member-states endorse UNGA Res. 51/48, positing Israel's illegal possession of nuclear weapons as a primary source of the threat of such armaments proliferating in the Middle East. The U.S. and Israel cast opposing votes.

Dec. 10: 131 member-states endorse UNGA res. 51/51, calling for immediate implementation of the Declaration of the Indian Ocean as an International Zone of Peace. The U.S. is 1 of 3 countries casting opposing votes.

Dec. 12: 159 member-states endorse UNGA Res. 51/82, reaffirming the right of the Palestinian people to self-determination. The U.S. and Israel cast opposing votes.

Dec. 12: 117 member-states endorse UNGA Res. 51/83, condemning the use of mercenaries to impede realization of human rights and self-determination in the Third World. The U.S. is 1 of 17 countries casting opposing votes.

Dec. 13: 159 member-states endorse UNGA Res. 51/124, calling for increased nonmilitary assistance to Palestinian refugees. Israel alone casts an opposing vote, while the U.S. is 1 of 2 countries abstaining.

Dec. 13: 157 member-states endorse UNGA Res. 51/126, reaffirming the right of return to Palestinians and other Arabs displaced by Israel's attack upon its neighbors in June 1967. Only the U.S. and Israel cast opposing votes.

Dec. 13: 159 member-states endorse UNGA Res. 51/128, commending and continuing activities undertaken by the UN Relief and Works Agency for Palestine Refugees in the Near East. Only the U.S. and Israel cast opposing votes.

Dec. 13: 159 member-states endorse UNGA Res. 51/129, reaffirming the right of Palestinians to recover properties from which they were displaced as a result of Israel's illegal expansion from 1948 onward, as well as all revenues derived therefrom. The U.S. and Israel cast the only opposing votes.

Dec. 13: 159 member-states endorse UNGA Res. 51/130, calling upon the Sec. Gen. to proceed with establishment of a University of Jerusalem (al-Quds) to serve Palestinian refugees. The U.S. and Israel cast opposing votes.

Dec. 13: 79 member-states endorse UNGA Res. 51/131, continuing the work of the Special Committee to Investigate Israeli Practices Affecting the Human Rights of Palestinians and Other Arabs of the Occupied Territories. Only the U.S. and Israel cast opposing votes.

Dec. 13: 156 member-states endorse UNGA Res. 51/132, reaffirming the applicability of the 1949 Geneva Convention IV to Israeli policies in the occupied territories of Palestine and Syria. Only the U.S. and Israel cast opposing votes.

Dec. 13: 152 member-states endorse UNGA Res. 51/133, denouncing Israeli settlements in the occupied territories as illegal. Only the U.S. and Israel cast opposing votes.

Dec. 13: 149 member-states endorse UNGA Res. 51/134, denouncing Israeli human rights violations in the occupied territories. Only the U.S. and Israel cast opposing votes.

Dec. 13: 153 member-states endorse UNGA Res. 51/135, calling upon Israel to resolve the issue of the Golan Heights in conformity with international law. Only Israel casts an opposing vote, while the U.S. is 1 of 9 countries abstaining.

Dec. 13: 143 member-states endorse UNGA Res. 146, calling for immediate implementation of UNGA Res. 1514 (XV)—the 1960 Declaration on the Granting of Independence to Colonial Countries and Peoples—in all non-self-governing territories. The U.S. and the U.K. cast the only opposing votes.

Dec. 13: 154 member-states endorse UNGA Res. 51/147, calling for increased dissemination of information on decolonization by UN agencies. Only the U.S. and the U.K. cast opposing votes.

Dec. 16: 133 member-states endorse UNGA Res. 51/190, reaffirming permanent Palestinian sovereignty over natural resources located in the West Bank and Gaza Strip, and Syrian sovereignty over those located in the Golan Heights. Only the U.S. and Israel cast opposing votes.

1997

Jan. 15: Plagued by severe unrest throughout the West Bank and Gaza Strip, and by increasing international criticism of his repudiation of the Oslo Accords, Israeli PM Netanyahu endorses the so-called Hebron Protocol.

Hailed by the U.S. as "a milestone in the Middle Eastern peace process," the Protocol embodies only the partial fulfillment of an Israeli withdrawal from the town of Hebron, which, according to the timetable established by the Cairo Agreement, was to have been accomplished months earlier. Creation of a zone allowing Palestinian "safe passage" from Gaza to the West Bank, which by the terms agreed at Cairo is supposed to occur in conjunction with the IDF's withdrawal from Hebron, is not undertaken at all. After completion of the transaction, Israel remains in complete control of 71% of the West Bank, and retains "security control" of another 23%, while Arafat's Palestinian Authority is left to preside over a mere 6%. The U.S. approves new loan guarantees for Israel, creating the financial base for expanded settlement activity.

Feb. 19: As "compensation" for his "concessions" under the Hebron Protocol, Israeli PM Netanyahu announces a program to build 6,500 residential units in a new settlement called Har Homa, in occupied East Jerusalem. In a side meeting with his cabinet, Netanyahu explains that "the Battle for Jerusalem" he is initiating is part of a broader plan to "revise" the Oslo Accords by "creating facts on the ground." Where Oslo posits the prospect of the Palestinians ultimately recovering some 90% of the land in the West Bank, Netanyahu's idea is that Israel should retain about two-thirds of the whole. Housing sales in the settlements surge by 50% over the first several months of 1997, while the number of settlers rises by 9% overall. Although British Foreign Min. Malcolm Rifkind publicly observes that the new construction, like all such Israeli activity, is illegal, the U.S. remains silent. Hamas therefore launches a new suicide bombing campaign, with major blasts occurring in Jerusalem on July 30 and Sept. 4.

Mar. 7: 14 of 15 Security Council member-states endorse draft res. 6335, ordering a halt to construction in all Israeli settlements in East Jerusalem. The U.S. employs its veto to override them (final vote: 14-1-0). The construction continues.

Mar. 13: 130 member-states endorse UNGA Res. 9225, denouncing Israeli attempts to alter the political status of East Jerusalem. Only the U.S. and Israel cast opposing votes.

Mar. 21: 13 of 15 Security Council member-states endorse draft res. 6345, ordering a halt to construction at Israel's Jabal Abu Ghneim settlement in East Jerusalem. The U.S. employs its veto to override them (final vote: 13-1-0). The construction continues.

Apr. 13: The U.S. Justice Dept.'s Inspector General releases a 517 page report to a considerable extent confirming chronic complaints that the FBI forensic laboratory has for decades been routinely manufacturing "scientific evidence" tailored to "prove" the guilt of those accused of crimes. At about the same time, a raft of studies confirm that numerous state, local and private crime labs, many of them staffed by personnel trained by the FBI, have been engaging in the same practice. Aside from a range of glaring violations of U.S. domestic law—notably America's vaunted constitutional guarantee of "due process"—the procedures at issue violate the Universal

Declaration of Human Rights (Articles 7-11), the International Covenant on Civil and Political Rights (Art. 9), and the American Convention on Human Rights (Art. 8). Despite the magnitude of the offenses involved, no officials are prosecuted (indeed, few are even removed from their positions). Worse still, virtually none of the several thousand falsely convicted prisoners involved are released from prison.

Apr. 24: The Senate votes to join 120 other countries by ratifying the 1993 Convention on the Prohibition of the Development, Production, Stockpiling and Use of Chemical Weapons and on Their Destruction. An amendment is added to the ratification, however, Section 307 of which states that "the President may deny a request to inspect any facility in the United States in cases where the President determines that inspection may pose a threat to the national security interests of the United States." The U.S. position on compliance is thus identical to that of Iraq, also a signatory to the 1993 Convention, a country whose posture U.S. officials routinely and vociferously denounce as "illegal."

Apr. 25: 134 member-states endorse UNGA Res. 9238, opposing further Israeli settlement in the occupied territories of Palestine. Only the U.S. and Israel, joined by the Federation of Micronesia, cast opposing votes. The settlement continues.

Sept. 14: Sec. of State Albright, making her first official visit to Israel, announces that "Palestinian terrorism" constitutes the "major obstacle to peace in the Middle East." No mention is made of the long history of Israeli terrorism, of Israel's sustained and ongoing violation of SC Resolutions 242 and 338, as well as the Oslo Accords; most specifically, there is no hint that Israel's accelerated settlement program might be generating the violence. Instead, Albright asserts that the mass arrest of Hamas activists by Arafat's Palestinian Authority should be considered a "fundamental precondition" for any resumption of the "peace process."

Oct. 23: Claiming that "tougher sanctions" are necessary to force Iraqi compliance with SC Res. 687, the U.S. pushes through SC Res. 1134. For the first time, an anti-Iraqi resolution is not passed unanimously; five countries, including France, Russia and China, abstain. France in particular points to the toll already taken by sanctions on Iraq's children (see the entry for May 12, 1996). Both France and Russia also point out that, while Iraq is undoubtedly cooperating less than fully with UNSCOM inspectors, the U.S. has itself been regularly exceeding the degree of force authorized in Security Council resolutions while engaging in enforcement of both the northern and southern Iraqi "no-fly zones."

Nov. 5: 143 member-states endorse UNGA Res. 52/10, calling for an immediate end to the U.S. embargo against Cuba. The U.S., Israel and Uzbekistan once again cast the only opposing votes. The embargo continues.

Nov. 7: A pair of Mossad agents disguised as Canadian tourists attempt to assassinate a mid-level Hamas leader named Khalid Meshal in Amman,

Jordan. The murder attempt is botched and the agents captured, a circumstance forcing the Israelis to exchange Sheikh Ahmed Yassin, Hamas' spiritual leader, arbitrarily imprisoned in Israel for several years, for their release. In the aftermath, it is discovered that the whole operation was personally approved by PM Netanyahu. Jordan's King Hussein also discloses that Hamas had made back-channel overtures concerning a ceasefire with Israel, and that his government had contacted the Israelis in a quiet effort to arrange it. Netanyahu's action is thus plainly intended to preclude any such result (since both the assassination and the ceasefire initiative were secret, it would also have been possible to cast Hamas' response to Meshal's murder as an "irrational escalation of violence"). Nonetheless, Netanyahu, joined by U.S. Sec. of State Albright, renews the demand that Arafat's Palestinian Authority perform a mass arrest of Hamas activists (see the entry for Sept. 14, 1997), this time adding "sympathizers" for good measure. Insofar as the intended victim was accorded diplomatic status by Jordan, the U.S.-backed Israeli murder attempt constitutes a patent violation of the 1973 Convention on the Prevention and Punishment of Crimes Against Internationally Protected Persons, Including Diplomatic Agents. The breach of Jordanian sovereignty involved in attempting the assassination in Amman represents an equally clear violation of the 1970 Declaration on Principles of International Law Concerning Friendly Relations and Cooperation Among States in Accordance With the Charter of the United Nations.

Nov. 26: 138 member-states endorse UNGA Res. 52/26, calling for implementation of the 1982 Law of the Sea. The U.S. alone casts an opposing vote.

Dec. 3-4: 129 UN member-states sign the Convention on the Prohibition of the Use, Stockpiling, Production and Transfer of Anti-Personnel Mines and Their Destruction ("Ottawa Treaty"). Of those countries represented at the conference, only the U.S., claiming "special needs," declines to endorse the measure. By March 1, 1999, when the treaty comes into force, more than 70 countries have submitted formal ratifications. As of this writing, there are over 100, while the U.S., alone among military powers worthy of the name, continues to refuse the law. The motive underlying U.S. recalcitrance in this regard has little to do with its publicly-stated "defensive" rationale ("securing" the perimeter of the Marine base at Guantánamo Bay, Cuba, for example, and "protecting" the demilitarized zone separating north from south Korea). Rather, it has everything to do with the fact that the cluster ordnance figuring so prominently in U.S. *offensive* capabilities might, under certain circumstances, be construed as containing antipersonnel mines.

Dec. 9: 131 member-states endorse UNGA Res. 52/38N, calling for declaration of the southern hemisphere as a nuclear weapons-free zone. The U.S. is 1 of 3 countries casting opposing votes.

Dec. 9: 109 member-states endorse UNGA Res. 52/39C, approving the draft text of a proposed convention prohibiting nuclear weapons. The U.S. casts an opposing vote.

Dec. 9: 147 member-states endorse UNGA Res. 52/41, declaring Israel's illegal possession of nuclear weapons to be a major cause of potential proliferation of such armaments in the Middle East. Only the U.S. and Israel cast opposing votes.

Dec. 9: 125 member-states endorse UNGA Res. 52/44, calling for immediate implementation of the Declaration of the Indian Ocean as an International Zone of Peace. The U.S. is 1 of 3 countries casting opposing votes.

Dec. 9: 115 member-states endorse UNGA Res. 52/49, continuing the work of the UN Committee on Exercise of the Inalienable Rights of the Palestinian People. Only the U.S. and Israel cast opposing votes.

Dec. 9: 113 member-states endorse UNGA Res. 52/50, calling for a Division of Palestinian Rights within the UN Secretariat. Only the U.S. and Israel cast opposing votes.

Dec. 9: 158 member-states endorse UNGA Res. 52/51, calling for a special informational program on the Question of Palestine. Only the U.S. and Israel cast opposing votes.

Dec. 9: 155 member-states endorse UNGA Res. 52/52, calling for a peaceful resolution of the Question of Palestine, in conformity with international law. Only the U.S. and Israel cast opposing votes.

Dec. 9: 92 member-states endorse UNGA Res. 52/54, calling upon Israel to rescind the extension of its domestic laws over the Golan Heights, and to withdraw its forces in conformity with SC Resolutions 242 and 338. Only the U.S. and Israel cast opposing votes.

Dec. 10: 159 member-states endorse UNGA Res. 52/57, calling for increased nonmilitary assistance to Palestinian refugees. Only Israel casts an opposing vote, while the U.S. is 1 of 2 countries abstaining.

Dec. 10: 158 member-states endorse UNGA Res. 52/59, reaffirming the right of persons displaced by Israel's June 1967 attack upon its neighbors to return to their homes. Only the U.S. and Israel cast opposing votes.

Dec. 10: 158 member-states endorse UNGA Res. 52/61, commending and continuing the UN Relief and Works Agency for Palestine Refugees in the Near East. Only the U.S. and Israel cast opposing votes.

Dec. 10: 158 member-states endorse UNGA Res. 52/62, reaffirming the right of Palestinians and other Arabs dispossessed by Israel's illegal expansion from 1948 onward to recover their property and revenues derived therefrom. Only the U.S. and Israel cast opposing votes.

Dec. 10: 158 member-states endorse UNGA Res. 52/63, calling upon the Sec. Gen. to proceed with the establishment of a University of Jerusalem (al-Quds) to serve Palestinian refugees. Only the U.S. and Israel cast opposing votes.

Dec. 10: 83 member-states endorse UNGA Res. 52/64, continuing the work of the Special Committee to Investigate Israeli Practices Affecting the Human Rights of Palestinians and Other Arabs of the Occupied Territories. Only the U.S. and Israel cast opposing votes.

Dec. 10: 156 member-states endorse UNGA Res. 52/65, reaffirming the applicability of the 1949 Geneva Convention IV to Israeli policies in the occupied territories. Only the U.S. and Israel cast opposing votes.

Dec. 10: 149 member-states endorse UNGA Res. 52/66, condemning Israel's illegal settlements in the occupied territories of Palestine and Syria. Only the U.S. and Israel cast opposing votes.

Dec. 10: 151 member-states endorse UNGA Res. 52/67, condemning Israeli human rights violations in the occupied territories. Only the U.S. and Israel cast opposing votes.

Dec. 10: 156 member-states endorse UNGA Res. 52/72, condemning economic and other activities impeding realization of self-determination in non-self-governing territories. The U.S. and the U.K. cast opposing votes.

Dec. 10: 139 member-states endorse UNGA Res. 52/78, calling for immediate implementation of UNGA Res. 1514 (XV)—the Declaration on the Granting of Independence to Colonial Countries and Peoples—in all non-self-governing territories. Only the U.S. and the U.K. cast opposing votes.

Dec. 10: 159 member-states endorse UNGA Res. 52/79, calling for dissemination of information on decolonization by UN agencies. The U.S. and the U.K. cast opposing votes.

Dec. 11: The U.S., along with what will soon be 178 other countries, signs the Kyoto Protocol, implementing the 1992 UN Framework Convention on Climate Change. Pres. Clinton does not submit the treaty to the Senate for ratification, however, and it therefore never enters into force in U.S. domestic law. By 2001, the U.S. is the only noncompliant state among the 38 countries who agree at Kyoto to reduce their overall level of greenhouse gas emissions.

Dec. 12: 113 member-states endorse UNGA Res. 52/112, condemning violations of human rights by mercenaries used to impede the realization of self-determination in non-self-governing territories. The U.S. is 1 of 18 countries casting opposing votes.

Dec. 12: 160 member-states endorse UNGA Res. 52/114, reaffirming the right of the Palestinian people to self-determination. Only the U.S. and Israel cast opposing votes.

Dec. 18: 109 member-states endorse UNGA Res. 52/181, condemning unilateral economic measures used as a means to politically/economically coerce Third World countries. The U.S. alone casts an opposing vote.

Dec. 18: 137 member-states endorse UNGA Res. 52/207, reaffirming the right of Palestinians to permanent sovereignty over natural resources in the occupied territories. Only the U.S. and Israel cast opposing votes.

1998

Mar. 2: The U.S. and Britain push through SC Res. 1154, providing that the U.S. in particular may "automatically" respond with military force to alleged Iraqi noncompliance with UN resolutions. Although vociferously opposed to this unprecedented assertion of the "principle of automaticity," all other permanent members of the Security Council abstain from voting. A day later, ignoring the refusal of Russia, France and China to endorse the resolution, Pres. Clinton falsely informs the public that "all members of the [Security] Council agree" that the U.S. holds the right to use force at its own discretion in imposing its will upon Iraq. This bold-faced lie represents a gross manipulation of Security Council procedures, and thus violates Chapters V, VI and VII of the UN Charter. More broadly, the U.S. posture completely contradicts a variety of other provisions contained in the 1970 Declaration on Principles of International Law Concerning Friendly Relations and Co-operation Among States in Accordance With the Charter of the United Nations and UNGA Res. 337A (V).

April 14: Citing "procedural default," the Supreme Court holds that Virginia can execute Paraguayan national Angel Francisco Breard despite the facts that he was denied his right to contact the Paraguayan consulate, Paraguay has brought suit before the ICJ, and the ICJ has ordered the U.S. to "take all measures at its disposal to ensure that [Breard] is not executed pending the final decision in these proceedings." Sec. of State Madeline Albright assures Virginia Gov. Gilmore that the ICJ order is "non-binding" (see the entries for Oct. 1, 1999, June 27, 2001 and Feb. 5, 2003).

June 7: A former Chairman of the Joint Chiefs of Staff, Admiral Thomas Moorer, appears on the CNN *NewsStand* program to disclose the Army's "Operation Tailwind," conducted in Sept. 1970. Therein, U.S. Special Forces personnel fighting in Laos used sarin nerve gas against a Pathet Lao base camp in an effort to kill a number of American defectors believed to be residing there (only 2 Americans were reportedly killed, along with "well over 100" Laotians, both military and civilian). Shortly thereafter, sarin was again used to destroy a mixed force of Pathet Lao and North Vietnamese regulars, again killing a number estimated to "run in the triple digits" (some of the Americans involved were also contaminated, and at least one suffers from degenerative neurological disorders diagnosed as having been caused by nerve gas exposure). These actions, which are well-documented, may not have been the only such undertaken in Laos. Be that as it may, they were plainly carried out in flagrant violation of the 1925 Geneva Protocol for the Prohibition of the Use in War of Asphyxiating, Poisonous or Other Gases.

June 26: 124 member-states endorse UNGA Res. 52/250, calling for participation of Palestinians in the work of the UN. The U.S. and Israel cast opposing votes.

July 17: 120 UN member-states vote to create an International Criminal Court (ICC) empowered to preside over cases involving genocide, crimes against humanity, war crimes and crimes of aggression (essentially the same venue as the Nuremberg Tribunal established at U.S. instigation under the 1945 London Charter). The U.S. joins China, India, Iraq, Israel, Libya, Sudan and Qatar in casting opposing votes. According to U.S. Senator Jesse Helms, the U.S. will never endorse the ICC until such time as it extends blanket immunity to all U.S. officials and military personal for all offenses, past, present and future. In effect, the U.S. position is that it will not "accept" ICC jurisdiction unless it is explicitly exempted from that same jurisdiction. It is obviously impossible to reconcile such a posture with the noble principles declaimed by Justice Jackson at Nuremberg, to the effect that the U.S. would never hold others to a standard of legality it was unwilling to accept for itself (see the entry for Nov. 20, 1945).

Aug. 19: Claiming that it is engaged in the illegal manufacture of chemical weapons, the U.S. bombs the Sudan's only pharmaceutical plant, al-Shifa, near Khartoum. In actuality there is no evidence whatsoever that any such activity is occurring, a matter readily borne out by the strenuousness of U.S. efforts to block a UN inspection of the sight in the aftermath. Shortly, it becomes clear that the primary U.S. objection to al-Shifa is that it was build in part with donations from Usama bin-Laden, a Saudi millionaire who, as nominal head of the al-Qaida terrorist network, is believed by the CIA to be responsible for recent attacks upon the U.S. embassies in Kenya and Tanzania, and the *U.S.S. Cole* in Yemen (frustrated at its inability to come to grips with bin-Laden himself, the U.S. is simply lashing out at *anything* associated with him). In reality, the al-Shifa plant was producing some 50% of the medicines available in the deeply impoverished Sudan, and its destruction left the country bereft of the chloroquinine used to treat malaria, drugs with which to treat tuberculosis, and most of the veterinary drugs needed to combat parasites. The "collateral" effect of the U.S. bombing—which was conducted in clear violation of the 1970 Declaration on Principles of International Law Concerning Friendly Relations and Co-operation Among States in Accordance With the Charter of the United Nations (esp. Chapters VI and VII), UNGA Resolutions 337A (V), 380 (V), 2131 (XX) and 2444, as well as the 1949 Geneva Convention IV—was thus the deaths of tens of thousands of Sudanese bystanders, the majority of them children. Given that the Sudan was already undergoing a vast humanitarian crisis at the time the bombing occurred, violation of Article II(c) of the Genocide Convention is also at issue.

Aug. 20: Still trying to lay a glove on the illusive Usama bin-Laden, the U.S. launches cruise missile strikes on what it believes are al-Qaida training camps in northeastern Afghanistan. The facilities turn out to occupied mostly by Pakistanis training to fight in India-controlled Kashmir; of the 20 killed and 30 wounded in the attack, none are members of al-Qaida. Afghanistan's Taliban government, which is in the process of easing al-Qaida out of the country—and which is at the time preparing to deport bin-Laden to Saudi Arabia, where he is wanted on a range of charges—immediately reverses its position(s), observing that "America is the biggest terrorist in the world." The U.S. strikes, undertaken without Security Council authorization, embody severe violations of the 1970 Declaration on Principles of International Law Concerning Friendly Relations and Co-operation Among States in Accordance With the Charter of the United Nations (esp. Chapters I, VI and VII), as well as UNGA Resolutions 337A (V), 380 (V) and 2131 (XX).

Oct. 14: 157 member-states, including Uzbekistan, endorse UNGA Res. 9479, calling for an immediate end to the U.S. embargo against Cuba. Only the U.S. and Israel cast opposing votes. The embargo continues.

Oct. 16: Police in London, where he has gone for medical treatment, arrest former Chilean dictator Augusto Pinochet, at the request of Spain, on charges of having ordered the torture and murder of Spanish citizens. A charge of genocide is also considered (see the entry for Sept. 11, 1973). The U.S. quietly intervenes through diplomatic back channels in behalf of its client, ultimately arranging for his "extradition" back to Chile, where, as a former head of state, he enjoys immunity from prosecution and, in any event, is adjudged to be too infirm to stand trial.

Oct. 23: Under mounting pressure from Hamas and the Islamic Jihad—and from his own constituents, now thoroughly disenchanted with his promises that their safety will be ensured by pursuit of ever-tougher policies against the Palestinians—Israeli PM Netanyahu signs the Wye River Memorandum, a U.S.-brokered understanding between his régime and Yasser Arafat's Palestinian Authority. Under terms of the Wye River accord, Israel agrees to resume the so-called Oslo Peace Process with a 3-stage withdrawal of its troops from an additional 13% of the West Bank. At the end of 3 months, the Palestinians are to be in "joint control" of some 40% of all West Bank territory. Reciprocally, Arafat agrees to launch a program, undertaken in collaboration with Israeli intelligence and monitored by the CIA, to halt the basing of Hamas and Jihad operations from areas under his control. There is strong indication that, although both the Jihad and Hamas object that the arrangement falls far short of Israel's meeting of its legal obligations, they agree to cooperate. On Dec. 20, however—although Arafat has fulfilled his end of the bargain, even going so far as to effect a formal cancellation on Dec. 14 of the long-obsolete Palestinian Charter of 1968 (which contained language concerning the destruction of Israel)—Netanyahu orchestrates a Knesset vote to suspend the withdrawal of Israeli troops from any portion of the West Bank until the Palestinians agree to 5 wholly new conditions. Although it is obviously the Israelis, not the Palestinians, who have scuttled the Wye River agreement, the U.S. sides, as always, with Israel. Hamas and the Islamic Jihad resume military operations.

Dec. 2: 154 member-states endorse UNGA Res. 9522, reaffirming that land-for-peace should be considered as a basis for resolution of the Mideast conflict. The U.S. and Israel cast the only opposing votes.

Dec. 3: 150 member-states endorse UNGA Res. 9525A, calling upon Israel to disarm Jewish settlers in the occupied territories of Palestine. The U.S. and Israel, joined by the Federation of Micronesia, cast the only opposing votes.

Dec. 3: 144 member-states endorse UNGA Res. 9525B, calling for a "final and complete" implementation of the UN's 1960 Declaration on the Granting of Independence to Colonial Countries and Peoples. The U.S. and the U.K. cast the only opposing votes.

Dec. 3: 156 member-states endorse UNGA Res. 9525C, calling for continued dissemination of information on decolonization by the UN Dept. of Public Information. The U.S. and U.K., joined by Israel, cast the only opposing votes.

Dec.3: 151 member-states endorse UNGA Res. 9525D, demanding that Israel cease all human rights violations against Palestinians. Only the U.S. and Israel cast opposing votes.

Dec. 3: 155 member-states endorse UNGA Res. 9525E, reaffirming the applicability of the 1949 Geneva Convention IV to Israeli policies in the occupied territories. Only the U.S. and Israel cast opposing votes.

Dec. 3: 150 member-states endorse UNGA Res. 9525G, calling upon Israel to comply with all relevant Security Council resolutions, especially SC Res. 497 (see the entry for Dec. 17, 1981). Only the U.S. and Israel cast opposing votes.

Dec. 3: 156 member-states endorse UNGA Res. 9525I, reaffirming the right of return of displaced Palestinians. Only the U.S. and Israel cast opposing votes. Israel publicly dismisses the idea that Palestinians are imbued with any such right as an "absurdity."

Dec. 3: 156 member-states endorse UNGA Res. 9525J, reaffirming the right of Palestinian refugees to recover their property, or revenues deriving therefrom, within the occupied territories of Palestine. Only the U.S. and Israel cast opposing votes.

Dec. 3: 157 member-states endorse UNGA Res. 9525K, calling upon Israel to comply with the terms and provisions of the UN Charter. Only the U.S. and Israel cast opposing votes.

Dec. 3: 156 member-states endorse UNGA Res. 9525L, calling upon Israel to remove all hindrances to the establishment of a university in East Jerusalem (al-Quds) serving Palestinians. Only the U.S. and Israel cast opposing votes.

Dec. 16: UNSCOM chief Richard Butler, having withdrawn the last of his personnel from Iraq, submits a report to the Security Council stating that the Iraqis had refused admission of inspectors to a number of "sensitive" installations (this is a conscious misrepresentation; Iraq had refused admission mainly to presidential palaces and other facilities deemed essential to "the dignity and sovereignty of the country"). On this pretext, and without Security Council authorization, Pres. Clinton orders the commencement of "Operation Desert Fox" the same evening. Over the next 4 days, more than 100 sites—several of them in Baghdad—are subjected to heavy bombing. As U.S. inspector Scott Ritter later observes, by that point, Iraq's existing stockpiles and capacity to produce weapons of mass destruction had *already* been completely destroyed. The U.S. airstrikes are thus plainly geared far more to impress upon the Iraqi government that it must do whatever it's told, than to "eliminate Iraq's chemical and biological weapons capabilities." In that sense, stripped of its trappings, "Desert Fox" is a clear violation of the 1970 Declaration on Principles of International Law Concerning Friendly Relations and Co-operation Among States in Accordance With the Charter of the United Nations. Given the nature of certain of the sites targeted, violations of the 1923 Hague Rules of Aerial Warfare, the 1949 Geneva Convention IV and UNGA Res. 2444 are also at issue.

1999

Mar. 24: Claiming it is necessary to halt yet another "humanitarian disaster"—this one centering upon a supposed Serbian "genocide" of ethnic Albanians—the U.S. completely disregards the UN by heading up a NATO air offensive to "liberate" Kosovo from the "criminal state" of Yugoslavia. Over the next 11 weeks, an "awesome array" of both "smart" and "dumb" aerial ordnance is expended not only against Yugoslav military forces, but such targets as "television stations, schools, hospitals, theaters, old folks homes" and other elements of the civilian infrastructures of both Kosovo and Yugoslavia itself. Even the Chinese embassy in downtown Belgrade is hit by a U.S. cruise missile. Thousands are killed, tens of thousands maimed, hundreds of thousands rendered homeless and made into refugees. By the time a peace accord is entered on June 3, making Kosovo into a NATO protectorate, an ad hoc group of international lawyers in Toronto has joined with the American Association of Jurists to file a complaint with the Hague War Crimes Tribunal charging that U.S.-led coalition forces have engaged in a range of crimes including "willful killing, willfully causing great suffering or serious injury to body or health, extensive destruction of property, not justified by military necessity and carried out unlawfully and wantonly, employment of poisonous weapons or other weapons to cause unnecessary suffering, wanton destruction of cities, towns, and villages, dwellings or buildings, destruction or willful damage done to institutions dedicated to religion, charity and education, the arts and sciences, [and] historic monuments, [as well as] open violation of the United Nations Charter, the NATO treaty itself, the Geneva Conventions and the principles of International

Law." Since the Tribunal is U.S.-sponsored, the charges—while entirely accurate—are quietly shelved (and go all but unreported in the media).

May 17: Binyamin Netanyahu is unseated as Israeli PM by Ehud Barak. Although this represents another of Israel's supposed "turns toward moderation"—e.g., Barak immediately announces that he will honor the Wye River agreement (see the entry for Oct. 23, 1998)—he also asserts categorically that "under no circumstances" will Israel be prepared to comply with SC Resolutions 242 and 338 by withdrawing to its 1967 borders. More specifically, he avows "every intention" of maintaining Israeli control over the whole of Jerusalem, and asserts that all Jewish settlements in the occupied territories of Palestine must be considered "permanent additions to the State of Israel." Although Barak's position is thus as flatly illegal as that espoused by any of his predecessors, it is enthusiastically endorsed by U.S. Pres. Clinton shortly announces increased economic assistance to Israel.

May 27: Even as it ignores charges filed against the U.S. and other NATO participants in the onslaught against Yugoslavia, the Hague Tribunal, to much fanfare, indicts President Slobodan Milosevic and five other top Serbian officials for war crimes and crimes against humanity. One problem is that even a team of 56 FBI forensic specialists dispatched by the Clinton Administration to gather evidence can find almost no indication that the grisly atrocities the Serbs are alleged to have committed against Kosovo Albanians ever occurred. Most spectacularly, a mine shaft near the town of Mitrovica widely reported to have been used as a mass grave for some 700 Albanians massacred by Serbian forces disgorges not a single corpse. At 30 other reputed "mass grave" sites, the FBI comes up with the bodies of fewer than 200 victims, the great majority of them apparently killed after NATO's "humanitarian intervention" had commenced. Ultimately, tales of the Serbs' "Nazi-like butchery" of Albanians prove as illusory as did those of their policy-driven mass rape of Bosnian Muslim women and the "new Belsen" they'd created at Trnopolje (see the entries for Aug. 5, 1992, and May, 2, 1996). Nonetheless, with his demonization firmly implanted in the public mind, Milosevic is eventually arrested and extradited to the Netherlands, where he is currently undergoing prosecution before the Hague Tribunal.

Oct. 1: The Inter-American Court of Human Rights issues Advisory Opinion OC-16/99, The Right of Information on Consular Assistance in the Framework of the Guarantees for the Due Process of Law, finding the U.S. in violation of Article 36 of the Vienna Convention on Consular Rights and Art. 14 of the International Covenant on Civil and Political Rights for executing Mexican national Mario Murphy despite having failed to notify him of his right to contact the Mexican consulate (see the entries for April 14, 1998, June 27, 2001, and Feb. 5, 2003).

Nov. 9: 155 member-states endorse UNGA Res. 9654, calling for an immediate end to the U.S. embargo against Cuba. Only the U.S. and Israel cast opposing votes. The embargo continues.

Dec. 6: 154 member-states endorse UNGA Res. 54/74, reaffirming the right of Palestinian refugees dispossessed as a result of Israel's illegal expansion from 1948 onward to recover their property and revenue derived therefrom. Only the U.S. and Israel cast opposing votes.

Dec. 6: 154 member-states endorse UNGA Res. 54/75, calling upon the Sec. Gen. to proceed with the establishment of a University of Jerusalem (al-Quds) to serve Palestinian refugees. Only the U.S. and Israel cast opposing votes.

Dec. 6: 84 member-states endorse UNGA Res. 54/76, continuing the work of the Special Committee to Investigate Israeli Practices Affecting the Human Rights of Palestinians and Other Arabs of the Occupied Territories. Only the U.S. and Israel cast opposing votes.

Dec. 6: 154 member-states endorse UNGA Res. 54/77, reaffirming the applicability of the 1949 Geneva Convention IV to Israeli policies in the occupied territories. Only the U.S. and Israel cast opposing votes.

Dec. 6: 149 member-states endorse UNGA Res. 54/78, condemning illegal Israeli settlements in the occupied territories of Palestine and Syria. The U.S. and Israel cast opposing votes.

Dec. 6: 150 member-states endorse UNGA Res. 54/79, condemning Israeli human rights violations in the occupied territories. Only the U.S. and Israel cast opposing votes.

Dec. 6: 150 member-states endorse UNGA Res. 54/80, calling upon Israel to rescind the extension of its domestic laws from the Syrian Golan Heights, and to comply with SC Resolutions 242 and 338. Only Israel casts an opposing vote, while the U.S. abstains.

Dec. 6: 153 member-states endorse UNGA Res. 54/85, condemning economic and other activities impeding the realization of self-determination in non-self-governing territories. Only the U.S. and the U.K. cast opposing votes.

Dec. 6: 141 member-states endorse UNGA Res. 54/91, calling for the immediate implementation of the 1960 Declaration on the Granting of Independence to Colonial Countries and Peoples in all non-self-governing territories. Only the U.S. and the U.K. cast opposing votes.

Dec. 6: 149 member-states endorse UNGA Res. 54/92, calling for increased dissemination of information on decolonization by UN agencies. Only the U.S. and the U.K. cast opposing votes.

Dec. 17: The U.S. and the U.K. pass SC Res. 1284, establishing new and far more stringent inspection criteria and extending sanctions against Iraq for an indefinite period. All other permanent members of the Security Council abstain from voting. While the resolution is promoted as being necessary to ensure that Iraq does not rebuild its inventory of chemical and biological weapons, or develop the capacity to produce nuclear weapons, U.S. officials concede to the *Wall Street Journal* that there is no evidence the Iraqis are planning, much less attempting, to do either. In a moment of candor, Sec. of State Albright concedes on the Jan. 2, 2002, edition of NBC's *Meet* *the Press* that concern over the possibility that Iraq might possess or acquire weapons of mass destruction is merely a pretext. The real object, she explains, is to force a "régime change," replacing Iraq's Ba'athist government with one preferred by the U.S. This being true, the U.S. manipulation of the Security Council embodied in Res. 1284 violates Chapter V of the UN Charter, as well as UNGA Resolutions 380 (V) and 2131 (XX).

Dec. 17: 100 member-states endorse UNGA Res. 54/151, condemning the use of mercenaries to impede realization of self-determination in non-self-governing territories. The U.S. is 1 of 16 countries casting opposing votes.

Dec. 17: 156 member-states endorse UNGA Res. 54/152, reaffirming the right of the Palestinian people to self-determination. The U.S. and Israel cast the only opposing votes.

Dec. 22: 94 member-states endorse UNGA Res. 54/200, condemning unilateral economic measures used as a means of political/economic compulsion against Third World countries. The U.S. and the U.K. cast the only opposing votes.

Dec. 22: 132 member-states endorse UNGA Res. 54/231, reaffirming the Palestinian right to permanent sovereignty over natural resources in the occupied territories. The U.S. and Israel enter opposing votes.

2000

Jan. 22: The Pentagon announces that it is "reluctantly willing to accept" a compromise worked out with prior signatories which would allow the U.S., uniquely, to enlist and train military personnel defined as children under the 1994 Convention on the Rights of the Child, so long as "every effort" is made to keep them out of combat until they reach their 18th birthday. Even this "breakthrough" proves insufficient to convince the Senate to ratify the Convention, however, since the U.S. continues to insist that it also holds a "sovereign prerogative" to declare children as young as 13 years of age "adults" for purposes of prosecution, imprisonment and potential execution. As of this writing, the U.S. and Somalia are the only two UN member-states refusing to accept universal protection of children's rights.

Mar. 27: The U.S. joins in approving SC Res. 1328, demanding that Israel immediately implement SC Resolutions 242 (1967) and 338 (1973). The condition for U.S. cooperation is, as always, that the resolution not include enforcement provisions of any sort. Israel, as always, simply ignores the resolution. As always, U.S. support to the offender continues undiminished.

July: Pres. Clinton convenes a "summit" between Israeli PM Barak and Palestinian Authority head Yasser Arafat at the U.S. presidential retreat at Camp David, Maryland, to "revise the working arrangement" between the two parties. Clinton and Barak describe in glowing terms the "breakthrough" embodied in Barak's offer to "concede part of East Jerusalem and "between 90 and 94 percent of the West Bank to the Palestinians." In actuality, what is offered adds up to only 50–60% of the area in question—that is, only marginally more than what was offered by Netanyahu—all of it broken up into a bewildering complex of separate cantons. In exchange, Arafat is expected to endorse outright Israeli annexation of 10% of the West Bank, and the idea that disposition of the remaining 40% should remain "under discussion"—that is, directly controlled by Israel—for an indefinite period. As Palestinian analyst Edward Said observes, "Israel took 78 percent of Palestine in 1948 and the remaining 22 percent in 1967. Only that 22 percent is in question now, and it excludes West Jerusalem... When we look at the 50-60 percent ["conceded" by Barak at Camp David] in terms of the former Palestine, it amounts to only about 12 percent of the land from which the Palestinians were driven in 1948." The vaunted Camp David initiative is thus a subterfuge through which the U.S. and Israel seek to cast an aura of legitimacy over the fruits of protracted Israeli aggression by presenting the situation as the opposite of itself. When Arafat refuses to accept Barak's proposition—which is plainly intended to circumvent SC Resolutions 242 and 338—both Barak and Clinton denounce him as an "obstacle to peace."

Sept. 28: Ariel Sharon, "guarded by about a thousand Israeli police and soldiers, [enters] Jerusalem's Haram al-Sharif...in a gesture designed to assert his right as an Israeli to visit a Muslim holy place." By Sept. 29, the Muslim Day of Prayer, substantial Palestinian protests have broken out in response to this blatant provocation by the "Butcher of Beirut" (see the entries for Sept. 14, 1982, and Feb. 7, 1983), and PM Barak dispatches "a massive and intimidating police and military" force to the al-Aqsa mosque. A day later, as the protests swell, IDF troopers shoot and kill 5 Palestinians, including 12-year-old Muhammad al-Durra, a child falsely accused of throwing rocks Thus begins the "Second Intifada" ("al-Aqsa Intifada"). By Oct. 1, a full-fledged slaughter is underway, with Israeli troops routinely firing on unarmed demonstrators and helicopter gunships firing missiles into buildings, apparently at random. Vehicles clearly marked as belonging to the Red Crescent Society—the internationally-recognized Arabic version of the Red Cross—are also targeted for systematic destruction by the IDF. The Israeli onslaught—which violates, among many other elements of international law, the 1949 Geneva Conventions I and IV—is condemned by a host of governments and virtually every international human rights organization. The U.S. response, announced on Oct. 4, is to approve an Israeli request for additional Apache attack helicopters and more advanced missiles to be fired from them. By early Nov., more than 170 Palestinians have been killed and upwards of 6,000 wounded by the IDF, while thousands of others have been placed under "preventive detention."

Oct. 20: 92 member-states endorse UNGA Res. 9793, demanding an immediate end to Israeli violence in the occupied territories of Palestine and implementation of the Sharem el Sheik Accords signed a few days previously. The U.S. and Israel, joined by the Federation of Micronesia, Nauru and Tuvalu, cast the only opposing votes.

Nov. 9: 167 member-states endorse UNGA Res. 9814, calling for an immediate end to the U.S. embargo of Cuba. The U.S. and Israel, joined by the Marshall Islands, cast the only opposing votes. The embargo continues.

Dec. 1: 157 member-states endorse UNGA Res. 55/36, calling for Israel to join 163 other signatory countries in accepting the Nuclear Non-Proliferation Treaty. The U.S. and Israel enter opposing votes.

Dec. 1: 96 member-states endorse UNGA Res. 55/51, condemning Israel for failure to comply with SC Res. 497 (1981) and nullifying Israel's attempt to extend its jurisdiction over the Golan Heights. The U.S. and Israel cast the only opposing votes.

Dec. 1: 106 member-states endorse UNGA Res. 55/52, authorizing a Special Committee on the Inalienable Rights of the Palestinian People. Only the U.S. and Israel cast opposing votes.

Dec. 1: 107 member-states endorse UNGA Res. 55/53, authorizing a Division of Palestinian Rights within the UN Secretariat. Only the U.S. and Israel cast opposing votes.

Dec. 1: 151 member-states endorse UNGA Res. 55/54, authorizing the Secretariat to conduct a special information program on the Question of Palestine. Only the U.S. and Israel cast opposing votes.

Dec. 1: 149 member-states endorse UNGA Res. 55/55, calling for a peaceful resolution of the Question of Palestine. Only the U.S. and Israel cast opposing votes.

Dec. 4: 170 member-states endorse UNGA Res. 55/87, reaffirming the right to self-determination of the Palestinian people. Only the U.S. and Israel cast opposing votes.

Dec. 8: 156 member-states endorse UNGA Res. 55/125, reaffirming the right of displaced Palestinians to return to their homes. Only the U.S. and Israel cast opposing votes.

Dec. 8: 157 member-states endorse UNGA Res. 55/127, calling upon Israel to abide by Articles 100, 104 and 105 of the UN Charter in its dealings with personnel employed by the UN Relief and Works Agency for Palestine Refugees in the Near East. Only the U.S. and Israel cast opposing votes.

Dec. 8: 156 member-states endorse UNGA Res. 55/128, reaffirming that Israel has no right to dispose of or profit from Palestinian properties expropriated from 1948 onward. Only the U.S. and Israel cast opposing votes.

Dec. 8: 156 member-states endorse UNGA Res. 55/129, authorizing the Sec. Gen. to "take all necessary steps" to establish a university in Jerusalem (al-Quds) serving Palestinian refugees. Only the U.S. and Israel cast opposing votes.

Dec. 8: 91 member-states endorse UNGA Res. 55/130, accepting the annual Report of the Special Committee to Investigate Israeli Practices

Affecting the Human Rights of Palestinians and Other Arabs of the Occupied Territories. Only the U.S. and Israel enter opposing votes.

Dec. 8: 152 member-states endorse UNGA Res. 55/131, reaffirming the applicability of the 1949 Geneva Convention IV to Israeli policies in the occupied territories of Palestine. Only the U.S. and Israel cast opposing votes.

Dec. 8: 152 member-states endorse 55/132, reaffirming the illegality of Israeli settlements in the occupied territories. The U.S. and Israel, joined by Nauru and Tuvalu, cast opposing votes.

Dec. 8: 150 member-states endorse UNGA Res. 55/133, condemning ongoing Israeli violence against the population of the occupied territories and demanding that Israel "cease all practices and actions violating the human rights of Palestinians." Only the U.S. and Israel cast opposing votes.

Dec. 8: 150 member-states endorse UNGA Res. 55/134, calling upon Israel to comply with SC Res. 497 (1981) by rescinding the imposition of its laws on the Golan Heights, and deploring Israeli violations of the 1949 Geneva Convention IV. Only Israel casts an opposing vote; the U.S. abstains.

Dec. 8: 150 member-states endorse UNGA Res. 55/138, condemning economic and other foreign entities impeding implementation of the 1960 Declaration on the Granting of Independence to Colonial Countries and Peoples. Only the U.S. and the U.K. cast opposing votes.

Dec. 8: 153 member-states endorse UNGA Res. 9838E, instructing the UN Dept. of Information to continue disseminating information on decolonization. Only the U.S. and the U.K. cast opposing votes.

Dec. 8: 125 member-state endorse UNGA Res. 55/146, proclaiming a Second International Decade for Eradication of Colonialism. Only the U.S. and the U.K. cast opposing votes.

Dec. 8: 138 member-states endorse UNGA Res. 55/147, calling for the immediate implementation of the Declaration on the Granting of Independence to Colonial Countries and Peoples in all non-self-governing territories. Only the U.S. and the U.K. cast opposing votes.

Dec. 13: A Human Rights Watch document entitled *Report on Israeli Settlement in the Occupied Territories* is released, detailing how, despite the fact that there were almost 8,000 unoccupied residential units in the settlements overall, the "pro-peace" government of Ehud Barak has underwritten construction of an additional 1,924 since July 1999. All told, it is shown that the settler population has nearly doubled since the Oslo Accords supposedly curtailed the rate of influx (see the entry for Sept. 13, 1993). The report also documents how Israel has contrived to "reserve" approximately 80% of the total water supply available in the occupied territories for use by Jewish settlers. While these findings, contested by neither Israel or the U.S., clearly underscore the magnitude of Israeli illegalities, U.S. support for the offender remains undiminished.

2001

Jan. 18: The National Security Council sends a cable to the U.S. delegation to an international conference convened to finalize the UN Draft Declaration of the Rights of Indigenous Peoples, emphasizing that the U.S. will accept no law according indigenous peoples the right to self-determination. Instead, the NSC instructs the delegation to propose "alternative language" in which native peoples are assured a right only to "internal self-determination," a concept previously unknown to international law. As explained by the NSC, this formulation would expressly deny to native peoples any "right to independence or permanent sovereignty over natural resources." The U.S. maneuver is thus designed and intended to nullify the "principle of equal rights and self-determination of peoples" articulated in Chapter I, Article 1(2) of the UN Charter, as well as the repeated guarantee that "all peoples have the right to self-determination" made in the Declaration on the Granting of Independence to Colonial Countries and Peoples, the International Covenant on Economic, Social and Cultural Rights (Art. 1(1)), the International Covenant on Civil and Political Rights (Art. 1(1)), the Declaration of the Right to Development (Art. 1.2) and elsewhere. At base, the U.S. effort to restrict indigenous peoples to exercise of a "right to internal self-determination" thus reduces to a thinly-veiled desire to formally legitimate internal colonialism (especially with regard to the structure of its own "domestic" relationship to Native North Americans; see the entry for Jan. 4, 1975).

Feb. 19: The newly-installed administration of Pres. George W. Bush, son of the earlier-mentioned Pres. Bush, approves the transfer of another $500 million worth of Apache attack helicopters to Israel. A day later, it is announced that the U.S. Army's Corps of Engineers will be spending a further $266 million in American tax dollars to build a major military base for the IDF in the Negev Desert. Leaving aside the implications of such transactions vis-à-vis Israel's ongoing denial of Palestinian rights—as well as those of Syria and Lebanon—it should be noted that the Israelis remain as much in violation of UNGA Res. 300 (IV) as they were when the resolution was passed in 1949.

Mar. 27: In a transparent replay of its maneuver regarding SC Res. 1328 exactly one year earlier, the U.S. joins in approving SC Res. 1381, demanding immediate implementation of SC Res. 338 (1973). Israel yawns and carries on with business as usual. This is because, on the same day, the U.S. vetoes a second resolution (S/2001/270; final vote: 9-1-4), this one jointly introduced by Ireland, Norway, Britain and France, to introduce UN observers to the occupied territories to monitor Israeli compliance. The U.S. claims not to object to observers, per se, but only to the resolution's "inappropriate" use of terms like "siege" and "occupied territories," and its "unfortunate" references to things like the concept of land for peace and the Geneva Conventions.

May 3: The U.S. is removed by vote of the members from the UN's Human Rights Commission. Various reasons are informally cited, including the adamant and persistent refusal of the U.S. to acknowledge the long record of systematic human rights violations by Israel, the persistent U.S. pattern of supporting other major human rights abusers around the world— as but a few examples, Suharto in Indonesia, Pinochet in Chile, the Guatemalan and Greek juntas, the Shah of Iran and the Salvadoran oligarchy—and its own abysmal record of human rights violations around the world. More formally, mention is made of the U.S. domestic posture, including conditions in its penal system and as its refusal either to abolish the death penalty or to endorse the Convention on the Rights of the Child.

May 17: Ariel Sharon displaces Ehud Barak as Israeli PM, announcing, predictably enough, that his policy will be to "take off the gloves" in dealing with the Palestinians. Although it is well documented that Sharon is a career war criminal—indeed, he proudly recounts many of his crimes in his autobiography—and has long been on record as a major proponent of state terrorism, his assuming the position of Israeli head of state generates no calls for a "régime change" by U.S. officials. On the contrary, Sharon is depicted by State Dept. spokespersons as being one of "America's oldest and strongest allies." In short order, the combination of Sharon's sordid background and his ratcheting up of Israeli repression prompts a major escalation in suicide bombings undertaken by Hamas and the Islamic Jihad, as well as a PLO offshoot calling itself the "al-Aqsa Martyrs Brigade." Sharon responds by ordering all-out IDF invasions of both the West Bank and Gaza Strip, devastating entire communities and, for a while, besieging Yasser Arafat in his Ramallah headquarters. In coming months, well over 100 Israelis and several hundred Palestinians are killed. Sharon's "methods" are so crude—not to mention, counterproductive—that even Pres. Bush openly demands that the Israeli offensive be halted "immediately." Sharon effectively thumbs his nose, ordering the operation to continue for another month. Palpably irritated by such insubordination, Bush nonetheless initiates no alteration in U.S.-Israeli relations.

June 27: The ICJ rules (14 to1) in the *LaGrand* case (*Germany v. U.S.*) that the U.S. has violated its obligations to Germany and to Karl and Walter LeGrand under Art. 36 of the Vienna Convention on Consular Relations by failing to inform them of their right to consular access. By this time Karl LeGrand has already been executed and the U.S. argues that the ICJ's Provisional Measures Order staying Walter's execution is not legally binding (precisely the opposite of argument before the ICJ when, suing Iran for redress relating to the 1979 hostage crisis, it pronounced an ICJ emergency order legally binding "as a matter of principle"). Walter LeGrand is executed on schedule (see the entries for April 14, 1998, Oct. 1, 1999, and Feb. 5, 2003).

July 9: U.S. Undersecretary of State for Arms Control and International Security John Bolton addresses the UN Conference on the Illicit Trade in Small Arms and Weapons in New York, informing assembled delegates that the U.S. does not consider its own trade in such materials to be problematic, and, correspondingly, that it will not support measures designed to strengthen curtailment of the arms trade on an across-the-board basis.

Aug. 31: The UN World Conference against Racism, Racial Discrimination, Xenophobia and Related Intolerance begins in Durban, South Africa. Israel, whose policies of discrimination against Palestinians are on the docket for considerable criticism in these connections, boycotts the proceedings. The U.S. delegation, discovering that it cannot suppress equation of zionism to racism in accordance with UNGA Res. 3379 (1975), also walks out.

Sept. 11: The sustained pattern of war crimes and crimes against humanity committed by the U.S. against the Iraqis, Palestinians, Libyans, Sudanese and many others is finally rejoined in kind when 19 members of al-Qaida commandeer 3 commercial airliners and, using them as "300,000-pound cruise missiles," level the twin towers of the World Trade Center in New York, and a wing of the Pentagon (a fourth airliner, reputedly aimed at either the Capitol Building or the White House, is shot down over Pennsylvania, killing all aboard). On Sept. 14, Congress passes a joint resolution authorizing Pres. Bush to use "all necessary and appropriate force against those nations, organizations, or persons he determines planned, authorized, committed, or aided" the attacks. Bush's resulting "war on terror" initially targets Afghanistan, in which al-Qaida maintains several training camps, demanding—despite the fact that the U.S. has never deigned to enter into an extradition treaty with it—that the county's Taliban government immediately turn over Usama bin-Laden. Publicly, Afghani head of state Mullah Omar asks only that the U.S. make an offer of proof that bin-Laden was actually involved in the 9-1-1 attacks; behind the scenes, he arranges in any event to deliver the al-Qaida leader to Pakistani intelligence agents, thence the U.S. His demand met in full, Bush nonetheless orders first an air assault, then a ground invasion of Afghanistan. As a means of combating "terrorism," the onslaught is absurd; nobody, including Bush himself has accused the Taliban of being "terrorist sponsors" per se, and the al-Qaida leadership, as well as most of the organization's fighters, simply to slip away during the course of the combat. In terms of forcing a "régime change"—that is, of replacing the fiercely independent Taliban with a much more malleable and western-oriented entity, one guaranteed to further U.S. oil interests in Central Asia—however, the campaign is entirely successful. In this sense, it is also a glaring violation of the1970 Declaration on Principles of International Law Concerning Friendly Relations and Co-operation Among States in Accordance With the Charter of the United Nations (esp. Chapters I, VI and VII), UNGA Resolutions 337A (V), 380 (V), 2131 (XX) and 3314 (XXIX), the International Covenant on Civil and Political Rights, and the International Covenant on Economic, Social and Cultural Rights. Additionally, the war is by and large fought with little regard for the requirements of either the 1949 Geneva Convention IV or UNGA 2444, and conspicuous violations of the 1949 Geneva Convention III occur when U.S.-aligned forces perpetrate a series of massacres and other atrocities against prisoners at Mazar-i-Sharif and elsewhere. Needless to say, while numerous Taliban leaders and soldiers are alleged to be "war criminals," no one aligned with the U.S. is similarly accused.

Sept. 28: In the wake of 9-1-1, the U.S. rams through SC Res. 1373, requiring that all UN member-states suppress the financing of and acquisition of weapons by international terrorist organizations, deny safe haven to terrorists, bring terrorists and all persons associated with them to justice, seal their borders against terrorist movements, and cooperate with all other member-states in pursuit of these goals. While the resolution seems reasonable on its face, the U.S. rather explicitly elects to define "terrorists" as any persons or groups it, and it alone, chooses, for whatever reason, to define as such. Neither the historical financing/equipage, nor the ongoing safe haven provided by the U.S. to innumerable terrorists—Nicaraguan contras, for example, and the aging Cuban exiles of Omega 7—counts, of course. The U.S. also insists that other governments are required to "freeze without delay" the assets of any individual or group it accuses of terrorism, or association with terrorists, rather than proceeding "in accordance with its domestic legal principles." Bringing terrorists to "justice" is construed as turning them over to the U.S. on demand, moreover; the U.S. at this point actively opposes the prosecution of *anyone* in whom it has an interest before the now-duly constituted ICC. In effect, a single element of law is being wielded as a means of voiding whole swaths of customary legal safeguards and protections, while the U.S. attempts to place itself in the position of supreme legal arbiter on a genuinely planetary basis.

Oct. 26: Pres. Bush signs the PATRIOT Act. On Sept. 12, while seeking to explain the reason underlying the 9-1-1 attack to the American people, he has explained that it's because "they hate our freedom." Thereafter, in apparent acknowledgement of the power "they" possess, he and selected congressional leaders team up to abolish what little remains of freedom in the U.S.—thereby presumably safeguarding the public against further such attacks—through the legislation in question. While nullifying the U.S. Constitution altogether, the PATRIOT Act also includes numerous provisions contrary to the Universal Declaration of Human Rights, the American Declaration of the Rights and Duties of Man, the American Convention on Human Rights, the International Convention on the Elimination of All Forms of Racial Discrimination, the International Covenant on Civil and Political Rights and UNGA Res. 33/173 (the Resolution on Disappeared Persons).

Nov. 10: Meeting in Morocco, the Congress of Parties to the 1997 Kyoto Protocol finalizes its program for reducing greenhouse gas emissions. By then, however, the U.S., alone among signatory states, has dropped out of the process. Although Pres. Bush included a plank on reducing carbon dioxide levels in the atmosphere in his 1999 campaign platform, his administration has to date introduced no viable plan by which to accomplish this goal. On the contrary, in June 2002, Bush refuses to so much as acknowledge the scientific consensus that human activities are primarily responsible for inducing global warming and other aspects of potentially catastrophic climate change. Unsurprisingly, given this official posture, the U.S. remains by far the worst offender on the planet in terms of per capita environmental impact.

Nov. 13: Pres. Bush signs a decree authorizing the creation of special military tribunals to try noncitizens suspected of terrorism against the U.S. In short order, this evolves into the proposition that since "terrorists"—a term construed so broadly as to encompass virtually anyone, anywhere, who for whatever reason and by whatever means takes concrete action to oppose U.S. policy, or indicates support for those who do—are "illegal combatants," their rights are protected by *neither* U.S. domestic nor international law. In effect, even a military tribunal is unnecessary: those accused, on whatever basis, of being involved with "international terrorism" can simply be held without a trial of any sort, for as long as the military desires, under any conditions the military wishes to impose upon them. The primary—but by no means the only—example of this procedure at work concerns some 660 Taliban soldiers and suspected al-Qaida fighters captured in Afghanistan, then sedated and flown half way around the world to be confined like zoo animals in outdoor cages at "Camp X-Ray," a specially-constructed facility within the U.S. Marine compound at Guantánamo Bay, Cuba (for an earlier counterpart facility, see the entry for Dec. 2, 1970). There, the Taliban captives, who are members of the armed forces of a recognized government, and are thus entitled to protection under the 1949 Geneva Convention III, have been conflated with the alleged al-Qaida captives, who are not. Actual members of al-Qaida—and there is clear evidence that at least some of those held under that heading at Camp X-Ray, including at least three children as young as 13 years of age, are not—are on the other hand properly classified not as "illegal combatants," but as "unprivileged combatants," and are thus entitled to protection under the 1949 Geneva Convention IV. As the matter is framed in the 1978 Fundamental Rules of International Humanitarian Law Applicable in Armed Conflicts, "*Everyone* shall be entitled to benefit from fundamental judicial guarantees. No one shall be held responsible for an act he has not committed. No one shall be subjected to physical or mental torture, corporal punishment or cruel or degrading punishment [emphasis added]." Thus, as things stand, the U.S., both in deed and in enunciated policy, stands in violation of every aspect of applicable international law. Indeed, both the actions and the policy violate U.S. law, wherein, to quote the Supreme Court in its 1866 *Milligan* opinion, constitutional requirements supposedly bind both "rulers and people, equally in war and in peace, covering with the shield of [their] protection *all* classes of men, at *all* times, and under *all* circumstances [emphasis added]."

Nov. 29: 151 member-states endorse UNGA Res. 56/24I, calling for conventional arms control at the regional and subregional levels. The U.S. alone casts an opposing vote.

Nov. 29: 153 member-states endorse UNGA Res. 56/27, describing Israel's illegal possession of nuclear weapons as a prime source of the risk of such armaments proliferating in the Middle East. The U.S. and Israel cast opposing votes.

Dec. 3: 130 member-states endorse UNGA Res. 56/31, calling upon Israel to resolve the dispute over Jerusalem in conformity with international law. The U.S. and Israel cast opposing votes.

Dec. 3: 90 member-states endorse UNGA Res. 56/32, calling upon Israel to comply with international law in resolving its dispute with Syria over the Golan Heights. The U.S. and Israel cast opposing votes.

Dec. 3: 106 member-states endorse UNGA Res. 56/33, continuing the Committee on Exercise of the Inalienable Rights of the Palestinian People. The U.S. and Israel cast opposing votes.

Dec. 3: 107 member-states endorse UNGA Res. 56/34, calling for a Division of Palestinian Rights within the UN Secretariat. The U.S. and Israel cast opposing votes.

Dec. 3: 153 member-states endorse UNGA Res. 56/35, calling for a special information program on the Question of Palestine. The U.S. and Israel cast opposing votes.

Dec. 3: 131 member-states endorse UNGA Res. 56/36, calling for a peaceful resolution of the Question of Palestine, in conformity with international law. The U.S. and Israel cast opposing votes.

Dec. 7: 134 member-states endorse UNGA Res. 56/49, calling for cooperation between the UN and the Preparatory Committee for a Comprehensive Nuclear Test-Ban Treaty. The U.S. alone casts an opposing vote.

Dec. 10: 151 member-states endorse UNGA Res. 56/52, calling for increased nonmilitary assistance to Palestinian refugees. Only the U.S. and Israel cast opposing votes.

Dec. 10: 151 member-states endorse UNGA Res. 56/54, reaffirming the right of Palestinians and other persons displaced by Israel's June 1967 attack upon its neighbors and subsequent hostilities to return to their homes. The U.S. and Israel cast opposing votes.

Dec. 10: 151 member-states endorse UNGA Res. 56/56, commending and continuing activities undertaken by the UN Relief and Works Agency for Palestine Refugees in the Near East. The U.S. and Israel cast opposing votes.

Dec. 10: 150 member-states endorse UNGA Res. 56/57, reaffirming the right of Palestinians dispossessed by Israel's illegal expansion from 1948 onward to recover their property and all revenues derived therefrom. The U.S. and Israel cast opposing votes.

Dec. 10: 151 member-states endorse UNGA Res. 56/58, calling upon the Sec. Gen. to proceed with establishing a University of Jerusalem (al-Quds) to serve Palestinian refugees. The U.S. and Israel cast opposing votes.

Dec. 10: 83 member-states endorse UNGA Res. 56/59, accepting the annual Report of the Special Committee to Investigate Israeli Practices Affecting the Human Rights of Palestinians and Other Arabs of the Occupied Territories. The U.S. and Israel cast opposing votes.

Dec. 10: 146 member-states endorse UNGA Res. 56/60, reaffirming the applicability of the 1949 Geneva Convention IV to Israeli practices and policies in the occupied territories of Palestine and Syria. The U.S. and Israel cast opposing votes.

Dec. 10: 145 member-states endorse UNGA Res. 56/61, condemning Israeli human rights violations in the occupied territories. The U.S. and Israel cast opposing votes.

Dec. 10: 147 member-states endorse UNGA Res. 56/62, calling upon Israel to comply with relevant UN resolutions and international law in resolving its dispute with Syria over the Golan Heights. The U.S. and Israel cast opposing votes.

Dec. 10: 147 member-states endorse UNGA Res. 56/66, condemning economic and other activities impeding realization of self-determination in non-self-governing territories. Only the U.S. and the U.K. cast opposing votes.

Dec. 10: 147 member-states endorse UNGA Res. 56/73, calling for increased dissemination of information on decolonization by UN agencies. Only the U.S. and the U.K. cast opposing votes.

Dec. 10: 132 member-states endorse UNGA Res. 56/74, calling for immediate implementation of the Declaration on the Granting of Independence to Colonial Countries and Peoples in all non-self-governing territories. Only the U.S. and the U.K. cast opposing votes.

Dec. 13: The U.S. submits notice that it is withdrawing, effective June 13, 2002, from its 1972 treaty commitments, originally entered into with the Soviet Union and subsequently transposed to Russia, to limit antiballistic missile systems. U.S. implementation precipitates an immediate withdrawal of Russia from its commitments under provision of the Strategic Arms Reduction Treaty (START II) signed on May 24, 2002. It also greatly increases the probability that China, Pakistan, North Korea, Iran, Syria and Libya—all of which are targeted for U.S. nuclear strikes in Pentagon contingency plans leaked to the *New York Times*—will feel an ever-greater need to develop increased nuclear capabilities of their own. Suffice it to say that the U.S. posture is directly contrary to the entire range of nuclear nonproliferation treaties, conventions and agreements the U.S. now claims it is dedicated to enforcing against other countries ("multilaterally where possible, unilaterally if necessary").

Dec. 14: 12 of 15 Security Council member-states endorse draft res. S/2001/1199, calling for the immediate withdrawal of Israeli forces from the occupied territories of Palestine. The U.S. employs its veto to override them (final vote: 12-1-2).

Dec. 15: 12 of 15 Security Council member-states endorse a draft res. condemning Middle East terrorism and calling for the introduction of a UN peacekeeping mission to the region as a means of alleviating the problem. The U.S., citing possible impairment of "Israeli sovereignty," employs its veto to override them (final vote: 12-1-2).

Dec. 19: 161 member-states endorse UNGA Res. 56/142, reaffirming the right of the Palestinian people to self-determination. Only the U.S. and Israel cast opposing votes.

Dec. 19: 123 member-states endorse UNGA Res. 56/150, reaffirming the right to development. The U.S. is 1 of 4 countries casting opposing votes.

Dec. 19: 169 member-states endorse UNGA Res. 56/155, reaffirming the right to food. The U.S. is 1 of 2 countries casting opposing votes.

Dec. 19: 100 member-states endorse UNGA Res. 56/179, condemning unilateral economic measures used as a means of political/economic compulsion against Third World countries. Only the U.S. casts an opposing vote.

Dec. 21: 148 member-states endorse UNGA Res. 56/204, reaffirming permanent Palestinian sovereignty over natural resources in the occupied territories. The U.S. and Israel cast opposing votes.

Dec. 24: 77 member-states endorse UNGA Res. 56/232, condemning the use of mercenaries to impede the right of self-determination in non-self-governing territories. The U.S. casts an opposing vote.

2002

Jan. 31: Pres. Bush uses his annual State of the Union address to announce that an "Axis of Evil" consisting of Iraq, Iran and North Korea have become targets in his "War on Terror." North Korea in particular seems dumbfounded, since it has neither been accused of sponsoring terrorism nor any particular affiliation with the other 2 countries, and has entered into an agreement with the U.S. to improve relations (with which the U.S., not Korea, has failed to comply; see the entry for Oct. 19, 1994). As to Iraq and Iran, they are notoriously hostile to one another. Themselves seemingly flummoxed by Bush's list, U.S. pundits scramble to explain that the "common denominator" joining the 3 countries is that all are engaged in developing nuclear and other weapons of mass destruction. This, however, does not square with the reality that U.S. allies like Israel, India and Pakistan, the latter only recently removed from the State Dept. list of terrorist sponsors, have illegally possessed nuclear arsenals/delivery systems for years. Thus, the actual common denominator defining the "Axis" is that the three constituents are among the countries most adamant in their refusal to accept U.S. dictates. Insofar as nothing resembling a Security Council authorization attends Bush's pronouncement, it can only be viewed as an abridgement of the1970 Declaration on Principles of International Law Concerning Friendly Relations and Co-operation Among States in Accordance With the Charter of the United Nations (esp. Chapters I, VI and VII), and a "Crime Against Peace," as defined in the London Charter. Certainly it violates both the letter and spirit of UNGA 337A(V).

Mar. 17: The U.S. joins in approving SC Res. 1381, demanding a halt to violence perpetrated by both Palestinians and Israelis (see the entry for May 17, 2001). As always, the U.S. condition for not vetoing a resolution involving Israel is that it not contain enforcement provisions of any sort. Unsurprisingly, U.S. support for Israel, both materially and diplomatically, continues undiminished despite a marked increase in Israeli military operations in the Palestinian territories immediately following the resolution's announcement.

Mar. 27: 134 member-states endorse UNGA Res. 56/266, calling for comprehensive implementation and follow-up on the World Conference against Racism, Racial Discrimination, Xenophobia and Related Intolerance (see the entry for Aug. 31, 2001). The U.S. and Israel cast the only opposing votes.

Mar. 30: The U.S. joins in approving SC Res. 1402, calling for a cease-fire and withdrawal of Israeli forces from Palestinian cities. The trade-off for U.S. endorsement is that the resolution lacks enforcement provisions.

Apr. 19: The U.S. joins in approving SC Res. 1405, expressing concern for the "dire humanitarian situation" suffered by residents of the Jenin refugee camp, in the West Bank, and calling upon Israel to lift restrictions imposed upon it by the IDF. U.S. endorsement is once again contingent upon the resolution's containing no enforcement provisions.

June 30: 13 of 15 Security Council member-states endorse draft res. S/2002/712, renewing the UN peacekeeping mission in Bosnia. The U.S. employs its veto to override them on the basis that the resolution would not specifically exempt U.S. personnel involved in the mission from ICC jurisdiction (final vote: 13-1-1).

Sept. 12: Pres. Bush addresses the UN General Assembly, informing it that it must henceforth either do as it is instructed by the U.S. or be consigned to "irrelevancy." In other words, its only function, from a Bushian perspective, is to legitimate *whatever* the U.S. decides to do at any given moment.

Sept. 24: The U.S. joins in approving SC Res. 1435, which demands that Israel "immediately cease measures in and around Ramallah including the destruction of Palestinian civilian and security infrastructure," as well as the "expeditious withdrawal of Israeli occupying forces from Palestinian cities [and] a return to the positions held prior to September 2000." The applicability of the 1949 Geneva Convention IV to Israeli policy is also reaffirmed. As always, the quid pro quo for U.S. cooperation in a resolution critical of Israel is that it contain no enforcement provisions.

Nov. 5: Under intense pressure from the U.S. delegation—which advances the premise that Iraq has secretly retained stockpiles of chemical and biological weapons/agents, and has resumed a program to develop nuclear weapons—the Security Council passes Res. 1441, requiring that the Iraqis, on pain of the "harshest consequences," accept "immediate and unconditional" UN inspections of all facilities in the country, including the private residences of its head of state. Former UN weapons inspector Scott Ritter, among others, derides such contentions as being absurd on their face (Ritter points out that there is absolutely no evidence that Iraq has acquired the technology necessary to resume its nuclear weapons program, and that any chemical weapons/agents it was still managing to hide when UN inspectors were withdrawn in 1998 would have long since have become inert). Iraq then admits a team of non-U.S. inspectors headed by a Norwegian, Hans Blix. After Blix submits several reports indicating that no "WMD" have been detected, Sec. of State Colin Powell goes before the General Assembly to present what he calls "proof" that the on-the-ground inspectors are wrong. Among Powell's "evidentiary submissions" is an aerial photograph of what he claims are specialized vehicles used to transport chemical weapons in the process of removing material from a warehouse (presumably to hide it). Although it is quickly demonstrated that the photo shows no more than regular trucks backed up to a loading dock, the U.S. launches a "diplomatic offensive" designed to obtain a Security Council resolution authorizing the use of military force against Iraq (which, at that point, is even destroying a handful of al-Samud missiles it has retained in its weapons inventory contrary to SC Res. 687). The effort fails spectacularly—France announces unequivocally that it will veto any such resolution, while Russia, China, Germany and Chile make it clear that they will not endorse it either—and the U.S. finally abandons it in Feb. 2003, claiming rather lamely that "all necessary authorization required for the use of force" is already embodied in SC Res. 1441 (a claim several other Security Council members vociferously deny).

Nov. 12: 173 member-states endorse UNGA Res. 57/11, calling for an end to the U.S. embargo on Cuba. The U.S. and Israel, joined by Uzbekistan, cast opposing votes. The embargo continues, despite this and a dozen other such resolutions.

Nov. 21: 128 member-states endorse UNGA Res. 57/49, calling for cooperation between the UN and the Preparatory Committee for the Comprehensive Nuclear Test-Ban Treaty. Only the U.S. casts an opposing vote.

Nov. 22: 120 member-states endorse UNGA Res. 57/58, calling for a reduction of nonstrategic nuclear fuel. The U.S. is 1 of 3 countries casting opposing votes.

Nov. 22: 125 member-states endorse UNGA Res. 57/59, calling for a new agenda to achieve a nuclear weapons-free world. The U.S. is 1 of 6 countries casting opposing votes.

Nov. 22: 105 member-states endorse UNGA Res. 57/63, calling for multilateralism in disarmament and nonproliferation of nuclear weapons. The U.S. is 1 of 12 countries casting opposing votes.

Nov. 22: 160 member-states endorse UNGA Res. 57/65, highlighting the relationship between disarmament and development. Only the U.S. casts an opposing vote.

Nov. 22: 160 member-states endorse UNGA Res. 57/73, calling for a nuclear weapons-free southern hemisphere. The U.S. is 1 of 3 countries casting opposing votes.

Nov. 22: 165 member-states endorse UNGA Res. 57/77, calling for conventional arms control at regional and subregional levels. The U.S. casts the only opposing vote.

Nov. 22: 156 member-states endorse UNGA Res. 57/78, calling for embarkation on the path to total elimination of nuclear weapons. The U.S. cast 1 of 2 opposing votes.

Nov. 22: 158 member-states endorse UNGA Res. 57/97, describing Israel's illegal possession of nuclear weapons as a main source of the risk that such armaments will proliferate in the Middle East. The U.S. and Israel cast opposing votes.

Dec. 3: 109 member-states endorse UNGA Res. 57/107, continuing the UN Committee on Exercise of the Inalienable Rights of the Palestinian People. The U.S. and Israel cast opposing votes.

Dec. 3: 108 member-states endorse UNGA Res. 57/108, calling for a Division of Palestinian Rights within the UN Secretariat. The U.S. and Israel cast opposing votes.

Dec. 3: 159 member-states endorse UNGA Res. 57/109, calling for a special information program on the Question of Palestine. The U.S. and Israel cast opposing votes.

Dec. 3: 160 member-states endorse UNGA Res. 57/110, calling for a peaceful resolution of the Question of Palestine, in conformity with international law. The U.S. and Israel cast opposing votes.

Dec. 3: 154 member-states endorse UNGA Res. 57/111, calling for Israeli compliance with relevant UN resolutions and international law in resolving the dispute over the disposition of Jerusalem. The U.S. and Israel cast opposing votes.

Dec. 3: 109 member-states endorse UNGA Res. 57/112, calling upon Israel to comply with relevant UN resolutions and international law in resolving its dispute with Syria over the Golan Heights. The U.S. and Israel cast opposing votes.

Dec. 11: 158 member-states endorse UNGA Res. 57/117, calling for increased nonmilitary assistance to Palestinian refugees. Only Israel casts an opposing vote, while the U.S. abstains.

Dec. 11: 155 member-states endorse UNGA Res. 57/119, reaffirming the right of Palestinians and other persons displaced by Israel's June 1967 attack upon its neighbors and subsequent hostilities to return to their homes. The U.S. and Israel cast opposing votes.

Dec. 11: 155 member-states endorse UNGA Res. 57/121, commending and continuing activities undertaken by the UN Relief and Works Agency for Palestine Refugees in the Near East. The U.S. and Israel cast opposing votes.

Dec. 11: 159 member-states endorse UNGA Res. 57/122, reaffirming the right of Palestinians dispossessed as a result of Israel's illegal expansion from 1948 onward to recover their property and revenues derived therefrom. The U.S. and Israel cast opposing votes.

Dec. 11: 155 member-states endorse UNGA Res. 57/123, calling upon the Sec. Gen. to proceed with establishment of a University of Jerusalem (al-Quds) to serve Palestinian refugees. The U.S. and Israel cast opposing votes.

Dec. 11: 86 member-states endorse UNGA Res. 57/124, accepting the annual Report of the Special Committee to Investigate Israeli Practices Affecting the Human Rights of Palestinians and Other Arabs of the Occupied Territories. The U.S. and Israel cast opposing votes.

Dec. 11: 155 member-states endorse UNGA Res. 57/125, reaffirming the applicability of the 1949 Geneva Convention IV to Israeli practices and policies in the occupied territories. The U.S. and Israel cast opposing votes.

Dec. 11: 154 member-states endorse UNGA Res. 57/126, condemning the illegality of Israeli settlements in the occupied territories of Palestine and Syria. The U.S. and Israel cast opposing votes.

Dec. 11: 148 member-states endorse UNGA Res. 57/127, condemning Israeli human rights violations in the occupied territories. The U.S. and Israel cast opposing votes.

Dec. 11: 155 member-states endorse UNGA Res. 57/128, calling for Israeli compliance with relevant UN resolutions and other elements of international law in resolving the issue of the Golan Heights. The U.S. and Israel cast opposing votes.

Dec. 11: 156 member-states endorse UNGA Res. 57/132, condemning economic and other activities impeding realization of self-determination in non-self-governing territories. The U.S. and the U.K. cast opposing votes.

Dec. 11: 154 member-states endorse UNGA Res. 57/139, calling for increased dissemination of information on decolonization by UN agencies. The U.S. and the U.K. cast opposing votes.

Dec. 11: 139 member-states endorse UNGA Res. 57/140, calling for immediate implementation of UNGA Res. 1514 (XV)—the 1960 Declaration on the Granting of Independence to Colonial Countries and Peoples—in all non-self-governing territories. The U.S. and the U.K. cast opposing votes.

Dec. 12: 132 member-states endorse UNGA Res. 57/141, calling for implementation of the 1982 Law of the Sea. The U.S. alone casts an opposing vote.

Dec. 18: 175 member-states endorse UNGA Res. 57/190, affirming the rights of the child. The U.S. and Somalia cast the only opposing votes.

Dec. 18: 173 member–states endorse UNGA Res. 57/195, calling for comprehensive implementation and follow-up on the World Conference against Racism, Racial Discrimination, Xenophobia and Related Intolerance (see the entry for Aug. 31, 2001). The U.S. and Israel cast opposing votes.

Dec. 18: 124 member-states endorse UNGA Res. 57/197, condemning the use of mercenaries to impede realization of self-determination in non-self-governing territories. The U.S. is 1 of 31 countries casting opposing votes.

Dec. 18: 172 member-states endorse UNGA Res. 57/198, reaffirming the right of the Palestinian people to self-determination. The U.S. and Israel cast opposing votes.

Dec. 18: 127 member-states endorse UNGA Res. 57/199, calling for adoption of the Optional Protocol Additional to the Convention Against Torture and Other Cruel, Inhuman or Degrading Treatment or Punishment (prohibiting the death penalty altogether). The U.S. is 1 of 4 countries casting opposing votes.

Dec. 18: 133 member-states endorse UNGA Res. 57/223, reaffirming the right to development. The U.S. is 1 of 4 countries casting opposing votes.

Dec. 18: 176 member-states endorse UNGA Res. 57/226, reaffirming the right to food. The U.S. alone casts an opposing vote.

Dec. 20: 155 member-states endorse UNGA Res. 57/269, reaffirming the right of the Palestinian people to exercise permanent sovereignty over the natural resources of the West Bank and Gaza Strip. The U.S. and Israel cast opposing votes.

Dec. 20: 12 of 15 Security Council member-states endorse a draft res. condemning Israel for its killing of several UN employees and destruction of a UN food warehouse in occupied Palestine. The U.S. employs its veto to override them (final vote: 12-1-2).

2003

Jan. 21: Mexico sues the U.S. before the ICJ for violating Art. 36 of the Vienna Convention on Consular Relations by denying consular access to its nationals charged with crimes. Commutation of the sentences of 54 Mexicans on death row is requested. On Feb. 5 the ICJ unanimously orders the U.S. to postpone the next 3 scheduled executions. The U.S. again ignores the order (see the entries for April 14, 1998, Oct. 1, 1999, and June 27, 2001). As of this writing, there are approximately 120 foreign nationals on death row and an untold number of others being held in indefinite post-Sept. 11 detention, most of whom have not been allowed to exercise their right to consular access.

Mar. 19: Without authorization, and therefore asserting its "inalienable right to defend itself" against the weapons of mass destruction supposedly hoarded by Saddam Hussein, the U.S. launches "Operation Iraqi Freedom," a fullscale invasion of Iraq. As of this writing—July 20, 2003—with the entire country having been under effective U.S. control for more than 3 months, the alleged "WMD" have been neither used nor found. Official justification for the conquest has therefore shifted to "the need to liberate the Iraqi people" by imposing "democracy" upon them. An "Iraqi interim government" selected by the Defense Dept. has been installed, making the U.S. a de facto member of OPEC and altering the geopolitical calculus of the entire Mideast region. The U.S. war constitutes a flagrant violation of the 1970 Declaration on Principles of International Law Concerning Friendly Relations and Co-operation Among States in Accordance With the Charter of the United Nations (esp. Chapters I, VI and VII) and UNGA Resolutions 337A (V) and 3314 (XXIX). Assuming the U.S. follows through on its announced intention to dictate the form of the postwar Iraqi government, its actions will violate UNGA Resolutions 380 (V) and 2131 (XX). Assuming further that the U.S. follows through on its express intent to use force to "preserve [for its own geopolitical reasons] the territorial integrity of the Iraqi state," irrespective of the desire of the Kurds to secede, it will also be in violation of Chapters XI and XII of the UN Charter, as well as the 1960 Declaration on the Granting of Independence to Colonial Countries and Peoples.

Apr. 10: Serious chatter is advanced in the media by Sec. of Defense Rumsfeld and other U.S. officials, present and former, about the prospect—since "we've already got sufficient forces on hand to do the job"—of extending the Iraq campaign into Syria as a means of compelling another "democratic régime change" there, thus "securing Israel's northern flank." The pretexts for invasion offered are that Syria "may" be harboring criminals from Iraq's deposed Ba'athist régime—as if the U.S. hasn't harbored the Shah of Iran and a multitude of other such criminals (see, e.g., the entries for Dec. 11, 1946 and Feb. 11, 1979)—and "concerns" that Syria is a sponsor of international terrorism—as if the U.S. hasn't sponsored groups like Omega 7 and the Nicaraguan contras (see the entries for Jan 1, 1959, and Mar. 16, 1986)—and "may" be in possession of weapons of mass destruction.

To its everlasting credit, Syria, uncowed by U.S. bellicosity, replies that it will be happy to see the Mideast cleared of WMD, and will therefore gladly participate in any serious initiative designed to relieve the Israelis of such illegal items. All things considered, the U.S. appears to be advancing one of its endlessly transparent deformations of legality as justification for launching yet another utterly illegal military onslaught. In any event, the entire U.S. posture vis-à-vis Syria is already contrary to the 1970 Declaration on Principles of International Law Concerning Friendly Relations and Co-operation Among States in Accordance With the Charter of the United Nations (esp. Chapters I, VI and VII) and UNGA Res. 337A (V).

Apr. 12: The news breaks that U.S. VP Dick Cheney is still on the payroll of Haliburton—he received $1 million in "deferred salary" in 2001, and holds some $8 million in stock options—the Texas-based oil corporation/defense contractor for which he served as CEO before resuming public office in 2000. The information adds to an already pronounced clucking attending the facts that Haliburton subsidiary Kellogg, Brown and Root was paid $33 million to build the Camp X-Ray prison facility at Guantánamo Bay, Cuba (see the entry for Nov. 13, 2001), has recently been awarded a lucrative no-bid contract to quell fires in the Iraqi oil fields, and seems likely to receive similar treatment with respect to an initial $1 billion contract to "rebuild Iraq" to Pentagon specifications (estimates of the overall cost outlays on this one run from $30-45 billion over the next decade). The issue is quickly "resolved" by allowing 4 other major defense contractors to sidle up to the trough, although, even as things stand, Haliburton was able to report a doubling of its gross revenues between mid-2001 and the beginning of 2003 (its stated income for 2002 was $1.6 billion). Actually, things are worse than they seem in the Cheney/Haliburton connection. As Defense Sec. in 1991, Cheney paid the corporation $4 million for a study of how it, along with its counterparts in the defense industry, might "help out" during a period of anticipated military downsizing. When Bill Clinton unexpectedly won the 1992 presidential election, Cheney immediately signed himself in to Haliburton's top slot, relying upon "stay behind" relationships to obtain at least $3.8 in defense contracts over the next 8 years (during Cheney's tenure, the corporation moved up in terms of revenues from 78th to 18th on the Pentagon's list of contractors). It should also be noted that during the 1990s—that is, during the otherwise draconian U.S. embargo of Iraq—Cheney managed to steer Haliburton into some $73 million in contracts with the Iraqi régime, helping to refurbish its oil production plant. In any event, those contending that the invasion/occupation of Iraq had nothing to do with WMD, terrorism, or "liberating the Iraqi people"—but was instead prompted by a desire for personal profit on the part of those in high policy-making positions—have an unimpeachable case. That any such employment of military force is illegal, and that those employing it are therefore criminals, goes without saying.

Apr. 15: Although Syria is not under UN sanction, the U.S. shuts off the flow of oil to the country from Iraq, from which it draws about 35% of its consumption. The U.S. motive is openly coercive, with American officials publicly exulting that the impact on Syria's economy will likely be sufficient to force its government to do their bidding. The unilateral U.S. embargo, using another country's natural resources to accomplish it, is in flagrant violation of the 1970 Declaration on Principles of International Law Concerning Friendly Relations and Co-operation Among States in Accordance With the Charter of the United Nations (esp. Chapters I and IX), UNGA Res. 337A (V), the Charter of Economic Rights and Duties of States, and both General Assembly Resolutions on Permanent Sovereignty Over Natural Resources (1962; 1973).

Apr. 24: The U.S. announces that it has begun production of a "whole new species" of low-yield—i.e., tactical—nuclear weapons, referred to as "bunker busters." Self-evidently, such production violates every nonproliferation treaty on the books, including those the U.S. has appointed itself to enforce against Iraq, North Korea and Iran. Given that the "collateral effects" of these "tack-nukes" is theoretically much less substantial than those attending the detonation of strategic nuclear weapons, the likelihood of their actually being used is astronomically greater. Insofar as this is true, it can be said that U.S. planners have consciously embraced a military doctrine in which violation of the 1972 Prohibition of the Use of Nuclear Weapons, the 1980 Resolution on the Non-Use of Nuclear Weapons, and an ICJ opinion holding use or threat of use of such weapons to be illegal, is deemed to be a matter of "discretion" (on the ICJ opinion, see the entry for July 8, 1996).

Apr. 29: Pres. Bush puts forth what he calls his "Roadmap for Peace in the Middle East." In substance, it proffers a land-for-peace arrangement in which Israel will be obliged to partially comply with SC Resolutions 242 and 338 and a Palestinian state will be established by mid-2005. The Palestinian National Congress immediately endorses the proposition, while the Sharon régime refuses it on its face. Under heavy pressure from the U.S., Sharon then reverses course, stipulating that it will cooperate only if Yasser Arafat relinquishes power and the PNC arranges a halt in military actions by Hamas and the Islamic Jihad (no mention is made of suspending Israel's military aggression). When Arafat accepts this proposition as well, and stepping aside in favor of Israeli-preferred Mahmoud Abbas, Sharon is placed in a quandary. For several weeks he manages to avert fulfillment of his own terms by ordering IDF actions against Hamas and the Jihad every time they appear ready to accept a Mahmoud-negotiated ceasefire. Finally, despite ongoing and blatant Israeli provocations, the pair of "terrorist organizations" agree to suspend operations for 90 days, leaving Sharon no viable alternative but to withdraw his troops from preselected locations in the West Bank and to initiate talks. The implications remain unknown as of this writing.

May 21: Responding to more than a decade of concerted U.S. pressure, the World Health Organization (WHO) adopts the Framework Convention on Tobacco Control, aimed in part at prohibiting smoking in public spaces worldwide as a means of reducing the supposed ill effects on public health of "environmental tobacco smoke" (ETS). The convention is adopted despite a broadbased study of the "problem" completed by the WHO in 1998 which revealed no evidence that ETS produces any negative health effects at all (on the contrary, possible health benefits to children were demonstrated). At about the same time, a 1993 study purporting opposite findings and published by the U.S. Environmental Protection Agency (EPA) was found to be scientifically invalid by federal courts in both the U.S. and Australia (an independent study conducted in California and released on May 16, 2003—involving more than 118,000 subjects over a 12-year period, it is the first genuinely largescale and sustained assessment yet carried out in the U.S.—has, moreover, reached essentially the same conclusions as the WHO study). For the U.S. government, which presently refuses to extend health care protection to more 40 million of its citizens, to pretend that its position on ETS has anything at all to do with a concern for "public health" is on its face preposterous. The more so, since—although a baby born in Los Angeles and never for a moment exposed to the alleged ravages of tobacco smoke reaches his/her EPA-established lifetime quota of inhaled toxins within 72 hours—this is the same government that refuses to accept the Kyoto Treaty's requirement that it reduce atmospheric pollutants within its own domain, and which insists that there is no correlation between the approximately 4,000 pounds of plutonium it has released into the environment and the rise in lung cancer rates among Americans over the past 50 years (*one* pound of plutonium, dispersed evenly through the earth's atmosphere, would be sufficient to induce lung cancer in every human being on the planet). Aside from the glaring aspects of social engineering embodied in U.S. antismoking policy—the social space/practices of poor, nonwhite and typically unruly people are being systematically abolished "for their own good" and/or the increased comfortability of their more privileged "betters"—it offers an ideal medium for diverting attention from the real problems it is designed to mask. That the subterfuge is being peddled on a worldwide basis speaks for itself. So, too, does the reality that the U.S., having sucked most other countries into participating in the travesty, has declined to sign off on its own antismoking convention. The reason? Certain provisions might impair its "free trade" in cigarettes (using "health" as a pretext to gouge the tobacco-buying public with increasingly astronomical taxes is one thing, after all, actually curtailing consumption of the products taxed, quite another).

July 7: The White House acknowledges for the first time what has been known in international circles since early March: Pres. Bush used "incomplete and possibly inaccurate information" in peddling the "case" for an immediate war against Iraq during his State of the Union Address (Jan. 28, 2003). Specifically at issue is his claim, attributed to "British intelligence," that Iraq had been trying to buy substantial quantities of uranium from Niger, presumably to pursue its alleged nuclear weapons program. The CIA, however, had already determined that "documentary evidence" of the purchase was forged—by whom has never been revealed—and had informed the White House of its findings. Similarly, Bush repeated a charge made by his National Security Advisor, Condoleezza Rice, that a shipment of aluminum tubing purchased by Iraq was "only suited for nuclear weapons programs," although the falseness of this claim, too, had already been reported by the CIA to the White House. And then there are the presidential assertions that proof of "a link between Saddam and al-Qaida" was iron-clad, an allegation flatly refuted by his own intelligence reports. In effect, like Lyndon Johnson with regard to the "Tonkin Gulf Incident" (see the entry for Aug. 4, 1964), and Ronald Reagan with regard to both El Salvador and Grenada (see the entries for Feb. 23, 1981 and Oct. 25, 1983), George W. Bush lied through his teeth as an expedient to obtaining congressional/public "consent" for a war he, for reasons unstated, wished to wage. It could, on this basis, be argued that the country has been/is being duped by the criminal prevarications of its chief executives. Neither Johnson nor Reagan suffered the least consequences of having been found out, however, and it's a sage bet that Bush won't either. In this sense, all "expressions of outrage" and other such dither notwithstanding, the Congress and the country are thoroughly complicit in the crimes.

July 18: The body of David Kelly, the British defense consultant alleged by the BBC to have blown the whistle on the fabricated documentation predicating his country's claim that Iraq was seeking to acquire uranium from Niger, is found in a London park. Although the death is designated a suicide, many are skeptical (some, perhaps, recalling such things as the 1959 finding by New Jersey officials that mobster Longy Zwillman committed suicide by first tying his hands together behind his back, then hanging himself in his garage, the official 2001 Mexican verdict that human rights activist Digna Ochoa had killed herself by shooting herself in the leg and head, and, of course, the astonishing number of prisoners throughout the "Free World" who, according to official sources, opt to beat themselves to death each year). Suffice it here to observe that Kelly's demise serves the interests both of Pres. Bush and his transatlantic lapdog, British PM Tony Blair, who was busily addressing a joint session of the U.S. Congress at the very moment the corpse was discovered. Whether the resulting "controversy" will have a lasting impact on either head of state remains to be seen, but the record provides ample reason to entertain serious doubts.

July 20: Federal District Judge Richard W. Roberts orders $653 million of $1.7 billion in Iraqi assets frozen in 1990 held for payment to 17 former U.S. POWs for "pain, suffering and mental anguish" allegedly suffered at the hands of their captors during the 1991 Gulf War. In 2002, the U.S., acting on the basis of a newly-enacted domestic statute—a provision of the 2001 USA PATRIOT Act by which the federal government unilaterally empowered itself to seize the assets of any country, group or individual it declared to be a "terrorist entity"—asserted outright "ownership" of the funds (the judge initially awarded the 17 plaintiffs nearly $1 billion—$653 million in compensatory and $306 million in punitive damages, but the U.S.-imposed dissolution of Iraq's Ba'athist government nullified the latter category). Undoubtedly, there are more than a few persons presently residing in cages at Guantánamo Bay and elsewhere who'd like to have a chat with the judge concerning the amounts *they* will be receiving *from* the U.S. in compensatory/punitive awards. So, too, any number of former Iraqi POWs, Panamanians, Grenadans and other such unfortunates stretching back in an unbroken line through the tiger cages of Con Son Island (see the entry for Apr. 14, 1971) to Korea. There are, for that matter, more than a few individuals in the U.S. itself who've documentedly suffered far worse at the hands of American penal authorities than anything experienced by the POWs—the name of Geronimo ji Jaga Pratt comes readily to mind (see the entry for Dec. 9, 1975)—without receiving anything remotely resembling the amount of compensation bestowed in this case. And, of course, there remains the issue of the thousands of Libyan, Iranian and comparable non-combatants of many other nationalities, *all* of whom have been denied standing in U.S. courts to press compensatory/punitive claims against the U.S. for damages demonstrably sustained as a result of its myriad violations of international law (see the entries for Apr. 14, 1986 and July 3, 1987, as examples). Equity being the first principle of valid jurisprudence, Judge Roberts' rulings embody a travesty amounting to state-sanctioned theft from the Iraqi people.

In the Alternative

Leaving the specifics of the U.S. record at this point to speak for themselves, it is worth noting that the process of international legal codification set in motion in 1945 has, however inadvertently from the perspective of its instigator, yielded some genuinely constructive results. Were the laws of war as they are now codified actually enforced, for example, many of the technological advantages presently enjoyed by the "world's only remaining superpower" in asserting its strategic superiority—this includes not only nuclear weaponry but the full range of "smart" ordnance calculated to produce specified amounts of "collateral damage" (read, civilian casualties)—would be nullified.[212] So, too, a dizzying array of tactical paraphernalia, from cluster bombs to depleted uranium munitions.[213] Even the use of such "non-lethal gases" as CS and CN, commonly employed for "crowd control" purposes in the U.S. itself, are illegal, and have been since the Hague Declaration 2 was promulgated in 1899.[214] Any such leveling of the military playing field— promising, as it does, a possible repetition of the "Vietnam Syndrome" besetting the U.S. during and immediately after its defeat in Indochina, every time it ventures to intervene in another country's affairs[215]— would go far towards deterring the kind of wanton aggression increasingly displayed by the U.S. over the past twenty years. At the very least, it would tend to wipe away the smug smirk perpetually adorning the lips of George W. Bush, and that in itself is a goal worth pursuing.

Absent the presently overwhelming potential of American firepower to impose order at the expense of law, the current drive of U.S. state/corporate élites to both systematize and fully globalize their position of economic dominance cannot be consummated.[216] On the contrary, restoration of a semblance of military parity to international power equations stands both to enable other "developed" countries to thwart U.S. ambitions over the short run, and, more importantly, to revitalize the sorts of Third World liberation movements that displayed so much promise during the period 1950-75.[217] In substance, enforcement of the now codified rule of international law would have the effect of repealing the endless expansion of their "share" of the planet's wealth/resources aspired to by American plutocrats, forcing them into an equally open-ended implosive spiral.[218] As U.S. military/economic power thus wanes, that of the rest of the world increases in relative terms. Each increment of the process, of course, serves to enhance the ability of the international community to compel U.S. compliance with the entire range of articulated covenants, conventions and United Nations resolutions (i.e., the longstanding U.S. policy of exempting itself and its "friends" from legal requirements and constraints would be consigned to history's dustbin).[219] Reciprocally, each turn of the legal ratchet accelerates the rate of decay evident within the structure of American suzerainty.

The process, if followed through to its logical culmination, would have the effect of at last actualizing the purpose for which the United Nations was from its inception theoretically intended: that of creating a truly democratic forum within which the rules and mechanics of international relations can be worked out in a manner preferred by, or at least acceptable to, the broadest possible range of constituents.[220] To this end, adjustments to the organization's internal configuration/procedures are plainly necessary, beginning with elimination of the prerogative wielded by select member-states to veto Security Council resolutions. The Council itself might best be redefined as something along the lines of a special committee, with implementation of its resolutions subject to vote by the General Assembly.[221] Likely, the U.S., as it has done before, will seek to avert such democratization of the UN by withholding payment of its dues.[222] This maneuver can be met head on by rescinding U.S. voting privileges in key areas—or altogether—until such time as it meets its obligations.[223] Should the U.S. attempt to withdraw from the UN under such circumstances—"going it alone," in defiance of international community—its assets abroad can be impounded, the proceeds used to offset its debt (both current and projected).[224]

The primary message to be conveyed is twofold, and of exceeding importance: first, that a body composed of 190 other member-states will no longer be bent to the will of a single member, and, second, that the U.S. holds substantially less right to secede from the UN than the Confederate States had to secede from the U.S.[225] Both perceptually and attitudinally, the U.S.—not only its leaders, but the population as a whole—are going to have to be left with no alternative but to accept the realization that their "manifest destiny" is to become a functioning part of rather than presiding over the community of nations,[226] that the role embraced by that community is to ensure the common good, and that the common good has long since been legally codified as devolving first and foremost upon the right of "all peoples to self-determination...by virtue of [which] they freely determine their political status and freely pursue their economic, social and cultural development" irrespective of the preferences of or the convenience of their choices to the U.S.[227] In other words, notwithstanding the triumphalist rhetoric of America's global profiteers—or the sense of overweening entitlement with which the average American yuppie asserts his/her imaginary "right" to possess a new Saab, or cellphone, or condo in Vail, no matter *how* many youngsters must elsewhere starve in the trade-off—socialism, not "free market capitalism," has been long and all but universally embraced as a normative legal requirement.[228] To pretend otherwise is thus not only to think/act in an antidemocratic manner, opposed to the fundamental freedoms of humanity, but criminally as well. And criminals, be it said, whether of the rational or the lunatic varieties, are always and everywhere quite rightly subject to corrective action by their more law-abiding peers.[229]

While the advantages to peoples elsewhere of finally being free to exercise their legal rights to sovereignty over their natural resources—and to organize their governments/economies as they themselves see fit—are to a considerable extent self-evident,[230] benefits accruing to the U.S. domestic populace may seem rather less clear. This is especially so, given the propensity of the American plutocracy to defray costs of retrenchment, whether long term or short, by passing them along to the poorest social sectors—primarily communities of color—as a matter of first resort.[231] Under existing international law, however, any such approach is patently illegal. Not only is the U.S. barred by the 1966 Convention on Elimination of All Forms of Racial Discrimination from undertaking such time-honored expedients to preserving profits, but it has become a matter of near-consensus among UN member-states that such things as adequate nutrition, health care and housing constitute fundamental human rights.[232] Hence, were U.S. élites to seek preservation of their privilege on the home front by resort to the usual "austerity measures," they could be subjected to international trade sanctions, the freezing of their assets abroad, and methods of convincing them that failure to meet their legally-defined obligations to the social welfare has become cost prohibitive.[233]

The bottom line is that the great majority of U.S. citizens would, like the rest of the world population, be materially better off were their government and its corporate counterparts leashed to the norms and standards of international legality rather than left to pursue "the U.S. national interest" however and by whatever means they might choose to define it at a given moment. This is true not only in the ways mentioned in the preceding paragraph, but also in terms of the rights acknowledged in international law as residing in children, women, prisoners, noncitizen migrant workers, and numerous others,[234] as well as the restraints imposed upon élites in employing force to sustain any order which has the effect of curtailing or abridging such rights.[235] So, too, the self-determining prerogatives inhering in U.S. external possessions like Guam and Puerto Rico,[236] not to mention the state of Hawai'i and the internal colonial archipelago of American Indian nations comprising in aggregate about a third of the area encompassed by the lower 48 states.[237] Ultimately, the only group likely *not* to benefit from the binding effects of international law are the U.S. plutocrats and the roughly five percent of the American population most closely aligned with them.

To be sure, it can quite reasonably be argued that, whatever its other advantages, the international legal system will have proven incapable of producing justice until Henry Kissinger, Madeleine Albright, Jesse Helms, Donald Rumsfeld, and other such scum are dangling on the gallows (or at least sitting in cells adjoining those of lesser thugs like Slobodan Milosevic).[238] Establishment of the International Criminal Court offers the tangible prospect of precisely this result, however, should ways be found to deliver America's myriad perpetrators of war crimes, genocide and other crimes against humanity to their chairs in the defendants' dock.[239] Indeed, the very existence of such a mechanism for adjudicating and punishing the powerful will undoubtedly have the effect of stimulating U.S. jurists to at last take seriously their obligation to ensure the conformity of their rulings and opinions with international rather than mere domestic legality.[240] This in itself could go far towards correcting many of the inequities afflicting American jurisprudence over the past two centuries.

It can also be argued, and rightly so, that in the final analysis control of state crime can be accomplished only by abolition of the state itself.[241] In this connection, it should be noted that no less unabashed a statist than nazi legal theorist Carl Schmitt viewed the kind of overarching legalism at issue herein as "state-destroying,"[242] at least in the usual Hegelian sense of the state as "the concrete order of orders, the institution of institutions."[243] Enforcing the rights of small states vis-à-vis large ones, and, more importantly, those of nonstatist indigenous nations vis-à-vis states of all sizes, can only have the effect of "hollowing out" the present configuration of world order,[244] engendering a dynamic of fragmentation/reduction in scale which renders statist forms of organization ever more unmanageable by virtue of their increasing incohesion and consequent incoherence.[245] It follows that there will be a growing quantity of "space," both figurative and literal, within which to actualize opposing forms of socioeconomic and political organization, thereby debunking in concrete terms the not-so-ancient myth that the state itself is any real way "necessary" to the wellbeing of humanity.[246] From such erosion, the dissolution of statism is an all but inevitable result.[247]

Answers to the question of how best to approach the task at hand are obviously complex, requiring a far more lengthy explication than is possible here. Suffice it for the moment to observe that the onus of responsibility for initiating the process indicated in the present section lies not with the international community, but with those of us residing within the belly of the proverbial beast. Upon us rests the burden set forth in the Nuremberg Doctrine, and explained more thoroughly by Karl Jaspers, of doing whatever may be necessary to force the government of the U.S. into obeying the requirements of international law (those, that is, of basic human decency).[248] To this end there can be no gentle or painless route. It must be grasped, first and foremost, by those who take seriously their responsibility to catalyze the desired socioeconomic/political transformation that it is absolutely pointless to expend time and energy "speaking truth to power."[249] Those in power aren't listening, largely because they are already far more aware of what is being said than are those saying it. After all, it is they who have quite deliberately created the very circumstances being addressed. Since only the most morally depraved—or psychopathically amoral[250]—could possibly choose to conduct themselves in this fashion, arguments to morality, no matter how eloquently posed, can/will have not the least effect upon their thinking, their behavior, or upon the ugly situations generated by combinations of the two.

It follows that success will not come through the writing of thoughtful letters to editors and congresspersons, petition drives and electoral "mobilizations" (no, the system cannot be voted out of existence—if it could, voting would be forbidden—and it matters not a whit which individual or party is selected to preside most visibly over its continued functioning).[251] Similarly, it can't be attained through undertaking the "right" legislative initiatives or by recourse to the courts (yes, any and all additions to the domestic statutory/regulatory structure serve simply to refine, reinforce and perpetuate the status quo, it is absurd to expect a judge to rule that the governing apparatus of which s/he is part must be abolished, and s/he would plainly lack the means of enforcing such a decree, even were s/he to enter it).[252] Nor can significant constructive change be accomplished through piecemeal activist boycotts—they don't really *care* whether you by Nikes as opposed to Adidas, boys and girls, and what's really so much "cleaner" about the other brands, anyway?—or the token strikes of a self-serving and long since bought-out "labor movement."[253] Success will not come, moreover, through the staging of rallies, no matter how large, or protests, no matter how symbolic; it will not accrue from the peace marches or the eternal "bearing of witness" at candle-lit prayer vigils;[254] it will not be gained by proliferation of community radio stations and alternative media more generally, or by devising better courses for the country's public schools and universities.[255] It cannot be had even by sporting the wittiest or most poignant of buttons and bumper stickers.

Changing up a bit, it seems worth noting that the American plutocracy can never be brought to heel by "cultural" means, including the establishment of viable "prefigurative relations" in one or another setting.[256] Textual deconstructions, no matter how profoundly insightful, have no material effect on the functioning of power,[257] nor does the now fashionable intellectual procedure of "resolving" the problems presently plaguing the world via the sophistry of consigning them to the past tense (as in, how about we actually complete the process of global decolonization *before* we announce our entry into "the postcolonial era"?).[258] At less rarified levels, the same holds true. The necessary objectives will not be reached through a perpetual replaying of Rage Against the Machine, Tupac Shakur, and Propagandhi cd's, deeper study of Hinduism and Tantra yoga, the building of better bike paths, or yet another alteration in hair styles, fashion statements and diets. Organic gardening won't fix things, nor will the wonders of natural child-birth, a further fetishizing of gender relations, or ever-more sweeping denunciations of "The Hierarchy".[259] Adding a few tattoos and body piercings will not do the job. There's no pill that can be taken to make things better, and, certainly pretending that there's some sort of "progressive" virtue in banning smoking—which is to say, the approximately one-third of the adult population of North America who are active smokers—from public spaces, *especially* the spaces supposedly devoted to "political organizing," is self-defeating to the point of outright idiocy.[260]

Skeptics might wish to explain exactly how and to what extent the nazis—Hitler *was,* after all, a duly elected anti-smoking ecologist vegetarian official influenced by Eastern mysticism and the occult[261]—might have been swayed in their policy-orientation by receipt of carefully-worded petitions. Nontheless, most of the things mentioned in the last two paragraphs—with the obvious exceptions of attempts to foistoff such drivel as "postmodernity"[262] and the glaringly elitist enthusiasm with which people who should, and probably do, know better have embraced the anti-smoking fad—are imbued with considerable value and utility, at least in their potentials (yes, even voting and candle-lit vigils can be tactfully useful exercises when properly contextualized[263]). Each of them embodies a certain capacity to convey truth, a matter which is of consequence, however, only when the truth invloved is addressed, consciously so, not "to power," but to *people,* in the *very teeth of power.* Put another way, the only "truth" which is actually true, and thus worthy of communication by those purporting to oppose the status quo, is that which is explicitly unacceptable to those in power; anything permitted by the powerful receives its license *only* because it serves in the final analysis to perpetuate the structure upon which their collective dominance depends.[264]

In this connection, the question may be reduced to a matter of how the "oppositionist message" is framed. The same information can invariably be deployed in ways leading people to the comfortable but utterly false conclusion that the system producing whatever horrors are under immediate discussion can be reformed in a manner eliminating the injustice/carnage involved—as if such outcomes were merely avoidable "byproducts" of an essentially sound social, economic and political order—or in ways making unequivocally clear the far less convenient facts that such results are inherent to the system, and that only through its complete eradication can an affirmative change in the offending conditions be achieved.[265] Reformist argumentation, and the constricted range of tactics attending it, will *always* be permitted and often welcomed by America's élites—though seldom really acted upon—under the cooptive veneer of liberal democracy with which they've larded the fascistic core of their dominion; arguments and tactics aimed at systemic eradication will never for a moment be countenanced.[266]

The implications of the distinction just posed can perhaps be most readily discerned by considering the effects of reforming the Third Reich in such a way as to expunge the policies leading to what is usually depicted as being the very worst of its crimes: its extermination of the European Jews.[267] Undeniably, this would have been a major victory in its own right. With that victory achieved, however, the nazi state would still have been the nazi state, and, since its policy of expansion was by no means contingent upon the Jewish genocide, it would still have launched a war of aggression claiming something over 40 million lives.[268] Averting the Jewish extermination, moreover, would have accomplished nothing at all in terms of protecting the Romani (Gypsies) and others subjected to entirely comparable modes of extermination.[269] Nor would it have done much to alleviate the suffering of the hundreds of thousands of communists, trade unionists, homosexuals and so on, who, although they were not exterminated outright, died like flies under the abysmal conditions prevailing in nazism's forced labor camps.[270] Only the most thoroughgoing destruction of the nazi system would ever have been sufficient to have prevented it from consummating itself as it did. And it is this that the German people are faulted for not have accomplished—or at least initiated—of their own volition.

The same rule applies to those of us residing within the U.S. Precisely how it must be acted upon is to a large extent rendered contingent by the terms of struggle imposed by the state as it mounts its internal defense. In this regard, the rampant growth in/militarization of the U.S. police/prison apparatus over the past quarter-century speaks loudly, as do recent relaxations of longstanding prohibitions against use of the military itself in preserving the domestic order.[271] The meaning of these developments must be taken for what it is, ways and means devised, skills developed, and—most of all—a consciousness inculcated among oppositionists that allows us not only to set about meeting the state's forces on their own terms, but to overcome them.[272] To this end, we must learn from the experiences of those who have confronted similar situations in the not-so-distant past, drawing the appropriate lessons from both their successes and their failures, bringing these lessons to bear on our own struggle, thus forging a strategy to win.[273] Here, there can be no pretence that "purity of principle" precludes the employment of particular tactics (e.g., that resort to arms is always and everywhere a philosophically inappropriate response to oppression[274], or, worse, that such responses are appropriate only when they occur somewhere—anywhere—but here[275]). To put it another way, as Malcolm

X did, it is not only our right but our obligation to proceed by any means necessary.[276]

This is the truth which must at this point be conveyed. It should not be mistaken for an assertion that everyone capable of lifting a weapon must suddenly "pick up the gun," storm some figurative bastille, and bring the state crashing to its knees.[277] It is unnecessary to "bring the motherfucker down" in the classic sense of the French and Russian revolutions, however alluring such imagery might seem. All that is necessary is that the U.S. be sufficiently destabilized—that is to say, weakened from within—for the rest of the world to enforce the rule of law against it (without having to fight World War III in the process).[278] At that point, the U.S. can be expected to begin to come apart in ways not dissimilar to those evidenced by the Soviet Union during the late 1980s.[279] Accomplishing this does not require vast numbers of guerrillas operating in the county's interior. Rather, it entails a clarity of consciousness on the part of those not engaged in combat capacities allowing them to both understand the necessity of armed struggle and provide essential material/psychological support to those who are, thus becoming, to paraphrase Mao Zedong, "the sea in which the guerrilla swims."[280] In effect, the petty ideological/philosophical bickering which currently divides the American opposition, and which has always divided it,[281] must be transcended in a manner enabling us to harness and coordinate all our tactical energies and resources, from ballots to bombs, in a concerted and collective drive to undermine/vanquish the enemy we so plainly share.

There will be many, no doubt, who view the preceding formulation with utmost skepticism, proclaiming either such unification of the opposition as is demanded, or its ability to seriously impair the functioning of the American state even if achieved, to be "unrealistic." To them, the only reasonable response is that this is *exactly* what those in power wish us to believe. The first line of defense of *any* oppressive system is situated primarily in the minds of the oppressed, a circumstance dictated by our indoctrination, virtually from birth, to see "the way things are" as being, if not exactly right or natural, then at least inevitable.[282] Correspondingly, we are left to conclude that substantive alterations in the status quo are impossible. It follows that allowing those in power to continue to occupy the station of defining "realism" for their self-proclaimed opponents means quite simply that reality will be constricted to perpetuation/refinement/intensification of the very modes of oppression the opposition purports to oppose. The "Archimedean point for [any] broader emancipation"[283] may thus be located with considerable precision in our embrace of a traditional anarchist premise, employed as a slogan by insurrectionary French students during the "almost revolution" of 1968 and given voice most recently by Jacques Derrida: to be "realistic," we must "demand the impossible."[284]

Notes

1. William H. Chrisman, *The Opposite of Everything is True: Reflections on Denial in Alcoholic Families* (New York: Quill, 1991).
2. I draw here upon the pioneering work undertaken in this connection during the 1930s by Wilhelm Reich. See Vincent R. Carfagno's translation of Reich's *The Mass Psychology of Fascism* (New York: Farrar Straus & Giroux, 1970). Also see Reich's *Listen, Little Man!* (New York: Noonday Press, 1948).
3. The phenomenon at issue is analyzed in part by Robert Jay Lifton and Eric Markusen in their *The Genocidal Mentality: Nazi Holocaust and Nuclear Threat* (New York: Basic Books, 1990). An excellent complimentary reading is R.D. Laing's *The Politics of Experience* (New York: Ballantine, 1967).
4. This can be considered "true," only in the most eurocentric sense imaginable. The Haudenosaunee (Six Nations Iroquois Confederacy) and numerous other American Indian peoples had developed highly-refined forms of democratic governance, used as models by the U.S. "Founding Fathers" in their designing of their republic. See Donald A. Grinde, Jr., *The Iroquois in the Founding of the American Nation* (San Francisco: Indian Historian Press, 1977); Bruce E. Johansen, *Forgotten Founders: How the American Indian Helped Shape Democracy* (Cambridge, MA: Harvard Common Press, 1982); Donald A. Grinde, Jr., and Bruce E. Johansen, *Exemplar of Liberty: Native America and the Evolution of Democracy* (Los Angeles: UCLA American Indian Studies Center, 1991).
5. Setting aside other problems—and they are many—this proposition is of course contingent upon who is ultimately defined as being fully "human." The U.S., not least in its juridical dimension, has always manifested acute sorts of difficulty in this regard. See, e.g., A. Leon Higgenbotham, Jr., *Shades of Freedom: Racial Politics and the American Legal Process* (New York: Oxford University Press, 1996).
6. *Marbury v. Madison*, 1 Cranch. (5 U.S.) 137 (1803).
7. *Downes v. Bidwell*, 128 U.S. 244, 280 (1901). The racial construction involved—i.e., the notion that "real" or "genuine" Americans "naturally" consist of White Anglo-Saxon Protestants (WASPs)—has from the outset been a cornerstone of U.S. jurisprudence and political reasoning. For background, see Reginald Horsman, *Race and Manifest Destiny: The Origins of American Racial Anglo-Saxonism* (Cambridge: Harvard University Press, 1981); Ian F. Haney-Lopez, *White by Law: The Legal Construction of Race* (New York: New York University Press, 1998).
8. See Deborah L. Madsen, *American Exceptionalism* (Oxford: University of Mississippi Press, 1998) esp. Chap. I, "Exceptionalism and American Cultural Identity," pp. 16-40.
9. It should be noted that it is precisely this fusion of state/corporate structures that many serious analysts have considered the feature most indicative of fascism. See, as examples, Michael Hurst, "What Is Fascism?" *Historical Journal*, Vol. XI, No. 1, 1968; Albert Szymanski, "Fascism, Industrialism and Socialism: The Case of Italy," *Comparative Studies in Society and History*, Vol. XV, No. 4, 1973; Zeev Sternhell, "Fascist Ideology," in Walter Laqueur, ed., *Fascism: A Reader's Guide* (Berkeley: University of California Press, 1976) pp. 315-76; Nicos Poulantzas, *Fascism and Dictatorship* (London: Verso, 1979).
10. Fraenkel describes the "Prerogative State [as a] governmental system which exercises unlimited arbitrariness and violence unchecked by legal guarantees." In contrast, he posits the "Normative State," which, he argues, consists of "an administrative body endowed with elaborate powers for safeguarding the legal order as expressed in statutes, decisions of the courts, and the activities of the administrative agencies." The U.S., like the Third Reich before it, is rightly viewed as being a mixture of the two. Ernst Fraenkel, *The Dual State: A Contribution to the Theory of Dictatorship* (New York: Oxford University Press, 1969) p. xiii.
11. For further insight, see Michael Stoelleis, *The Law Under the Swastika: Studies on Legal History in Nazi Germany* (Chicago: University of Chicago Press, 1998).
12. Perhaps the most insightful study of the logical contortions involved is Robert Stanley's *Dimensions of Law in the Service of Order: Origins of the Federal Income Tax, 1861-1913* (New York: Oxford University Press, 1997). Also see Mark Neocleous, *The Fabrication of Order: A Critical Theory of Police Power* (London: Pluto Press, 2000); Howard Zinn, *Disobedience and Democracy: Nine Fallacies of Law and Order* (Cambridge, MA: South End Press, 2002).
13. For an entirely representative articulation of the belief that the demands of order should trump even the most basic protections of constitutional and international human rights law—this from the top "law enforcement officer" in a small American city—see Chief Ruben Greenberg, *Let's Take Back Our Streets!* (Chicago: Contemporary Books, 1989). There are a multitude of studies on where this mentality leads in practice. Among the better are Paul Chevigny, *Edge of the Knife: Police Violence in the Americas* (New York: New Press, 1995); Christian Parenti, *Lockdown America: Police and Prisons in the Age of Crisis* (London: Verso, 1999);Andrea McArdle and Tanya Erzen, eds., *Zero Tolerance: Quality of Life and the New Police Brutality in New York City* (New York: New York University Press, 2001); Tom Burghart, ed., *Police State America* (Toronto/Montréal/San Francisco: Arm the Spirit/Solidarity, 2002).
14. An excellent study of how the process is supposed to work will be found in Francis Anthony Boyle's *The Foundations of World Order: The Legalist Approach to International Relations, 1898-1922* (Durham, NC: Duke University Press, 1999).
15. Nebrija's 1492 observation that language might serve as "a perfect companion to empire" is quoted in Patricia Seed, *Ceremonies of Possession in the Conquest of the New World, 1492-1640* (Cambridge, U.K.: Cambridge University Press, 1995) p. 8. On law serving the purpose suggested in my paraphrase, see SaidiyaV. Hartman, *Scenes of Subjugation: Terror, Slavery, and Self-Making in Nineteenth-Century America* (New York: Oxford University Press, 1997).

16. Jürgen Habermas, *Between Facts and Norms: Contributions to a Discourse Theory of Law and Democracy* (Cambridge, MA: MIT Press, 1996); James L. Marsh, Unjust Legality: *A Critique of Habermas's Law* (Lanham, MD: Rowman & Littlefield, 2001).

17. Generally speaking, the procedures at issue here are covered in Noam Chomsky, *Necessary Illusions: Thought Control in Democratic Societies* (Boston: South End Press, 1989). Also see William Graeber, *The Engineering of Consent: Democracy and Authority in Twentieth-Century America* (Madison: University of Wisconsin Press, 1987); Edward S. Herman and Noam Chomsky, *Manufacturing Consent: The Political Economy of the Mass Media* (New York: Pantheon, 1988).

18. David Cole and James X. Dempsey, *Terrorism and the Constitution: Sacrificing Civil Liberty in the Name of National Security* (New York: New Press, [2nd ed.] 2002).19. This is in many ways the standard by which all the rest must be measured. Although, after a quarter-century of increasingly intensive research, there remains absolutely no scientific evidence supporting the notion that "second-hand" tobacco smoke poses a "health hazard," public or otherwise, a well-organized "antismoking lobby," working in collaboration with CNN, launched a media offensive during the early 1990s to peddle the exact opposite belief. On this pretext, with the EPA having arbitrarily declared such smoke a "Class-A Carcinogen," the practice of smoking itself—in effect, the typically unruly and less than affluent social milieux associated with it—has been banned from all modes of commercial transport and virtually all public space in the U.S. (including the smog-engulfed sidewalks outside such airports as O'Hare, LAX and San Francisco International). In many cities—and several entire states, starting with California—it has also been prohibited by law in all restaurants, bars and workplaces (foundries, welding shops and the like included). A standard refrain throughout has been the collective obligation to "protect our kids" from the respiratory ravages allegedly inflicted upon them by the irresponsible behavior of a minority—actually, about a third of the adult population—without once addressing such obvious questions as when, precisely, it was decided that a child's place is in a saloon? Meanwhile, it is officially claimed that the roughly 4 tons of plutonium missing from U.S. inventories, much of it presumably dispersed in the environment, has no bearing on America's epidemic lung cancer rate. Similarly, the fact that a child born in Los Angeles reaches his/her EPA-established lifetime quota for "safely" inhaling toxins—including carcinogens—within 2 weeks of birth, apparently fails to register on the average antismoking soccer mom as she drives endlessly about the LA freeways, delivering "the kids" to an equally endless series of meaningless activities. The upshot is a country that rejects the Kyoto Protocol while simultaneously refusing to allow foreign airliners to land at its airports unless their passengers have been forbidden to smoke en route. For the most current compilation scientific data on the effects of second-hand tobacco smoke, see Ronald R. Watson and Mark Witten, eds., *Environmental Tobacco Smoke* (Boca Raton, FL: CRC Press, 2000). A thorough debunking of the continuous stream of falsehoods emitting from the antismoking "movement" will be Jacob Sullum, *For Your Own Good: The Anti-Smoking Crusade and the Tyranny of Public Health* (New York: Free Press, 1998). On the effects of plutonium dispersal in the environment, see Helen Caldicott, *The New Nuclear Danger: George W. Bush's Military-Industrial Complex* (New York: New Press, 2002) esp. pp. 62-5. The effects of other radioactive contaminants are well-covered in Jay M. Gould, *The Enemy Within: The High Cost of Living with Nuclear Reactors* (New York; Four Walls Eight Windows, 2002). With regard to the quantity/effects of non-tobacco-related atmospheric pollutants more generally, see, e.g., Eric Mann, *L.A.'s Lethal Air: New Strategies for Policy, Organizing, and Action* (Los Angeles: Labor/Community Strategy Ctr., 1991).

20. On the "wars" against the San Francisco and New York homeless populations, see Parenti, *Lockdown America*, pp. 100-6; Heather Barr, "Policing Madness: People with Mental Illness and the NYPD," in McArdle and Erzan, *Zero Tolerance*, pp. 60-3.

21. The reference here is to New York Mayor Rudolph Giuliani's much-remarked "war on jaywalkers." For a survey of the effects of this and similar aspects of the mayor's "zero tolerance" policies in NYC, see Judith A. Greene, "Zero Tolerance: A Case Study in Police Policies and Practices in New York City," *Crime and Delinquency*, Vol. 45, No. 2, 1999.

22. See Marc Mauer, *The Race to Incarcerate* (New York: New Press, 1999); Tara Herival and Paul Wright, eds., *Prison Nation: The Warehousing of America's Poor* (New York: Routledge, 2003).

23. One wonders, for instance, exactly when it was that a wave of road workers was mowed down by speeding motorists. It *must* have happened. How else to explain the fact that signs have suddenly sprouted in every road repair/construction zone in the country—a description that with equal suddenness has begun to apply to virtually all transit routes from expressways to back country blacktops each summer—informing drivers that fines are therein "doubled for speeding"? In actuality, there were a total of 65 vehicle-related fatalities in 1999, only 9 of them caused by drivers passing through construction zones (the rest involved being crushed by heavy equipment, and the like). Of the 9 deaths caused by "civilian" traffic, none are shown to have involved speeding. The same pattern holds true for the entire period, 1992-99: of 564 vehicle-related fatalities among road construction workers, "only 170 involved traffic vehicles moving through a work zone," and speeding is not indicated as a factor in any of them; Stephanie G. Pratt, David F. Fosbroke and Suzanne M. Marsh, *Building Safer Highway Work Zones: Measures to Prevent Worker Injuries from Vehicles and Equipment* (Cincinnati, OH: NIOSH Pub. # 2001-128, 2001). Absent an actual precipitating incident or set of incidents, repetition of which an across-the-board lowering of speed limits can be tangibly shown to avert, the motive underlying the state's doubling of fines for violations committed in road construction zones can only be seen as generating an influx of revenues (that is, to impose an undeclared/unapproved tax under the pretext of "increasing public safety"). These monies, in turn, are typically used to underwrite enforcement of other, equally arbitrary rules and regulations, all of them marked by the imposition of ever more exorbitant fines and fees (e.g., the "court costs" now attaching to most traffic citations, including those in which the offense

originally alleged is dismissed). The upshot is a spiraling degree of behavioral—read, social—regimentation, quite literally all of it passed off as being "for the public good." Analysis of the sadism imbedded in analogous rationalizations/attitudes manifested at an individuated level will be found in Alice Miller's *For Your Own Good: Hidden Cruelty in Child-Rearing and the Roots of Violence* (New York: Farrar, Straus and Giroux, 1983). At the societal level, see Reich, *Mass Psychology of Fascism.*

24. Part of this assessment is purely experiential. I have traveled fairly widely over the past three decades, spending time both in such ostensibly "totalitarian" settings as Libya and Cuba, and in such order-fixated "democracies" as Germany. In no country have I observed the degree of fetish evident in the U.S.—and, to a lesser extent, Canada—with painting lines on the street at every intersection, dictating where supposedly functional adult pedestrians are and are not allowed to cross from curb to curb. A less subjective standard of measure obtains in simply weighing the aggregation of volumes containing U.S. statutory and regulatory codes and comparing the result to the gross weight of the comparable aggregations obtaining in other countries.

25. This is, of course, a primary tenet of anarchism, articulated endlessly in the literature. For an excellent and very succinct enunciation of the thesis, see Robert Paul Wolff, *In Defense of Anarchism* (Berkeley: University of California Press, [2nd ed.] 1998).

26. Witness the fact that it is no longer possible to find a stretch of road, no matter how remote, anywhere in the U.S. which is not subject to being patrolled/monitored by radar and laser technology to ensure that motorists abide by maximum speed limits, arbitrarily assigned, as always, in the name of "public safety." This, despite the fact that there is not—and has never been—a statistically discernable distinction in open road accident rates when the speed limit is set at, say, 55 mph, as opposed to 65, 70 or 75 mph (or, even, as was demonstrated in Montana a few years back, when no speed limit is posted at all).

27. Doubters should try taking a nap on bench along a public sidewalk—or in a public park—some afternoon, or sleeping overnight in a public campground without doing so in the assigned spot, and after paying the requisite fee.

28. See, e.g., Milton Mayer, *They Thought They Were Free: The Germans, 1933-45* (Chicago: University of Chicago Press, 1955).

29. In nazi jurisprudence, individual "rights against the state were theoretically abolished... The autonomous space left to the individual had [thus] become—concurrent with the collapse of the idea of legal protection—a concession by the [state] that could be further restricted at any time"; Stolleis, *Law Under the Swastika,* pp. 107–8. For a detailed examination of certain of the extreme sorts of codified inequalities engendered by this construction of "legality," see Richard Lawrence Miller, *Nazi Justiz: Law of the Holocaust* (Westport, CT: Praeger, 1995). For liberal philosophical explication of the ostensible U.S. "countermodel ," see John Rawls, *A Theory of Justice* (Cambridge, MA: Harvard University Press, [rev. ed.] 1999); *Justice as Fairness: A Restatement* (Cambridge, MA: Harvard/Belknap, 2001). An interesting exploration of the ways in which the equity principle has been incorporated into the Law of Nations will be found in Thomas M. Franck's *Fairness in International Law and Institutions* (Oxford, UK: Clarendon Press, 1995).

30. There were, to be sure, those who disagreed even with this. Alexander Hamilton, for one, advocated at the Constitutional Convention that both the President and the Senate should be appointed for life, largely to offset the popularly-elected House of Representatives; Howard Zinn, *A People's History of the United States* (New York: HarperPerennial, 1995) p. 95.

31. The issue was/is at least as much structural as attitudinal. In the insurgent Maryland Constitution of 1776, for example, it was required that anyone running for governor demonstrate ownership of at least 5,000£ of property, those running for state senator, 1,000£. Upwards of 90 percent of all adult Euroamerican males were thus precluded from even attempting to hold such offices. Ultimately, the U.S. Constitution was drafted in such a way as to forestall violent responses from the body politic by sharing power "equally" between the 10 percent of the white male population occupying the top tier of America's socioeconomic life on the one hand, and all remaining white men on the other; Zinn, *People's History,* pp. 81, 96. The fruition of this fundamental disequilibrium was charted nearly two centuries later by G. William Domhoff, in his *Who Rules America?* (Englewood Cliffs, NJ: Prentice-Hall, 1967; New York: McGraw-Hill, [4th ed.] 2001).

32. *Dred Scott v. Sandford* (60 U.S. 393 (1856)). For background, see Don Fehrenbacher, *The Dred Scott Case: Its Significance in American Law and Politics* (New York: Oxford University Press, 1978).

33. *U.S. ex. Rel. Standing Bear v. Crook* (25 F, Cas. 695, C.C.D. Neb. (1879)). For background, see Thomas Henry Tibbles, *The Ponca Chiefs: An Account of the Trial of Standing Bear* (Lincoln: University of Nebraska Press, 1972 reprint of 1879 original).

34. *Chae Chan Ping v. U.S.* (130 U.S. 581 (1889)). For background, see Louis Henkin, "The Constitution and United States Sovereignty: A Century of Chinese Exclusion and Its Progeny," *Harvard Law Review,* No. 100, 1987.

35. E.g., *Jean v. Nelson* (727 F.2d 957 (1985)); *Reno v. Flores* (507 U.S. 202 (1993)). For background, see Victoria Cooke Capitaine, "Life in Prison Without Trial: The Indefinite Detention of Immigrants in the United States," *Texas Law Review,* No. 79, 2001.

36. See generally, D. Kelly Weisberg, *Women and the Law: A Social Historical Perspective* (Cambridge, MA: Schenkman, 1982); Marylynn Salmon, *Women and the Law of Property* (Chapel Hill: University of North Carolina Press, 1989).

37. C. Vann Woodward, *The Strange Career of Jim Crow* (New York: Oxford University Press, [3rd ed., rev.] 1974).

38. *Plessy v. Ferguson* (163 U.S. 537 (1896)). For background, see A. Leon Higginbotham, Jr., *Shades of Freedom: Racial Politics and Presumptions of the American Legal Process* (New York: Oxford University

Press, 1996).

39. Anonymous, "George L. Jackson, September 23, 1941-August 21, 1971," introduction to *Soledad Brother: The Prison Letters of George Jackson* (Chicago: Lawrence Hill, [2nd ed.] 1994) p. ix.

40. James B. Stewart, *Den of Thieves* (New York: Simon & Schuster, 1991) pp. 441-2. For further background, see Connie Bruck, *The Predators' Ball: The Inside Story of Drexel Burnham and the Rise of the Junk Bond Raiders* (New York: Penguin, 1989).

41. Mauer, *Race to Incarcerate*, p. 152; citing William N. Brownsberger, *Profile of Anti-drug Enforcement in Urban Poverty Areas in Massachusetts* (Cambridge, MA: Harvard Medical School, 1997) p. 21.

42. In *McClesky v. Kemp* (481 U.S. 279 (1987)), the Supreme Court concluded that such a glaring racial disparity in imposition of the death penalty is permissible, since comparable disparities pertain to all other aspects of sentencing in the U.S. as well; see "McClesky v. Kemp, 1987: A Racially Disproportionate Death Penalty System Is Not Unconstitutional," in Hugo Adam Bedau, *The Death Penalty in America: Current Controversies* (New York: Oxford University Press, 1997) pp. 254-67. On Georgia, see American Civil Liberties Union, *Race and the Death Penalty: Georgia and the Nation* (Washington, D.C.: ACLU, 1987).

43. To illustrate, between 1976 and 1986, although African Americans suffered homicide at 6 times the rate of whites, only 5 percent of all executions in the U.S. resulted from the murder of a black, and no white person was executed for such a crime; reported by Michael Kroll in the New York Times, Apr. 24, 1987. Such differential rates have also applied historically to instances in which capital punishment has been imposed for nonlethal offenses: 89% of all those executed for rape between 1930 and 1967, for example, were black men convicted of assaulting white women; Amnesty International, United States of America: The Death Penalty (London: Amnesty International, 1987) p. 19. Also see Michael E. Enders, *The Morality of Capital Punishment: Equal Justice Before the Law?* (Mystic, CT: Twenty-Third Publications, 1985).

44. Christopher J. Mumola and Allen J. Beck, *Prisoners in 1996* (Washington, D.C.: U.S. Dept. of Justice, Bureau of Justice Statistics, June 1997) p. 11. Also see Mauer, *Race to Incarcerate*, pp. 152-3.

45. In 1993, African American males of this age-group suffered an incarceration rate of over 3,000 per 100,000, while young black men in South Africa were imprisoned at a rate of 729 per 100,000; Alan Ryan, "Preparing for the Twenty-First Century Blues," New York Review of Books, May 13, 1993.

46. On Latinos born in 1991, some 16% of whom can expect to be imprisoned before their 30th birthday—as compared to about 4% of whites—see Thomas P. Bonzar and Allen J. Beck, *Lifetime Likelihood of Going to State or Federal Prison* (Washington, D.C.: U.S. Dept. of Justice, Bureau of Justice Statistics, 1997). For the most detailed information on Native American incarceration rates, see Luana Ross, *Inventing the Savage: The Social Construction of Native American Criminality* (Austin: University of Texas Press, 1998).

47. In 1995, the U.S. incarcerated 600 persons per 100,000, Russia, 690 per 100,000. Such rates might be usefully compared to Slovenia's 30 persons per 100,000, Japan's 37, Iceland's 40, Norway's 55, Greece's 55, Ireland's 55, Finland's 60, Denmark's 65, Sweden's 65, the Netherlands' 65, Belgium's 75, Switzerland's 80, Germany's 85, Austria's 85, Italy's 85, England's 100, Spain's 105, Scotland's 110 and Canada's 115. For further details, see Marc Mauer, *Americans Behind Bars: U.S. and International Rates of Incarceration*, 1995 (Washington, D.C.: Sentencing Project, 1997).

48. African Americans, to offer the salient example, comprise only 13% of the U.S. population, but, by 1988, over half of all persons incarcerated were black (up from 30% in 1955); Mauer, Race to Incarcerate, p. 121.

49. Actually, crime rates fail to account for U.S. incarceration rates in any way at all. Overall, the U.S. imprisons its citizens at nearly 1000% the rate of Sweden, for example, but the two countries' rates of victim-producing—as opposed to victimless—crime are identical; Pat Mayhew and Jan J.M. Van Dijk, *Criminal Victimization in Eleven Industrial Countries* (Netherlands: Ministry of Justice, 1997).

50. See the chapter entitled "What's Class Got to Do With It?" in Mauer, *Race to Incarcerate*, pp. 162-70. Also see Sabina Virgo, "The Criminalization of Poverty," in Elihu Rosenblatt, ed., *Criminal Injustice: Confronting the Prison Crisis* (Boston, MA: South End Press, 1996) pp. 47-60.

51. "[I]t is well settled that corporations are persons within the provisions of the Fourteenth Amendment of the Constitution of the United States"; *Gulf, California and San Francisco Railway v. Ellis* (165 U.S. 150, 154 (1897)). "The edification of the corporation to the status of a person is one of the most enduring institutions of the law and one of the most widely accepted legal fictions"; Sanford A. Schane, "The Corporation is a Person: The Language of a Legal Fiction," *Tulane Law Review*, No. 61, 1987, p. 563.

52. Boesky, known as "Ivan the Terrible," was a key player in Michael Milken's stock fraud conspiracy, charged with a multitude of crimes. On Dec. 20, 1987, having been allowed to enter a guilty plea to a single felony count—which nonetheless involved the theft of hundreds of millions of dollars—he was sentenced to serve a mere 3 years in a minimum-security prison. He was also required to pay $100 million fines and penalties. Prior to announcing its case against him, however—thus precipitating an entirely predictable plunge in stock prices—prosecutors allowed him to liquidate at least $200 million in stock holdings—estimates run as high as $440 million— much of it illegally attained, at full "value." The proceeds from this government-approved insider trade obviously left Boesky quite a tidy "nest egg" once the authorities had taken their cut; Stewart, *Den of Thieves*, pp. 359-60, 295-7.

53. Availing himself of the Reagan administration's deregulation of the Savings and Loan "industry," which, as a top Republican economic policy consultant, he'd helped usher in, Keating used his position as president of the Los Angeles-based Lincoln Savings and Loan to orchestrate a scheme in which S&Ls across the country extended billions in fraudulent loans to Michael Milken and other corporate raiders, financing their heavily leveraged buyouts and artificially inflating stock prices in exchange for

a variety of kickbacks. In 1992, after his own and scores of other S&Ls were shown to be on the verge of collapse, Keating was convicted in California of defrauding investors in Lincoln's bond issues, and sentenced to 10 years imprisonment. Then, in 1993, he was convicted in federal court on 73 counts—including several devolving upon RICO conspiracy—and sentenced to another 10. In 1996, however, after he'd served only 50 months, the latter convictions were overturned on the basis that the prior California conviction might have "prejudiced" federal jurors against the defendant. Protracted "negotiations" then resulted in an arrangement wherein Keating finally entered a guilty plea to 4 counts of fraud—involving a mere $1 million—in exchange for a sentence of time served; *U.S. v. Keating* (147 F.3d 895 (1998)); the plea was actually entered on Apr. 6, 1999. All told, he spent barely 4 years behind bars for taking the lead role in a scam that cost taxpayers an estimated $500 billion—to underwrite the so-called S&L bailout—one of the larger undeclared transfers of public wealth to the country's economic élite in American history. In the bargain, it appears that he was allowed to keep an estimated $24 million in "personal funds" he'd stashed in offshore accounts before his first trial. For background, see Michael Benstein and Charles Bowden, *Trust Me: Charles Keating and the Missing Billions* (New York: Random House, 1993).

54. Anderson was CEO of Union Carbide when, as a "cost efficiency measure" the corporation ignored safety procedures that would have prevented the deaths of some 16,000 people caused by an untended gas leak at its plant near Bhopal, India, in 1984. Although the U.S. has an extradition treaty with India, and India has repeatedly submitted a valid demand that Anderson be handed over for prosecution, the U.S. has for two decades—i.e., during the administrations of four successive presidents—remained adamant in its refusal to do so; Noam Chomsky, *9-11* (New York: Seven Stories Press, 2001) p. 103.

55. Mimi Schwartz and Sherron Watkins, *Power Failure: The Inside Story on the Collapse of Enron* (Garden City, NY: Doubleday, 2003); "Former Qwest execs charged with fraud," Chicago Sun Times, Feb. 26, 2003; Rebecca Blumenstein and Susan Pulliam, "WorldCom Fraud Was Widespread: Ebbers, Many Executives Conspired to Falsify Results in Late 1990s, Probe Finds," *Wall Street Journal*, June 10, 2003; Barbara Lee Toffler and Jennifer Reingold, *Final Accounting: Ambition, Greed, and the Fall of Arthur Anderson* (New York: Broadway Books, 2003); Alex Berenson, "Accounting at Mortgage Concern is Under a Criminal Investigation," *New York Times*, June 12, 2003.

56. "It is a sad fact that underworld crime pales in comparison to the institutionalized abuses of the upper-world... Sociologist Edwin Sutherland, who coined the term white-collar crime, [defining it as] bribery, kickbacks, payoffs, computer crime, consumer and banking fraud, [imposition of] unsafe working conditions, illegal competition, deceptive practices, embezzlement, pilferage, and securities theft...pointed out that 'white-collar criminals are by far the most dangerous to society of any type of criminals in terms of effects on private property and social institutions [and] concluded that these 'established entrepreneurs' 'make Mafias and crime syndicates look like pushcart operations'... Sociologist Stanley D. Eitzen determined that the monetary impact of white collar crime surpassed all forms of street crime by a factor of ten. More important, the American system of justice consistently gives the flagrant white-collar offenders virtual carte blanche, while plastering the nation's front pages with tales of arrests of bank robbers, gambling bosses, bookies...labor racketeers [and drug dealers]. This feat of prestidigitation [has] served the purpose of engaging the [public] with tales of Capone and [Gotti], while distracting them from the far bigger story of massive, routinely sanctioned white collar crime"; Gus Russo, *The Outfit: The Role of Chicago's Underworld in the Shaping of Modern America* (New York: Bloomsbury, 2001) pp. 491-3. For corroboration, see, as examples, Stewart, *Den of Thieves*; Bruck, *Predators' Ball*; Benstein, *Trust Me*. An excellent, if decidedly partial, historical overview with be found in Matthew Josephson's *The Robber Barons* (New York: Harcourt, Brace, Jovanovich, 1962 reprint of 1934 original).

57. This involved the speculative sale of "public lands" in Georgia. Leaving aside fact that most of the land at issue belonged to various American Indian peoples rather than Georgia or the U.S.—and the obvious problems with any policy wherein public property is discounted in bulk to monied buyers with the intent that they then parcel it out at a substantial profit to poorer buyers—the swindle devolved upon the peddling of deeds to nonexistent tracts. Although only 8,717,960 acres were available, a total of 29,097,866 acres were ostensibly deeded; C. Peter McGrath, *Yazoo: Law and Politics in the New Republic* (Providence, RI: Brown University Press, 1966) p. 3.

58. "Of the public scandals during Grant's second term, the Credit Mobilizer attracted the most attention. This was a company organized by supporters of the Union Pacific in order to divert the profits of railway construction to themselves. Fearing lest Congress intervene, the directors placed large blocks of stock 'where they would do the most good'; that is, in the hands of congressmen. Vice President Schuler Colfax and several Republican senators were also favored... A 'Whisky Ring' in St. Louis was [then] found to have defrauded the government of millions in taxes, with the collusion of treasury officials and the President's private secretary, General Orville E, Babcock... Even the Indians, who had little to lose, were victimized; General William W. Belknap, Grant's second term secretary of war, received a 'kickback' of almost $25,000 from the post trader whom he had appointed at Fort Sill. Corruption in the post office and interior department stopped just short of the President... Navy yards, regarded by spoilsmen as part of their patronage, were riddled with graft; payrolls were padded with the connivance of Grant's navy secretary... [A] million feet of lumber purchased by the Boston navy yard simply disappeared, and...the famous yacht America [was] remodeled for [financier] Benjamin F. Butler at taxpayers' expense"; Samuel Eliot Morison, *The Oxford History of the American People* (New York: Oxford University Press, 1965) pp. 730-1.

59. Pres. Warren G. Harding died of embolism in San Francisco on Aug. 2, 1923, shortly after it was dis-

covered that his director of the Veterans Bureau, a Col. Forbes, had been receiving kickbacks on new hospital construction. Almost before the ink was dry on Forbes' resignation letter, it was revealed that "Albert B. Fall, secretary of the interior, with the connivance of Edwin N. Denby (a complete nonentity whom Harding had made navy secretary) had entered into a corrupt alliance with the Doheny and Sinclair oil interests to turn over to them valuable oil deposits, which President [Woodrow] Wilson had reserved for the navy. The Elk Hill oil reserve in California was leased to Doheny and the Teapot Dome oil reserve in Wyoming to Sinclair. In return for these favors they built some oil storage tanks for the navy in Pearl Harbor; but Fall got at least $100,000 from Doheny and $300,000 from Sinclair. The [ensuing] Senate investigation forced both secretaries to resign, the oil leases were canceled, and the government recovered $6 million. Criminal prosecutions sent Fall and Sinclair to prison for short terms, but the rest got off." Meanwhile, Harding's appointee to head up the Justice Dept., "Harry Daugherty, who regarded the office of attorney general as an opportunity to reward friends…was dismissed for misconduct involving the illegal sale of liquor permits and pardons"; Morison, *History of the American People*, pp. 932-3.

60. The whole story on Nixon, who was forced to resign his presidency on Aug. 8, 1974, is not and will likely never be known, given his refusal to honor subpoenas—he was disbarred in 1976, after being convicted of obstructing justice in New York (no prison time, of course)—and the fact that he was pardoned a priori by his successor, Gerald Ford, for any violations of the federal statutory code he may have committed (thereby aborting several ongoing investigations). A good survey of what is known in the connection(s) at issue will be found in Anthony J. Lucas, *Nightmare: The Underside of the Nixon Years* (New York: Penguin, 1988). Also see *The Offenses of Richard M. Nixon: Bribery and Other High Crimes and Misdemeanors* (Chicago: Public Issues/Quadrangle, 1974).

61. The most recent concerns current Vice President Dick Cheney's relationship to Halliburton, Enron and other energy corporations. On July 10, 2002, for instance, the BBC aired a segment titled "Cheney Accused of Corporate Fraud." Like Nixon before him, Cheney is presently refusing to honor subpoenas on the basis of "executive privilege."

62. An interesting survey on this score will be found in Hank Messick's *The Politics of Prosecution: Jim Thompson, Marje Everett, Richard Nixon and the Trial of Otto Kerner* (Ottawa, IL: Caroline House, 1978).

63. A classic example is that of Adm. John M. Poindexter, forced to resign his position as Ronald Reagan's National Security Advisor, then convicted in 1986 of conspiracy, perjury, obstruction of justice and defrauding the federal government (the convictions were overturned in 1991 on the basis of immunity granted in exchange for Poindexter's testimony before Congress during the Iran-Contra hearings, despite the fact that he'd demonstrably lied while testifying). Afterwards, he was quickly hired as a vice president by Syntec, a major defense contractor, and retained as a consultant by several other such firms. In Feb. 2002—despite his record—Poindexter was again hired by the government itself, this time as director of the Pentagon's newly-established Office of Information Awareness; see John Markoff, "Chief Takes Over New Agency to Thwart Attacks on U.S.," *New York Times*, Feb. 13, 2002.

64. Fred J. Cook, *The Crimes of Watergate* (New York: Franklin Watts, 1981).

65. In Mar. 1988, Marine Col. Oliver North, who had served on Reagan's National Security Council staff since 1981, was, along with his boss, Adm. John Poindexter, indicted on 16 felony counts resulting from his role in the Iran-Contra operation and subsequent coverup. Although four of the most serious charges were shortly dropped on national security grounds, North was convicted on 3 of the remaining 12 counts in May 1989. His conviction was vacated on July 20, 1990, however, on the basis that he'd been granted immunity in exchange for congressional testimony; *U.S. v. North* (910 F.2d (1990)). On Poindexter, see note 63. For background, see Peter Kornbluh, Malcolm Byrne and Theodore Draper, eds., *The Iran-Contra Scandal: The Declassified History* (New York: New Press, 1993); Lawrence E. Walsh, *Firewall: The Iran-Contra Conspiracy and Cover-Up* (New York: W.W. Norton, 1998).

66. U.S. Senate, Select Committee to Study Government Operations with Respect to Intelligence Activities, *Book II: Intelligence Activities and the Rights of Americans* (Washington, D.C.: 94th Cong., 2nd Sess., USGPO, 1976).

67. Actually, there was one case, the outcome of which is instructive. Former FBI Director L. Patrick Gray, former Acting Associate Director W. Mark Felt, former Assistant Director for Domestic Intelligence Edward S. Miller, and John Kearny, former head of the New York Field Office's Squad 47 (COINTELPRO Section) were indicted in 1978 for having committed a variety of crimes during the Bureau's pursuit of WEATHERFUGS (Weatherman fugitives) during the early-70s; Nicholas Horrock, "Gray and Two Ex-FBI Aides Indicted in Conspiracy in Search for Radicals," *New York Times*, Apr. 11, 1978. Charges were dropped against Gray, essentially on the basis that he was too highly-placed and too transient in his position to have been responsible for the misdeeds of his underlings. Kearny, on the other hand, received a directed verdict of acquittal on the basis that he'd too lowly-placed and had thus merely followed the orders of his superiors (the so-called "Nuremberg Defense," supposedly invalid in U.S. courts). Felt and Miller were, however, convicted in 1980. Their appeal was preempted by pardons bestowed by Ronald Reagan in April 1981; Tony Poveda, *Lawlessness and Reform: The FBI in Transition* (Pacific Grove, CA: Brooks/Cole, 1990) p. 83. For overviews of what went altogether unprosecuted, see U.S. Senate, Select Committee to Study Government Operations with Respect to Intelligence Activities, *Book III: Final Report: Supplementary Detailed Staff Reports on Intelligence Activities and the Rights of Americans* (Washington, D.C.: 94th Cong., 2nd Sess., USGPO, 1976); Harry Blackstock, *COINTELPRO: The FBI's Secret War on Political Freedom* (New York: Monad Press, [2nd ed.] 1987); Ward Churchill and Jim Vander Wall, *The COINTELPRO Papers: Documents from the FBI's Secret Wars Against Dissent in thee United States* (Cambridge, MA: South End Press, [Classics ed.] 2002).

68. U.S. Dept. of Justice, Office of the Inspector General, *The FBI Laboratory: An Investigation into the*

Laboratory Practices and Alleged Misconduct in Explosives-Related and Other Cases (Washington, D.C.: U.S. Dept. of Justice, Apr. 1997). For further details, see John F. Kelly and Phillip K. Wearne, *Tainting the Evidence: Inside the Scandals at the FBI Crime Lab* (New York: Free Press, 1998).

69. As one veteran New York police officer put it, "Cops are almost taught how to commit perjury when they are in Police Academy. Perjury to a policeman—or to a lawyer, by the way—is not a big deal. Whether they are giving out speeding or parking tickets, they are almost always lying"; quoted in Alan Dershowitz, *The Best Defense* (New York: Random House. 1983) p. 377. Former Kansas City Police Chief Joseph McNamara concurs, noting that police perjury is so common that "hundreds of thousands of law-enforcement officers commit felony perjury every year testifying about drug arrests" alone; Joseph McNamara, "Has the Drug War Created an Officers' Liars Club?", *Los Angeles Times*, Feb. 11, 1996. The problem is hardly new, and by no means restricted to the waging of the so-called War on Drugs; see Irving Younger, "The Perjury Routine," *Nation*, May 3, 1967. When police misconduct of any sort is at issue, it is all but invariably present and tacitly condoned by "oversight" officials; see, e.g., Ed Quillan, "The Double Standard on Perjury," *Denver Post*, Jan. 26, 2003. For one of the better overviews, see Christopher Slobogin, "Testifying: Police Perjury and What to Do About It," *University of Colorado Law Review*, No. 67, 1996.

70. The official figures will be found in National Institute of Justice, *Police Use of Force: Collection of National Data* (Washington, D.C.: U.S. Dept. of Justice, Bureau of Justice Statistics, 1997). For interpretation, see Chevigny, *Edge of the Knife*; Peter A. Love and Gabriel Torres, *Police Brutality and Racism in the United States: Race Convention Report to the United Nations* (New York: Center for Constitutional Rights, 1998); Jill Norton, ed., *Police Brutality* (New York: W.W. Norton, 2000).

71. On the night of Feb. 4, 1999, Diallo was shot 19 times by four NYPD undercover cops from a range of 15-20 feet—a total of 41 shots were fired in 8 seconds—under the conditions described. The angle at which several bullets entered the victim's body indicate that the police kept firing even after he was prostrate. The shooters were charged in this case—largely because of the magnitude of public protest—but the location of their trial was moved from NYC to Albany, New York, a veritable police retirement community. There, on Feb. 25, 2000, they were acquitted on all counts. Federal authorities then began an ostensible investigation into possible violations of Diallo's civil rights. On Jan. 31, 2001, however, Acting Attorney General Eric Holden announced that the case had been closed because the Justice Dept. "could not prove beyond a reasonable doubt that the officers willfully deprived Mr. Diallo of his constitutional right to be free from the use of unreasonable force." See generally, "Amadou's Ghost," *Village Voice*, Mar. 8, 2000; Julia Vitullo-Martin, "The Legacy of Amadou Diallo," *Gotham Gazette*, Feb. 4, 2002.

72. The most comprehensive available overview of the recent death toll will be found in *Stolen Lives: Killed by Law Enforcement* (New York/Los Angeles: Anthony Baez Foundation/National Lawyers Guild/October 22nd Coalition, [2nd ed.] 1999). For further details on the context in which the slaughter has occurred, see Allyson Collins, *Shielded from Justice: Police Brutality and Accountability in the United States* (New York: Human Rights Watch, 1998).

73. See, as examples of official findings U.S. Department of War, *Report of the Secretary of War: The Sand Creek Massacre* (Washington, D.C.: Sen. Exec. Doc. 26, 39th Cong., 2d Sess., 1867); U.S. Senate, Committee on the Philippine Islands, *Hearings Before the Senate Committee on the Philippine Islands* (Washington, D.C.: S. Doc. 331, 57th Cong., 1st Sess., 1902); *Citizen's Commission of Inquiry, The Dellums Committee Hearings on War Crimes in Vietnam* (New York: Vintage, 1972). There are, of course, many others.

74. For a reasonably comprehensive overview, see the essay entitled "'To Judge Them by the Standards of Their Times': America's Indian Fighters, the Laws of War and the Question of International Order," in my *Perversions of Justice: Indigenous Peoples and Angloamerican Law* (San Francisco: City Lights Books, 2003) pp. 303-403.

75. Calley was convicted by a military tribunal on Mar. 29, 1971, of having been responsible for the murders of "at least 102 Oriental human beings" at a Vietnamese hamlet known as My Lai 4 on Mar. 16, 1968. He was initially sentenced, with much fanfare, to serve "life at hard labor." Spared the labor while he appealed, his sentence was reduced, five months after his conviction, to twenty years imprisonment. In Apr. 1974, Secretary of the Army Howard H. Callaway cut it to ten years, and the conviction itself was reversed on Sept. 24. In the interim, Calley remained on "house arrest," and thus never set foot in prison. For background, see Joseph Goldstein, Burke Marshall and Jack Schwartz, *The My Lai Massacre and Its Cover-Up: Beyond the Reach of the Law?* (New York: Free Press, 1976); Michael Bilton and Kevin Sim, *Four Hours at My Lai* (New York: Viking, 1992).

76. plu-toc-ra-cy \plü-täk-re-së\ n, pl –cies [Gk ploutokratia, fr. ploutos wealthy; akin to L pluere to rain] (1652) 1 : government by the wealthy 2 : a controlling class of the wealthy — plu-to-crat \plüt-e-krat\ n — plu-to-crat-ic \plüt-e-krat-ic\ adj — plu-to-crat-i-cal-ly \-i-k(e)lë\ adv; *Webster's Ninth New Collegiate Dictionary* (Springfield, MA: Meriam-Webster, 1983) p. 906. The definition should be compared to the content of Domhoff's *Who Rules America?* On racism and sexism, see Higginbotham, *Shades of Freedom;* Catherine A. MacKinnon, *Feminism Unmodified: Discourses on Life and Law* (Cambridge, MA: Harvard University Press, 1987).

77. See, e.g., Lennox S. Hinds, *Illusions of Justice: Human Rights Violations in the United States* (Iowa City: School of Social Work, Iowa State University, 1978). More broadly, see Chomsky, *Necessary Illusions.*

78. Glenn T. Morris, "Vine Deloria, Jr., and the Development of a Decolonizing Critique of Indigenous Peoples and International Relations," in Richard A. Grounds, George E. Tinker and David E. Wilkins, eds., *Native Voices: American Indian Identity and Resistance* (Lawrence: University Press of Kansas, 2003) p. 121.

79. As stated in its Charter (Chap. IV, Art. 13, 1(a)), the first responsibility of the UN is "promoting inter-

national co-operation in the political field and encouraging the progressive development of international law and its codification"; Burns H. Weston, Richard A. Falk and Anthony D'Amato, *Basic Documents in International Law and World Order* (St. Paul, MN: West, 1990) p. 24. Pres. Franklin D. Roosevelt first brought up the idea of creating such an entity when discussing terms of their Atlantic Charter with Winston Churchill in 1941. The term "United Nations" was then employed in the Washington Declaration of Jan. 1, 1942, and endorsed by the heads of 26 states. Details were then worked out at U.S. instigation during the Moscow and Teheran meetings between Roosevelt, Churchill and Stalin in 1943, and consummated during the Yalta conference of Feb. 1945; Phyllis Bennis, *Calling the Shots: How Washington Dominates Today's UN* (New York: Olive Branch Press, 2000) p. 3.

80. This is covered rather well in Edwin Tetlow, *The United Nations: The First 25 Years* (London: Peter Owen, 1970).

81. See generally, F.P. Walters, *A History of the League of Nations* (New York: Oxford University Press, 1960).

82. Indeed, "the thesis developed that if the willfully obstructionist U.S. Senate had ratified the Treaty of Versailles, which contained the League of Nations Covenant, the Second World War would never have occurred"; Boyle, *Foundations of World Order*, p. 139.

83. This backdrop is well-described in Noam Chomsky's *Towards a New Cold War: Essays on the Current Crisis and How We Got There* (New York: Pantheon, 1982) pp. 1-59. For the official iterations upon which Chomsky bases much of his analysis, see Thomas H. Etzold and John Lewis Gaddis, eds., *Containment: Documents on U.S. Foreign Policy and Strategy, 1945-1950* (New York: Columbia University Press, 1978).

84. The rhetoric attending this supposed "foundational goal" of the UN is well-represented in the opening chapter of Gareth Evans, *Cooperating for Peace: The Global Agenda for the 1990s and Beyond* (London: Allen & Unwin, 1993).

85. Eugene Davidson, *The Trial of the Germans: Nuremberg, 1945-1946* (New York: Macmillan, 1966);Arnold C. Brackman, *The Other Nuremberg: The Untold Story of the Tokyo War Crimes Trials* (New York: Quill, 1987). Also see Roy Palmer Domenico, *Italian Fascists on Trial, 1943-1948* (Chapel Hill, NC: University of North Carolina Press, 1991). Additional context, especially with regard to the "lesser" trials of Germans conducted during the late-40s, will be found in John Alan Appleman, *Military Tribunals and International Crimes* (Westport, CT: Greenwood Press, 1954).

86. See generally, Kevin Danaher, ed., *Fifty Years is Enough: The Case Against the World Bank and the International Monetary Fund* (Boston, MA: South End Press, 1994).

87. Roosevelt proposed exactly this arrangement at the 1944 Dunbarton Oaks conference attended by representatives of Great Britain, the USSR and China. French agreement was added in Feb. 1945. This group, known as the "Big Five," comprised the permanent members of the Security Council; Bennis, *Calling the Shots*, pp. 4-5.

88. A significant part of this concerned the degree to which European powers like France and Germany, and to a lesser extent Britain, were dependent upon the U.S. for aid in rebuilding their shattered infrastructures, the quid pro quo for which was rather clearly enunciated in Sec. of State George C. Marshall's "European Recovery Program" ("Marshall Plan"), beginning in 1946. Even at that, however, the U.S. hedged its bets, pursuing all manner of clandestine efforts to subvert, coopt and otherwise subordinate the recipients of U.S. assistance; see Sallie Pisani, *The CIA and the Marshall Plan* (Lawrence: University Press of Kansas, 1991).

89. "[U]nder the regime of the United Nations Charter, neither the organization itself nor any of its member states was supposed to remain 'neutral' in the face of an unjustified threat or use of force (article 2(4)), nor when confronted by the existence of a threat to peace, breach of the peace, or act of aggression by one state against another state (Chapter VII and article 39). According to article 2 (5), all members were to give the organization every assistance in any action it took in accordance with the Charter, and they must refrain from giving any assistance to any state against which the organization took preventive or enforcement action... [A]rticle 24 gave the Security Council 'primary responsibility' for the maintenance of international peace and security, and article 25 required all members of the UN 'to accept and carry out' the decisions of the Security Council"; Boyle, *Foundations of World Order*, p. 140.

90. "Article 2 (6) even empowered the organization to act against nonmembers 'so far as may be necessary for the maintenance of international peace and security'"; ibid.

91. Contrary to official mythology, the U.S. nuclear bombings of Hiroshima and Nagasaki at the end of World War II were dictated by no military necessity (the Japanese had been attempting to surrender for months). Rather, the whole point was to "send a message" to the Soviets that, as Pres. George Herbert Walker Bush would put it 45 years later, "what we say, goes." For amplification and exhaustive detail, see Gar Alperovitz, *Atomic Diplomacy: The Use of the Atomic Bomb and the American Confrontation with Soviet Power* (New York: Penguin, [2nd ed.] 1985); *The Decision to Use the Atomic Bomb and the Architecture of an American Myth* (New York: HarperCollins, 1995).

92. See Mark Seldon, *China in Revolution: The Yenan Way Revisited* (Armonk, NY: M.E. Sharpe, 1995 rev. of 1971 original).

93. For delineation of the concept, see, as examples, Lin Piao, "People's War," and Vo Nguyen Giap, "War of Liberation," both in John Gerassi, ed., *The Coming of the New International: A Revolutionary Anthology* (New York: World, 1971) pp. 122-38, 168-80. Also see Che Guevara, *Guerrilla Warfare* (New York: Monthly Review Press, 1961).

94. Mao Zedong popularized the term during the 1955 Bandung Conference; Robert Young, *White Mythologies: Writing History and the West* (New York: Routledge, 1990) p. 11. For context, see Peter Worsely, *The Third World* (London: Weidenfeld & Nicholson, [2nd. ed.] 1967).

95. "[R]espect for the principle of equal rights and self-determination of peoples" is set forth in Article 55 of the UN Charter. Tellingly, the article itself falls under "Chapter IX: International Economic and Social Co-operation." The requirement and procedures for decolonization are spelled out under "Chapter XI: Declaration Regarding Non-Self-Governing Territories" (Articles 73-4), "Chapter XII: International Trusteeship System" (Articles 75-85) and "Chapter XIII: The Trusteeship Council" (Articles 86-91); for text, see Weston, Falk and D'Amato, *Basic Documents*, pp. 24, 27-31. For explication, see W. Ofuatey-Kodjoe, *The Principle of Self-Determination in International Law* (Hamden, CT: Archon Books, 1972); Antonio Rigo-Sureda, *The Evolution of the Right to Self-Determination: A Study of United Nations Practice* (Leiden, Netherlands: A.W. Sijhoff, 1973); Michla Pomerance, *Self-Determination in Law and Practice* (The Hague: Marinus Nijhoff, 1982).

96. Even the Europeans were deceived by the degree of cynicism and duplicity imbedded in the U.S. posturing. "France worried that the U.S. effort to establish a Trusteeship Council within the UN, couched as it was in rhetorical commitment to the colonies' evolution towards...independence, threatened Paris's control over its 'overseas departments.' While the British government, [which] hoped to rely on its own colonies for a return to economic power after the war, initially shared those concerns, London was quickly reassured by the U.S. Then, seeking to persuade the French that Washington had no real anti-colonial intentions, British Foreign Secretary Anthony Eden reminded France's provisional foreign minister, Georges Bidault, that although the trusteeship plan was an American one, it was not really designed to challenge colonialism at all, but in fact to 'permit the United States to lay hands chastely on the Japanese islands in the Pacific. The system is not to be applied to any region in Europe nor to any colonies belonging to the Allied countries' ... Thus encouraged that Washington had no greater commitment to decolonization than its colony-holding allies, and in fact intended to establish its own quasi-colonial control over former Japanese-controlled territories, the French relaxed and accepted creation of the Trusteeship Council." Soon, however, it became apparent that both countries had been had. Not only were "the efforts of the rising U.S. superpower coming into conflict with British and French attempts to [retain] some control [over] their dwindling colonies"—which were now formally delegitimated—but when "decolonization [really] took hold throughout the 1960s and 1970s, the U.S. [was well positioned to dominate] ostensibly 'independent' post-colonial governments," a matter which "gave Washington important new leverage over its old-fashioned colonial allies"; Bennis, *Calling the Shots*, p. 6. For good overviews of the process, see Franz Ansprenger, *The Dissolution of Colonial Empires* (New York: Routledge, 1989); David D. Newsom, *The Imperial Mantle: The United States and the Third World* (Bloomington: Indiana University Press, 2001). On the U.S. relationship to its southern neighbors, see Eduardo Galeano, *The Open Veins of Latin America: Five Centuries of the Pillage of a Continent* (New York: Monthly Review, 1973).

97. An excellent survey will be found in Norman Miller and Robert Aya, eds., *National Liberation: Revolution in the Third World* (New York: Free Press, 1971). Also see Frantz Fanon, *The Wretched of the Earth* (New York: Grove Press, 1963); Régis Debray, *Revolution in the Revolution?* (New York: Grove Press, 1967); the chapters on Vietnam, Algeria and Cuba in Eric R. Wolf, *Peasant Wars of the Twentieth Century* (New York: Harper Torchbooks, 1969); Amilcar Gabral, *Revolution in Guinea: Selected Texts* (New York: Monthly Review, 1969); Gérard Chaliand, *Revolution in the Third World: Myths and Prospects* (New York: Viking, 1977).

98. Such support was entirely consistent with certain tenets of marxist-leninist ideology; see the essays collected by Gerassi in *The Coming of the New International*; also those collected in William J. Pomeroy, ed., *Guerrilla Warfare and Marxism* (New York: International, 1968).

99. At issue here is what one seminal study aptly referred to as "superprofits"; Richard J. Barnet and Ronald E. Müller, *Global Reach: The Power of the Multinational Corporations* (New York: Simon and Schuster, 1974).

100. The best overview of the political machinations at issue, and the methods employed in pursuing them, will be found in Noam Chomsky's and Edward S. Herman's *The Political Economy of Human Rights, Vol. 1: The Washington Connection and Third World Fascism* (Boston, MA: South End Press, 1979). On U.S. weapons peddling, see Michael T. Klare, *American Arms Supermarket* (Austin: University of Texas Press, 1984; John Tirman, *Spoils of War: The Human Cost of America's Arms Trade* (New York: Free Press, 1997).

101. See generally, Richard J. Barnet, *Intervention and Revolution: America's Confrontation with Insurgent Movements Around the World* (New York: New American Library, [2nd ed.] 1972); Peter L. Hahn and Mary Ann Heiss, *Empire and Revolution: The United States and the Third World since 1945* (Columbus: Ohio State University Press, 2001). The diplomatic backdrop is described in Newsom, *Imperial Mantle*, pp. 147-58.

102. For all its rhetoric about self-determination, a clear indication of how far the U.S. actually was in 1945 from intending any sort of across-the-board decolonization is that when it erected the UN headquarters in New York, the building was designed to accommodate an eventual total of only 70 member-state delegations, including that of the Vatican; Bennis, *Calling the Shots*, p. 8.

103. On the whole, it seems to be fairly well understood that covenants and conventions—at least those the U.S. has endorsed—are binding, and that violating them can be reasonably construed as "breaking the law." The same cannot be said with regard to customary law, which, since it by definition remains uncodified, and thus comprises a set of "unwritten rules," tends to be treated by the American public, when they're aware of it at all, more as a set of optional guidelines than as a body of law with which their government is obligated to comply. The inaccuracy of this view is delineated quite clearly in Michael Byers' *Custom, Power and the Power of Rules: International Relations and Customary International Law* (Cambridge, UK: Cambridge University Press, 1999).

104. See "'The Law Stood Squarely on Its Head': U.S. Doctrine, Indigenous Self-Determination, and the Question of World Order," in my *Acts of Rebellion: The Ward Churchill Reader* (New York: Routledge, 2003) pp. 3-22.

105. See "The Tragedy and the Travesty: The Subversion of Indigenous Sovereignty in North America," in my *Struggle for the Land: Native North American Resistance to Genocide, Ecocide and Colonization* (San Francisco: City Lights, [2nd ed.] 2003) pp. 37-92. Also see the essays collected in my *Perversions of Justice: Indigenous Peoples and Angloamerican Law* (San Francisco: City Lights, 2003).

106. A written plan was submitted to the Congress by George Washington, even before he became president, in which the "Father of his Country" recommended using treaties with Indians in much the same fashion Hitler would later employ them against his adversaries at München and elsewhere (i.e., to lull them into a false sense of security or complacency which placed them at a distinct military disadvantage when it came time to confront them with a war of aggression). "Apart from the fact that it was immoral, unethical and actually criminal, this plan placed before Congress by Washington was so logical and well laid out that it was immediately accepted practically without opposition and immediately put into action"; Allan W. Eckert, *That Dark and Bloody River: Chronicles of the Ohio River Valley* (New York: Bantam, 1995) p. 440.

107. Apart from the 400-odd treaties with American Indian peoples ratified by the Senate between 1787 and 1871, the federal executive negotiated a slightly larger number that went unratified. The latter, despite the fact that they never entered into force in the U.S.—meaning that the U.S. never accepted or attempted to meet the obligations delineated therein—have nonetheless been routinely interpreted by federal courts as effecting a legal transfer of indigenous land title to the U.S. (e.g., 21 unratified treaties serve as the predication of U.S. title claims over most of California). For treaty texts, see Charles J., Kappler, ed., *Indian Treaties, 1778-1883* (New York: Interland, 1973); Vine Deloria, Jr., and Raymond J. DeMallie, *Documents of American Indian Diplomacy: Treaties, Agreements, and Conventions, 1775-1979*, 2 vols. (Norman: University of Oklahoma Press, 1999; information on the California treaties will be found at p. 745).

108. Known as the "last in line" or "last in time" principle, this facet of U.S. juridical doctrine—set forth most clearly in *Whitney v. Robertson* (124 U.S. 190 (1888))—was never valid. The applicable element of customary treaty law, as codified under Article 27 of the Vienna Convention on the Law of Treaties (1969), is that a country "may not invoke the provisions of its internal law as justification for its failure to perform a treaty"; Weston, Falk and D'Amato, *Basic Documents*, p. 98. On the Vienna Convention being the codification of customary law rather than a promulgation of new legal principles, see Ian Sinclair, *The Vienna Convention on the Law of Treaties* (Manchester, UK: Manchester University Press, [2nd ed.] 1984) pp. 1-28.

109. With regard to American Indians, this was first accomplished via the 1885 Major Crimes Act (ch. 341, 24 Stat. 362, 385, now codified at 18 U.S.C. 1153); for context, see Sidney L. Harring, *Crow Dog's Case: American Indian Sovereignty, Tribal Law, and United States Law in the Nineteenth Century* (Cambridge, UK: Cambridge University Press, 1994). This unilateral extension of its jurisdiction over indigenous nations, recognized as such through ratified treaties, established the template upon which are based such bizarre manifestations of U.S. criminal arrogance as its 1989 assertion that it held a "legitimate right" to invade Panama in order to enforce its drug laws against head of state Manuel Noriega; see generally, *Independent Commission of Inquiry on the U.S. Invasion of Panama, The U.S. Invasion of Panama: The Truth Behind Operation "Just Cause"* (Boston: South End Press, 1991).

110. In the connection at hand, the U.S. juridical doctrine of a "plenary"—i.e., complete and unchallengeable—power inhering under certain circumstances in the federal government is articulated most clearly in *U.S. v. Kagama* (118 U.S. 375 (1886)) and *Lone Wolf v. Hitchcock* (187 U.S. 553 (1903)). For explication, see Natsu Taylor Saito, "Asserting Plenary Power over the 'Other': Indians, Immigrants, Colonial Subjects and Why U.S. Jurisprudence Needs to Incorporate International Law," *Yale Law and Policy Review*, Vol. 20, No. 2, 2002.

111. The classic illustration in this regard concerns the opinions rendered in *Cherokee Nation v. Georgia* (30 U.S. (5 Pet. 1 (1831)) and *Worcester v. Georgia* (31 U.S. (6 Pet.) 551 (1832)), wherein the Supreme Court in some respects upheld the rights and interests of American Indians vis-à-vis those asserted by the federal government and the state of Georgia. Upon hearing of the high court's conclusion in the second case, Pres. Andrew Jackson is reputed to have responded, "Justice Marshall has rendered his decision. Now let him enforce it." With that, Jackson proceeded, in open defiance of the court's ruling, to do what he'd set out to do in the first place; for context, see Jill Norgren, *The Cherokee Cases: The Confrontation of Law and Politics* (New York: McGraw-Hill, 1996). Self-evidently, Jackson's 1832 posture prefigured that of Ronald Reagan in 1985, when he responded to an adverse finding in *Nicaragua v. U.S.* by repudiating the jurisdiction/authority of the International Court of Justice; Abraham Sofaer, "The United States and the World Court," *Current Affairs*, No. 769, Dec. 1985.

112. In his opening statement at Nuremberg, the lead defense counsel argued, in essence, that the charges brought against the defendants devolved upon 1) violations of international covenants and conventions Germany had never endorsed (and to which they, as German officials, could therefore not reasonably be held accountable), 2) violations of law which had not been codified at the time of the defendants' alleged offenses (thus breaching the prohibition against prosecution on the basis of ex post facto application of law), and which, in any event, 3) "strung [the accused] together into a conspiracy by legal concepts rooted in Anglo-Saxon law and alien to us"; Hermann Jahrreiss, "Statement Before the Nuremberg Tribunal," in Jay W. Baird, *From Nuremberg to My Lai* (Lexington, MA: D.C. Heath, 1972) pp. 84-91. The Tribunal effectively rebutted each point, in turn, by recourse to the binding effect of customary law upon all states, whether or not they have specifically embraced it; Quincy Wright, "The Law

of the Nuremberg Trial, Pt. II," Sheldon Gleuck, "The Nuremberg Trial and Aggressive War," Henry L. Stimson, "The Nuremberg Trial: Landmark in Law," and Herbert Wechsler, "The Issues of the Nuremberg Trial," all in ibid., pp. 30-43, 91-8, 114-25, 125-36.

113. In considerable part, the Soviet collapse was precipitated by the spiraling costs of attempting to maintain a degree of parity with the U.S. in terms of weapons technology, a fully "planned" sector of America's "free enterprise" economy into which the Reagan administration diverted approximately one-third of the public wealth aggregate during the 1980s (all of it withdrawn from social welfare and healthcare programs, support to all levels of education, and maintenance of critical physical components of the country's civilian infrastructure). Given the differences in scale between the two countries' economies, it has been calculated that while the U.S. military to civilian production ratio was 50:100 in 1988, the USSR was forced to adopt a 370:100 ratio to keep pace; Seymore Melman, "Rossiya—ne Weimar," *Vsemirnoe slovo*, No. 8, 1995, pp. 79-80. Overall, see Ken Jowitt, *New World Disorder: The Leninist Extinction* (Berkeley: University of California Press, 1992).

114. Exhaustion had set in among the liberationists well before the end of the 1970s, largely as a result of the relentlessness with which the U.S. had prosecuted "low intensity" wars against them; see Gérard Chaliand, *Revolution in the Third World: Myths and Prospects* (New York: Viking, 1977); Col. John S. Pustay, *Counterinsurgency Warfare* (New York: Free Press, 1965); Michael T. Klare and Peter Kornbluh, *Low Intensity Warfare: Counterinsurgency, Proinsurgency, and Antiterrorism in the Eighties* (New York: Pantheon, 1988). For good overviews of the results, see Paul Harrison, *Inside the Third World: The Classic Account of Poverty in the Developing Countries* (New York: Penguin, [3rd ed.] 1993); Michael Chossudovesky, *The Globalization of Poverty: Impacts of IMF and World Bank Reforms* (London: Zed Books/Third World Network, 1997).

115. Bennis, *Calling the Shots*, p. 11. On the "police action" itself, see I.F. Stone, *The Hidden History of the Korean War, 1950-1951* (Boston: Little, Brown, [2nd ed.] 1988).

116. With regard to the demand for self-exempting status, consider as but two examples, the U.S. posture vis-à-vis the 1997 treaty banning the use of antipersonnel mines and the 1998 statute authorizing creation of an International Criminal Court; Bennis, *Calling the Shots*, pp. 279-80, 274-9. It should also be noted that when, in 1988, the U.S. finally purported to ratify the 1948 Convention on Prevention and Punishment of the Crime of Genocide, it did so only after attaching a "sovereignty package" in which it claimed a "right" to exempt itself from complying with any provision it found to be in conflict with U.S. domestic law; Lawrence J. LeBlanc, *The U.S. and the Genocide Convention* (Durham, NC: Duke University Press, 1991) esp. pp. 239-40.

117. To quote former UN ambassador/Sec. of State Madeline Albright, the U.S. "will behave multilaterally when we can, unilaterally when we must"; statement on NBC's *Meet the Press*, Jan. 2, 2000.As French Foreign Minister Hubert Vedrine framed the situation, "the predominant weight of the United States and the absence for the moment of a counterweight...leads it to hegemony, and the idea it has of its mission to unilateralism"; quoted in John Vinocur, "Going It Alone: The U.S. Upsets France so Paris Begins a Campaign to Strengthen Multilateral Institutions," *International Herald-Tribune*, Feb. 3, 1999. The dynamic at play was being analyzed at book length years earlier; see Jochen Hippler, *Pax Americana? Hegemony or Decline* (London: Pluto Press, 1994). For the most current assessments, see John Feffer, ed., *Power Trip: U.S. Unilateralism and Global Strategy After September 11* (New York: Seven Stories Press, 2003).

118. See, e.g., "Russia, France to Veto New UN Resolution on Iraq," *People's Daily*, Mar. 11, 2003.

119. Madeleine Albright, a Democrat, quoted by Catherine Toups in the *Washington Times*, Dec. 13, 1995. Four years later, North Carolina's Republican Sen. Jesse Helms, a veritable Cro-Magnon reactionary, repeated Albright's ostensibly more "liberal" characterization almost verbatim when addressing the Security Council, asserting that the function of the UN is to serve as an "effective instrument" of the U.S.; quoted in Barbara Crossette, "Helms, in Visit to UN, Offers Harsh Message," *New York Times*, Jan. 21, 2000.

120. For a good selection of quotes to this effect from Pres. Bush, Sec. of Defense Rumsfeld and other officials—including comparisons of the possible fate of the UN to that of the League of Nations—see Col. Dave Smith, "Irrelevance and Credibility: The Bush Administration, the United Nations and NATO," *Counterpunch*, Feb. 15, 2003.

121. Bennis, *Calling the Shots*, p. 52.

122. Noam Chomsky, for example, is quite prone to mentioning U.S. vetoes of Security Council resolutions and/or defiance of resolutions promulgated by the General Assembly without giving such details as when and by what votes they were/were not effected. As illustration, see his *The Fateful Triangle: The United States, Israel and the Palestinians* (Boston, MA: South End Press, 1983) pp. 27-8, 50, 67, 72, 114-5, 158, 184, 189, 215, 249, 344, 426.

123. Consider, e.g., John Prados' *The President's Secret Wars: CIA and Pentagon Covert Operations from World War II through Iranscam* (New York: William Morrow, [2nd. ed.] 1986). While the book provides a truly rich history of its subject matter, almost nothing is said with regard to the legality of what is recounted.

124. I tend to rely primarily on three: Weston's, Falk's and D'Amato's, *Basic Documents*; Adam Roberts' and Richard Guelff's *Documents on the Laws of War* (Oxford, UK: Clarendon Press, 1982); and Ian Brownlie's *Basic Documents on Human Rights* (Oxford, UK: Clarendon Press, [3rd ed.] 1992).

125. Bennis, *Calling the Shots*, pp. 52, 27.

126. See, overall, Anjali V. Patil, *The UN Veto in World Affairs, 1946-1990* (New York: UNIFO/Mansell, 1992).

127. Bennis, *Calling the Shots*, pp. 16-7. The sanctions were restricted to arms, trade and investment matters. The U.S. a prime violator on all counts; see Sean Gervasi, *The United States and the Arms*

Embargo Against South Africa: Evidence, Denial, and Refutation (Binghamton: Fernand Braudel Ctr. for the Study of Economics, Historical Systems, and Civilizations, State University of New York, 1978); Desaix Myers III with Kenneth Propp, David Hauk and David M. Liff, *U.S. Business in South Africa: The Economic, Political, and Moral Issues* (Bloomington: Indiana University Press, 1980). In this, Israel was an avid accomplice; see Richard P. Stevens and Abdelwahab M. Elmessiri, *Israel and South Africa: The Progression of a Relationship* (New Brunswick, NJ: North American, [2nd ed.] 1977); Benjamin Beit-Hallahmi, *The Israeli Connection: Who Israel Arms and Why* (New York: Pantheon, 1987) esp. pp. 108-74.

128. "I think I should say now [Reagan] is a racist pure and simple... Get rid of constructive engagement, apply to South Africa the policies you apply to Nicaragua, and viola, apartheid will end"; quoted in the *Washington Post*, Sept. 10, 1985.

129. In addition, the U.S. and Israel will be seen to have on a half-dozen occasions cast the only opposing votes on resolutions calling for a closer working relationship between the UN and the Arab League. For context, see Chomsky, *Fateful Triangle*; Naseer Aruri, *Obstruction to Peace: The United States, Israel, and the Palestinians* (Monroe, ME: Common Courage Press, 1995); Nur Masalha, *Imperial Israel and the Palestinians: The Politics of Expansion* (London: Pluto Press, 2000).

130. Ramsey Clark, ed., *The Impact of Sanctions on Iraq: The Children are Dying* (Washington, D.C.: Maisonneuve Press, 1996); *Challenge to Genocide: Let Iraq Live* (Washington, D.C.: International Action Center, 1998).

131. At his daily press briefings in early March 2003, carried live on CNN, Fox News and MSNBC, Rumsfeld consistently referred to "14 UN [or Security Council] resolutions." By mid-month, although no new resolutions had been passed, he was just as consistently using "17" as his preferred number.

132. Ronald W. Walters, *South Africa and the Bomb: Responsibility and Deterrence* (Lexington, MA: Lexington Books, 1987) esp. pp. 138-46. For more on Israeli collaboration, see Seymore M. Hersh, *The Samson Option: Israel's Nuclear Arsenal and American Foreign Policy* (New York: Random House, 1991) pp. 263-8, 271-83. Also see Ronald W. Walters, "U.S. Policy and Nuclear Proliferation in South Africa," in Western Massachusetts Association of Concerned African Scholars (WMACAS), *U.S. Military Involvement in Southern Africa* (Boston: South End Press, 1978) pp. 172-96.

133. On Israel's nuclear weapons, Hersh, *Samson Option*; Israel Shahak, *Open Secrets: Israeli Nuclear and Foreign Policies* (London: Pluto Press, 1997); Avner Cohen, *Israel and the Bomb* (New York: Columbia University Press, 1998). "Israel is [also] believed to maintain a sophisticated biological weapons programme...includ[ing] anthrax and more advanced agents in weaponized form"; *Sify News*, Apr. 24, 2003.

134. As of 1996, the declared U.S. stockpile of chemical weapons consisted of 30,599.55 tons of unitary (single component) agent and 680.19 tons of binary components, little of which—despite a U.S. agreement to destroy it all by early 2004—has actually been "decommissioned." Meanwhile, Pres. Clinton halted the announced destruction of U.S. inventories of weaponized smallpox virus—estimated as comprising as much as 80% of the world's supply—in 1999. In 2002, it was revealed that research on a new, vaccine-resistant strain of anthrax—also an airborne strain—was underway, along with a new, grenade-sized "delivery system" for dispensing biowarfare agents. Indeed, it is generally suspected that the U.S.—which adamantly refuses international inspection of such WMD facilities—is presently constructing a new and highly secret bioweapons production facility. See Jonathan B. Tucker, "Should This Killer be Put to Death?" *Washington Post*, Nov. 30, 1998; "Smallpox Virus Destruction: Why Change Course?" *Biodefense Quarterly*, Vol. 1, No. 1, June, 1999; Jonathan Power, "The U.S. and Russia have been hypocritical about biological weapons," *Transnational*, Jan. 24, 2003; Jonathan Borger, "U.S. Weapons Secrets Exposed," *Guardian*, Oct. 29, 2002.

135. The range of U.S. charges against Iraq were laid out by Pres. Bush in his speech before the General Assembly on Sept. 12, 2002. It should be noted that however abominable Iraq's treatment of its Kurdish minority, that accorded them by neighboring Turkey, a clearcut U.S. client, was/is far worse. Much of the Ba'athist animus towards the Kurds, moreover, was generated by their deployment as sacrificial pawns in a U.S. covert program, carried out during the 1970s and designed to destabilize the Baghdad government; see Gerard Chaliand, *A People Without a Country: The Kurds and Kurdistan* (New York: Olive Branch Press, [2nd ed.] 1993) esp. pp. 169-77.

136. See Richard Leonard, *South Africa at War: White Power and the Crisis in Southern Africa* (Westport, CT: Lawrence Hill, 1983).

137. An excellent set of maps depicting the original UN partition plan, Israel's 1948 expansion into Palestine, and the results of its 1967 war of expansion are provided at the end of Maxime Rodinson's *Israel: A Colonial-Settler State?* (New York: Monad Press, 1973). Also see Simha Flapa, *The Birth of Israel: Myths and Realities* (London: Croom Helm, 1987); Benny Morris, *The Birth of the Palestinian Refugee Problem, 1947-1949* (Cambridge, UK: Cambridge University Press, 1987); Zeev Sternhell, *The Founding Myths of Israel: Nationalism, Socialism, and the Founding of a Jewish State* (Princeton, NJ: Princeton University Press, 1998).

138. For overviews, see Masalha, *Imperial Israel and the Palestinians*; Michael Palumbo, *Imperial Israel: The History of the Occupation of the West Bank and Gaza* (London: Bloomsbury, [2nd ed.] 1992); Benny Morris, *1948 and After: Israel and the Palestinians* (Oxford, UK: Clarendon Press, 1990) and Avi Shlaim, *The Iron Wall: Israel and the Arab World* (New York: W.W. Norton, 2000). For ideology, see Baruch Kimmerling, *Zionism and Territory: The Socio-Territorial Dimensions of Zionist Politics* (Berkeley: Inst. of International Studies, University of California, 1983).

139. "Israel is a Jewish state with a minority of non-Jewish citizens. It is [however, declaratively] not the state of its citizens, but of the Jewish people... The consequences of [this] arrangement...for the lives

of non-Jewish citizens are considerable... We would hardly consider similar arrangements in a 'White State' or a 'Christian State' as an illustration of 'unique moral standards'"; Chomsky, *Fateful Triangle*, pp. 156-7, 158. For details, see Sabri Jiryis, *The Arabs in Israel* (New York: Monthly Review Press, 1976); Elia T. Zureik, *The Palestinians in Israel: A Study in Internal Colonialism* (London: Routledge & Kegan Paul,1979); Nur Masalha, ed., *The Palestinians in Israel* (Nazareth: Galilee Ctr. for Social Research, 1993); Edward W. Said and Christopher Hitchens, eds., *Blaming the Victims: Spurious Scholarship and the Palestinian Question* (London: Verso, [2nd ed.] 2001); Roane Carey, *The New Intifada: Resisting Israel's Apartheid* (London: Verso, 2001).

140. The literature is again copious. For a good sampling, see David Schnall, *Beyond the Green Line* (New York: Praeger, 1984); Abu Shakra and Jan Demarest, *Israeli Settler Violence in the Occupied Territories, 1980-84* (Chicago: Palestine Human Rights Campaign, 1985); Zachary Lockerman and Joel Beinin, eds., *Intifada: The Palestinian Uprising Against Israeli Occupation* (Boston, MA: South End Press, 1989); Robert L. Friedman, *Zealots of Zion: Inside Israel's West Bank Settlement Movement* (New York: Random House, 1992); Edward W. Said, *The Politics of Dispossession* (London: Chatto & Windus, 1994) and *The Question of Palestine* (New York: Vintage, [2nd ed.] 1992); Nur Masalha, *A Land Without People: Israel, Transfer and the Palestinians, 1948-1998* (London: Faber and Faber, 1997); Said and Hitchens, *Blaming the Victims*; Carey, *New Intifada*.

141. The acknowledgment was made by the U.S. Indian Claims Commission in its 1978 final report. For details and analysis, see the essay entitled "Charades Anyone? The Indian Claims Commission in Context," in my *Perversions of Justice*, pp. 125-52. Also see "The Earth Is Our Mother: Struggles for Indian Land and Liberation in the Contemporary United States," in my *Acts of Rebellion*, pp. 65-110.

142. See Noel J. Kent, *Hawaii: Islands Under the Influence* (Honolulu: University of Hawaii Press, [2nd ed.] 1993); Haunani-Kay Trask, *From a Native Daughter: Colonialism and Sovereignty in Hawai'i* (Honolulu: University of Hawai'i Press, [2nd ed.] 1999).

143. On Puerto Rico in particular, see Ronald Fernandez, *Prisoners of Colonialism: The Struggle for Justice in Puerto Rico* (Monroe, ME: Common Courage Press, 1994). For the full panorama, see Arnold H. Leibowitz, *Defining Status: A Comprehensive Analysis of United States Territorial Relations* (The Hague: Kluwer Law International, 1989).

144. See Holly Sklar's "Brave New World Order," and my own "On Gaining 'Moral High Ground': An Ode to George Bush and the 'New World Order'," both in Cynthia Peters, ed., *Collateral Damage: The 'New World Order' at Home and Abroad* (Boston, MA: South End Press, 1992) pp. 3-46, 359-72.

145. Commission of Inquiry, *U.S. Invasion of Panama* (see note 109).

146. For a "patriot's-eye" view of this travesty, see Maj. Mark Adkin, *Urgent Fury: The Truth Behind the Largest U.S. Military Operation Since Vietnam* (Lexington, MA: Lexington Books, 1989).

147. Holly Sklar, *Washington's War on Nicaragua* (Boston, MA: South End Press, 1988).

148. For background, see Robert Armstrong and Janet Shenk, *El Salvador: The Face of Revolution* (Boston, MA: South End Press, 1982); Mark Danner, *The Massacre at El Mozote* (New York: Vintage, 1994).

149. Jonathan G. Taylor, *Indonesia's Forgotten War: The Hidden History of East Timor* (London: Pluto Press, 1991); Ernest Harsch and Tony Thomas, *Angola: The Hidden History of Washington's War* (New York: Pathfinder Press, 1976); John Stockwell, *In Search of Enemies: A CIA Story* (New York: W.W. Norton, 1978); Jennifer Harbury, *Searching for Everardo: A Story of Love, War and the CIA in Guatemala* (New York: Warner Books, 1997).

150. Bennis, *Calling the Shots*, pp. 161-5. Also see Marc Weller, "Libyan Terrorism, American Swagger," *New York Times*, Feb. 15, 1992; Paul Lewis, "U.S. Tightens Sanctions Against Libya," *New York Times*, Nov. 12, 1993.

151. For the standard interpretation, see Karen Bornemann *Spies, Pan Am Flight 103: Terror over Lockerbie* (Berkeley Heights, NJ: Enslow, 2003).

152. Among the dead was the adopted infant daughter of Libyan head of state Muamar al-Qadaffi. The U.S. claimed the strikes were in retaliation for Libya's sponsorship of bombings at the Rome and Vienna airports on Dec. 27, 1985, in which a single American child, 11-year-old Natasha Simpson, was killed. Instructively, both the Italian and Austrian intelligence agencies stated unequivocally that Libya had nothing to do with the attacks. A second pretext was that Libya was behind the April 5, 1986 bombing of the La Belle discothèque in Berlin, in which a U.S. serviceman was killed, although German intelligence was equally adamant that there was no "Libyan connection" at issue (instructively, U.S. military intelligence shared this view); Noam Chomsky, *Pirates and Emperors: International Terrorism and the Real World* (New York: Claremont, 1986) pp. 135, 148. On the refusal of U.S. courts to consider the victims' claims, see William Blum, *Rogue State: A Guide to the World's Only Remaining Superpower* (Monroe, ME: Common Courage Press, 2000) p. 230.

153. See note 54. For further information, see Larry Everest, *Behind the Poison Cloud: Union Carbide's Bhopal Massacre* (Chicago: Banner Press, 1986); Dominique Laspierre, Javier Moro and Kathyrine Spink, *Five Past Midnight in Bhopal: The Epic Story of the World's Deadliest Industrial Disaster* (New York: Warner, [2nd ed.] 2003).

154. Bennis, *Calling the Shots*, p. 162-3.

155. For a handy overview of the embargo and its effects in terms of international relations, see Michael Krinsky and David Golove, eds., *United States Economic Measures Against Cuba: Proceedings of the United Nations and International Law Issues* (Northampton, MA: Aletheia Press, 1993). On material effects, see Peter Schwab, *Cuba: Confronting the U.S. Embargo* (New York: Palgrave Macmillan, 2000).

156. Leo Huberman and Paul M. Sweezy, *Cuba: Anatomy of a Revolution* (New York: Monthly Review Press, 1961).

157. See, e.g., the 1994 statement of Madeleine Albright, quoted in Bennis, *Calling the Shots*, p. 161.

158. This is still the case in Cuba, although the collapse of the socialist bloc during the early-90s, combined with a tightening of the U.S. embargo during the same period, has made it much more difficult—"Cuba spent $45 million in 1991...to buy the powdered milk it once [obtained] from the German Democratic Republic in a barter exchange for high-protein Cuban animal feed"—and rationing has become necessary "to assure across-the-board distribution of ever-scarcer [foodstuffs]"; Gail Reed, *Island in the Storm: The Cuban Communist Party's Fourth Congress* (Melbourne/ New York: Ocean Press/Ctr. for Cuban Studies, 1992) pp. 6-7. On the U.S. situation, see Loretta Schwartz-Nobel, *Growing Up Empty: The Hunger Epidemic in America* (New York: HarperCollins, 1999). On U.S. votes against the idea of food as a right, see as examples the entries herein for Dec. 14, 1981; Dec. 18, 1982; Dec. 16, 1984; Dec. 19, 2001.

159. On the Cuban health care system, see Julie Margot Feinsilver, *Healing the Masses: Cuban Health Politics at Home and Abroad* (Berkeley: University of California Press, 1993); Theodore H. MacDonald, *Developmental Analysis of Cuba's Health Care System since 1959* (Lewistown, NY: Edwin Mellen Press, 1999). On its U.S. counterpart, see Panchetta Wilson, *Inside the HMO: America's Health Care Crisis* (Winter Park, FL: FOUR-G, 1999). On U.S. votes against the idea of health care as a right, see the entries for Dec. 14, 1981; Dec. 18, 1982; Dec. 16, 1984, herein.

160. The problem arose during the mid-80s, when Ronald Reagan, as a "cost-cutting measure," began to shove entire categories of mental patients out of institutions and onto the streets; E. Fuller Torrey, *Nowhere to Go: The Tragic Odyssey of the Homeless Mentally Ill* (New York: HarperCollins, 1985). The results of such "frugality" are addressed by the material cited in note 20. Also see Judith Lynne Failer, *Who Qualifies for Rights? Homelessness, Mental Illness and Civil Commitment* (Ithaca, NY: Cornell University Press, 2002). Such horrors are, of course, hardly inflicted by the U.S. and likeminded states upon the mentally ill alone; see *Children on the Streets of the Americas: Globalization, Homelessness and Education in the United States, Brazil and Cuba* (New York: Routledge, 2002). What Cuba accomplishes with so little stands in stunning contrast to how little the U.S. is willing to do with so much.

161. For background on the development of Cuba's exemplary educational system, see Karen Wald, *Children of Che: Childcare and Education in Cuba* (Palo Alto, CA: Ramparts Press, 1978). More recent information will be found in Theodore H. MacDonald's *Making a New People: Education in Revolutionary Cuba* (Vancouver, BC: New Star Books, 1996). For background on the situation in the U.S., see the classic analyses offered by Rudolph Franz Flesch in his *Why Johnny Can't Read* (New York: HarperCollins, 1955) and *Why Johnny Still Can't Read* (New York: HarperCollins, 1985). For more current information, see Bruce M. Mitchell and Robert S. Salsbury, *Unequal Opportunity: A Crisis in America's Schools* (Westport, CT: Bergin and Garvey, 2002).

162. The foundations for this and all other aspects of Cuba's social welfare efforts had been firmly established before the end of the 1960s; see generally, Carmelo Mesa-Lago, *Revolutionary Change in Cuba* (Pittsburgh, PA: University of Pittsburgh Press, 1974). A more up-to-date summary will be found in Marifeli Pérez-Stable, *The Cuban Revolution: Origins, Course, and Legacy* (New York: Oxford University Press, 1999) pp. 91-4. Probably the best current overview is provided by Cuban premier Fidel Castro in his *On Imperialist Globalization: Two Speeches* (London: Zed Books, 1999) esp. pp. 36-45.

163. See the chapter entitled "Carrying the Big Stick: SWAT Teams and Paramilitary Policing," in Parenti, *Lockdown America*, pp. 111-38. Also see Peter B. Kraska and Victor E. Kappler, "Militarizing American Police: The Rise and Normalization of Paramilitary Units," *Social Problems*, Vol. 44, No. 1, Feb. 1997; Peter Cassidy, "The Rise in Paramilitary Policing," *Covert Action Quarterly*, Fall 1997.

164. For backdrop, see Alexander C. Lichtenstein and Michael A. Kroll, *The Fortress Economy: The Economic Role of the U.S. Prison System* (Philadelphia: American Friends Service Committee, 1990).

165. The description was employed by noted penal psychologist Richard Korn in his "Report on the Effects of Confinement in the HSU," attached to National Prison Project, *Report on the High Security Unit for Women, Federal Correctional Institution, Lexington, Kentucky* (New York: American Civil Liberties Union, Aug. 25, 1987). Also see Mike Ryan, "Solitude as Counterinsurgency: The U.S. Isolation Model of Political Incarceration," and Fay Dowker and Glenn Good, "From Alcatraz to Marion to Florence: Control Unit Prisons in the United States," both in my and J.J. Vander Wall's coedited *Cages of Steel: The Politics of Imprisonment in the United States* (Washington, D.C. Maisonneuve Press, 1992) pp. 83-109, 131-51.

166. See the chapter entitled "Big Bucks from the Big House: The Prison-Industrial Complex and Beyond," in Parenti, *Lockdown America*, pp. 211-44. Also see Daniel Burton-Rose, Dan Pens and Paul Wright, eds., *The Celling of America: An Inside Look at the U.S. Prison Industry* (Monroe, ME: Common Courage Press, 1998).

167. According to a 2002 survey conducted by *Business Week*, the disparity isn't just between top U.S. executives and their workers. The average U.S. CEO compensation rate—$7,452 per hour, or about $60K per 8-hour day—is 10 times that of their counterparts in Japan, 11 times that of CEOs in Germany and South Korea, 16 times that paid in France, 19 times that in Italy, 25 times that in Britain, 38 times that in Hong Kong, 45 times that in Mexico, and 57 times that in Brazil. Also see Jake Ulick, "CEO salaries, bonuses keep rising," *CNN/Money*, Mar. 25, 2003.

168. Such enterprises have a long and sordid history in the U.S.; see Daniel E. Bender and Richard A. Greenwald, eds., *Sweatshop USA: The American Sweatshop in Historical and Global Perspective* (New York: Routledge, 2003). Also see Mary E. Williams, ed., *Child Labor and Sweatshops* (San Diego: Greenhaven Press, 1999); Ellen Israel Rosen, *Making Sweatshops: The Globalization of the U.S. Apparel Industry* (Berkeley: University of California Press, 2002).

169. The mechanisms by which this is accomplished are well and succinctly described in Danahur, 50 Years is Enough. An excellent, if somewhat dated, survey of the results in terms of police buildups, etc., will be found in Edward S. Herman's *The Real Terror Network: Terrorism in Fact and Propaganda* (Boston,

MA: South End Press, 1982). Other effects are surveyed in Harrison, *Inside the Third World.*
170. Reed, *Island in the Storm*, pp. 97-8. Also see Feinsilver, *Healing the Masses.*
171. Medea Benjamin, "On Its Own: Cuba in the Post-Cold War Era," in Phyllis Bennis and Michel Moushabeck, eds., *Altered States: A Reader in the New World Order* (New York: Olive Branch/Interlink, 1993) p. 419.
172. "The General Assembly, determined to encourage strict compliance with the purposes and principles enshrined in the Charter of the United Nations [and] concerned about the continued promulgation and application by Member-States of laws and regulations whose extraterritorial effects affect the sovereignty of other States and the legitimate interests of entities or persons under their jurisdiction, as well as the freedom of trade and navigation, [and] concerned with the adverse effects of [such] measures on the Cuban population...urges States that have such laws or measures to take the necessary steps to repeal or invalidate them"; GA Res. A/48/L.14/Rev. 1 (Nov. 24, 1992).
173. Pres. William Jefferson Clinton, quoted in the *Miami Herald*, Oct. 17, 1997.
174. The Charter constraints will be found under Chapter IX: International Economic and Social Cooperation (Articles 55-60); for text, see Weston, Falk and D'Amato, *Basic Documents*, pp. 24-5.
175. On sabotage, see Blum, *Rogue State*, p. 108.
176. Bennis, *Calling the Shots*, p. 160.
177. Noam Chomsky, *Deterring Democracy* (New York: Hill and Wang, 1992). Also see the chapters entitled "The Perils of Democracy" and "The Fledgling Democracies," in Chomsky's *The Culture of Terrorism* (Boston: South End Press, 1988) pp. 131-68, 225-49.
178. The idea is framed very well in the section entitled "Constructive Bloodbaths in Vietnam," in Chomsky and Herman, *Third World Fascism*, pp. 299-337.
179. See, e.g., the chapter entitled "The Threat of a Good Example," in Chomsky, *Culture of Terrorism*, pp. 217-24. The supposed benefits of such a policy to its victims was actually theorized during the early-70s by behavioral psychologist B.F. Skinner, in his *Beyond Freedom and Dignity*, a book accorded considerable attention by U.S. élites and their academic apologists. The latest edition of Skinner's 1971 "classic" was released by Hackett in 2002.
180. One of the better overviews of what was done to Vietnam, Laos and Cambodia, is presented in Noam Chomsky's and Edward S. Herman's *The Political Economy of Human Rights, Vol. II: After the Cataclysm: Postwar Indochina and the Reconstruction of Imperial Ideology* (Boston: South End Press, 1979).
181. See the entries for Dec. 17, 1950, and Apr. 13, 1967, herein. For further background, see William Blum, *The CIA: A Forgotten History* (London: Zed Books, 1986) pp. 31-7, 243-50.
182. See the entry for Aug. 19, 1953, herein. For further background, see Kiddi, *Roots of Rebellion*, pp. 132-41, 142; Blum, *CIA*, pp. 67-76; Kennet Love, *The American Role in the Pahlavi Restoration of 19 August 1953*, unpublished mss. among the Allen Dulles papers stored at Princeton University; excerpted in *Counterspy*, Sept./Oct., 1980.
183. See the entry for June 18, 1954, herein. For further background, see Stephen Schlesinger and Stephen Kinzer, *Bitter Fruit: The Untold Story of the American Coup in Guatemala* (New York: Doubleday, 1982).
184. See the entry for Jan. 17, 1961, herein. For further background, see Blum, *CIA*, pp. 174-80; John Raneleigh, *The Agency: The Rise and Decline of the CIA* (New York: Touchstone Books, 1987) pp. 339-44.
185. See the entries for Apr. 29 and Oct. 1, 1965, herein. For further background, see Chomsky and Herman, *Third World Fascism*, pp. 205-7; 242-51; Carlos María Gutiérrez, *The Dominican Republic: Rebellion and Repression* (New York: Monthly Review Press, 1972).
186. See the entry for Feb. 24, 1966, herein. For further background, see Peter Barker, *Cold Chop: The Coup that Toppled Nkrumah* (Accra: Ghana Publishing House, 1969).
187. See the entry for Sept. 11, 1973, herein. Background will be found in Les Evans, ed., *Disaster in Chile: Allende's Strategy and Why It Failed* (New York: Pathfinder Press, 1974).
188. For background, see Harsch and Thomas, Angola; Stockwell, *In Search of Enemies*; Blum, *CIA*, pp. 284-91.
189. See the entries for Mar. 16 and June 27, 1986, herein. For further background, see Sklar, *Washington's War Against Nicaragua*; Reed Brody, *Contra Terror in Nicaragua* (Boston: South End Press, 198?).
190. Among the better overviews are Chomsky's and Herman's *Third World Fascism*; Blum's *CIA*; and John Prados' *Presidents' Secret Wars: CIA and Pentagon Covert Operations from World War II Through Iranscam* (New York: Quill Morrow, 1986).
191. See the entries for June 26, 1945, Feb. 16, 1949, Oct. 21, 1949, and June 25, 1950, herein. For further background, see Stone, *Hidden History of the Korean War*; Clay Blair, *The Forgotten War: America in Korea, 1950-1953* (New York: Times Books, 1987).
192. See the entry for Sept.-Oct. 1949, herein. Further background on the period at issue will be found in Blum, *CIA*, pp. 15-23. For deeper background on U.S. relations with Chiang Kai-shek, see Barbara W. Tuchman, *Stillwell and the American Experience in China, 1911-45* (New York: Macmillan, 1970).
193. "The struggle against Batista had started on the morrow of his coup in March 1952. In the years that followed it seemed plain to people all over the world that Batista was a thief and a murderer who should be shunned by decent persons. It was plain to the people of Cuba who had suffered the loss of 20,000 of their finest sons and daughters at the hands of Batista's torturers. But...the United States ambassadors...were the dictator's pals [and] the State Department...disregarded the pleas of eminent Cubans that it stop the shipment of arms to the unlawful government in power. Not until March 1958 [barely nine months before Batista was overthrown] was an embargo of arms declared [and] even after the embargo was declared, rockets were delivered to Batista's air force"; Huberman and Sweezy,

Anatomy of a Revolution, pp. 65-6.
194. "By 1975, the Congo strongman, regarded by the [CIA] as one of its 'successes' in Africa, had ruled over his hapless , impoverished subjects for 10 long years. In the process, with a flair for conspicuous corruption that ranks with the best this century has to offer, Mobutu amassed a personal fortune estimated to run into the billions of dollars sitting in the usual Swiss, New York, etc., banks, while most of the population suffered from severe malnutrition... It can be said as well that his corruption was matched only by his cruelty"; Blum, *CIA*, p. 292.
195. On the U.S. relationship with Reza Shah Pahlavi after 1953, see Bahman Niumand, *The New Imperialism in Action* (New York: Monthly Review Press, 1969); Amin Saikhal, *The Rise and Fall of the Shah* (Princeton, NJ: Princeton University Press, 1980).
196. James Ferguson, *Papa Doc, Baby Doc: Haiti and the Duvaliers* (Oxford, UK: Blackwell, 1987); Paul Farmer, *The Uses of Haiti* (Monroe, ME: Common Courage Press, 1994).
197. For background on U.S. support to the Somoza family, see Henri Weber, *Nicaragua: The Sandinista Revolution* (London: Verso, 1981) pp. 15-9; Gregorio Selser, *Sandino* (New York: Monthly Review Press, 1981) pp. 181-96.
198. Robert D. Crassweller, *Trujillo: The Life and Times of a Caribbean Dictator* (Santo Domingo, D.R.: n.p., 1979).
199. See the entries for Sept. 11, 1973 and Oct. 16, 1998; Apr. 29, 1965, Dec. 22, 1975, and Apr. 22, 1976, herein. For further background on the Suharto régime, see Taylor, *Indonesia's Forgotten War*. On Pinochet, see Mary Helen Spooner, *Soldiers in a Narrow Land: The Pinochet Regime in Chile* (Berkeley: University of California Press, 1994); Hugh O'Shaughnessy, *Pinochet: The Politics of Torture* (New York: New York University Press, 2000).
200. On the nature of the Stroessner régime, see Richard Arens, ed., *Genocide in Paraguay* (Philadelphia: Temple University Press, 1976).
201. On Greece, see Blum, *CIA*, pp. 246-50; Amnesty International, *Torture in Greece: The First Torturers' Trial in 1975* (London: Amnesty International, 1977). On Guatemala, see Harbury, *Searching for Everardo*; Jean-Marie Simon, *Guatemala: Eternal Spring, Eternal Tyranny* (New York: W.W. Norton, 1987).
202. Michael Klare and Eric Pokesch, "Evading the Embargo: How the U.S. Arms South Africa and Rhodesia," in WMACAS, *U.S. Military Involvement in Southern Africa*, pp. 157-71.
203. On the Argentine junta, see Jo Fisher, *Mothers of the Disappeared* (Boston: South End Press, 1989); on U.S. support, see pp. 80-1. Also see Sandy Vogelgesang, *American Dream, Global Nightmare: The Dilemma of U.S. Human Rights Policy* (New York: W.W. Norton, 1980) pp. 220-1, 229; Lars Schoultz, *Human Rights and U.S. Policy Towards Latin America* (Princeton, NJ: Princeton University Press, 1981).
204. See the entry for Feb. 23, 1981, herein. For further background, see Carolyn Forche and Philip Wheaton, *History and Motivation of U.S. Involvement in the Control of the Peasant Movement* (Washington, D.C.: EPICA, 1980); Arnon Hadar, *The United States and El Salvador: Political and Military Involvement* (Berkeley, CA: U.S.-El Salvador Research and Information Ctr., 1980); Thomas Anderson, *War of the Dispossessed: Honduras and El Salvador* (Lincoln: University of Nebraska Press, 1981).
205. "It was of course understood that Saddam Hussein was one of the world's most savage tyrants. But he was 'our gangster,' joining a club in which he could find congenial associates. Repeating a familiar refrain, Geoffrey Kemp, head of the Middle East section in the National Security Council under Reagan, observed that 'We weren't really that naïve. We knew that he was an SOB, but he was our SOB.' '[Saddam] was a natural ally....,' senior Reagan-Bush NSC official Peter Rodman comments in retrospect, 'The fact that [he] was a murderous thug didn't change that'"; Noam Chomsky, "'What We Say Goes': The Middle East in the New World Order," in Peters, *Collateral Damage*, pp. 62-3. For extensive details on the U.S. relationship with Saddam Hussein during the 1980s, see Alan Friedman, *Spider's Web: The Secret History of How the White House Secretly Armed Iraq* (New York: Bantam Books, 1993); Bruce W. Jentleson, *With Friends Like These: Reagan, Bush, and Saddam, 1982-1990* (New York: W.W. Norton, 1994). On U.S. relations with Noriega, see Peter Dale Scott and Jonathan Marshall, *Cocaine Politics: Drugs, Armies and the CIA in Central America* (Berkeley: University of California Press, 1991) pp. 65-78.
206. See Russ Bellant, *Old Nazis, the New Right, and the Republican Party* (Boston: South End Press, 1988).
207. The extent to which members of the SS and other nazi fugitives useful to the U.S. in terms of intelligence gathering, covert operations, scientific research, etc., were shielded from charges war crimes/crimes against humanity and employed by the U.S.—often in the U.S. itself—is well documented; see Christopher Simpson, *Blowback: America's Recruitment of Nazis and Its Effect on the Cold War* (New York: Collier Books, 1988). The same procedure applied with respect to Japanese scientists and technicians, all of them guilty of war crimes/crimes against humanity, deemed useful to the U.S. program to develop its own biowar capabilities; see Sheldon H. Harris, *Factories of Death: Japanese Biological Warfare, 1932-1945, and the American Cover-Up* (New York: Routledge, 1994).
208. Indeed, most of those tried, convicted and sentenced to anything short of capital punishment—and sometimes them as well—were shortly released from prison to resume their places in the Cold War struggle of the "Free World" against "communist totalitarianism." In 1952, a "parole process was created by the Americans that was designed to release what the State Department described as 'hardcore' German war criminals long before their sentences had expired. In April 1958, an Allied parole board released the final four war criminals in Western captivity. Three of the four had been Einsatzkommando members originally sentenced to death by an American tribunal at Nuremberg in 1949"; Peter Maguire, "Nuremberg: A Cold War Conflict of Interest," in Belinda Cooper, *War Crimes:*

The Legacy of Nuremberg (New York: TV Books, 1999) pp. 67-8. For further contextualization, see the chapter entitled "I.G. Wins the Peace," in Joseph Borkin, *The Crime and Punishment of I.G. Farben* (New York: Free Press, 1978) pp. 157-63. On the nature of the crimes perpetrated by those whose death sentences were commuted, see Richard Rhodes, *Masters of Death: The SS-Einsatzgruppen and the Invention of the Holocaust* (New York: Alfred A. Knopf, 2002).

209. Bennis, *Calling the Shots*. Also see Richard Falk, *Predatory Globalization: A Critique* (Oxford, UK: Polity Press, 1999); Andrew Basevic, *American Empire: The Realities and Consequences of U.S. Diplomacy* (Cambridge, MA: Harvard University Press, 2002).

210. Rumsfeld is quoted in Max Boot, "American Imperialism? No need to run away from the label," *USA Today*, May 5, 2003.

211. For use of the term in this fashion, see Blum, *Rogue State*; Noam Chomsky and Edward W. Said, *Acts of Aggression: Policing "Rogue" States* (New York: Seven Stories Press, 1999); Noam Chomsky, *Rogue States: The Rule of Force in World Affairs* (Cambridge, MA: South End Press, 2000); Clyde Prestowitz, *Rogue Nation: American Unilateralism and the Failure of Good Intentions* (New York: Basic Books, 2003).

212. See generally, Michael Howard, George J. Andropoulos and Mark R. Shulman, eds., *The Laws of War: Constraints on Warfare in the Western World* (New Haven, CT: Yale University Press, 1994). For texts, see Roberts and Guelff, *Documents on the Laws of War*; W. Michael Reisman and Chris T. Antoniou, eds., *The Laws of War: A Comprehensive Collection of Primary Documents on International Laws Governing Armed Conflicts* (New York: Vintage, 1994). On nuclear weapons, specifically, see Francis A. Boyle, *The Criminality of Nuclear Weapons* (Santa Barbara, CA: Nuclear Age Foundation, 1983); Martin Feinrider and Arthur Miller, eds., *Nuclear Weapons and the Law* (Westport, CT: Greenwood Press, 1984); Leon Vickman, *Why Nuclear Weapons Are Illegal* (Santa Barbara, CA: Nuclear Age Foundation, 1988); N. Singh and Edward McWhinney, *Nuclear Weapons and Contemporary International Law* (The Hague: Martinus Nijhoff, 1989); Robert Jay Lifton and Richard Falk, *Indefensible Weapons: The Political and Psychological Case Against Nuclearism* (New York: Basic Books, [2nd ed.] 1991).

213. Unexploded cluster "bomblets" remain "live" and thus constitute the same hazard to children and other noncombatants as land mines. The use of such ordnance is therefore proscribed under the 1997 Land Mines Convention; Blum, *Rogue State*, pp. 100-3. On depleted uranium munitions, see John Catalinotto and Sara Flounders, eds., *Metal of Dishonor: How the Pentagon Radiates Soldiers and Civilians with DU* (New York: International Action Project, 1997); Akira Tashiro, Discounted Casualties: The Human Cost of Depleted Uranium (Hiroshima: Chugoku Shimbun, 2001).

214. "The Contracting Powers agree to abstain from the use of projectiles the object of which is the diffusion of asphyxiating or deleterious gases"; Hague Declaration IV (2) Concerning Asphyxiating Gases (1 A.J.I.L. (Supp.) 157 (1907), signed July 27, 1899); passage in Reisman and Antoniou, *Laws of War*, p. 57.

215. On the "syndrome's" political dimensions, see Paul Joseph, *Cracks in the Empire: State Politics in the Vietnam War* (Boston: South End Press, 1981). On its military effects, see Richard Boyle, *Flower of the Dragon: The Breakdown of the U.S. Army in Vietnam* (San Francisco: Ramparts Press, 1972); Cincinnatus, *Self-Destruction: The Disintegration and Decay of the United States Army during the Vietnam Era* (New York: W.W. Norton, 1981). On the subsequent "rehabilitation of American confidence," see Chomsky and Herman, *After the Cataclysm*; Michael T. Klare, *Beyond the "Vietnam Syndrome": U.S. Interventionism in the 1980s* (Washington, D.C.: Institute for Policy Studies, 1981).

216. For background, see Falk, *Predatory Globalization*, pp. 48-63. Also see Noam Chomsky, *Profits Over People: Neoliberalism and Global Order* (New York: Seven Stories, 1999); James Petras and Henry Veltmeyer, *Globalization Unmasked: Imperialism in the 21st Century* (London: Zed Books, 2001); Wayne Ellwood, *The No-Nonsense Guide to Globalization* (London: Verso, 2002).

217. For a quick sketch, see Ash Narain Roy, *The Third World in the Age of Globalization: Requiem or New Agenda?* (London: Zed Books, 1999). Backdrop will be found in Gerassi, *Coming of the New International*.

218. In other words, the "fundamental contradictions of international capitalism" will finally bear much of the fruit predicted by marxian economists a half-century and more ago. See, e.g., Paul A. Baran, *The Political Economy of Growth* (New York: Monthly Review Press, 1957). Also see Baran's posthumously published *The Longer View: Essays Toward a Critique of Political Economy* (New York: Monthly Review Press, 1969). For a more recent view, see Jochem Hippler, *Pax Americana? Hegemony or Decline* (London: Pluto Press, 1994).

219. For a more "moderate" argument positing essentially the same objectives, see Erskine Childers and Brian Urquhart, *Towards a More Effective United Nations* (Uppsala, Sweden: Dag Hammarskjold Foundation, 1994).

220. For amplification on this point, see Terrance Edward Paupp, *Achieving Inclusionary Governance: Advancing Peace and Development in the First and Third Worlds* (New York: Transnational, 2000). For additional perspectives, see Peter J. Fromuth, ed., *A Successor Vision: The United Nations of Tomorrow* (New York: United Nations Assoc., 1988); Richard A. Falk, Robert C. Johansen and Samuel S. Kim, eds., *The Constitutional Foundations of World Peace* (Albany: SUNY Press, 1993).

221. See the chapter entitled "Democratizing the UN," in Bennis, *Calling the Shots*, pp. 233-44. Also see William Stassen, *United Nations: A Working Paper for Restructuring* (Indianapolis: Lerner, 1994). Additional useful arguments are advanced in Childers and Urquhart, *Towards a More Effective United Nations and Renewing the United Nations System* (Uppsala, Sweden: Dag Hammarskjold Foundation, 1992).

222. Bennis, *Calling the Shots*, pp. 18-9, 58-9, 70, 90, 99, 299-302.

223. There is precedent for this, as when the U.S. was removed from the UN Human Rights Commission;

Barbara Crossette, "US is Voted Off Rights Panel of the UN for the First Time," *New York Times*, May 4, 2001.

224. The U.S. itself has set ample precedent for such a procedure, most recently when a federal district judge ordered payment of nearly $1 billion in frozen Iraqi assets—over which the U.S. asserted outright "ownership" under provision of its own domestic law in 2002—to 17 former U.S. POWs for the "pain, suffering and mental anguish" the experienced at the hands of their captors during the 1991 Gulf War; see the entry for July 20, 2003; William C. Mann, "Judge Orders U.S. to Retain Iraqi Assets," *Guardian Unlimited*, July 20, 2003.

225. Setting aside the red herring of slavery—the North had no more desire to abolish the institution than did the South, and, as should be evident in the present chronology, has maintained it in a range of altered forms ever since the American Civil War—the southern states had every legal right, both constitutionally and under the Law of Nations, to pursue popular sovereignty by seceding from the Union; see, e.g., Clifford Dowdy, *The History of the Confederacy, 1832-1865* (New York: Barnes & Noble, 1955) pp. 25-42; Samuel Elliot Morison, *The Oxford History of the American People* (New York: Oxford University Press, 1965) pp. 607-8. It is worth noting that Lincoln openly condemned the southerners' refusal to knuckle under to the dictates of the central government as "anarchy"; quoted in Page Smith, *The Nation Comes of Age: A People's History of the Ante Bellum Years* (New York: McGraw-Hill, 1981) p. 1184. As concerns the northern view of the enslavement of blacks, another statement by the "Great Emancipator" should prove clarifying: "[I] have no purpose to directly or indirectly interfere with the institution of slavery in the States where it now exists. I believe I have no lawful right to do so, and I have no inclination to do so. I have no purpose to introduce political and social equality between the white and black races. There is a physical difference between the two, which in my judgment will probably forever forbid their living together upon the footing of perfect equality... I, as well as [the most devout southern racist] am in favor of the race to which I belong having the superior position"; quoted in Juan F. Perea, Richard Delgado, Angela P. Harris and Stephanie M. Wildman, *Race and Races: Cases and Resources for a Diverse America* (St. Paul: West Group, 2000) p. 129. Far more interesting than perpetually circling the stale proposition that blacks were "freed" by preservation of the Union, is consideration of how differently history might have evolved had the Confederate States—within which chattel slavery could not have lasted much longer in any event—been victorious, thus irrevocably precluding consolidation of the U.S. monstrosity in its present form.

226. It should be noted that the 19th century articulation of America's "destiny" to possess the property of Others was always as much racist as it was imperialist; see Horsman, *Race and Manifest Destiny*. It therefore served as the ideal platform for subsequent articulation of the Hitlerian doctrine of *lebensraumpolitik* (politics of living space); see Frank Parella, *Lebensraum and Manifest Destiny: A Comparative Study in the Justification of Expansionism* (Washington, D.C.: MA Thesis, Dept. of International Affairs, Georgetown University, 1950). To have the matter in Hitler's own words, see Adolf Hitler, *Mein Kampf* (New York: Reynal and Hitchcock, 1939) pp. 403, 591; *Hitler's Secret Book* (New York: Grove Press, 1961) pp. 46-52.

227. The language quoted appears, among other places, in Art. 2 of the Declaration on the Granting of Independence to Colonial Countries and Peoples (U.N.G.A. Res. 1514 (XV),15 U.N. GAOR, Supp. (No. 16) 66, U.N. Doc. A/4684 (1961)), Art. 1 (1) of the International Covenant on Economic, Social and Cultural Rights (U.N.G.A. Res. 220 (XXI), 21 U.N. GAOR, Supp. (No. 16) 49, U.N. Doc. A/6316 (1967)), and Art. 1 (1) of the International Covenant on Civil and Political Rights (U.N.G.A. Res. 2200 (XXI), 21 U.N. GAOR, Supp. (No. 16) 52, U.N. Doc. A/6316 (1967)). For text, see Weston, Falk and D'Amato, Basic Documents, pp. 344, 371, 376.

228. In addition to many of the works already cited, see the essays collected in W. Michael Reisman and Burns H. Weston, *Toward World Order and Human Dignity: Essays in Honor of Myers S. McDougal* (New York: Free Press, 1976); Frederick E. Snyder and Surakiart Sathirathai, eds., *Third World Attitudes Toward International Law: An Introduction* (The Hague: Martinus Nijhoff, 1987). Also see Richard Falk, *Revitalizing International Law* (Ames: Iowa State University Press, 1989); Ellen M. Wood, *Democracy Against Capitalism: Renewing Historical Materialism* (Cambridge, UK: Cambridge University Press, 1995); John Gray, *False Dawn: The Delusions of Global Capitalism* (New York: New Press, 1998); Paul Farmer, *Infections and Inequalities: The Modern Plagues* (Berkeley: University of California Press, 1999).

229. For ways and means of approaching this issue, see Jeffrey Ian Ross, ed., *Controlling State Crime: An Introduction* (New York: Garland, 1995). Also see Edward M. Wise and Ellen S. Podgor, eds., *International Criminal Law: Cases and Materials* (New York: Lexis, 2000).

230. See the essays collected in Barbara Stallings, ed., *Global Change, Regional Response: The New International Context of Development* (Cambridge, UK: Cambridge University Press, 1995), and Roberto Mangabeira Unger's *Democracy Realized: The Progressive Alternative* (London: Verso, 1998). Also see Pomerance, Self-Determination in Law and Practice; Fidel Castro, "The Battle for Sovereignty is a Battle for Culture, Too," in his *On Imperialist Globalization*, pp. 81-156.

231. For a succinct overview, see Martin Carnoy, *Faded Dreams: The Politics and Economics of Race in America* (Cambridge, UK: Cambridge University Press, 1994).

232. See generally, Philip Alston and Katarina Tomayevski, eds., *The Right to Food* (The Hague: Martinus Nijhoff, 1984). For a more subtle—and accurate—placement of the question of food within the context of human rights than that presently offered by the UN, see Gustavo Esteva and Madhu Suri Prakash, *Grassroots Post-Modernism: Remaking the Soil of Cultures* (London: Zed Books, 1998) pp. 52-67.

233. Such action would be quite in line with the Charter of Economic Rights and Duties of States (U.N.G.A. Res. 3281 (XXIX), 29 U.N. GAOR, Supp. (No. 31) 50, U.N. Doc. A/9631 (1975)), as well as International

Covenant on Economic Social and Cultural Rights; see William F. Felice, *Taking Suffering Seriously: The Importance of Collective Human Rights* (Albany: SUNY Press. 1996). For the framework for potential additional applications of the antidiscrimination conventions, see Paul G. Warren, *Power and Prejudice: The Politics and Diplomacy of Racial Discrimination* (Boulder, CO: Westview Press, 1988); Jürgen Habermas, *Inclusion of the Other: Studies in Political Theory* (Cambridge, MA: MIT Press, 1998).

234. For children, this would devolve upon enforcement of the 1994 Convention on the Rights of the Child (U.N.G.A. Res. 44/25 Annex, 44 U.N. GAOR, Supp. (No. 49) 167, U.N. Doc. A/44/49 (1995)). For women, it would devolve upon enforcement of the Inter-American Convention on the Prevention, Punishment and Eradication of Violence Against Women (33 Int. Leg. Mat. (1994)) and the Convention on the Elimination of All Forms of Discrimination Against Women(U.N.G.A. Res. 34/180 (XXXIV), 34 U.N. GAOR, Supp. (No. 46) 194, U.N. Doc. A/34/380 (1979)). For prisoners, it devolves, among other things, upon enforcement of the UN Standard Minimum Rules for the Treatment of Prisoners (E.S.C. Res. 663 (XXIV) C, 24 U.N. ESCOR, Supp. (No. 1) 11, U.N. Doc. E/3048 (1957)) and the Convention Against Torture and Other Cruel, Inhuman or Degrading Treatment or Punishment (U.N.G.A. Res. 39/46 Annex, 39 U.N. GAOR, Supp. (No. 51) 197, U.N. Doc. E/CN.4/1984/72 (1984)). For migrant workers, it devolves upon enforcement of the International Convention on the Protection of the Rights of Migrant Workers and Members of Their Families (U.N.G.A. Res. 45/158, *reprinted* in 30 ILM 1517 (1991)). Also at issue is enforcement of the Universal Declaration of Human Rights (U.N.G.A. Res. 217 A (III), U.N. Doc. A/810, at 71 (1948)) and the American Convention on Human Rights (O.A.S. Treaty Ser., No. 36, O.A.S. Off Rec. OEA/Ser. L/V/II.23 doc. 21 rev. 6 (1979)).

235. Arguably, given the extent to which the U.S. "law enforcement" apparatus has been militarized over the past 20 years, its actions are subject to the provisions of the 1949 Geneva Convention IV Relative to Protection of Civilian Persons in Time of War. In addition to the sources cited in note 163, see Peter B. Kraska, ed., *Militarizing the American Criminal Justice System: The Changing Roles of the Armed Forces and the Police* (Boston: Northeastern University Press, 2001).

236. On Puerto Rico, see Fernandez, *Prisoners of Colonialism.* For further details, see Christina Duffy Burnett and Burke Marshall, eds., *Foreign in a Domestic Sense: Puerto Rico, American Expansionism, and the Constitution* (Chapel Hill, NC: Duke University Press, 2001). On Guam, see Robert F. Rogers, *Destiny's Landfall: A History of Guam* (Honolulu: University of Hawaii Press, 1995) esp. pp. 271-7.

237. For backdrop, Kent, Hawaii; the essays entitled "Stolen Kingdom: The Right of Hawai'i to Decolonization" and "Charades, Anyone? The Indian Claims Commission in Context," both in my *Perversions of Justice*, pp. 73-124, 125-52. Also see the essays collected in my *Struggle for the Land.*

238. A template of sorts is provided by Christopher Hitchens in his *The Trial of Henry Kissinger* (London: Verso, 2001). Under its 1993 Law Concerning Grave Breaches of International Humanitarian Law, Belgium quite properly asserted universal jurisdiction over such offenses, and therefore indicted former U.S. Pres. George H.W. Bush, now Vice Pres. Dick Cheney, now Sec. of State Colin Powell, and retired army Gen. Norman Schwartzkopf for war crimes committed during the 1991 Gulf War. More recently, when indictments were formulated against Pres. George W. Bush, Gen. Tommy Franks and others as a result of the 2003 war against Iraq, the U.S. threatened "severe diplomatic consequences." At that point, Belgium caved in, amending its law on May 7, 2003, quashing the current indictments, and relinquishing jurisdiction in the others; see Mike Wendling, "Belgium Scrambles to Change Law Before Potential Bush Indictment," *CNS News*, Mar. 26, 2003. On Milosevic, see Summary of *Milosevic v. The Netherlands* (The Hague Dist. Ct., KG 01/975), *International Law in Brief*, Aug. 31, 2001.

239. The U.S. has presently extracted agreements from 98 countries not to honor ICC extradition requests vis-à-vis its military personnel. As of July 1, 2003, it suspended aid to a further 35 countries until such time as they, too, accept such agreements; "U.S. Cuts Off 35 Nations Over World Criminal Court," *Washington Post*, July 2, 2003. The prospects for the ICC nonetheless look bright. On Oct. 10, 2001, the Council of Europe—composed of NATO members, which, along with Australia, Canada, New Zealand and selected other states, are statutorily exempt from U.S. sanctions—adopted the Declaration on the International Criminal Court, unequivocally endorsing it. As of mid-2002, 139 countries had signed the Rome Statute establishing the ICC, and 76—including most U.S. allies—had ratified treaties accepting its jurisdiction; "Q&A: The International Criminal Court," *BBC News*, July 13, 2002. Under such circumstances, it is unlikely that U.S. obstruction can be effectively sustained over the long run.

240. Although U.S. jurists habitually refuse to admit arguments based on international law into domestic proceedings, the notion that they are obliged to do so is hardly radical. Indeed, the obligation has been repeatedly conceded by the Supreme Court, as in its *Paquete Habana* opinion (175 U.S. at 700 (1900)): "International law is part of our law, and must be ascertained and administered by the courts of justice of appropriate jurisdiction, as often as questions of right depending upon it are duly presented for their determination. For this purpose, where there is no treaty, and no controlling executive act or judicial decision, resort must be had to the customs and usages of civilized nations." For explication, see Saito, "Asserting Plenary Power Over the 'Other'" and "Will Force Trump Legality After September 11? American Jurispudence Confronts the Rule of Law," *Georgetown Immigration Law Journal*, Vol. 17, 2003. On a different but related tack, see Francis Anthony Boyle, *Defending Civil Resistance Under International Law* (Dobbs Ferry, NY: Transnational, 1988).

241. Brian Martin, "Eliminating State Crime by Abolishing the State," in Ross, *State Crime*, pp. 389-417.

242. Gopal Balakrishnan, *The Enemy: An Intellectual Portrait of Carl Schmitt* (London: Verso, 2000) p. 35. For an interesting corroboration, coming from an entirely different direction, see Rahmattulah Kahn, "The Thickening Web of International Law," *Issues in Global Governance: Papers Written for the Commission on Global Governance* (New York: Kluwer Law International, 1995).

243. Carl Schmitt, *Über die drei Arten des rechtswissenschaftlichen Denkens* (Hamburg: HAVA, 1934) p. 17;

this conception of the state was set forth by Hegel in his *The Philosophy of Right*; Balakrishnan, *The Enemy*, p. 197. For further amplification of this theme, see Alexander B. Murphy, "International Law and the Sovereign State System: Challenges to the Status Quo," in George J. Demko and William B. Wood, eds., *Reordering the World: Geopolitical Perspectives on the 21st Century* (Boulder, CO: Westview Press, [2nd ed.] 1999) pp. 227-43. Another worthwhile read in this connection is Richard Falk's *Law in an Emerging Global Village: A Post-Westphalian Perspective* (Oxford, UK: Polity Press, 1998).

244. This was a prospect pointed out by Richard Falk fully 20 years ago, in a little-noticed essay entitled "Anarchism and World Order," included in his *The End of World Order: Essays in Normative International Relations* (New York: Holmes & Meier, 1983) pp. 277-98. Also see Herbert Read, *Anarchy and Order* (Boston: Beacon Press, 1971); William I. Robinson, *Promoting Polyarchy: Globalization, U.S. Intervention and Hegemony* (Cambridge, UK: Cambridge University Press, 1996); Harvey Starr, *Anarchy, Order, and Integration: How to Manage Interdependence* (Ann Arbor: University of Michigan Press, 1999). As an aside, it should be noted that, contrary to the corruptions of popular usage, the words "nation" and "state" are not synonymous. The first implies a "natural" human affinity, the second a centralized form of governance; see, e.g., Hugh Seton-Watson, *Nations and States: An Inquiry into the Origins of Nations and the Politics of Nationalism* (Boulder, CO: Westview Press, 1977). For application of the distinction in an indigenous context, see Bernard Nietschmann, "The Fourth World: Nations versus States," in George J. Demko and William B. Wood, eds., *Reordering the World: Geopolitical Perspectives on the 21st Century* (Boulder, CO: Westview Press, 1994) pp. 225-42; Ali A. Mazrui, *A World Federation of Cultures: An African Perspective* (New York: Free Press, 1976).

245. These are themes fruitfully explored by Leopold Kohr in his *The Breakdown of Nations* (New York: E.P. Dutton, 1975) and *The Overdeveloped Nations: The Diseconomies of Scale* (New York: Schocken Books, 1978). In both cases, by "nations," Kohr means "states." Other useful readings will be found in Howard J. Ehrlich, ed., *Reinventing Anarchy, Again* (San Francisco: AK Press, 1996) and John Borneman's *Subversions of International Order: Essays in the Political Anthropology of Culture* (Albany: SUNY Press, 1998).

246. The idea here goes far beyond that expounded by Hakim Bey in his useful but overly-celebrated *T.A.Z.: The Temporary Autonomous Zone* (Brooklyn, NY: Autonomedia, 1985, 1991). For elucidation of a range of more substantial models/concepts, see Melvyn Dubofsky, *We Shall Be All: A History of the IWW* (Chicago: Quadrangle, 1969); Pierre Clastres' *Society Against the State: The Leader as Servant and the Humane Uses of Power Among the Indians of the Americas* (New York: Urizen Books, 1977); Harold Barclay, *People Without Government: An Anthropology of Anarchism* (London: Kahn & Averill/Cienfuegos Press, 1982); Juan Gómez Casas, *Anarchist Organization: The History of the F-A-I* (Montréal: Black Rose Books, 1986). Among the better theoretical refutations of the notion that the state is in some sense necessary and other aspects of statist mythology are Ernst Cassirer's *The Myth of the State* (New Haven, CT: Yale University Press, 1946); Frank Harrison's *The Modern State* (Montréal: Black Rose Books, 1983) and Robert Paul Wolff's *In Defense of Anarchism* (Berkeley: University of California Press, [2nd ed.] 1998). Also see Kirkpatrick Sale, "The 'necessity of the state'," in Ehrlich, *Reinventing Anarchy*, pp. 38-55.

247. Statists tend to understand the reality of this dynamic, even if many anarchists do not; see the waking nightmares inscribed by Robert D. Kaplan in his *The Coming Anarchy: Shattering the Dreams of the Post Cold War* (New York: Random House, 2000).

248. It should be noted, first of all, that the U.S. took the lead role in formulating the legal doctrine applied at Nuremberg; Bradley F. Smith, *The Road to Nuremberg* (New York: Basic Books, 1981). Although U.S. Supreme Court Justice Robert H. Jackson, his country's lead prosecutor during the proceedings, disavowed the idea that it was intended "to incriminate the whole German people...the indictments were [by nature] directed against" the Germans in their collectivity. Somewhere between "a quarter and a half of the German population [was] involved in the indictments" of the Nazi Party, the SA, and the SS, and convicted of complicity in offenses against the peace and humanity after the tribunal concluded the evidence was sufficient to warrant their designation as "criminal organizations"; Eugene Davidson, *The Trial of the Germans, 1945-1946* (New York: Macmillan, 1966) pp. 7, 555-6. Jaspers' philosophical validation of the doctrine—which was adopted by the UN in its 1946 Affirmation of the Principles of International Law Recognized by the Nuremberg Tribunal (U.N.G.A. Res. 95 (I), U.N. Doc. A/236)—is even more sweeping, encompassing as it does virtually every German not demonstrably engaged in concrete resistance to the nazi régime; Karl Jaspers, E.B. Ashton and Joseph W. Koterski, *The Question of German Guilt* (New York: Fordham University Press, 2002 reprint of 1945 original). In any event, the U.S. is forever bound to the principles applied to the Germans by Justice Jackson's stipulation, advanced to counter defense objections that certain of the charges against the accused had no precedent, that, "We are not prepared to lay down a rule of criminal conduct against others which we are not willing to have invoked against us"; quoted in Bertrand Russell, *War Crimes in Vietnam* (New York: Monthly Review Press, 1967) p. 125.

249. For samples of the standard formulation, see Aaron B. Wildavsky, *Speaking Truth to Power: The Art and Craft of Policy Analysis* (New Brunswick, NJ: Transaction, 1987); Manning Marable, *Speaking Truth to Power: Essays on Race, Resistance and Radicalism* (Boulder, CO: Westview Press, 1998); Paul A. Bove, ed., *Edward Said and the Work of the Critic: Speaking Truth to Power* (Durham, NC: Duke University Press, 2000).

250. This is not intended rhetorically. Serious analysis has suggested that the term is clinically appropriate in describing certain heads of state, and may well be applicable to others; see Robert G.L. Waite, *The Psychopathic God: Adolf Hitler* (New York: Basic Books, 1977). Also see Walter C. Langer, *The Mind of Adolf Hitler* (New York: Basic Books, 1973); Richard A. Koenigsberg, *Hitler's Ideology: A Study in*

Psychoanalytic Psychology (New York: Library of Social Sciences, 1975). In juxtaposition, see the analysis offered in Jeffrey Kimball, *Nixon's Vietnam War* (Durham, NC: Duke University Press, 2002). More broadly, see Robert Jay Lifton and Eric Markusen, *The Genocidal Mentality: Nazi Holocaust and Nuclear Threat* (New York: Basic Books, 1990).

251. Witness the results of the highly effective campaign conducted by the Civil Rights Movement to register disenfranchised African American voters and obtain passage of the 1965 Voting Rights Act. By 1969, almost two-thirds of all eligible blacks had been registered, and, where in 1959 almost none held office, 1,125—994 men and 131 women—had been elected. By 1975, the number of Afroamerican elected officials had almost tripled, to 3,499—2,969 men and 530 women—including 18 members of the Congress, 281 state legislators and 135 mayors. During the period of this rather substantial electoral success, however, "the social and economic conditions for the [vast] majority of blacks remained the same, and in some respects grew worse"; Manning Marable, *Race, Reform and Rebellion: The Second Reconstruction in Black America, 1945-1982* (Jackson: University of Mississippi Press, 1984) pp. 134, 172-3. The trend was neither "anomalous" nor indicative of "normal lag time" in generating results. As of 1999, there were 8,936 black elected officials in the U.S.—a third of them women—including 39 members of Congress; "Number of black elected officials shows modest increase," Associated Press, Dec. 12, 2000. Yet the socioeconomic circumstances afflicting more than 80% of all African Americans remain as bad or worse than they were in 1965; see generally, Andrew Hacker, *Two Nations: Black and White, Separate, Hostile, and Unequal* (New York: Scribner's, 1992). As the saying goes, "If voting could change anything, it would be illegal."

252. This is, of course, one of the primary problems embodied in the sort of "Green" politics embodied in this country by Ralph Nader and Winona LaDuke, in Germany by Rudolph Bahro and the late Petra Kelly. What, exactly, might be expected of a newly-elected Pres. Nader other than an avalanche of constrictive regulations and statutes—that is, a tremendous reinforcement of statist control mechanisms—is a bit unclear. On the German Greens, who are rather more interesting than their U.S. counterparts, see Rudolph Bahro, *From Red to Green: Interviews with New Left Review* (London: Verso, 1984); Petra Kelly, *Fighting for Hope* (Boston: South End Press, 1984); Werner Hülsberg, *The German Greens: A Social and Political Profile* (London: Verso, 1988).

253. The sellout of organized labor may be dated from 1934, when, to secure statist legitimation, the leadership of most unions endorsed the Roosevelt administration's National Recovery Act, an initiative "designed to take control of the economy through a series of codes agreed on by management, labor, and the government, fixing prices and wages, limiting competition. From the first, the NRA was dominated by big businesses and served their interests." By the time the NRA was declared unconstitutional by the Supreme Court in 1935, the labor leadership had already accommodated itself to the Wagner Act, which guaranteed the right to organize in exchange for acceptance of sharp constraints upon the right to strike; Zinn, *People's History*, pp. 383, 386.

254. For the best—or at least most exhaustive—elaboration of the method/strategy underlying these and related tactics, see Gene Sharp's *The Politics of Nonviolent Action*, 3 vols. (Boston: Porter Sargent, 1973). For a comprehensive survey of applications in the U.S., see Staughton and Alice Lynd, eds., *Nonviolence in America: A Documentary History* (New York: Orbis, 1995).

255. The entirely reasonable proposition put forward by New Leftists during the late 1960s that campuses might serve as centers of both cadre organizing and a broader inculcation of revolutionary consciousness has plainly been used for purposes never intended by those who made it; Carl Davidson, *The New Radicals in the Multiversity and Other SDS Writings* (Chicago: Charles H. Kerr, 1990); Noam Chomsky, "The Responsibility of Intellectuals," in his *American Power and the New Mandarins* (New York: Pantheon, 1967) pp. 323-66. At the present juncture, the great majority of academic leftists appear to subscribe to the notion advanced by the celebrated "cultural theorist" Homi K. Bhabha that any form of concrete engagement must by definition be "counterproductive," and that writing/teaching are the only truly valid modes of revolutionary activity; Homi K. Bhabha, "Interrogating identity: Frantz Fanon and the postcolonial prerogative," in his *The Location of Culture* (New York: Routledge, 1994) pp. 40-65; "Remembering Fanon: Self, Psyche, and the Colonial Condition," in Nigel C. Gibson, ed., *Rethinking Fanon: The Continuing Dialogue* (Amherst, NY: Humanity Books, 1999) pp. 179-98. As Bart Moore-Gilbert points out, Bhabha consciously "inflates the critic's role at the expense of the obviously much more critical role played by both armed resistance and conventional forms of political organization in ending the system of formal imperialism and challenging the current system of neocolonialism"; *Postcolonial Theory*, p. 138. For similar critiques of Bhabha, see Aijaz Ahmad, *In Theory: Classes, Nations, Literatures* (London: Verso, 1992) esp. pp. 68-9; Neil Lazarus, "Disavowing Decolonization: Fanon, Nationalism, and the Problematic of Representation in Current Theories of Colonial Discourse," *Research in African Literatures*, Vol. 24, No. 2, 1993; Benita Parry, "Signs of Our Times: A Discussion of Homi Bhabha's The Location of Culture," *Third Text*, Nos. 28-9, 1994. For a broader, and very well shaped critique of academic leftism, see John Patrick Diggins, *The Rise and Fall of the American Left* (New York: W.W. Norton, [2nd ed.] 1992) pp. 279-306. Fortunately, a countering tendency has lately taken hold, which may serve to restore the potential the New Leftists had in mind. See, as examples, Cary Nelson, *Manifesto of a Tenured Radical* (New York: New York University Press, 1995); Henry A. Giroux, *Pedagogy and the Politics of Hope* (Boulder, CO: Westview Press, 1997); Peter McLaren, *Revolutionary Multiculturalism: Pedagogies for Dissent in the New Millennium* (Boulder, CO: Westview Press, 1997); Linda Tuhiwai Smith in her *Decolonizing Methodologies: Research and Indigenous Peoples* (London/Dunedin: Zed Books/University of Otago Press, 1999); Arundhati Roy, *Power Politics* (Cambridge, MA: South End Press, 2001) esp. the statement offered at pp. 11-2. Overall, the "good stuff," both in the 1960s and now, conforms rather closely to the values/methods described

by the late Paulo Freire in his *Pedagogy of the Oppressed* (New York: Herder and Herder, 1972) and *Education for Critical Consciousness* (New York: Continuum, 1982).

256. The concept is Gramscian in origin, although it has become thoroughly garbled in its current applications. On the original intent, see *Antonio Gramsci: Selections from Political Writings, 1910-1920* (New York: International, 1977). Also see Carl Boggs, *The Two Revolutions: Gramsci and the Dilemmas of Western Marxism* (Boston: South End Press, 1984) esp. pp. xi, 8, 107-8, 246, 276, 289-91.

257. See, e.g., J. Claude Evans, *Strategies of Deconstruction: Derrida and the Myth of the Voice* (Minneapolis: University of Minnesota Press, 1991); John Ellis, *Against Deconstruction* (Princeton, NJ: Princeton University Press, 1989).

258. For two of the best overviews of the field, see Bart Moore-Gilbert, *Postcolonial Theory: Contexts, Practices, Politics* (London: Verso, 1997); Robert J.C. Young, *Postcolonialism: An Historical Introduction* (London: Blackwell, 2001). For critique, see Anne McClintock, "The Angel of Progress: Pitfalls of the Term 'Post-colonialism'," in Patricia Williams and Laura Chrisman, eds., *Colonial Discourse/Post-Colonial Theory: A Reader* (New York: Columbia University Press, 1994) pp. 291-304; Stuart Hall, "When was 'the Post-colonial'? Thinking at the Limits," in Iain Chambers and Lidia Curti, eds., *The Post-Colonial Question: Common Skies/Divided Horizons* (London: Routledge, 1996) pp. 242-60; Arif Dirlick, *The Postcolonial Aura* (Boulder, CO: Westview Press, 1997).

259. Although I take issue with his formulation in some respects, I find I have to align to a considerable extent with the argument advanced by Murray Bookchin in his *Social Anarchism or Lifestyle Anarchism: An Unbridgeable* Chasm (San Francisco: AK Press, 1995). As to "The Hierarchy," I share Terry Eagleton's view that it "is a mistake to confuse hierarchy with elitism... 'Hierarchy,' a term which originally denoted the three categories of angels, has come to mean any kind of graduated structure, not necessarily a social one. In its broadest sense, it refers to something like an order of priorities. In this broad sense, everyone is a hierarchist, whereas not everyone is an elitist. Indeed, you [undoubtedly] object to elites because they offend your order of priorities... As Charles Taylor puts it, 'To know who you are is to be oriented in moral space, a space in which questions arise about what is good and bad, what is worth doing and what is not, what has meaning and importance for you and what is trivial and secondary'... [In effect,] radical politics is necessarily hierarchical in outlook, needing some way of calculating the most effective distribution of its limited energies over a range of issues. It assumes...that some issues are more important than others, that some places are preferable starting-points to other places, that some struggles are central to a particular form of life and others are not"; Terry Eagleton, *The Illusions of Postmodernism* (Oxford, UK: Blackwell, 1996) pp. 93-5; quoting Charles Taylor, *Sources of the Self* (Cambridge, UK: Cambridge University Press, 1989) p. 28.

260. Among the leading antismoking groups is "Action on Smoking and Health" (ASH), an outfit that has grossly distorted or fabricated virtually every piece of "data" it's released over the past decade and openly advocated such tactics as injecting cyanide into the cigarettes of unwary smokers. The records of organizations like "Americans for Nonsmokers Rights" (ANR) and "Group Against Smokers' Pollution" (GASP) are no better on the information front. Suffice it to observe that if the antismoking lobby—funded, as it is, in large part by evil pharmaceutical cartels—had anything resembling a valid case to make, it wouldn't have to lie about it so consistently. For a perfect crystallization of the mentality at issue here, see Patrick Griffin, *Let's Ban Smoking Outright! OK, It's a Stupid, Fascist, Unnecessary, Unworkable, Historically Discredited Idea, but, Besides That, What's Wrong With It?* (Berkeley, CA: Ten Speed Press, 1995).

262. On Hitler's election, see, e.g., Joachim C. Fest, *Hitler* (New York: Harcourt Brace Jovanovich, 1973) pp. 299-326. On his vegetarianism and pathological aversion to smoking, see Waite, *Psychopathic God*, pp. 19, 27, 154; Ian Kershaw, *Hitler, 1889-1936*: Hubris (New York: W.W. Norton, 1999) pp. 261-2, 343. On his preoccupation with ecology, see Robert A. Pois, *National Socialism and the Religion of Nature* (London: Croom Helm, 1986); Janet Biehl and Peter Staudemaier, *Eocofascism: Lessons from the German Experience* (San Francisco: AK Press, 1995). On his preoccupation with Eastern mysticism, see Nicholas Goodrick-Clarke, *Hitler's Priestess: Savitri Devi, the Hindu-Aryan Myth, and Neo-Nazism* (New York: New York University Press, 1998). On his preoccupation with the occult, see Louis Pauwels and Jacques Bergier, *The Morning of the Magicians* (New York: Stein and Day, 1964); Jean Michael Angebert, *The Occult and the Third Reich: The Mystical Origins of Nazism and the Search for the Holy Grail* (New York: Macmillan, 1974); Nicholas Goodrick-Clarke, *The Occult Roots of Nazism: Secret Aryan Cults and Their Influence on Nazi Ideology* (New York: New York University Press, 1994).

263. The late Stokely Carmichael (Kwame Turé) once explained to me that, although he didn't believe voting could accomplish anything constructive, and had therefore never voted in his life, he'd been arrested 38 times and done time on Parchman Farm for insisting upon the right of rural blacks in the Deep South to vote. The reason, he said, was to demonstrate to those denied the right that they didn't have to take "no" for an answer, not with regard to voting, or by extension, with regard to anything else. The sense of both personal and group empowerment embodied in the first lesson, he believed, led to an ability to realize actual power with the second. The issue of voting was thus important, although voting itself was not. The approach is partially revealed in Carmichael's and Charles V. Hamilton's *Black Power: The Politics of Liberation in America* (New York: Vintage, 1967). Also see Clayborne Carson, *In Struggle: SNCC and the Black Awakening of the 1960s* (Cambridge, MA: Harvard University Press, 1981); James Forman, *The Making of Black Revolutionaries* (Seattle: University of Washington Press, 1997 reprint of 1972 original).

264. At issue is the theme of cooptation, a theme explored rather well by Marcuse in his essay, "Repressive Tolerance," in Robert Paul Wolff, Barrington Moore, Jr., and Herbert Marcuse, *A Critique of Pure Tolerance* (Boston: Beacon Press, [2nd ed.] 1969) pp. 81-123. Also see Marcuse's *An Essay on Liberation*

(Boston: Beacon Press, 1969).

265. The seminal exploration of this polarity was offered by Georg Lukács in the collection of essays enti- tled *History and Class Consciousness: Studies in Marxist Dialectics* (Cambridge, MA: MIT Press, 1971 trans. of 1922 original). Also see Joseph Gabel, *False Consciousness: An Essay on Reification* (New York: Harper Torchbooks, 1975).

266. Marcuse is again instructive; see his *Essay on Liberation and Counter-Revolution and Revolt* (Boston: Beacon Press, 1972).

267. To offer but one sample quote from the myriad, "extermination of the Jews [is] the most intolerable part of Hitler's legacy"; George Victor, "Foreword," in William H. Schmaltz, *Hate: George Lincoln Rockwell and the American Nazi Party* (Washington, D.C.: Brassey's, 1999) p. xi. The mainstays underpinning this emphasis are Raul Hilberg's *The Destruction of the European Jews* (Chicago: Quadrangle, 1961) and Lucy S. Dawidowicz's *The War Against the Jews* (New York: Free Press, [2nd ed.] 1985).

268. The great bulk of these fatalities—as many as 27 million—where, under their Generalplan Ost, the nazis pursued an outright war of extermination; G.F. Krivosheev, ed., *Soviet Casualties and Battle Losses in the Twentieth Century* (London: Greenhill Books, 1997) pp.83- 280. For backdrop, see Barry Leach, *German Strategy Against Russia, 1939-1941* (Oxford, UK: Clarendon Press, 1973) pp. 63-123; Alexander Dallin, *German Rule in Russia, 1941-1945* (New York: St. Martin's, 1957).

269. Donald Kendrick and Grattan Puxon, *Gypsies Under the Swastika* (Hertfordshire, UK: University of Hertfordshire Press, 1995); Guenter Lewy, *The Nazi Persecution of the Gypsies* (New York: Oxford University Press, 2000).

270. See generally, Michael Berenbaum, ed., *A Mosaic of Victims: Non-Jews Persecuted and Murdered by the Nazis* (New York: New York University Press, 1990); Edward L. Homze, *Foreign Labor in Nazi Germany* (Princeton, NJ: Princeton University Press, 1967). It should be noted that the death rate in the infamous nazi concentration/labor camp at Dachau was 36%. At Buchenwald, another notorious example, it was 19%. At Mauthausen, "the harshest...of all the concentration camps," the death rate was 58 %; Michael Burleigh, *Ethics and Extermination: Reflections on the Nazi Genocide* (Cambridge, UK: Cambridge University Press) p. 211. Before Americans begin to cluck too loudly on the matter, however, not one prisoner is known to have survived a 10-year sentence under Mississippi's convict leasing system, which prevailed from 1866 to1890; David M. Oshinsky, *"Worse Than Slavery": Parchman Farm and the Ordeal of Jim Crow Justice* (New York: Free Press, 1996) p. 46. Also see Matthew J. Mancini, *One Dies, Get Another: Convict Leasing in the American South, 1866-1928* (Columbia: University of South Carolina Press, 1996); Alex Lichtenstein, *Twice the Work of Free Labor: The Political Economy of Convict Labor in the New South* (London: Verso, 1996).

271. The barriers against employing the military for domestic policing purposes that prevailed under the 1877 Posse Comitatus Act (18 USC § 1385) began to be seriously eroded with the advent of Ronald Reagan's "War on Drugs" during the mid-1980s (see the amendments codified at 10 USC § 371 and 32 USC § 112). More ominous still is a classified protocol, adopted by Reagan and referred to as the "Praetor Guideline," under which the chief executive has claimed the self-assigned "discretion" to sim- ply—and secretly—"waive" statutory constraints altogether, employing élite military units like the Army's Delta Force to "neutralize" selected domestic targets; David T. Hardy with Rex Kimball, *This is Not an Assault: Penetrating the Web of Official Lies Regarding the Waco Incident* (San Antonio, TX: Xlibris, 2001) p. 85.

272. If war, as Clausewitz famously put it, is "policy by other means," then politics are war by other means and thus subject to the principles set for by Sun Tsu in his classic, *The Art of War* (Blue Unicorn Editions, 1998). For development of the idea, see Che Guevara, *Guerrilla Warfare* (New York: Vintage, 1961); Robert Taber, *The War of the Flea: The Classic Study of Guerrilla Warfare* (Dulles, VA: Brassey's, 2002 reprint of 1965 original) pp. 149-72. Also see Abraham Guillén, *Philosophy of the Urban Guerrilla* (New York: William Morrow, 1973); Carlos Marighella, *Mini-Manual of the Urban Guerrilla* (Boulder, CO: Paladin Press, 1985 reprint of 1967 original). For the complete formulation on law/politics, see Carl von Clausewitz, *On War* (Princeton, NJ: Princeton University Press, 1976) p. 87.

273. See generally, Bill Ayers, "A Strategy to Win," in Harold Jacobs, ed., *Weatherman* (San Francisco: Ramparts Press, 1970) pp. 183-95. Bearing in mind that that the object is to separate wheat from chaff, a good initial selection of background readings includes Régis Debray, *Revolution in the Revolution? Armed Struggle and Political Struggle in Latin America* (New York: Grove Press, 1967); Gérard Chaliand, *Armed Struggle in Africa: With the Guerrillas in "Portuguese" Guinea* (New York: Monthly Review Press, 1969); James Robert Ross, ed., *The War Within: Violence or Nonviolence in the Black Revolution* (New York: Sheed and War, 1971); George L. Jackson, *Blood in My Eye* (New York: Random House, 1972); Maria Esther Gilio, *The Tupamaros Guerrillas: The Structure and Strategy of the Urban Guerrilla Movement* (New York: Saturday Review Press, 1972); Vin McClellan and Paul Avery, *The Voices of Guns* (New York: G.P. Putnam's Sons, 1977); J. Bowyer Bell, *Terror Out of Zion: The Shock Troops of Israeli Independence* (New York: Discus, 1977); Alessandro Silj, *Never Again Without a Rifle: The Origins of Italian Terrorism* (New York: Karz, 1979); John Castelluci, *The Big Dance* (New York: Dodd, Mead, 1986); Joseba Zulaika, *Basque Violence: Metaphor and Sacrament* (Reno: University of Nevada Press, 1988); Jim Fletcher, Tanaquil Jones and Sylvère Lotringer, *Still Black, Still Strong: Survivors of the U.S. War Against Black Revolutionaries* (Brooklyn, NY: Semiotext(e), 1993); Hala Jaber, *Hezbollah: Born with a Vengeance* (New York: Columbia University Press, 1997); Daniel Castro, *Revolution and Revolutionaries: Guerrilla Movements in Latin America* (Wilmington, DE: SR Books, 1999); Ciaran de Baroid, *Ballymurphy and the Irish War* (London: Pluto Press, [rev. ed.] 2000); Shaul Mishal and Avraham Sela, *The Palestinian Hamas: Vision, Violence, and Coexistence* (New York: Columbia University Press, 2000); Jalil Muntaqim, *We Are Our Own Liberators: Selected Prison Writings*

(Toronto: Arm the Spirit/Abraham Guillen Press, 2003); Hans Joachim Klein, *The German guerrilla: terror, reaction, and resistance* (Minneapolis: Soil of Liberty, n.d.).

274. Most of this comes through some rather profound misinterpretations/deliberate distortions of Gandhi. First of all, Gandhi himself displayed some rather serious departures from reality. "Civil disobedience as a strategy of political opposition can succeed only with a government ruled by conscience. In 1938, after Kristallnacht, when Gandhi advised the Jews in Germany to employ *Satyagraha*, the Indian version of passive resistance, he disclosed his inability to distinguish between English and German political morality"; Dawidowicz, *War Against the Jews*, p. 274. Second, the "purity" of Gandhi's own views on nonviolence were hardly those typically attributed to him by proponents in the U.S. Consider the following: " I do believe that, where there is only a choice between cowardice and violence, I would advise violence. Thus when my eldest son asked me what he should have done, had he been present when I was almost fatally assaulted in 1908, whether he should have run away and seen me killed or whether he should have used his physical force which he could or wanted to use, and defend me, I told him that it was his duty to defend me even by using violence"; Krishna Kripalani, *All Men Are Brothers: Life and Thoughts of Mahatma Gandhi as Told in His Own Words* (Ahmedabad: Navajina, 1950) p. 138. Or try these: "my creed of non-violence not only does not preclude me but compels me to associate with anarchists and all who believe in violence" (p. 108); "taking life may be a duty...even man-slaughter may be necessary in certain cases" (p. 121); "In life, it is impossible to eschew violence completely. Now the question arises, where is one to draw the line? The line cannot be the same for every one" (p. 121); "[I would rather] risk violence a thousand times than the emasculation of an entire race" (p. 135); "I would rather have Indian resort to arms [than] remain a helpless witness to her own dishonour" (p. 138). For these reasons he openly advocated "training in arms," not only "for those who believe in the method of violence," but even for those embracing nonviolence as a method (p. 138). This was because "*non-violence presupposes ability to strike. It is a conscious, deliberate restraint*" adopted by people fully capable of dispensing violence in the same manner it is dispensed by their opponents/oppressors (emphasis added; p. 134).

275. This goes to the time-honored practice of the U.S. "peace movement" in professing "solidarity" with those engaged in armed struggle elsewhere—notably Vietnam, El Salvador and Nicaragua—while itself avoiding all forms of confrontation involving serious physical risk. See my and Mike Ryan's *Pacifism as Pathology: Reflections on the Role of Armed Struggle in North America* (Winnipeg: Arbeiter Ring, 1998).

276. See George Breitman, ed., *By Any Means Necessary: Speeches, Interviews, and a Letter* (New York: Pathfinder Press, 1970); the interview with Les Crane published as "Whatever is Necessary to Defend Ourselves," in Bruce Perry, ed., *Malcolm X: The Last Speeches* (New York: Pathfinder Press, 1989) esp. p. 88. For a useful survey of ways in which the idea took hold, see Peter Stansill and David Zane Mairowitz, eds., *BAMN [by any means necessary]: Outlaw Manifestos & Ephemera, 1965-1970* (Brooklyn, NY: Autonomedia, 1999 reprint of 1971 original).

277. Although it achieved a number of breakthrough insights, this was a fundamental error in the organizing strategy adopted by the RYM I faction of SDS; see Ron Jacobs, *The Way the Wind Blew: A History of the Weather Underground* (London: Verso, 1997) esp. pp. 24-65.

278. This is the precondition for the kind of positive outcome called for by most analysts; see, as examples, Falk, *Beyond World Order*, pp. 299-314; Bennis, *Calling the Shots*, pp. 233-49; Taupp. Inclusionary Governance, pp. 462-5. Also see the interview of Noam Chomsky by David Barsamian published in *Monthly Review* (Vol. 53, No. 6, 2001) under the title "The United States is a Leading Terrorist State."

279. On the Soviet unraveling, see Alexander J. Notyl, ed., *The Post-Soviet Nations: Perspectives on the Demise of the USSR* (New York: Columbia University Press, 1992). That the same devolutionary potential existed in the U.S. during the late-60s peak of resistance to business as usual, is evident in the very title of William L. O'Neill's *Coming Apart: An Informal History of America in the 1960s* (Chicago: Quadrangle, 1971). Unfortunately, far too many radicals opted to embrace one or another explicitly statist "solution" to the problems posed by the American state, thus squandering the momentum that had been attained; see Max Elbaum, *Revolution in the Air: Sixties Radicals turn to Lenin, Mao and Che* (London: Verso, 2002). Among those who didn't, and who as a consequence began to lay a theoretical groundwork for a popular resurgence of the devolutionary impulse, were Murray Bookchin, *Post-Scarcity Anarchism* (San Francisco: Ramparts Books, 1971), André Gorz, *Farewell to the Working Class: An Essay on Post-Industrial Socialism* (Boston: South End Press, 1982), Raoul Vaneigem (see his *The Revolution of Every Day Life* (Seattle: Left Bank Books, [2nd ed.] 1994)), and John Zerzan (see his *Elements of Refusal* (Columbia, MO: CAL Press/Paleo Editions, [2nd ed.] 1999)).

280. "Most people think it impossible for guerrillas to exist for long in the enemy's rear. Such a belief lacks comprehension of the relationship that should exist between the people and the troops. The former may be likened to water and the latter to the fish who inhabit it"; Robert B. Asprey, *War in the Shadows: The Guerrilla in History* (Garden City, NY: Doubleday, 1975) p. 360; quoting Mao Tse-tung, *On Guerrilla Warfare* (New York: Praeger, 1962).

281. See generally, Diggins, *Rise and Fall of the American Left*; Christopher Lasch, *The Agony of the American Left* (New York: Alfred A. Knopf, 1966); David Zain Mairowitz, *The Radical Soap Opera* (New York: Discus Books, 1974).

282. At issue, of course, is the Gramscian conception of hegemony; see Boggs, *Two Revolutions*, pp. 153-98; Walter L. Adamson, *Hegemony and Revolution: A Study of Antonio Gramsci's Political and Cultural Theory* (Berkeley: University of California Press, 1980) pp. 170-9.

283. Marcuse, "Repressive Tolerance," p. 111.

284. As Derrida put it, "We must do and think the impossible. If only the possible happened, nothing would happen. If I only did what I can do, I wouldn't do anything"; see "No One is Innocent: A Discussion with

Jacques Derrida About Philosophy in the Face of Terror" *The Information Technology War and Peace Project*, 2 (www.watsoninstitute.org/infopeace/911/derrida_innocence.html). On the formulation's place within the anarchist tradition, see Peter Marshall, *Demanding the Impossible: A History of Anarchism* (London: Fontana Press, 1992). On French student usage, see Allan Priaulx and Sanford J. Ungar, *The Almost Revolution: France-1968* (New York: Dell, 1969); Open Assembly of June 13-14, 1968, "The Appeal from the Sorbonne," in Carl Oglesby, ed., *The New Left Reader* (New York: Grove Press, 1969) pp. 267-73; George Katsiaficas, *The Imagination of the New Left: A Global Analysis of 1968* (Boston: South End Press, 1987) pp. 87-116.

Sources Used in Preparing the Chronologies

Adams, Nina S., and Alfred W. McCoy, eds., *Laos: War and Revolution* (New York: Harper Torchbooks, 1970).

Ali, Tariq, ed., *Masters of the Universe? NATO's Balkan Crusade* (London: Verso, 2000).

Alperovitz, Gar, *Atomic Diplomacy: Hiroshima and Potsdam—The Use of the Atomic Bomb and the American Confrontation with Soviet Power* (New York: Vintage, 1967).

Andrist, Ralph K., *The Long Death: The Last Days of the Plains Indian* (New York: Macmillan, 1964).

Arnove, Anthony, ed., *Iraq Under Siege: The Deadly Impact of Sanctions and War* (Cambridge, MA: South End Press, 2000).

Aruti, Naseer, ed., *Palestinian Refugees: The Right of Return* (London: Pluto Press, 2001).

Association of Concerned African Scholars, *U.S. Military Involvement in Southern Africa* (Boston: South End Press, 1978).

Axelrod, Alan, *Chronicle of the Indian Wars from Colonial Times to Wounded Knee* (New York: Prentice Hall, 1993).

Baird, Jay W., ed., *From Nuremberg to My Lai* (Lexington, MA: D.C. Heath, 1972).

Ball, Howard, *Justice Downwind: America's Atomic Testing Program in the 1950s* (New York: Oxford University Press, 1986).

Bamford, James, *Body of Secrets: Anatomy of the Ultra-Secret National Security Agency* (New York: Anchor Books, 2002).

Barker, Peter, *Operation Cold Chop: The Coup that Toppled Nkrumah* (Accra: Ghana Publishing Corp., 1966).

Barkman, Elazar, *The Guilt of Nations: Restitution and Negotiating Historical Injustices* (New York: W.W. Norton, 2000).

Barnet, Richard J., and Ronald E. Müller, *Global Reach: The Power of the Multinational Corporations* (New York: Touchstone Books, 1974).

Beit-Hallahmi, Bejamin, *The Israeli Connection: Who Israel Arms and Why* (New York: Pantheon, 1987).

Bell, J. Bowyer, *Terror Out of Zion: The Shock Troops of Israeli Independence* (New York: Discus, 1977).

Bennis, Phyllis, *Calling the Shots: How Washington Dominates Today's UN* (New York: Olive Branch Press, 2000).

————, "Veto," *The Link*, Vol. 36, No. 1, Jan.–Mar. 2003.

Benvenisti, Eyal, *The International Law of Occupation* (Princeton, NJ: Princeton University Press, 1993).

Blum, William, *The CIA: A Forgotten History* (London: Zed Books, 1986).

_____, *Rogue State: A Guide to the World's Only Remaining Superpower* (Monroe, ME: Common Courage Press, 2000).

Bolger, Daniel P., *Savage Peace: Americans at War in the 1990s* (San Francisco: Presidio Press, 1995).

Brackman, Arnold C., *The Other Nuremberg: The Untold Story of the Tokyo War Crimes Trials* (New York: Quill-Morrow, 1987).

Brownlie, Ian, ed., *Basic Documents on Human Rights* (Oxford, UK: Clarendon Press, [3rd ed.] 1992).

Buchheit, Lee, *Secession: The Legitimacy of Self-Determination* (New Haven, CT: Yale University Press, 1978).

Burnett, Christine Duffy, and Burke Marshall, eds., *Foreign in a Domestic Sense: Puerto Rico, American Expansion, and the Constitution* (Durham, NC: Duke University Press, 2001).

Byers, Michael, *Custom, Power and the Power of Rules: International Relations and Customary International Law* (Cambridge, UK: Cambridge University Press, 1999).

Chaliand, Gerard, ed., *A People Without a Country: The Kurds and Kurdistan* (New York: Olive Branch Press, [2nd ed.] 1993).

Carey, Roane, ed., *The New Intifada: Resisting Israel's Apartheid* (London: Verso, 2001).

Chomsky, Noam, *For Reasons of State* (New York: Vintage, 1973).

_____, *Towards a New Cold War: Essays on the Current Crisis and How We Got There* (New York: Pantheon, 1979).

_____, *The Fateful Triangle: The United States, Israel and the Palestinians* (Boston: South End Press, 1983).

_____, *The Culture of Terrorism* (Boston: South End Press, 1988).

_____, *Deterring Democracy* (New York: Hill & Wang, 1991).

_____, *The New Military Humanism: Lessons from Kosovo* (Monroe, ME: Common Courage Press, 1999).

_____, *Rogue States: The Rule of Force in International Affairs* (Cambridge, MA: South End Press, 2000).

_____, *9-11* (New York: Seven Stories Press, 2001).

Churchill, Ward, *Struggle for the Land: Native North American Resistance to Genocide, Ecocide and Colonization* (San Francisco: City Lights, [2nd ed.] 2003).

_____, *Perversions of Justice: Indigenous Peoples and Angloamerican Law* (San Francisco: City Lights, 2003).

Churchill, Ward, and Jim Vander Wall, *The COINTELPRO Papers: Documents from the FBI's Secret Wars Against Dissent in the United States* (Cambridge, MA: South End Press, [Classics Ed.] 2002).

Churchill, Ward, and J.J. Vander Wall, eds., *Cages of Steel: The Politics of Imprisonment in the United States* (Washington, D.C.: Maisonneuve Press, 1992).

Citizens Commission of Inquiry, eds., *The Dellums Committee Hearings on War Crimes in Vietnam: An Inquiry into Command Responsibility in Southeast Asia* (New York: Vintage, 1972).

Clark, Ramsey, et al., *War Crimes: A Report on United States War Crimes Against Iraq* (Washington, D.C.: Maisonneuve Press, 1992).

Cohen, Avner, *Israel and the Bomb* (New York: Columbia University Press, 1998).

Cole, David, and James X. Dempsey, *Terrorism and the Constitution: Sacrificing Civil Liberties in the Name of National Security* (New York: New Press, [2nd ed.] 2002).

Collier, Ellen C., *Instances of Use of United States Armed Forces Abroad, 1798-1989* (Washington, D.C.: Congressional Research Service, 1989).

Collins, John M., *America's Small Wars* (McLean, VA: Brassey's, 1991).

Cooley, John K., *Unholy Wars: Afghanistan, America and International Terrorism* (London: Pluto Press, 1999).

Crawford, James, *The Creation of States in International Law* (Oxford: Clarendon Press, 1979).

Creighton Miller, Stuart, *"Benevolent Assimilation": The American Conquest of the Philippines, 1899-1903* (New Haven, CT: Yale University Press, 1982).

Davidson, Eugene, *The Trial of the Germans: Nuremberg, 1945-1946* (New York: Macmillan, 1966).

Dinges, John, and Saul Landau, *Assassination on Embassy Row* (New York: Pantheon, 1980).

Dominico, Roy Palmer, *Italian Fascists on Trial, 1943-1948* (Chapel Hill: University of North Carolina Press, 1991).

Dower, John W., *War Without Mercy: Race and Power in the Pacific War* (New York: Pantheon, 1986).

Duffet, John, ed., *Against the Crime of Silence: Proceedings of the International War Crimes Tribunal* (New York: Clarion Books, 1970).

Falk, Richard, *Human Rights and State Sovereignty* (New York: Holmes and Meier, 1981).

_____, *Predatory Globalization: A Critique* (Cambridge, UK: Polity Press, 1999).

Falk, Richard, ed., *The Vietnam War and International Law* (Princeton, NJ: Princeton University Press, 1968).

Feher, Michel, *Powerless by Design: The Age of the International Community* (Durham, NC: Duke University Press, 2000).

Fisher, Jo, *Mothers of the Disappeared* (Boston: South End Press, 1989).

Flounders, Sara, ed., *NATO in the Balkans: Voices of the Opposition* (New York: International Action Ctr., 1998).

Franklin, H. Bruce, *M.I.A., or Mythmaking in America* (Brooklyn, NY: Lawrence Hill, 1992).

_____, *Vietnam and Other American Fantasies* (Amherst: University of Massachusetts Press, 2000).

Friedman, Alan, *Spider's Web: The Secret History of How the White House Illegally Armed Iraq* (New York: Bantam, 1993).

Gavel, Mike, ed., *The Pentagon Papers: The Defense Department History of United States Decisionmaking on Vietnam*, 5 vols. (Boston: Beacon Press, 1971).

Goldstein, Robert Justin, *Political Repression in Modern America, 1870 to the Present* (Cambridge/New York: Schenkman/Two Continents, 1978).

Hannum, Hurst, *Autonomy, Sovereignty and Self-Determination* (Philadelphia: University of Pennsylvania Press, 1990).

Hardy, David T., with Rex Kimball, *This Is Not An Assault: Penetrating the Web of Official Lies Regarding the Waco Incident* (San Antonio, TX: Xlibris, 2001).

Harris, Sheldon H., *Factories of Death: Japanese Biological Warfare, 1932-45, and the American Cover-Up* (New York: Routledge, 1994).

Harsch, Ernest, and Tony Thomas, *Angola: The Hidden History of Washington's War* (New York: Pathfinder Press, 1976).

Herivel, Tara, and Paul Wright, eds., *Prison Nation: The Warehousing of America's Poor* (New York: Routledge, 2003).

Herman, Edward S., *The Real Terror Network: Terrorism in Fact and Propaganda* (Boston: South End Press, 1982).

Hersh, Seymour M., *The Samson Option: Israel's Nuclear Arsenal and U.S. Foreign Policy* (New York: Random House, 1991).

Higginbotham, A. Leon, Jr., *Shades of Freedom: Racial Politics and the Presumptions of the American Legal Process* (New York: Oxford University Press, 1996).

Hinkle, Warren, and William Turner, *The Fish is Red: The Story of the Secret War Against Castro* (New York: Harper & Row, 1981).

Howard, Michael, George J. Andropolous and Mark R. Shurman, eds., *The Laws of War: Constraints on Warfare in the Western World* (New Haven, CT: Yale University Press, 1994).

Hoyt, Edwin P., *America's Wars and Military Incursions* (New York: McGraw-Hill, 1987).

Independent Commission of Inquiry on the U.S. Invasion of Panama, *The U.S. Invasion of Panama: The Truth Behind Operation "Just Cause"* (Boston: South End Press, 1991).

Keddie, Nikki R., *Roots of Revolution: An Interpretive History of Modern Iran* (New Haven, CT: Yale University Press, 1981).

Kent, Noel J., *Hawaii: Islands Under the Influence* (Honolulu: University of Hawaii Press, [2nd ed.] 1993).

Klare, Michael T., *Beyond the "Vietnam Syndrome": U.S. Intervention in the 1980s* (Washington, D.C.: IPS Books, 1981).

_____, *The American Arms Supermarket* (Austin: University of Texas Press, 1984).

Klare, Michael, and Peter Kornbluh, eds., *Low Intensity Warfare: Counterinsurgency, Proinsurgency and Antiterrorism in the Eighties* (New York: Pantheon, 1988).

Korman, Sharon, *The Right of Conquest: The Acquisition of Territory in International Law and Practice* (Oxford, UK: Clarendon Press, 1996).

Langguth, A.J., *Hidden Terrors: The Truth About U.S. Police Operations in Latin America* (New York: Pantheon, 1978).

LeBlanc, Lawrence J., *The United States and the Genocide Convention* (Durham, NC: Duke University Press, 1991).

Lee, Martin A,, and Bruce Shlain, *Acid Dreams: The Complete Social History of LSD: The CIA, the Sixties, and Beyond* (New York: Grove Press, 1992).

Lens, Sidney, *The Forging of the American Empire* (New York: Thomas Y. Crowell, 1971).

Leonard, Richard, *South Africa at War: White Power and the Crisis in Southern Africa* (Westport, CT: Lawrence Hill, 1983).

Lewallen, John, *Ecology of Devastation: Indochina* (New York: Penguin, 1970).

Lockman, Zachary, and Joel Beinin, eds., *Intifada: The Palestinian Uprising Against Israeli Occupation* (Boston: South End Press, 1989).

Maclear, Michael, *The Ten Thousand Day War: Vietnam, 1945-1975* (New York: St. Martin's Press, 1981).

MacKenzie, Angus, *Secrets: The CIA's War at Home* (Berkeley: University of California Press, 1999).

Marks, John, *The Search for the "Manchurian Candidate": The CIA and Mind Control* (New York: W.W. Norton, 1979).

Masalha, Nur, *Imperial Israel and the Palestinians: The Politics of Expansion* (London: Pluto Press, 2000).

McCoy, Alfred W., with Cathleen B. Read and Leonard O. Adams, II, *The Politics of Heroin in Southeast Asia* (New York: Harper Torchbooks, 1972).

Meron, Theodor, *Human Rights and Humanitarian Norms as Customary Law* (Oxford, UK: Clarendon Press, 1989).

Molina, Alejandro Luis, ed., *USA on Trial: The International Tribunal on Indigenous Peoples and Oppressed Nations in the United States* (Chicago: Editorial El Coquí, 1996).

Morris, Benny, *The Birth of the Palestinian Refugee Problem, 1947-1949* (Cambridge, UK: Cambridge University Press, 1987).

Myers, Desaix, III, *U.S. Business in South Africa: The Economic, Political, and Moral Issues* (Bloomington: Indiana University Press, 1980).

Nincic, Djura, *The Problem of Sovereignty in the Charter and Practice of the United Nations* (The Hague: Marinus Nijhoff, 1979).

Olshansky, Barbara, *Secret Trials and Executions: Military Tribunals and the Threat to Democracy* (New York: Seven Stories Press, 2002).

O'Shaughnessy, Hugh, *Pinochet: The Politics of Torture* (New York: NYU Press, 2000).

Plaster, John L., *SOG: The Secret Wars of America's Commandos in Vietnam* (New York: Simon & Schuster, 1997).

Pomerance, Michla, *Self-Determination in Law and Practice* (The Hague: Marinus Nijhoff, 1982).

Pomeroy, William J., *Apartheid, Imperialism, and African Freedom* (New York: International, 1986).

Prados, John, *The President's Secret Wars: CIA and Pentagon Covert Operations from World War II through Iranscam* (New York: William Morrow, [2nd. ed.] 1986).

Rai, Milan, *War Plan Iraq: Ten Reasons Against War on Iraq* (London: Verso, 2002).

Raneleigh, John, *The Agency: The Rise and Decline of the CIA* (New York: Touchstone, 1987).

Rashid, Ahmed, *Taliban: Militant Islam, Oil and Fundamentalism in Central Asia* (New Haven, CT: Yale University Press, 2000).

Ratner, Steven R., and Jason S. Abrams, *Accountability for Human Rights Atrocities in International Law: Beyond the Human Rights Legacy* (New York: Oxford University Press, 2001).

Rigo-Sureda, Antonio, *The Evolution of the Right to Self-Determination: A Study of United Nations Practice* (Leiden, Netherlands: A.W. Sijhoff, 1973).

Ritter, Scott, *Endgame: Solving the Iraq Problem Once and For All* (New York: Simon & Schuster, 1999).

Roberts, Adam, and Richard Guelff, eds., *Documents on the Laws of War* (Oxford, UK: Clarendon Press, 1982).

Robertson, Geoffrey, *Crimes Against Humanity: The Struggle for Global Justice* (New York: New Press, 2000).

Rogers, Robert F., *Destiny's Landfall: A History of Guam* (Honolulu: University of Hawaii Press, 1995).

Rosenberg, Howard I., *Atomic Soldiers: American Victims of Nuclear Experiments* (Boston: Beacon, 1980).

Said, Edward W., *The Question of Palestine* (New York: Vintage, [2nd ed.] 1992).

Sartre, Jean-Paul, and Arlette El Kaïm-Sartre, *On Genocide and a summary of the evidence and judgments of the International War Crimes Tribunal* (Boston: Beacon Press, 1968).

Scott, Peter Dale, and Jonathan Marshall, *Cocaine Politics: Drugs, Armies and the CIA in Central America* (Berkeley: University of California Press, 1991).

Shawcross, William, *Sideshow: Kissinger, Nixon and the Destruction of Cambodia* (New York: Simon and Schuster, 1979).

Shelton, Dinah, *Remedies in International Human Rights Law* (New York: Oxford University Press, 1999).

Shlaim, Avi, *The Iron Wall: Israel and the Arab World* (New York: W.W. Norton, 2000).

Simpson, Christopher, *Blowback: America's Recruitment of Nazis and Its Effect on the Cold War* (New York: Collier Books, 1988).

Sinclair, Ian, *The Vienna Convention on the Law of Treaties* (Manchester, UK: Manchester University Press, [2nd ed.] 1984).

Sklar, Holly, *Washington's War on Nicaragua* (Boston, MA: South End Press, 1988).

Smith, Bradley F., *Reaching Judgment at Nuremberg* (New York: Basic Books, 1977).

_____, *The Road to Nuremberg* (New York: Basic Books, 1981).

Stavens, Ralph, Richard J. Barnet and Marcus G. Raskin, *Washington Plans an Aggressive War* (New York: Random House, 1971).

Stenehjem Gerber, Michele, *On the Home Front: The Cold War Legacy and the Hanford Nuclear Site* (Lincoln: University of Nebraska Press, 1992).

Stevens, Richard P., and Abdelwahab M. Elmissiri, *Israel and South Africa: The Progression of a Relationship* (New Brunswick, NJ: North American, [2nd ed.] 1976).

Stockholm International Peace Institute, *Incendiary Weapons* (Cambridge, MA/Stockholm: MIT Press/Almquist & Wiksell, 1975).

Suter, Keith, *An International Law of Guerrilla Warfare: The Global Politics of Law-Making* (New York: St. Martin's Press, 1984).

Tashiro, Akira, *Discounted Casualties: The Human Cost of Depleted Uranium* (Hiroshima: Chugoku Shimbum, 2001).

Taylor, John G., *Indonesia's Forgotten War: The Hidden History of East Timor* (London: Zed Press, 1991).

Taylor, Telford, *Nuremberg and Vietnam: An American Tragedy* (Chicago: Quadrangle, 1970).

Tebbel, John, and Keith Jemison, *The American Indian Wars* (New York: Harper & Row, 1960).

Timmerman, Kenneth R., *The Poison Gas Connection: Western suppliers of unconventional weapons and technologies to the Middle East* (Los Angeles: Simon Wiesenthal Center, 1993).

Uhl, Michael, and Tod Ensign, *G.I. Guinea Pigs: How the Pentagon Exposed Our Troops to Dangers More Deadly Than War* (New York: Playboy Press, 1980).

Valentine, Douglas, *The Phoenix Program* (Lincoln, NE: Authors Guild, 1990).

Vidal, Gore, *Perpetual War for Perpetual Peace: How We Got to be So Hated* (New York: Nation Books/Thunder's Mouth Press, 2002).

Vodelgesang, Sandy, *American Dream, Global Nightmare: The Dilemma of U.S. Human Rights Policy* (New York: W.W. Norton, 1980).

Walker, Martin, *The Cold War: A History* (New York: Owl Books, [2nd ed.] 1995).

Walters, Ronald W., *South Africa and the Bomb: Responsibility and Deterrence* (Lexington, MA: Lexington Books, 1987).

Weisberg, Barry, *Ecocide in Indochina: The Ecology of War* (San Francisco: Canfield Press, 1970).

Welsome, Eileen, *The Plutonium Papers: America's Secret Medical Experiments in the Cold War* (New York: Dial Press, 1999).

Weston, Burns H., Richard A. Falk and Anthony D'Amato, eds., *Basic Documents on International Law and World Order* (St. Paul, MN: West, [2nd ed.] 1990).

Wilcox, Fred A., *Waiting for an Army to Die: The Tragedy of Agent Orange* (New York: Vintage, 1983).

Williams, T. Harry, *The History of American Wars from 1745-1918* (Baton Rouge/London: Louisiana State University Press, 1981).

Woodward, C. Vann, *The Strange Career of Jim Crow* (New York: Oxford University Press, [3rd ed.] 1974).

Ya-Otto, John, with Ole Gjerstad and Michael Mercer, *Battlefront Namibia: An Autobiography* (Westport, CT: Lawrence Hill, 1981).

Zinn, Howard, *A People's History of the United States* (New York: HarperCollins, 1990).

Ordering Information

AK Press
674-A 23rd Street,
Oakland, CA 94612-1163,
USA
Phone: (510) 208-1700
E-mail: akpress@akpress.org
URL: www.akpress.org

Please send all payments (checks, money orders, or cash at your own risk) in U.S. dollars. Alternatively, we take VISA and MC.

AK Press
PO Box 12766,
Edinburgh, EH8 9YE,
Scotland
Phone: (0131) 555-5165
E-mail: ak@akedin.demon.uk
URL: www.akuk.com

Please send all payments (cheques, money orders, or cash at your own risk) in U.K. pounds. Alternatively, we take credit cards.

For a dollar, a pound or a few IRC's, the same addresses would be delighted to provide you with the latest AK catalog featuring several thousand books, pamphlets, zines, audio products and stylish apparel published & distributed by AK Press. Alternatively, check out our websites for the complete catalog, latest news and updates, events, and secure ordering.

AK Press

Radical Priorities by Noam Chomsky, ed. C.P. Otero
$18.95. ISBN 1 902593 69 3
In *Radical Priorities*, C.P. Otero sets out to "provide relatively easy access to Chomsky's libertarian philosophy and political analysis". Taken from a wide variety of sources, many never widely published—some never in a book at all and spanning four decades, the reader is furnished with a truly comprehensive window into Chomsky's anarchist convictions. Convictions which, while ever-present in his analysis are left largely misunderstood or worse—ignored.

The Politics of Anti-Semitism ed. by Alexander Cockburn and Jeffrey St. Clair
$11.95. ISBN 1 902593 77 4
How did a term, once used accurately to describe the most virulent evil, become a charge flung at the mildest critic of Israel, particularly concerning its atrocious treatment of Palestinians? Edited by Cockburn and St. Clair of the print and online journal *Counterpunch* and includes contributors Edward Said, Robert Fisk, Michael Neumann, Norman Finklestein, Yuri Avneri and Yigal Bronner.

No Gods No Masters (2 vols.) by Daniel Guerin
Vol. I $18.95. ISBN 1 873176 64 3
Vol II $16.95. ISBN 1 873176 69 4
This is the first English translation of Guerin's monumental anthology of Anarchism. It details, through a vast array of hitherto unpublished documents, writings, letters and reports, the history, organization and practice of the anarchist movement—its theorists, advocates and activists.
Book I includes the writings of Max Stirner, Pierre-Joseph Proudhon, Mikhail Bakunin, James Guillaume, Max Nettlau, Peter Kropotkin, Emma Goldman and Cesar de Paepe amongst others
Book II includes work from the likes of Malatesta, Emile Henry, Emile Pouget, Augustin Souchy, Gaston Leval, Voline, Nestor Makhno, the Kronstadt sailors, Luigi Fabbri, and Buenaventura Durruti

Moving Forward by Michael Albert
$11.95. ISBN 1 902593 41 3
If not capitalism, then what? In *Moving Forward*, Albert argues that we have to change how we conceive of work and wages, rewarding effort and sacrifice rather than output, and moving from heirarchical workplce structures to worker self-management. From here he moves to a proposal for how we might organize the larger functions of the economy in workers' councils and a general discussion of how our society might look with a participatory economy.

Also Available from AK Press:

What is Anarchism? by Alexander Berkman $13.95 ISBN 1 902593 70 7

Addicted to War by Joel Andreas $8.00 ISBN 1 902593 57 X

Workers' Councils by Anton Pannekoek $15.00 ISBN 1 902593 56 1

Controlled Flight Into Terrain by John Yates $10.95 ISBN 1 902593 67 7

Philosophy of Punk by Craig O'Hara $12.00 ISBN 1 873176 16 3

The Spanish Anarchists by Murray Bookchin $19.95 ISBN 1 873176 04 X

Facing the Enemy by Alexandre Skirda $17.95 ISBN 1 902593 19 7

2/15: The Day The World Said NO To War $24.95 ISBN 1 902593 85 5

A New World In Our Hearts: 8 Years of Writings from the Love and Rage Revolutionary Anarchist Federation by Roy San Fillipo (ed.) $11.95 ISBN 1 902593 61 8

Direct Action: Memoirs Of An Urban Guerilla by Ann Hansen $19.95 ISBN 1 902593 48 0

Beneath the Paving Stones: Situationists and the Beach, May 68 by Dark Star Collective (ed.) $15.00 ISBN 1 902593 38 3

Orgasms of History: 3000 Years of Spontaneous Revolt by Yves Fremion and Volny $18.95 ISBN 1 902593 34 0

Reinventing Anarchy, Again by Howard Ehrlich (ed.) $24.95 ISBN 1 873176 88 0

AK Audio

Doing Time: The Politics of Imprisonment CD by Ward Churchill
$14.98 ISBN 1 902593 47 2

In this cd Ward Churchill exposes the Criminal Justice System's role as an agent of social control. This lecture, recorded at the Doing Time Conference at the University of Winnepeg, focuses on the prison system's compliance with the FBI in subverting and neutralizing movements for social change. Churchill also attacks the Prison Industrial Complex, the mushrooming rate of incarceration in the U.S., and debunks the media's whitewash of prison injustice.

In a Pig's Eye: Reflections on the Police State, Repression and Native America
2XCD by Ward Churchill
$19.98 ISBN 1 902593 50 2

In this keynote lecture, Churchill weaves together the themes for which he has become hailed as an activist and scholar—genocide, repression, and resistance—and amply demonstrates why the fate of Leonard Peltier, the current state of Native America, and the long, sordid history of the state clampdown on dissent have ramifications across the globe.

Pacifism and Pathology in the American Left CD by Ward Churchill
$14.98 ISBN 1 902593 58 8

Liberal activism often embraces non-violent resistance in reponse to state-sponsored terrorism at home and abroad. In this emotional critique, Churchill urges activists to support any and all tactics in order to stop the tyranny of the state. Churchill argues that the terrorist attack of 9/11 disrupted U.S. global capitalism more radically than any peaceful protest the Left has been able to organize. Recorded at a packed and fired up AK Press warehouse in Oakland.

Life in Occupied America CD by Ward Churchill
$14.98 ISBN 1 902593 72 3

In this trenchant, and often bitingly acerbic lecture, coupled with a fiery question and answer session, Native activist scholar Ward Churchill lays out the current state of Native America. From the first recorded instance of biological warfare (a written order from the British commander Lord Amherst in 1763 to utilizing small-pox infected blankets as a means of cleansing his rebellious subjects) to a Native population today living in conditions of Third World poverty (a life expectancy on the Reservations for a man of less than 50 years, 60% unemployment, and outbreaks of the Bubonic Plague, for example), Churchill tracks the effects, causes and consequences of 500 years of wars, broken treaties, duplicity, exploitation, environmental degradation, genocide and colonisation—life in occupied America (in the words of John Trudell) since predator came.

Also available from AK Audio:

The Emerging Framework of World Power: Everlasting War CD by Noam Chomsky $14.98. ISBN 1 902593 75 8
Propaganda and Control of the Public Mind 2XCD by Noam Chomsky $20.00. ISBN 1 873176 68 6
Come September CD by Arundhati Roy $14.98. ISBN 1 92593 80 4
The New War on Terrorism: Fact and Fiction CD by Noam Chomsky $14.98. ISBN 1 902593 62 6
Case Studies In Hypocrisy: U.S. Human Rights Policy 2XCD by Noam Chomsky $20.00. ISBN 1 902593 27 8
Free Market Fantasies: Capitalism in the Real World CD by Noam Chomsky $13.98. ISBN 1 873176 79 1
An American Addiction: Drugs, Guerillas, Counterinsurgency—U.S. Intervention in Colombia CD by Noam Chomsky $13.98. ISBN 1 902593 44 8
Prospects For Democracy CD by Noam Chomsky $14.98 ISBN 1 873176 38 4
Artists in a Time of War CD by Howard Zinn $14.98. ISBN 1 902593 65 0
Beating the Devil CD by Alexander Cockburn $14.98 ISBN 1 902593 49 9
A People's History of the United States: A Lecture at Reed College 2XCD by Howard Zinn $20.00 ISBN 1 873176 95 3
Taking Liberties: Policing, Prisons and Surveliance in an Age of Crisis CD by Christian Parenti $14.98 ISBN 1 902593 63 4
All Things Censored CD by Mumia Abu-Jamal $14.98 ISBN 1 902593 06 5
Prisons on Fire: George Jackson, Attica & Black Liberation CD by the Freedom Archives $14.98 ISBN 1 902593 52 9
The Prison Industrial Complex CD by Angela Davis $14.98 ISBN 1 902593 22 7
Heroes and Martyrs: Emma Goldman, Sacco & Vanzetti and the Revolutionary Struggle 2XCD by Howard Zinn $20.00 ISBN 1 902593 26 X